AMERICAN MUSIC
A PANORAMA

Second Concise Edition

Daniel Kingman

Assisted by Lorenzo F. Candelaria
University of Texas, Austin

THOMSON

SCHIRMER

Australia • Canada • Mexico • Singapore • Spain
United Kingdom • United States

THOMSON

★

SCHIRMER

Publisher, Music: Clark G. Baxter
Assistant Editor: Kasia Zagorski
Editorial Assistant: Jonathan Katz
Technology Project Manager: Jennifer Ellis
Marketing Manager: Mark Orr
Marketing Assistant: Justine Ferguson
Advertising Project Manager: Brian Chaffee
Project Manager, Editorial Production: Emily Smith
Print/Media Buyer: Jessica Reed

Permissions Editor: Joohee Lee
Production Service: Greg Hubit Bookworks
Text Designer: Rokusek Design
Photo Researcher: Terri Wright
Copy Editor: Carole Crouse
Cover Designer: Jeanne Calabrese
Cover Image: Art Resource, New York
Compositor: TBH Typecast, Inc.
Cover and Text Printer: Phoenix Color Corp.

For more information about our products, contact us at:
Thomson Learning Academic Resource Center
1-800-423-0563
For permission to use material from this text, contact us by:
Phone: 1-800-730-2214
Fax: 1-800-730-2215
Web: http://www.thomsonrights.com

Library of Congress Control Number: 2002112002

ISBN 0-534-59832-3

Wadsworth/Thomson Learning
10 Davis Drive
Belmont, CA 94002-3098
USA

Asia
Thomson Learning
5 Shenton Way #01-01
UIC Building
Singapore 068808

Australia
Nelson Thomson Learning
102 Dodds Street
South Melbourne, Victoria 3205
Australia

Canada
Nelson Thomson Learning
1120 Birchmount Road
Toronto, Ontario M1K 5G4
Canada

Europe/Middle East/Africa
Thomson Learning
High Holborn House
50/51 Bedford Row
London WC1R 4LR
United Kingdom

Latin America
Thomson Learning
Seneca, 53
Colonia Polanco
11560 Mexico D.F.
Mexico

Spain
Paraninfo Thomson Learning
Calle/Magallanes, 25
28015 Madrid, Spain

To Louise

Panorama

The *panorama* was a popular form of didactic art in the larger frontier cities of America in the mid-1800s. It was an exhibition of the painter's art done on a mammoth scale. A huge canvas, twenty feet high or more, would slowly pass before the assembled audience, moving, scroll-like, from one large roll to another. The paying spectators would see vast scenes unrolling before their eyes in a sort of primitive motion picture—battle scenes, or the course of the Mississippi River between two points. Often this was done to the accompaniment of music.

CONTENTS

CHAPTER 8

CHAPTER 9

PART III

POPULAR SACRED MUSIC

CHAPTER 10

AUTHOR'S GUIDE
TO THE PANORAMA

From a vantage point high enough, the eye can sweep over the whole far-flung, sundry, teeming, and boisterous panorama that is American music. With this volume we place in your hands a guide to that panorama—a metaphor that remains for me a useful and compelling one, reflecting my view of American music as a number of more or less distinct but parallel streams. Some are at full flood stage; some have dried to a narrow rivulet. All are constantly changing—overflowing their banks, retreating from them, dividing into separate branches, or yielding their flow to neighboring streams. What we eventually realize is that they are all interconnected. And as would be incumbent on any guide, I will often encourage the reader to take in the wider view, as well as observing with fascination the rapids and shoals of the single tributaries.

The fundamental organization of the book into individual streams gives it a flexibility that can be useful in designing a course. In addition to the six parts devoted to those streams, I have kept from previous editions a brief Post-Chapter that samples the heterogeneous music of my own geographic area and is designed to encourage the reader to get outside the book and take a look around in his or her "own backyard," so to speak, and observe there the encompassing diversity.

A WORD ABOUT THE STREAMS

The unconventional ordering of the richly complex panorama of American music into more or less parallel streams imposes a responsibility on me as the author. It is incumbent upon me at the very outset to explain as clearly as possible how I define those streams.

I see a basic distinction in character and function between three kinds of music—folk and ethnic (considered together), popular, and classical, or fine art. Let us make a momentary digression into the visual art of painting, where we can observe these distinctions in another medium.

Folk art is sometimes referred to as "naïve" or "innocent" art. Look for a moment at *Blacksmith Shop*, by the American artist, Francis A. Beckett. We do not know why it was painted. Perhaps it was done to document a particular blacksmith shop. It does, in fact, show us the design of the bellows and forge, the tools used, the type of work—making wagon wheels—and even

Blacksmith Shop by Francis A. Beckett

{below} "Blacksmith's Boy—Heel and Toe," by Norman Rockwell. *The Saturday Evening Post*, November 2, 1940.

possibly the identity of the blacksmiths.) Or perhaps it was painted simply for the joy of doing it. It was probably not created for any public beyond the artist's own immediate community. Though it unquestionably *may* have interest and even aesthetic appeal to those outside the community, that was probably not its purpose. The technique, though by no means absent, is relatively unschooled—rather meticulous in detail, but, to the critical observer, deficient in proportions and perspective. And there is no sense of action; the painting does not convey the feeling that these men are actually at work. Like the folk ballad, it simply gives us the facts, without comment or emotion.

Popular art, on the other hand, is created by highly skilled professionals, and for a public broad enough to support its production. The illustration for *The Saturday Evening Post* by Norman Rockwell not only is flawlessly executed but has entertainment value as well. The characters have unmistakable individuality, and the painting illustrates a story—of a blacksmithing contest, on which bets are placed. More than just giving us the facts, through conveying the obvious intensity of both the blacksmiths and the spectators, the painting draws us into the scene and, to a certain extent, dictates our reaction to it. This is popular art at its most persuasive.

The *fine arts* tend to have a quality of detachment. Even when there is obvious subject matter, we are aware of what is called an *aesthetic distance* from the subject. It is not so much the subject that we see as the artist's *vision* of the subject. Imagination and fantasy play a significant role. *The Carnival of Harlequin* by Juan Miró is clearly an interior (not a blacksmith shop, to be sure, though there is one wheel in there with deformed spokes), but it is an interior filled with fantastic images *suggesting* animals, fish, insects, and the instruments and

The Carnival of
Harlequin,
by Joan Miró.

symbols of music. *The Carnival of Harlequin* might be said to interpret the *commedia dell'arte* character of Harlequin the way Virgil Thomson and Gertrude Stein's "Pigeons on the Grass Alas" might be said to interpret St. Ignatius's Vision of the Holy Ghost (CD 5/19, p.438).

To return to our subject, *folk music* evolves within fairly close-knit homogeneous communities possessing a strong sense of group solidarity. It is music known to and enjoyed by a large proportion of the community, who identify it as "their music," made by and for themselves. Many of the members of the community—a much higher proportion than in the population at large—perform the music themselves, with varying degrees of skill. To take the ballad as an example, the relatively large number of those in the community who sing the ballads may have indifferent qualifications *as singers*, but it is not the singer, or the quality of the singing, that is the center of attention; it is the ballad itself. (Just as in the first painting, it is the blacksmith shop itself that is the focus of attention; the identity of the painter is obscure and unimportant.)

Folk communities in the past tended to be rural and geographically isolated, though this is no longer an important defining factor. Folk music is highly conventional in style, with stylistic boundaries of acceptance fairly rigid, and with changes from outside influences coming slowly. A factor that *is* still important is its dissemination mainly by oral tradition, but this must now include by extension radio, recordings, television, and film. *Ethnic musics* may share some of folk music's characteristics, but the term is applied to those musics that originated in societies whose homeland was outside the United States (excepting, of course, American Indian music) and—an important defining distinction—in cultures in which the principal language is not English. However, I have made no attempt to draw a hard-and-fast distinction between folk and ethnic musics. Furthermore, for the sake of organizational convenience, I have included in Part I the consideration of music of Hispanic, French, Scandinavian, Asian, and American Indian origins that has overlapped into the realm of either popular or classical music. The streams are, I hope, fairly distinct, but it would be a serious mistake to regard them as either isolated or insulated one from another.

Popular music is music created for and enjoyed by the vast majority of the people, undefined by region. No specific ethnic background is requisite to fully appreciate or identify with it. It is primarily (though not exclusively) music for entertainment, and as such it makes only modest demands on its listeners' musical knowledge and experience. It tends to adopt sounds from both folk and classical music that have become sufficiently familiar to the wider public. It is produced by skilled professionals whenever and wherever a critical mass of population exists to support its commercial production and distribution. Disseminated in the beginning mainly by print notation, as sheet-music sales declined popular music became, for all intents and purposes, oral-tradition music. Its popularity (as measured in today's world by a highly influential system of "charts") is in itself the most widely recognized measure of its worth.

Classical music has evolved out of a tradition of cultivation both longer and broader than that of either folk or popular music, and encompasses music from a variety of historical periods, by no means excluding the present. As culti-vated music it rewards a certain degree of musical experience in the listener, though its devotees are not defined by any intellectual, social, economic, regional, or racial classification. In our time it is less bound by convention than the music of the other streams, and it encompasses a wider variety of media, forms, textures, harmonies, rhythms, and styles. Classical music has an almost unique ability to absorb, quote from, or treat as "subject matter" any other kind of music. Although a piece of classical music may *become* popular (a con-dition to which few of its composers would object), one point of distinction from popular music is that it does not *depend for its existence* on mass appeal.

A few more details of the book's organization may call for some explana-tion. "The prodigious offspring of the rural south" are treated together as regional musics that made the transition from folk to popular music—country and blues beginning with the advent of radio and recordings, and rock coming out of both in the late 1940s.

A further source of diversity in the panorama is found in the distinction between sacred and secular music, with one frequently influenced by the other.

Jazz is a special case. Emerging from African American roots (in both sacred and secular music) at the turn of the last century, it has become in my view arguably a form of classical music, despite the undoubted influence on popular music of jazz-related rhythms, styles, and orchestration. But it is a classical music set apart by virtue of its having retained certain identifying and obligatory stylistic traits (mainly rhythmic), and on being uniquely dependent upon, and shaped by, its traditional ingredient of improvisation.

A WORD ABOUT THE CD SET

In response to the valuable suggestions of user reviewers, we have expanded the CD supplement and, wherever possible, included complete works in place of the shortened versions used heretofore. This should make the supplement much more inviting on its own. In general the complete lyrics of the vocal works, including translations, are printed in the text. *Listening Guides* are pro-vided for some examples. References to the CD selections appear in the margins alongside their discussions in the text. Cross-referencing to CD tracks in other chapters is done wherever it may amplify a topic or point out interesting relationships.

No practical CD supplement could include all the examples relevant to the subject. Furthermore the profit-oriented (in contrast to education-oriented) policies of much of the commercial music industry made unavailable the rights to many relevant examples, particularly of popular music. The *Additional Listening* section at the end of each chapter is meant to alleviate those limitations by identifying current recordings. Music department record libraries can help, especially with anthologies such as the New World Records and, in jazz, the venerable Smithsonian Collection of Classic Jazz (still in many libraries, though unfortunately no longer being produced). And the private libraries of teachers and students can fill in some gaps. Opera buffs, for example, will want to illustrate the points made about *Porgy and Bess* in Chapter 22 with a recording of the complete opera.

A WORD ABOUT THE PRINTED MUSIC IN THE TEXT

The songs that are printed in the text are intended to be *sung* and are pitched with that in mind. There is hardly any substitute for this experience. Many can be listened to in authentic re-creations, or versions by traditional singers, including "Chester" (p. 181, CD 2/35), "Jesus Wept" (p. 183, CD 2/36), "'Tis the Gift to Be Simple" (p. 194, CD 3/2), "The Wildwood Flower" (p. 112–113, CD 2/15), "Wabash Cannon Ball" (p. 113, CD 2/16), and "Wondrous Love" (p. 187, CD 3/1).

Music notation without text and CD track is rare. Where it appears, it illustrates musical terms or concepts, such as the blues scale in Chapter 2, the Latino rhythms in Chapter 4, the rock harmony examples in Chapter 9, and the ragtime syncopations in Chapter 15.

Special attention is drawn to the complete Roy Harris Third Symphony in Chapter 19. Here I have taken advantage of the opportunity afforded by a longer CD set to have students listen to, and study, longer works in their entirety. This memorable seventeen-minute work in one movement is, in my opinion, one of the most important American symphonies. The printed examples in the text are designed to give insight into the characteristics of the musical "language" employed but also some sense of how a longer work is put together—how long extended melodic lines can function, how what is done in one part can be referred to in another, how the two demands of unity and variety are met.

A WORD ABOUT THE PROJECTS

The suggestions for *Projects* have been kept and revised from previous editions. They are intended to give the student an opportunity to investigate further, on her or his own, many different aspects of American music. Even a tiny scrap of knowledge that one discovers, with a little effort, for oneself can become a cherished corner of the whole subject, forever one's own. Even if not actually undertaken as projects, they can tease out fresh insights into the subjects.

A WORD ABOUT WHAT'S IN THE BACK OF THE BOOK

References are a legal necessity and a scholarly obligation. But in this case they are more. With their annotations they serve as reading lists. The lists of *Additional Reading* are just that; they do not duplicate material in the *References*.

ACKNOWLEDGMENTS

My able assistant, Dr. Lorenzo Candelaria, has provided help in many of the numerous tasks associated with this edition; he has created captions, researched the bibliography and discography, and performed valuable help updating many areas, besides assembling the Glossary and the Index. These jobs are often unsung, but sorely missed when they are not done thoroughly.

Lise Waxer, a published scholar in her field, furnished valuable specifics for Chapter 4, which enabled me to present more detailed descriptions of Latino forms and rhythms than are found in many general works. Patricia Shifferd, Program Director of Continental Harmony, a project of the American Composers Forum, supported the inclusion of the projects in Chapter 17, and the four composers represented—Phillip Bimstein, Jaron Lanier, Steve Heitzeg, and Anne LeBaron—were generous with information, materials, and permissions regarding their compositions.

I wish especially to thank the users of this book who consented to write detailed and quite helpful peer reviews: David Borgo, James Madison University, Virginia; Mary Campbell, Las Positas College, California; Julie Dunbar, Edgewood College, Wisconsin; Karen Fosheim, Delta State University, Mississippi; Robert I. Holst, Lewis University, Illinois; Donna Cardamone Jackson, University of Minnesota; Donald C. Meyer, Lake Forest College, Illinois; Jeffrey J. Noonan, Southeast Missouri State University; Kay Norton, Arizona State University; Jennifer S. Peters, McKendree College, Illinois;

Paula Savaglio, Hope College, Michigan; and Helena Simonett, Vanderbilt University, Tennessee. Many of their suggestions have been incorporated in this edition, and consequently quite a few of what I consider to be definite improvements, both small and large, were inspired by the points they made.

Every book has an editor, but I cannot resist the opportunity to conclude by saying that few authors are fortunate enough to have an editor as understanding, patient, supportive, and gifted with the ability to convey that rare but essential ingredient of *enthusiasm* as Abigail Baxter. She was my assistant editor for the very first edition, and I can truly say that had I not found to my pleasant surprise that she had returned to Schirmer, I not only could not, but also *would* not, have undertaken this fourth version of *American Music: A Panorama*.

PART I   FOLK AND ETHNIC MUSICS

A scanning of the vast panorama of American music can begin nowhere more logically than with our folk and ethnic musics—musics that have been previously defined for our purposes in the Author's Guide. America's music, throughout its broad spectrum, is so relatively new as to have remained closer to folk sources than is the case in almost any other country. The professional sector of American musical life has never gone for very long without returning to refresh and revitalize itself at the fount of folk culture. Masterpieces as diverse as *Porgy and Bess* and *Appalachian Spring* (both by highly sophisticated composers) bear witness to this, as do large amounts of music in popular culture, from Dan Emmett to Bob Dylan and Paul Simon.

Yet this very closeness of America's music to its folk and ethnic roots is attended by a paradox. There is probably no other country in the world in which the soil of folk culture has been so thoroughly broken up, and either eroded away or rendered sterile. The all-pervasive media not only have spread commercial urban music exhaustively but also have put music largely into the hands of the professional entertainer. Continuous and extensive migration has broken down and emasculated regional character. And affluence, spectacular in comparison with most of the rest of the world, has put the appliances and products of the media into the hands of virtually everyone, so that the need, ability, or desire to make one's own music has lessened, where it has not actually disappeared.

So it would appear that the rich humus of folklore has provided us with nourishment but has proved to be fragile as well. Yet the realization of its fragility has made us more aware of its value and has encouraged us to make efforts not only to conserve it but also to keep its cultivation alive and relevant. And American folk and ethnic musics do live on in the space-and-communications age. Perhaps that is because, faced with the formidable challenge to human values and human scale posed by technology, and with the disorientations of an unstable world, we have come to realize both our need for the sense of community that a living connection with the past provides and the benefits of keeping alive, through adaptation to the world we live in, an oral tradition that is simple, direct, and unflinchingly honest in its expression.

Photo by David Gahr

The fiddler's expression vividly captures the enduring joyous spirit of American folk music.

The Anglo-Celtic-American Tradition

The Anglo-Celtic-American tradition of folk music, its origins traceable to England, Scotland, and Ireland, is best epitomized in the ballad, that venerable storytelling convergence of poetry and music. The ballad occurs in the United States in three strains: the *imported ballad*, little changed from its old-country forms; the *naturalized ballad,* still recognizable as descended from the old-country versions, in spite of having adopted the trappings of its new cultural surroundings; and *native ballads,* wholly new stories indigenous to the United States.

IMPORTED BALLADS

We begin with one of the most widespread and popular of the imported ballads.

"Barbara Allen" as a Prototype of the Anglo-Celtic-American Ballad

CD 1/1 (3:15) "Barbara Allen," H. J. Beeker, vocal and guitar. Recorded by John A. Lomax in Boone, North Carolina, 1936.

It might seem unlikely that the tale of a man who, spurned by a cold-hearted woman, actually dies of his love for her should have so enduringly engaged ballad singers and listeners from the seventeenth century in Scotland (its first recorded emergence) to the twenty-first century in America. Yet that has been the history of "Barbara Allen." Oliver Goldsmith wrote in 1765, "The music of the finest singer is dissonance to what I felt when an old dairy-maid sung me into tears with . . . 'The Cruelty of Barbara Allen'" (Child 2: 276). It had the same effect in 1938 on the singer Bob Brown, an old-timer who lived at the edge of the Big Thicket in east Texas. When Brown came to the line "Young man, I think you're dying," folk-song collector William Owens reports that "tears filled his eyes and he brushed at his wrinkled cheek with the back of his hand."

Owens writes, "If I were asked to name the ballad most deeply ingrained in the heart and thinking of the American folk, 'Barbara Allen' would be my choice. I have heard it up and down the country against backgrounds ranging from expensive nightclubs to sharecroppers' shacks" (Owens 23).

The tune heard on CD 1/1 (see Transcription 1.1) resembles in *shape* if not in note-to-note detail many other tunes associated with this ballad. These tunes constitute a tune family. The addition of a very rudimentary guitar accompaniment (using the three basic chords known to every beginning guitarist) makes this version sound like the conventional idea of folk music.

Transcription 1.1 "Barbara Allen"

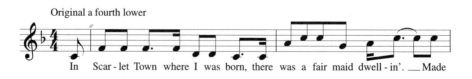

Original a fourth lower

In Scar-let Town where I was born, there was a fair maid dwell-in'. __Made

ev - 'ry youth cry well a - way, _   Her name was Bar - bara All - en.

Pentatonic scale

2. It was all in the month of June,
   All things there were bloomin'.
   Sweet William lay on his deathbed
   O'er the love of Barbara Allen.

3. And death was painted on his face,
   O'er his heart was stealin'.
   Oh hasten away to comfort him,
   Oh lovely Barbara Allen.

4. He sent his servant to the town
   Where Barbara was a-dwellin'.
   "My master's sick and sends for you
   If your name be Barbara Allen."

5. Slowly, slowly she got up,
   Slowly she came nigh him.
   All she said when she got there,
   "Young man, I think you're dyin'."

6. "Oh I am sick, very sick,
   Death on me is stealin'.
   No better, no better I never can be
   If I can't have Barbara Allen."

7. "Oh yes, you're sick, very sick,
   Death on you is stealin'.
   No better, no better you never can be
   For you can't have Barbara Allen."

8. "Oh don't you remember in yonder town
   You were at the tavern.
   You drank a health to the ladies all around
   And slighted Barbara Allen."

Text, "Barbara Allen."
(The first stanza appears
in Transcription 1.1.)

9. As she was on her highway home
   The birds they kep' a-singin'.
   They sang so clear and seemed to say,
   "Hard-hearted Barbara Allen."

10. Looked to the east, looked to the west,
    Spied his coach a-comin'.
    "Lay down, lay down that corpse of clay
    That I may look upon him."

11. "Oh Mother, Oh Mother, go make my bed,
    Make it long and narrow.
    Sweet William died for pure, pure love,
    And I shall die for sorrow."

12. She was buried in the old church yard.
    He was buried nigh her.
    On William's grave there grew a red rose,
    On Barbara's grew a green brier.

13. The rose and the brier they grew so high
    They could grow no higher.
    They met and formed a true love knot,
    The rose wrapped around the brier.

The version of "Barbara Allen" sung by Mr. Beeker is a fairly complete one and incorporates most of the events found in other versions. An almost invariable element of this ballad is the "rose-and-brier" motif, with the plants growing up out of the graves to become entwined in a lovers' knot. This sentimental device, rooted in old beliefs that the soul, upon death, either passes into or becomes a plant expressing the character of the dead person, occurs in other ballads as well (Wimberly 39–43).

FEATURES COMMON TO MOST BALLADS

A closer look at this version of "Barbara Allen" can acquaint us with features common to many other ballads, and in fact to much folk music throughout the world. Most ballads are in strophic form: that is, all the stanzas are sung to the same tune. There are as many stanzas as it takes to tell the story, or as many as the singer cares to sing or can remember. The lyrics are in what is commonly called ballad meter. Each stanza consists of four lines; each two-line part, arranged as four-plus-three, has the same succession of stressed and un-stressed syllables (called *poetic feet*):

   /   /   /   /
In **Scar**let **Town** where **I** was **born,**

      /   /   /
There **was** a **fair** maid **dwel**lin'.

     /   /   /   /
Made **every youth** cry **well** away,

   /   /   /
Her **name** was **Bar**bara **All**en.

The standard poetic foot is *iambic*—that is, comprising an unstressed fol-lowed by a stressed syllable. But in the informal world of ballad-making and singing, extra syllables are frequently crammed in to fit the needs of the sense. This is particularly noticeable in "John Hardy," the lyrics of which are on page 10.

Ballad meter (ta-**da**-ta-**da**-ta-**da**-ta-**da**; ta-**da**-ta-**da**-ta-**daa**) can be found in many contexts besides that of the ballad. Many hymns, such as "There Is a Land of Pure Delight," are in ballad meter, also called Common Meter.

Ballads are frequently sung without accompaniment. CD 1/2 is a slower, more expressive version of the ballad, from that other mountain repository of folklore and music, the Ozarks of Missouri and Arkansas. Notice that the absence of any accompaniment gives greater rhythmic and emotive freedom to the singing. This version uses an alternative tune, from another tune family, that is also associated with "Barbara Allen." No ballad is apt to have only a sin-gle tune indissolubly wedded to it. Neither is any given tune always exclusively associated with only one ballad. Charles Seeger puts it both accurately and col-orfully when he writes that "both spouses are frequently unfaithful to their common-law kind of union" (Seeger 122).

CD 1/2 (1:17)
"Barbara Allen," May Kennedy McCord, Ozark folksinger, vocal. Recorded by Sidney Robertson Cowell in Springfield, Missouri, 1936.

Tune Sources and Scales

Many ballad tunes exhibit characteristics of antiquity, particularly those com-ing from the Appalachians. Much of this antique flavor can be attributed to the scales on which they are based. One scale frequently encountered is the penta-tonic, a scale of five (rather than the more familiar seven) notes to the octave. (See Transcription 1.1.) This scale is the basic building material of much folk and ethnic music worldwide; we hear it in American Indian music and in the music of Africa, the Orient, and central Europe. It occurs in our popular music as well; the first two phrases of two of Stephen Foster's best-known songs, "Old Folks at Home" and "Oh, Susannah," are pure pentatonic. Both of the preceding versions of "Barbara Allen" use the pentatonic scale. (You can hear the sound of the pentatonic scale by playing only the black keys of the piano.)

Dispersion and Variation with the Passage of Time

"Barbara Allen" has traveled far and wide. As of 1962, the Library of Congress Archive of American Folk Song contained 243 transcribed versions of this ballad, picked up from twenty-seven states, from Maine to Florida to California. The essence of the story, sometimes referred to as the *emotional core,* endures in all versions. But less vital elements are subject to considerable variation. Traditional folksingers do not intentionally alter a song, but in the course of oral transmission changes become inevitable. Simple forgetting is a constant factor. Another source of change is a misunderstanding of elements of language as the ballad ages.

Difficult or ambiguous words, or words and phrases no longer in current usage, are very vulnerable to change. "The Gypsy Laddie" (see "Gypsy Davy," CD 1/3) is a Scottish ballad in which the lady of the castle, in her lord's absence, is abducted by a band of gypsies who appear at the castle, cast a spell on her (or give her nutmeg and ginger, considered to be aphrodisiacs), and abduct her. One old version of the ballad, still retaining aspects of the supernatural, says of the gypsy band that as they saw the lady "They coost their glamourie owre her." A later, garbled version says of the gypsies that "They called their grandmother over"! Not only has the word *glamourie* ("glamour") been misunderstood, but also its older meaning as an actual spell to be cast over someone has been lost, to the impoverishment of the ballad.

Interpreting the Ballads

The early attention given to ballads was directed almost exclusively to their texts, and indeed "the ballad as literature" is a prominent branch of study. There are many ways to approach the interpretation of ballads. Using "Barbara Allen" as an example, one could pursue the *historical* context. Was Barbara a real person? One theory is that the ballad was a popular libel on Barbara Villiers, the famous mistress of Charles II of England (1630–85). Or, to take another road (admittedly less traveled by), one could explore the *social-psychoanalytical* dimensions of the ballad, as noted folklorist Alan Lomax (1915–2002) has done, viewing Barbara Allen as "frigid western woman humbling and destroying the man whom she sees as her enemy and antagonist" (171).

Before we take our leave of the elusive Barbara, it is suggested that you find and listen to other versions of this famous ballad, including renditions by professional folksingers such as Pete Seeger, and even popular singers such as Josh White. (See Additional Listening.) This will enable you to compare the role of the professional singer with that of the (usually amateur) traditional singer, the authentic "carrier" of the tradition.

NATURALIZED BALLADS

Old ballads, transplanted in time and place, usually retain their emotional core but become "naturalized" in their details. Changes in place names are common; the "Oxford girl" easily becomes the "Knoxville girl," for example. Other details that surround us in daily life are adapted as well. Nowhere is this more strikingly illustrated than in Woody Guthrie's version of "The Gypsie Laddie," known as "Gypsy Davy"(CD 1/3).

CD 1/3 (2:46)
"Gypsy Davy," Woody Guthrie, guitar and vocal. Recorded by Alan Lomax in Washington DC.

The core of the story is that the lord, on returning to the castle, rides after the gypsies who have abducted his lady. In some versions he is successful in bringing her back; in others he is not. (The ballad has been viewed as a parody on the Greek myth of Orpheus and his attempt to bring Eurydice back from the underworld.) The original Scottish version dates from the time of Shakespeare, when king and parliament sought to drive the gypsies out of Scotland.

A comparison of Guthrie's version with an older Scottish one shows some interesting instances of naturalization as the ballad traveled from the highlands of Scotland to the western prairie of America. The Scottish lord has become the "boss"; his black steed has become the "buckskin horse with the hundred-dollar saddle"; and instead of riding east and riding west in search of the abducted lady, "till they cam' to yonder boggie," the boss finds wagon tracks (as might be expected on the western plains) that lead to a gypsy encampment, and a campfire with gypsies singing to the "sound of a big guitar." Also noteworthy is the presence of a child, the "blue-eyed babe," a typically American addition not in the older Scottish version.

1. It was late last night when my boss come home
   Asking about his lady;
   The only answer he received:
   "She's gone with the Gypsy Davy
   Gone with the Gypsy Dave."

Text, Guthrie version of "Gypsy Davy"*
(Words and new music adaptation by Woody Guthrie. TRO – © copyright 1961 (renewed) and 1963 (renewed) Ludlow Music, Inc., New York, NY. Used by permission.)

*This printed version differs from what you will hear on CD1/3, because the copyright owner insisted on the use of a version copyrighted for print twenty years after Woody Guthrie sang and recorded the original version.

2. Go saddle for me my buckskin horse
   And a hundred dollar saddle.
   Point out to me their wagon tracks
   And after them I'll travel,
   After them I'll ride.

3. Well, I had not rode 'til the midnight moon,
   I saw their campfire gleaming.
   I heard the notes of the big guitar
   And the voice of the gypsy singing
   The song of the Gypsy Dave.

4. It was there in the light of the camping fire
   I saw her fair face beaming,
   Her heart in tune to the big guitar
   The song of the gypsy singing
   That song of the Gypsy Dave.

5. "Have you forsaken your house and home?
   Have you forsaken your baby?
   Have you forsaken your husband dear
   To go with the Gypsy Davy?
   And sing with the Gypsy Davy
   The song of the Gypsy Dave."

6. "Yes, I've forsaken my husband dear
   To go with the Gypsy Davy,
   And I've forsaken my mansion high
   But not my blue-eyed baby,
   Not my blue-eyed babe."

7. She smiled to leave her husband dear
   And go with the Gypsy Davy;
   But the tears come a-trickling down her cheeks
   To think about the blue-eyed baby,
   To think about the blue-eyed babe.

8. Take off, take off your buck-skin gloves
   Made of Spanish leather;
   Give to me your lily-white hand
   And we'll ride home together
   And home again we'll ride.

9. No, I won't take off my buckskin gloves,
   Made of Spanish leather.
   I'll go my way from day to day
   And sing with the Gypsy Davy
   The song of the Gypsy Dave.

A frequent modification of ballad meter is the extension of the last line by repetition. Compare this with the African American ballad "John Henry" on page 32–33, CD 1/15. For more on Woody Guthrie, see pages 99–100.

NATIVE BALLADS

Whereas the older English and Scottish ballads, even in adaptation, have not entirely concealed their archaic style and medieval atmosphere (part of their charm for singers of our time, no doubt), the native ballads have more realistic immediacy. They have known authors in many cases, and they are much more apt to be based on actual occurrences, even though assigning an exact time and place to the events may present fascinating and nearly insoluble problems. (The searches for the factual basis of the railroad ballad "Casey Jones" and the lumberjack ballad "The Jam on Gerry's Rock" are cases in point.) In contrast to the older British ballads, American ballads tend to be more about occupations—buffalo hunters ("The Buffalo Skinners," see Additional Listening at the end of the chapter), cowboys ("Little Joe the Wrangler"), railroading ("The Wreck of Old 97"), lumberjacks ("The Jam on Gerry's Rock"), sailors ("The Bigler's Crew"), and criminals ("Jesse James"). They frequently involve fatal physical disasters ("The Avondale Disaster," "The Titanic") or a more or less journalistic recounting of murders and executions ("Pearl Bryan," "Little Omie Wise," "John Hardy") rather than dwelling on more psychic, introverted, or pathological themes such as supernatural phenomena, fatal jealousy, or incest. Malcolm Laws finds in native ballads a more subjective, sympathetic approach to their heroes or heroines—evidence of a "tender humanity toward all who are faced with tragedy"—and concludes that native balladry "may be rugged and colorful or commonplace and sentimental; much of it may be inept, some even illiterate, but above all it shows compassion, neighborliness, and concern for other men's misfortunes" (111).

Native ballads, like most lead stories on the evening news, have tended to be about crimes (murders or assassinations), or disasters such as floods, train wrecks, ship sinkings, or mine disasters. Although both the perpetrator and the victim in "John Hardy" were black men, this murder ballad has ordinarily been sung by white singers in the southern Appalachians. This recording by the Carter Family (CD 1/4) presents only a small fraction of the details, factual

CD 1/4 (2:50) "John Hardy," the Carter Family. Recorded in 1930.

or made up, associated with this famous ballad. (78-rpm phonograph records became a major means for making the ballads known, but the time limits imposed made for the dissemination of very truncated versions.) The only verifiable information relating to this ballad is the existence in the courthouse at Welch, McDowell County, West Virginia, of an order for the execution of one John Hardy on January 19, 1894, for murder. A witness at the trial stated that Hardy worked for the Shawnee Coal Company and that one payday night he shot a man in a crap game over twenty-five cents.

Text, "John Hardy"

1. John Hardy was a desperate little man,
   He carried two guns every day,
   He shot a man on the West Virginia line,
   And you ought to seen John Hardy getting away.

2. John Hardy got to the East Stone Bridge,
   He thought that he would be free,
   But up stepped a man and took him by his arm
   Saying, "Johnny, walk along with me."

3. He sent for his poppy and his mommy too,
   To come and go his bail.
   But money won't go a murdering case,
   And they locked John Hardy back in jail.

4. John Hardy had a pretty little girl,
   The dress that she wore was blue,
   As she came tripping through the old jail hall
   Saying, "Poppy I've been true to you."

5. John Hardy had another little girl,
   The dress that she wore was red.
   She followed John Hardy to his hanging ground
   Saying, "Poppy, I would rather be dead."

6. "I've been to the East and I've been to the West,
   I've been this wide world around.
   I've been to the river and I've been baptized,
   And it's now I'm on my hanging ground."

7. John Hardy walked out on his scaffold high,
   With his loving little wife by his side.
   And the last words she heard poor John-o say,
   "I'll meet you in that sweet by and by."

The bare and grim facts are relieved by human touches, however, such as the introduction of John Hardy's little daughters into the story, one dressed in blue and the other in red. Such touches would not be found in the more stark Old World ballads. Remember that Woody Guthrie introduced a "blue-eyed babe" into his naturalized version of the "Gypsy Davy," a gentle touch not found in older versions. By the time "John Hardy" came into existence, the phrase "sweet by and by" had become commonplace. For more on the very popular gospel song of that name written in 1867, see pages 197–99.

"Tom Joad" (CD 1/5) is an instance of a native ballad based on a novel, in this case John Steinbeck's *Grapes of Wrath*. Woody Guthrie wrote the lengthy ballad of at least seventeen known stanzas after having watched the movie version several times in a row. It was one of Guthrie's famous *Dust Bowl Ballads*. (See Additional Listening for Chapter 6.) The tune is taken from the Carter Family's recording of "John Hardy" (CD 1/4). The harmonica is the only wind instrument portable enough to be useful in either folk or early country music. A harmonica holder, hung around the neck, enables a performer to play both the harmonica and the guitar simultaneously.

CD 1/5 (1:24)
"Tom Joad" (3 stanzas), Woody Guthrie, vocal. Recorded by Alan Lomax in Washington DC, 1940.

PRINT AND THE BALLAD

Oral tradition—human memory as the conservator and the human voice as the "publisher"—still retains among folklorists its preeminence as the *ideal* medium of folk song, and whether a ballad can be found to be in oral tradition is still regarded as a valid test of its "folkness," regardless of its origins. But print has long had a hand in ballad conservation and dissemination, and more recently so have other media, such as recordings. The older a ballad is, the more likely it is to have been in and out of print over the course of its history. Furthermore, it is likely that its printed versions have had an influence both on the state in which it exists today and on its geographical distribution.

The broadside (a single-sheet, cheap, printed version of the words only) and the songster (a small collection of such texts, also cheaply printed for popular sale) have long figured in ballad history, both here and in the British Isles. Broadside ballads were usually hastily written (using preexisting material liberally) by hack writers for quick sale to capitalize on current public events, such as hangings. James W. Day, a blind Kentucky musician who used the pseudonym Jilson Setters, told of writing a ballad about a convicted murderer named Simpson Bush. He took it to the hanging and recalled, "I had my pockets plum full of my song-ballet [*sic*] that I had made up about Bush and that a printer had run off for me on a little hand press at the county seat. I sold every one I had" (Thomas 136–38; Laws 44–45). The broadside appeared in a more up-to-date medium during the famous Scopes trial of 1925, when sixty thousand phonograph recordings of a ballad on the subject were sold on the steps of the courthouse in Dayton, Tennessee, while the trial was going on (Cohen and Seeger).

One example of the interaction between print and sound media on the one hand and oral tradition on the other will close our brief consideration of this complex and fascinating subject. In 1925 Polk Brockman, an early country-music talent scout, heard of a cave death in Kentucky and wired the Reverend Andrew Jenkins in Atlanta, in effect "ordering" a song on the subject. Brockman paid Jenkins twenty-five dollars for the song, plus another twenty-five dollars to make a recording of it, which became popular. This was the origin of the ballad "Floyd Collins," later collected from oral tradition in Virginia, North Carolina, Tennessee, Kentucky, New York, and Utah (Laws 51, 223–24).

OTHER ASPECTS OF THE BALLAD

Before we leave the ballad, there are three other things that are essential to know about it. The first is that ballad-making does not belong solely to the past. The folk movement has many active performers who are not only collectors and compilers but poets and composers as well. One interesting example is the ballad "South Coast," a gambler's tale of love and death written in the 1920s by Lillian Bos-Ross, its setting not the Hebrides but the wild coast of California in the colonial days of the vaquero.

The second thing to realize is that an absolutely integral part of folk song is the style in which it is sung. This includes many aspects, such as tone quality, vocal inflection and embellishment, and subtle variations in rhythm and pitch—all of which are practically impossible to put into printed notation. This points up the importance of field recordings, such as those heard in CDs 1/1 and 1/2, in preserving intact the essence of ballads as sung by traditional carriers.

This brings us to the third important aspect—the distinction, already hinted at, between the *traditional* and the *professional* singer. It is important to understand and distinguish the role of each. Traditional singers are themselves part of the tradition, and their memory constitutes the reservoir of this tradition. Professionals must reach a larger audience and must please and entertain that audience. In doing so they may find it necessary to make changes, large or small, that compromise the tradition somewhat.

But professionals have positive contributions to make as well. They may stimulate interest in, and thus help to preserve, traditional music that would otherwise be lost. They bring to their performances a proven degree of musical talent inherently greater than that of the average "carrier" of the tradition. And their renditions are not going to be marred by the lapses of memory that mutilate many a ballad in the hands of traditional singers. It is true that in rare cases the traditional singer may *become* professional (as did Jean Ritchie, for example), but the two *roles* remain distinct.

FIDDLE TUNES

There is probably no form of rural homespun music so indelibly associated in the popular mind with the American folk scene as the familiar *hoedown*. The fiddle and its tunes provided music to dance to, and the fiddle was long the dominant instrument in rural America.

Hoedowns are rapid dance tunes in duple meter, relatives of the reels and hornpipes of the British Isles. The names and tunes of the most popular hoedowns are well known to any square-dance enthusiast or frequenter of fiddlers' contests: "Lost Indian," "Soldier's Joy," "Devil's Dream," "Leather Britches," "Wag'ner" ("Wagoner"), "Old Joe Clark," "Give the Fiddler a Dram," "Natchez under the Hill," "Sourwood Mountain," and so on.

State Historical Society of Missouri, Columbia

PIONEER LIFE IN MISSOURI IN 1820.

A fiddler's music accompanies the daily activities of a typical Missouri family on the frontier in the early nineteenth century. The fiddle was long the dominant instrument in rural America.

CD 1/6 (1:00)
"Soldier's Joy," Marion
Summer, fiddle, with
guitar and mandolin
backup. Recorded in
Hazard, Kentucky.

"Soldier's Joy" (CD 1/6) like most fiddle tunes, is in binary form—that is, a structure with two distinct parts, or strains, each of which is repeated. Often the first strain is in the middle or low range of the fiddle, and the second, or "high," strain is higher in pitch and played on the top two strings. The following Listening Guide, with timings, will help you to follow the form.

"Soldier's Joy"   LISTENING
                                                                                        GUIDE

0:00   "Warm-up"
        introduction

0:02   First strain

0:08   First strain repeated

0:15   Second ("high") strain

0:22   Second strain repeated

0:29   Return to first strain

0:35   First strain repeated,
        with variation

0:43   Second strain

0:50   Second strain repeated

0:57   Closing tag

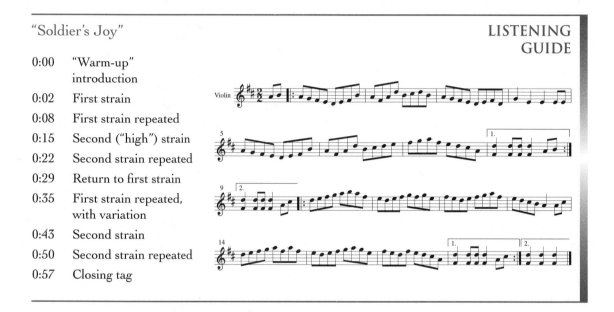

The transcription in the Listening Guide is reasonably close to the way each strain of "Soldier's Joy" is played—at least once! But careful and repeated listening rewards the listener with a growing sense of the fluidity and vitality of oral tradition. A performance in oral tradition is like a Polaroid snapshot of a piece *as it exists in the hands of that particular performer at that particular moment.* Marion Summers hardly plays even a single strain exactly twice in the same way. How does a fiddler think of a fiddle tune? Perhaps as a concept—a *shape* to be roughly but very freely followed; certainly not as a set of written-down notes. "Girl, they ain't no music to them tunes. You jes' play 'em," says the fiddler (Thede 11).

The term breakdown, also frequently applied to this type of fiddle tune, is but one illustration of the frequent exchange between the often parallel musical traditions of blacks and whites. It was a name used in the nineteenth century for any dance in African American style, but especially those popular with white boatmen on the Ohio and the Mississippi (Nathan 92; Twain, Chap. 3).

The jigs are there, too (called in some areas quadrilles)—lively tunes in 6/8 time like "The Irish Washerwoman." The waltz, a seemingly unlikely transplant from central Europe, has wide currency among country fiddlers. Less surprising are the occasional schottisches, with their characteristic dotted rhythms like those of the Scottish *strathspey*. The fiddler's repertory, especially in the lowlands and in the West, has come to include rags and blues. The bulk of Anglo-American fiddle tunes, however, have come more or less directly from the thriving body of reels and hornpipes used for dancing in the British Isles, especially in Scotland and Ireland.

Some individual tunes not in any of these categories have interesting histories. Both "Jordan Is a Hard Road to Travel" and "Old Dan Tucker" were written by Dan Emmett for the professional minstrel stage. And the famous "Bonaparte's Retreat" is a kind of reminiscence of the Battle of Waterloo — possibly, as the solemn drone indicates, having reached the fiddle repertory by way of a bagpipe air.

For an example of country fiddling as practiced in colonial times, listen to "The College Hornpipe" (p. 219, CD 3/13). For accompaniment to a protest song of the 1890s, listen to "The Farmer Is the Man That Feeds Them All" (p. 97, CD 2/8). For an example of fiddling in country ragtime, listen to "Dill Pickles Rag" (p. 292, CD 4/4).

Print and the Fiddle Tune

The complex intertwining of print and oral tradition that we have observed in the case of the ballad has also been at work with the fiddle tune. Despite many fiddlers' independence of, or honest aversion to, notated music, the fact is that fiddle tunes have been collected in written form, at first in manuscript and later to appear in published collections, since at least the early nineteenth century. Elias Howe, a New England fiddler, published in 1840 *The Musician's Companion*, a collection of fiddle tunes that he sold from door to door. He published numerous and ever-larger collections over the next half-century, culminating in a joint venture with Sydney Ryan in 1883 — *Ryan's Mammoth Collection of 1050 Jigs and Reels*. This was reissued by M. M. Cole in 1940 as *1000 Fiddle Tunes*. Sold initially through the Sears Roebuck stores across the nation, it has since become firmly established as the "fiddler's bible."

The Instruments

"Violin" and "fiddle" are usually used as contrasting terms to describe the contrasting uses to which the same instrument is put in the fine-art and folk traditions, respectively. Interestingly enough, the two words come from the same root. The fiddler's instrument may be "store-bought," possibly from a mail-order house. (An old catalog lists "Our Amati Model Violin" for $7.25, while the "Special Stradivarius Model" sells for $9.25, the latter including bow, case, an extra set of strings, an instruction book, and a fingerboard chart (see Christeson, endpaper). But fiddles were often homemade as well.

The standard violin tuning in perfect fifths was used, but so were a number of variants, and for various reasons. To secure a low "drone" string, the G string was sometimes tuned down to an E or even a D; open strings were sometimes duplicated for resonance in a given key. (The standard tuning for "Bonaparte's Retreat," for example, uses three D strings!)

Such were (and are) the marvelous eccentricities and nonconformities of country fiddles and fiddlers. We can say "are" with a degree of assurance that would have seemed unfounded optimism as recently as the 1960s. The old-timers are leaving the scene, to be sure. But there is currently enough interest among younger performers to inspire reasonable confidence that the highly social and contagiously joyous art of country fiddling will not perish for some time to come.

PLAY-PARTY SONGS OR GAMES

Another type of Anglo-Celtic-American folk music occupies a unique niche somewhere between the ballad and the fiddle tune. There are songs that became widely used for a form of organized dancing called the play-party, and so became known as play-party songs or play-party games. They have their origin in the prohibition, in some religious traditions, against dancing as such, but especially against the use of the fiddle, considered an instrument of the devil. (This is nowhere more effectively dramatized than in the short story "Eric Hermannson's Soul" by Willa Cather, which has been made into an opera by American composer Libby Larsen [see pp. 445–47, CD 5/21].)

At the play-party games, the fiddle was banned. Even the word "dance" was forbidden. Vance Randolph describes the events in the Ozarks: "The party-games are really dances, of course, but there is no orchestra; the players furnish their own simple music by singing 'swing-arounds' as they go through their figures, while the spectators clap their hands and stamp their feet as the spirit moves them" (394ff). Play-party games were transcribed, and the games described as they were danced in the Appalachians by Cecil Sharp (P. 2, 367–417).

This derivative of a play-party song (CD 1/7) shows its relation to the dance in the lines "Ladies step forward and the gents fall back" and "First to the left and then to the right" (see Transcription 1.2). The miller was tradition-ally a character of dubious reputation in the community, and the line "One hand on the hopper and the other in the sack" refers to his practice of helping himself to a portion of the meal he was grinding. The song is a combination of

CD 1/7 (1:50)
"Old Man at the Mill," Clint Howard, vocal and guitar; Fred Price, fiddle; Doc Watson, guitar

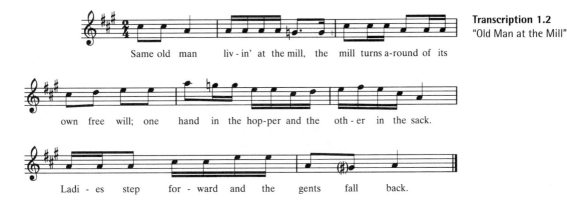

Transcription 1.2
"Old Man at the Mill"

two songs: "The Jolly Miller," a children's game-song that was played over a hundred years ago, and "The Bird Song," collected in the Appalachians in the early years of the twentieth century.

1. "Down," said an owl with its head all white,
   "A lonesome day and a lonesome night.
   Thought I heard some pretty girl say,
   'Court all night and sleep next day.'"

   Refrain

2. Then said a raven, and she flew,
   "If I was a young man I'd have two,
   One for to git and the other for to sow,
   I'll have a little string to my bow, bow, bow."

   Refrain

3. My old man's in Kalamazoo
   And he don't wear no—"Yes, I do!"
   First to the left and then to the right
   This old mill grinds day and night.

   Refrain

Text, "Old Man at the Mill." See Transcription 1.2 for text to the refrain.

(From Folkways Recordings.)

Listen carefully for the musical pitch on the word "mill." It is flatter than the conventional seventh degree of the scale. This is a vestige of the old *modes* (in this case the one called Mixolydian). The modes incorporate certain tones in their scales that differ from those found in the conventional major or minor scales. The Mixolydian, with its flatted seventh degree, is frequently found in folk music, and hence in early country music, and in the harmonies of folk-derived rock, and therefore of much popular music.

▰ PROJECTS

1. Find an example of a traditional ballad sung by a present-day professional singer, and compare it with a version in a printed collection (either words or music, or both).
2. Find some traditional ballads in collections of folk music from your own region. Libraries in your region will emphasize local collections.
3. Make a collection and comparison of ballad refrains, noting the presence or absence of apparently meaningless syllables, words, or phrases.
4. Read Charles Seeger's thought-provoking article "The Folkness of the Non-Folk vs. the Non-Folkness of the Folk," in Jackson Bruce, ed. *Folklore and Society* (Hatboro, PA: Folklore Associates, 1966). Write a brief essay setting forth *your* interpretation of "folkness" and "non-folkness," drawing examples from the life and culture you see around you.

▰ ADDITIONAL LISTENING

Anglo-American Ballads, vol. 1, Rounder CD 1511.

Anglo-American Songs and Ballads. Library of Congress: AFS L14.

Versions and Variants of Barbara Allen. Library of Congress: AFS L54. A sampling of the many versions of the ballad "Barbara Allen" can be gained from the above archival issues from the Library of Congress (one has been reissued by Rounder Records). Audio-cassettes of AFS L14 and AFS L54 are available at http://lcweb.loc.gov/folklife/folkcat.html. Listen to other versions by professional folksingers—for example, Pete Seeger, *God Bless the Grass*, Smithsonian/Folkways CD 37232.

"The Buffalo Skinners" is one of the earliest ballads of the West, predating the advent of the cowboys. Several versions are available. One sung by an actual cowboy is included in *Slim Critchlow: Cowboy Songs*, Arhoolie CD 479; one sung by a famous collector, John Lomax, is on *Cowboy Songs, Ballads, and Cattle Calls from Texas*, Rounder CD 1512; and one sung by a famous professional, Pete Seeger, is on *Industrial Ballads*, Smithsonian/Folkways CD 40058.

CHAPTER

2 The African American Tradition

AFRICAN MUSIC AND ITS RELATION TO BLACK MUSIC IN AMERICA

As we begin our study of African American music, two questions occur immediately: To what extent is it African, and what evidence do we have of its African-ness? (This question is not new. A title such as "The Survival of

African Music in America" has a contemporary ring: actually, it is the title of an article published in 1899 [Murphy]).

In the Western Hemisphere, African survivals are strongest on the north and east coasts of South America, and in the islands of the Caribbean (the latter including, culturally, French-dominated Louisiana until the twentieth century). These were areas of large plantations, with a high percentage of blacks in the population, where minimal attempts were made during slavery to control the activities of blacks when not at work. In what is now the United States, African traits survived less vigorously, for a variety of reasons; among them were the smaller ratio of blacks to whites, their more direct supervision by slave masters, their conversion in fairly large numbers to Christianity, and the attempts to repress African customs by those who regarded them (especially the dancing, which is nearly inseparable from music in African culture) as lascivious, immoral, and pagan.

Nevertheless, African culture unquestionably persisted, and there were early opportunities to observe its survival in the customary celebrations on special occasions. In the South under slavery, Christmas and Easter were traditionally occasions for "jubilees," and before the mid–nineteenth century colorful public festivities such as 'Lection Day in New England (in May or June), Pinkster (which immediately followed Pentecost, or *Pinksteren* in Dutch) in New York, and the Sunday afternoon dancing in Congo Square in New Orleans furnished ample evidence of the survival of African music and dance in antebellum America. (For further information on African survivals, see Southern, *Music*; Southern, *Readings*; Epstein; Maultsby.)

One geographical area in the United States noted for its exceptional preservation of African music, language, and customs is that of the sea islands off the coast of Georgia and South Carolina. Here, in relative isolation, numbers of black people, often living in extreme poverty, retained Africanisms in music, speech, and customs well into the twentieth century. This area has been a rich mine for folklorists and anthropologists.

African music is vast and complex. Continentwide it is far from homogeneous. The greatest influence in America has been from West Africa. Certain outstanding traits that have marked correspondences with black music in America are very audible in "Music in Praise of a Yoruban Chief" (CD 1/8). Most obvious is the dominance of *rhythm*, manifested in a number of ways: a highly developed metronome sense—the sense of an inexorably steady pulse governing the music; a high degree of rhythmic complexity and diversity; and the corresponding dominance of percussion instruments. Another trait, having to do with musical form, is the use of short vocal phrases, repeated and varied, against a continuous rhythmic background. The choral singing in this example gives further evidence of the predominance worldwide of the pentatonic scale.

CD 1/8 (2:00)
"Music in Praise of
a Yoruban Chief."
Recorded by Moses Asch.

Transcription 2.1
"Music in Praise of a Yoruban Chief"

(See pp. 3, 5–6.) The persistent pattern of the choral phrases is shown in Transcription 2.1.

Harold Courlander, in the liner notes for this source recording, explains the importance of the Yoruba as a cultural group of the Guinea Coast of West Africa, concentrated primarily in southwestern Nigeria. Their drumming styles, and even versions of the drums themselves, are to be found in Cuba and Trinidad, and are a significant influence in the Latin/Caribbean music of New York City. (See pp. 77–78.)

RELIGIOUS FOLK MUSIC: THE SPIRITUAL

CD 1/9 (1:02)
"Sheep, Sheep, Don't You Know the Road" (excerpt), Sea Island Singers, Bessie Jones, leader. Recorded by Alan Lomax on St. Simons Island, Georgia, 1961.

There is no better introduction to the spiritual than "Sheep, Sheep, Don't You Know the Road" (CD 1/9). It illustrates musical traits common to the music of both West Africa and African America. The metronome sense is evident, and even though there are no percussion instruments, the basic "drumbeat" is present in the foot tapping that is heard and in the backbeat that is clapped. (This offbeat *reaction* to the beat is typical of African American music, especially very rhythmic vocal music; it is a frequent audience response to the beat.) Call-and-response is a common trait of both African and African American music. Transcription 2.2 shows this typical pattern, and also shows again the use of the pentatonic scale.

Transcription 2.2
"Sheep, Sheep, Don't You Know the Road"

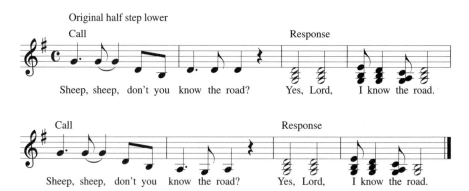

Photo by Frederick Ramsey

Members of Holiness Church near Marion, Alabama participate in the choral singing of spirituals. The rhythmic background is provided here by percussive instruments (the cymbals) and by clapping.

This is the first known recording of this spiritual. After it was made, the Sea Island Singers, with the help of Alan Lomax, were organized and toured in the United States for a decade.

Another example of the folk spiritual is "Low Down the Chariot and Let Me Ride" (CD 1/10). This beautiful spiritual illustrates both the call-and-response pattern and the metronome sense, whereby the rhythmic pulse is present without any percussion (although the foot-tapping beat is barely audible).

CD 1/10 (2:03). "Low Down the Chariot and Let Me Ride," Dock Reed and Vera Hall. Recorded by Harold Courlander in Alabama in the early 1950s.

Text, "Low Down the Chariot and Let Me Ride"

(Call)	*(Response)*
1. Let me ride,	. . . let me ride
Oh let me ride,	. . . let me ride,
Oh let me ride,	. . . let me ride,
Oh low down the chariot and let me ride.	

2. I'm humble to ride

3. Got a right to ride

4. Got a ticket to ride

5. My mother done rid

6. Train coming

7. I'm a soldier

8. My father done rid

Notice that the "chariot" symbol from biblical imagery becomes transformed into the "train," a frequent image in both the spiritual and the blues ("Train coming . . . Got a ticket to ride . . . my mother done rid . . ."). Some listeners may be able to detect that Vera Hall's response to the first call on what would be the seventh degree of the scale is slightly flat according to conventional tuning. Here we make the acquaintance of the "blues seventh," such a characteristic inflection in the spirituals, in gospel music, in the blues, and in jazz. The flatted seventh degree of the scale was pointed out in "Old Man at the Mill" (CD 1/7) as a frequent feature of Anglo-Celtic music as well. But in African American music, as the blues seventh, it is more flexible and subject to "bending." The validity of mutual influence between the blues scale and the European modal scales is dubious.

The term spiritual (derived from a shortening of the New Testament phrase "spiritual songs") has been applied to two related bodies of folk music that began to flourish notably in the nineteenth century—one black and the other white, with a great deal of interchange between them. (An example of a white spiritual, "Wondrous Love," is found on p. 187, CD 3/1. A similar African American spiritual, with the same words, was found in a collection published in 1882. See Jackson 177.)

The African American spiritual came into being following the conversion of significant numbers of slaves to Christianity. The religious singing of blacks in colonial times is reported in a few contemporary observations, of which the often-quoted one by Rev. Samuel Davies in the mid-1700s is representative:

> I can hardly express the pleasure it affords me to turn to that part of the Gallery where they sit, and see so many of them with their Psalm or Hymn Books, turning to the part then sung, and assisting their fellows who are beginners, to find the place; and then all breaking out in a torrent of sacred harmony, enough to bear away the whole congregation to heaven.

This describes the singing of blacks in the context of a formal religious service. But the spiritual itself was born under far less formal circumstances. The real spiritual represents not so much an *adaptation* of the Methodist and Baptist hymns and formal services as a thoroughly African *response* to them.

Many accounts confirm that the "sperichils" were not at first a part of the formal services but belonged to the *shout* that took place *after* these services, when the benches were pushed back to the wall and the worshipers stood in the middle of the floor. The shouters were really in a sense dancers, forming a *ring* in which they circled in a kind of shuffling movement to the sound of singing and hand clapping. The ring itself was significant as a distinctly

African heritage. The shout could last well into the night. "Run, Old Jeremiah" is a vivid example of this (see Additional Listening). The shout was viewed with disapproval by pious whites, and even by the African Methodist Episcopal Church itself, which tried to curb the shout (called by some the "Voodoo Dance") and the spirituals themselves, which were labeled "corn-field ditties."

The Discovery, Publication, and Adaptation of the Spirituals

The Civil War and its aftermath brought whites from the North, many of them abolitionists, into direct contact with black people for the first time. Even before the war's end, events such as the formation of black regiments fighting for the Union cause, and the famous "Port Royal experiment," began the process of acquainting Northerners with the songs of the slaves. (In the Port Royal experiment teachers and missionaries from the North were recruited to teach and supervise thousands of African Americans on Carolina Sea Island plantations abandoned by white owners and overseers as a result of the Union blockade of the coast.) Written accounts of the singing appeared in northern periodicals, some with texts of spirituals. In 1867 the first collection of African American spirituals was published in book form, *Slave Songs of the United States* (Allen, Ware, and Garrison). This justly famous collection includes a number of spirituals well known today, although some are more familiar in later variants. These include "Roll, Jordan, Roll," "Michael, Row the Boat Ashore," "Nobody Knows the Trouble I've Had," and "Good News, Member." There were also a number of secular songs, among them work songs ("Heave away, Heave away! I'd rather court a yellow gal than work for Henry Clay") and a number of Louisiana Creole songs in patois French. Altogether a rather broad collection!

After the Civil War a number of schools and colleges were established in the South, under the auspices of the Freedmen's Bureau and various church and missionary groups, to begin the great task of educating the newly freed slaves. The Fisk Jubilee Singers, from Fisk University, had an important role in letting the spirituals be heard, first in their Nashville community, then throughout the northern states, and finally in Europe. Their moving story, with its trials and triumphs, inspired other colleges and choral groups (Southern, *Music* 225–28).

Solo singers also performed spirituals. Although white soloists began including them in their programs in the 1920s, it was great black artists such as Roland Hayes, Paul Robeson, and Marian Anderson who sang them with the greatest effectiveness and meaning, and established their stature in the repertoire of solo song.

CD 1/11 (3:00) "Jacob's
Ladder," Paul Robeson,
vocal

Paul Robeson (1898–1976) was a noted actor as well as a singer. He played in Eugene O'Neill's *The Emperor Jones* in 1925, the same year he began giving concerts as a bass-baritone. He was famous as an actor for his playing of Shakespeare's Othello, and as a singer for his singing of "Ol' Man River" in Jerome Kern's *Showboat,* and especially for his performances of black spirituals.

Thus the spiritual, in what might be termed its concert phase—written down, harmonized, arranged, and provided with a piano accompaniment—was launched. Though valid and highly moving music, it should not be confused with African American religious folk song as it originally existed, or as it has continued to exist down to our own time in the churches and camp meetings of the South.

The Words of the Spiritual

Not all African American folk music is religious. Many black people regard the blues as sinful music, and even if we view their condemnation as the product of a particular tradition of religious orthodoxy, we can also recognize that between the broad epic and moral connotations of "Go Down, Moses" and the self-centered eroticism of "The Black Snake Moan" there is indeed a great gulf fixed. Nevertheless, the lines of demarcation between sacred and secular are far from rigid. Thus, the biblical imagery so pervasive in the spiritual may also appear in the work song (see CD 1/14).

> Well, God told Norah.
> Hammer, ring . . .
> You is a-goin' in the timber.
> Hammer, ring . . .

It may even occasionally crop up in the blues.

> I went down in Death valley, nothin' but the tombstones and dry bones,
>   (repeated)
> That's where a poor man be, Lord, when I'm dead and gone.

No image was either too humble or too intimately connected with daily life to be used.

> Cryin' what kind o' shoes am dose you wear, . . .
> Cryin' dese shoes I wear am de Gospel shoes, . . .
> I know my robe's gwinter fit me well,
> I'm gwinter lay down my heavy load.
> I tried it on at de gates of hell,
> I'm gwinter lay down my heavy load.

Spirituals have drawn deeply upon a thorough acquaintance with biblical narrative and symbol, as dramatized through the generations by many a gifted and anonymous backwoods preacher. So immense is their number and range that they constitute *in toto* an epic re-creation, in folk fashion, of virtually the entire Bible, from Genesis:

> He made the sun an' moon an' stars,
> To rule both day an' night;
> He placed them in the firmament,
> An' told them to give light.

to Revelation:

> De Lord spoke to Gabriel,
> Fare you well, Fare you well;
> Go look behin' de altar,
> Fare you well, Fare you well.
> Take down de silvah trumpet,
> Fare you well, Fare you well.
> Blow yo' trumpet Gabriel;
> Fare you well, Fare you well.

Instances abound of the vivid pictorial imagery brought to their subjects by anonymous black poets.

> Dark clouds a-risin'!
> Thunder-bolts a-bustin'!
> Master Jesus comes a-ridin' by
> With a rainbow on his shoulder.

The generally assumed anonymity of the authors was not universal; the existence of individual African American "bards" in the late nineteenth century has been documented. James Weldon Johnson describes "Singing" Johnson, who went from church to church making up, singing, and teaching new songs to the congregation. (Johnson and Johnson, Preface).

It was once commonly believed that spirituals represented solely an otherworldly view, that they expressed the consolation that African Americans found in religion for their intolerable worldly conditions, and that the promises and hopes referred only to life in the hereafter. Evidence for a contrasting view, however—a view of spirituals' *concrete relationship* to contemporary conditions—began to be put forward in the nineteenth century by abolitionist writers and others.

In this view spirituals express (or cloak) in biblical terms not only the wretchedness of slavery but also hopes and plans for an escape from its bondage in this life. This could come about either through northern intervention (thus "de Lord" could stand for a collective embodiment of "de Yankees") or through escape ("steal away") to the North ("heab'n") or to Canada ("Canaan"). The secret meetings to which the faithful were called ("Go down in de lonesome valley") kept hope and morale alive, spread news, and laid plans. The yearning for a "home" encouraged by the colonization projects could be expressed as a reliance on the "old ship of Zion" that would "take us all home"—or even as the hope for a Moses who would smite and divide the broad waters ("deep river") so that the slaves could miraculously pass over— back to Africa. The figure of Moses was quite naturally a very central one. The Israelites were the slaves, longing for deliverance; Pharaoh represented the slaveowners; Egypt (or alternatively Babylon) was the South and slavery. The famous "Go Down, Moses" hardly needs interpretation to see its relevance to the black people in slavery.

> When Israel was in Egypt's land,
> Let my people go.
> Oppressed so hard they could not stand,
> Let my people go.
> Go down, Moses,
> 'Way down in Egypt's land;
> Tell ole Pharaoh,
> Let my people go.

The Music of the Spiritual

As with all folk music, what we see in print cannot convey anything like the full effect of the music as sung. As William Francis Allen wrote in 1867,

> The best we can do, however, with paper and types, or even with voices, will convey but a faint shadow of the original. The voices of the colored people have a peculiar quality that nothing can imitate; and the intonations and delicate variations of even one singer cannot be reproduced on paper. And I despair of conveying any notion of the effect of a number singing together, especially in a complicated shout, like "I can't stay behind, my Lord," or "Turn, sinner, turn O!" There is no singing in *parts*, as we understand it, and yet no two appear to be singing the same thing—the leading singer starts the words of each verse, often improvising, and the others, who "base" him, as it is called, strike in with the refrain, or even join in the solo, when the words are familiar. When the

"base" begins, the leader often stops, leaving the rest of his words to be guessed at, or it may be they are taken up by one of the other singers. And the "basers" themselves seem to follow their own whims, beginning when they please and leaving off when they please, striking an octave above or below . . . or hitting some other note that chords, so as to produce the effect of a marvelous complication and variety, and yet with the most perfect time, and rarely with any discord. And what makes it all the harder to unravel a thread of melody out of this strange network is that, like birds, they seem not infrequently to strike sounds that cannot be precisely represented by the gamut, and abound in "slides from one note to another, and turns and cadences not in articulated notes." (Preface)

This description tells us much about the singing, in fact. It confirms at least four distinct points. First, the subtlety and variety of vocal delivery is noted: the "intonations and delicate variations," the "sounds that cannot be precisely represented by the gamut," the "slides from one note to another." Second, we are definitely reminded that this is communal singing; unlike the more solitary blues, it calls for the participation, the interaction, of a closely knit society of singers, all feeling the same impulsion to break into song. Third, though it is choral singing, there is usually a leader to whom the rest of the group responds, although not with the drilled rhythmic precision of trained choirs. And fourth, we are reminded of the important role of improvisation—the spur-of-the-moment variations wrought spontaneously by the singers. This is a trait particularly associated with black music. "No two African performances are identical," says A. M. Jones, and the description applies equally to American blues, American jazz, and the African American spiritual.

One further observation, implicit in early descriptions, must be added; there was, in most cases, no accompaniment by instruments. The use of piano, guitar, tambourine—even, in some cases, trumpet or trombone—was a later addition belonging more to gospel songs.

The Survival of the Folk Spiritual

Folk spirituals have indeed survived in popular culture, and the description deduced from Allen's observation of 1867 may be reviewed as a quite accurate description of rural spiritual singing as it has survived into our own time. Fortunately, some of this old-style singing was recorded in the 1930s and 1940s. The spiritual has provided material and inspiration for many subsequent forms. Though it is still cultivated to some extent in the old style as a folk form, it was inevitable that African American religious music would over time reflect changing social and cultural patterns. The story is continued in Chapter 11, which deals with the emergence of gospel music.

SECULAR FOLK MUSIC

Cries, Calls, and Hollers

A kind of musical expression among black people that is at once primordial and evocative is found in the cries, calls, and hollers. Early observers described these occasionally. Frederick Olmsted, reporting on a journey through the South in 1853, tells of being awakened in his railroad car in the middle of the night by a gang of black workmen enjoying a brief break around a fire.

> Suddenly one raised such a sound as I had never heard before, a long, loud, musical shout, rising, and falling, and breaking into falsetto, his voice ringing through the woods in the clear, frosty night air, like a bugle call. As he finished, the melody was caught up by another, then by several in chorus. (Courlander 81–82)

These cries and calls—of the field, the levee, the track—were highly individualized expressions, for communication, for relieving loneliness, for giving vent to feelings, or simply for expressing the fact of one's existence. Their city counterparts, the street cries, were more utilitarian: they advertised goods and services. Both types have all but disappeared from their original setting. A few have been recorded. Musically, they are florid, melismatic vocalizations, based on a single interval, a single chord, or a pentatonic or modal scale, with embellishing tones and often certain "blue" notes of variable pitch. In fact, the embryonic blues scale is so apparent in some of these calls that it will be well to introduce its main features here. This will serve as a reminder of the close relation between some of these solitary, highly individualized calls and hollers and the primitive rural blues. For this purpose, we shall examine one call in some detail. It is a cornfield holler, or *arwhoolie* (are-hoo´-lee), specifically a "Quittin' Time Song."

CD 1/12 (0:33)
"Quittin' Time Song,"
Thomas J. Marshall

"Quittin' Time Song," heard on CD 1/12, may be notated (though only approximately!) as shown in Transcription 2.3. It will be noted that there are only three essential pitch areas: a high one (which may be called the *dominant*), on which nearly all the phrases begin; a low one (which may be called the *final*), on which they all end; and an important area a third above the final, a *mediant*. The first two are relatively stable in pitch, but the mediant is variable. It sometimes gives a definite impression of major (marked with a sharp); sometimes it sounds minor, and sometimes ambiguous (indeterminately in between major and minor).

Transcription 2.3
"Quittin' Time Song"

If we were to add to this scale a second area of variable pitch a third above the dominant, we would have the bare bones of the traditional blues scale.

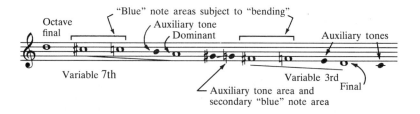

Transcription 2.4
Complete blues scale

Playing this music on an instrument of fixed and equal temperament such as the piano gives a highly conventionalized and falsified impression of its subtly inflected and extremely fluid nature as performed by the voice, whether in spirituals, hollers, or blues. Thus our conventional concept of this variable-pitched scale is a somewhat mechanized and secondhand one.

Incipient Blues

CD 1/13 (1:10)
"I Don't Mind the Weather," Jim Henry. Recorded in Parchman, Mississippi, 1937.

African American cries, calls, and hollers were intensely personal expressions, and this is also one of the most important characteristics of the blues. When we listen to "I Don't Mind the Weather" (CD 1/13), we realize how this kind of elemental song gradually approaches the rural blues in proportions, and in range and explicitness of expression.

Text, "I Don't Mind the Weather"

Mmmm _____
Boys, I've got a boychild in Texas, he ought to be 'bout grown
O _____
Go marchin' to the table, O Lord, find the same old thing.
Ummm _____
Boys, I'll be so glad when payday comes.
O _____
Captain, captain, when payday comes,
I'm gonna catch that Illinois Central, O Lord, goin' to Kankakee.
Mmmm _____

Note that this field holler, and incipient blues, begins with the blues seventh. (See Transcription 2.4.) The subjective impulses evident in both this and the previous example—the spontaneous reflection, either on the immediate situation (darkness coming on, the prospect of a tasteless meal, waiting for payday) or on deeper longings or regrets ("I've got a boychild in Texas, he ought to be 'bout grown")—are typical of what later became the blues. In a more tightly knit stanza form of four repeated lines, still unaccompanied, is the rather haunting "Another Man Done Gone" (see Additional Listening). Both songs are about prison life—the first from a man who looks forward to getting out and leaving the South, the second reporting in enigmatic language about the escape of a man from a county chain gang. The blues themselves are treated in Chapter 8.

Work Songs and Ballads

The use of singing to coordinate and lighten physical work, acting as both a coordinator of effort and a lifter of spirits, is practically universal among men who must engage in hard communal labor, on land or sea. Work songs were prevalent among black laborers during slavery; even spirituals could be used in this way, and some of the earliest collected songs (such as "Michael, Row the Boat Ashore") had this duality of function about them. After the Civil War, work songs were needed wherever gang labor was used, especially in the work of building railroads. There had to be a leader, of course; this called for a special skill involving not only a firsthand knowledge of the work and its pacing and a gift for timing but also the ability to infuse into the work the balm of rhythm and song. A few of the recordings we possess of genuine work songs communicate this sense of rhythm and spirit. With increased mechanization the work song almost disappeared. The only conditions under which it survived were those that closely duplicated conditions under slavery—that is, in the prisons and on the work farms, where, indeed, practically all the field recordings of work songs were made.

The ballad and the work song are dissimilar in function. However, the leader's need to prolong the work song to fit the task at hand often led to the adoption of the ballad, or storytelling, method, with its possibilities for improvisation and its indefinite proliferation of stanzas. "Hammer, Ring," a work song used in railroad building to coordinate the driving of spikes to fasten the long steel rails to the ties, is a long-drawn-out balladlike song that recounts the story of "Norah" and the building of the ark.

CD 1/14 (0:50) "Hammer Ring," Jesse Bradley and group, vocal. Recorded in southern United States between 1933 and 1940.

Refrain Won't you ring, old hammer.	Hammer ring! [2X]
Broke the handle on my hammer.	Hammer ring! [2X]
Got to hammerin' in the Bible.	Hammer ring! [2X]
Refrain Won't you ring, old hammer.	Hammer ring! [2X]
Goin' to talk about Norah. [Noah]	Hammer ring! [2X]
Well God told Norah,	Hammer ring! [2X]
You argue some Bible.	Hammer ring! [2X]
Refrain Oh, ring, old hammer.	Hammer ring! [2X]

Text, "Hammer Ring" (excerpt)

"John Henry" (CD 1/15) is the best known of all African American ballads. It is the ballad of a folk hero, although the theme of "man versus machine" is not always explicit. Songs about John Henry are of two general types: ballad or, in truncated form, "hammer" song (frequently a blues), which includes lines referring to some feature of the ballad. In this particular version it is sung as a combination of ballad and work song, similar to "Hammer, Ring" cited earlier.

The tale has been identified with an actual event: the construction of the Big Bend Tunnel on the Chesapeake & Ohio Railroad near Hilton, West Virginia, in 1870–72. At a mile and a quarter in length, it was the largest tunnel ever built up to that time. A steel drill had to be hand-driven to make a deep

CD 1/15 (2:53). "John Henry," Arthur Bell, vocal. Recorded by John A. and Ruby T. Lomax at Cumins State Farm, Gould, Arkansas, 1939.

hole in the solid rock for a blasting charge. The construction of the Big Bend Tunnel may have been the occasion of the introduction of a newly invented steam drill to do this work, and a contest between hand driving and steam driving may well have occurred—a contest that the hero won at the cost of his life. On the other hand, John Henry may actually have died in one of the frequent cave-ins that occurred.

This version of "John Henry" (CD 1/15), coming from farther west, in Arkansas, changes the job from that of driving a blasting-hole in a tunnel to lining track. Note the wandering filler line "the dress that she wo' was red," which, as in "John Hardy" (CD 1/4), conveniently provides a rhyme for "dead." The last two stanzas of this version of "John Henry" are both rare and puzzling. For more information and speculation on this ballad, see Alan Lomax, *Folk Songs of North America*, pages 551–53, in References for Chapter 1.

1. Well, every Monday mornin',
   When the bluebirds begin to sing,
   You can hear those hammers a mile or more,
   You can hear John Henry's hammer ring, O Lordy!
   Hear John Henry's hammer ring.

2. John Henry told his old lady,
   "Will you fix my supper soon?
   Got ninety miles o' track I've got to line,
   Got to line it by the light of the moon, O Lordy!
   Line it by the light o' the moon."

3. John Henry had a little baby,
   He could hold him out in his hand;
   Well, the last word I heard that po' child say,
   "My daddy is a steel-drivin' man, O Lordy!
   Daddy is a steel-drivin' man."

4. John Henry told his old captain,
   Said, "A man ain't nothin' but a man;
   Before I let your steel gang down
   I will die with the hammer in my hand, O Lordy!
   Die with the hammer in my hand."

5. John Henry told his captain,
   "Next time you go to town
   Uh-jes' bring me back a ten-pound maul
   For to beat your steel-drivin' down, O Lordy!
   Beat your steel-drivin' down."

6. John Henry had a old lady,
   And her name was Polly Ann.
   John Henry tuck sick and he had to go to bed;
   Pauline drove steel like a man, O Lordy!
   'Line drove steel like a man.

7. John Henry had a old lady,
   And the dress she wo' was red.
   Well, she started up the track and she never looked back,
   "Goin' where my man fell dead, O Lordy!
   Where my man fell dead."

8. Well, they taken John Henry to Washington,
   And they buried him in the sand.
   There is peoples from the East, there's peoples from the West
   Come to see such a steel-drivin' man, O Lordy!
   See such a steel-drivin' man.

9. Well, some said-uh he's from England,
   And some say he's from Spain;
   Bu-uh I say he's nothin' but a Lou's'ana man,
   Just a leader of the steel-drivin' gang, O Lordy!
   Leader of the steel-drivin' gang.

The metric structure of this version of "John Henry" invites comparison with the Anglo-Celtic-American ballads in Chapter 1. Here the succession of stressed syllables is 3-3-4-3.

     /   /   /
Well, every Monday mornin',

       /   /   /
When the bluebirds begin to sing,

       /   /   /   /
You can hear those hammers a mile or more,

      /   /   / [extension]
You can hear John Henry's hammer ring, O Lordy!

[extension]
Hear John Henry's hammer ring.

This is called Short Meter in hymnody, and the arrangement of the stressed syllables is that of the limerick. The singer's extensions at the ends of the stanzas are similar to Woody Guthrie's in "Gypsy Davy" (pp. 7–9, CD 1/3).

Students of the African American ballad such as Malcolm Laws have pointed out the fecundity of invention that manifests itself in improvisation. This propensity to improvise may account for the inclusion of apparently incoherent additions such as can be noted in the version of "John Henry" above. But improvisation also gives rise to greater variety and spontaneity in ballad creation and singing by African Americans.

Laws also notes, in comparison with white balladry, a greater empathy with the often unfortunate subjects of the ballads. This is nowhere more evident than in the number and variety of ballads on the sinking of the *Titanic*. The black *Titanic* ballads, unlike the white versions, often invoke a religious interpretation; "God moves on the water" is a frequent phrase. Versions in print are found in Sandburg (254) and Lomax and Lomax (26). The clearest, most coherent, and complete recorded version is a seven-stanza one in *Georgia Sea Island Songs* (NW 80278). Laws writes that the black balladeer "is so keenly aware of the truth and realism of the story he tells that he holds his listeners by his own sincerity" and adds that "these narrative folksongs of the Negro are moving and intense, and they have added immeasurably to the richness of American balladry" (94). In the memorializing of great public disasters in ballads, is it possible that we might look for more moving and intense balladry, black or white, on the even greater disaster of September 11, 2001?

◼ PROJECTS

1. Write a short paper on the South Carolina and Georgia Sea Islands as repositories of black folklore, speech, and song. Include whatever you can find out about conditions there today.
2. Review some of the significant studies that have been made of African survivals in American black music. Some of these are by Melville Herskovits, Alan Merriam, Harold Courlander, Richard Waterman, and Paul Oliver (*Savannah Syncopators*).
3. Write a short paper on textual themes in African American spirituals, including the double meanings they contain. (John Lovell's *Black Song: The Forge and the Flame*, his article in Katz, *The Social Implications of Early Negro Music in the United States*, and Sterling Brown, *Negro Poetry and Drama* could serve as points of departure.)
4. Compare a traditional version of a spiritual (as found in an early collection such as Allen et al., *Slave Songs of the United States*) with a concert version as sung by a recitalist or a trained concert choir. Discuss the advantages and disadvantages of such concert arrangements.

◼ ADDITIONAL LISTENING

"Another Man Done Gone." *Afro-American Blues and Game Songs*. Rounder CD 1513.

"Run, Old Jeremiah." *Afro-American Spirituals, Work Songs, and Ballads*. Rounder CD 1510.

The American Indian Tradition   3

Our First People have the right to be called by their proper names—names that belong to their own individual tribes or nations: Navajo, Kiowa, Lakota, Miwok, and so on. It is where a collective name is needed (a need that did not arise before the arrival of the white man) that we are faced with a dilemma. The term "native American," still in many quarters dutifully accepted as socially and politically correct, is a cumbersome designation whose actual meaning is wide of the mark. The primary meaning of "native" is simply "being the place or environment in which a person was born" ("Native," def. 1). Everyone is a native of someplace, and there are by now hundreds of millions of us who are natives of nowhere else but the United States of America—and therefore native Americans. The name "Indian" is, in its genesis, a geographical misnomer. Though a mistake of history, it has by this time the weight and dignity of history, and is in fact the name used by the First People themselves. Until a more suitable name can be found, by an age less obsessed with well-meaning but inaccurate euphemisms, we shall in this book continue the precedent set by previous editions, and take our cue from the name of the Smithsonian Institute's long-awaited National Museum of the American Indian.

It is estimated that at the time of the first European exploration and colonization, some three million people lived in North America, between one and two million of them north of what is now Mexico. The population consisted of a thousand different tribal units, each generally having its own language, belonging to one of approximately sixty language families. The cultural complexity resulting from the 25,000-year history of the aborigines in North America is largely accounted for by the fact that the waves of migration from Asia were widely separated in time. This is illustrated by the fact that the language families are not necessarily identified or coincident with the culture areas, as defined in the next paragraph. The Navajo and the Apache of the desert Southwest, for example, have a language related to that of the tribes of the far north of Canada and Alaska.

The music of the North American Indians has many characteristics shared by all; this fact has given a limited validity to the concept of generic, or pan-Indian, music. But there are significant distinctions as well—characteristics that can be identified more or less successfully with eight roughly defined culture areas: Southeast and Northeast (both east of the Mississippi), Plains, Southwest (including most of California), Great Basin, Northwest Coast (from northern coastal California to and including coastal Alaska), Plateau (north of the Great Basin, between the Northwest Coast area and the Rocky

Mountains), and North (Arctic and Sub-Arctic, including the Athapaskan and Inuit, or Eskimo, peoples). (See Nettl, *North American;* Nettl, "Indians.") The culture area of origin, if not the actual tribe, from which each of the musical examples in this chapter originates can be read from the CD designations, and the musical characteristics will be noted briefly; however, the reader should be warned that generalizations drawn solely from so few examples are not well supported.

When we study Indian music, we are dealing with the music of indigenous societies that once were aboriginal cultures but are so no longer. In the 300-odd years during which the whites completed their westward advance across the continent, aboriginal Indian life was thoroughly disrupted. Indigenous societies were dispossessed and their populations drastically reduced by disease and warfare; some tribal groups were destroyed, and most others were relocated or confined on reservations, where they were first treated as a conquered, subject population. As a consequence, large elements of aboriginal cultural ways, including some musical elements, disappeared—destroyed, discarded, lost, or altered beyond modern recognition. One of the most remarkable things about American Indian musical culture is that a significant remnant of it has indeed survived.

Not only has it survived, but it has also entered a new phase of cultivation. It will therefore be necessary to treat American Indian music in two distinct, though related, aspects: first, what can be learned of it as an integral part of the culture of an aboriginal people; and second, Indian music as it exists today.

MUSIC IN ABORIGINAL INDIAN LIFE

There are two ways to view an artistic artifact. The first is as a thing of interest and beauty in and of itself. The second is as a component of the complete context of the society that brought it forth, having essential meaning only in that context. These views are never absolutely separate; we experience every art object with some mixture of the two. But the closer we get to art in the aboriginal state, the more necessary it becomes to take into account the second view. Though never abandoning the study and apprehension of a work of art intrinsically, we must give a much greater proportion of our effort to understanding what the lives of those who made the art were like, and what place and meaning it had for them. This is in no case more imperative than with the music of the Indian people.

Whatever one's immediate reaction to Indian music, one must realize that it was never created to be experienced in the essentially passive way in which we listen to music in the concert hall or on recordings. Its ambience determines its essence. As Willard Rhodes has said, "Primitive music is so inextricably bound up in a larger complex, ceremonial or social, that it is practically non-existent out of its functional context" (132). (The word "primitive" is here used in the *anthropological* sense as "... having cultural or physical similarities with their early ancestors" ["Primitive," def. 4].)

Here is a condensation of a description of a Hopi ceremony that included music, as in fact do most Indian ceremonies:

> With a Hopi acquaintance I drove one July morning to Bakabi, to see the final ritual of the *Niman*. When I arrived in the village, I found that most of the Hopis had ascended to the line of roof tops, from which they could watch the ceremony in the plaza below. . . . The sky was cloudless and intensely blue. Sunshine flooded everything, illuminating the white walls of the houses along the plaza's farther side. . . . Soon a file of fifteen or twenty men came slowly into the plaza. . . . Each man's body, bare above the waist, was painted brown and marked with white symbols. Behind his right knee was fastened a rattle, made of a turtle shell. With each step that he took, the rattle gave out a hollow, muffled sound. In his right hand he carried a gourd rattle. . . . But the striking feature was the mask that each man wore. This covered his head completely and came down to his shoulders. The front was white and was inscribed with block-like figures, which suggested eyes, nose, and mouth. . . . Immediately, the ceremony began. With measured, rhythmic step the long single file moved slowly forward, in time with a subdued chant. . . . With every step the turtle-shell rattle fastened behind the right knee contributed its hollow accent, sometimes suddenly magnified when all the dancers in unison struck the right foot sharply against the ground. Now and then the gourd rattles were shaken for two or three seconds, giving a curious accompaniment of elevated

Photo by R. H. Lowie/American Museum of Natural History

Hopi Indians in full ceremonial dress. Gourd rattles (held in the right hand) and rattles made of turtle shell (tied behind the right knee) accent measured, rhythmic steps as these celebrants slowly move forward in a single file. This scene closely resembles the eyewitness account given above.

sound in contrast to the low, chanting voices. . . . When it was all over, I came away with the feeling that I had witnessed an ancient rite that was rich in symbolism and impressive in its significance. (O'Kane 186–91)

Even if a recording of this music had been made, how much could it convey to us, abstracted from its context?

CONCRETENESS AND EFFICACY OF SONGS

Music in Indian life had also a *concreteness* unknown to sophisticated societies. The abstraction *music* would have been an unfamiliar and useless concept; it was only *this song* that had meaning. The important thing about a song is not its *beauty* but its *efficacy*. Frances Densmore, one of the pioneering authorities on Indian music, has written, "The radical difference between the musical custom of the Indian and our own race is that, primarily, the Indians used song as a means of accomplishing definite results"(63). The following incident illustrates that this view of music is by no means dead. For a recent recording of gambling songs by the Yurok and Tolowa tribes of northern California, translations of the words could not be made because "to do so would put the songs' luck in jeopardy" (Heth).

The degree of concreteness with which Indian songs are viewed is further illustrated by the fact that in many cases they are treated as strictly personal possessions, which may be transmitted to others only by being sold or given away. One old man, after being persuaded to record a noted war song, said that he would not live long now that he had given away his most valuable possession. There is a sense of tangible reality, of magical power, of "presence," in *all* manifestations of what we would term "art" among aboriginal peoples. In the nineteenth century, after an eastern artist had been among the Plains Indians sketching the buffalo, an old Indian complained to a white friend that there were no longer so many buffalo on their range—a white man had put a great number of them in a book and taken them away with him. Is this not indeed an expression of the same magic-imbued worldview that inscribed on rocks and in caves those often remarkably impressionistic likenesses of beasts the hunters needed to kill? It is this world we must be prepared to enter if we would understand what music originally meant to our First People.

"REAL" SONGS AND SONGS FOR RECREATION

Songs of great power, sung chiefly by medicine men or women, would be used in communal ceremonies and would be very carefully passed on in oral tradition. For example, extreme accuracy was (and is) crucial to the efficacy of the songs of the Navajo. There could also be new songs, belonging to men who had acquired them in the course of "vision quests"—self-imposed ordeals of courage and self-denial that were known among virtually all tribes in their aboriginal state. Lonely fasts, often carried out in locations and conditions of extreme discomfort and danger, and lasting as long as four days, would, when successful, result in what appeared as tangible communication with the spirit dwelling in some animal or some natural phenomenon. With the imparting of the vision (which identified the seeker forever afterward with the particular animal, if that were the apparent source) would often come what was received as a new song.

These, then, were the "real" songs—the property either of individuals or of the tribe. A clear distinction was made in most tribes between these songs, which had inherent power, and songs that either were borrowed from other tribes or were made up—consciously composed—and used to enhance various forms of recreation. In recent years, under the pressures of acculturation, the old songs have decreased in importance in the repertory of most tribes. Many that are known to have existed have been lost altogether. The older ceremonial songs are heard in their purer form on the early recordings, sung often by old men whose memories stretch back to a time on the Plains and farther west when little acculturation had yet taken place. It is in this context that one should listen to the oldest recorded song here included, "Pigeon's Dream Song" (see next section).

TYPES OF SONGS ACCORDING TO PURPOSE

Dream Songs and Songs to Heal the Sick

A very important class of songs are those used for healing the sick. These are among the "real" songs. One example is from the Menominee, an Algonquian tribe that at the time this song was collected in the late 1920s, was still living along the Menominee River in Wisconsin, an area they had inhabited for at least three centuries. "Pigeon's Dream Song" (CD 1/16, Transcription 3.1) was used for healing, and was sung by Louis Pigeon.

This song shows the attributes of the Plains style in its descending "terraced" melodic line. Except for a single note, the scale is a very rudimentary four-tone, or tetratonic, scale. The repetition of short phrases as heard in the example is a feature of nearly all North American Indian music.

Frances Densmore recorded this song on portable cylinder equipment in the field. Of Louis Pigeon she says that "when he was a boy he sometimes fasted for two days at a time, abstaining from both food and drink. At last he

CD 1/16 (0:40) "Pigeon's Dream Song," Louis Pigeon. Menominee, Northern Plains.

Transcription 3.1
"Pigeon's Dream Song"

Tetratonic scale (four-tone scale, excluding octave duplications)

secured a dream that gave him power to treat the sick, and said that his own advanced age showed the power of his dream. Two birds [a crow and a raven] gave him songs in this dream." A free translation of the words is "Your tribe will come to you to be cured of sickness."

Ceremonial Dances

CD 1/17 (1:30)
"Cherokee/Creek Stomp Dance," Eastern Woodlands. Recorded in Oklahoma.

The Stomp Dance (CD 1/17) is a series of dances as part of a ceremonial event. Typical of the music of the Southeast is the responsorial form, or *"call-and-response"* procedure, of African American music, but with shorter phrases or shouts. In contrast with the tetratonic scale of "Pigeon's Dream Song," the melodic lines tend to move up and down in thirds and even triads, this contributing to a sense of tonality that gives it a more familiar sound to non-Indians. The singing style is more relaxed than that typical of the Plains tribes. Because of the forcible removal of most of the Cherokee to Oklahoma over a century and a half ago, we find the music native to the Southeastern United States being performed and recorded in the prairies of the southern Midwest.

Songs for Success in War, Hunting, or Agriculture

CD 1/18 (1:30)
"Butterfly Dance," San Juan Pueblo, New Mexico

The Pueblo Indians of the Southwestern deserts, including the Hopi, the Taos, and the Zuni, have the most complex societies to be found north of Mexico, and hence their music is also the most varied and complex. Most noticeable are the frequently changing drum patterns. The phrases are longer and more intricate than those in other Indian music. The scale is pure pentatonic—the scale we have already encountered in Anglo-Celtic-American song (Transcription 1.1, p. 3) and in African music (Transcription 2.1, p. 20). The voices, typically for Pueblo singing, are low and growling in tone. The text metaphorically traces the life cycle of the corn plant, on which the Pueblo people are highly dependent.

Songs for Gambling

Gambling songs apear from the earliest recorded collections to the present. The gambling usually takes the form of a guessing game between two opposing teams. A guesser from one team must choose the location of a marked object (a stick, a bullet, a prune pit, etc.) that has been hidden by the opposing team among like unmarked objects concealed in the hands, under overturned moccasins, and so on. Songs were sung to bring luck; the singer might have assistants, or "seconds," to sing with him if he wished. Gambling was mostly restricted to men, and the stakes could be very high. Regional characteristics apply less to the ubiquitous gambling songs than to other kinds of music. The beat of the drum is fast, and the voice is tense and fairly high in range. The drum heard in this example (CD 1/19), used for gambling songs among the Yurok and the Tolowa, is a square double-headed one, of elk hide stretched on a frame of redwood—of unique design, made from readily available local materials.

CD 1/19 (1:17) "Gambling Song," Yurok, Northwest California

Love Songs

The "love songs" were not, as in our popular culture, for the expression of sentimental feelings but were, rather, "lucky" songs, to secure success in love through the invocation of magical power. The Indian flute was associated almost exclusively with these courtship songs, but they could also be sung, as we hear in this example (CD 1/20). The song has the terraced descending shape associated with the music of the Plains Indians. It has a range of an octave, and the scale is, again, tetratonic.

CD 1/20 (1:43) "Sioux Love Song," Lakota, Plains, John Coloff, flute and vocal

The making and playing of the traditional Indian flute had, until recently, become a thing of the past. Its revival has been marked by the emergence of concertizing and recording flutists such as R. Carlos Nakai, who have expanded its use to include new music composed for it in a variety of styles, both popular and classical. (See CD 1/27.)

Transcription 3.2
"Sioux Love Song"

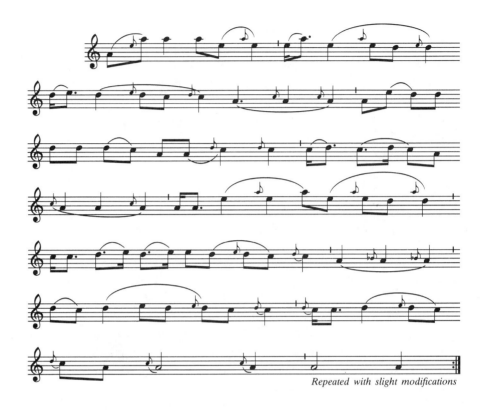

Repeated with slight modifications

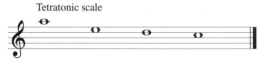

Tetratonic scale

Songs to Accompany Work

CD 1/21 (1:39)
"Corn-Grinding Song,"
Navajo, Southwest.
Recorded at Chinle
(Canyon de Chelly),
Arizona, 1975.

Songs related to work (women's work, that is) exist, as in the Corn-Grinding Songs, though these are not work songs in the sense of those in the African American tradition. Among the Navajo these are sung by the men while the women grind the corn, to imbue it with spiritual quality so that it can be used in ceremonies. Typical of the Navajo is the light singing style, with some pulsations, and the use of intervals from natural overtone series (that is, octaves, fifths, and fourths), giving a tonal sound to the music. Instruments used are a ceremonial basket turned upside down and used as a drum, and a hand rattle.

Social Songs

There are songs for other social functions: to welcome and bid farewell to guests (very elaborate along the northwestern coast); to honor warriors and chieftains; and to use in contests and other purely social ceremonies. Social dancing, with its own music, was originally relatively unimportant, though it has now become much more prevalent—one manifestation of the changes that have come over Indian life.

The "Rabbit Dance" (CD 1/22) is a social dance, in which men and women are allowed to dance together. Though the singing style is clearly that of the Plains, with high, tense, pulsated vocal quality and the phrases shaped in gradually descending lines, it was recorded in California by The Los Angeles Northern Singers—testimony to the extensive relocation of Indians to urban centers such as Denver and Los Angeles. The use of English in one section is possibly satirical. A *forty-nine song* is a particular kind of humorous, often derisive, song with English words. (For a forty-nine song of another Plains tribe, the Comanche, see Additional Listening.)

CD 1/22 (0:55)
"Rabbit Dance,"
Northern Plains

> Hey, sweetheart, I always think of you.
> I wonder if you are alone tonight.
> I wonder if you are thinking of me.

CHARACTERISTICS OF INDIAN MUSIC

Through listening to the preceding, or similar, examples, you will have acquired a practical introduction to the characteristics of Indian music. These can be summed up briefly as follows:

Though Indian music is predominantly vocal, singing is usually accompanied by a drum or some sort of rattle, or both. The basic unit of the music is the song, which may last anywhere from less than a minute to several minutes. When the song accompanies dancing, as it very often does, there is a good deal of repetition; it is common to sing a song four times.

The scales used in Indian music are found generally to correspond to our familiar diatonic scale—that is, the basic scale structure available on the white keys of the piano. Some form of the pentatonic scale (that obtainable on the black keys) is also very common, as is the further reduced four-tone, or tetratonic, scale. Singing in other than the unison (or the octave, if the women sing also) is extremely rare, though not unknown.

Indian instruments include drums, whistles, flutes, hand-shaken rattles, and ornaments worn by dancers (made of shell, bone, or some kind of metal), which produce a rhythmic kind of rattling during the dance. The drums range in size from small handheld ones to quite large ones resting on the ground, or suspended between posts in the ground, and played by several people at once. They are made in a variety of ways and are even improvised from inverted baskets, washtubs or kettles covered with skin, or wooden boxes. Flutes are usually fashioned from some straight-grained wood or cane, but in the Southwest they can be made of clay. Rattles are nearly universal, are of many types, and are often worn on the ankles while dancing. The use of drums alone, without singing, is virtually unknown; this is in distinct contrast to African, and hence to West Indian, tradition. The rhythms of drum and rattle are simple, the impulses usually grouped in pairs in a relation that ranges from perfectly even pulses to those that alternate long-short or heavy-light. Longer songs may be divided into clearly defined sections, with definite tempo changes. The tempo of the drum is sometimes independent of that of the voice.

Since the music is nearly all vocal, the question of the words arises. The songs are very often not in the language of speech. Vocables—simple vocal sounds—often either are interpolated between actual words or replace them altogether. (The fa-la-la refrains of Anglo-American ballads are an interesting parallel.) To call these syllables meaningless is not quite correct; they may have private or ritual significance, or they may be sounds whose original meaning has been lost, either through changes in the language or because they were borrowed from other tribes. Whatever their origin, the vocables are not improvised but belong to the given song and are reproduced with complete consistency.

INDIAN MUSIC AND ACCULTURATION

Acculturation has gone on continuously since the first contacts with the white man. The French Huguenots were teaching the Florida Indians to sing psalms in the sixteenth century, and the Franciscans who traveled to the Rio Grande Valley with the settlers and their military escorts brought Spanish religious festivals and music to New Mexico in the seventeenth century. At the Zuni pueblo of Hawikuh, in western New Mexico, Fray Roque de Figueredo in 1630 was teaching not only Gregorian chant and counterpoint but also bassoon, cornett, and organ (portable organs were brought on expeditions by the Franciscans). Indian music and musicians were perfectly capable of assimilating non-Indian tunes, as a Hopi version of "Dixie" and a Chinook version of "Jesus Loves Me" attest. (See Additional Listening.)

The length of time that the indigenous Americans have been exposed to the white man's culture varies widely from area to area. We know the least about aboriginal Indian music in the eastern United States, where the cultural pressures, and the dispossessions and dispersions, began earliest and were most severe. A single example of a major uprooting has already been alluded to: between 1830 and 1842, Indians from five tribes (the Choctaw, the Creek, the Cherokee, the Chickasaw, and the Seminole) were forced to move (in an episode known as the "Trail of Tears") from the southeastern states to an area west of the Mississippi known as the Indian Territory—and formally so designated until its admission to the Union as the state of Oklahoma in 1907. After the Civil War the western portion of the Indian Territory became home for many Indians from the northern and central Plains as well. This kind of dislocation brought tribes from greatly separated regions into contact, and this contact marked the beginnings of the pan-Indian movement.

The Ghost Dance and the Peyote Religion

Two singular developments in the West since the encroachment of white civilization grew out of that cataclysm, directly or indirectly. The first of these was the spread of the Ghost Dance, with its accompanying music. Originating in the Great Basin area, the Ghost Dance cult represented a kind of messianic religious belief in the appearance of a savior and the expulsion of the white man, accompanied by the resurrection of dead Indian leaders and the return of the buffalo and of the old ways. In the 1880s the Ghost Dance spread rapidly, especially among Plains tribes. It was outlawed by the Bureau of Indian Affairs, and its repression by the United States Army culminated in the tragic massacre of Sioux Ghost Dance devotees at Wounded Knee in South Dakota in 1890. As an active cult and ritual, a vehicle of a fanatical hope, the Ghost Dance died out as rapidly as it had spread. Its songs persisted, however, and were recorded among Plains tribes as late as the 1940s. A Pawnee "Ghost Dance Song"(CD 1/23) is representative.

The Ghost Dance was a pan-Indian cultural phenomenon; Ghost Dance songs of various tribes show similar characteristics, of Great Basin origin, that are often markedly different from those of their own indigenous tribal music. Songs of the Great Basin tribes tended to be simple and of small range, and to consist of short paired phrases (AA BB CC and so on) in a descending line, as can readily be heard in this example.

CD 1/23 (1:07)
"Ghost Dance Song,"
Pawnee, Plains

A second, and not unrelated, development has been the spread of the peyote religion (the Native American Church), the rites of which include the use of the hallucinogenic buttons of the peyote cactus. Originating apparently in pre-Columbian Mexico, it had spread northward into the Rio Grande and Gila River basins by the eighteenth century, where it was known among the Apache. The religion reached the Plains about 1870. Taking on there a somewhat different form, it became a group or community rite, with a well-defined ceremonial that incorporated some elements of Christian theology and symbolism. The spread of the peyote religion has been rather carefully documented, and is still going on; it reached the Navajo in the 1930s, and the Indians of Canada and Florida in the mid–twentieth century. Singing is an integral part of the meetings at which the peyote buttons are consumed, and although any songs, including Christian hymns, may be used, special peyote songs have evolved.

CD 1/24 (0:54)
"Peyote Song,"
Lakota (Sioux), Plains

The musical form of the peyote song is similar to that of the Ghost Dance songs described previously. The example in CD 1/24 is in two parts; in the second part JESUS ONLY is spelled out.

The relation of the peyote religion to the vanished Ghost Dance, and to the severe upheaval to which the American Indians and their aboriginal culture generally have been subjected in the modern world, is summed up by David McAllester:

> The wide spread of the Ghost Dance must have contributed to the receptivity of the Indians to peyote. After the brief currency of the former the Indians were left with little sense of spiritual direction, although the conditions of radical change and insecurity that fostered the Ghost Dance were intensified after its collapse. . . . In place of resistance a philosophy of peaceful conciliation and escape rose. . . . The vision, all-important on the Plains, was made easily available by the use of the cactus. (85)

Further Instances of Acculturation

The greatest degree of integration of Indian and non-Indian elements in music and dance has taken place in the Southwest, especially in New Mexico, where Hispanic and Indian culture, language, and religion exist side by side, sometimes interpenetrating, but always distinct. Hispanic influence is evident in the *matachines* of New Mexico—pageants of dance and drama derived from quite old Spanish fiestas (possibly introduced to the Pueblo Indians by the Franciscans as early as the seventeenth century) that are associated with the Christian observances of Easter and Christmas. J. Donald Robb notes an interesting instance of borrowing that still maintains the distinctness of the two cultures; he points out that at times these dances appear in two distinct versions: "a Spanish version with fiddle and guitar imported from a nearby Spanish village and an Indian version with Indian music, chorus, drums, and costuming, which nevertheless follows generally the plot, the dance evolutions, and other aspects of the traditional matachines dance" (6). See "Cultural Interaction in New Mexico as Illustrated in the Matachines Dance" (Lornell and Rasmussen 155–85). (See Additional Listening.)

A more recent absorption, wholly in the secular domain, is represented by the popular dance music among the Papago, Pima, and Yaqui tribes in southern Arizona known as *waila*, or more commonly as "chicken scratch." Chicken scratch bands use combinations of such instruments as guitar, accordion, saxophone, and drum set (non-Indian) to play waltzes, two-steps, and polkas that show resemblances to Mexican mariachi music, Texas-Mexican norteña music, German band music, and even Louisiana zydeco.

"Enis Special" (CD 1/25) a polka by Mike Enis and Co. (a small ensemble from the Tucson, Arizona area), is representative. The instrumentation includes alto saxophone, and the button accordion adopted from the musica norteña tradition, and native also to the cajun tradition farther east. (See Chapters 4 and 5, and "*Waila*: The Social Dance Music of the Tohono O'odham" by James Griffith, in Lornell and Rasmussen, 187–208.)

CD 1/25 (0:35)
"Enis Special" (excerpt),
Papago, from San
Xavier Reservation

The State of Indian Music Today

American Indian music today can best be described as a renovated art—that is, an art renewed in a way that consciously preserves tradition while adapting it in a manner that allows it to survive, and even thrive, in the conditions under which Indians live in the modern world. Twentieth-century influence is seen in an altered view of the *function* of music. Although its religious function has by no means disappeared, it coexists with both a recreational and an entertainment function. There exist sizable communities of Indians not only in virtually every small city in the West but also in and around large urban areas, particularly Chicago, Denver, Los Angeles, and the San Francisco Bay area, especially Oakland. These urban Indian communities regularly enjoy large social gatherings, at which Indian songs and dances are performed—in Los Angeles, for example, by such groups as The Los Angeles Northern Singers, made up of members of the Sioux, Arikara, Hidatsa, and Northern Arapaho tribes. At these gatherings, not only are the tribal songs and dances found to be flourishing, but along with the new emphasis on the social function of the music there are preserved unmistakable traces of the older attitude toward music as well. These can be seen, for example, in the custom of "sponsoring" an entertainment in honor of a person or an event (which had its aboriginal counterpart in customs such as the *potlatch*) and in surviving manifestations of the concepts that certain songs are private possessions and that certain songs bring luck.

In spite of the pressures of professionalism and commercialization, music has been part of a serious movement of cultural revival since the 1950s. The intertribal powwows held annually on the Plains (especially in Oklahoma) are today great social events, but they are important cultural events as well. They include contests, both for "straight dancers" and for "fancy dancers," the latter giving an opportunity for the display of prodigious virtuosity in dancing, and elaborateness of costume. A live recording of a "Contest Song for Fancy Dancers"(CD 1/26) conveys some of the excitement and spirit of this event, and gives convincing evidence of the energy of present-day revivalism in American Indian culture.

CD 1/26 (1:18)
"Contest Song for Fancy
Dancers," Ponca, Plains

Another aspect of Indian music today is the opportunity afforded Indian musicians with a creative bent to function as composers, using Indian culture as a basis for the creation of individual works within, and with meaning for, the Indian community—an opportunity that did not exist in the older tribal society. Indian performers on native instruments have also found, or created, increased opportunities for concertizing and recording. As the numerous CD offerings available in record stores attest, the popularity of this "new" Indian music has spread to a portion of the general public as well. The revival of the Indian flute has already been mentioned in connection with the work of R. Carlos Nakai, of Navajo/Ute descent. (See p. 41.) Nakai and other professional Indian performers have recorded fusion music that blends elements of Indian musical styles, and especially the sound of the Indian flute, with jazz and rock. Performers such as flutist/singer/composer Robert Mirabal have effectively capitalized on popular "new age" sounds as well. Less frequent has been the incorporation of the Indian flute into classical ensembles; an example of this is the *Two World Concerto* (CD 1/27).

Note that while the orchestra makes use of the full gamut of the European American chromatic scale of twelve tones to the octave, the Indian flute, an instrument with five tones to the octave, naturally uses the same pentatonic scale we have encountered in so much of the music so far. This, together with its distinctive tone quality and its ability to "bend" the pitch, serves to separate the Indian flute from the orchestra as a distinct voice.

We conclude by drawing attention to an approach to revivalism that seeks to emphasize not the *externals* of indigenous American culture but its *inner, esoteric* meaning for the members of a tribe today; that is, instead of trying to recreate their musical past, it seeks "to create their musical present." This kind of musical *revitalization*, as it has been called, has taken place among the Choctaw in the Ardmore, Oklahoma, area. As Victoria Lindsay Levine, who has studied this revival extensively, has put it, "In revitalizing their musical culture, the Ardmore Choctaw did not attempt to reproduce their historic dance events as such, but they did seek to recreate the spirit of early dances in contemporary performance contexts." These contexts involve a "de-emphasis on the more external aspects of performance," including dance costumes—a de-emphasis that allows for a high degree of individuality. This would seem a promising "Native American strategy for cultural survival" (391–409).

CD 1/27 (2:15)
Two World Concerto for Native American flute and orchestra. First movement, *Spirit Call:* "paint for us the times to come" (excerpt, by James DeMars). 1993. R. Carlos Nakai, Native American flute with the Canyon Symphony Orchestra, James DeMars conducting.

■ PROJECTS

1. Talk with some people of Indian descent—at least two, if possible—about the current state of Indian culture from their point of view. Should it be preserved, and if so for what reasons? In what ways should the preservation of traditional ways compromise

and adapt to modern society, and in what ways should it retain its distinctness and integrity?

2. Write an essay discussing what you, or what non-Indians in general, might have to learn from the way Indians traditionally used and regarded music.

3. Do some research into the curriculum of one or more Indian colleges (Navajo Community College, for example); try to determine the extent to which traditional Indian music is being studied and taught there.

■ ADDITIONAL LISTENING

Music of the American Indian Series from the Library of Congress American Folklife Center, Archive of Folk Culture (AFS). The following recordings are available on audio-cassette at *http://lcweb.loc.gov/folklife/folkcat.html.*

Delaware, Cherokee, Choctaw, Creek, L 37 (Peyote songs).

Great Basin: Paiute, Washo, Ute, Bannock, Shoshone, L 38 (Ghost Dance songs).

Kiowa, L 35 (Ghost Dance and peyote songs).

Navajo, L 41 (Peyote songs).

Northwest (Puget Sound), L 34 (Chinook version of "Jesus Loves Me").

Plains: Comanche, Cheyenne, Kiowa, Caddo, Wichita, Pawnee, L 39 (Ghost Dance songs, forty-nine song).

Pueblo, Taos, San Ildefonso, Zuni, Hopi, L 43 (Hopi version of "Dixie").

Sioux, L 40 (Ghost Dance songs, peyote song).

Songs of the Pawnee and Northern Ute, L 25 (Ghost Dance songs).

Spanish and Mexican Folk Music of New Mexico. Smithsonian Folkways CD 04426. Includes two matachines dances.

Two World Concerto. Perf. R. Carlos Nakai. Cond. James DeMars. Canyon Records CR-7016.

Various releases, New World Records: CDs 80246, 80297, 80301, 80337, 80343, and 80406.

CHAPTER

The Hispanic and Latin Traditions

4

The complexities confronting anyone investigating music coming from "south of the border" can be traced to the fact that this music represents a complicated overlaying and blending of cultures from four continents — North and Central America, South America, Europe (specifically the Iberian peninsula), and West Africa. The distinction the author makes between the Hispanic tradition and what has become known as the Latin tradition has to do with both the *sources* and the *routes of entry* of the complex influences of each. The Hispanic strain came overland into the Southwest from Mexico, with an ingredient of Indian influence, hence of *mestizo* culture. The Latin strain (ultimately largely Hispanic as well, with ingredients of African influences) came by sea from the Caribbean, especially from Cuba.

THE HISPANIC TRADITION

We begin our exploration of this complex subject with the impact of Spanish conquest and colonization in the Western Hemisphere. The first persistent European presence in America was that of the Spaniards. In the generation following the voyages of Columbus, Spain, the foremost European power of the time, entered upon a period of phenomenal exploration and conquest. By the mid–sixteenth century the Spanish had begun extensive exploration by land and by sea from Florida to the northern California coast, and by 1565 (at St. Augustine, Florida) the first attempts at colonization in what is the present area of the United States had begun. Although Florida was the first point of contact, Spanish influence in what is now the southeastern United States was not destined to be significant in the long term. In the Southwest, on the other hand, it was decisive. Beginning with military expeditions and conquests in the 1540s, and culminating with the high-water mark of Spanish penetration in the California mission period of the late eighteenth and early nineteenth centuries, the foundation was laid for Hispanic influence, which is still of the greatest importance culturally in that part of the country and which has been reinforced in all periods by almost continuous migrations from Mexico.

SACRED MUSIC FROM MEXICO

The first musical influences were religious. Spanish sacred music reached the highest point of its development in the prosperous sixteenth century, rivaling in its excellence and in the intensity of its cultivation that of Rome itself. It was Spanish sacred music from that era that traveled with the *conquistadores,* and music was found to be one of the priests' most powerful tools for converting and teaching the Indians. A survival of this influence into the twentieth century was cited in Chapter 3, in the matachines dance-drama among the Indians and Mexicans of New Mexico (see p. 46). Before the end of the sixteenth century, vocal and instrumental music were intensively cultivated in Mexico by both Indians and Spanish, accompanied by the manufacture of musical instruments and the printing of music.

New Mexico

Taking into account the earliest missions and small colonial settlements in the upper Rio Grande Valley of New Mexico as early as 1598, New Mexico is the area of the oldest sustained Hispanic influence in the United States. And because of its subsequent relative isolation (from the Re-Conquest after the Pueblo Revolt of the 1680s to the testing of the atomic bomb in the 1940s), this influence has until recently persisted with little interference, especially in the valleys of the upper Rio Grande and the Pecos River. The opening of the Santa Fe Trail in 1821 and the conquest and annexation of the area by the United States in 1846–48 had little effect on life in the remote villages, much of which centered on their churches.

It is almost certain that during the seventeenth century Spanish religious music, coming by way of Mexico, was performed in the missions of New Mexico. However, during the Pueblo Revolt nearly all records from the missions were destroyed. As a result, the religious music of New Mexico that we know the most about today is the relatively simple folklike music cultivated and preserved by a devout people worshiping for generations in relative isolation. Of particular antiquity and interest is the music of *La Fraternidad Piadosa de Nuestro Padre Jesús Nazareno*, (The Pious Brotherhood of Our Father Jesus of Nazareth), more familiarly known as *Los Hermanos Penitentes* (The Penitent Brotherhood), or simply *Los Penitentes*.

The most characteristic form of music cultivated by the Penitentes was the *alabado*, a religious folk song in free meter sung in unison. The alabado, whose currency is not limited to the Brotherhood, has indeed been called the "backbone of congregational singing since the sixteenth century" and has been and still is sung in Hispanic Catholic churches throughout the Southwest (Fernández). The alabados of New Mexico are seemingly unrelated to those of Spain, and the origins of neither the words nor the melodies are known at this time. Most of the alabados sung by the Penitentes are lengthy strophic songs commemorating aspects of the Passion of Christ, such as the Stations of the Cross, which are reenacted in pageant form. They are unaccompanied except by the florid improvised interjections of the *pito* (a homemade flute played only during Holy Week), which are said to represent the lamenting cries of the Virgin Mary. Many of the alabados (of which "Al Pie de Este Santo Altar" (CD 1/28) is an example) have been preserved, having been recorded about 1950 in their many variants from village to village (Robb).

CD 1/28 (1:35)
"Al Pie de Este Santo Altar," Luis Montoya, vocal; Vicente Padilla, pito (flute). Recorded in Santa Fe, New Mexico, 1952.

Al pie de este santo altar	At the foot of this holy altar
le Virgen quedó llorando	the Virgin stood weeping
por Jesús, su Hijo divino,	for Jesus, her divine Son,
y en su pasión contemplando.	in contemplation of His Passion.

Text, "Al Pie de Este Santo Altar"

En su santísimo llanto,	In her most holy sorrow,
clama y dice: "¡Ay, mi Jesús!	she calls out and says: "Ah, my Jesus!
¿Qué haré sola en este mundo?	What am I to do alone in this world?
¿Quién lo baja de la cruz?"	Who will bring Him down from the cross?"

CD 1/29 (1:42)
Song from *Las Posadas,*
sung by Franquilino
Miranda and group.
Recorded by John A.
and Alan Lomax in
Cotulla, Texas, 1934.

A more widespread form of religious folk song is that associated with the Christmas play *Los Pastores* (The Shepherds), and its prelude, *Las Posadas* (The Lodgings). They are related to the mystery plays, liturgical dramas prevalent in Europe from the ninth through the sixteenth centuries. Possibly written by the Franciscans in Mexico, they made their ways by separate routes to California, New Mexico, and Texas. *Las Posadas* commemorates Mary and Joseph seeking lodging.

Text, song from
Los Posadas

1. [Venimos] a casa
   del Ave María,
   pidiendo posada
   por un solo día.

   [We come] from the house
   of the "Hail Mary" [Annunciation]
   asking for lodging
   but for one day.

2. Y aquí, en esta casa,
   posada no damos,
   que es mucha familia
   y apenas entramos.

   And here, in this house
   we give no lodging,
   for our family is large
   and we barely fit ourselves.

3. Posada pedimos
   por esta ocasión,
   y a mi esposa amada
   tener un rincón.

   We seek lodging
   for this occasion,
   and for my beloved wife
   to have a small corner of the house.

4. Posada no damos
   por esta ocasión;
   pasen adelante,
   que hay otras mejor.
   [This last line sounds different on the recording.]

   We give no lodging
   for this occasion;
   Go on ahead,
   for there are better lodgings elsewhere.

5. Hermosos los pobres,
   no tenemos dinero
   ni prendas valiosas
   para el mesonero.

   Lovely are the poor,
   we have neither money
   nor valuable garments
   for the innkeeper.

Many versions of *Los Pastores* were recorded in New Mexico about the middle of the twentieth century, and some have been painstakingly transcribed (Stark). The *Los Pastores* singing group heard here (CD 1/29) performed the play every Christmas in Cotulla, Texas, which Lomax described as "a little cattle town down in the mesquite thickets of south Texas near the Mexican border." He tells us that "entire scripts—words, tunes, and stage directions—have been handed on by word of mouth from father to son in a number of communities." Note the singing in parallel thirds and sixths in this folk rendition. This dominant trait of Mexican music can be heard in the performance of corridos (CD 1/32) and in mariachi music (CD 1/31).

California

An echo of the greatness of Spanish church music belatedly reached California in the late eighteenth and early nineteenth centuries. It is now known that during the brief flourishing of the Franciscan missions in California from 1769 to their secularization beginning in 1834, there was a rather considerable musical culture and that music was integral to mission life. Both vocal and instrumental music were taught to the Indians, who made up the choirs and small orchestras. The range of music extended from folklike hymns and alabados to elaborate settings of the Mass for chorus with instrumental accompaniment. Inventories made after their secularization show that at least nine of the missions had collections of instruments; Santa Barbara, possibly the most prosperous, had forty-three instruments in 1834, including a fairly large organ. The presence of these instruments, the training and dedication to music of *padres* Juan Sancho, Narciso Durán, Arroyo de la Cuesta, and Junipero Serra himself, and the fact that visitors reported the existence of orchestras and choruses of over thirty musicians and were much impressed by the quality of their music make it reasonable to assume that at some of the missions, on special occasions, there was performed elaborate polyphonic music such as the recently discovered Mass in D major by Ignacio de Jerúsalem, who was chapel master of the Mexico City Cathedral from 1749 to 1769. (See Additional Listening.)

Spanish California was not a cultural backwater. The Franciscan missions and their attendant *presidios* and secular communities, though remote, were for the most part very prosperous centers—prosperous even compared with towns in Spain and in the United States of the time. They were situated in a naturally fertile land with a mild climate, with abundant livestock and food supplies, and with abundant labor supplied by an essentially captive population. It was only after Mexican independence, and with it the secularization of the missions and the departure of the Franciscan priests, that mission music declined and virtually disappeared. Such manuscripts as existed (consisting wholly of liturgical music) were destroyed or forgotten, and what little was preserved of a musical culture went over into oral tradition. Under the circumstances, it is remarkable that any survived; it is therefore rather surprising to come upon a photograph of the last Indian choir of Mission San Buenaventura, taken in 1860, with each of the Indians holding what appears to be a homemade instrument — a flute, for example, fashioned from an old gun barrel. That the singing of the Indian choirs survived even longer in some cases, without losing its intensity or meaning, is attested to by Robert Louis Stevenson's account of a festival at Mission San Carlos Borromeo (Carmel) in 1879: "I have never seen faces more vividly lit up with joy than the faces of these Indian singers. It was to them not only the worship of God, nor an act by which they recalled and commemorated better days, but was besides an exercise of culture, where all they knew of art and letters was united and expressed" (496).

SECULAR MUSIC FROM MEXICO

Secular folk music from Latin America has been far more widespread and influential in the culture of the United States than has sacred music. To begin to understand the nature and sources of this music, it is important to realize that the mestizo folk culture of Latin America is everywhere a blend of Spanish, Indian, and African elements, the mix varying from region to region. African influence is strongest in the Caribbean (especially Cuba, Jamaica, and Hispaniola) and in the Caribbean and Brazilian coastal areas of South America, though it is not to be discounted in Mexico itself. It has been estimated that in the seventeenth century, for example, there were more Africans than Spaniards in Mexico (Stevenson, *Music* 231; Geijerstam 11).

In the secular music from Mexico (as indeed from all of Latin America), dance and song are closely associated. (Koegel, "Spanish and Mexican Dance

A fiddle player accompanies dancers at a *fandango* in San Antonio, Texas, 1844. While dancing a *vals* might have been the main attraction for most, others were content to drink, carouse, or even fire pistols in the air!

Courtesy DRT Library, The Alamo, San Antonio

Music"). Many kinds of music can be used for either. For example, the corrido (or ballad) can be danced as well as sung, and the *huapango,* originally a dance from Veracruz, can also be sung. Dancing was a very important pastime from the earliest times in rural Hispanic communities, and there are numerous accounts of *bailes* or *fandangos* (both refer to dances) in the *salas* (halls) of the towns or villages of New Mexico and California, to the accompaniment of fiddle and guitar. Popular Mexican dances were the *el jarabe, la jota,* and *la bamba.* European dances, arriving either from Mexico itself or, in California, from Anglo-American sailors, were *el vals* (the waltz), *la polca* (the polka), *el chotís* (the schottische), and *el cutillo* (the cotillion or square dance). Both the waltz and the quadrille (*las cuadrillas*) owe their presence in Mexico to French influence in the nineteenth century, especially during the French occupation of 1862–67.

"El Chotís" (CD 1/30) like the fiddle tune "Soldier's Joy" (see p. 14), is in binary form. As in all dance music, the repetition of individual strains is practically universal, to provide enough continuous music. An interesting feature of "El Chotís" is the irregularity of the phrase lengths; instead of consisting of the usual four measures, standard in commercial popular music, some phrases have been extended to five or even six measures. These extra measures, superimposed on the "template" of four-measure regularity that we subconsciously impose on dance music, produces a slight jolt, like an extra heartbeat, and adds interest to the flow of the music.

CD 1/30 (1:30)
"El Chotís," Melitón Roybal. Recorded by Reed Cooper in El Rancho, New Mexico, 1970.

Transcription 4.1
"El Chotís"

This informality, with the player or singer beginning the next phrase whenever he or she feels ready to, is found in much folk music, including early country music. The standardization of phrase lengths is one of the symptoms of the transition from folk to popular music.

El Rancho is a small Spanish farming community near the San Ildefonso pueblo on the road to Los Alamos. Anita Gonzales Thomas has written (in the album notes for "El Chotís") that "*bailes* were held in every town or village, in salas, halls, with whitewashed walls lit by tallow candles." Melitón Roybal, who was 72 at the time this recording was made, had been playing for bailes and weddings for fifty years.

Another point to observe about secular music coming from Mexico is that other cultures have made their own marks on it, either here or in Mexico itself. It must not be assumed that these cultural mixings occurred only north of the border. As Geijerstam has pointed out, the waltz, the polka, the mazurka, and the schottische were imported into Mexico itself in the nineteenth century, reaching Mexico City mostly from Paris (16). The mixture of Austrian, German, Czech, and Anglo-American influences can be seen in the types of dances cited above and in their names. In the border region the German influence (its chief contributions being the polka and the button accordion) proved to be decisive.

Although genuine regional musics, as enjoyed by the mostly rural people in the highly differentiated parts of Mexico, have existed and continue to exist, they have been overshadowed by a kind of "generic" Mexican music, perpetuated as part of a professionalized "cultural front." This development is similar to, but much older than, that of the pan-Indian music described in Chapter 3. In the 1880s, for example, during the Díaz regime, *orquestas típicas*, made up of professional musicians dressed in charro costumes, were formed, and were supported by the government as a means of promoting Mexican culture abroad. (The term *charro* refers to the highly skilled rope artists who performed in rodeos, or *chareadas*, and who wore the distinctive costumes from which the costumes of the mariachi musicians have been adapted.) Orquestas típicas, led by directors such as Carlos Curtí, toured the United States and Europe before the turn to the twentieth century, and since then such ensembles have been important, both as tourist attractions in the large Mexican cities and as exporters of "typical" Mexican music. This has become the function of the more recent trumpet mariachi ensembles. With the advent of broadcasting and recording, the production of popular music based on folk styles but performed by professional musicians began in Mexico City, in the same kind of development that produced "country music" from regional folk styles in the United States.

The Mariachi

The result of this popularization and consequent standardization has been the emergence of two dominant types of instrumental ensemble, used to accompany either dancing or singing. One is the *mariachi*, which in its current popular form consists of trumpets, violins, a *vihuela* (a smaller five-string guitarlike instrument), a guitar, a *guitarrón* (bass guitar), and optionally a harp of a particular design from the state of Jalisco.

Even though mariachi's country of origin is Mexico, it has become a thoroughly naturalized music of the Unites States. By now it is performed, studied, and taught not only in the Southwest, where its cultivation is extensive, but throughout the country, as Daniel Sheehy points out in his article "Mexican Mariachi Music: Made in the U.S.A." (Lornell and Rasmussen 131–54). With its rhythms, its trumpets playing in parallel thirds, and not least the typical charro costumes of its musicians, it has become a kind of convenient symbol of "Mexicanness." Professional mariachis in the United States have become highly skilled and versatile show and recording bands, with as many as fourteen musicians who both sing and play. Although they have broadened both their repertory and their musical styles to reach a larger musical public, they have never abandoned their musical roots, to which they consistently pay homage. For example, Mariachi Cobre of Tucson, a professional band that has been performing for years at the Epcot Center in Disney World, Florida, recently recorded "Las Abajeñas" ("The Lowland Women"), a *son* that can be traced as far back as a recording made in Mexico before 1908.

The transcription in the listening guide for "Las Abajeñas" shows the notation for a rhythmic characteristic of the Mexican *son* —a deft flipping back and forth between 3/4 and 6/8 meters. This typical Hispanic device can be heard in pieces such as "America" in *West Side Story*. Note parallel thirds and sixths, as heard in the song from *Las Posadas* (CD 1/29) and in the corrido (CD 1/32).

CD 1/31 (2:21) "Las Abajeñas" ("The Lowland Women"), Mariachi Cobre, Tucson, Arizona

---

Traditional *son:* "Las Abajeñas"
Mariachi Band: 2 trumpets, 6 violins, vihuela, guitar, and guitarrón

LISTENING
GUIDE

0:00   Instrumental introduction

Stanza 1

| 0:17 | Lines 1–4 | Me gustan las abajeñas
por altas y presumidas.
Se bañan y se componen,
y siempre descoloridas. | I like the lowland women
because they're tall and regal.
They bathe and dress up,
and always look pale. |
| 0:25 | Lines 1–4 | *(repeat)* | |

(continued)

LISTENING GUIDE

(continued)

0:33	Lines 5–8	Mariquita, mi alma, yo te lo decía que tarde o temprano, mi vida, habías de ser mía.	Mariquita, my love, I told you that sooner or later, by my life, you had to be mine.
0:41	Lines 5–8	*(repeat)*	

Instrumental

0:49 Ritornello

0:57 Trumpet passage

1:04 Ritornello repeats

Stanza 2

1:13	Lines 1–4	Me gustan las abajeñas que saben la ley de Diós. Que largan a sus maridos, por irse con otros dos.	I like the lowland women who live in God's good graces. They send their husbands off, so they can be with another two.
1:20	Lines 1–4	*(repeat)*	
1:29	Lines 5–8	Dejala que vaya, ella volverá; si amores la llevan, mi vida, celos la traerán.	Go ahead and let her leave, she will return; for if loves take her away, by my life, jealousies will bring her back.
1:37	Lines 5–8	*(repeat)*	

1:44 Ritornello again (see transcription)

1:52 Trumpet passage

2:02 Coda [repeat of introduction]

2:13 Traditional mariachi ending

Musica norteña

The other dominant Mexican American instrumental ensemble is the *conjunto* of the *musica norteña*. This distinctively regional ensemble, coming from the lower Rio Grande Valley shared by Texas and the far northeastern part of

Mexico (hence the adjective *norteña,* "northern"), consisted in its early stages of only the button accordion, endemic to the region, with an accompaniment of guitar or *bajo sexto* (a form of twelve-string guitar). Beginning in the 1950s, a saxophone was frequently added (often doubling the accordion in thirds, a typically Mexican device also used with voices and with mariachi trumpets), as well as a jazz-type drum set and a bass—more recently an electric one. The differences between mariachi music and musica norteña are not so much distinctions in repertory—they may perform the same songs or dances—as distinctions in their instrumentation and style of performance. Musica norteña most often has as its rhythmic basis either the "oompah oompah" of the adopted polka or the "oompah-pah oompah-pah" of the adopted waltz, whereas the mariachi ensemble is more apt to retain the complex rhythms and cross-rhythms of the Mexican *son.* The musica norteña style is exemplified in the corrido described in the next section.

Conjunto music is probably the more widely popular of the two among Mexican Americans themselves, especially the younger generation. It evolved into a distinctive and regionally very influential style at the hands of accordionists, most notably in the beginning Narciso Martinez ("El Huracán del Valle"). The music was spread throughout the Southwest by a more recent generation of performers, including Flaco Jiménez and the guitarist-singers Freddy Fender (Baldemar Huerta), Doug Sahm (an Anglo with the acquired name of Doug Saldaña), and José Maria De Leon ("Little Joe") Hernández. (See Additional Listening.) Acquiring political overtones to some degree, and associated with the ethnic pride and aspirations of Chicanos, musica norteña has become identified throughout the West as Chicano music.

Since the subject of Chicano music and identity has been introduced, it will be worthwhile to sort out briefly here the complexity of the Mexican American populace. Making up an increasingly large percentage of the population of the United States, especially in the Southwest, people of Mexican descent constitute a complex cluster of three or four fairly distinct groups. *Mexican Americans* are those who were born here or have lived here long, identify themselves most strongly as Americans, and have become thoroughly assimilated into mainstream American life—business, political, and social. Sometimes identified as a separate, and much smaller, group are *Hispanic Americans,* whose ancestors settled in Texas, New Mexico, or California (the *californios*) before Anglo settlement and domination came to those areas. They may even regard their cultural heritage as coming more from Spain than from Mexico, especially the Hispanic New Mexicans (*"Spanish Americans"*). A third group are *Chicanos,* whose identity as a cultural group was born in the 1960s. These tend to be young Mexican Americans who have rediscovered and are celebrating their ethnic identity. In varying degrees activist and militant, they are impatient with what they see as discrimination against their race (La Raza) and may, in the extreme, look upon the United States as a country of oppression and racism. The overt extreme was expressed in the dress (the zoot suit) and the stance of the *pachuco,* the young Mexican "gang" member. As Steven Loza has said, "The Los Angeles Chicano movement reflected the general spirit of young people who rejected the term *Mexican American* in favor of *Chicano,* a word that symbolized defiance of the notions of cultural assimilation and represented an expression of pride" (47). Their cultural focus tends to be definitely not Spanish (except in language), and not so much Mexican as pre-Columbian Indian, and even pre-Aztec. (The mythical Aztlán, placed somewhere in the American Southwest, is regarded as the birthplace of all native American races. According to this view, the migrations northward from Mexico in historical times are regarded as a *return* to a legendary homeland.) A fourth group are *Mexicanos,* or Mexican immigrants, both documented and undocumented. They form a large and mobile population. Although many, if not most, of them do not intend to stay in this country and resist assimilation, they account for a significant part of the constant replenishment of Mexican culture that comes through the continuous immigration from Mexico (Contreras; *Aztlán*).

The Corrido

Of all the folk forms now popular, none is more distinctive or more interesting than the *corrido.* The Hispanic love of poetry, and especially the commemoration of people and events in poetry, here finds expression in what is still a vital tradition. The corrido is the equivalent of the folk ballad—a narrative strophic song. As distinguished from the older *romance,* of Spanish origin, it deals with actual people and events, often of immediate and topical concern, in an earthy, frank, and unembellished way. It had its origins in Mexico in the turbulent mid–nineteenth century, when it was often political and satirical. Before the advent of recordings and, later, radio, corridos were circulated by itinerant *corridistas* or *trovadores* (troubadours), going from hacienda to hacienda, or singing in marketplaces and on street corners. As with the Anglo-American ballad, corridos were cheaply printed as broadsides, with words only (see p. 11).

The corrido of the southwestern United States is nearly as old as its Mexican forebear. An area rich in the production of corridos and other folklore has been the valley of the lower Rio Grande, from the two Laredos to the Gulf. A fertile valley in the midst of an arid plain, overlooked in early exploration and colonialization, largely ignored by Spain and Mexico, and spurned by the United States, it was inhabited by people of a fiercely independent spirit. When in 1836 Texas declared its independence from Mexico, the valley suddenly became a border area, and a period of unrest, oppression, and bloodshed began that was to last intermittently for nearly a century. Like many strife-torn border areas—that between England and Scotland, for example—it bred its heroes and its villains, and its ballads to commemorate them. An early corrido was "El Corrido de Kiansis," known in the border area by 1870. It describes the experiences and hardships of the Mexican *vaqueros* in the cattle drives of the late 1860s and early 1870s from Texas to the western terminus of the railroad in Kansas.

The corridos are ballads, and invite comparison with the ballads as presented and discussed in Chapters 1 and 2. They are similar in their typical form of four-line rhymed stanzas, or *coplas*. But the meter of the corrido is different: approximately eight syllables to a line, and only three stressed syllables, are set to music that is often irregular in its metrical structure, as is not unusual in folk music. One of the most famous corridos, still sung today, is "El Corrido de Gregorio Cortez" (CD 1/32).

Note the singing in parallel thirds, as was heard in the song from *Las Posadas* (CD 1/29) and "Las Abajeñas" (CD 1/31). Use of the accordion marks this as typical of Texas-Mexican border style, or musica norteña. This version of the corrido was probably shortened to fit a single side of a 78-rpm recording. Some versions run to twenty stanzas.

CD 1/32 (2:42)
"El Corrido de Gregorio Cortez," Los Hermanos Banda ("The Banda Brothers"). Recorded in Monterrey, N.L., Mexico, about 1958.

1. En el condado del Carmen
   miren lo que ha sucedido,
   Murió el *sherife* mayor
   quedando Román herido.

   In Cameron County (Texas)
   look what has happened.
   The sheriff died,
   leaving Román wounded.

2. Otro día por la mañana
   cuando la gente llegó,
   Unos a los otros dicen
   no saben quien lo mató.

   The following morning
   when the people arrived,
   Some said to the others
   they don't know who killed him.

3. Se anduvieron informando
   como tres horas después,
   Supieron que el malhechor
   era Gregorio Cortéz.

   They were investigating
   and about three hours later
   They found out that the wrongdoer
   was Gregorio Cortéz.

4. Insortaron a Cortéz
   por toditito el estado.
   Vivo o muerto que se aprehenda
   porque a varios ha matado.

   Cortéz was wanted
   throughout the state.
   Alive or dead may he be apprehended
   for he has killed several.

5. Decía Gregorio Cortéz
   con su pistola en la mano,
   «No siento haberlo matado
   al que siento es a mi hermano.»

   Said Gregorio Cortéz
   with his pistol in his hand,
   "I'm not sorry for having killed him,
   It's for my brother that I feel sorry."

Text, "El Corrido de Gregorio Cortez"
(Used by permission. From the booklet accompanying Arhoolie CD 7019/20: Corridos y Tragedias de la Frontera. www.arhoolie.com)

6. Decía Gregorio Cortéz con su alma muy encendida, «No siento haberlo matado la defensa es permitida.»	Said Gregorio Cortéz with his soul aflame, "I'm not sorry for having killed him, self defense is permitted."
7. Gregorio le dice a Juan, «Muy pronto lo vas a ver, anda hablale a los *sherifes* que me vengan a aprender.»	Gregorio says to Juan, "Very soon you will see, go and talk to the sheriffs that they should come and arrest me."
8. Decían los americanos «Si lo vemos que le haremos si le entramos por derecho muy poquitos volveremos.»	The Americans said, "If we see him what shall we do to him; If we face him head on very few will return."
9. Ya agarraron a Cortéz, ya terminó la cuestión; la pobre de su familia la lleva en el corazón.	Now they caught Cortéz, now the case is closed; His poor family he carries in his heart.

The incident took place in 1901. Gregorio Cortéz was a young Mexican who, having been falsely accused of horse stealing, shot and killed in self-defense the sheriff who had fatally wounded his brother. After a dramatic chase, he was captured and, after multiple trials, was acquitted of murder. He was convicted of another murder, however, and served time in Huntsville Penitentiary. Given a conditional pardon, he went to Mexico to take part in the Revolution, was wounded, returned to Texas, and died there in 1916. Américo Paredes wrote a book about the man, the legend, and the corrido, titled "With His Pistol in His Hand" (a line from the corrido), and the ballad became the basis for a movie.

In the corrido we encounter a ballad tradition still very much alive. In the days of the 45-rpm single, the common currency of popular music in the 1960s and 1970s, local radio stations could be playing a newly composed and recorded corrido within twenty-four hours of the event (often a violent crime or scandal) it commemorated. The almost journalistic immediacy of the corrido resulted in some lawsuits against record companies. Corridos of protest were, and are, common. Many are *homenajes*, lamenting the deaths of popular heros. Since the 1970s there have been many corridos on César Chávez and Dolores Huerta and the farm labor movement in California. A typical modern corrido from south Texas is "La Muerte de Martin Luther King" ("The Death of Martin Luther King").

Gentlemen, I am going to sing for you
About the glory of a valiant man,
Who, while trying to save his country,
Found death in his pathway. *(Translation by Joaquin Fernandez. Reprinted by
permission of RAMMS Music, A Division of House of Falcon, Inc.)*

The early corridos were performed and recorded as *duetos*—two singers
with guitar. Later, by the mid-1940s, they were performed by conjuntos, with
their distinctive additions of accordion, and sometimes saxophone, thus
becoming part of the norteño repertoire.

The Canción

The *canción* is lyrical and often sentimental, in contrast to the narrative and
even epic quality of the corrido. The term *canción* is used to cover a broad
range of songs, of which songs about love are only one type. In the category of
folk songs in oral tradition, J. Donald Robb has printed many canciones from
New Mexico alone, including such traditional songs as "Cielito Lindo" and "La
Golondrina." Two soldiers' songs are "La Cucaracha," of which there are many
satirical parodies, and "La Adelita," both extremely popular during the revolutionary period of 1910–20. These songs, together with the two conciones mentioned above, have interesting histories and great meaning for Mexicans and
Mexican Americans alike. Belonging to a large and variously defined category
of songs are the *canciones rancheras*—part of the "country music revival" glori-
fying the peasantry after the Revolution. The best-known survivor, probably
written for a film by the same name, is "Allá en el Rancho Grande."

Corresponding roughly to the romantic ballad of American popular music
is the *bolero,* usually a lament about lost love. Lydia Mendoza (b. 1916), "La
Alondra de la Frontera" (the Meadowlark of the Border) and "La Cancionera
de los Pobres" (the Songstress of the Poor), sang many of these, accompanying
herself on the twelve-string guitar. The story of her life gives some insight into
Mexican American music throughout the Southwest, and *tejano* (Texas) border
music in particular, and the lives of those who made, and still make, this music.
She was a member of a musical family that in the 1920s was traveling from
town to town in the lower Rio Grande Valley, trying to make a living from
their singing and playing. Like many Mexican families, they had fled the violence and turmoil of the prolonged Mexican Revolution. Lydia was only 12
when La Familia Mendoza made their first recording in 1928, at a time when
record companies were first beginning to realize the potential market that
existed for recordings of regional folk music. (There are many parallels with
the Carter Family of Virginia, who began recording what eventually became
"country music" about the same time. The music of the Carter Family, who

actually did some of their recording in San Antonio, was being broadcast over powerful radio stations in Texas, and later in northern Mexico, about the same time that La Familia Mendoza was popular. (See pp. 115–16 and "The Carter Family on Border Radio," *American Music* 14. 2 [Summer 1996], pp. 205–17.)

The hardship and discrimination the Mendozas endured was typical of the experience of most immigrant musicians and their families. Lydia Mendoza's first success was the recording of a canción "Mal hombre" ("Cold-Hearted Man") in 1934.

CD 1/33 (3:29)
"Mal Hombre"
("Cold-Hearted Man"),
Lydia Mendoza, vocal,
with twelve-string
guitar. Recorded in San
Antonio, Texas, 1934.

Text, "Mal Hombre"
(P. D.—Arranged by
Lydia Mendoza—from
Arhoolie CD490—
www.arhoolie.com)

Era yo una chiquilla todavia	I was but a young girl
cuando tu casualmente me encontraste	when, by chance, you found me
y a merced a tus artes de mundano	and with your worldly charm
de mi honra el perfume te llevaste.	you crushed the flower of my innocence.
Luego hiciste conmigo lo que todos	Then you treated me like all men
los que son como tu con las mujeres,	of your kind treat women,
por lo tanto no extrañes que yo ahora	so don't be surprised now that I tell you
en tu cara te diga lo que eres.	to your face what you really are.

Refrain	Mal hombre,	Cold-hearted man,
	tan ruin es tu alma que no tiene nombre;	your soul is so vile it has no name;
	eres un canalla, eres un malvado,	you are despicable, you are evil,
	eres un mal hombre.	you are a cold-hearted man.

A mi triste destino abandonada	Abandoned to a sad fate
entable fiera lucha con la vida,	my life became a fierce struggle,
ella recia y cruel me torturaba	suffering the harshness and cruelty of the world
yo mas debil al fin cai vencida.	I was weak and was defeated.
Tú supistes a tiempo mi derrota,	In time you learned of my downfall,
mi espantoso calvario conociste,	how my life had become a road to hell,

te dijieron algunos: «Ve a
salvarie»
y probando quien eres te
reiste.

Refrain
Poco tiempo despues en el
arroyo
entre sombras mi vida
defendia
una noche con otra tu
pasaste
que al mirarme senti que
te decia:

«¿Quien es esa mujer? ¿Tú
la conoces?»
«Ya la ves- respondiste –una
cualquiera.»
al oír de tus labios el ultraje

demonstrabas también lo
que tú eras.

our friends advised you, "You can
help her,"
but being who you are, you just
laughed.

Refrain
A short time later,

I defended my life in a shadowy
world.
One night you passed by with
another woman
and upon seeing me, I heard her say:

"Who is that woman? Do you know
her?"
and you answered, "You can see for
yourself, she's a nobody."
When you humiliated me with that
insult
you proved once again who you are.

Recordings brought increased personal appearances, and eventually Mendoza became what some consider the most important and historic pioneer recording artist in the entire field of Mexican American music. Her recorded repertoire is certainly representative of this field; it includes mostly canciones, but also corridos, rancheras, boleros, valses, and tangos, recorded not only "con su guitarra" but also with leading conjuntos in Texas and with Mariachi Vargas de Tecalitlan, the most famous mariachi in Mexico.

A canción of powerful significance to Chicanos in recent years, especially those in the farmworker movement in California, is "De Colores" (Transcription 4.2). It was originally an old Spanish folk song. Most of the five verses that are extant, including the two that are widely known and sung, express an appreciation of nature. Other verses introduce a religious dimension, with special reference to the *cursillos,* intensive three-day "courses" sponsored by the Catholic Church that have been particularly popular in the Spanish-speaking Southwest. "De Colores" became associated with the farm labor movement under the leadership of César Chávez, and it was certainly sung during the historic march from Delano to Sacramento in 1966. Though with its theme of harmony and unity it has been effective in organizing workers, it is not a militant song. Literal translation fails to convey the essence of the simple words, which invoke light, color, and the harmony of nature, using the images of the colors of the fields in spring, the colors of birds that come from afar, and the colors that are seen in the rainbow. It has assumed the character of a deeply meaningful hymn.

Transcription 4.2
"De Colores"

De co - lo - res,____ de co - lo - res se vis-ten los cam-pos en la pri - ma - ve - ra;____ de co - lo - res,____ de co - lo - res son los pa - ja - ri - llos que vie - nen de fue - ra.____ De co - lo - res,____ de co - lo - res es el ar - co i - ris qu ve - mos lu - cir,____ y por e - so los gran-des a - mo - res de mu - chos co - lo - res me gus - tan a mi,____ y por e - so los gran-des a - mo - res de mu-chos co - lo - res me gus - tan a mi.

Los Angeles

Los Angeles, with a Mexican population exceeded in number only by that of Mexico City itself, has its own distinctive Mexican musical history and culture. Founded in 1781 and a part of Mexico until 1848, El Pueblo de Nuestra Señora la Reina de Los Angeles (The City of Our Lady the Queen of the Angels) had a lively tradition of bailes, fandangos, feasts, and processions, all accompanied by music. Among the californios of all classes, music was an important part of life, and there were few who could not sing or play an instrument. After California was annexed by the United States, emigration from Mexico decreased while that from the rest of the States increased dramatically. Mexican cultural and political influence declined overall but did not by any means disappear. Records of the period show a flourishing musical life for the Spanish-speaking public in Southern California in the last half of the nineteenth century. For the cultivated society there were the bailes, in homes or hotels, for which there were printed invitations. Less formal were the fandangos of the cantinas and the saloons. There were many open air band concerts; and touring virtuosi and opera and theatrical companies came from Mexico City, and even from Spain (Koegel, *Inter-American Music Review*).

The demographics of Southern California started to change early in the twentieth century, as immigration from Mexico began the inexorable, if uneven, rise that continues to this day. This was due in the early years of the century to the turmoil associated with the Mexican Revolution, and subsequently to the increased industrialization of Southern California, and the gap in wages between the two countries. Mexican settlement tended to concentrate around the oldest part of the city, much of it on the lowlands along the river that bears the city's name. Out of this *barrio* (literally "district," or "neighborhood") emerged in the 1930s numerous corridos in the Hispanic tradition, not only corridos about tragedies such as the suicide in prison of Juan Reyna, but also satirical corridos such as "El lavaplatos" ("The Dishwasher"), "Consejos al maje" ("Advice to the Naive"), and "Se acabó el WPA" ("The WPA Has Ended") commenting on social and economic conditions affecting Mexicans. These began to be recorded about the same time that local Spanish-speaking radio stations began to flourish. (A popular ensemble of singers and guitarists, Los Madrugadores [The Early Risers], performed on the radio between 4 and 6 a.m. beginning in the 1930s.) The World War II years saw the emergence among young Mexican Americans, partly as a defensive reaction to the rising prejudice against them, of a sense of pride and uniqueness in their race—*La Raza*.

Many musicians and groups emerged to celebrate this identity—this "Chicano experience," as documented by *La Opinión*, a venerable Spanish-language newspaper published in Los Angeles. Probably the most influential group of the last twenty years is Los Lobos (The Wolves). Referring to his extensive documentation of groups and individuals in the Los Angeles scene, Loza says, "More than any of the other case studies analyzed here, Los Lobos reflect the musical diversity and processes of change, maintenance, and adaptation among the Mexican/Chicano people of Los Angeles" (233). Their range of styles and subjects has included Spanish-language rancheras, conciones, corridos, and boleros in more or less traditional style, as heard in their albums, *Just Another Band from East L. A.* and *La Pistola y El Corazón*. Their songs in the 1980s and 1990s have been mostly in English, and use an adapted heavy-metal style, but with consistently interesting use of instrumental color. An effective piece of social commentary, on the plight of the illegal immigrant, is "Will the Wolf Survive" (see Additional Listening).

Nueva Canción

At a time when protest music in the United States had gone off in many directions, there was a movement in the same hemisphere that reached a degree of intensity and focus in the 1970s and 1980s not seen here (except for the civil rights movement) since the Depression and its aftermath. This was the *nueva canción,* or New Song movement. Political in its nature and its message, it was spawned in various Latin countries, spontaneously and sometimes simultaneously, to oppose by means of song oppression and murder, and to better the lives of the common people. It emerged in Chile in the 1960s, with Violetta Parra and Victor Jara (who was murdered in 1973); in Argentina with Mercedes Sosa (exiled in 1978); in Cuba (where it is called *nueva trova)* with Silvio Rogríguez and Pablo Milanés; and in Nicaragua and El Salvador. As the movement grew, there were festivals in Nicaragua, Peru, Argentina, and Brazil. Its relation to folk song in the United States has been peripheral but not negligible. It certainly had its antecedents in the Peoples Song movement in the 1930s and 1940s. It has engaged the redoubtable Pete Seeger and, on an occasional basis, younger singers such as Holly Near. In keeping with its democratic ideals, nueva canción has placed its emphasis not on folk "stars" but on groups, chief of which, in its greatest area of influence in the Southwest, have been Los Peludos (The Hairy Ones) in San Francisco, Los Perros (The Dogs) in Los Angeles, and Los Alacranes Mojados (The Wet Scorpions) in San Diego. Its guiding tenets have been the eschewing of commercialism and the use of native acoustic instruments indigenous to all areas of the Western Hemisher (Titon 388–400).

Hispanic Musical Theater: The Zarzuela

The *zarauela* is a form of Spanish musical theater introduced to the Americas 150 years ago. It has become increasingly popular in Hispanic theaters in the United States during the last twenty years. Like popular English-language musical theater, it combines spoken dialogue (usually in English) with song (in Spanish) and dance. A blend of popular and elite, it is musical comedy in an operatic style. To paraphrase Janet Sturman, where Los Lobos may be said to be "a mouthpiece for Chicano concerns, [zarzuela] typically speak[s] for, and to, a more broadly defined Hispanic population" (9).

THE LATIN TRADITION

Music from the Caribbean and South America reached the United States by sea, the chief ports of entry having been New Orleans in the nineteenth century and New York City in the twentieth. It has come from areas as far away as Argentina and as close as Cuba, and from cultures reflecting individually unique mixtures of Spanish, Portuguese, and African influences. (All are in the final analysis importations, since the influence of native Indian musics from these regions has been, until recently, negligible. But see the nueva canción movement, described earlier.)

New York City has long been a magnet for emigration from the Caribbean, and its Latin populations make up small cities within the supercity. Emigration from Puerto Rico (ceded to the United States after the Spanish-American War in 1898 and given commonwealth status in 1952) has been significant ever since United States citizenship was granted to Puerto Ricans in 1917, and it reached a peak in the 1940s and early 1950s. Emigration from Cuba has been less extensive, but an important ingredient in *la salsa* in New York City has been the presence of Cubans of the poorer classes, especially black Cubans who came to the United States before the Revolution of 1959. Thus for two generations New York has echoed with the strongly flavored music of the Caribbean: the Spanish-derived forms of the danza, the *seis,* and the *aguinaldo,* and the African-influenced plena and bomba of Puerto Rico, the Cuban *son* and *guajira,* the Afro-Cuban rumba, and the music of the Yoruban *lucumí* ritual (in Spanish *santería*).

A Survey of Latin Musical Forms by Geographical Origins

The multitudinous forms of Latin music have blended with and influenced one another throughout the last century and a half, especially after this music reached New York City, the virtual "melting pot" of Latin music from the Caribbean and Central and South America. Nevertheless, the countries and the cultures of origin still have enough significance to constitute perhaps the best key to organizing and understanding the whole panorama of the manifold and often overlapping forms of Latin music that have existed and still exist.

A starting point will be the nineteenth century Cuban *contradanza,* or *habanera,* which influenced the Puerto Rican danza, one of the most European and formal of Latin dances in the New World. Its basic rhythm (see Transcription 4.3) permeated much ethnic music in the Western Hemisphere. (For more on the origin of the danza, see Aparicio 8.)

CD 1/34 (1:10)
"Borinquen" (excerpt), Israel Berrios, composer and vocal. Performed by the Sextetto Criollo Puertoriqueño.

Transcription 4.3
The rhythmic pattern of *danza* and *habanera*

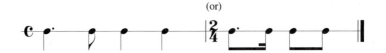

The nineteenth century pianist and composer Louis Moreau Gottschalk (see pp. 340–42) composed his *Danza* for piano, employing this rhythm, in Puerto Rico in 1857. Bizet used it in the "Habanera" for his opera *Carmen* in 1875. It is the basis for the Mexican *danza,* and was the "Spanish tinge" that Jelly Roll Morton noted as being an important and overlooked ingredient in jazz. It was used by Scott Joplin in his rag titled "Solace: A Mexican Serenade" (CD 4/2, p. 289) and is the underlying rhythm of the second strain of W. C. Handy's "St. Louis Blues." The ensemble for the danza on CD 1/34 consists of two guitars, two *cuatros* (small guitarlike instruments), and a güiro. (For a description of the instruments used in Latin music, see pp. 77–78.)

Puerto Rico[1]

> *plena:* A Puerto Rican style mixing African and European elements, developed in the working-class neighborhoods of Ponce during the early twentieth century. Played on small round frame drums called *panderetas,* plena is characterized by topical and satirical lyrics — it is sometimes referred to as the "singing newspaper." *Plena* is performed at medium-fast tempi; the basic rhythmic pattern follows.

Transcription 4.4
The rhythmic pattern of *plena.*

In the 1950s, Rafael Cortijo adapted *bomba* and *plena* to a Cuban-influenced dance band style that became enormously popular and influenced the development of *salsa.* Listen to *El Safacón de la 102nd St.,* New World 244 *Caliente = Hot.* For additional listening see: Cortijo y su Combo, *Baile con Cortijo y su Combo* (Seeco); Plena Libre, *Más Libre* (Ryko).

Aparicio, in her highly class-and-gender-oriented study, characterizes the distinction in milieu between the danza and the plena as "a white lady called the danza" as compared with "a sensual mulatta called the plena."

---

[1]For the rest of this section, the author is indebted to Lise Waxer, an eminent authority on Latin music, for her excellent "A Quick Guide to Latin Music," portions of which she kindly furnished for this edition.

bomba: Afro–Puerto Rican genre dating back to the colonial era, developed by slaves on the sugar plantations of Puerto Rico. Performed on three barrel-shaped drums called *barriles,* and accompanied by vocals and small percussion. *Bomba* ranges from medium to fast tempi, and features a very volatile and kinetic dance style characterized by interplay between the lead solo drum and dancers. The basic pattern follows.

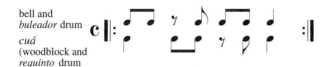

bell and
buleador drum

cuá
(woodblock and
requinto drum

Transcription 4.5
The rhythmic pattern
of *bomba.*

Listen to *Bomba Calindé,* New World 244. For additional listening see: Rafael Cepeda, *El Roble Mayor* (Balele Records); Cortijo y su Combo, *Baile con Cortijo y su Combo* (Seeco).

Cuba

danzón: Elegant mid-tempo salon dance of Cuban origin, developed in the 1870s, derived in part from the European semi-classical *contradanza* but with African-influenced rhythmic principles. Traditionally performed by the flute-and-violin *charanga* ensemble, danzón had a strong influence on the Puerto Rican *danza,* which also dates from this period. In the late 1930s, a *montuno*-like section was added to the end of the *danzón,* which was called "mambo"—this eventually gave rise to the big brass dance band *mambo.* See: Arcaño y sus Maravillas, *Danzón Mambo 1944–51* (Tumbao).

bolero: Romantic Cuban ballad form dating to the 1880s, characterized by a slow tempo and lyrics of lost love and heartbreak. Popularized widely after the advent of sound recording and radio in the early twentieth century, important sub-styles of bolero developed in Argentina and Mexico in the 1930s and 40s. See: Trio Los Panchos, *Los Mejores Boleros de Los Panchos, vols. 1 & 2* (Blue Moon).

mambo: Popular upbeat 1940s and 50s Cuban dance genre, emphasizing dynamic brass and energetic dancing. The term possibly comes from an African (Bantu?) word meaning "to speak." The mambo was created in 1938 by Orestes López, who developed an improvisatory *montuno*-like section added at the end of the danzón, but soon the mambo stood on its own, as a separate genre. By the late 1940s, the mambo had been adapted from the flute-and-violin *charanga* ensembles to jazz-style big bands by such Cuban artists as Machito (based in New York) and Damaso Pérez Prado (based in Mexico City). The mambo had a bigger impact in North America than in its native Cuba, crossing over into mainstream American society to become a huge dance craze of the 1950s, along with the *chachachá* (see below). For additional listening see: Machito and his Afro-Cubans, *Tremendo Cumban 1949–52* (Tumbao).

CD 1/35 (3:23)
"Para Los Rumberos,"
Tito Puente, 1956

"Para Los Rumberos" (CD 1/35), a mambo that is a salsa "standard," is here heard in a big-band version featuring a virtuoso performance on the timbales by Tito Puente, a composer, arranger, and performer who was a dominant figure in both Latin and jazz in New York for fifty years. The clave (see p. 77) is often difficult to find in the complex rhythms of the Latin rhythm section. In this case, the fast 3 + 2 clave is frequently spelled out in the band, especially in the very last section.

Mambo: "Para Los Rumberos"

LISTENING GUIDE

0:00   Introduction

0:09   Alternation of three 8-bar chorus refrains with two 8-bar instrumental phrases

0:42   20-bar section, including 8-bar variation on chorus refrain by baritone saxophone

1:00   Alternation of six 8-bar chorus refrains with five 8-bar phrases on timbales

2:10   Extended solo on timbales, including cross-rhythms

2:49   Eight statements of clave by timbales, with whole band joining in unison

3:03   Coda, or ending

---

chachachá: Variant of the danzón, invented in Cuba by Enrique Jorrín with his 1949 composition "La Engañadora." Characterized by a medium-slow tempo and a strong downbeat accent, the dancers' feet emphasize the rhythm "cha-cha-**cha.**" Through the 1950s, the chachachá became a widely popular dance genre both in Cuba and abroad. Listen to *Guataca*, from *Tito Puente: 50 Years of Swing* (RMD 3–82050). For additional listening see: Orquesta Aragón, *That Cuban Cha Cha Chá* (BMG Tropical).

rumba: Athough *rumba* generally denotes "a party" in general Latin American usage, in Cuba the term refers specifically to an Afro-Cuban musical style performed on conga drums and other percussion. It is not to be confused with the North Americanized term "rhumba," which referred to a simplified form of Cuban *son* popular during the 1930s. Afro-Cuban rumba is subdivided into three main sub-genres: *yambú* (slow), *guaguancó* (mid-tempo), and *columbia* (fast). For additional listening see: Los Muñequitos de Matanzas, *Rumba Caliente 77/88* (Qbadisc).

CD 1/36 (3:03) "La Polemica" (rumba), Los Muñequitos de Matanzas

son: Predominant form of Cuban popular music and the primary basis for *salsa,* son is a mid-tempo style forged from African and European elements in the late 19th century in the eastern part of Cuba and developed through successive stylistic periods in the 1920s–30s (in Santiago) and the 1940s–50s (in Havana). Traditionally played by small *conjuntos* (bands), son is characterized by a two-part structure consisting of (1) formal verses and, (2) an improvisatory, call-and-response section called the *montuno.* A simplified form of *son* called *"rhumba"* (not to be confused with Afro-Cuban *rumba)* was introduced into North America in 1930 and replaced the Argentine *tango* (see below) to become the Latin dance craze of the 1930s and 40s, succeeded by the *conga, mambo,* and *chachachá.* For additional listening see Conjunto Chappotín, *Los Tres Señores del Son—Cuní, Chappotín, Lilí* (Egrem).

CD 1/37 "Fuego en el 23" (0:00). Composed by Arsenio Rodriguez. Performed by Sonora Poncena.

montuno: The dynamic, improvisatory call-and-response section that constitutes the second half of typical salsa and Cuban *son* and *rumba* pieces. The term is also used to refer to the catchy syncopated vamp played by the piano in salsa and Cuban music.

salsa: A popular Latin dance style based primarily on the *son* and other Afro-Cuban genres, developed in New York City and Puerto Rico during the 1960s and 70s; it also incorporates Afro–Puerto Rican elements from *bomba* and *plena* and influences from North American jazz (especially via the *mambo*). Early forms of 1960s salsa included the sprightly *pachanga* and the slower *boogaloo,* which fused African-American r&b with Cuban *son.* The dynamic and heavily percussive sound of classic 1960s-70s salsa is often referred to as *salsa dura* ("heavy/hard" salsa), *salsa brava* (fiery salsa) or *salsa gorda* ("fat" salsa), in distinction to the smoother, pop-ballad sound of *salsa romántica* (romantic salsa), which predominated in the late 1980s and 1990s. Classic 1960s and '70s salsa

(*salsa dura*) featured much social commentary; songs from the more contemporary 1980s-90s style (*salsa romántica*) focuses primarily on love and romance. See CD 1/37, "Fuego en el 23."

The term *salsa* has a variety of meanings. For a discussion of these, see page 78.

tumbao: The basic rhythmic patterns played by the conga drums, bass, and piano in salsa and Cuban music (the patterns for each instrument are different, but can be referred to by the same term). See transcription. The term can also refer to the general swing or feel of a piece.

Transcription 4.6
The rhythmic patterns of *tumbao*

conga: Popular uptempo Latin dance craze of the late 1930s, based on the traditional Afro-Cuban Carnival *comparsa* (processional) dance of the same name, allegedly introduced into North America in 1938 by percussionist and television star Desi Arnaz. Characterized by a strong accent on beat 4, mirrored by a "one-two-three-**kick**" dance step.

Dominican Republic

merengue: Principal popular dance genre of the Dominican Republic, characterized by a fast duple rhythm, sprightly horn choruses, and catchy refrains. Began to achieve strong international prominence in the 1970s and 80s, displacing salsa's popularity in many Latin American countries. Songs are usually picaresque but can also be topical, commenting on current political and social themes; merengue is criticized by some for the sexist objectification of women in many contemporary tunes. Traditional merengue (*típico*) uses a basic rhythm notated below, but since the 1960s, most commercial merengue tunes have used the *maco* rhythm. See various artists, *Made in Dominicana* (Kubaney).

merengue
típico
(tambora)

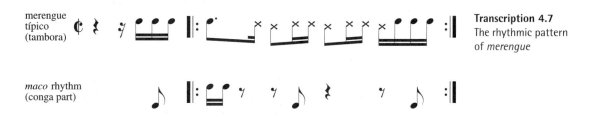

Transcription 4.7
The rhythmic pattern
of *merengue*

maco rhythm
(conga part)

bachata: Popular lyric song form from the Dominican Republic, characterized by a medium-slow tempo, twangy guitar picking, and lyrics that deal with betrayal and lost love. Became very popular in Puerto Rico and among U.S. Latins in the late 1990s. See: Blas Durán, *Bachata Dulce* (Mas Music).

Colombia

cumbia: The national genre of Colombia, based on Afro-Colombian forms from the country's Caribbean Coast, and characterized by a strong pulse on 2 and 4 in the following rhythm.

Transcription 4.8
The rhythmic pattern
of *cumbia*

A simplified variant of cumbia music (referred to as *raspa* in Colombia) spread internationally to Mexico, Central America, Ecuador, Peru, and Bolivia. In Mexico, cumbia has been adopted as a national genre, somewhat displacing the *ranchera* and other popular Mexican styles. See: Various Artists, *Colombia* (Putomayo).

Brazil

samba: Important Afro-Brazilian popular dance style developed in Salvador da Bahia in the 19th century and carried to Rio de Janeiro in the early 20th century, where it became the key musical genre associated with Carnival. Characterized by an upbeat duple meter, catchy interlocking polyrhythms, a plethora of percussion instruments, and scintillating footwork, samba is marked by a strong bass-drum accent on beat "3" of the bar:

Transcription 4.9
The rhythmic pattern of *samba*

Samba provided an important basis for the development of *bossa nova* (the "new rhythm") in Rio de Janeiro during the 1950s, which was a "cooler," slower version of samba using more complex, jazz-influenced harmonic vocabulary. Bossa nova had a tremendous impact on North American listeners during the early 1960s, thanks to the collaboration of jazz saxophonist Stan Getz with bossa nova pioneers Antonio Carlos Jobim and João Gilberto. Many bossa nova tunes have now become jazz standards. See: Various Artists, *Brasil, Samba de Carnaval;* Antonio Carlos Jobim, *Verve Jazz Masters 13* (Verve).

Argentina

tango: Important Argentine dance style from the turn of the last century, which became a major Latin dance craze in Europe and North America from the 1900s to 1920s. The ensemble includes the lush, trademark sound of the *bandoneon* (accordion-like instrument), piano, violins and other European instruments. Tango's mid-tempo rhythm is marked by a marchlike, 4-beat pattern. See: Various Artists, *Tango (Motion Picture Soundtrack)* (Deutsche Grammophon).

Transcription 4.10
The rhythmic pattern of *tango*

The Rhythms of Caribbean Music

A basic rhythmic ingredient of Cuban music is the *clave,* a rhythmic pattern whose constant repetitions unify the piece. At its simplest it is two measures in length, and consists in its skeletal form of five strokes distributed over two measures, as either "3 + 2" or "2 + 3."(See Transcription 4.11.)

As Waxer has put it, "In Cuban music, all the rhythmic patterns, melodic lines, horn accents, and even the syllables of the lyrics must line up with the clave. . . . Clave is not explicitly used in other Latin American dance styles (for

example, cumbia, merengue, bachata, bomba, plena, samba, tango), although a subtle 'clave sense' emerges from similar rhythmic patterns and principles of syncopation and ostinato (repeated grooves) in these forms." The clave, as played on the *claves*, is a familiar sound in Latin music; but the clave is by no means invariably performed on that instrument, nor is it always overtly stated in its simplest form. Listen again to "Para Los Rumberos" (CD 1/35) for the explicit sounding of the 3 + 2 clave, especially at the very end.

The Instruments of Latin Music

In contrast with the music of Mexico, Latin-Caribbean music, and especially that from Cuba and Hispaniola, shows much more African influence. (The influence of Cuban and African music on that of Mexico must not be overlooked, but *in the main* this generalization holds true.) This influence is apparent in the greater role of percussion and in the vast array of percussion instruments. The drums are of primary importance, and there are several families of them, each family associated with a particular genre of Latin music. The *congas*, single-headed drums with tapered barrel shape and used primarily in the Cuban-derived rumba, consist of the *quinto*, the *segundo*, and the *tumba* (or *tumbadora*). In the Puerto Rican-derived bomba and plena, the drums are the *requinto* and the *seguidora*. The ensemble for the plena may add the *pandereta*, a frame drum like a tambourine without the metal discs. Associated with the Yoruban lucumí religion are the *batá* drums, consisting of the *okónkolo*, the *itótele*, and the largest, or "mother," drum, the *iyá*, which communicates directly with the *orishas*, or spirits. In each drum family, the instruments are listed from small to large. The largest and deepest routinely have the role of providing the basic support, while the smaller, higher drums improvise around the basic pattern, or clave (see Transcription 4.11). In Latin popular music the *timbales*, a pair of shallow, cylindrical tuned drums, are used extensively and played as featured solo instruments by virtuosos such as the late Tito Puente. In addition to the drums are the smaller handheld percussion instruments, including the claves (two hardwood sticks struck together), the *maracas* (gourd-shaped, with seeds or shot in them), the *güiro* (a slotted gourd scraped with a piece of metal), the *campanas* (cowbells), and thin sticks struck against a hard surface such as a drum shell, called in the Cuban rumba a *cás-cara,* and in the Puerto Rican bomba a *cuá.* This partial list of Latin percussion instruments is given simply to convey the importance of rhythm in this music—an importance that is readily confirmed on hearing it.

The Meanings of Salsa

It is important to note that the term *salsa,* so commonly heard in relation to the Latin music of New York City, is a sensitive word that is subject to varying interpretations. As we saw earlier, in its strict usage "salsa" refers to a popular style based on the Cuban *son.* In another usage it is simply a marketing label (much like "soul" in African-American popular music), and was denigrated as such by Tito Puente, and in references to the "salsa industry" by others. But there is a third sense in which, again like "soul," the word is used both to describe the feeling performers put into their playing (*con salsa,* that is, "with sauce") and as a key word in defining cultural identity, especially by Puerto Ricans. In the ethnic sense, salsa is seen as the music of immigrants and the urban working class, produced mostly by black and mulattto musicians, and tied to the social functions of the Puerto Rican bomba and plena. Before the Cuban revolution of 1959, which brought Fidel Castro to power, Latin music in New York City was heavily Cuban. After the Cuban embargo that followed the revolution, the word "salsa," in sociological terms, came to apply to the attempt by Puerto Rican musicians to wrest the identity of their music from the dominance of Cuban musical influences. (See Aparicio 78ff.)

Ethnic Music of the Caribbean in New York City

In dealing with this music, it is important to note the distinction between the *ethnic* music, with what John Storm Roberts has referred to as its "undiluted Latin styles," and the adaptations of it by and for American popular music.

An important aspect of the importation of Latin music to the United States is its service to the Latin immigrants themselves, in their own lives and communities. To quote Roberts in full: "The presence of a large Latin community in New York—and later in other U.S. cities—provided a demand for authenticity, a place for musicians to play undiluted Latin styles, and, perhaps most important, a doorway for innovations from Cuba and other Latin countries" (57).

Roberts's point about the "demand for authenticity" deserves attention. Just as Chicano music has become a symbol and focus of ethnic pride for those of Mexican descent in the Southwest, so has Afro-Cuban, Afro–Puerto Rican, and Afro-Dominican music performed the same function for those of Cuban, Puerto Rican, and Dominican origin in New York City. They illustrate, in the words of one writer, "the proclivity of people to seize on traditional cultural symbols as a definition of their own identity" (Bennett, in Singer 183).

But Latin musicians are no different from other musicians in that they do not *automatically* "seize on traditional cultural symbols" in making their music; these must usually be learned, in one way or another. The Afro-Caribbean music played in New York is essentially a music played by ear and therefore aurally transmitted. But the personal contact between musicians that is traditionally associated with aural transmission has been to a considerable degree replaced by learning from records. In that regard, it is interesting to note the role played by men such as René López and Andy González—who have large record collections and who are also effective social and political historians, educators, impresarios, record producers, and even performers themselves—in educating other Latin musicians as to what their "traditional cultural symbols" are, their history, and the importance of their authenticity if they are to serve to "define their own identity."

Caribbean Influences in American Popular Music

The "Latin tinge" from the Caribbean has had a perennial influence on American popular music over the past century, usually by way of popular dance. The habanera around the turn of the century was followed in the 1910s and 1920s by the tango, which arrived from Argentina by way of Paris! In the 1930s came the rhumba, from the Cuban *son,* and after this the samba (Afro-Brazilian), the mambo (Afro-Cuban), the chachachá (Cuban), the merengue (Dominican), and in the 1960s the bossa nova (Brazilian). These successive waves of popular Latin genres have been initiated mostly as professional musicians, steeped in their own traditions, moved into the arenas of American jazz or popular music, bringing their traditional styles with them but adapting them to cater to broad popular taste.

Iberian-Afro-Indian music from the south has influenced what may be regarded as "mainstream" American music in ways far less superficial than the successive waves of popular Latin dance fashions. The "Latin tinge," therefore, is an important, if largely unacknowledged, hue in much of our music.

▬ PROJECTS

1. Attend a concert by a professional mariachi show band, and write a review. Comment on, among other things, the makeup of the audience, the things the audience reacted most strongly to, and the relationship of the music played to traditional Mexican music.
2. Write a paper on the state of Chicano music today. Include a discography and a list of poet-musicians active in Chicano circles. The periodicals *Aztlán* and *Latin American Music Review* may be helpful.

3. In *Listening to Salsa*, Frances Aparicio writes that the conflicting views on salsa "dramatize the central role of popular music as a site for the formation and definition of national identity" (66). In a short essay, develop your own opinion as to whether or not popular music can form and define national identity. Explain why, in your opinion, it either can or cannot. If you believe it can, give other examples of popular music defining national identity (of the United States or any other country).

4. Identify and write a brief informative paragraph on three women performers of Latin-Caribbean music. The books by Aparicio, Steward, and Waxer (see References) should be helpful. Present the facts and *your* opinions; do not quote flowery press-agent-like prose. Include two songs each that you think show them at their best, and explain your choices.

ADDITIONAL LISTENING

The Best of Flaco Jiménez. Arhoolie CD 478.

Dark and Light in Spanish New Mexico. NW 80292. Includes alabados and bailes.

Caliente = Hot: Puerto Rican and Cuban Musical Expression in New York. NW 244.

Freddie Fender: Canciones de Mi Barrio. Arhoolie CD 366.

Mass in D major. By Ignacio de Jerúsalem. *Mexican Baroque.* Teldec 4509-96353-2.

Mexican-American Border Music, Vol. 1. Arhoolie Folklyric CD 7001. Includes "Que me gano con llorar" and is a good additional example of the early phases of musica norteña.

Mexican-American Border Music, Vol. 3. Arhoolie CD 7016. Includes Narciso Martínez.

Mission Music of California: A 200-year Anthology. Mission San Luis Rey, [760] 757-3651.

Spanish Mexican Folk Music of New Mexico. Smithsonian/Folkways P-426. Includes a polka and a waltz.

"Will the Wolf Survive." *Just Another Band from East L. A.* Perf. Los Lobos. Slash/Warner Bros. 9 45367-2.

CHAPTER

5 Other Traditions: French, Scandinavian, Asian

LOUISIANA AND THE FRENCH INFLUENCE

Louisiana is a land of sultry climate, dominated largely by the complex outflow, through shifting channels and bayous, of one of the largest river systems in the world. It has a complex cultural pattern as well—albeit one that is fairly stable, the main ingredients of its mix having been established for over a century. To an indigenous Indian population was added that of French colonizers and settlers beginning in the early eighteenth century. There was scant Spanish immigration during the period of Spanish rule (1764–1800). An important factor in the cultural mix of Louisiana was the dramatic rise in the African American population, coming mostly from the West Indies, at the end of the eighteenth century. Black people were brought to Louisiana in significant numbers by planters escaping the revolution in Haiti in the 1790s. The cultural ties of Louisiana with the West Indies, especially Haiti, have been important ever since. After the Louisiana Purchase in 1803, American influence and immigration naturally increased, and the substantial black population made possible, in part, the rapid growth of the sugar plantations. Italians, Hungarians, Slovenians, Germans, and Irish have since been added to the mix in smaller numbers. The dominant cultural (and therefore musical) patterns of Louisiana, however, are the result of a complex interaction between those of French and African descent.

French American Music of Louisiana

French people began settling Louisiana early in the eighteenth century, some coming directly from France, and others arriving after a stopover of a few generations in the West Indies. Many were families of means and belonged to the aristocracy, and they soon constituted a wealthy planter class. Their cultural inclinations were urban and sophisticated; this was manifested in the establishment of French opera in New Orleans as early as the 1790s.

At the other end of the economic scale was the French-descended refugee population that came to Louisiana from Acadia (now Nova Scotia) in the latter part of the eighteenth century. A few Acadians had reached Louisiana before the Expulsion, but the great flow took place after 1755, when the victorious English, in a cruel episode known as the Dérangement, began to expel all Acadians who would not take an oath of allegiance to the British crown. The Acadians began arriving in Louisiana some ten years later, after stopovers in France and in the American colonies. These people, mostly farmers and fishermen whose families had come from Brittany and Normandy, were regarded with contempt by the upper-class French, who excluded them from New Orleans but allowed them to settle upstream, along a stretch of the right bank of the Mississippi that became known as the "Acadian coast." The "Cajuns" were regarded as inferior—an attitude that still persists—but the colony benefited from the presence of these industrious people, in their raising of crops and livestock to feed New Orleans, and their ability to construct the all-important dikes to control the rivers and bayous.

The Cajuns suffered a "second expulsion" after the Purchase and the coming of the Americans, when it was found that the land they occupied was ideal for raising sugar. They moved farther south and west, into the bayous and swamps of the coastal regions, and into the prairies of the west. Thus they came to occupy the "French triangle," with its base along the Gulf coast, and its apex around Alexandria. Tracing their lineage back two centuries to the first Acadian families (the Moutons, the Arceneaux, the Bernards, the Broussards, the Guidrys), they occupy the largest area of French-derived culture and language in the United States. There are now approximately one million people, roughly a quarter of the population of Louisiana, who identify themselves as Cajuns.

Louisiana Folk Songs from France

CD 1/38 (2:45) "Sept ans sur mer" ("Seven Years at Sea"), sung by Elida Hofpauir and her sister. Recorded by John A. and Alan Lomax in New Iberia, Louisiana, 1934.

Text, "Sept ans sur mer"

There are some charming and quite old folk songs that Irène Thérèse Whitfield has distinguished from Cajun songs as having been brought directly from France (24). "Sept ans sur mer" (CD 1/38), an old, possibly medieval, sailor's ballad is very widespread. It is sung in French Canada as well as in Louisiana. Originating in Brittany and Poitou, and following the seacoasts, it is found in versions in Icelandic, Norwegian, Danish, Catalan, Spanish, and Portuguese.

1. On a resté six ans sur mer,
   Sans pouvoir border la terre. [2X]

   On stormy seas we six years sailed,
   And never once green land we hailed.

2. Au bout de la septième année.
   On a manqué de provisions. [2X]

   The bitter seventh year came on.
   We found our stores at last were gone.

3. On a mangé souris et rats
   Jusque le touvre du navire. [2X]

   We ate the mice, we ate the rats
   And through the hold we ran like rats.

4. On a tiré la courte paille
   Pour voir lequel qui serait mangé. [2X]

   And then at lots we took a try
   To see which one of us would die.

5. "En voilà, p'tit Jean, s'il tombe-z-au cas,
   Ça serait p'tit Jean qui serait mangé.
   O voilà, p'tit Jean, qu'il tombe sur toi,
   Ça serait p'tit Jean qui serait mangé.

   "Look, little John, if chance does will,
   It's you we'll take, it's you we'll kill.

   Look, little John, so chance does will,
   It's you we'll take, it's you we'll kill."

6. "O p'tit Jean, ça fait du mal."   "Too bad, little John," they cried,
   Il crie, "Courage, mes camarades."   "Oh, courage, comrades," he replied
   [2X]

7. "Je vois la terr' sur toutes côtés,   "For I see land on every side
   Trois pigeons blanc qui s'a voltigé.   And three white pigeons toward
   [2X]   us fly.

8. "Je vois aussi trois filles du père   "And I see lovely sisters three
   Qui se promenaient au bord du   Come walking down all by the sea;
   rivage. [2X]

9. "O si jamais je mets pieds sur terre   "And if I set my foot on land
   La plus jolie je l'épouserai." [2X]   I'll ask the fairest for her hand."

Cajun Music

"J'ai passé devant ta porte" (CD 1/39) illustrates two characteristics of Cajun music, the use of the button accordion, and waltz meter. The song is asserted to be "still one of the best-known and best-loved of the Cajun songs" (album notes). It is included in the often-cited collection *Louisiana French Folk Songs* (Whitfield 88). As to the lyrics, the album notes give the following commentary: "Sudden death was not unusual in South Louisiana, or anywhere else, fifty or sixty years ago. A neighbor, reminiscing, told me about being in love with a girl, and coming back from a week's visit to his parents, to find the she had died and was buried without his knowing" (Catherine Blanchet, notes to *Louisiana Cajun Music*, Vol. 2. Arhoolie LP109).

CD 1/39 (2:57)
"J'ai passé devant ta porte" ("I passed in front of your door"), Cleoma B. Falcon, vocal and guitar; Joseph Falcon, accordion; Ophy Breaux, fiddle

J'ai passé devant ta porte,   I passed in front of your door,
J'ai crié, "By-bye, la belle,"   I cried, "Bye-bye, sweetheart,"
Y a personne qu'a pas répondu,   Nobody answered,
O yé-yaïe, mon coeur me fait mal.   O ye-yaie, my heart hurts.

Je m'ai donc mis, oui, à observer,   I then set myself to observe,
Moi, j'ai vu une petite lumière allumée, I saw a little light lighted,
Y a quelque chose qui me disait   Something told me I should be
   j'aurais pleuré   crying,
O yé-yaïe, mon coeur me fait mal.   O ye-yaie, my heart hurts.

Quand j'ai été cogner à la porte,   When I went to knock at the door,
oui, ils m'ont ouvert la porte,   yes, they opened the door,
Moi, j'ai vu des chandelles allumées   Me, I saw the candles lighted
Tout autour de ton cercueil.   All around your coffin.

Text, "J'ai passé devant ta porte"

The fiddle was the basic Cajun instrument from the earliest times, being used for the enduring pastime of dancing. A dance lasting late into the night, to which the children are brought and bedded down, is known as a *fais do-do* (French: "go beddy-bye"). In the 1920s the accordion (possibly making its way into the area with German settlers) began to be adopted, as it was farther west in the musica norteña of the Texas-Mexico border (see Chapter 4). By the time the Cajun accordionist Joseph Falcon and his wife, née Cleoma Breaux, recorded "J'ai passé devant ta porte," the accordion had become an integral part of the Cajun band, which consisted, in addition, of fiddle, guitar, and, in the early days, triangle, or *'tit fer*. Listening to early recorded sources, we find a music that is lighthearted in mood and theme, with a marked predilection for love songs, and a repertory consisting mostly of waltzes, pieces in duple meter related to hoedown music, and pieces related to the blues. The vocal style is unique and unmistakable, though difficult to describe. Vocal tone is somewhat flat and nasal, at times only approximating the pitch, with frequently interjected yells and wails.

Cajun music began to be recorded in the 1920s. This was the time when major record companies realized that there was a considerable market for regional folk music, and began to record not only Cajun music but also early country music (marketed as "old-time music"—see Chapter 7), spirituals, work songs, and blues (see Chapters 2 and 8), ballad singers (see Chapter 1), religious groups and preachers (see Chapter 11), and many other types of ethnic music. In fact, one notable archive of folk and ethnic music, the *Anthology of American Folk Music*, consists entirely of early commercial recordings.

In the late 1930s and the 1940s, with the expansion of the oil industry and the influx of workers from the rural Southeast, Cajun music lost many of its earlier distinctive characteristics and was nearly swamped in the flood of country-and-western music. It was about this time that the Hawaiian steel guitar, which had recently become popular in country music, joined the Cajun band. And one hears in "Le cote farouche de la vie" a Cajun adaptation of the country-music song "It Wasn't God Who Made Honky-Tonk Angels," to the tune of "I'm Dreaming Tonight of My Blue-eyes" (see Additional Listening). Many of the recordings of this period take on the character of hillbilly music sung in patois.

CD 1/40 (3:20) "Le Two-Step à Midland," Michael Doucet, fiddle and vocal, and Beausoleil. Recorded Lafayette, Louisiana, 1981.

Since the 1950s there has been a resurgence of the older styles; the accordion is back, and so are some of the older songs. With musicians such as Michael Doucet (who has revived Cajun fiddle playing) and his group Beausoleil, Cajun music has undergone a full-fledged revival and a reconnection with its traditions. The long instrumental passages in both CD 1/39 and 1/40 remind us that Cajun music is intended for dancing.

Elemore Morgan, Jr.

A resurgence of older styles in Cajun music since the 1950s brought back the distinctive sound of the accordion (played here by Nathan Abshire).

O chere bébé, gardez-donc mais quoi tu m'as fait	O darling, look what you've done to me	Text, "Le Two-Step à Midland"
T'as fait la misère, o chagrin	You've caused me misery, oh pain	
Ouais chagrin que moi j'ai eu	Oh, the pain that I've felt	
O hé 'tit coeur, 'y a pas personne qui veut les voir.	Oh little heart, nobody knows.	
Mais moi j'ai seul à la maison	I'm all alone at my house	
Veux t'en allez ouais avec moi?	Do you want to go with me?	

O, mais gardez donc le chagrin que tu m'as fait	Oh, look at the pain you've caused me
Chere bébé, mais je mérite pas ça	Babe, I don't deserve that
Oui catin malheureux	Heartless woman
O ouais plus belle t'es plus belle	Your beauty isn't pretty any more
Pourquoi faire mais les misères	Why do you make me miserable
Mais ouais dans moi	Oh me
Et moi tout seul je t'espérais.	All alone I waited for you.
O 'y a pas longtemps, 'y a pas longtemps	It wasn't long, it wasn't long ago
Que moi je t'ai vue, chère bébé	That I saw you, baby
Mais moi t'ai donc emmenée	But I'd like to take you with me
Pour aller ouais ensemble.	To go away together.

AFRICAN AMERICAN MUSIC OF LOUISIANA

People of African descent have played a major role in Louisiana history and culture. Like the French, they have been stratified into a complex ranking of caste and lineage. High in the social order were the "gens de couleur libre" ("free persons of color"), of whose presence in Louisiana there are records from the early eighteenth century. From 1725 on they either entered free, were freed in recognition of merit and loyalty, were given their freedom by a white parent or lover, or purchased their own freedom. (American Indians also had the status of "free persons of color.") Many became wealthy and influential, owning land and slaves. At the other end of the social scale (though not as low as the Cajuns) were the black slaves from Africa and the West Indies.

There is ample evidence of African-based music-making in and around New Orleans in the nineteenth century. Seven songs in dialect French, and given the name "creole," were included at the end of the famous *Slave Songs of the United States*, edited by William Allen, Charles Ware, and Lucy Garrison, and published in 1867. (The term *creole* is plagued with the ambiguity of multiple meanings and is no longer used, except in quotes, to apply to African Americans or their music in Louisiana.) Place Congo, opposite the Vieux Carré (and on the present-day site of Louis "Satchmo" Armstrong Park), was the scene of weekly black festivities and ceremonies, from which whites were traditionally excluded. As was true in Africa itself, there was (and is) a nearly inseparable association of music and dance. The bamboula, the *counjaille*, the *calinda*, the habanera—these were types of songs, but they were also dances.

The *bamboula* was named for a small drum made from a section of the huge bamboo that grows in the West Indies; the drum accompanied both song and dance. The dance itself was vividly described in a much-quoted article "The Dance in Place Congo," by George Washington Cable, which included the music (Cable).

Transcription 5.1
"Bamboula"

The first measure has a rhythm basic to much Latin American music—and, presumably via New Orleans, to much American black music as well—that of the habanera or danza, which could be either song or dance (see pp. 69–70). Two examples of the melody incorporated into classical music are "Bamboula," by Louisiana-born Louis Moreau Gottschalk (see pp. 340–42), and "The Dance in Place Congo," by Henry F. Gilbert. (See Additional Listening.)

A pervading influence among the blacks of French Louisiana—and not unknown among whites, as well—was *voodoo*, known in New Orleans as *hoodoo*. Originating principally among the Dahomeans in Africa, voodoo had become intermingled with the liturgy and ritual of Roman Catholicism (despite the general opposition of the Church) among the blacks of the French West Indies, especially San Domingo and Martinique. Hoodoo ceremonies were marked by rhythmic drumming, chanting, and dancing. The bamboula was associated with it. The goal seemed to be a kind of ecstatic possession by one of the hoodoo deities. According to eyewitness accounts, this possession was not unlike that to be seen at primitive revival meetings.

Much of the African American music of Louisiana we have just described contained some of the important seeds of jazz, and it was jazz that was the culminating musical form to be developed by black musicians from the rich variety of influences present in turn-of-the-century New Orleans. (See Stearns, especially Chaps. 3, 4, and 5.)

Zydeco: Cajun Rhythm-and-Blues

African American musicians in Cajun country have produced a rhythm-and-blues translation of Cajun music known as *zydeco* (or *zodico* or *zarico*). The term *zydeco* is said to have come from the pronunciation of "les haricots" (beans) in the early Cajun song "Les haricots sont pas sale." On the Louisiana-Texas Gulf Coast, the term *zydeco* can also refer to a party (like the term *fais do-do*), or to a gumbo dish. Zydeco music retains and features the accordion (in this case the piano-accordion) but adds to the band the piano, the electric guitar, the electric bass, drums, and sometimes saxophones; usually leaves out the fiddle; often adds a characteristic "rub board" (which has the function and sound of the washboard of the early jug and blues bands); and has a strong rhythm-and-blues flavor.

CD 2/1 (3:10)
"Zydeco sont pas sale,"
Clifton Chenier,
vocal and accordion;
Cleveland Chenier, rub
board; Madison Guidry,
drums. Recorded in
Houston, Texas, 1965.

Clifton Chenier (1925–1987), the "king of zydeco" (he had many publicity photos taken wearing an actual crown), was a versatile musician who in the 1960s and 1970s performed both zydeco, singing in Cajun-French, and out-and-out Gulf Coast rhythm-and-blues, which he sang in English. Chenier's "Zydeco sont pas sale" ("The snap beans aren't salty"), from about 1965, is representative of early zydeco.

Important performers of zydeco in an older style, closer to Cajun music, are the accordionists Freeman Fontenot and Alphonse "Bois-sec" Ardoin, and the fiddler Canray Fontenot. The newer style, closer to rhythm-and-blues, is represented by accordionists John Delafose, Rocking Dopsie, Rocking Sidney, Stanley "Buckwheat" Dural, and Doozoo Chavez. White musicians such as Wayne Toups and Zachary Richard are also performing zydeco.

THE UPPER MIDWEST AND THE SCANDINAVIAN INFLUENCE

We have examined briefly the French-Iberian-African culture at the mouth of the Mississippi. At the source of this great river, and across the upper Midwest, we find a land that in its climate, its topography, and the ethnic background of its people is in utter contrast. In the geological day-before-yesterday, the land was scoured by glaciers, which left behind many lakes and a rich glacial soil, supporting vegetation that varied from prairie in the south to dense forest in the north. It lies right in the center of the North American continent, and although its early Scandinavian settlers (especially the Swedes and the Finns) found the topography similar to that of their homeland, the Norwegians found the harsh continental climate much more extreme. As a Norwegian immigrant wrote home from Wisconsin in 1857, "The winter here is shorter than in Norway, but it is usually much colder, and when the summer comes, that in turn is much warmer. . . . Many people not adjusted to the climate break down" (Bergmann 52).

The first inhabitants encountered by the Europeans were the Chippewa and the Dakota Sioux. Throughout the seventeenth, eighteenth, and early nineteenth centuries, a tenuous white presence was maintained by the successive establishment of forts and trading posts by first the French, then the English, and finally the Americans, all of whom were interested primarily in furs. But the beginning of permanent settlement had taken place well before the Civil War, by which time a series of land-grabbing treaties and military operations had practically driven out the Indians, to make way for a rapid influx of prospective farmers.

Scandinavian immigrants began settling in Wisconsin in the 1840s, and in Minnesota in the 1850s. The Swedes, the most numerous group, began as farmers but later moved to the cities, to be outnumbered in farming by the Norwegians, the next most numerous. The Norwegian immigrant man, bringing with him a strong attachment to the land, would characteristically progress from hired hand to shareman to landowning farmer. Other immigrant peoples, also from northern or central Europe, were the Germans (notably in Wisconsin), the Danes, the Finns, the Poles, and the Czechs. But by the last quarter of the century it was the Scandinavians whose presence was decisive in determining the cultural makeup of the upper Midwest.

Scandinavian American Music in the Upper Midwest

The kind of regional music most in evidence in this area is music for dancing. The music, the instruments, and the dances themselves occur in layers, based on their antiquity. The oldest dances from Norway, such as the *halling* (in which the dancer kicks a hat off a vertically held pole), the *springer*, or the *gangar*, belong to a bygone era and are encountered only in deliberate and costumed revivals. The same is true of the instruments that were brought direct from Norway, and were associated with the old dances. Chief among these was the Hardanger fiddle (*Hardangfele*), an instrument that has, beneath the four strings played with the bow, a set of sympathetic strings that vibrate in resonance with the bowed strings.

As the old dances and the old instruments went out of general use, they were replaced by the three dances most popular among Scandinavian Americans today—the schottische (CD 2/2), the waltz (CD 2/3 and the polka (CD 2/4). (For a look at the Slavic—specifically Czech—polka picture in the Upper Midwest, see Lornell and Rasmussen 25–47.)

CD 2/2 (0:48)
"Hejsan Grabbar"
("Hey! Boys"),
schottische (excerpt)

CD 2/3 (0:35)
"Drømmen om Elin"
("Dream of Elin"),
waltz (excerpt)

The most popular instruments for dances are now the regular fiddle and the accordion, accompanied by guitar, piano, pump organ, or banjo, as available. In rural areas, dances took place at house parties in homes, or in the cleared-out second-floor lofts of roomy barns. More recently, barns that have never housed hay or cattle have been built especially for "barn dances." In the towns and cities, public dances are held in various social halls.

CD 2/4 (1:05)
"Banjo, Old Time,"
polka (excerpt)

CD 2/5 (0:50)
"Nikolina" (excerpt,
two verses),
Olle i Skratthult
(Hjalmar Peterson)
with ensemble

In the first years of the twentieth century, commercial recordings of Scandinavian music began to be made by professional and semiprofessional bands. As early as 1915 the Swedish immigrant musician and entertainer Hjalmar Peterson (who adopted the stage name "Olle i Skratthult") recorded his love song "Nikolina" (Transcription 5.2), which became immensely popular and was performed in many variants both as a song and as an instrumental piece.

Transcription 5.2
"Nikolina"

Att va - ra Kär_____ dä ä en rys - lig pi - na den som för - sökt dä sä - ger in - te nej. Jag var så rys - ligt kär i Nik - o li - na, å Nik - o - li - na li - ka Kär i mej.

Text translation
"Nikolina," first stanza

When you're in love you're in an awful torture,
Who ever has tried it will not disagree,
I was so very fond of Nikolina
And Nikolina was as fond of me.

The impact of recordings, radio, the jukebox, traveling vaudeville (Olle i Skratthult himself was "on the road" for years with his band of entertainers), and movies was to force changes in Scandinavian American music, and a decline in home music-making—a familiar pattern everywhere. But it was, ironically, through the very medium of the old recordings that the "old-time" styles of the early twentieth century were ultimately preserved—also a familiar pattern wherever there has been a revival of old-time music. State agencies and programs such as the Folk Arts Program of the Minnesota State Arts Board are engaged in actively encouraging the documentation and preservation of "people's arts." (Most of the fifty states now have such programs, under various titles.) Closely related to this preservation movement are ethnic gatherings such as the annual Nordic Fest in Decorah, Iowa, and widespread celebrations of Syttende Mai (May 17, Norwegian Independence Day). Practically all ethnic groups everywhere in America have similar gatherings to celebrate their original national holidays—the Mexican Cinco de Mayo is another example. The work of LeRoy Larson, folklorist, scholar, banjo player, and record producer, together with his Minnesota Scandinavian Ensemble, typifies what is being done in the way of contemporary live performance. His work, like that of Michael Doucet in Louisiana, Justin Bishop in Colorado, and many others, is not simply to preserve but also to re-create, to reinterpret, and to create anew in traditional styles, and thus to demonstrate their vitality and validity as an effective alternative to the progressive homogenization of American culture. Were it not for them, and people like them in virtually every state, this chapter would have been confined to simply chronicling the decline and death of regional musics in this country.

THE ASIAN INFLUENCE

Compared with other ethnic musics we have so far considered, the influence of Asian music in America, and on American music, has occurred fairly recently—mostly after World War II. For obvious reasons its impact has been far greater on the West Coast than on other parts of the country. There are other factors as well that make the story of Asian influence quite different from that of the European-derived cultures from Spain, France, and Scandinavia. We shall be concerned specifically with the music of India, Indonesia, and Japan. In each case not only does their music come out of traditions that are among the oldest in the world, but also their music is much less familiar to Western ears than the music that reached us from Europe. It shares this unfamiliarity with the music of the American Indians—ultimately from Asia as well! It must be recognized, however, that this lack of familiarity is disappearing under the impact of the "world music" movement. As a manifestation of this happy broadening of our cultural frontiers, there is an ever-swelling flood of recordings on the market of ever more specialized music of hitherto obscure places and cultures (*Betawi and Sundanese Music of the North Coast of Java: Topeng, Betawi, Tanjidor, Ajeng; Kalimantan: Dayak Ritual and Festival Music;* and *Yoshitsune: Songs of Medieval Hero Accompanied by the Biwa* are but samples of what is available.)

In considering Asian American music, we must distinguish Asian music performed by Asians in the United States (such as that re-created in practically its original form by recent arrivals from Vietnam, Laos, and Cambodia) from the products of the syncretization of Asian and American musical elements—in other words, we must distinguish mere transplantation from the blending of two musics. It is the latter that will be our focus here.

The Music of India

Classical Indian music is a formidably difficult art with a venerable history, demanding long apprenticeship for its mastery. Despite that, it is being taught in the United States as well as in India, and a number of gifted American musicians have dedicated themselves to learning it. Beginning in the thirteenth century, classical Indian music resolved itself into two styles, which have become two separate but related disciplines: the Hindusthani of the north and the Carnatic of the south. To attempt to launch into anything like an adequate explanation or description of this music is out of the question. All that can be ventured at this point is to say that the beginning listener to this music will be aware of a texture consisting of a sinuous melodic line, either vocal or played on a plucked stringed instrument such as the *sitar.* The melodic line is governed by one of number of *ragas.* These can be compared to, but are more complex than, the modes in Western music (major, minor, Mixolydian, and so on). The characteristics of the ragas include not only particular scales but also melodic patterns, motives, ornaments, and even emotional character. The melodic line is supported by drumming of considerable variety and complexity, and a continuous drone on the pitches of an open fifth, played either by a stringed instrument (a *tambura*) or by a bellows-driven reed instrument. (There are by now electronic substitutes for both.)

Our focus here will be not on Indian music itself (there are numerous recordings and live performances available) but on the attempts, past and present, to achieve a syncretism between East Indian music and Western music of various styles. Illustrative of the syncretism with Western classical music is the *Concerto for Sitar and Orchestra* by the renowned sitarist Ravi Shankar, and the famous collaboration between Shankar and the violinist Yehudi Menuhin on *West Meets East* (see Additional Listening). An interesting parallel with this is the *Two World Concerto* for native American flute and orchestra with virtuoso R. Carlos Nakai on the (American) Indian flute. (See CD 1/27, p. 48.)

A well-known example of syncretism with popular music was illustrated by George Harrison's recording with the Beatles of his "Love You To" on the album *Revolver* (1966) (see Additional Listening). Reflections of Indian music occur in Harrison's opening solo on the sitar, after which a tambura-like drone is established, to which is added a *tabla*-like drumbeat, before the entry of the voices. Harrison was a student of Ravi Shankar and became a devotee of Indian music and philosophy.

The Music of Indonesia

Indonesia is a curved string of hundreds of islands, straddling the equator, and extending for over three thousand miles from the Malay Peninsula on the Southeast Asian mainland to New Guinea, just north of Australia. It includes the islands of Sumatra, Java, and (in part) New Guinea and Borneo. It has been independent only since the defeat of the Japanese at the end of World War II.

The basic musical ensemble in Indonesian music is the *gamelan*. The gamelan consists basically of sets of gongs, either hung in the familiar manner or resting horizontally in a wooden frame, and sets of metal slab instruments, set up and played in the manner of the Western vibraphone, but low to the ground and always played sitting down cross-legged. There are also plucked or bowed stringed instruments, and drums. There can be singing as well, with a high nasal sound. But the basic sound of the gamelan is that of a rich variety of sounds of struck metal. To many Western ears it is a pleasing and intriguing sound, and its popularity has led to the setting up of many gamelans throughout the country, many in academic music departments. This has been accompanied by the teaching of gamelan, and Indonesian music in general, and the founding of many gamelan ensembles.

Each gamelan has its own makeup and character, including its own unique version of one of the two basic tunings, *pélog* (a scale with seven pitches to the octave) and *sléndro* (with five). Though to the casual ear the tuning may seem to approximate some form of the Western seven-tone diatonic scale, none corresponds exactly, and each gamelan will have its own version of one (or both in the case of a full *sléndro pélog* gamelan) of the tunings. So individual are gamelans that each may have its own name, and their instruments are not interchangeable.

The whole *behavior* of Indonesian music (and indeed of most Asian music) is unfamiliar to Western ears. It has a static quality. Once set in motion, it doesn't seem to "go anywhere" or "do anything." It just keeps on, and eventually stops. There can be gradual changes in tempo but few or no changes in volume and timbre (brought about in Western music by changes in instrumentation), and the climaxes are very subtle. This musical behavior has appealed to some composers, and Asian music furnished one of the sound models for minimalism (see pp. 422–27). The implied philosophical implications of this behavior have also been cited by those who hold that music is not actually *supposed* to "do" anything or "go" anywhere, but simply to "be" (or not to be). John Cage espoused this point of view, and he and his followers have contrived a great deal of music based on the idea of simply "letting sounds be themselves" (see p. 414).

With all the recorded "world music" available today, it is easy to hear Indonesian gamelan music in its authentic form. (See Additional Listening, especially *Worlds of Music.*) Our focus here will be, as with the music of India, on the syncretism of Indonesian and Western music. Here, as we have seen in the case of both East Indian and American Indian music, the *concertante* form, which combines a soloist or soloists with some kind of instrumental ensemble, is a practical procedure.

CD 2/6 (3:00)
Threnody for Carlos Chavez (excerpt), by Lou Harrison. 1978.

Lou Harrison, a California composer who lives at America's very western edge, as close as he can to the sea that separates American from Asian, is an authority on, and a builder of, gamelans, as well as a skilled gamelan performer (see pp. 401–2). As a composer, he has brought East and West together in many compositions. In *Threnody for Carlos Chavez* (CD 2/6), he reverses the usual procedure of bringing together an "exotic" solo instrument and a conventional Western orchestra; in this piece it is the soloist who plays a Western instrument (the viola), accompanied by an entire gamelan "orchestra." Carlos Chávez (1899–1978) was a noted Mexican classical composer who wrote many works based on Mexican musical idioms.

The Music of Japan

Japan has been open to the West for less than a century and a half, and sizable Japanese immigration to the United States began only a century ago; therefore, Japanese influence on our music and culture is far more recent than the Hispanic, French, or Scandinavian. But more than that, the Japanese have come to represent a significant portion of our population, and that makes the influence of their culture a weightier matter, with political overtones as well, as we shall see. Japanese Americans identify themselves as *issei*, first-generation immigrants born in Japan; *nisei*, second generation; or *sansei*, third generation. There are certain characteristics associated with each. The issei tended to perpetuate the musical traditions they brought with them. The nisei were intent on assimilation and on adapting to the culture of their new homeland. The sansei are more thoroughly assimilated but at the same time tend to want to reclaim their heritage by recovering certain cultural aspects of Old Japan, including the music, in accord with what has been called "the law of the return of the third generation" (Lornell and Rasmussen 260). Some of the sansei also tend to become socially involved in advocacy for Japanese ethnic identity and civil rights.

Traditional Japanese music has come down to the present day in at least two strains: the *gagaku*, or highly cultivated classical court dance and music, and the *minyo,* or folk music and dance. A third strain is the popular music, growing out of the folk style but already heavily influenced by Western popular music, even in Japan itself. All three are present among Japanese Americans. The court music and dance is taught and cultivated, particularly in Los Angeles and San Francisco. The minyo, the dances of which are more easily learned than those of the gagaku, is more broadly cultivated by amateur dance groups. (See Chapter 23.)

The pitch material of traditional Japanese music consists of two pentatonic scales. The scale used in traditional music for the *shakuhachi* (an endblown flute made of bamboo), the *shamisen* (a three-stringed plucked lute), and the *koto* (a thirteen-stringed zither) contains semitones, and could be approximated by playing the notes D E♭ G A B♭. The scale used in folk and popular music is the less exotic-sounding pentatonic scale found worldwide, and is the one available on just the black notes of the piano. We have already encountered it in Anglo-Celtic-American folk music, in African American music, and in American Indian Music. It is used in African and Chinese music as well.

Nobuko Miyamoto, born in Los Angeles in 1939, is a sansei who has become a "socially and politically active songster." (Lornell and Rasmussen 264ff). Her early training included European classical music and jazz. As an activist, she became a songster for the Asian American movement in the 1970s, and as such met and worked with African American and Hispanic activists, and took part in the nueva canción movement (see p. 68). Her song "Tampopo" ("Dandelion"), written for the Japanese American community, is a Japanese-style folk song sung in English, with choruses in Japanese.

CD 2/7 (3:01) "Tampopo" ("Dandelion") (excerpt), by Nobuko Miyamoto. 1994.

The instruments are the traditional Japanese flute, shamisen, and taiko drum, with the addition of an acoustic bass. The scale is pure pentatonic. The pitchless spoken calls are characteristic of Japanese folk music. American elements are the plucked acoustic bass and, most notably, the swing rhythm in all the parts. (Miyamoto, the singer, was a jazz vocalist.) Susan Asai has written that "Miyamoto's songs have a didactic Buddhist message that is intended as an expression of Japanese Buddhist culture. The song implies learning to hear and receive the Truth through the practice of 'just dancing,' as interpreted by the Jodo Buddhist sect" (Lornell and Rasmussen 271).

▬ PROJECTS

1. Find out about any holidays or festivals that are celebrated by French American, Scandinavian American, or Asian American groups in your community, and attend and report on them.

2. Find out about and report on the support your own state government gives to folk, ethnic, or regional arts, through a state folklorist or through a state arts board or arts council.

▬ ADDITIONAL LISTENING

"Bamboula," by Louis Moreau Gottschalk. *The Banjo and other Creole Ballads*. Eugene List, piano. Vanguard Classics OVC 4050.

Concerto for Sitar and Orchestra. By Ravi Shankar. Angel/EMI Classics 69121-2.

"The Dance in Place Congo." By Henry F. Gilbert. NW 80228.

Cajun Honky Tonk. Arhoolie CD 427. "Le cote farouche de la vic."

Revolver. By the Beatles. Capitol CD 46441, 1966 (re-released 1990).

West Meets East. Perf. Ravi Shankar and Yehudi Menuhin. Angel 67180-2.

Worlds of Music. Ed. Jeff Todd Titon. 4th ed. New York: Schirmer Books, 2002. Set of 4 CDs accompanying.

For Japanese examples see Lornell and Rasmussen 284–85.

Various releases by Arhoolie Records, 10341 San Pablo Ave., El Cerrito, CA 94530.

CHAPTER

6 Folk Music as an Instrument of Advocacy

The use of music in the service of a cause is nothing new. John Powell, American composer and folk-music scholar, has called attention to an anecdote about the ingenuity and zeal of Saint Aldhelm, seventh-century abbot of Malmsbury:

> According to this story, the Saint would station himself on a bridge in the guise of a gleeman and would collect an audience by singing popular songs. He would then gradually insert into his entertainment the words of the holy scriptures and so lead his hearers to salvation. (Jackson, vii)

From Saint Aldhelm in the seventh century to the CIO labor organizer, the civil rights advocate, or the environmental activist in the twenty-first, the method is the same—adapting an already known and accepted song, or song style, so as to transform it into an instrument of advocacy. "Protest songs," the name frequently applied to songs of advocacy, have been sung in the United States since colonial times, mostly as *broadsides*, cheaply printing the words only, to be sung to an existing tune. (See "Print and the Ballad," pp. 11–12.) The opening verse of the "Junto Song" of 1775, satirizing what was seen as British avarice in taxing the colonists ("'Tis money makes the member vote, And sanctifies our ways; It makes the patriot turn his coat, And money we must raise"), is startling in its applicability to today's debates on reforming politics! (For the whole song, see p. 229 and CD 3/17.)

The plight of the farmer has seldom been the subject of protest songs, but the Populist movement in the 1890s produced "The Farmer Is the Man That Feeds Them All" (CD 2/8). Fiddlin' John Carson was the first musician to record commercially what was at first called "old-time music," and later "country music" (see p. 114).

CD 2/8 (3:01)
"The Farmer Is the Man That Feeds Them All," Fiddlin' John Carson, vocal and fiddle. Recorded in New York, 1923. NW245.

Text, "The Farmer Is the Man That Feeds Them All"

> If you'll only look and see, I know you will agree,
> That the farmer is the man that feeds them all.
> While the women uses snuff, and they never get enough,
> But the farmer is the man that feeds them all.
> When the farmer comes to town, with his wagon broken down,
> The farmer is the man that feeds them all.

Chorus The farmer is the man, the farmer is the man,
> Buys on credit until fall.
> Then they'll take him by the hand, then they'll lead him through
>   the land,
> And the merchant he's the man that gets it all.

> While the judge on his bench, he will scratch his head and wink,
> But the farmer is the man that feeds them all.
> And the lawyer, I'll declare, will tell a lie and swear,
> But the farmer is the man that feeds them all.

(Chorus)

> Oh, the doctor hangs around, while the blacksmith whups his iron,
> But the farmer is the man that feeds them all.
> And the preacher and the cook, they'll go trolling on the brook,
> But the farmer is the man that feeds them all.
> If you'll only look and see, I know you will agree,
> That the farmer is the man that feeds them all.

(Chorus)

THE URBAN FOLK-SONG MOVEMENT OF THE 1930s AND 1940s

The Depression period of the 1930s ushered in a new era of American folk song as an instrument of advocacy. As D. K. Wilgus said, "The use of folksong for political purposes is an old device: what is new is the use of the folk concept, the magic term *folk*" (228).

The "magic" inherent in the term *folk* has been described by R. Serge Denisoff as "Folk Consciousness."

> Folk Consciousness refers to an awareness of folk music which leads to its use in foreign (urban) environment in the framework of social, economic, and political action. The addition of social and organizational themes to traditional tunes, the emulation of rural attire, and the idealization of folk singers as "people's artists" are all aspects of Folk Consciousness. (99)

CD 2/9 (1:22)
"I Am a Union Woman" (excerpt), Aunt Molly Jackson, vocal

When northern labor organizers went into the South to organize mine and textile-mill workers, they found that the tradition of folk singing, which was still vital in the rural South, was already at work providing songs to rally the workers in the bitter struggle. In Harlan County, Kentucky, scene of violent labor disputes in the coal mines in 1931, Aunt Molly Jackson (born Mary Magdalene Garland; 1880–1960), a larger-than-life heroine who was midwife, doctor, union organizer, and ballad singer for the coal miners, and who had lost brother, husband, and son in the mines, was singing:

Text, "I Am a Union Woman"

I am a union woman, just as brave as I can be.
I do not like the bosses and the bosses don't like me.

Refrain   Join the CIO, come join the CIO.

I was raised in Kentucky, in Kentucky borned and bred.
And when I joined the union, they called me a Rooshian Red.

Refrain

When my husband asked the boss for a job, this is the words he said:
"Bill Jackson, I can't work you, sir, your wife's a Rooshian Red."

Refrain

If you want to join a union as strong as one can be,
Join the dear old NMU and come along with me.
If you want to join a union, step in and come along.
We'll all be glad to have you, we are many thousand strong.

Refrain

When the union organizers and their supporters and chroniclers, such as John Dos Passos and Theodore Dreiser, returned to the North, they brought with them not only many of the songs but also some of the singers, including Aunt Molly Jackson herself, who had been banished, in effect, from Kentucky. Thus began the urban phase of the urban folk-song movement. In addition to singers from the Kentucky coal mines, there was Leadbelly (Huddie Ledbetter, 1885–1949), whose talents were discovered in a Louisiana prison by folklorists John and Alan Lomax, who secured his parole and brought him to New York. There was Harvard dropout and durable activist Pete Seeger, son of the distinguished ethnomusicologist Charles Seeger. And there was Woody Guthrie.

Woody Guthrie

Woody Guthrie (1912–67) was a highly individual and somewhat enigmatic figure. His Oklahoma background was certainly folk in any sense of the term, and his absorption of this heritage is evident in his early recordings of traditional ballads, including "Gypsy Davy," encountered in Chapter 1. (See pp. 7–9, and CDs 1/3 and 1/5.) The broad and varied experiences of his life, the first thirty years of which are so colorfully set forth in his somewhat fictionalized autobiography, *Bound for Glory*, gave him abundant contact with the common people. His identification with them, and his sympathies for them, resulted in a spontaneous flood of songs (only a small proportion of which have been preserved), and of poems and sketches. Many of the songs, even those that became broadly popular, had a hard and determined edge of protest to them, though that edge was somewhat muted in popular versions. "So Long, It's Been Good to Know Ya," for example, reveals its original context, as a song about the Dust Bowl, only in its spontaneous, rambling, talking-and-singing version by Woody himself. (See Additional Listening.) Certainly songs like this and "Hard Travelin'" have their roots in his personal experience. But some of the songs, especially the ones he wrote on commission, such as those written for the Bonneville Power Administration and the set on the famous Sacco and Vanzetti case, show the effects of their separation from a definable folk community. This is seen in the broadly inclusive "This Land Is Your Land." The Dust Bowl Ballads (including the ballad "Tom Joad," treated in chapter 1 and heard on CD 1/5), written after the fact, were neither sung nor known by the migrant workers themselves who left the area for California in the 1930s. Yet his enormous talent, when brought to bear on an immediate event, could produce a truly great song, through his faculty of making us sense at once the human dimension. "The Sinking of the *Reuben James*," about the seamen lost in the first American ship torpedoed in World War II,

Woody Guthrie personifies the urban folksong movement more than any other musician of his generation. The sign featured prominently on his guitar underscores the inseparable elements of music, politics, and activism in his ballads.

Photo courtesy of the New York Library for the Performing Arts

was probably the best ballad to come out of that conflict. (See Additional Listening for versions by both Woody Guthrie and Pete Seeger.)

A man of shrewd intelligence and diverse talents (he read voluminously and was a very prolific writer apart from his songs, and an artist as well), Guthrie was no simple "man of the soil." Yet he often found himself having to deny his own acute perceptions and conceal his intellect behind a mask of simplistic doggerel in trying to fulfill his most difficult job of all—which was largely thrust upon him—that of being a kind of universal "folk poet" of the common man.

Pete Seeger and the Almanac Singers

CD 2/10 (1:15)
"Pittsburgh," Pete
Seeger, vocal and banjo.

Pete Seeger (b. 1919) is the son of ethnomusicologist Charles Seeger (pp. 5, 18 [Projects]). His sister Peggy and his brother Mike are prominent folk performers and scholars. Pete himself, the quintessential folk activist, has been the perennial survivor of many of the urban folk-song movement's phases. Early in 1941 Seeger assembled a group of folk-song enthusiasts then active in New

York's left-wing circles, and formed a group called the Almanac Singers. (See Additional Listening.) From time to time Woody Guthrie joined this group. On a trip together that happened to take them through Pittsburgh, Guthrie and Seeger came up with one of the earliest political/environmental songs, "Pittsburgh" (CD 6/3).

Pittsburgh town is a smoky old town, Pittsburgh, [2x]
Pittsburgh town is a smoky old town,
Solid iron from McKeesport down, in Pittsburgh,
Lord, God, Pittsburgh.

All I do is cough and choke in Pittsburgh, [2x]
All I do is cough and choke
From the iron filings and the sulphur smoke in Pittsburgh,
Lord, God, Pittsburgh.

What did Jones and Loughlin steal in Pittsburgh, [2x]
What did Jones and Loughlin steal,
Up and down the river just as far as you could see, in Pittsburgh,
Lord, God, Pittsburgh.

From the Alleghany to the Ohio in Pittsburgh, [2x]
From the Alleghany to the Ohio,
They're joining up in the C.I.O. in Pittsburgh,
Lord, God, Pittsburgh.

"Pittsburgh" is another example of protest music's habitual method of appropriating existing folk tunes for the production of parodies. The tune is that of the familiar children's song "Crawdad" ("You get a line, and I'll get a pole, and we'll go down to the crawdad hole"). Pittsburgh has now cleaned itself up, and all is forgiven, because the song is now popular in an official version, with the words "Pittsburgh Town is a great old town."

PROTEST AND FOLK SONG IN THE 1960s

Bob Dylan

The protest-song movement was somewhat muted in the decade and a half following World War II. When it reemerged in the 1960s it presented a marked contrast to the movement of the 1930s and 1940s. The career of Bob Dylan (Robert Zimmerman, b. 1941) is illustrative. Dylan emerged into prominence from the same Greenwich Village milieu that had launched his idol, Woody

Guthrie, into the role of protester and "folk poet." But the men, their backgrounds, and their times were different. As a folk musician, Guthrie never had consciously to adopt a style and never felt it necessary to change his style—in fact, there is no indication that he was ever much *aware* of such a thing as style. Dylan, coming along at a later and more self-conscious period for folk music, had already gone from rock 'n' roll to acoustic folk by the time he went to New York; he was to change his style, his sound, and his type of material many times thereafter. Because of Dylan's popularity and the force of his talent, each of his changes from the 1960s on sent waves of influence, and alienation, through the folk and rock worlds. As Wayne Hampton has put it, Dylan, the "self-proclaimed 'song and dance man,'. . . has continued to seek new audiences and to alienate old ones" (194, 199).

Dylan did create some memorable songs and ballads of protest, especially in his early career. Some are explicit as to the issues:"The Lonesome Death of Hattie Carroll" and "Seven Curses" (the corruption of justice); "Only a Pawn in Their Game" and "Oxford Town" (the machinations of racial prejudice); "Masters of War" and "With God on Our Side" (war); "Let Me Die in My Footsteps" (bomb shelters). He also produced some very realistic ballads that are not overt protest songs, in that the target, as a defiantly general human condition, is less readily assailable, as in "The Ballad of Hollis Brown" and "North Country Blues" (poverty). Others are more highly distilled and convey more generalized feelings about the future: "Blowin' in the Wind" and "The Times They Are a-Changin'."

Some songs display that surrealistic kind of private imagery that marks much of the poetry of the 1960s and 1970s, and is a sign of a distinct departure from the old tradition in the direction of the esoteric ("A Hard Rain's a-Gonna Fall" and "Subterranean Homesick Blues").

Dylan has absorbed many influences. His debt to African American blues is readily apparent. Less obvious is his relationship to the Anglo-American ballad tradition treated in Chapter 1, and to the cultural milieu (including the religious) that nourished it. His "Girl of the North Country" is an offshoot of a perennial ballad. The tune of "Masters of War" is basically that of the haunting "Nottamun Town," a song from the Appalachians. (His source for the tune was Appalachian folksinger Jean Ritchie and her family, which source he at first failed to credit. Woody Guthrie similarly borrowed tunes from the Carter Family's recordings, as we noted in Chapter 1. See p. 11.) The question-and-answer incipits to the stanzas of "A Hard Rain's a-Gonna Fall" are an adaptation from the Scottish ballad "Lord Randall." "Who Killed Davy Moore?" is a modern version of "Cock Robin," "When the Ship Comes In" draws on the imagery of the revival spiritual, and "I Pity the Poor Immigrant" has the parallel construction of the Old Testament canticles.

Wayne Hampton, writing in the mid-1980s a perceptive summation of Dylan's work, sees "a congruence underneath the chaos of Dylan's public images" that he identifies as "two interpenetrating themes." The first is that of "the outcast, the rolling-stone drifter . . . fleeing conformity and convention." The second is that of "the seer in quest of visions" whose roots "seem to be an eclectic brand of Christianized mysticism." These two themes are combined in characterizations of the "real Bob Dylan" as "Bible-toting hobo," "mystery tramp," and "mystical drifter" (194–95).

One of Dylan's most familiar songs, which resonated with the times, is "The Times They Are a-Changin'" (1963). With it's advice to ". . . please get out of the new [road] if you can't lend a hand . . ." has an interesting parallel in "Get Off the Track," a famous abolitionist song of 1844 by the Hutchinson Family, protest singers of pre–Civil War days. (See pp. 263–65, and CD 3/29.)

FREEDOM SONGS, AND THE CIVIL RIGHTS MOVEMENT IN THE SOUTH

For all the differences between the 1930s and the 1960s, there was an interesting parallel. In the 1930s, labor sympathizers who went into the South to help organize the miners found a sturdy singing tradition already at work furnishing songs for the workers. In the early 1960s, protest folksingers from the North who went into the South at the time of the early civil rights struggle also found a southern tradition, in this case based on African American religious singing, already furnishing songs for those engaged in marches, mass meetings, sit-ins, and prayer vigils, and for those in jails.

"Ain't Gonna Let Nobody Turn Me Around" (CD 2/11) is an adaptation of a traditional song, of a type sung at revival or camp meetings, in which verses could be multiplied by simply changing one word. Thus "nobody" (in "Ain't gonna let nobody, Lordy, turn me around" is changed to "segregation," "jailhouse," and so on. (See Transcription 10.6, p. 192, "Way Over in the Promised Land.")

Of these songs from an indigenous tradition, "We Shall Overcome," based on the African American church song "I'll Overcome Some Day," with words by the gospel hymnodist C. Albert Tindley, is the best known, and it is sung today all over the world. It had been adapted from the religious song as early as 1945 by union workers in Charleston, South Carolina. It was the "theme song" of Highlander Folk School, in Tennessee, whence it was introduced into the civil rights movement. As many times as you have heard or sung this song, you are invited to be moved afresh by it as you listen to it sung at a reunion concert of the Freedom Singers in Washington DC in 1988 (CD 2/12).

CD 2/11 (0:55)
"Ain't Gonna Let Nobody Turn Me Around" (3 verses). The SNCC (Student Non-violent Coordinating Committee) Freedom Singers, Albany, Georgia, 1962.

CD 2/12 (2:07)
"We Shall Overcome" (traditional), SNCC Freedom Singers

CONTINUITY AND CHANGE IN THE FOLK STYLE OF ADVOCACY FROM THE 1970s TO THE 2000s

Although the writing and singing of protest songs has not attracted the attention in the last quarter of the century that it did in the 1960s, it continues to exist, though in changed form. The single big issues, such as civil rights and the Vietnam War, with the capacity to galvanize a significant portion of the public, have been replaced by issues that are far more diverse and complex, including racism in its more subtle forms, help for the aging and the disabled, and the widespread malaise of overconsumption and preoccupation with "lifestyle" that exists among the haves in our society, the many manifestations of environmental degradation, and the unimaginably long-term problems associated with nuclear energy and its waste.

CD 2/13 (4:28)
"Gonna Be an Engineer," by Peggy Seeger. Peggy Seeger, vocal and guitar.

Among these complex issues, one that has not lacked attention is women's rights, and indeed the whole question of the role of women in all walks of life. This is more than ever an issue in the new millennium, worldwide. An unabashed feminist song dealing with the enforced role of women in the family and the job market, is the hard-hitting, no-holds-barred "Gonna Be an Engineer," by Peggy Seeger (CD 2/13). It has the proportions of a ballad and was a pioneering topical song.

Among some singer-composers active since the 1970s, protest has been expressed in ways more subtle and indirect, often achieving impact through understatement and satire. To name a few examples, in the early 1970s John Prine, in a Dylan style and approach, produced an unsurpassed classic protest against the degradation of the Appalachians by strip mining in his "Paradise"—a paradise that Mr. Peabody has hauled away in his coal train. Racism is treated with a sadder, gentler touch by Pierce Pettis in "Legacy." Humor is evident in the anecdotal treatment of the immigrant problem in David Massengill's "My Name Joe." Poverty is treated in a low-key way in Nanci Griffith's "Down 'n' Outer." (See Additional Listening.)

Although protest is now more sophisticated, it is interesting to note that releases of recordings from an earlier era—songs by Woody Guthrie, Pete Seeger and the Almanacs, and so on—occupy a considerable position in the market. This may represent either a nostalgia for the days when the issues, the supposed solutions, and the songs themselves were clearer and more straightforward, or simply an affection for what happened when you just put Woody Guthrie and his guitar in front of a microphone any place that was handy and recorded whatever came out.

Granted that their messages are often exaggerated, crudely expressed, and simplistic, and are made only by the committed few, protest songs *can* express the gut concerns of the many. In that sense they are part of a long and healthy tradition of dissent that has contributed to the character of American culture and its music. And there is gold in the songs themselves, as the ephemeral dross is discarded: "We Shall Overcome" (from black hymnody), "So Long, It's Been Good to Know You" (Woody Guthrie), "Where Have All the Flowers Gone" (Pete Seeger), and "Blowin' in the Wind" (Bob Dylan) are as much a part now of our oral tradition as the songs of Stephen Foster or the favorites of Tin Pan Alley.

▰ PROJECTS

1. Attend a meeting or a rally (either as participant or as observer) and note what role, if any, is played by actual songs (as opposed to chanted slogans). If their role is minimal or totally absent, speculate as to why this is so, and what might make gatherings devoted to advocacy different in the 2000s from those in any period in the past you might choose (the civil rights movement, for example).
2. R. Serge Denisoff has contrasted what he called the "magnetic" song—that is, the song that advocates a specific action ("join the union" or "join the march," for example) with the "rhetorical" song, which simply dramatizes an issue. Looking through past issues of either *Broadside* or *Sing Out!* or a collection such as the Greenway, the Fowke and Glazer, or the Lomax *Hard-Hitting Songs* . . . as listed in Additional Reading, find one song of each type, analyzing and contrasting their stances.

▰ ADDITIONAL LISTENING

"Down 'n' Outer." By Nancy Griffith. *Late Night Grande Hotel.* MCA Records MCAD 10306.

Dust Bowl Ballads. Smithsonian/Folkways CD FH 2481. More by Woody Guthrie.

"Legacy." By Pierce Pettis. *While the Serpent Lies Sleeping.* Windham Hill WD-1087.

"My Name Joe." By David Massengill. *Coming up for Air.* Flying Fish CD 70590.

"Paradise." By John Prine. *John Prine.* Atlantic SD 8296.

Pete Seeger and the Almanac Singers. Smithsonian/Folkways CD FH 3864.

Sing for Freedom: Civil Rights Movement Songs. Smithsonian/Folkways CD 40032.

"Sinking of the *Reuben James,* The" (reissue). By Woody Gutherie. *Woody Guthrie. That's Why We're Marching: World War II and the American Folk Song Movement.* Smithsonian/Folkways CD 40021.

"So Long, It's Been Good to Know Ya" (reissue). By Woody Guthrie. *Woody Guthrie. That's Why We're Marching: World War II and the American Folk Song Movement.* Smithsonian/Folkways CD 40021.

Voices of the Civil Rights Movement. Smithsonian/Folkways CD 40084.

PART II · THREE PRODIGIOUS OFFSPRING OF THE RURAL SOUTH

The rural American South, in its former isolation and conservatism, fathered two musical offspring, reared in private within its confines and long unknown outside: the country music of white people and the blues of black people. Though unlike in significant ways, they share a patrimony and a native soil. Both have become in our time mighty musical nations with half a century of commercial success behind them. Long segregated, they have both played their part in producing a third prodigious, electrified, urbanized offspring: rock.

How did the South come to father these prodigies? What were their musical and cultural antecedents? What are their enduring characteristics? We shall explore these questions and then trace the first two genres as they emerged from the isolation of folklore into the bright public arena of popular culture, from which emerged the third.

The South has constituted the largest and richest reservoir of folklore we have. In the latter half of the twentieth century, great changes came to this region, so that it is no longer what it once was. But if we are seeking the origins of its folklore, we have to look at the South not as it is now but as it existed for three centuries before our own time. The two key words are isolation and conservatism. The isolation was not only geographic (of the lowlands as well as the highlands) but also demographic—an isolation of the southern people, largely, from the greater mass of the American people. For once the frontier had passed through and moved on west, there was emigration *from* the South but, until our time, little significant immigration *to* the South. The conservatism owed a good deal to this isolation but also to the almost exclusively agrarian economy; to the hierarchical (if not actually aristocratic) social and political structure; to the defensive attitude assumed almost monolithically by southern whites toward the institution of slavery and its equally problematic sequel, white supremacy; and, last but by no means least, to the prevailing orthodox religious modes of thought. Out of this soil, then, sprang the two most pervasive forms of rural music America has ever produced and, as a second generation, a citified but visceral amalgamation that has revolutionized popular music throughout the world.

Southern Historical Society/University of North Carolina at Chapel Hill

The fiddle, mandolin, and banjo were prominent in the rural American South. The low position of the fiddle is typical, and recalls the seventeenth-century technique of playing the violin against the upper arm and chest rather than on the shoulder.

CHAPTER

Country Music

7

The latent popularity of "hillbilly" music, fully revealed only after it had spread beyond its original geographical limits in the 1930s and 1940s, was one of the surprises of the twentieth century, at least to city-bred entrepreneurs and savants of popular culture. Its base of popularity was found not only in the rural South and, as might be expected, among its people who had immigrated to the cities and to other parts of the country, but also among rural white people elsewhere who had no cultural ties with the South at all. We are dealing, then, with the closest thing to a universal "people's music" that rural white Americans have had. (The term *hillbilly*, like so many labels in art that have stuck, was originally derogatory. The first recorded use of the term appeared in a New York periodical in 1900, as follows: "A Hill-Billie is a free and untrammelled white citizen of Alabama, who lives in the hills, has no means to speak of, dresses as he can, talks as he pleases, drinks whiskey when he gets it, and fires off his revolver as the fancy takes him" [Green 204–28]. The term *old-time music,* an early euphemism for marketing purposes, was used for a time, before the adoption of the now-universal designation "country music.")

ENDURING CHARACTERISTICS OF THE WORDS

Words are of paramount importance in country music. They exhibit certain pervasive traits that have consistently characterized this genre through its half-century of change.

Fundamental Attitudes

Country music is steeped in a paradoxical blend of realism and sentimentality. The realism reveals itself in a readiness to treat any human situation in song and to deal unflinchingly with any aspect of life that genuinely touches the emotions. It shows up in extreme cases — for example, in the depicting of such grim scenes as the following:

Text, "Snow Dove" (see Additional Listening)

He went upstairs to make her hope
And found her hanging on a rope.

A later song, "Wreck on the Highway" by Roy Acuff, updates this penchant for furnishing grisly details. Such unsparing realism (a characteristic of the ballad tradition) contrasts strikingly with the conventionalized subject matter and treatment of most urban commercial song before 1950, and identifies country music as one progenitor of the subsequent "revolution" in American popular music.

The obverse of this realism is a nearly universal tendency toward sentimentality — a sentimentality that may often strike one outside the tradition as excessive and tainted with self-pity. (For a provocative discussion of sentimentality as a characteristic attitude of the South, and some speculation as to its origins, see Cash 82–87, 126–30.)

Text, "No Letter in the Mail" (see Additional Listening)

Walking down this lonesome road,
I'll travel while I cry.
If there's no letter in the mail,
I'll bid this world goodbye.

The sentimentalizing of objects is common, especially in the "weepers" of the later, more commercial phase of country music, such as "Send Me the Pillow You Dream On."

Perennial Themes

The subjects of country songs and ballads, though diverse, group themselves around certain perennial themes. One is love.

> Tell me that you love me, Katy Cline.
> Tell me that your love's as true as mine.

Text, "Katy Cline" (see Additional Listening)

Another is death.

> There's a little black train a-coming,
> Fix all your business right;
> There's a little black train a-coming
> And it may be here tonight.

Text, "Little Black Train" (see Additional Listening)

Still another is religion.

> I am bound for that beautiful city
> My Lord has prepared for his own,
> Where all the redeemed of all ages
> Sing, "Glory!" around the white throne.

Text, "No Disappointment in Heaven" (see Additional Listening)

And a fourth is nostalgia.

> There's a peaceful cottage there,
> A happy home so dear.
> My heart is longing for them day by day.

Text, "'Mid the Green Fields of Virginia" (see Additional Listening)

Trains figure prominently in country music, as they do in blues.

> I'm riding on that New River train,
> I'm riding on that New River train,
> The same old train that brought me here
> Is going to carry me away.

Text, "New River Train" (see Additional Listening)

The railroad train and the life of the rambler were both romanticized in rural thought. In recent times the truck and even the jet airplane have figured in country songs, but they have not seized the imagination with anything like the vivid intensity that the train has been able to evoke.

Songs about events were once an important part of country music, and any country singer could make up his or her own songs on important happenings of the day.

> Come all you fathers and mothers,
> And brothers, sisters too,
> I'll relate to you the history
> Of the Rowan County Crew.

Text, "Rowan County Crew" (see Additional Listening)

This trait shows country music's relation to the earlier ballad tradition. Many songs and ballads collected by Cecil Sharp in the southern highlands in 1916–18 appear in country-music recordings of the 1920s and 1930s. The ballad "John Hardy" (see CD 1/4, p. 10) was collected by Sharp in 1916 and was recorded commercially by the influential Carter Family in 1930.

The ballad tradition was kept alive as event songs continued to be written. With the coming of commercialism, it became vital to hit the market as soon after the event as possible. A song based on General Douglas MacArthur's speech before Congress in 1951, after President Harry Truman removed him from command in Korea, was written and recorded by Gene Autry within hours of the event, and a song on the assassination of Senator Huey Long of Louisiana in 1935 was written two years *before* his death—and was even sung to him by its author (Gentry 65–70).

Dialect and Other Regionalisms

The early country singers naturally retained not only their regional accent in their songs but their dialect as well, with such usages as "a-going," "a-coming," "rise you up," and "yonders." With the first wave of commercial success and the broadening of country music's public, there was a tendency (on the part of singers such as Jimmie Rodgers) to drop the dialect and substitute standard English. In more recent country music, a few vernacular survivals, such as the well-nigh universal "ain't" and the dropping of the final *g*'s of the *-ing* suffix ("ramblin'," "cheatin'"), have become clichés. The loss of an authentic vernacular, together with the introduction of such devices as more sophisticated rhymes ("infatuation," "sensation," "imagination"), has introduced an artificial conventionality to latter-day country music, which has already lost many of its distinctive regional characteristics in the general process of homogenization.

ENDURING CHARACTERISTICS OF THE MUSIC

Despite evolution and change, certain enduring musical characteristics have been identified with country music. The choice of instruments, the style of singing, the melody, and the harmony are all distinctive.

The Instruments

Country music is basically music for string band, originally played on those stringed instruments that were easily portable. The dominant instrument in traditional country music is the *fiddle*, which takes the lead not only in dance music but often also in the instrumental breaks in songs. The *mountain dulcimer* and the *autoharp* belong more to the folk origins of this music, and with a few exceptions did not survive long into country music itself. The *banjo* (possibly acquired in the lowlands, through contact with African Americans and black-face minstrels) became an early mainstay of country music. In the second quarter of the twentieth century, it was almost supplanted by the *guitar*, a more resonant instrument with a greater range. The *mandolin* entered country music in the 1930s, being at first associated with Bill Monroe and subsequently with the whole style known as "bluegrass," which also introduced a revival of the banjo. With its thin but penetrating tone, the mandolin competes with the banjo for the lead parts. Less easily portable is the *string bass* (always plucked rather than bowed), but it became established in country music as early as the 1930s and has been essential in the bluegrass band since the 1940s.

An exotic addition to the hillbilly band came from as far west as Hawaii, probably by way of the Hawaiian bands that were so popular in the United States in the early decades of the twentieth century. The Hawaiian *steel guitar*, with its sliding, wailing sound, was appropriated by country musicians as far back as the 1920s and 1930s. (Similar sliding effects were obtained by many early African American blues guitarists, stopping the strings with broken bottles or knife blades.) A guitar with a built-in resonator, which served to amplify the sound mechanically before the advent of the electric guitar, was known as the *dobro*.

The piano, drums, saxophones, and trumpets, essentially alien to country music, were introduced in the country/jazz hybrid "western swing" in the 1930s. With "rural electrification" came the electric guitar in the 1940s (primarily associated with the need for a louder sound in honky-tonk music) and eventually, in the late 1960s, electric keyboards. Acoustic stringed instruments, however, remain the basis for any country music committed to its tradition.

The Style of Singing

A characteristic manner of singing characterizes traditional country music. A direct carryover from the folk singing of the rural South, it is typified (as heard in bluegrass music) by a high, nasal, and somewhat strained tone. The "lonesome," impassive manner of delivery is suited to the impersonality of the ballad tradition. The clear, vibratoless tone so akin to that of the country fiddle also lends itself to the kind of vocal ornamentation familiar in this music: short slides and anticipatory flourishes heard in advance of the principal notes, especially in slow tunes such as "Wayfaring Stranger," as sung by traditional singer Roscoe Holcomb (CD 2/14). The thin, penetrating timbre of the banjo matches the tone quality of the singer. This high, tense, rigid vocal quality was later modified under southwestern influence.

CD 2/14 (0:37) "Wayfaring Stranger" (excerpt), Roscoe Holcomb, vocal and banjo

Essential to any consideration of vocal style is that utter sincerity of delivery without which country music is not genuine. Hank Williams, Sr., expressed it vividly when asked about the success of country music:

> It can be explained in just one word: sincerity. When a hillbilly sings a crazy song, he feels crazy. When he sings, "I Laid My Mother Away," he sees her a-laying right there in the coffin. He sings more sincere than most entertainers because the hillbilly was raised rougher than most entertainers. You got to know a lot about hard work. You got to have smelt a lot of mule manure before you can sing like a hillbilly. (Malone 242)

(For an anecdote on the relation between experience and sincerity, see Gentry 60.)

Melody and Harmony

The folk music of the English and Scottish ballad tradition, as we saw in Chapter 1, tended to preserve the old modal scales, with their attendant archaic-sounding melodic patterns and harmonies. A vestige of the old modality, in the form of the flatted seventh degree of the scale, can be heard in "The Old Man at the Mill" (CD 1/7; see p. 17 for notation). As country music sought to expand its public, the old modal tunes began to lose favor. Singers brought up in the older tradition still sang them privately but were reluctant to record them or to sing them for "outsiders." (Clarence Ashley, an old-time musician, recorded almost as an afterthought during one session in 1930 his version of "The House Carpenter," a venerable English and Scottish ballad from the Child canon. It turned out to be one of his most memorable recordings. See Additional Listening.) New tunes came into use—tunes with harmonies of the utmost simplicity that made them well adapted to guitar accompaniment. The melodies of two of the best-known songs in the repertoire will illustrate the harmonic vocabulary of most country music tunes. They imply the same three basic chords only; further, both tunes follow the outlines of their clearly implied harmonies. The first is "Wildwood Flower" (CD 2/15, Transcription 7.1).

CD 2/15 (1:26)
"Wildwood Flower"
(2 verses), the Carter
Family

Transcription 7.1
"Wildwood Flower,"
last verse

(Taken from the New Lost
City Ramblers Song Book
[Smithsonian-Folkways
40036].)

Oh, he taught me to love him and called me his flower

That was bloom-ing to cheer him through life's drea-ry hour;

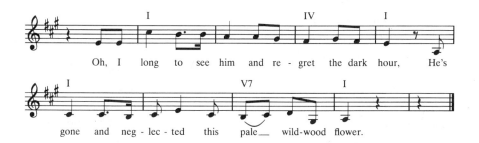

Oh, I long to see him and re - gret the dark hour, He's

gone and neg - lec - ted this pale __ wild-wood flower.

The tune of the second song, "Wabash Cannon Ball" (CD 2/16, Transcription 7.2), follows its chord outlines even more faithfully; only seven tones in the entire tune do not belong to the prevailing chords.

CD 2/16 (2:33)
"Wabash Cannon Ball,"
Roy Acuff, vocal

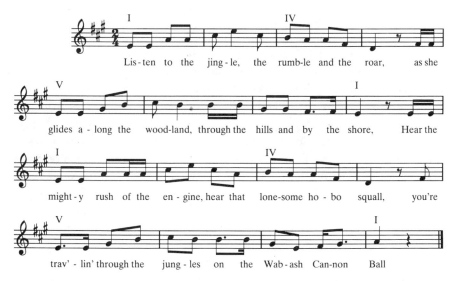

Lis - ten to the jing - le, the rumb - le and the roar, as she

glides a - long the wood-land, through the hills and by the shore, Hear the

might - y rush of the en - gine, hear that lone-some ho - bo squall, you're

trav' - lin' through the jung - les on the Wab - ash Can - non Ball

Transcription 7.2
"Wabash Cannon Ball,"
last verse

(Adapted from Vance
Randoph, *Ozark Folksongs,*
edited and abridged by
Norm Cohen [Urbana:
University of Illinois Press,
1982], pp. 385–386. Used
by permission.)

Though "Wildwood Flower" has been unmistakably a country song ever since the Carter Family recorded it in the 1920s, the melody can be traced to sources outside the rural South—in this case, as in many others, to a parlor song of the previous century. As the scholar D. K. Wilgus has said, "A good percentage of the lyric songs of the early hillbilly tradition seem to derive from the nineteenth century sentimental parlor song—and are often considerably improved in the process" (Gentry 229). Parlor songs (see Chapter 14) were extremely popular with amateur singers. Many of them were published, and therefore no doubt sung, with guitar accompaniment as an alternative to the piano; this early adaptation to the guitar must have made even easier their later passage into the repertoire of country musicians. "Listen to the Mocking Bird," published in 1855, became a favorite with country fiddlers. "Lorena," perhaps the most popular love song of the Civil War, was published in 1857 in versions for both guitar and piano accompaniment, and became in the 1950s a country-music standard.

In country music, as in folk music, tunes are freely borrowed and adapted to make new songs. The tune of "Wildwood Flower" became the basis for Woody Guthrie's "The Sinking of the *Reuben James*"; and "Wabash Cannon Ball" furnished the model for "Footprints in the Snow," a favorite among blue-grass performers.

COMMERCIAL BEGINNINGS: EARLY RECORDINGS, RADIO, AND THE FIRST STARS

We first encounter country music proper as it emerged from folk tradition into the realm of popular music in the 1920s. Although commercial phonograph recording was established before the turn of the century, its application to jazz, blues, and hillbilly music did not come for another two decades, principally because recording executives either were only dimly aware that those genres existed or were unsure as to whether there was a market for such recordings — ironic in view of later developments! When recording companies did move into the area of hillbilly music (camouflaging it at first under such names as "old-time music" or "old familiar tunes"), they did so at least partly in response to growing competition from that other powerful new medium of the day, radio. Thus the roles of radio and phonograph recording in the dissemination and popularization of country music were elaborately intertwined from the start — and still are.

In 1923 Georgia moonshiner, circus barker, and political campaign per-former Fiddlin' John Carson (who had recently become a locally popular radio performer) recorded "The Little Old Log Cabin in the Lane" (see Addi-tional Listening) and "The Old Hen Cackled and the Rooster's Going to Crow." (Fiddlin' John can be heard on CD 2/8, p. 97, singing and fiddling an early populist song, "The Farmer Is the Man Who Feeds Them All.") This recording proved to be phenomenally and prophetically successful, and the move to record hillbilly music was on. Recording companies made excursions into the South, set up temporary studios, and began recording country musi-cians by the score, either singly or in groups. In other cases, the newfound artists were brought to New York to record. A few who were recorded in the 1920s became the stars of the ensuing period. These included Uncle Dave Macon (from Tennessee), the Carter Family (from Virginia), and Jimmie Rodgers (from Mississippi).

Radio broadcasting, until then an amateur's plaything, suddenly came of age in the 1920s. As receiving sets came within the economic reach of more and more Americans, broadcasting stations appeared and multiplied, and with them grew the demand for performers to cater to the new invisible audience. Some stations in the South began almost immediately to broadcast country music by local musicians. In 1925 WSM in Nashville began a show, with two unpaid performers and without a commercial sponsor, that was to evolve into *Grand Ole Opry*. The early radio programs, like the early recordings, presented a highly traditional country music, still close to its folk origins. (The *Anthology of American Folk Music* of Smithsonian/Folkways illustrates this phase of "old-time music.") But its very popularity generated winds of change.

Of the three stars of early country music mentioned earlier, the first two are representative of performers who never essentially changed their style or material to consciously appeal to a larger audience. David Harrison ("Uncle Dave") Macon (1870–1952), a wagoner from Tennessee, got his professional start playing banjo and singing in local fairs, tent shows, and traveling medicine shows, and the basis of his style and repertory was his background in nineteenth-century minstrel, circus, and vaudeville songs and routines. "Johnny Gray" ("Blow You Winds of Morning"), a quasi ballad of unknown origin with an old refrain, shows his lively banjo style. (See Additional Listening.) He was a favorite performer on *Grand Ole Opry* from 1925 to 1952.

The Carter Family (Alvin Pleasant, 1891–1960; his wife, Sara, 1898–1979; and his sister-in-law Maybelle, 1909–78) came from a Virginia mountain background. Their varied repertory (which included not only nineteenth-century parlor songs but also early Tin Pan Alley songs and gospel hymns, as well as ballads and other folk material) made them very influential, as did their

Frank Driggs Collection

The Carter Family— Maybelle Addington Carter (guitar), Sarah Carter (autoharp), and Alvin Pleasant Carter. Commercial recordings by the Carter Family were influential in promoting the short-lived popularity of the autoharp in country music.

distinctive sound and style, with Sara Carter playing autoharp, and Maybelle Carter playing the melody on the bass strings of the guitar and the harmony and the rhythm on the upper strings. See CD 1/4, p. 10, "John Hardy"; CD 2/15, pp. 112–13, "Wildwood Flower"; and CD 3/5, p. 199, "Can the Circle Be Unbroken."

CD 2/17 (2:55) "Mule Skinner Blues" (Blue Yodel #8), Jimmie Rodgers, vocal and guitar. (Compare Jimmie Rodgers's original with the famous bluegrass version by Bill Monroe, CD 2/21.)

Jimmie Rodgers (1897–1933) based his career on music he had actually grown up with, but he contributed enormously to the popularization of that music, and in the process wore a number of different country hats. He recorded many types of songs: sentimental love songs, melancholy nostalgic songs, cowboy and railroad songs, white blues. He was able to put across a great variety of material by the force of his sincerity and personality. His eclecticism was bound to lead him away somewhat from traditional country songs and traditional country style. He introduced the famous "blue yodel" (of which his "Mule Skinner Blues" is representative) into country music and was really one of the first popular crooners.

With the advent of Jimmie Rodgers, the attention and emphasis in country music shifted to the solo singer. The "Singing Brakeman" of Meridian, Mississippi, had an extremely short career as a performing and recording artist. But in a mere six years (from his first trial recording in 1927 to his death in 1933), he recorded 111 songs, sold 20 million records, became internationally famous, and led country music into greener pastures than it had ever dreamed existed.

The interaction between the commercial country music of the 1930s and what was held to be "folk music" shows how complex the relationship between the two had become after the advent of radio and recordings. Folklorists traveling through the South in the 1930s, in the first wave of collecting on behalf of the Library of Congress and others, "discovered" and collected songs that their singers had learned from the commercial recordings of Jimmie Rodgers!

Hillbilly music's native soil was the upland South, and it is the music from this hill country—played with banjo, acoustic guitar, mandolin, fiddle, string bass, dobro, and harmonica, and sung with a straight, unembellished vocal tone and unaffected regional accent—that has come to be unmistakably identified with the country music of the Southeast. But meanwhile the West was being heard from.

THE WEST: THE COWBOY IMAGE

America has long pursued a love affair with its own romantic conception of the West and the cowboy. The western branch of country music has played its part in the propagation of this romanticism. For just as the Southwest is in large degree a cultural extension of the South, so is "western" music an extension and adaptation of hillbilly music.

The link is Texas. Here the southern influence, especially in east Texas, is notably strong. The country was settled primarily by southern planters, and slavery and the raising of cotton flourished, along with southern religion, culture, and folklore. But Texas is also, as the song goes, "where the West begins." The dry and spacious topography, the open range and the raising and transporting of cattle to the new railroads, and ultimately the industrialization following the oil boom, produced a distinctive Texan economy. The influence of Mexican, Louisiana Cajun, and midwestern American culture distinguished Texas from the old South.

Authentic Cowboy Music

There is a rich store of authentic cowboy and frontier songs that were actually sung in the old West. "The Buffalo Skinners," a pre-cowboy song from the days of the buffalo, is one of the oldest (see Additional Listening). These were among the first folk songs, after African American spirituals, to be collected and published in the United States, the earliest dating from 1908. Early singers such as Jules Verne Allen and Harry "Haywire Mac" McClintock, who really had been cowboys, and Carl T. Sprague and Powder River Jack Lee, who learned songs at first hand from cowboys, made recordings of these songs in the 1920s. But the cowboy image did not loom large in American popular culture until the advent of western movies and the "singing cowboy."

The Cowboy Image on Records and Film

The "western" part of the trade designation "country-and-western" was added as cowboy life began to be romanticized. Ken Maynard was perhaps the first singing cowboy; he sang two traditional songs in *The Wagon Master* as early as 1929. The genre—and the image—was well launched in the 1930s. Jimmie Rodgers, already a star as the "Singing Brakeman" from Mississippi, adopted the ten-gallon hat, Texas as his home state, and the role of singing cowboy. Native Texans such as Gene Autry, Ernest Tubb, and Woodward Maurice "Tex" Ritter soon capitalized further on this image. (Their background was the farm rather than the range, but farm life has never been successfully romanticized in America.) Ritter's recording of the traditional "A-Ridin' Old Paint" (see Additional Listening) is representative. The Sons of the Pioneers, which included Leonard Slye (later Roy Rogers), was among the earliest singing groups. Rubye Blevins moved from her native Arkansas to California and became, as Patsy Montana, the first singing cowgirl. Her own song, "I Want to Be a Cowboy's Sweetheart" (see Additional Listening), became very popular and marked a significant entry of women into the ranks of country singers.

Few actual cowboy songs went into country-and-western repertoire. The country music entertainer adopted cowboy dress (often in fancy and exaggerated form) and continued to sing country songs. Cowboy films made in Hollywood spurred the writing of popular songs based on western *themes*. Songs such as "Tumbling Tumbleweeds" and "Cool Water" (see Additional Listening), by Bob Nolan (a Canadian by birth), and "The Last Roundup," by Billy Hill (who was born and grew up in Boston), became prototypes of the "western" song.

THE WEST: REALISM AND ECLECTICISM

Honky-Tonk Music

The occupation of cowboy has not gone out of existence. The chronicling, in song, poem, and story, of the lives and traditions of real-life cowboys, as they have changed and adapted over the years, continues. (The vitality of cowboy poetry, always an important adjunct to cowboy song, is illustrated in the surprising growth of events such as the annual Cowboy Poetry Conference in Elko, Nevada, and its numerous progeny springing up elsewhere in the West.) But the open range, with its freely roaming cows and cowboys, was largely fenced and gone by 1900, and the great cattle drives ended more than a century ago. A more realistic ambience of the West, particularly in Texas, has been for half a century that of small farm towns and oil-boom towns, of truck stops and taverns; its more realistic heroes and heroines the oil "boomers," the truck drivers, and their women. A new kind of "western" music evolved to fit this environment—the environment of the honky-tonk. The honky-tonk, which Malone has described as a "social institution," was a generic term for the neon-light-emblazoned bars, taverns, saloons, dance halls, ballrooms, and nightclubs that grew up, generally on the outskirts of towns. The music evolved for this environment had to emphasize the louder and more incisive instruments; the electric guitar began to be used in the 1940s, as did that distinctly urban instrument, the piano. Malone has pointed out that country musicians "found receptive audiences in the oil communities," but in the absence of live performers the music reached its consumers by means of the ubiquitous jukebox.

The music was no longer concerned with nostalgia for rural life, home, or family, or with traditional religion or mores; it dealt with harsh realities, preeminently loneliness and infidelity ("slippin' around"). "Walking the Floor Over You," as recorded by Ernest Tubb, with its use of the steel guitar and the addition of a honky-tonk piano, typifies the genre (see Additional Listening). Texans have been the main purveyors of honky-tonk. In the 1970s and 1980s the Austin, Texas, "outlaw" wing of country-and-western music reincarnated the honky-tonk sound, style, subject matter, and spirit.

Hybridization with Jazz: Western Swing

Texas, at the crossroads of a variety of influences, was hospitable to bands that were more innovative and eclectic in their instrumentation and repertory than those of the more traditional Southeast. It is not surprising, then, that Texas was the locale where hybridization took place between country music and big-band jazz. The introduction of such hitherto alien instruments as saxophones, drums, and later trumpets into the string band of fiddles, mandolins, and guitars began as early as the 1930s.

Bob Wills, most closely associated with this development, started his famous Texas Playboys in 1934. His "Cotton Eyed Joe" has been described as the "meeting of frontier fiddle and big-band swing." Based on an old square-dance fiddle tune with the nonsensical words typical of the play-party song (see p. 16), it is framed by Wills's fiddling over a "boom-chuck" accompaniment. The breaks introduce, successively, jazz steel guitar and jazz piano, before the return of the fiddle.

CD 2/18 (2:36) "Cotton Eyed Joe," Bob Wills and His Texas Playboys, 1946

Wills's "Steel Guitar Rag" of 1936, though not as well known as his "San Antonio Rose," helped to make the steel guitar a prominent instrument in country, and especially honky-tonk, music. (See Additional Listening.) By the early 1940s the popularity of this eclectic blending of styles and repertory allowed Wills to move the band's base of operations from Texas to California, whence he toured and recorded extensively.

The mix became known as "western swing," and other bandleaders, such as Milton Brown, Spade Cooley, Tex Williams, and Hank Penny, cultivated it as well. California, more than Texas, nurtured this hybrid genre; Bakersfield-born Merle Haggard, among others, has been responsible for its recent revival.

POSTWAR DISSEMINATION AND FULL-SCALE COMMERCIALIZATION

The migrations and upheavals that attended both the Depression in the 1930s and World War II in the 1940s had the effect of spreading country music far beyond the provincial soil that had given it birth, dispersing its devotees to the cities and their suburbs, and to all parts of the country. This regional music thus acquired nationwide popularity, and became altered—de-regionalized—in the process. This set the stage for its full-scale commercialization in the decades that followed.

Mainstream Stars of the 1950s and 1960s

The use of the suspect term *mainstream* here is prompted by the fact that the country music stars mentioned below clearly came out of, and continued to cultivate, the dominant characteristic traditions of country music.

Of these, Alabama-born Hank Williams (1923–53) probably shone the brightest and cast the longest shadow—all the more remarkably since his career, like that of Jimmie Rodgers twenty years earlier, was brief (essentially 1947–52). He called his band the Drifting Cowboys. (The pervasiveness of the western image is seen in the name Williams gave his band and the stylized cowboy costume he sometimes wore, even though he had virtually no cowboy songs in his repertory.) It had a traditional instrumentation of fiddle, guitars, steel guitar, bass, and occasional mandolin. His vocal style could be relaxed and rhythmic or highly intense, depending on his material, and his technique included such traditional effects as a modified yodel (as in "Lovesick Blues"; see Additional Listening), and an almost-sobbing break on emotion-laden songs (as in "I'm So Lonesome I Could Cry").

CD 2/19 (2:45) "I'm So Lonesome I Could Cry," Hank Williams, 1949

This song furnishes a striking example of an extreme form of the sentimentality noted previously as an attribute of country music—the pathetic fallacy. Animals—the whippoorwill or the robin—or even inanimate objects such as a train, the moon, a star—are endowed with the capacity for human feelings and even the ability to manifest them visibly.

Many of Williams's songs reflect his own very troubled life. In spite of that, his range was broad. It is characteristic of country singers (as of blues and rock singers) that, unlike most of those in the fields of pop, jazz, or classical music, they write many of their own songs. Williams excelled in this regard; his memorable songs include "Your Cheatin' Heart," "Move It on Over," "Kawliga," "Honky-Tonkin'," and "Hey, Good Lookin'." Also placing him in the mainstream of country musicians is the fact that he wrote and recorded religious songs, including his well-known "I Saw the Light," based on an earlier gospel song.

Other stars who worked in an essentially traditional vein during country music's postwar surge of popularity were Hank Snow (Canadian-born, and known best for "I'm Moving On"), Johnny Cash (from Arkansas, basically traditional despite his early association with rockabilly, and his "high media visibility"), and Tennessee Ernie Ford (actually from Tennessee, and known for his performance of Merle Travis's "Sixteen Tons," and for his subsequent turn to gospel music). Of more recent popularity are Loretta Lynn (from Kentucky, known for her autobiographical song "Coal Miner's Daughter"), and Merle Haggard, who came to prominence after his release from San Quentin prison in 1960. (See Additional Listening for all songs in this paragraph.)

"With the emergence of Patsy Cline, the modern era of women country singers really began" (Malone 263). Cline (born Virginia Patterson Hensley, in Winchester, Virginia, in 1932) had a versatility of style that enabled her, in the late 1950s and early 1960s (she was killed in a plane crash in 1963), to lead what Malone has called the "merger of country and pop among women singers." (And this without particularly wanting to; she dressed as a cowgirl, and always wanted to yodel on her records.) She became the first of the crossover stars mentioned later. Her vocal power and expressive flexibility is shown in "I'm Blue Again" (CD 2/20) which shows her considerable distance from that other pioneer Patsy (Montana) of a quarter-century earlier. The accompaniment is in a kind of halfway mode between country and pop; the steel guitar reminds us of Hank Williams, but the use of vocal backup group and drum set are distinctly pop.

CD 2/20 (2:04) "I'm Blue Again," Patsy Cline

Rockabilly and a New Generation of Performers and Fans

The influence of African American musical styles has never been absent from country music; blues have been in the repertory from the beginning, and the debt of Dock Boggs, the Delmore Brothers, Jimmie Davis, Jimmie Rodgers, Bob Wills, and many others to blues and jazz is clear. In the 1950s a few white performers then in their twenties (principally Carl Perkins, Elvis Presley, and Jerry Lee Lewis, and to a lesser extent Buddy Holly and Johnny Cash) began copying the material and style of black blues and rhythm-and-blues singers such as Arthur Crudup, Little Richard, and Otis Blackwell. The nascent rock 'n' roll had a heavy impact on country music itself, splitting its constituency (many fans and performers alike left traditional country for rock, some to return later) and leaving its mark on Nashville and commercial country music, in the form of the rock beat, the electrification of the instruments, and the studio-produced sound.

The immediate progeny of this cross-fertilization was *rockabilly*—according to Gary Giddins, "an amalgamation of honky-tonk, country, blues, gospel, and boogie-woogie jack-hammered by white performers . . . [and] largely the creation of Sun Records, operated by Sam Phillips" (Giddins). The mixture of ingredients in this music, which had such overwhelming appeal for youthful fans, is complex, as Giddins's summary indicates. (In connection with the gospel ingredient in rockabilly, it is interesting to note that both Presley and Lewis came out of a Pentecostal [specifically, Assemblies of God] background.)

The persistent influence of rock on subsequent commercial country music is attributable in large part to the historic background and tastes of many country fans who grew up in the rockabilly era of the 1950s and 1960s. On the other hand, a somewhat different, and largely urban, generation of youth brought up on the folk rock of Bob Dylan were introduced to country music when Dylan visited it briefly in the late 1960s in the albums *John Wesley Harding* (1968) and *Nashville Skyline* (1969, with Johnny Cash).

Nashville and the Sound of Pop

The major changes in the move toward pop music had to do with the sound of the instrumental accompaniment—changes that were primarily associated, for a variety of reasons, with Nashville, Tennessee. Nashville had an early lead in establishing itself as a center for the commercial production and dissemination of country music, thanks to the presence there since 1925 of radio station WSM and *Grand Ole Opry*. Recording began as a sideline in conjunction with the station in the 1940s. The availability of talent in the area, together with the increasing market for country music, caused major record companies to begin recording there instead of in New York or Chicago, and ultimately to establish their own studios in Nashville. Independent record companies also sprang up, and as more and more records were produced there the city acted like a magnet for performers from all over the South. The cycle of growth went on, and the combination of superbly equipped studios and an abundance of skilled engineers and versatile musicians available as session players led to the expansion of the Nashville recording industry to include all types of popular music. The city is also the home of a number of television studios, publishing houses, and booking agencies. The new Grand Ole Opry House is in the center of a huge amusement park.

The characteristics of the "Nashville sound," which began to be evident in the 1950s, include the regular use of drums (which, except in the jazz-hybrid western swing, had been foreign to country music), electric bass (sometimes pounding out a fairly heavy beat reminiscent of rock or boogie), a background of strings (definitely violins and not country fiddles!), and the use of female singers (often tightly disciplined gospel groups) to provide an impersonal, anonymous kind of vocal backup. Studio techniques such as echo effects and overdubbing (adding material in later recording sessions) became standard. A common device for sustaining interest in popular arrangements—raising the pitch a half step when material is repeated—was adopted in Nashville productions; easy for today's facile session players, it sounds oddly out of place in country music, which has its roots in traditional tonality and ways of playing the instruments. (Loretta Lynn's "Coal Miner's Daughter," a Nashville production number as recorded in 1969, is an example of this. See Additional Listening.) The occasional whine of the steel guitar, the very occasional faint sound of a fiddle or a banjo (often overdubbed), simple diatonic harmonies and melodies, and above all lyrics that still exude an inbred and ineradicable sentimentality—these are virtually all that remain to distinguish thoroughly "Nashvillized" country music from any other kind of "easy listening" fare.

Austin, Texas: "Outlaws" and Honky-Tonk

An alternative to the Nashville sound and concept is the neo-honky-tonk ("cosmic cowboy") music emanating from Texas, where honky-tonk began. Austin has a unique ambience that combines ranchers and cowboys with college students at the University of Texas. As a result, in Bill Malone's words, "a musical culture emerged which enveloped them all, and one which reflected a curious combining of images and symbols: hippie, Texan, and, above all, cowboy . . ." (394). The best-known country musician to be associated with the Austin musical scene is Willie Nelson (b. 1933). After his move to Austin in 1972, his symbolic abandoning of the Stetson for a headband, earrings, and long hair, while he went on purveying a brand of uncomplicated, pre-Nashville honky-tonk music, ensured his appeal to the three constituencies Malone referred to: the hippie, the Texan, and the cowboy. (Nelson's 1975 recording of "Blue Eyes Crying in the Rain," a song that had been recorded thirty years earlier by Roy Acuff, is an example of what Malone has called, the "clean, uncluttered country music" that was a characteristic of Austin in this period. See Additional Listening.)

Country Music's Identity Crisis: Crossovers and Superstars

The identity of country music is precisely what was imperiled in the 1970s and 1980s. In the wake of its tremendous commercial success, the country-music industry has, in Malone's words, "discovered that its best interests lie in the distribution of a package with clouded identity, possessing no regional traits . . . a music that is all things to all people. . . ." This is a capsule description of country pop, which reflects the music's "ambivalence about its rural past" and the determination of its producers that it "not reek too strongly of rural or working-class life" (Malone 369, 378). As the music itself has become more bland and less regional, many of its performers have tended to move out and away from both the context and the material of country music. Tammy Wynette, Barbara Mandrell, and Dolly Parton achieved superstar status in crossing over into pop styles and into the media of television and movies. In the other direction, pop singers such as Kenny Rogers successfully crossed over and achieved a measure of identification as country singers—though exactly what that designation now means, and to whom, is no longer as clear as it once was, since the identity of the audience for country music has also undergone a considerable shift.

At the turn of the millennium, there is little left to distinguish what is marketed as country from what is marketed as pop—except a trace of rural accent, a few death-songs (usually the best), and, one might risk the facetiousness of saying, the way the singers are dressed. (Here the image is by this time thoroughly Western, rather than Southern. Long, long gone are the unposed photos of fiddlers in denim overalls, and of old wooden rockers on delapidated porches. George Strait, for example, appears on album covers in immaculate Western garb—not just *clean*, but also obviously *brand new*, and from the most expensive shops.) The sound is studio-clean as well, and the studio groups produce a backup virtually indistinguishable from that of other Nashville-packaged pop. Bluegrass (to which we turn next) is now marketed in a separate category; banished from country pop is the sound of the fiddle or the banjo—even the guitar or the steel guitar is rare. What is the public buying and listening to? A recent survey of the largest record store in the author's city showed, in the section labeled "country," the most display space devoted to boxed sets and re-issues of—Patsy Cline! Next came the same for Johnny Cash, Merle Haggard, and Willie Nelson, and the reissues went all the way back to the Carter Family, and even the historic Bristol, Tennessee/Virginia sessions of 1927!

THE PERSISTENCE AND REVIVAL OF TRADITIONAL STYLES

Bluegrass

The strongest bastion of the musical tradition of the rural southeastern United States is bluegrass music. Yet bluegrass music as we know it today is scarcely fifty years old. Its origins, well documented, are within the living memory of many, and some of its originators are still playing and singing. It is less a literal *revival* of an older style than it is a new, highly demanding, highly professional virtuoso style *based* on and evolved from the music of the old string bands. The term *bluegrass* stands for an acoustic-string-band sound (fiddle, mandolin, banjo, guitar, and bass) and a singing style that stresses a high-pitched, straight tone. What has been repeatedly described as the "high, lonesome sound" is further enhanced by the choice of the "open-sounding" intervals of perfect fourths and perfect fifths in the harmony parts in the choruses. There is also a pronounced blues influence, palpable not only in the presence of blues numbers in the repertory but also in the frequent blues inflections in fiddle and banjo passages.

There are slow, mournful bluegrass songs, but its most characteristic tempo is fast—often breathtakingly so. Bluegrass shares with bebop jazz (a revitalization of jazz by virtuosos that evolved about the same time) the distinction of being the fastest vernacular music we have—pushed to its limits by phenomenal players.

The one man who, more than any other, was responsible for the evolution of bluegrass, and whose group, the Blue Grass Boys, gave it its name, was Bill Monroe (1911–96). Monroe was a gifted mandolin player, guitarist, and singer who began his professional career performing with his two brothers and proceeded, with persistence and integrity, to develop a style that was true to the old-time music. Monroe was not from the bluegrass country but from farther west in Kentucky. Nor did the style evolve there; it came into being slowly, by degrees, in Atlanta (where the Blue Grass Boys were first assembled) and in Nashville (where they became part of *Grand Ole Opry*). Monroe's high, clear singing style and his mandolin playing were important hallmarks of the genre, as was the reinstatement of the fiddle. His most requested piece, and the first one he performed on his debut on *Grand Ole Opry* in 1939, was his famous rendering of Jimmie Rodgers's "Muleskinner Blues."

A trademark of bluegrass in the popular mind is the incisive tone of the five-string banjo, played with virtuoso technique. The banjo had all but disappeared in country music by the 1940s, but it had a dramatic revival in a picking style native to western North Carolina, as exemplified in the phenomenal playing of Earl Scruggs (b. 1924). Scruggs joined the Blue Grass Boys in 1945. His tenure with them was fairly brief; it is in the nature of professional careerdom that rising potential stars do not stay long with their mentors but leave to form their own groups. But it was in the three years when Scruggs and Monroe were playing together (along with three other outstanding performers: Lester Flatt, guitarist and singer; Chubby Wise, fiddler; and Howard Watts, bassist) that the "bluegrass sound" was essentially established. Flatt and Scruggs left in 1948 to form the Foggy Mountain Boys; they, the Stanley Brothers, the Lilly Brothers, Jim and Jesse McReynolds, Mac Wiseman, and Jimmy Martin, among others, continued the cultivation and evolution of bluegrass music. Bluegrass has shown a capability of reinterpreting African American ballads as well as blues. CD 2/22 is a fast-paced rendition of "John Henry" that invites comparison with the version presented in Chapter 2, CD 1/15, pages 32–33.

Bluegrass has for some time, possibly because of its strict loyalty to acoustic instruments, had an existence independent of the more mass-audience-oriented and ambivalent country music. But the style has also by this time spawned substyles, branching off in several directions. The group Seldom Scene has purveyed a smooth honky-tonk bluegrass (as in "Bottom of the Glass" of 1974), and the Osborne Brothers were already producing in the 1960s a kind of neo-bluegrass (as in "Rocky Top" of 1967), adding piano and drums, sophisticated

CD 2/21 (2:44) "Muleskinner Blues," Bill Monroe and His Blue Grass Boys, Atlanta, 1940. It is interesting to compare this with Jimmie Rodgers's original, CD 7/4.

CD 2/22 (2:38) "John Henry," Lilly Brothers, 1957

harmonic progressions, and lyrics that, with their corny references to such stereotypical images as moonshine, were pseudohillbilly. (See Additional Listening.) But traditional bluegrass flourishes as well, especially in the many summer festivals that have been taking place since the early 1960s and that encompass all the many styles the genre has produced.

Other Aspects of Traditionalism

Mike Seeger, John Cohen, and the New Lost City Ramblers took a different course in relation to traditional music—that of establishing a repertory ensemble that, among other things, would keep alive older styles and older songs, such as those that had hitherto survived only on recordings from the 1920s and 1930s. Their recordings for Folkways and their *New Lost City Ramblers Song Book* embodied this approach. And groups such as Horse Sense (led by Justin Bishop) have specialized in researching and keeping alive traditional cowboy music.

In the year 1974 two interesting signposts appeared, pointing in opposite directions. *Grand Ole Opry"* in Nashville, Tennessee, moved from the historic Ryman Auditorium to its opulent new state-of-the-art home in Opryland. And Garrison Keillor, who had written a piece on *Grand Ole Opry* for the *New Yorker,* started his own radio show in St. Paul, Minnesota, *A Prairie Home Companion.* This return to the format and feeling of old-time radio, with its audience becoming involved as part of the show, was partly satirical and partly serious. The program has included jazz, ragtime, blues, gospel, ethnic music, and high school bands and choirs, as well as old-time country music and bluegrass, and the featured performers have been consistently either older traditional musicians such as Ralph Stanley, mid-generation established stars such as Emmylou Harris, or younger performers such as Peter Strushko, who played and sang out of a genuine understanding of and love for the music they were recreating. In spite of Keillor's gifts as a storyteller, the enormous popularity of the program could not have been due to him alone; it was an indication that an increasing number of people were growing tired of the slick, homogenized productions, the hype, and the packaging of the pop-music industry (including country pop), and responded to the freshness and the down-to-earth lack of pretension of a kind of music that had not been stripped of the flavor or the eccentricities of either the region or the culture from which it had come. It is significant that this recognition and response could come even from those whose own background was very different from that of a Ricky Skaggs, or whose chronological age was far removed from that of a Ralph Stanley or a Bill Monroe. It is in the nature of youth to seek innovation and change, but it has also been the young in great numbers, both performers and audience, who in our time have recognized the value of the traditional aspects of our culture, and have been enthusiastic in cultivating them and keeping them fresh.

▬ PROJECTS

1. Interview a number of people, from varied backgrounds, on the subject of country music, with a view to ascertaining the degree of correlation (if any) between a like or dislike of country music and a basically rural or urban background and orientation. It may be well to play some recorded examples as part of the interview. Include yourself as one respondent if you like.
2. Compare the treatment of the man-woman relationship in a typical honky-tonk song of the 1940s with that of a typical popular song (Tin Pan Alley–Hit Parade type) of the same period.
3. Do a survey of two or three performances of *A Prairie Home Companion* on public radio as to the range of music and performers presented.
4. Review the film *O Brother Where Are Thou* with regard to the music. Do you know any of the songs? In what ways does the use of "old-time music" contribute to the atmosphere and sense of place?

▬ ADDITIONAL LISTENING

"A-Ridin'Old Paint." See *Back in the Saddle Again.*

Back in the Saddle Again. New World 80314. Contains many early recordings of cowboy songs.

"Blue Eyes Crying in the Rain." See *Classic Country Music.*

"Bottom of the Glass. See *Classic Country Music.*

"Buffalo Skinners, The." *Slim Critchlow: Cowboy Songs.* Arhoolie 479.

Classic Country Music: A Smithsonian Collection. Smithsonian Collection of Recordings RD 042. A basic collection.

"Coal Miner's Daughter." See *Classic Country Music.*

"Cool Water." See *Classic Country Music.*

"House Carpenter, The." *Anthology of American Folk Music,* vol. 1 Smithsonian/Folkways 40090.

"I'm Moving On." See *Classic Country Music.*

"I Want to Be a Cowboy's Sweetheart. See *Classic Country Music* and *Back in the Saddle Again.*

"Johnny Gray" ("Blow You Winds of Morning"). *Uncle Dave Macon.* Smithsonian/Folkways RF051.

"Katy Cline." *Mountain Music Bluegrass Style.* Smithsonian/Folkways 40038.

"Little Black Train." *Dock Boggs: His Folkways Years, 1963–1968.* Smithsonian/Folkways 40108.

"Little Old Log Cabin in the Lane, The." See *Classic Country Music.*

"Lovesick Blues." See *Classic Country Music.*

"'Mid the Green Fields of Virginia." *Carter Family: 1927–34.* JSP Records 7701.

"New River Train." See "Katy Cline."

"No Disappointment in Heaven." See "Little Black Train."

"No Letter in the Mail." See "Katy Cline."

"Rocky Top. See *Classic Country Music.*

"Rowan County Crew." See "Little Black Train."

"Sixteen Tons." See *Classic Country Music.*

"Snow Dove" (also known as "The Butcher Boy"). See "Katy Cline."

"Steel Guitar Rag." See *Classic Country Music.*

"Tumbling Tumbleweeds." See *Classic Country Music.*

"Walking the Floor Over You." See *Classic Country Music.*

CHAPTER

8   Blues and Soul: From Country to City

THE SPIRITUAL AND THE BLUES

The spiritual, as discussed in Chapter 2, began in slavery; the blues (as described there in their embryonic form) could have evolved only afterward, with the profound changes that affected the lives of African Americans in the South after the Civil War. These changes had to do with the new, albeit severely circumscribed, dimension of leisure; with a new degree of solitude; with the confrontation with an entirely new set of social and economic problems, not the least being the need for money; with broader contacts and experiences; with a much greater fluency in the American language; and finally with a new mobility. (See Baraka, Chapter 6.) This mobility was forced in most cases by the relentless (and new) necessity of finding employment— much harder for the men than for the women. Among these were the blind street musicians who had gravitated to the larger cities; making street music was the prime means of livelihood and independence available to those with even a modicum of talent. Thus it happened that the blues were propagated by a class of musicians who were to a degree outcasts, even among their own race—rejected at least by its more settled and established members, especially the most devoutly religious, to whom the blues were "devil songs." The black author Richard Wright writes in his preface to Paul Oliver's *The Meaning of the Blues:*

> All American Negroes do not sing the blues. These songs are not the expression of the Negro people in America as a whole. I'd surmise that the spirituals . . . came from those slaves who were closest to the Big Houses of the plantations where they caught vestiges of Christianity whiffed to them from the Southern Whites' cruder forms of Baptist or Methodist religions. If the plantations' house slaves were somewhat remote from Christianity, the field slaves were almost completely beyond the pale. And it was from them and their descendants that the devil songs called the blues came—that confounding triptych of the convict, the migrant, the rambler, the steel driver, the ditch digger, the roustabout, the pimp, the prostitute, the urban or rural illiterate outsider. (Oliver 10)

It was perhaps inevitable, for a variety of reasons, that the prisons came to hold more than their share of bluesmen; many field recordings were made in the penitentiaries and prison farms of the South in the 1930s and 1940s, and some important blues singers were discovered there.

BLUES SUBJECTS

The subjects treated in the blues encompass a wide range. No area of commonly shared human experience is excluded. Some blues speak of a nameless depression.

> Early this morning the blues came walking in my room.

Some are about work—

> I worked all summer, yes, and all the fall
> Going to spend Christmas in my overalls.

or the lack of it.

> I'm goin' to Detroit, get myself a good job,
> Tried to stay around here on this starvation farm.

Some sing of gambling—

> Jack of Diamonds, you appear to be my friend
> But gamblin' gonna be our end.

of crime, of the law, of prisons —

Judge gave me life this mornin' down on Parchman Farm

of prostitution, of enslaving addiction, or of the necessity or the irresistible urge to move on.

When a woman gets the blues, she hangs her head and cries.
But when a man gets the blues, he flags a freight train and rides.

But the greatest number are in some way about the fundamental man-woman relationship. As the blues singer Robert Pete Williams said, "Love makes the blues. That's where it comes from" (Cook 40). The man-woman relationship is displayed in the blues in a great variety of aspects — from a comment on the power of a woman's attraction —

Well, a long, tall woman will make a preacher lay his Bible down

or the exhilaration of being in love —

Well, I feel all right and everything is okay.
Yes, I feel all right, everything is okay.
It's the love of my baby, oh, makes me feel this way.

to a scornful comment on infidelity —

High yeller, she'll kick you, that ain't all,
When you step out at night 'nother mule in your stall.

or the painful fact of separation —

My man left this morning, jest about half past four,
He left a note on his pillow, sayin' he couldn't use me no more.

or the most bitter rejection.

If I was cold and hungry, I wouldn't even ask you for bread,
I don't want you no more, if I'm on my dying bed.

Blues language is keen, apt, and colorful, and is given to the use of irony, metaphor, and double entendre. No subject is off limits, and although broad social comment is foreign to such a personal medium, the blues poet finds a way to relate the most topical subject to an earthy metaphor with a telling phrase.

Uncle Sam ain't no woman, but he sure can take your man away.

THE FORM AND MUSIC OF THE BLUES

The incipient blues, related to field calls and field hollers, were sung unaccompanied, as was heard in "I Don't Mind the Weather" (CD 1/13, p. 30). But at some undefined early date, the guitar was adopted as the natural instrument for accompanying the sung laments and comments that were the blues. Blues harmony may consist simply of a single chord with embellishments, as we hear in "Levee Camp Moan" (CD 2/23).

> Mmmmmm_____
> Lord, they accused me of murder; I haven't harmed a man. [3x]
> Oh, they accused me of forging; I can't write my name. [2x]

CD 2/23 (1:08) "Levee Camp Moan" (excerpt), Texas Alexander, vocal and guitar

Note that, in contrast with "I Don't Mind the Weather," the guitar participates here as a full partner in the development of the melodic line.

The melodic material of the blues has already been set forth in Transcription 2.4, page 29, with the areas of variable pitch noted. But a sense of clearly defined pitch may be further obscured by a wide variety of highly personalized vocal techniques. In the blues, the words themselves are not as important as they are in the ballad. The blues may thus be shouted (a manner of delivery related to the primitive field holler, which has been taken over successively by rhythm-and-blues and rock 'n' roll). They may be hummed; they may be sung in falsetto, or with falsetto breaks; they may be sung with the gravelly tone of the false bass voice; they may be chanted in the manner of a recitative; they may even be spoken. In the folk blues, words and even lines may be left unfinished. As for melodic contour, there are many individual variations, but the general tendency is to start the phrase high and proceed downward, ending with a dropping inflection, as in the "Quittin' Time Song" (field holler) transcribed in Chapter 2 (Transcription 2.3, p. 29, and CD 1/12).

The form of the blues is often described as though it were invariably conventionalized. Actually the rural blues is often quite free in form. The sung portions do not always arrange themselves into three-line stanzas, but many consist of a varying number of lines, often unequal in length. The standard form—a line, repeated, followed by a different concluding line—should be considered, in the country blues, as a tendency only.

> My mama told me before I left home,
> My mama told me before I left home,
> You better let them Jacksonville women alone.

It was perhaps first crystallized in the published blues that began appearing as early as 1912 and that certainly influenced subsequent blues performers.

The standard musical phrase is four bars long—hence the standard "12-bar blues" form. But in the case of the blues in its folk phase, single phrases could be four and a half, five, or seven bars long, with the singer beginning the next line whenever he or she felt like it. (In the rural blues, it was almost invariably he.) (This irregularity of phrase lengths in folk music is a common feature and has been noted in Hispanic folk music, p. 55, and in Anglo-Celtic folk music and hence in early country music, pp. 112–13.) When there is instrumental accompaniment, which is nearly always, the sung line never takes up the whole musical "space," so to speak. The voice comes to its cadence about halfway through, and the phrase is always completed by an instrumental *break*. This paces the song, gives the singer time to think of the next line, and provides the opportunity for some more-or-less fancy and often highly individual instrumental playing. The blues song is always introduced by an instrumental "warm-up," which may be the length of an entire stanza.

The usual harmonic plan of the blues involves the use of the three principal chords of the key in a pattern that *tends* toward the following:

1st phrase	I	—	—	I^7
2nd phrase	IV$^{(7)}$	—	I	—
3rd phrase	V^7	(IV)	I	—

"Weary Worried Blues" (CD 2/24) is a fully developed 12-bar blues. The harmonica is the singer's partner and alter ego, performing a complete 12-bar introductory chorus, completing each phrase after the singer and taking a complete solo chorus after two vocal choruses. This foreshadows the later use of the saxophone in the blues band, as can be heard in the rhythm-and-blues number "Good Rockin' Tonight" (CD 2/29, p. 158), and as B. B. King uses his guitar in "Sweet Little Angel" (CD 2/28, p. 143).

CD 2/24 (2:45) "Weary Worried Blues," Brownsville Son Bonds, vocal and guitar; Hammie Nickerson, harmonica. 1934.

Skillful players developed their own individual sounds and techniques, some of which passed into general currency. Sliding between tones, for example, was made possible by the use of the back of a knife blade on the strings of the guitar, or the broken top of a bottle (with the jagged edge annealed) worn on the little finger. This "bottleneck" style, perhaps suggested by the Hawaiian guitar, overrode the rigid tuning imposed by the frets and provided a flexibility that made it possible for a skillful performer to match the sliding and wailing of the voice. The playing of Robert Johnson in "Preachin' Blues" illustrates this (see Additional Listening).

Other instruments were used as auxiliaries to the ubiquitous guitar. The harmonica, as heard in "Weary Worried Blues," was fairly cheap and very portable, and this "blues harp" became, in the hands of virtuosos such as Sonny Terry, a very flexible and expressive instrument, capable of shadings and bendings that approached the subtlety of the voice.

Improvised instruments were common. The jug served as a kind of substitute tuba. The washboard, fitted out with auxiliary metal pans and lids attached, was a whole rhythm section. The inverted washtub, with a piece of rope stretched between a hole through its center and a broom handle, was a substitute bass (and was a relative of the African earth bow). Jug bands and washboard bands incorporating these instruments were sometimes recorded commercially, so that their sounds have come down to us.

The Blues as Popular Music

Admittedly it is difficult to draw a very precise line between the blues as folk music and the blues as essentially popular music, with professional entertainers catering to a "public" instead of casual music-makers performing within a closely knit community. But the distinction exists, nonetheless. Amiri Baraka has written:

> Socially, classic blues and the instrumental styles that went with it represented the Negro's entrance into the world of professional entertainment and the assumption of the psychological imperatives that must accompany such a phenomenon. . . . It was no longer strictly the group singing to ease their labors or the casual expression of personal deliberations on the world. It became a music that could be used to entertain others *formally*. The artisan, the professional blues singer, appeared; blues-singing no longer had to be merely a passionately felt avocation, it could now become a way of making a living. An external and sophisticated idea of performance had come to the blues, moving it past the casualness of the "folk" to the conditioned emotional gesture of the "public." (81–82)

The blues began as, and in a certain sense still is, the lament, the comment, often mocking or ironic, of the solitary individual, bereft of the support of tribe or close-knit society, facing *alone*, on personal terms, a hostile or indifferent world. Yet long before our time the lament had become an entertainment, the solitary singer's comment had crystallized into a form that could be printed and sold, and the lone cry had become a commodity. It had become, in a word, popular music—even before the first recordings of it appeared. But the legacy of its folk beginnings remained to characterize the blues indelibly: the way the voice is handled, the blues intonation, the range and treatment of its subjects, and, above all, the basic blues feeling that has its roots in a solitary experience and view of life. Those who were to become its first professionals had, like their white hillbilly counterparts, served their apprenticeship in traveling tent shows and minstrel and medicine shows, or in playing and singing for all-night parties and dances, or even (as many blind singers did) in performing for passersby in front of country stores or on city streets.

EARLY PUBLISHED BLUES

It was inevitable that a type of music being sung and played in cities and small towns in the lowland South from the Piedmont to Texas should eventually find its way into print. This happened first in 1912, when by coincidence within a period of two months blues were published in St. Louis ("Baby Seals Blues"), Oklahoma City ("Dallas Blues"), and Memphis ("Memphis Blues"). "Memphis Blues" had been widely played in that city for three years before its publication, by the enterprising composer-bandleader who, more than any other early professional, was to promote the blues as popular music and bring it to a wide public — William C. Handy. Handy's early experiences with the performance and publication of these compositions are interestingly set forth in his autobiography, *Father of the Blues*. In the beginning, "Memphis Blues" netted him fifty dollars, with the real profits for years going to others. But Handy was to learn quickly. If the nickname "father of the blues" is something of an exaggeration (Bruce Cook has said that a more accurate one would be "rich uncle"), his place in blues history is still important, and his ties with its roots are perfectly genuine (Cook 122).

The Form and Texts of Published Blues

By the time the blues was being composed and arranged for broad popular consumption, the musical form had been developed and extended. It came to include at least two and sometimes three strains, often in the relationship of verses-with-chorus. The three-phrase, 12-bar pattern with its usual harmonic plan (see p.134) was standard for at least one of the strains, but there were also strains cast in the standard European 16-bar form. These early published blues, as a matter of fact, showed a mixture of influences. The blues elements were often quite attenuated, and the music was sometimes pure ragtime, with its more elaborate European harmonies, as in the second strain of Handy's "Memphis Blues." At times still other influences were evident; the best-known strain of the most famous blues of all, the "St. Louis Blues," is actually, as Handy wrote it, a 16-bar habanera! As he notes in his autobiography, the effect of this habanera rhythm — the "Spanish tinge" of which Jelly Roll Morton spoke — on black dancers for whom he played was not lost on the observant Mr. Handy, and he used it again in his "Beale Street Blues" and "Aunt Hagar's Children."

The blues as published for general public consumption were distinct from the earthy blues of the tent shows that were later to become so popular on recordings. Each had its own public and its own standards for admissible subject matter and language, but there was some commonality of musical and textual ideas. The recently invented telephone was an irresistible metaphor in blues, as it was in early gospel music. The "Hello Central" motif appears in Handy's "The Hesitating Blues," published in 1915 (see Handy, 100–103); Ma Rainey's "Sissy Blues" (see p. 137), recorded in 1926; and Lightnin' Hopkins's poignant "Hello Central," recorded in 1950. Handy made a practice of noting down folk phrases he heard here and there ("Goin' where the Southern cross' the Dog"; "Ma man's got a heart like a rock cast in de sea") and incorporating them into his songs. But in the published blues of Handy and others the rhymes are more exact, the lyrics more facile, employing clever plays on words, and the subjects (as in Handy's "Wall Street Blues," of 1929; see Handy 111) artificially remote from the soil in which the blues had germinated.

CLASSIC BLUES

The blues as a more or less standardized form of popular music for a large public (mostly black, but with a growing white element) enjoyed what has been called its "classic" period from 1920, when the first recordings were made and sold, until the onset of the Depression in the early 1930s. Personal-appearance tours (mostly on vaudeville circuits) and nightclub appearances were a mainstay for the more popular blues singers, and there were some radio performances and even some films. But the principal medium for the propagation of the blues was the phonograph recording. In a development parallel to that of instrumental jazz and white hillbilly music, thousands of blues performances by hundreds of singers were recorded, and millions of copies sold.

The period of the classic blues was dominated by the female blues singer. Various reasons have been advanced for this, but the most likely ones have to do with the nature of show business at the time and the success of the women singers in tent and vaudeville shows. The recording of blues was regarded at the outset as a risky venture. The first singers recorded were not really blues singers but professional entertainers with experience in cabaret and vaudeville singing in styles much like those of popular white singers. Mamie Smith made the famous first recording ("That Thing Called Love" and "You Can't Keep a Good Man Down") in 1920. After that recording's promising success, she recorded the famous "Crazy Blues," and the potential became unmistakable. Real blues singers in the southern tradition began to be recorded a few years later. Of these by far the best known and most influential were Gertrude "Ma" Rainey (1886–1939) and Bessie Smith (1894–1937), both of whom began recording blues in 1923.

Ma Rainey's early career sheds light on the milieu in which the classic blues evolved. Both her parents were in the minstrel-show business, and she herself was singing on the stage by the time she was 14. She acquired her familiar nickname "Ma" when, at age 18, she married William "Pa" Rainey, a minstrel performer, and they began touring with their song-and-dance routine. (She herself preferred to be called "Madame" Rainey.) Thus she had had more than twenty years of professional experience in touring circus, variety, and minstrel shows by the time she made her first blues recording. Of all the classic blues singers, she remained closest to the vernacular blues tradition. She never sang professionally outside the South, except to make recordings in New York and Chicago during a four-year period that ended in 1928. By then, a recording executive is said to have expressed the opinion that Ma's "down-home" material had gone out of fashion. During that brief period she recorded with some of the leading jazz musicians, but also with a traditional Southern jug, kazoo, washboard, and banjo band.

Ma Rainey's lyrics reflected the country blues range of subject matter and went beyond the perennial types of man-woman themes to touch on poverty, alcoholism, prostitution, homosexuality, and topical references (as in "Titanic Man Blues"). Here are some samplings of her frankly earthy material. Her "Hustlin' Blues" treated prostitution.

A rare photo of Ma Rainey with her Georgia Jazz Band. "Georgia Tom" Dorsey, who enjoyed a dual career as a "bluesman" and gospel singer, is at the piano.

It's rainin' out here and tricks ain't walkin' tonight, [2x]
I'm goin' home, I know I've got to fight.
If you hit me tonight, let me tell you what I'm going to do, [2x]
I'm gonna take you to a court and tell the judge on you.
I ain't made no money, and he dared me to go home, [2x]
Judge, I told him he better leave me alone.
He followed me up, and he grabbed me for a fight, [2x]
He said, girl do you know, you ain't made no money tonight.
Oh, Judge, tell him I'm through, [2x]
I'm tired of this life, that's why I brought him to you.

Text, "Hustlin' Blues"

Her "Sissy Blues" treated homosexuality.

I dreamed last night I was far from harm,
Woke up and found my man in a sissy's arms.

Text, "Sissy Blues"

Chorus

Hello Central, it's bound to drive me wild,
Can I get a number, or will I have to wait a while?
Some are young, some are old,
My man says sissies got good jelly roll.

(Chorus)

My man's got a sissy, his name is "Miss Kate,"
He shook that thing like jelly on a plate.

(Chorus)

Now all the people ask me why I'm all alone
A sissy shook that thing and took my man from home.

(Chorus)

The unflinching realism of much of Ma Rainey's material was a far cry
from the smirking double entendre typical of the sleazier vaudeville shows—a
type of lyric exploited in both city and country blues by record companies
eager to bolster sales in the early years of the Depression, when the amazingly
prosperous era of the classic blues was waning. This was the kind of material
Bessie Smith was forced to record in her last years.

Ma Rainey recorded in Chicago and New York with a pickup group that
included many of the important blues and jazz performers of the time. In
"Countin' the Blues"(CD 2/25), her Georgia Jazz Band includes Louis Armstrong and Fletcher Henderson.

CD 2/25 (3:09)
"Countin' the Blues,"
Ma Rainey and her
Georgia Jazz Band.
Recorded in New York,
1924.

Contemporary accounts and pictures indicate that she was a stocky, somewhat ugly woman, imbued with what must have been an imposing stage presence and an uncanny degree of what can best be described by that much-abused term "charisma." In her surviving recordings what we hear, dimly transmitted through primitive recording techniques, is a voice and a kind of singing devoid of the slightest trace of artificiality.

Bessie Smith, eight years younger than Ma Rainey, began her career as the latter's protégée, though she declined to acknowledge that in later years. She and Ma Rainey began recording about the same time, but Bessie Smith eventually became far better known and was undoubtedly a more versatile singer. She became identified wholly with the sophisticated city blues tradition, and her material was tailored largely for that market.

CD 2/26 (2:56)
"Mama's Got the Blues,"
Bessie Smith, vocal;
Fletcher Henderson,
piano. 1923.

Like Ma Rainey, she worked with the leading jazz musicians, and recorded with piano (with Fletcher Henderson, for example), with piano and one instrument (quite often with Joe Smith or Louis Armstrong playing muted blues cornet), with a small jazz combo, and even with choral background in some early "production numbers." "Mama's Got the Blues" (CD 2/26), recorded with Fletcher Henderson as pianist, is a typical 12-bar slow blues, with lyrics traditional for the period. Her mastery of the idiom and the forcefulness and directness of her delivery are undisputed. But Bessie Smith, too, was out of fashion by the time she made her last recordings in 1933.

Other singers in the classic blues tradition included Ida Cox, Bertha "Chippie" Hill, Clara Smith, Sippie Wallace, and Victoria Spivey, all of whom performed with major jazz musicians of the 1920s and 1930s. It was the day of the woman blues singers, and although there have been eminent black female popular singers since (Ella Fitzgerald, Billie Holiday, Sarah Vaughan, Aretha Franklin), none after the classic period has been so exclusively identified with the blues. The dominant role in blues singing has since passed largely to men.

BLUES AND JAZZ

As we have seen, the blues had evolved structurally in such a way as to demand the complementing role of an answering voice (or instrument) at the end of each sung line. This manifestation of call-and-response is a distinguishing feature of the blues. The solitary blues singer filled in his own breaks on his guitar; in the city blues the piano, and later the collaborating instrumentalist, took up this function. An interesting example of distinctive jazz breaks provided by a small combo can be heard in Ma Rainey's "Countin' the Blues" (CD 2/25), in which each break in the three-line blues form is taken in turn by cornet, clarinet, and trombone. These collaborations provide some of the finest moments in early jazz.

At this time "blues" and "jazz" were taken by some to be one and the same. Although they are distinct traditions, their parallel development is a rather complex history of periodically strong influence and identification. At the same time that the rural blues was slowly taking shape, something like its urban counterpart was having a hand in the early formation of jazz. By 1900 there were bands in New Orleans (and possibly in Memphis and other cities as well) playing music that was called "blues." We will never know what the blues played by these early bands sounded like. But the identification of blues with jazz remained exceptionally close through the classic blues period we have been examining. Then, in the 1930s, began a gradual divergence; the blues declined somewhat, and jazz evolved in other directions. Although the blues as a harmonic and formal design can be heard in all ages of jazz, the blues references, as we advance through the so-called modern period, become increasingly attenuated. Recently, under the impact of the reenergized urban blues and the synthesis called *soul music,* jazz has been forcibly pulled back to a closer relation with its blues roots. But in fact the blues, in both form and feeling, has never been wholly absent from jazz, which has produced thousands of blues, all of them variations in some respect on the "given" blues premises. Three examples, each from a different period and style of jazz, show the recurring influence of the blues: "Dippermouth Blues" (1923; CD 4/11, pp. 306–7), "Ko-ko" (1940; CD 4/13, p. 314), and "Parker's Mood" (1948; in the *Smithsonian Collection of Classic Jazz,* as are the other two examples as well).

BOOGIE-WOOGIE

Boogie-woogie and ragtime are essentially solo piano forms, but they are quite distinct from each other in origin and style. (See pp. 289ff. for the contrasting origins of ragtime.) The progenitor of boogie-woogie is the blues. Its sound is unforgettable—a driving left hand with a hypnotically repeated pattern (the musical term for this, *ostinato,* is related to our word "obstinate"); the right hand often insisting equally obstinately on its own repeated figures; and, underlying all, blues form and harmony. It was spawned as piano entertainment in bars, nightclubs, and related establishments. Generically, boogie-woogie was probably an adaptation of what blues singer-guitarists had been doing, with their intricate, ostinatolike accompaniments. Early boogie-woogie soloists would often sing along, or talk to their audience, while they were playing.

Boogie-woogie, transferred out of the environment of its origins, went through a period of short but intense popularity in the late 1930s. This is apt to obscure the fact that it is a much older phenomenon. Jelly Roll Morton (see p. 297) said that many piano performers in his early days (shortly after the turn of the century) played in what must have been something like this style of piano blues with heavy ostinatolike left hand. W. C. Handy mentions adopting and orchestrating for his group a type of piano music played in the bordellos of the Mississippi delta region about the turn of the century. It was called "boogie-house music."

There is a relationship between boogie-woogie and the big bands of the 1930s, especially in Kansas City, where the "jump" style was in many ways a translation of boogie idioms to the jazz band, just as the idioms of ragtime had been transferred to traditional jazz a generation earlier. (See p. 308.) Although the craze for it subsided somewhat in the 1940s, boogie-woogie remained a potent musical style. With its driving ostinato and blues form, it was to emerge as a major influence on rock 'n' roll in the 1950s, as can be heard, for example, in the work of Jerry Lee Lewis.

CD 2/27 (2:57) "Mr. Freddie Blues," Meade "Lux" Lewis, piano. Recorded in Chicago, 1936.

Boogie-woogie's resources are limited. Nevertheless, within those limitations a considerable amount of variety is found—variety of tempi (not all boogie is fast), of left-hand patterns, and of general feeling. In "Mr. Freddie Blues" (CD 2/27), a boogie-woogie treatment by Meade "Lux" Lewis of an earlier blues by J. H. Shayne, the typical ostinato bass and the 12-bar blues form are exceptionally clear.

THE ABSORPTION OF COUNTRY BLUES INTO POPULAR MUSIC

Recordings of city blues by female singers in the early 1920s were very successful, as we have noted. As the business of selling records by mail grew, it was realized that a large market existed among the black people of the rural South for recordings of their own singers. The ice was broken for male blues singers when Papa Charlie Jackson recorded his "Lawdy Lawdy Blues" in Chicago in 1924. (The piece was not really a blues, nor was Jackson a blues singer but a minstrel- and medicine-show performer from New Orleans, who accompanied himself on a six-string banjo.) The parallel with the first female singers to record blues commercially is interesting. (See pp. 135–36.) When this yielded an encouraging amount of commercial success, the search for traditional country blues performers was on, and there soon followed recordings by singers from across the entire South, from Florida (Blind Blake) to Texas (Blind Lemon Jefferson).

Race records was the trade term used for several decades for recordings by black musicians intended for black consumers. For the earliest recordings, singers were brought to Chicago, where they worked in "studios" often primitive even by the standards of the time. But expeditions through the South with recording equipment were also undertaken. The engineering and production of the records were for the most part as cheap as the promotional material was crass, and usually little attempt was made to preserve the masters. The records themselves, especially those made in the 1920s, became very rare indeed. With few exceptions the singers themselves were exploited while being treated with disdain.

A few country-blues singers, survivors in a harsh environment, did eventually become well known and frequently recorded, the beneficiaries of two developments in the cities: the urban folk-song movement of the 1930s and 1940s (see Chapter 6), which brought Leadbelly (Huddie Ledbetter) into prominence, and, in the 1960s, the folk-song revival movement, with its attendant folk festivals, at which country-blues performers such as Robert Pete Williams, Mississippi John Hurt, Lightnin' Hopkins, Son House, and the team of Sonny Terry and Brownie McGhee appeared. Terry and McGhee went on to successful careers in New York.

URBAN BLUES

There is no music that better epitomizes the harsher aspects of urban life, especially for African Americans, than the urban blues. The heartwood of the blues is rural, but at the layer where it is continuing to add living tissue it is wholly of the city. Thus the blues, like a great proportion of the black populace whose music it is, made the move from country to city.

The move toward modern urban blues was signaled by the introduction of that quintessentially urban instrument, the piano, into the ensemble. The combination of piano and guitar was used by the influential team of Leroy Carr and Francis "Scrapper" Blackwell in the 1930s (their "Blue Night Blues" is representative, see New World 290), and the piano almost invariably figured in Chicago blues recordings of the period. The style of piano playing, except for traces of ragtime, was, not surprisingly, essentially that of the blues-related boogie-woogie, with its heavy and incessant left-hand ostinatos clearly presaging the main features of rock 'n' roll. Also to be noted was the addition of drums to many of the Chicago groups. But this was a transitional period in the citification of the blues; some recordings still included such down-home instruments as the harmonica and even the washboard. The blues, just before World War II, had one foot in the city and one still in the country. (See *Blues Roots/Chicago—the 1950s* in Additional Listening.)

In the 1950s and 1960s, a number of blues singers born in the South, and with strong blues roots there, began recording, mostly in Chicago, a brand of hard-driving blues with a strong beat, backed by electric guitar (which they often played themselves), bass, drums, and sometimes electric organ and/or piano. This blues was strongly influenced by the gospel tradition, a background from which many of the singers came. These include Howlin' Wolf (born Chester Arthur Burnett; 1910–1976), Muddy Waters (born McKinley Morganfield; 1915–1983), and John Lee Hooker (1917–2001), all from Mississippi, and Willie Mae "Big Mama" Thornton, from Alabama (1926–1984). Muddy Waters's 16-bar blues "Hoochie Coochie Man" is typical (New World 261). These artists defined a type of urban blues that was very influential on later blues and rock musicians, especially in England, where many of them toured.

Meanwhile in the West, typically Kansas City, blues singers were often backed by jazz bands, with heavily pounding rhythm sections, and featuring prominently the wind instrument that became the blues singer's alter ego, the saxophone. The wailing, honking, screaming saxophone often took a complete chorus after the singer had sufficiently established the mood. That in turn affected vocal style. The modern blues singer has a microphone, of course, but the shouting style that Midwest blues singers such as Joe Turner (whose "Shake, Rattle and Roll" became a musical icon of nascent rock 'n' roll) and Jimmy Rushing had to adopt to be heard, unamplified, over the big-band sounds of Kansas City, remains as a characteristic of much blues singing today. (For an example of rhythm-and-blues, listen to CD 2/29, "Good Rockin' Tonight.") As Amiri Baraka has put it,

> These Southwestern "shouters" and big blues bands had a large influence on Negro music everywhere. The shouter gave impetus to a kind of blues that developed around the cities in the late thirties called "rhythm and blues," which was largely huge rhythm units smashing away behind screaming blues singers. (168)

The symbolic distortion forced upon that most sensitive of all musical instruments, the human voice, by the stridency and abrasiveness of a stark urban milieu is summed up by Baraka: "Blues had always been a vocal music . . . but now the human voice itself had to struggle, to scream, to be heard" (171–72). The guitar, by now invariably electric, remained as an element of continuity in the blues band.

If we add to this a small vocal ensemble, usually female, for the blues singer to "play" to, which gave the responses to his or her calls and echoed the key phrases, we have virtually described the medium of the urban blues that, by the early 1950s, had been given the commercial designation *rhythm-and-blues*. Rhythm-and-blues, like the earlier race records, is a vast commercial category. Charlie Gillett has written, "As a market category . . . 'rhythm and blues' was simply a signal that the singer was black, and recording for a black audience" (130).

"A Fool in Love" (in *Roots: Rhythm and Blues*, see Additional Listening), with its 8-bar verses and a vocal group taking over the role of the blues saxophone in the 12-bar choruses, is illustrative. This rhythm-and-blues, especially as conventionalized by such entertainers as Chuck Berry and Bo Diddley, was still performed by black musicians for an almost exclusively black audience, reached either in person or by means of recordings—a market which rivaled that for the race recordings of city and country blues thirty years earlier. But it also unquestionably formed the basis for the music—rock 'n' roll—that won a vast young white audience from the mid-1950s on. So closely, in fact, did early rock 'n' roll performers imitate black models that the early recordings of the white singer Elvis Presley (who spent his adolescent years in the blues ambience of Memphis) sold primarily to black audiences.

THE SOUL SYNTHESIS

A broader synthesis of black musical styles, and one embodying many elements of the blues, is embraced in the concept of "soul." According to Charles Keil, "'Soul' may be partly defined as a mixture of ethnic essence, purity, sincerity, conviction, credibility, and just plain effort" (160). The ethnic orientation of "soul" is clear; it began to evolve, as Keil points out, after the Supreme Court's school desegregation decision of 1954, one of the landmarks in a decade that saw the aspirations of African Americans take a definite turn toward strengthening racial and cultural *identity*, rather than achieving integration per se. As a concept, soul embraces a wide spectrum of life's aspects, from religion to sex to food; indeed, it emphasizes a kind of synthesis of everything, and the communication and sharing of experience and strong emotion. (In this regard, it is similar to, and has been compared to, the concept of "salsa" in Latin/Caribbean music. See p. 78.) As Keil has said, "For many Negroes, life is one long sacrificial ritual. The blues artist, in telling his story, crystallizes and synthesizes not only his own experience but the experiences of his listeners" (161).

Musically, soul is a synthesis as well—of blues, jazz, and gospel. Its foremost artists among blues singers have been Ray Charles, B. B. King, Bobby Blue Bland, Junior Parker, Aretha Franklin, and Ike and Tina Turner. Of their performances, Keil has said, "The word 'ritual' seems more appropriate than 'performance' when the audience is committed rather than appreciative" (164). No better example of this can be cited than B. B. King's "Sweet Little Angel," as recorded live at the Regal Theater, a famous blues venue in Chicago, in 1964 (CD 2/28). It consists of five choruses of 12-bar blues, the

CD 2/28 (3:45) "Sweet Little Angel," B. B. King

first and last featuring King's electric guitar. The audience reaction gives a feeling for the ritual of an authentic performance of soul.

BLUES AT THE TURN OF THE CENTURY

Many changes have affected blues in the 1990s and into the new century. The recordings that are being produced are both fewer and technologically and stylistically slicker. As Mary Katherine Aldin has noted, "The good old days of producing on a shoestring and selling records at gigs have all but disappeared." Live concerts have become more expensive and more gargantuan. "The juke joints of the 1930s and even the folk clubs of the 1960s have been replaced," as Aldin has pointed out, "by blues festivals that draw tens of thousands. . . . The audience usually cannot get closer than binocular distance, and the sense of immediacy, urgency, and intimate communication so essential to the blues experience has all but disappeared" (Cohn 390, 392).

Aldin further calls attention to more fundamental changes as well when she asserts that

> . . . . not a single young artist is carrying on the tradition of, say, John Lee Hooker or Son House . . . one reason is that the young people growing up today come from a different background. They don't learn field hollers, don't pick cotton, aren't sharecroppers. They work city jobs, even in the small towns, and the music of the auto mechanic or car-wash operator is, by its very nature, going to be a more urbanized sound, so that what David Evans called "the solo work song that for years provided blues with its basic vocal and melodic material" no longer exists. (Cohn 398–99)

Gender and racial shifts are noteworthy as well. White male blues singers such as Johnny Winter and William Clarke have come into prominence, as has the interracial women's group "Saffire: The Uppity Blues Women."

Among bluesmen and blueswomen prominent today (some of whom are already in their fifties or older) are Johnny Copeland, Robert Cray, and Albert Collins, who, although each a full-fledged artist on his own, formed a very successful trio); Clarence "Gatemouth" Brown; James Cotton; KoKo Taylor; Taj Mahal; Joe Lewis Walker; Son Seals; and Kenny Neal.

Reflecting many of these changes, as well as ties to the past and its traditions, is "We're Outa Here," by Clarence "Gatemouth" Brown, recorded in 1991 (see Additional Listening). It consists of twenty 12-bar blues choruses in a fast tempo over a pronounced boogie-bass pattern—one that was already old in the 1930s. The fairly large band includes winds that play jazz riffs. There are solo choruses for guitar and piano, but only three choruses with vocals! The whole exhibits a virtuosity which is a match for that of bebop jazz and blue-grass breakdowns.

Whatever the present and future state of the blues, there can be no doubt of its importance up to this point. Blues authority Paul Oliver has called it "one of the richest and most rewarding of popular arts and perhaps the last great folk music that the western world may produce" (168).

PROJECTS

1. Collect recorded examples of at least three blues guitarist-singers. Describe and compare their original guitar techniques and styles, especially their treatment of the "breaks."
2. Collect recorded examples of blues illustrating at least four of the textual themes identified and treated this chapter or, alternatively, in Paul Oliver, *The Meaning of the Blues.*
3. Using W. C. Handy's autobiography, *Father of the Blues* (and any other sources you can find) as your basis, describe in a brief essay what life was like for a black musician in the Deep South in the first quarter of the twentieth century.
4. Assemble a list of at least five male and five female blues singers (besides Ma Rainey and Bessie Smith) who recorded between 1920 and 1930, with a brief biographical sketch of each. Cite at least one recording for each, and listen to as many others as you can.

ADDITIONAL LISTENING

Blues Roots/Chicago—the 1930s. Smithsonian/Folkways RF016.

"Preachin' Blues." *The Country Blues,* vol. 1. Smithsonian/Folkways RF001.

Roots: Rhythm and Blues. Smithsonian/Folkways RF020.

"We're Outta Here." *No Looking Back.* Alligator Records ALCD 4804.

CHAPTER

9

Rock: A Panorama in Itself

The vast sweep of American popular music (and by now we can truthfully say *world* popular music) over the past half-century is an extensive panorama in itself. The single term *rock* is hardly sufficient to cover all its manifestation, but

Jefferson Starship at the Great American Music Fair in Syracuse, NY, 1975. The vast sweep and mass popularity of rock music are reflected here by an audience that extends out to a vanishing point.

Roger Ressmeyer/CORBIS

that is the name on the door that opens out to the view. The inciting style of the revolutionary panorama was essentially white "rock and roll," coming out of essentially black rhythm-and-blues. (See CDs 2/29 and 2/30, and Smithsonian/ Folkways *Roots: Rhythm and Blues* RBF20.) Rock and roll has never really gone away, and continues to be a cherished favorite with many of the very musicians who were themselves responsible for its replacement by later styles, including John Lennon and Bob Dylan. But the late 1960s (the era of the emergence of Dylan, the Rolling Stones, and the Beatles) is often cited as the time when rock and roll began to yield to a broader spectrum of performing and arranging styles, and so was born the often-cited distinction between rock and roll, and the vast array of musics now still covered under the umbrella term *rock*.

One utterly transforming feature of this new rock panorama of the past half-century is the fact that the *recording* of a work has taken complete precedence over the *performance* of that work—a performance that, in relation to the recording, may in fact never have even existed. As Carl Belz wrote in 1972:

> Although jazz and other types of folk music exist on records, they did not originate in that medium. For the most part, they originated and developed through live performances. Rock, it seems to me, has generally done the opposite. Records were the music's initial medium. (viii)

The more one thinks about it, the more revolutionary this appears. At one level, whereas a recording used to exist to capture and make permanent a performance, now the performance—in fact, a whole tour of performances—may exist to promote a recording. (Of course, that doesn't apply just to concerts of popular music; at virtually every public performance, or even at lecture appearances, don't we almost certainly encounter the table of CDs for sale?)

At another level, there arises the even more fundamental question of what exactly *is* the work of art. Is it *a* performance, or is it *the* recording. Most rock artists spend far more time in the studio *creating* the work than they do onstage performing it. The honing of a work before a succession of live audiences has been replaced by hours, and even days, weeks, and years, of intensive overdubbing, and so on, in the studio. The record itself, not a live performance (which will almost certainly not be capable of duplicating what is heard on the record), is the end product. (For an exploration of this whole question in some depth, including the matter of what is original and what is a "forgery," and the distinctions between autographic and allographic works, see Gracyk, especially the first three chapters.)

Some of the vast array of musics known as rock will be dealt with in due course (see pp. 157–69), in roughly chronological procession—a procession that has been traced many times by many writers and that is by now familiar to many readers. But the many kinds of music grouped roughly, and often uncomfortably, under the rock umbrella have enough in common to make useful some general observations. Gracyk has suggested three characteristics that most of these performance styles share: having some basis in African American popular music, being rooted in song [as opposed to being basically instrumental music, which most jazz is], and paradigmatically existing as *recorded* music, as noted earlier (7). As we did with the other two "prodigious offspring of the rural South" (country music and the blues), we shall take a look first at the words (since they are all in a sense word-oriented) and then at the music.

CHARACTERISTICS OF THE WORDS

Do the words matter in rock? Depending on whom you ask, and which kind of rock you're talking about, the answers vary widely. On the one hand, there are rock fans, and even some performers themselves (who are not singers), who say that they never pay attention to the lyrics. In a sense, the *sound* of rock is the emotive *message* of rock. At times the very sound may in fact overwhelm the lyrics, either rendering them inaudible or reducing them to elemental fragments or vocal ejaculations, building with the sound to an intense climax. The lyrics are in fact sometimes the last ingredient to be added to the mix that has been described as "less typically a song than an arrangement of recorded sounds" (Gracyk 1).

On the other hand, there is a sense in which rock, like country music, and like the folk music that was the source of them both, is fundamentally word-oriented; its vehicle *is*, when all is said and done, the song. This has given rise to a close scrutiny of rock lyrics, and to books with titles such as *The Poetry of Rock* (ed. Goldstein) and *Performed Literature: Words and Music by Bob Dylan* (Bowden).

Rock Lyrics and the Blues

Early rock 'n' roll, coming as it did directly out of rhythm-and-blues, naturally reflected this patrimony in its lyrics. From Roy Brown's "Good Rockin' Tonight," as recorded by Wynonie Harris in 1947 (CD 2/29), to Chuck Berry's "Rock 'n' Roll Music" a decade later (see Additional Listening), the family likeness is clear: a celebration of energy, of vitality, of movement, of sex, of the very act of making the music itself. Like rhythm-and-blues, it was music for dancing. The classical blues form itself (*aab*) did appear in rock 'n' roll, as it had in rhythm-and-blues; its repetition of a single line followed by a concluding line can be found as a kind of relic of classical blues in the choruses of such early rock 'n' roll songs as "I Can't Go On" (Fats Domino), "Good Golly, Miss Molly" (as performed by Jerry Lee Lewis), and "Maybellene" (Chuck Berry), all on NW 249. But the broader range of blues lyrics was missing from early rock 'n' roll, which was basically music to dance to. In general, the growing popularization of rock 'n' roll, and the subsequent evolution of rock, created a widening separation from blues lyrics in both form and content.

Rock Subject Matter

Love, Romantic, Real-Life, and Altruistic   Many rock songs are about love-in-real-life, whether joyous, poignant, or painful. These songs express the same emotions in varying degrees of poetic sophistication, from the simple and straightforward:

> Oh please say to me, you'll let me be your man.
> And please say to me, I want to hold your hand . . .
> And when I touch you I feel happy inside
> It's such a feeling that my love I can't hide.

to the more graphically metaphorical:

> I feel the earth move under my feet,
> I feel the sky tumbling down,
> I feel my heart start tremblin' whenever you're around.

to the more philosophical implication of

> And so you see I have come to doubt
> All that I once held as true;
> I stand alone without beliefs,
> The only truth I know is you.

There is another class of lyrics that go still further and treat love as a more universal and at the same time more subjective feeling—love of fellow beings, love of the earth, love of life itself. Perhaps a manifestation of the same impulses that motivated the "flower children," and closely related to pro-environment, antiviolence, antidiscrimination, and antiwar sentiments, these songs have come from a wide range of composers and lyricists, from the Beatles ("Mother Nature's Son," who is sitting beside a mountain stream) to Bob Marley ("One Love," 1977).

> One love, one life,
> Let's get together and be all right.

The epic Woodstock gathering in 1969 drew from folk-rock singer-composer Joni Mitchell the advice to "get back to the garden" (of Eden) in "Woodstock."

A new altruism manifested itself beginning in the 1980s, addressing humanitarian issues in a positive manner. This has been associated with the production of large-scale benefit concerts and recordings, including the 1979 series of concerts presented by the Musicians United for Safe Energy (MUSE, against nuclear power), Band Aid, in 1984, to raise money for the underprivileged in Ethiopia, and the 1985 superstar album *We Are the World*, produced as a project to raise money for the relief of hunger in Africa. But by far the greatest outpouring of benefits has come (and is still coming) in the aftermath of the September 11, 2001, attacks that destroyed New York's World Trade Center, with horrendous loss of life, and severely damaged the Washington Pentagon. Representative of live concerts was "The Concert for New York City," which took place on October 20, 2001, at Madison Square Garden, and included David Bowie, Eric Clapton, Destiny's Child, Mick Jagger, Keith Richards, Billy Joel, Elton John, Paul McCartney, and The Who. A historic telethon, "America: A Tribute to Heroes," included Sheryl Crow, Willie Nelson, Paul Simon, Bruce Springsteen, Stevie Wonder, and U2. These, and many more, have been issued as CDs.

Sex   Folk blues, as we saw in the previous chapter, treated sexual themes in a frank, matter-of-fact way; rhythm-and-blues tended to do the same. When this music began to reach a wider young public, it encountered heated opposition from the older generation in general, and from parents in particular. Those interested in producing it on a commercially profitable scale began to censor — by disguising or transmuting — references to sex, often in metaphors such as dancing or automobile driving — images common enough in the culture, to be sure. This is especially apparent in the "cover" versions of black rhythm-and-blues songs. The much-cited example of successive versions of Hank Ballard's "Work with Me, Annie" makes this point. The original, from 1954, had a blues form with a strong backbeat. Its code phrase, "work with me," was thereafter laundered to "rolling with me" (as sung by Etta James) and then to "dancing with me" (as sung by Georgia Gibbs).

The reappearance of overtly sexual lyrics in rock was due again to the influence of the blues. The young British groups that emerged in the 1960s were greatly influenced by American blues singers such as Howlin' Wolf, Muddy Waters, and Bo Diddley. The new groups, best typified in this regard by the Rolling Stones, introduced a more direct treatment of sex into rock — in particular, the aggressiveness and bravado illustrated, for example, by Muddy Waters's "Hoochie Coochie Man" (NW 261), and as reflected in such Stones songs as "Satisfaction," "Parachute Woman," and "Play with Fire." The early (1964) "I'm a King Bee" was a reworking of an actual blues number.

Sex-in-and-of-itself has been expressed more explicitly since the mid-1970s, beginning with disco and exemplified by Donna Summer's "Love to Love You Baby" (a "seventeen-minute orgasm"). Prince (Rogers Nelson) in albums of the early 1980s preempted the breaching of a broad range of taboos, from masturbation to group sex, oral sex, and incest. Beginning in the 1980s heavy-metal groups such as Kiss, the Who, AC/DC, Judas Priest, and especially Motley Crüe have purveyed both sex and violence, often combined and rendered still more explicit by visual promotional material and videos.

Dissent   Much of rock is "good-time" music; much of it is eminently music to dance to; in its lyrics, much of it is concerned with the man-woman relation. These aspects (though certainly not its *sound*) rock shares with the popular music whose beginnings preceded it by more than a century. But it differs from previous forms of mass entertainment in being to a greater extent an expression of revolt. It is also fair to say that rock is essentially the product and expression of urban culture — some have said of "street culture." The titles of two fairly early books on rock, both dating from the early 1970s, express these aspects of revolt and urban ("street") ambience. George Melly's *Revolt into Style* deals primarily with the British scene but takes its title from a comment that Elvis Presley had turned "revolt into a style." Charlie Gillett's *The Sound of the City* begins with an introduction subtitled "Dancing in the Street," wherein Gillett writes that "rock and roll was perhaps the first form of popular culture to celebrate without reservation characteristics of city life that had been among the most criticized. In rock and roll, the strident, repetitive sounds of city life were, in effect, reproduced as melody and rhythm" (1). Simon Frith, however, writes that "Rock 'n' Roll . . . has celebrated street culture both for its participants and for its suburban observers, and by the mid-1960s such a celebration meant more to the latter group" ("Folk or Popular?" 168). Although the "street" has never been the home of rock performers or of most of their devotees, rock is nevertheless as distinctly an outgrowth and expression of urban life and values as country music is of rural life and values. Traceable ultimately to common origins in the rural South, these two have grown apart, musically and socially (and one might almost say politically), and have become the musical property of two distinctly different constituencies that are still identifiable, in a cultural if not a literal sense, as *city* and *country*. Together they account for the major portion of our popular music.

There is a sense in which rock was born as an underground form. Its forebear, rhythm-and-blues, was to many a cultural outcast. When it was popularized and adopted by the mass of youth as "rock 'n' roll," in the 1950s, its threatening aspects diminished. But its identity as a vehicle of protest has been periodically reasserted since. Events of broad public concern have been reflected in rock songs. The Vietnam War was addressed by Country Joe and The Fish

> Come on all of you big strong men,
> Uncle Sam needs your help again.
> He's got himself in a terrible jam,
> Way down yonder in Vietnam.
> So put down your books and pick up a gun;
> We're gonna have a whole lotta fun.

Text, "I-Feel-Like-I'm-Fixin'-to-Die Rag" (Joe MacDonald, 1967)

and by Jefferson Airplane in "Volunteers" (1969).

The tragic killing of demonstrators at Kent State brought a response from Crosby, Stills, Nash, and Young in "Ohio." The rap of the 1980s and 1990s brought out explicit warning protests about conditions of ghetto life, such as the "The Message" by Grandmaster Flash and the Furious Five (1981).

There has been a ratcheting up over the years of the degree of rancor expressed; at times it has approached a vicious level of alienation and hatred. On the subject of parents, for example, we need only compare the relatively good-natured antiparental satire of "Yakety-Yak" of the 1950s (in which youth objects to having to do household chores to receive an allowance) with the more sober challenge posed by Bob Dylan's "The Times They Are a-Changin'" of 1963 (in which parents are asked if they wouldn't please get out of the new road if they didn't find themselves able to help), and then with the threatening vitriol of Ozzy Osbourne's "Rock 'n' Roll Rebel" (1983), who threatens his parents that if they try to make him conform, he will make them regret that they had been born. Another kind of dissent (as in "grunge" or punk) is that which is extremely introverted, expressing resignation, self-doubt, self-deprecation, and a kind of desperate and nihilistic malaise—a strain of modernism that Martha Bayles has described, in a much broader context, as "perverse modernism" (41ff). An example is Richard Hell's "Blank Generation" of the mid-1970s. (Lyrics are quoted in *Best of New Wave Rock*, New York, Warner Brothers, c. 1978, p. 51.)

The Psychedelic and the Surreal   When rock left the realm of simple good-time music in the 1950s and confronted the troubled 1960s with increased sophistication, the imagery of some of its lyrics became less direct, less rooted in the obvious realities of a tangible, everyday world, and more given to the exploration of the visionary and the surreal, as experienced in a subjective mental state denoted by the term *psychedelic*. For a comparatively brief period (the late 1960s), rock lyrics found their way into paths explored by poetry and painting three-quarters of a century earlier, creating and juxtaposing fantastic images with obscure or subliminal significance—a carefree life beneath the waves in a yellow submarine ("Yellow Submarine," by Lennon and McCartney for the Beatles); a dreamworld of ambulatory chessmen and a smoking caterpillar that we enter by falling down a rabbit hole—one mapped out for us a century ago by Lewis Carroll ("White Rabbit," by Grace Slick for the Jefferson Airplane); or a courtroom scene in which an electric guitar, victim of a highway accident, is brought before a jury ("Electric Guitar," by David Byrne for the Talking Heads).

Though the rock ambience of the 1960s began to include (and indeed to imply) the widespread use of drugs everywhere, it was the street and drug culture of San Francisco that most explicitly expressed and came to typify it. But the "acid-rock" phase was relatively short-lived, and it cannot be maintained that *all* psychedelic images or mental states in rock lyrics refer to the use of drugs.

Rock Lyrics as Poetry, and Rock as Art

The claims of rock lyrics to the status of poetry are based on their creating an *aesthetic distance* from the subject, a distance which sacrifices that directness of approach to a subject—that complete lack of *art-consciousness*—that is the very attribute by which we recognize folk art. It is the difference between the unabashed, unreflective, sensual exuberance of Roy Brown's "Good Rockin'

Tonight" (CD 2/29) and the obscure, ambiguous introversion of David Byrne's "Memories Can't Wait," in which the party is in the mind. Rock, in its Apollonian aspect, has replaced folkness with artfulness. Since rock has its very roots in folkness, this artfulness presents an interesting paradox. Simon Frith has noted, "The irony was that it was on the basis of its folk conventions that rock developed its claims as a 'high art' form" (*Sound Effects* 10).

CHARACTERISTICS OF THE MUSIC

The Basic Makeup of the Rock Band

Underlying the profuse variety of sounds in rock's fifty-year history, there is a basic aggregation of three sound sources. Since rock, like its progenitors, blues and country music, has as its basic vehicle the song, the *human voice*, invariably amplified (the microphone is one of the icons of rock) is indispensable. A second indispensable element is the amplified sound of plucked strings—invariably the *guitar* (or guitars), nearly always electric, usually backed up by its larger and most obligatory cousin, the electric bass. The third indispensable element is the *drum set*. These three constitute an irreduceable core of sound; they are all that are needed for rock's sound signature, and often all that are present. (The jazz ensemble, even the smallest, has likewise its own irreduceable core of instruments: piano, bass, and drums—again, sometimes all that is present.)

Of the optional additions, first in importance would be the keyboard instruments—at first the traditional piano, now usually electronic keyboard(s). The next most frequently heard option is the saxophone, exemplifying rock's relation to the rhythm-and-blues. To this core whatever else is added (banjos, sitars, flutes, violins, a brass section, a full symphony orchestra) is essentially frosting on the cake.

Style Traits

Rhythm   The most obligatory rhythmic element of rock is the beat, as maintained by the drummer and the bass player, sometimes with the assistance of the rhythm guitarist and the keyboard player. Forthright, loud, and insistent, this rhythmic ground often incorporates a simple melodic figure in the bass, called a bass riff, which is obsessively repeated, and which shows rock's strong relationship to blues-derived boogie-woogie. (See CD 2/27, pp. 139–40.) This is apt to be most noticeable in the music of those black artists whose work comes directly out of rhythm-and-blues, from Chuck Berry in the 1950s to

Prince in the 1980s. (See Lloyd Price's "Mailman Blues" and Little Richard's "Every Hour," both in the classical 12-bar blues form, and both on NW 249.)

A second rhythmic feature of rock that is close to its roots is the prominent backbeat—the strongly marked offbeat *reaction* to the basic pulse that is so typical a feature of black music-making, in which the drummer has simply picked up and imitated the hand-clapping, for example, of black audiences, sacred and secular. It can be heard in pieces as otherwise dissimilar as "Maybellene" (1955), by Chuck Berry (NW 249), and "Born in the USA" (1985), by Bruce Springsteen.

A third contributor to rock rhythm is that of the Latin band. (See Leiber and Stoller's "What About Us?" written for the Coasters. Dating from 1959, this was perhaps rock 'n' roll's first protest song. See also "New Orleans." Both are also on NW 249. For much more on Latin/Caribbean rhythm, see pp. 69–79.)

Harmony   Most rock music is just as much in a key as are the popular tunes of a hundred years ago, and therefore possesses tonality, but the chords used in rock to define that tonality, and hence the harmonic progressions ("chord changes"), owe much more to both the blues scale and the modes of Anglo-Celtic folk music than they do to the harmonies and the progressions of the European-derived popular music of Broadway and Tin Pan Alley, which rock largely replaced. Harmony is perhaps a difficult aspect of music for the uninitiated to grasp, but it is by no means trivial or esoteric; it affects profoundly the way music sounds to us, whether we realize it or not. At the risk of oversimplifying a subtle and complex aspect of music, it might be useful to consider the harmony of what was formerly popular music (including not only Tin Pan Alley but also much of Gershwin and "classical" jazz) as tending to use chords from the "sharp side" of the key—that is, chords that approach the tonic by descending in fifths. Transcription 9.1 shows these chords first in sequential order, and then as embellished in a progression, the last four chord g which are in fact identical with the "changes" of the chorus of "Harvest Moon," that good old favorite from the barbershop period.

Transcription 9.1
Chords from the Tin Pan Alley period

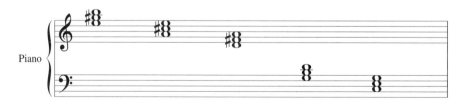

Harmonies from what might be called the "rock period," on the other hand, tend to use chords that are on the "flat side" of the key—that is, that are related to the tonic in fifths below, rather than above. Transcription 9.2 shows these chords first in sequential order, and then as embodied (though not in the same order) in an actual set of "changes" from the second part of "Riverwide" by Sheryl Crow. It is worthy of note that these chords involve two of the most prominent blue notes from the blues scale—that is, the flat seventh (in this case B-flat) and the flat third (in this case, E-flat). These are also the distinctive notes from modes most commonly found in Anglo-Celtic folk music (specifically the Mixolydian and the Dorian).

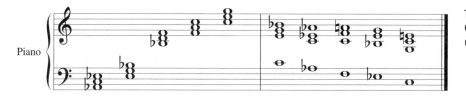

Transcription 9.2
Chords from the
rock period

Vocal Styles

The heritage of the blues is apparent in the vocal styles used in rock; the shout, the cry, the groan (of either pain or ecstasy), use of falsetto, the mumbled slur deliberately "throwing away" portions of the lyrics—all these have their roots in blues and gospel singing. Although these are basic resources of rock singing, it is also true that vocal styles in popular music tend to be highly individual; tone quality, inflection of the voice, manner of delivery, even accent become identifying "trademarks" of a particular singer. The highly individualized styles of extremely popular singers become prototypes, imitated by those who follow. Black blues singers such as Joe Turner, Muddy Waters, and John Lee Hooker were influential on early rock 'n' roll vocalists; there developed subsequently a Bob Dylan type of delivery, a Beatles style of singing and inflection, a David Byrne manner of monotone half-recitation, and so on.

"Body Language": The Kinesics of Rock

We cannot consider our treatment of rock's style traits *as a comprehensive whole* to be complete without taking into account what Larry Worster has called attention to as "the movement of the body in the rock experience" (Worster). To see a rock performance, either live or on film or video, is to recognize that rock is music not only for the ear, the mind, and the emotions but for the body as well. This is apparent in the total *involvement* of the audience, but it applies to the performers themselves in the very act of performance. The gestures of playing the guitar (the electric guitar is, along with the microphone, the other indispensible icon of rock) can be exaggerated into a sensational mime show in itself, with the strings intimately caressed, savagely attacked, or even (apparently) played with the teeth. The bodily response to the beat can be magnified and endowed with a degree of energy that can erupt into a full-scale kind of onstage choreography of volcanic proportions.

The *Apollonian* and the *Dionysian* in Rock

Mention of "body language" leads to a consideration of the relationship between the Apollonian and the Dionysian aspects of experience. The German philosopher Friedrich Nietzsche (1844–1900), in *The Birth of Tragedy*, put forth as two contrasting temperaments, those of the Greek gods Apollo and Dionysus. Apollo can be said to represent the orderly, the rational, and the controlled, and to be associated with light (Apollo was the god of the sun) and with the intellect. Dionysus, the god associated with the introduction of wine and viniculture, can be said to represent the emotional, the ecstatic, the dark, and the irrational, and to be associated with orgiastic rites reminiscent of the phenomena of *possession*. (Dionysus was torn to shreds at birth by the Titans, and reconstituted by his grandmother Rhea. The nighttime revels in the forest of his female devotees were said to climax in the capture and eating raw of wild animals. With reference to this mythological episode, it is difficult not to be reminded of the killing of live animals onstage by Alice Cooper and Ozzy Osbourne.) It was natural, beginning in the 1960s, to apply this dichotomy to the various aspects of rock as they diverged from each other, and several writers have made such application. Walter Breen makes the obvious connection between the Dionysian and the psychedelic drug trips of the 1960s (Eisen 16ff). Of course, no single group and no single performance can be labeled as purely one or the other. As in the human experience itself, this dichotomy is more constructively viewed not as an immutable division but as a continuum. In the center is a kind of balance of Apollonian and Dionysian tendencies—

tendencies present in the work of every artist. But if the distinction is to have any meaning, it will have to be related to specific examples.

In terms of tendencies, the two principal British "invaders" of the 1960s can be regarded as typifying this dichotomy. The Beatles can be thought of as representing the Apollonian temperament—*relatively* calm, poised, and disciplined, in later songs addressing the intellect, whereas the Rolling Stones can be thought of as representing the Dionysian—undisciplined, frenzied, orgiastic. To cite more recent examples, we might compare the Talking Heads, as disciples of Apollo, with the Sex Pistols or Kiss, as disciples of Dionysus.

In general terms, the Apollonian can be said to be represented by minimal (though by no means absent) gesturing in performing, no extremes of visible *effort* in performing, a sound volume *relatively* moderate, an absence of an overt "working" of the audience, stage dress not significantly different from that of the audience (e.g., The Grateful Dead, Bruce Springsteen, current rap artists). By contrast, the Dionysian can be said to be represented by exaggerated gestures in performing the music (especially in the case of guitarists) and an often violent stage choreography (for example, Elvis Presley—with whom, possibly, it all began—Jerry Lee Lewis, Jimi Hendrix, The Rolling Stones, The Who, and others), extreme visible effort expended in performing—sweating, and so on (for example, Bruce Springsteen), extremely loud sound volume as an indispensable, even possession-inducing, element of the performance event, an obvious "working" of the audience (as one performer put it, "work them up almost to the point of orgasm, and then keep working until you drop"), exaggerated costuming. (Costuming is, of course, integral to most performing, with the exception of folk music, country blues, and rap; it became a trademark of country music as soon as that music became commercial. But what is meant here is, for example, the exaggeration of "glitter" rock and some "new wave"— of David Bowie, Elton John, Alice Cooper, Kiss, and others.)

A BRIEF HISTORY OF ROCK'S TIMES AND STYLES

In the chapter thus far, our task has been to identify and discuss characteristics, both textual and musical, that can apply to any subgenre that goes by the generic name of rock. If this part of the chapter has done its work reasonably well, it can furnish the conceptual tools with which to examine whatever future styles and subgenres may emerge. It is now time to conclude with a necessarily brief summary of the subject by placing its times and styles in a chronological framework.

Roots in Black Music

CD 2/29 (2:26) "Good Rockin' Tonight," Wynonie "Blues" Harris, vocal, with group

Recordings of rhythm-and-blues, the taproot of rock 'n' roll, had a somewhat narrow market in the early 1950s, largely racially defined. Had this music remained, as it began, nearly the exclusive province of a young black audience, the history of American popular music would have been different. As it happened, black rhythm-and-blues, played on black radio stations in the large cities, and recorded and sold through outlets primarily intended for the black public, began to become popular with an increasingly large group of white youth. This coincided with a period of low inventiveness and pallid offerings from the established white popular music industry, and of increased independence and dissatisfaction with conventionality on the part of many young whites. "Good Rockin' Tonight" (CD 2/29) of 1947 was a very popular rhythm-and-blues number, with its boogie-woogie bass (for more on boogie-woogie, see pp. 139–40 and CD 2/27) and honking blues saxophone.

It was a disc jockey on a Cleveland radio station, Alan Freed, who first realized the potential inherent in the popularity of black rhythm-and-blues among white adolescents. In 1951 he began programming the music extensively. (It is possibly true that he invented the name "rock 'n' roll"; his early radio program was called "Moondog's Rock and Roll Party.") He also arranged live stage shows of black rhythm-and-blues performers for predominantly white audiences. In 1954 he moved to New York as disc jockey for WINS, which quickly became the city's leading popular music station.

By 1954 white groups were "covering" (recording their own versions of) popular black rhythm-and-blues recordings; Bill Haley's "Shake, Rattle, and Roll" of that year, a version of an earlier recording by the blues singer Joe Turner (NW 249), was among the first of the very popular covers. But rock 'n' roll, as a new form of white popular music *based on* black rhythm-and-blues, began to evolve as a distinct music, and the black artists who were among the most popular with the growing constituency of whites were those whose styles were closest to the new idiom—Chuck Berry (b. 1926; his "Maybellene" has already been cited), Bo Diddley (Elias McDaniel; b. 1928), Fats Domino (b. 1928), and Little Richard (Richard Penniman; b. 1935). Conversely, rock 'n' roll as a primarily white phenomenon began with those white performers who most closely patterned their work on black models—men such as Bill Haley (1925–81), whose "Rock Around the Clock" (1955) has been recognized as the first white rock 'n' roll hit, and Elvis Presley (1935–77), who was strongly imprinted with the blues ambience of Memphis.

CD 2/30 (2:50) "Hound Dog," Willie Mae "Big Mama" Thornton, vocal

It was Presley (whose coming was presaged by his early producer's search for a "white boy who could sing colored") who most forcefully exemplified the combination of black and white influences that constituted early rock. His famous "Heartbreak Hotel" (1956) accomplished the symbolic feat of achieving popularity in both black (rhythm-and-blues) and white (country-and-western) markets. A comparison of the rhythm-and-blues hit "Hound Dog" as sung by Willie Mae "Big Mama" Thornton in 1952 (CD 2/30) with the cover by Elvis Presley in 1956 shows both the similarities and the differences, as rhythm-and-blues gave rise to rock and roll. (Presley's "Hound Dog" was unavailable for inclusion in the CD set. See Additional Listening.)

"Hound Dog" is obviously a woman's song, and retains its original bite only when sung by a woman, as subsequent performances by blues singers such as Etta James attest. The gender change makes the cover version weak by comparison; the power of the metaphor of the woman's rejection of the man as a "hound dog snoopin' around my door" is hardly matched by "you ain't never caught a rabbit and you ain't no friend of mine." All that is left is the force of the music itself—an example that lends credence to the notion that the words in rock and roll often hardly matter at all.

White Country Music and Early Rock

If black rhythm-and-blues was the taproot of rock, white country music also played an important part. Country music evolved out of folk roots as a conservative regional music. By the 1950s, however, its public was no longer so narrowly limited. The electric guitar had long been used in country music, and the singing guitarist, as basic to white country music as to black country blues, became the mainstay of the early rock ensemble, as typified by performers such as Bill Haley, Elvis Presley, Carl Perkins (b. 1932), and Buddy Holly (1936–59), all of whom were identified with rockabilly (see pp. 121–22).

Rock and the Recording Industry

Given the new technology that allowed recordings to be produced nearly anywhere in the country, early rock belonged to the "indies"—small independent record companies that had been mainly responsible for supplying the hitherto limited black rhythm-and-blues market, and now expanded and multiplied to meet the new demand for rock 'n' roll. This market was extremely volatile. Hits would zoom into prominence overnight, and disappear almost as fast. As in the early publishing days of Tin Pan Alley, a single hit would be enough to establish a company. The major companies, representing the conservative and declining Tin Pan Alley tradition, found themselves left out of this market. This fact had more than economic significance. As Larry Worster has pointed out, "Independence from the major corporations meant independence from the control of 'normal' mores, values, or ideological alliances. Hence Elvis and the other 'sexy' stars of the 50s were able to rise to stardom despite their controversial images; they were not controlled by the corporations" (Worster).

The "Clean Teen" Market and the Reentry of the Majors

By the early 1960s a vast teenage market had emerged to be catered to. It was in catering to this market that the major record companies regained their dominance. This younger market had its own concerns to be addressed. Its preoccupation with cars, for example, was reflected in any number of "hot rod" songs, such as "Little Deuce Coupe," which, in a manner curiously typical of folk art, combines vernacular expressions with oddly technical descriptions of the car's mechanical features. From California came surfing songs (best represented, probably, by the highly successful and polished recordings of the Beach Boys, whose "Surfin' U.S.A." became a classic). The surfing cult spread rapidly across the country, having little to do, ultimately, with the actual practice of the sport; as Belz remarks, "The surf itself had been obviated as an essential ingredient" (97).

New Infusions and Developments of the 1960s

The British Influence   The pervasive and continuous influence of English artists and groups on American rock since the 1960s fits a pattern of the long historical interdependence of British and American popular music. In one direction, English ballad opera was a staple in America in colonial times; the English music hall provided songs and a song style for American musical comedy in the nineteenth century; and Gilbert and Sullivan has been almost as popular in the United States as in England. British folk music, a subtly pervasive presence in nearly all English music, was a source of one of the most important strains of American folk music. In the other direction, American blackface comedy, ragtime, blues, and jazz were each, in its heyday, exports that were much in demand. A broad segment of the younger British public has always followed avidly developments in American popular music—especially the fruits of black popular culture. There have been times when the devotion to some particular phase was stronger in England than in America generally. The 1960s was such a time. The earthier manifestations of the blues, which no longer enjoyed very wide popularity in the United States, were being assiduously cultivated by a segment of British youth. Muddy Waters, Big Bill Broonzy, Howlin' Wolf, Sonny Terry, and Brownie McGhee were known in England not only from their recordings but also from personal tours. As adherents of a later style, such men as Chuck Berry and Bo Diddley were well known and influential in England after they had been largely supplanted in America. As Muddy Waters said to an American college audience, "I had to come to you behind the Rolling Stones and the Beatles. I had to go England to get here!" (Shaw, *Honkers* 526). What the English groups gave back to America turned out to be America's own black rhythm-and-blues, filtered through the temperament and experience of British youth, and giving off echoes, when the beat was a little less relentless, of the music hall and, further in the background, of English folk music.

The Rolling Stones explored and extended the somewhat limited range staked out by the shouting, "bragging" blues, producing aggressive statements (and becoming effective personal symbols) of revolt, nihilism, and sexual bravado. The other group transcended the limiting range of the hard-edged blues. The Beatles (John Lennon, 1940–80; Paul McCartney, b. 1942; George Harrison, 1943–2001; and Ringo Starr [Richard Starkey], b. 1940) began their meteoric journey across the mid-century skies of popular culture by a reintroduction of innocence—an infectious pleasure in music-making akin to what was felt in the folklike singing and playing of early black rock 'n' roll artists such as Chuck Berry, and of white rockabilly singers such as the Everly Brothers. (Indeed, such questions as the probable influence of the vocal style and close harmonies of the Everly Brothers' songs of the early 1960s on the Beatles cannot be ignored; the British "invasion" brought with it much that was already our own.)

This innocence is nowhere more apparent than in their famous "I Want to Hold Your Hand" of 1964. It proved to be the quality that opened the way to a much broader range of expression for the Beatles, which their collective talent enabled them to explore. In the process came, inevitably, sophistication but also musical and poetic development.

Their work, from folk beginnings, gradually came to acquire that aesthetic distancing from its subject that gave it a genuine *art*-stance. The *Sgt. Pepper's Lonely Hearts Club Band* album (1967), in its entirety, probably best signaled that development, of which even segments of the world of fine-art music had to take notice. Writing from the vantage point of this world, musicologists such as Wilfred Mellers and composers such as Ned Rorem could regard the Beatles' work as almost pointing the way toward a kind of salvation for fine-art music, or at least one avenue of escape from the paralyzing dilemma of noncommunication in which it found itself in the 1960s. The eclecticism that the Beatles' work came to embody — running the gamut from synthesized sound to Renaissance music and Indian ragas (see pp. 92–93) —was widely imitated and has become endemic. From the mid-1960s on, so interwoven are the stories of British and American rock that it is impossible to trace native rock music without nearly constant references to what British groups were doing.

Folk Rock, Protest Rock, and Psychedelic Rock   In the United States the protest movements of the 1960s, as expressed in the folk and neo-folk music treated in Chapter 6, created their resonances in rock. This was evidenced in the *folk rock* of the Byrds (whose "Turn, Turn, Turn" was a version of Pete Seeger's adaptation from the book of Ecclesiastes) and in much of the work of the Grateful Dead and other San Francisco groups. Folkness, protest, and the use of drugs were combined aspects of the mammoth outdoor festival at Woodstock, New York, in August 1969, which created, however briefly, a sense of community (a "Woodstock Nation"), not only among the half million young people who attended but among the like-minded young throughout the world. Unfortunately, the negative potential of such mass gatherings was tragically revealed by the violence at the Altamont, California, concert by the Rolling Stones in December of that same year, which dealt a severe blow to the aspirations, and the acceptance by the broader public, of the "Woodstock Nation."

CD 2/31 (2:25) "Cold Sweat" (excerpt), James Brown, vocal. 1967.

Black Rock: Soul and Motown   African American rhythm-and-blues, the dominant parent of rock, continued to evolve among black musicians in the "soul synthesis" treated in the preceding chapter. Arnold Shaw has written that in the 1960s, "black music became blacker than it had ever been, more gospel-oriented than it had ever been. The development came with an intensification of the struggle for equality, the rise of black nationalism, the growth of black pride—'Black is Beautiful'—and the emergence of a black-power movement" (*Dictionary* 364). The blues shouting, screaming, and grunting over a rock band backup of a bass riff and a strong backbeat of James Brown's "Cold Sweat" of 1967 (CD 2/31) are representative of this aspect of the *soul* of the 1960s.

CD 2/32 (2:45) "You Can't Hurry Love," Diana Ross and the Supremes. 1965.

In contrast to this, Motown (derived from Motor Town—Detroit) was represented by the Supremes, who were, to use Brock Helander's words, "prime purveyors of the sophisticated, highly commercial, and sometimes bland black vocal group sound of Motown . . . [that achieved] massive popularity with both black and white audiences" (666). "You Can't Hurry Love" by Diana Ross and the Supremes, from 1966 (CD 2/32) is representative.

The Complexities and Diversities of Rock from the 1970s to the Present

Hard Rock and Heavy Metal   The loud, aggressive, Dionysian aspects of rock were continued and exaggerated in hard rock and heavy metal. (The aptly descriptive designation "heavy metal" is said to have come from the lyrics to a 1968 song performed by the group Steppenwolf that included the phrase "heavy metal thunder.") The beginnings of hard rock can be detected in the sound, actions, and *stance* of Elvis Presley himself in his cover of "Hound Dog" and in Jerry Lee Lewis and Little Richard. Hard rock emerged more overtly in those British bands who were following in the footsteps of the American hard-edged blues performers blues such as Howlin' Wolf and Muddy Waters—principally the Rolling Stones, but also Cream, with Eric Clapton. As hard rock became more the "mainstream" in the early 1970s, with performers such as Bob Seeger, the aggressive fringes adopted the features associated with heavy metal. As Joe Stuessy describes the distinction:

> If hard rock was loud, heavy metal was louder; if hard rock was simple and repetitive, heavy metal was simpler and more repetitive; if hard rock singers shouted, heavy metal singers screamed; if hard rockers experimented with distortion and feedback, heavy metalers distorted everything; if hard rock favored long instrumental improvisations, heavy metal offered longer, louder, and more dazzling instrumental solos; if hard rock was *countercultural,* heavy metal would come to specialize in the *anticultural.* (306)

The British seemed to lead in this development, with groups such as Led Zeppelin (whose "Whole Lotta Love" of 1970, with its heavy bass riff and obsessive repetition in the main sections, its electronic manipulation and sound effects in a middle section, and the explicit sexuality of its lyrics, is representative). Presently Led Zeppelin and other British groups, principally Black Sabbath and Judas Priest, took heavy metal a further step out of the mainstream by introducing and capitalizing on occult themes of black magic, witchcraft, and devil worship, as well as the darker aspects of Celtic and Greek mythology, and of medieval lore, all of which were more familiar to British youth, who grew up surrounded by castles and whose cultural heritage included dark myths and legends, than to Americans, for whom the scariest themes were those from horror movies. These themes were exaggerated, of course, in the cover art and promotional posters and advertising. American heavy-metal groups of the 1970s included Iron Butterfly, Blue Cheer, Van Halen, MC5, and The Blue Öyster Cult.

A further step away from mainstream rock were the visual and theatrical aspects of some heavy metal. Black leather and elaborate hardware, including chains, had become familiar in costuming. Makeup contributed to the creation of fantastic and abnormal stage personae. Alice Cooper (the name of the band, as well as the stage name of the lead singer, Vincent Furnier, was derived from the name of a woman allegedly burned at the stake for witchcraft in the 1500s) featured black eye makeup. Kiss, another group, used full character makeup, personifying what one observer has identified as "the bloody, ghoul-like image of a cat, a lover, a spaceman, and a devil" (Charlton 164). The fascination engendered in a jaded public by the sensational packaging of androgynous stage personae, such as David Bowie's Ziggy Stardust, and Boy George, must account in part for their success. Stage action pursued a demonic path from the routine destruction of musical instruments (by The Who and others) to the previously mentioned killing of live animals onstage.

Although heavy metal, to qualify as such, incorporates much of the time the loudness, the pounding beat, and the distortion that is its trademark, this frequently masks musical sophistication and virtuosity, especially on the electric guitar. In Blue Öyster Cult's "(Don't Fear) The Reaper" (the Grim Reaper being death itself) of 1976, there can be heard, over and between the statements of the obsessive four-note bass riff, guitar solos of considerable complexity. Classically trained Edward Van Halen brought a new level of performance to the electric guitar; any of the Van Halen albums illustrate this, but the famous "Eruption" of 1978 is an astounding display of virtuosity, which includes a transformed quote from a famous Kreutzer study known to every student of the violin.

A recent example of heavy metal's absorption of the media of classical music was the live performance and recording of some of the orchestrated earlier releases of Metallica ("the world's most powerful rock band") in combination with the San Francisco Symphony in 1999. The resultant album, *Metallica S & M*, produced what the liner notes described as a "mood provoking storm of sound." ("Of Wolf and Man" was not available for inclusion in the CD set.)

Punk, Hardcore, and New Wave   In a popular art form fed from the underground, there is always a *new* underground ready to emerge when the current underground becomes generally accepted. In the 1960s, 1970s, and 1980s there were a succession of these. The British group the Sex Pistols has been described as the "archetypal punk rock band," noted "for their adamantly incompetent playing, cynically vituperative and anti-commercial, and deliberate onstage vulgarity" (Helander 615). At the grassroots level, punk was the music of teenage "garage bands"—bands with little musical skill but with energy and an attitude, overwhelmingly negative. Nowhere is this "nihilistic punk metabolism" more evident than in the names of the groups, which call up images normally considered aberrant, repulsive, or destructive—the Mutants, the Ghouls, Wierdos, Circle Jerks, Flesheaters, Twisted Sister, Crime, Damage, Slash, Search and Destroy, and Black Flag (a symbol for anarchy but also a well-known poison).

The 1980s brought changes to the underground scene. *Hardcore,* though still expressing dissent in a rough-edged and purposely unimaginative musical style, presents songs that focus on specific issues, rather than anger for its own sake. Lyrics could be found that dealt, for example, with the use of live animals in scientific experiments ("Mad Scientists' Ball" by Dead Silence), with the environment ("Progress" by Clown Alley), and with tyranny and oppression ("Dr. Harley" by Rhythm Pigs). (Lyrics are typically so difficult to understand in performance that they are published on lyric sheets that accompany the records, or in fan magazines known as "fanzines.")

Heavy satire was heard in "Kill the Poor" (1980) by The Dead Kennedys, a San Francisco group. The lyrics "satirically praise the U.S. government for developing the neutron bomb that can kill people and leave property undamaged and suggest that, in order to save money otherwise wasted on welfare, the bomb be used to kill poor people" (Charlton 207–8). (As a similar instance of vitriolic satire, Katherine Charlton cites Irish satirist Jonathan Swift's *A Modest Proposal,* from the eighteenth century, in which he suggested that the English solve the problem of starvation in Ireland by eating Irish children.)

Also out of punk there came a movement more sophisticated in both music and lyrics, known as *new wave.* It was best represented in the work of David Byrne, leader of Talking Heads (turn off the sound on a TV discussion program, and especially in fast forward, this is all you are aware of). As a measure of the musical and textual sophistication, the backup vocal group has its own material, sometimes creating a kind of counterpoint in which solo singer and vocal group or groups sing contrasting material, either sequentially or simultaneously. "Once in a Lifetime" (1980), from *Remain in Light,* is illustrative. The satire, instead of attacking a political target, was turned to more quasi-philosophical questions—for example, the individual in modern society—and couched in the obscure language and metaphors of some contemporary poetry. This intellectual stance drew the attention both of a public not previously known for its devotion to rock and of the mass media. David Byrne widened his range from that of singer-guitarist-composer for a band with quasi-punk beginnings to being film director, actor, designer, photographer, and writer.

More Hospitable Aspects of Mainstream Rock at the Turn of the Century

All the attention just given to the more flamboyant Dionysian forms of rock music should not tempt us to ignore the more humane and sensitive offerings in the mainstream. The works of composer-poet-singers such as Nanci Griffith and Sheryl Crow deal in their lyrics with the woman-man relationship, of course, and in sensitive ways, but they also treat, for example, the plight of the underprivileged, as in Nanci Griffith's "The Power Lines" and "Down 'n' Outer." (For a single example of the many contributions made by many artists in the wake of September 11, see p. 149 for an account of Sheryl Crow's singing for the American Express workers who had lost so many colleagues.) Musically, this new Apollonian mainstream tends to relate more to rock's roots in folk music, with a less driving beat, more intimate combos and arrangements, and a tendency to use more acoustic instruments.

Reggae   American rhythm-and-blues, reaching the Caribbean island of Jamaica through radio and records, became very popular about the mid-1950s with the predominantly black population. The Jamaican reggae (an outgrowth of the earlier *ska*), which evolved from this influence, spread to the United States, and indeed worldwide, in the 1970s and early 1980s. The rhythm of reggae, like that of Calypso music from another part of the West Indies (Trinidad), is strongly Caribbean in its patterned elaboration of the beat. The heavy relentless beat of hard rock is replaced by a more melodious ostinato, and the offbeats are ornamented with a complex overlaying of cross-rhythms, performed with a variety of Latin percussion sounds, either acoustic or synthesized. Yet it is quite distinct from the Cuban and Puerto Rican salsa heard in New York as described in Chapter 4. The lyrics of many of the songs express concern for the poor and downtrodden but usually without the angry and threatening tone of heavy metal, and often in the storytelling form of the ballad (as in "Buffalo Soldier," about the conscripting of black men into the Union Army to kill Indians). The most popular group was Bob Marley and the Wailers, whose "Get Up Stand Up" (1973) is representative of the style and the positive nature of their "message" songs (see Additional Listening).

The Rock Video   Until the 1980s the visual presentation of rock songs — apart from live performances, which had become spectacularly elaborate in the case of superstars — had been confined to films. Rock remained primarily an aural form, with radio and records its prime media. But with the combined advance of videotape technology and the multiple channels available on cable TV, this changed. In August 1981, MTV, the first all-rock channel on cable television, began broadcasting. Record-album promoters, who had long been in the habit of sending free albums to radio stations for airplay, now hastened to produce and send free video versions of new songs to MTV, and to the other TV stations that soon began to broadcast rock videos. The video became a powerful new weapon in the endless battle to promote artists and records. Rock videos are not intended *primarily* for sale themselves, but are designed to sell the records they are "about." As such, they provide consumers with an elaborately crafted visual *iconography* of the performer, with his or her image built up to larger-than-life proportions. Sometimes they are merely visually edited presentations of live performances (similar in effect to TV coverage of a football game), with close-ups of the performers and shots of the frenzied audience, including girls rushing the stage to kiss the male star, and others "stage diving"—a Dionysian ritual of jumping on stage and then diving into the audience waiting to catch them.

"Conceptual" videos, on the other hand, use intercutting to outside scenes, sometimes actual filmed footage (as in Bruce Springsteen's "Atlantic City" [1982] or "Born in the U.S.A." [1984]), and sometimes featuring the star in some imaginary story situation (which may illustrate the song's "plot" or meaning, or be unrelated to it). In the more elaborately "staged" videos, such as those of Michael Jackson, there is a rapidly paced collage of fantasy images, placing the star in a series of exotic surroundings. At times this results in segments with a sustained mood; at other times there is a breakneck pace, the eye bombarded with the kaleidoscope of fast-changing images using all of the manipulative techniques available—slowed-down or speeded-up motion, superimposed images, rapid zooming, distortion, "morphing" (where one image changes into another), and cartooning. These are devices familiar from the TV commercial, with which the rock video, which is also a sales pitch, has much in common.

There are some rock videos, such as Pearl Jam's "Jeremy," which deal in social commentary, with comment or interpretation, beyond what is in the song itself, added visually. But for the most part rock videos, like the records they are designed to sell, deal in entertainment, not real life. It has been pointed out, with justification, that the more sexually oriented videos (produced and directed by men) present a male "dream world" in which women (numerous, attractive, and afflicted with nymphomania) are presented as devoid of individuality, uniqueness, humanity, or any capacity for genuine feelings.

Rap and Hip Hop   In concluding our survey of rock, we find that we are confronting once again, as we did with blues, gospel, and rhythm-and-blues, the potency of African American musical styles in American popular music—this time, in the 1980s and 1990s, with the emergence of rap. Rap does not *transcend*, but rather *celebrates* (in the minds of some black writers), the *separateness* of black culture and black popular music. As with much of the music that is the subject of this chapter, the social aspect looms in importance. "To really delve into rap, the honest, intimate expression of a marginalized underclass, one embarks on a journey beyond music" (Fernando xxiii). It has been hailed as bringing together "a tangle of some of the most complex social, cultural, and political issues in contemporary American society" (Rose 2). Of the rhymed couplets constituting the lyrics, Fernando writes: "Rap bloomed in the depths of the ghetto, a place characterized by overarching poverty, violence, and crime. Though currently reflecting a diversity of lifestyles, opinions, and feelings, rap responds directly and indirectly to the trials and tribulations of a life at the bottom, and for the most part remains true to the gritty reality of the streets that produced it" (xviii).

Rap emerged from the street culture of the South Bronx in New York City in the mid-1970s, specifically from the dances. For dancers, the best parts of the songs played on the phonographs for dances were the "breaks," where just the instruments were let loose to jam. Since these breaks were too short, the idea of using two turntables playing the same record emerged as a solution, with the disc jockey cutting back and forth to make an extended version. This was the role of the "DJ" in providing music for "break dancing." To this was added the role of the rapper, a role related to that of the African *griot*, or storyteller, the talking blues or boogie-woogie piano player, or the Jamaican "toasting," or speaking over recorded music, called "deejaying" there. There is, in fact, a close relationship between rap and reggae, which rap recognizes as one of its roots.

Arnold Shaw has called rap "rhymed street slang delivered at breakneck speed" (*Dictionary* 302). Although it would seem like breakneck speed to the inexperienced trying to replicate it, actually the tempo is very steady, comfortable for the rapper, and for most pieces within a fairly narrow range of between 108 and 116 beats per minute. It is bass-heavy music, it usually has a very strong backbeat, and the rhythmic background is kept simple to allow the words, which are its essence, to be clearly articulated and understood. Often there is a bass riff (repeated pattern), and in the breaks between the long spoken stanzas, a syncopated melody fills in. The music is now mostly electronic. A single solo rapper is usual, but there is some interplay with other rappers.

Rap was originally recorded by small independent record companies, and their release of "Rapper's Delight" in 1979 brought it into broader notice. ("Rapper's Delight" was not available for inclusion in the CD set, but see Additonal Listening.) An early and by now classic hit was "The Message" (1981) by Grandmaster Flash and the Furious Five. "The first rap to break away from boasting and deal with reality, it described the hopelessness of the urban condition" (Fernando 19).

Rats in the front room, roaches in the back,
Junkies in the alley with a baseball bat.
I tried to get away but I couldn't get far
'Cause the man with the tow truck repossessed my car.

Text, "Rapper's Delight"

In its purest form, it is rhythm and speech at its sparsest. It remains distanced from rock. Perhaps it is more related to the talking blues; perhaps its narrative aspect marks it as some kind of extension of the ballad. Wherever placed, rap certainly is, as Rose has said, "a black cultural expression," and as such cannot be well understood apart from this culture. The term *hip hop* (which appeared first in the lyrics of "Rapper's Delight": "With a hip, hop, the hipit, the hipidipit, hip, hip, hopit, you don't stop") evidently has multiple meanings. Hyphenated as *hip-hop*, it has been defined as a primarily electronic subgenre of rap, of which "The Message" is cited as an example. But *hip hop*, unhyphenated, is also used (by Rose) to denote the culture itself, of which the major components are graffiti, break dancing, and rap.

With this we bring to a close our brief treatment of a varied and prodigious topic—a treatment long for the book but far too short for the subject, which is hardly less than the world's popular music.

■ PROJECTS

1. Interview a local disc jockey, and produce a paper profiling the job (both positive and negative aspects) and recording his or her opinions or current trends in popular music, the influence and responsibilities of the disc jockey, and so on.
2. Interview the manager, or a knowledgeable employee, of a local record store, and produce a paper on a topic such as (1) the buying habits of the local publics (for example, percentages for rock, for country, for classical, for folk, for soul, for "underground," and so on); (2) any recognizable characteristics (e.g. apparent age, occupation, dress, behavior, etc.) of the various publics; (3) the store's handling of "underground" recordings; (4) the effect of rock videos on the sales of specific albums; (5) his or her experiences in the handling of hit albums (the predictability of hits, the buying rush—how strong and how *long*, etc.); or make up your own approach.
3. If you have some background or interest in English literature, assemble a small collection of rock lyrics and try to confront the question of rock "poetry"—the quality and consistency of the imagery, the extent to which it can stand on its own as poetry, and so forth.
4. Tipper Gore's *Raising PG Kids in an X-rated Society* (Nashville: Abingdon Press, 1987) and Robert Walser's *Running with the Devil: Power, Gender, and Madness in Heavy Metal Music* (Hanover & London: Wesleyan Univ. Press, 1993), Chapter 5, present opposing views on a topic of importance to parents. Read both, make up your own mind, and then present your own views in a paper.

■ ADDITIONAL LISTENING

"Born in the U.S.A." Bruce Springsteen. *Born in the U.S.A.* Sony 38653.

"(Don't Fear) The Reaper." Blue Öyster Cult. *Don't Fear the Reaper: The Best of Blue Öyster Cult.* Sony 65918.

"Down 'n' Outer." Nanci Griffith. *Late Night Grande Hotel.* MCAD 10306.

"Electric Guitar." Talking Heads. *Fear of Music.* Warner Bros. 6076.

"Eruption." Van Halen. *Van Halen.* Warner Bros. 47737.

"Get Up Stand Up." Bob Marley. *Legend.* Polygram Records 846210.

"Hound Dog." Elvis Presley. *The Number One Hits.* RCA Victor 6382-2-R.

"I Feel Like I'm Fixin' to Die Rag." Country Joe & The Fish. *The Collected Country Joe & The Fish.* Vanguard Records 111.

"I Feel the Earth Move under My Feet." Carole King. *Tapestry.* Sony 65850.

"I Want to Hold Your Hand." The Beatles. *Beatles One.* Capitol 29325.

"Kathy's Song." Simon & Garfunkel. *The Columbia Studio Recordings, 1964–1970.* Sony 63815.

"Kill the Poor." The Dead Kennedys. *Fresh Fruit for Rotting Vegetables.* Alternative Tentacle 1.

"Little Deuce Coupe." The Beach Boys. *Greatest Hits,* vol. 1. Capitol 21860.

"Love to Love You Baby." Donna Summer. *The Donna Summer Anthology.* Polygram Records 518144.

"Memories Can't Wait." Talking Heads. *Fear of Music.* Warner Bros. 6076.

"Message, The." Grandmaster Flash. *Message from Beat Street: The Best of Grandmaster Flash.* Rhino Records 71606.

"Of Wolf and Man." Metallica. *Metallica S & M.* Elektra 62463-2 CD.

"Ohio." Crosby, Stills, Nash, and Young. *So Far.* Atlantic 82648.

"Once in a Lifetime." Talking Heads. *Remain in Light.* Warner Bros. 6095.

"One Love." Bob Marley. See "Get Up Stand Up."

"Power Lines, The." Nanci Griffith. *Late Night Grande Hotel.* MCAD 10306.

"Rapper's Delight." *The Best of Sugarhill Gang.* Rhino R2 71986.

"Riverwide." Sheryl Crow. *The Globe Sessions.* Interscope Records 490404

"Rock 'n' Roll Music." Chuck Berry. *Anthology.* MCA 112304.

"Rock 'n' Roll Rebel." Ozzy Osbourne. *Bark at the Moon.* Sony 67238.

"Satisfaction." The Rolling Stones. *Hot Rocks, 1964-1971.* ABKCO 6667.

"Surfin' U.S.A." The Beach Boys. *Greatest Hits,* vol. 1. Capitol 21860.

"Times They Are a-Changin', The." Bob Dylan. *The Best of Bob Dylan.* Sony International 424037.

"Turn, Turn, Turn (To Everything There Is a Season)." The Byrds. *The Byrds' Greatest Hits.* Sony 66230.

"Volunteers." Jefferson Airplane. *White Rabbit and Other Hits.* RCA 2078.

"White Rabbit." Jefferson Airplane. *White Rabbit and Other Hits.* RCA 2078.

"Whole Lotta Love." Led Zeppelin. *Early Days: The Best of Led Zeppelin,* vol. 1. Atlantic 83268.

"Work with Me, Annie." Hank Ballard. *Sexy Ways: The Best of Hank Ballard & The Midnighters.* Rhino Records 71512.

"Yakety-Yak." The Coasters. *20 Greatest Hits.* Deluxe 7786.

"Yellow Submarine." The Beatles. *Beatles One.* Capitol 29325.

America is still too young to have been able to nurture such highly cultivated worship music as is represented, for example, by the rich flowerings of Gregorian chant, elaborate settings of the Roman Catholic Mass, or the Lutheran cantata. Nor, the question of time aside, have the conditions been present that could have produced such flowerings. The reasons are many—America's broad spectrum of denominations, her inbred distrust of the ecclesiastical organization and wealth that are indispensable for building a tradition of highly refined religious art, and her increased secularization. The intensity of focus has been lacking in America that in Europe, from the Middle Ages up to the time of the social and industrial revolutions, could have put large resources of talent at the service of the church, and produce, at the apex, a *Notre Dame Mass* or a *St. Matthew Passion.* Thus America's output of what might be called cultivated religious music has been meager, and up to now mostly derivative.

At the relatively unconscious and unlearned level of folk, or near-folk, art, on the other hand, Americans have produced sacred music that, in accord with its homely character, has become deeply embedded in the culture of a broad segment of the people. Thus the most significant of America's religious music is that which has remained closest to folk sources. Like popular music (and it is popular music in the sense of the large market it has had for a century and a half, and the commercial establishment that has grown up to serve this market), it draws its significance not primarily from its aesthetic value but from its meaning in the lives of those who sing it and from the response it evokes. Indeed, immediacy and depth of response, without the distancing of any art-consciousness, are part and parcel of the phenomena of both folk and popular art. Charles Ives, one of America's most significant composers but also a perceptive thinker, pointed up in the epilogue to his *Essay Before a Sonata* the importance of this near–folk music to those whose music it is. He is speaking to the American composer, but his words have substance for anyone who would understand American music.

> The man "born down to Babbitt's Corners" may find a deep appeal in the simple but acute Gospel hymns of the New England "camp meetin'" of a generation or so ago. He finds in them—some of them—a vigor, a depth of feeling, a natural-soil rhythm, a sincerity—emphatic but inartistic—which, in spite of a vociferous sentimentality, carries him nearer the "Christ of the people" than does the *Te Deum* of the greatest

Dorothea Lange/Library of Congress

A devout young couple worships in modest surroundings through simple song.

cathedral . . . [If] the Yankee can reflect the fervency with which "his gospels" were sung—the fervency of "Aunt Sarah," who scrubbed her life away for her brother's ten orphans, the fervency with which this woman, after a fourteen-hour work day on the farm, would hitch up and drive five miles through the mud and rain to "prayer meetin'," her one articulate outlet for the fulness of her unselfish soul—if he can reflect the fervency of such a spirit, he may find there a local color that will do all the world good. If his music can but catch that spirit by being a part with itself, it will come somewhere near his ideal—and it will be American, too.

CHAPTER

10

From Psalm Tune to Rural Revivalism

PSALMODY IN AMERICA

Probably the first musical sounds from the Old World that the indigenous inhabitants heard in what is now the United States were the psalm tunes sung by Protestant settlers and sailors. French Huguenots were singing psalms from their psalter in Florida half a century before the landing of the English Separatists at Plymouth. At the other edge of the continent, the California Indians were fascinated by the psalm singing of Sir Francis Drake's men in 1579. (For a brief account of psalm singing among the Indians, see Stevenson 3–11.) When the first permanent settlements in Massachusetts were established, psalters were an important part of the few precious possessions brought over. The Separatists (Pilgrims) who founded the Plymouth Colony in 1620 brought with them the psalter (*The Book of Psalmes: Englished both in Prose and Metre*) that Henry Ainsworth had published for the Puritan exiles in Amsterdam in 1612. The version of Psalm 100, the tune of which is familiar to many as the Doxology, appears in Figure 10.1. Readers of music will note the absence of barlines and the use of the tenor clef, with "c" on the fourth line.

Other psalters used by the early colonists include the older Sternhold and Hopkins, and especially the psalter by Thomas Ravenscroft (London, 1621), used by the Puritans of the Massachusetts Bay Colony.

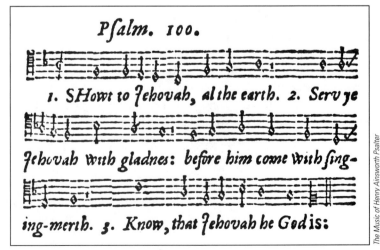

Figure 10.1
Psalm 100 from the
Ainsworth Psalter, 1612.

The Music of Henry Ainsworth Psalter

All hymns, like ballads, are in strophic form. (See p. 4.) Hymns are cataloged according to syllables per line, so that a four-line hymn with ten syllables per line would have the numbers 10 10.10 10 printed above the first line. Psalm 100, in Figure 10.1, has eight syllables per line—88.88. This is known as Long Meter (L.M.). The metric pattern 86.86 is identical with ballad meter, as described in Chapter 1 (pp. 4–5), which in hymnody is called Common Meter (C.M.). ("Amazing Grace," a folklike melody of unknown origin, is in Common Meter, or ballad meter. See CD 2/34.) The only other meter used with sufficient frequency to be given a name is Short Meter, which is 66.86 and has the same pattern of *stressed* syllables as does the familiar *limerick*. A "D." (for "double") following the meter indicates that the pattern is gone through twice for each verse. This cataloging of meters is useful in allowing different tunes to be used for the same hymn text. Any hymn in Common Meter, for example, can be sung to any tune in the same meter. Check your local hymnal for verification.

Psalm tunes were the most important body of religious music in constant use throughout those colonies founded by the English and the Dutch, almost until the time of the Revolution. They were subsequently largely replaced by the music of hymns, anthems, and fuging tunes, but many of the old psalm tunes have survived, and tune names such as "Toulon," "Windsor," "York," "Bristol," "Old 104th," "Old 112th," "Old 120th," and the famous "Old 100th" bespeak their presence in every major modern hymnal.

Calvinism and the Psalms

A glance at a map of Europe, together with some understanding of the situation there at the time of the Reformation, will make clear why it was the psalm tune, rather than the Lutheran chorale or the venerable and cultivated music of the Roman Catholic Church, that dominated early religious music on the eastern seaboard of the United States and, with its related progeny, left its mark on American sacred music for three hundred years. We cannot here fill in the background; suffice it to say that most of the earliest permanent settlers there brought with them not only their psalters and their psalm tunes but also their pronounced aversion to state religion and temporal ecclesiastical hierarchy and power—all of which, to them, was summed up in one word: "popery." This was to have a profound effect on the development of American consciousness and culture.

Calvinism dominated the religious practices of a large portion of the early settlers on the east coast of the United States. Music in the Calvinist churches was rather severely limited to the unaccompanied unison singing of metrical versions of the psalms. This was but one manifestation of the ancient and ever-present dichotomy that exists between the musician and the theologian on the question of music in worship. The musician wishes to use the utmost skill and craft, and give the music free rein; the theologian wishes to keep music simple and ensure its subordination to the worship itself. The controversy is nearly as old as the Christian church itself, and the history of church music is the history of the swinging of the pendulum back and forth between the two positions. The church recognized, as the Greeks had long before, the power of music over human emotions. As two recent writers have aptly summarized the situation, "The Christian church has carried on a long, often fruitful relationship with music, governed, however, by the kind of uneasy truce man had struck with fire" (McKay and Crawford 8). It so happened that in the sixteenth century the pendulum swung decisively to the side of strict control of music, in both the Roman Catholic Church and the new Reformed Church, but much more drastically and completely in the latter. In the Reformed Church, the new broom had no weight of musical tradition to encumber it. Psalm singing, then, was the product of a musical simplicity enforced on theological grounds. (For an honest and detailed account of all aspects of life in New England from 1674 to 1729, there is no better source than the diary of Samuel Sewall. See Additional Reading.)

Psalm Tunes and Psalters

With John Calvin's exhortation to psalm singing came the need for metered and rhymed versions of the psalms, and tunes to which they could be sung by entire congregations and not by trained choirs. This need was met by a series of psalters, the first published in Strasbourg in 1539. The sixteenth century thus saw the establishment of two great bodies of sacred tunes, the Lutheran chorales and the psalmody of the Reformed Church. They share similar characteristics (as well as some of the same tunes): they are easily singable melodies of fairly simple construction, with vestiges of the old modal scales already encountered in our study of folk music.

The most significant psalter, for us, was the first book printed in what is now the United States, *The Whole Booke of Psalmes Faithfully Translated into English Metre*, published in Boston in 1640 and nicknamed the Bay Psalm Book. It was no mean achievement for a community of fewer than twenty thousand people that had established itself on the edge of the American wilderness scarcely more than a decade before. The motive of these scholars is revealed in characteristic words at the close of the preface (Figure 10.2).

> If therefore the verses are not alwayes
> so smooth and elegant as some may desire
> or expect; let them confider that Gods
> Altar needs not our pollishings: Ex. 20. for
> wee have respected rather a plaine transla-
> tion, then to smooth our verses with the
> sweetnes of any paraphrase, and soe have
> attended Confcience rather then Elegance,
> fidelity rather then poetry, in tranflating
> the hebrew words into englifh language,
> and Davids poetry into englifh meetre;
>
> that foe wee may fing in Sion the Lords
> fongs of prayfe according to his owne
> will; untill hee take us from hence,
> and wipe away all our teares, &
> bid us enter into our mafters
> ioye to fing eternall
> Halleluiahs.

Figure 10.2
From the preface of the Bay Psalm Book, 1620—the first book printed in the American colonies. Citing the authority of Exodus 20 (where God demands that His altar be made of unhewn stone), the Psalm translators emphasized substance over elegance of expression.

Two Divergent "Ways"

By the 1720s a hundred years of psalm singing in America had produced two discernible traditions, simultaneous but widely divergent. They amounted to a written and an oral practice. In the written practice, the tunes would be sung as they were notated in the psalmbooks of the time. But psalmbooks were few, and few in the congregations, especially in rural areas, could read music. This led to the practice of lining out, in which the deacon, or precentor, sang or recited each line before it was sung by the congregation. This oral practice, called the Usual Way, led to a severe shrinking in the number of tunes in common use and a marked slowing of the tempo. (One observer noted, "I myself have twice in one Note paused to take Breath.") This folk practice in singing the psalms has persisted to this day in the parts of the Old World from which it came, as a sampling of Gaelic Psalmody as sung in the Free Church of Scotland on the Isle of Lewis, in the Outer Hebrides, will illustrate (CD 2/33).

CD 2/33 (1:10)
Psalm 56, verse 12. Sung in Gaelic. Recorded in Stornoway, Isle of Lewis, Scotland, 1978.

Two aspects of the Usual Way have persisted to the present, especially in rural areas. The first is the independence of, or even the absence of, a printed hymnal—hence singing from memory. In some traditions this is felt to be essential. A deacon in a rural Baptist church in Appalachia said, "You know,

CD 2/34 (1:02)
"Amazing Grace" (one
verse). Recorded at Old
Regular Baptist Church
at Jeff, Kentucky.

that's the secret in not having the notes to these [hymns]: a fellow can just sing it . . . however his heart feels" (Patterson 168).

The second is the persistence of the practice of lining out. This practice is preserved in rural hymn singing, even when the congregation obviously knows the words by heart. For an example of the survival of the Usual Way in the United States, we could listen to the singing in some rural churches in the South, especially in the Appalachians. In "Amazing Grace" as sung in a Baptist church in Kentucky, for example (CD 2/34), we can hear the lining out and the slow, individualized singing.

Reform and Instruction

Opposition to the Usual Way on the part of a more musically literate portion of the populace grew more outspoken as time went on, and came to a head in the 1720s. What the reformers, or proponents of what was called *Regular Singing*, wanted to make happen could be accomplished only by teaching people to read music. This is exactly what they set out to do. Instruction books such as *An Introduction to the Singing of Psalm Tunes in a Plain and Easy Method* (Rev. John Tufts) appeared in the 1720s and went through many editions. As intimated in their titles, these books represented only the first of a long series of assaults by American ingenuity on the perennial problem of how to make music easier for the uninitiated. From *An Introduction . . . in a Plain and Easy Method* through *Ragtime in Ten Easy Lessons*, this elusive goal has been pursued—often with some success.

But no one has ever learned to perform music just by reading a book. The need for instruction by a "master," and for practicing together under his tutelage, produced one of the most important and pervasive musical and social institutions in our early history—the singing school.

THE SINGING-SCHOOL TRADITION

That uniquely American institution, the singing school, may have had its beginnings in New England, but ultimately it spread far and wide. In the cities its descendants are represented by the numerous choral societies, great and small. In rural areas it retained its original characteristics longest; here, as a social as well as a musical gathering, it brightened the routine of lives that were otherwise all too often harsh and dreary. The firm place and meaning of the singing school in rural American life before the twentieth century can hardly be better attested to than by the following excerpt from the reminiscences, in folk-verse form, of a pioneer woman writing of her life in Sangamon County, Illinois, in the mid–nineteenth century.

We had so few things to give us pleasure
The memories of such times I love to treasure.
Our singing school, where we looked forward to meet
Our beloved teacher, and his pupils to greet.
Our singing books, few here now, ever saw
The old patent notes, fa, sol, la, sol, fa, me, la.
There were some good voices to lead the rest,
All long since gone to the home of the blest.
I seem to hear their voices now singing, loud and clear
And almost feel their presence hovering near.

How the Singing Schools Worked

From the 1720s on, the singing-school movement gradually picked up momentum, and the period 1760 to 1800, encompassing the Revolution and the founding of the new nation, saw its greatest activity, especially in New England. The singing school was a private venture, taught by an itinerant master. The school would be advertised in advance in the community, and subscriptions taken. The singing school itself was not a denominational institution, and in fact the instruction did not always take place in the church; a room in a schoolhouse or local tavern was sometimes used. Two or three meetings a week for three months seems to have been a common schedule. If the singing master had published a tunebook, the pupils would be expected to buy and use it, thus somewhat augmenting his income, which was seldom large. There is evidence that singing masters sometimes took their pay in produce — Indian corn, for example. For this and many other interesting details of the New England singing-school tradition, see Buechner.

The solmization syllables (fa, sol, la, mi) were invariably taught as a basis for learning to sing the correct pitches, and the words of the pieces were not allowed to be sung until the syllables had been mastered. As an ingenious device for getting the tempo exact, homemade pendulums (of a length carefully specified) were recommended, and William Billings gives the following directions for making them in the preface to his *Continental Harmony:*

> Make a pendulum of common thread well waxed, and instead of a bullet take a piece of heavy wood turned perfectly round, about the bigness of a pullet's egg, and rub them over, either with chalk, paint or whitewash, so that they may be seen plainly by candle-light.

(It was usually stipulated that the students bring their own candles.) At the close of the term, there was almost always a public concert, or "exhibition."

The pupils thus got a chance to show off what they had learned; the singing master then moved on to another community.

Contemporary accounts show that the pupils were mostly young people. It seems, from the directions for the conduct of a singing school that have survived, that the teacher's ability to keep order was at least as important as his ability to teach music—an observation that has a familiar ring. Yet there is little doubt that the singing schools generally accomplished their objectives very well. After the term was over, one or more of the ablest pupils might start teaching themselves, or even try their hand at composing psalm settings, anthems, or fuging tunes. Thus the singing schools, in addition to raising the general level of musical literacy and expanding the repertory of music available, played a vital part in encouraging the development of native composers.

Billings of Boston and His Contemporaries

Not every singing master became a composer, of course, but the number that did is substantial. In fact, the singing-school movement gave us our first school of indigenous American composers, who worked under the most fruitful conditions a composer can experience: writing music for which there is a clear demand and appreciation on the part of a well-defined public. This fruitful period for America's first native composers did not last long—near-ideal conditions for art never do—but the productivity was intense (one scholar has termed it a "golden age"), for one authority has estimated that by 1800 there were over a thousand compositions in print in American tunebooks, most of them by native composers.

The singing masters and composers were for the most part humble craftsmen, artisans, or small businessmen, who composed and taught in addition to plying their trades. The names and trades of these native pioneers read like a litany of eighteenth-century New England names and occupations, and perhaps help to give the flavor of the singing-school movement in a way nothing else can: Supply Belcher, tavernkeeper; David Belknap, farmer and mechanic; William Billings, tanner; Amos Bull, storekeeper; Oliver Holden, carpenter; Jeremiah Ingalls, cooper; Jacob Kimball, lawyer; Abraham Maxim, farmer and schoolteacher; Justin Morgan, horse breeder; Timothy Swan, hatter.

William Billings (1746–1800), the best known among these, was also the most prolific, inventive, and enthusiastically dedicated. In 1770, at the age of 24, he published the first tunebook in America consisting entirely of music by a single composer; his *New-England Psalm-Singer* contained more than 120 compositions. In the next quarter-century he brought out five more books, whose titles give something of their flavor and usage: *The Singing Master's Assistant*

(1778), *Music in Miniature* (1779), *The Psalm-Singer's Amusement* (1781), *The Suffolk Harmony* (1786), and *The Continental Harmony* (1794).

Billings became quite well known in his time. Yet he was never able to give up his tanning trade permanently, and in fact records show him to have held down several civil posts to help make ends meet for himself and his family—even to jobs that had to do with keeping hogs off the streets and keeping the streets clean in Boston's Eleventh Ward. He died in severe poverty.

Billings, a friend of Samuel Adams and Paul Revere, was an ardent patriot, and his patriotic song "Chester"(CD 2/35, Transcription 10.1) was one of the most popular songs of the Revolution. With its first stanza, it appeared in 1770 in *The New-England Psalm-Singer;* during the Revolution, further stanzas were added, with the names of five British generals and the boast that "Their Vet'rans flee before our Youth,/ And Gen'rals yield to beardless Boys"—and it was in this form that it appeared in *The Singing Master's Assistant* of 1778.

CD 2/35 (1:53)
"Chester," by William Billings. The Old Sturbridge Singers, Sturbridge, Massachusetts. 1964.

Transcription 10.1
"Chester," by William Billings

The foe comes on with haughty Stride,
Our troops advance with martial noise;
Their Vet'rans flee before our Youth,
And Gen'rals yield to beardless Boys.

What grateful Off'ring shall we bring,
What shall we render to the Lord?
Loud Hallelujahs let us Sing,
And praise his name on ev'ry Chord.

Text, "Chester," with its original capitalization

Billings was a colorful and energetic writer of prose as well, as his salty, conversational, and sometimes lengthy prefaces to his tunebooks attest. His philosophical approach to music, as well as to politics, was one of independence and self-reliance. Oft-quoted statements of his—such as "Nature is the best Dictator"; "I don't think myself confin'd to any Rules for Composition laid down by any that went before me"; and "I think it best for every Composer to be his own Carver"—may, taken out of their own context and the context of his work, suggest a degree of rebellious iconoclasm far beyond Billings's actual intent, or what his works show. Nevertheless, he was among the first to sound a note of independence that was more fully orchestrated half a century later by Emerson, and again a full century later by Charles Ives.

Perhaps the best summation of Billings as man and composer is contained in an entry in the diary of the Reverend William Bentley of Salem, made a few days after Billings's death. Bentley, one of America's best-educated men of his time (Jefferson had thought of him for the presidency of the University of Virginia), moved in circles unfamiliar and even inaccessible to Billings. Nevertheless, his insight into Billings's work and importance moved him to write, "Many who have imitated have excelled him, but none of them had better original power. . . . He was a singular man, of moderate size, short of one leg, with one eye, without any address, & with an uncommon negligence of person. Still he spake & sung & thought as a man above the common abilities." (The phrase "without any address" should not, despite his poverty, be taken as meaning that Billings was among the homeless. This usage of the word "address" is now uncommon, and describes Billings as one who lacked either the capacity for "skillful management" or a tactful and cultivated manner of speaking, or possibly both.)

Yankee Tunebooks by the Hundreds

Billings was but one among many. An examination of the singing-school period during its golden age gives an impression of tremendous activity and vitality. By 1810 about three hundred of the distinctive tunebooks, homely in appearance and typography, had been published. Their oblong shape gave rise to the terms "long boys" and "end-openers." The titles of these old books tell us much. Some show the classical education or aspirations of their compilers: *Urania; Harmonia Americana*. Some of the titles show clearly the books' use and purpose: *The Musical Primer; The Easy Instructor; The Psalmodist's Assistant; The Psalmodist's Companion; The Chorister's Companion*. Many bespeak their own locale: *The Massachusetts Compiler; The Vermont Harmony; The Harmony of Maine; The Worcester Collection of Sacred Harmony; The Essex Harmony*. The word "harmony" was widely used: *The American Harmony, The Northern Harmony; The*

Union Harmony; The Federal Harmony; The New England Harmony; The Christian Harmony; and, as a final distillation, *The Harmony of Harmony.* To close the list, there appeared (with singular appropriateness to their environment) *The Rural Harmony* and *The Village Harmony.*

The Music of the Tunebooks

The venerable psalm tunes are well represented in some of the earlier collections (*Urania,* for example), but along with these appear the tunes for the short nonscriptural hymns to original texts, and the larger and more ambitious anthems—more elaborate settings of scriptural texts, adapted scriptural texts, or original texts. It is evident that by this time hymnody had fairly well succeeded in replacing psalmody.

The *canon* (or *round*) does not appear frequently, although Billings has given us a beautiful example in his first publication, the justly famous "Jesus Wept" (CD 2/36, Transcription 10.2).

CD 2/36 (2:08)
"Jesus Wept," by
William Billings. The
Old Sturbridge Singers,
Sturbridge, Massachu-
setts. 1964.

Transcription 10.2
"Jesus Wept," by
William Billings

Of particular interest are the famous *fuging tunes.* (The term, though derived from *fugue,* was very possibly pronounced "fudging" in contemporary usage.) Alan Buechner describes it simply as a piece that "begins like a hymn and ends like a round." It was the second section, or *fuge,* that was distinctive, with its rather informally constructed homespun imitative entrances of the voices. The fuging tune was very popular in its day: the effect of hearing the

CD 2/37 (0:45)
"Amity" (one verse),
by Daniel Read. The
Old Sturbridge Singers,
Sturbridge, Massachu-
setts. 1964.

successive entrances coming from different parts of the U-shaped meeting-house gallery must have thrilled singers and congregation alike. Billings describes these pieces as being "twenty times as powerful as the old slow tunes." Although he composed many himself, there were other composers of the time who favored them even more, and it has been found that over a thousand were published by 1810. The fuging tune later fell into disfavor among reformers of church music, who urged that it was both too crude and too lively as music for worship. But its appeal among the rural folk persisted, and fuging tunes in considerable numbers appear in the shape-note songbooks of the nineteenth century. "Amity," by Daniel Read, a Revolutionary War soldier who became a storekeeper and maker of combs, is an excellent example of this popular form (CD 2/37).

Text, "Amity"
(Daniel Read)

How pleasant is to see
Kindred and friends agree,
Each in their proper station move,

(Fuging section)
And each fulfill their part,
With sympathizing heart,
In all the cares of life and love.

A number of the larger anthems and set pieces were written for specific occasions or observances—for Thanksgiving, for a Fast Day, for Ordination, for Christmas, for Easter, for thanksgiving "after a victory," to commemorate the landing of the Pilgrims, and so on. (It is not clear in what circumstances and by whom Billings's Christmas pieces were sung, since the Puritans had suppressed traditional Christmas customs as "Prophane and Superstitious" in the seventeenth century, and this proscription was in effect until the mid–nineteenth century, at which time Christmas was still a regular working day in Boston. See McKay and Crawford 144–45.) Some were of a still more topical nature, as illustrated by Billings's famous "Lamentation Over Boston," a spirited paraphrase of Psalm 137 commemorating the British occupation of the city during the war.

The End of an Era and the Suppression of the Indigenous Tradition in the Urban East

America's expansion, which began in earnest with the opening of the nineteenth century, manifested itself in two directions at once: in the growth of her cities in size, complexity, and sophistication; and in the continuous rolling westward of her frontier. Both had profound effects on American thought, life, and art—including indigenous religious music. By 1810 an "anti-American" reform movement had successfully established a trend away from the native, unschooled, innocent art of the pioneer tradition, and toward the closer imitation of European models. The fuging tune especially was castigated. In 1807 the preface of a new compilation characterized the fuging tunes as "those wild fugues, and rapid and confused movements, which have so long been the disgrace of congregational psalmody." The reformers prevailed, to the extent that the editor of the *Boston Courier* lamented in 1848 "the good old days of New England music have passed away, and the singing-masters who compose and teach it, are known only in history as an extinct race" (Stevenson 85 n).

THE FRONTIER AND RURAL AMERICA IN THE NINETEENTH CENTURY

That the music of the New Englanders was in fact far from extinct is now clear to us. As is often the case, in the rural areas the "old ways"—and the old music—were tenaciously clung to long after they had been replaced in the cities. And the frontier, southwestward into the long valleys of the Appalachians and beyond into the broad river valleys of the Ohio and the Tennessee, was an extension of rural America. We can follow the movement of the singing-school tradition along these paths just by tracing the continued appearance of its odd oblong books of tunes. Moving out of Boston and Philadelphia, we find compilations being made in Harrisburg, Pennsylvania; in the Shenandoah Valley of Virginia; in Hamilton, Georgia; in Spartanburg, South Carolina; in Lexington, Kentucky; in Nashville, in Cincinnati, in St. Louis. The titles tell a story of both continuity and movement. As lineal descendants of *The New England Harmony* and *The Harmony of Maine*, we find *The Virginia Harmony, The Kentucky Harmony, The Knoxville Harmony, The Missouri Harmony, The Western Lyre, The Southern Harmony,* and, finally, the famous *Sacred Harp.* These books clearly revealed their ancestry—in their shape and appearance; in their prefatory introductions to the "Rudiments of Music"; in their continued use of the four solmization syllables (fa, sol, la, mi); in their hymns in three and four parts, with the melody buried in the middle of the texture in the tenor voice; and in their sprinkling of more ambitious anthems and fuging tunes. Pieces by Billings himself were almost invariably included; far from being "extinct," as the Boston editor lamented in the middle of the nineteenth century, William Billings and some of his contemporaries have turned out to be the most continuously performed composers in American history. Indeed, their music has already entered its third century. The singing schools continued to flourish in the nineteenth century, fulfilling their dual musical and social function much as they had done in New England in colonial times. (See the folk verse from Sangamon County, Illinois, on p. 179.) Later came the institution of annual gatherings, or "singings," some lasting two or three days, with "dinner on the grounds" a fixed feature.

Thus we see that the "old ways" did not die. Two important additions were made, however, as the native tradition moved out of the East into the South and the West. One was the development of the famous shape-notes, and the other was the infusion of the folk element into the music.

The Shape-Notes

John Tufts's *An Introduction . . . in a Plain and Easy Method* in the early eighteenth century was only the first of many attempts to simplify and speed up the process of teaching people to read music. There appeared in 1801 a book by William Little and William Smith called, appropriately, *The Easy Instructor,* which introduced a simple but ingenious device that proved to be eminently practical. This consisted of the use of differently shaped notes for each of the four syllables then in use to indicate degrees of the scale. In the key of F major, for example, the scale with its syllables would look like Transcription 10.3.

Transcription 10.3
The shaped notes

Fa   Sol   La   Fa   Sol   La   Mi   Fa

The device appears to have caught on rather quickly and well. *The Easy Instructor* was reissued in various editions for thirty years; by the time it ceased publication, there were at least eighteen other songbooks in print using the same device. *The Easy Instructor* was first published in the urban East (Philadelphia). The shape-note method was so readily adopted by the compilers of the traditional rural songbooks, however, that its vast literature—for so long all but unknown to outsiders—has taken on the name "southern shape-note hymnody."

Infusion of the Folk Element

Another important development as this rural hymnody moved southwest at the beginning of the nineteenth century was a fresh infusion of the folk element into the tune collections. Folk or folkish tunes of Anglo-Celtic cast, given sacred words and spare, austere harmonic settings, were found in the new books, alongside the established hymn tunes, anthems, and fuging tunes. This had already begun in New England. The "borrowing" of folk tunes to supply the needs of sacred music—"plundering the carnal lover"—is a venerable practice. The great body of Lutheran chorale tunes, for example, contains its share of melodies that began life as folk or popular tunes, in some cases love songs.

The harmony of these hymns abounds in austere open consonances (octaves, fifths, fourths). The spare openness of the harmonic texture contributes as much as the modality of the tunes to the distinctiveness of this music, which must be actually *heard* (preferably live) to be appreciated. This style is nowhere better illustrated than in the three-voice setting of the famous folk hymn "Wondrous Love," as found in *The Southern Harmony* (CD 3/1). The folk tune is in the middle, or tenor, voice. Figure 10.3 shows the entire folk hymn "Wondrous Love" in shape-note notation.

CD 3/1 (0:33) "Wondrous Love" (one verse), singers at the Alabama Sacred Harp Singing Convention, Birmingham, Alabama

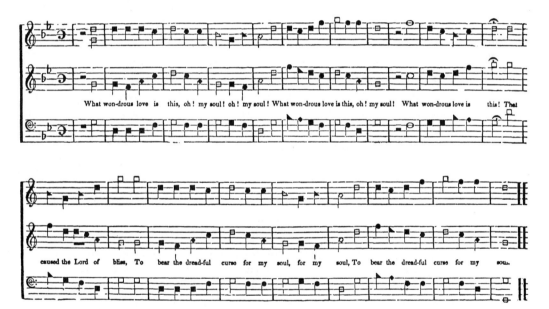

Figure 10.3 The hymn based on "Wondrous Love," in three-part harmony and written in shape-note notation. The popular folk tune is in the middle voice.

It is interesting to note that some American composers in the 1930s and 1940s, such as Aaron Copland and Virgil Thomson, writing at a time when American classical music had begun to find its own voice, would tend to adopt similarly lean textures and sounds.

Revivalism and the Camp Meeting

Successive waves of religious revivalism have swept America since 1800. Their impact on our indigenous religious music was most pronounced in the period of the expanding frontier before the Civil War, for it was on the frontier that revivalism nurtured its most striking manifestation: the camp meeting. The camp meeting in turn nurtured, for its own needs, one of our most distinctive forms of religious music: the revival spiritual. To understand the origin, nature, and function of the revival spiritual, let us turn our attention briefly to the camp meeting itself.

The colonial South was far from being a devout society. The fundamentalist faith that later became so ingrained there was established as a result of two factors. One was the hardship of what amounted to a frontier existence throughout the antebellum South for the "plain folk" who made up the bulk of the population—mostly white subsistence farmers, who were continually forced to move and take up less arable land as the large slave-worked plantations spread into the fertile lowlands. This kind of existence bred a need for the reassurance and consolation that could be supplied by an evangelical religion—a religion that held out the promise in the hereafter of all the good that was so elusive and pitifully transient in the here-and-now. The other factor was the unremitting effort of the three most popular denominations after the Revolution: the Presbyterians, the Baptists, and the Methodists (the last most especially, with their organized hierarchy and their corps of indefatigable circuit-riding preachers). These two factors set the stage for the Great Revival of the early nineteenth century.

At its beginning it was called the Kentucky Revival, for that state was its fertile seedbed. Of all the newly opened territories west of the Appalachians, Kentucky was the first to attract settlers, and it acted as a kind of staging area for those who were eventually to move on. By 1800 it was a "boom" state, having a greater population (over 200,000) than all the other states and territories outside the original thirteen colonies combined. It was about this time that revivalism in its most sensational form came to this raw frontier state.

The early camp meetings of the Kentucky revival were huge, chaotic, turbulent affairs. Many people traveled for days to get there. The famous camp meeting of August 1801 at Cane Ridge, in the gently rolling country of Bourbon County, northeast of Lexington, lasted six days, and estimates of the number in attendance ran between ten and twenty-five thousand. The preaching, praying, shouting, and singing went on day and night. According to one of the many eyewitness accounts,

> The noise was like the roar of Niagara. The vast sea of human beings seemed to be agitated as if by a storm. I counted seven ministers, all preaching at one time, some on stumps, others in wagons, and one . . . was standing on a tree which had, in falling, lodged against . . . another. Some of the people were singing, others praying, some crying for mercy in the most piteous accents, while others were shouting most vociferously. . . . A strange supernatural power seemed to pervade the entire

mass of mind there collected. . . . Soon after I left and went into the woods, and there I strove to rally and man up my courage.

After some time I returned to the scene of excitement, the waves of which, if possible, had risen still higher. The same awfulness of feeling came over me. I stepped up on to a log, where I could have a better view of the surging sea of humanity. The scene that presented itself to my mind was indescribable. At one time I saw at least five hundred swept down in a moment as if a battery of a thousand guns had been opened upon them, and then immediately followed shrieks and shouts that rent the heavens. (Johnson 64–65)

There was many a strange and disquieting sight to be viewed on the American frontier, and none more so at times than the camp meeting. But in spite of the undenied excesses of the early ones, their emphasis on emotionalism, and the dubious significance of many of the "conversions," most careful observers now conclude that the positive influence of the camp meetings outweighed the negative. As Charles Johnson has summed it up, "Among all of the weapons forged by the West in its struggle against lawlessness and immorality, few were more successful than the frontier camp meeting. This socioreligious institution helped tame backwoods America"(Johnson vii).

The Revival Spiritual

Singing was a vital part of revivalism from the beginning. Another account of Cane Ridge tells of the powerful impulse of song: "The volume of song burst all bounds of guidance and control, and broke again and again from the throats of the people." Still another eyewitness reported that at the camp meetings the "falling down of multitudes, and their crying out . . . happened under the singing of Watts's Psalms and Hymns, more frequently than under the preaching of the word" (Johnson 57). All agree that the singing was loud. "The immediate din was tremendous; at a hundred yards it was beautiful; at a distance of a half a mile it was magnificent" (Chase 204).

What was sung at the camp meetings? Since it was for so long a matter of purely oral tradition, evidence must be pieced together. The reference above to "Watts's Psalms and Hymns" refers to the words; certain hymns, and bits and pieces of hymns, of eighteenth-century English divines such as Isaac Watts were much used. Though pocket-sized "songsters" with just the words began to appear about 1805, the tunes were not written down and published until the 1840s. From these later collections we can form some notion of the camp-meeting repertory, since we know what the hallmarks of the true revival spiritual were. The tunes had to be lively and easily learned. There was

Courtesy of the New York Historical Society, New York City

The simple music, tents, and makeshift podiums of an outdoor Methodist camp meeting in New York around 1837 offer a deliberate contrast to the highly cultivated religious musics and great cathedrals of the European tradition.

an almost unvarying reliance on the verse-chorus form; everyone could at least join in on the choruses, even if they didn't know. the verses, or if the leader introduced unfamiliar ones or even made them up on the spot. A further development along the line of what has been called "text simplification," for the sake of mass participation, was the single-line refrain, interpolated after a couplet of original text or even after every line. With the crowds joining in on the refrains, this turned the singing into the familiar call-and-response pattern. Indoor church hymns could be transformed into revival spirituals by this process.

It is interesting to observe this at work in the case of one of the most popular hymn texts of the time. The original hymn "Canaan," by the English clergyman Samuel Stennett (1727–95), describes in Blakean imagery the beauties of heaven. The first of many verses runs thus:

Text, "Canaan"
(Samuel Stennett)

> On Jordan's stormy banks I stand,
> And cast a wishful eye,
> To Canaan's fair and happy land,
> Where my possessions lie.
> O, the transporting rapturous scene,
> That rises to my sight!
> Sweet fields array'd in living green,
> And rivers of delight.

In the revival-song version shown in Transcription 10.4, only one couplet at a time is used, with a typical chorus added, spelling out in more homely language of action and urgency the conviction that the believer is actually *going* to the promised land so poetically described. The result is a spirited and popular revival spiritual that was first printed in William Walker's *Southern Harmony* in 1835.

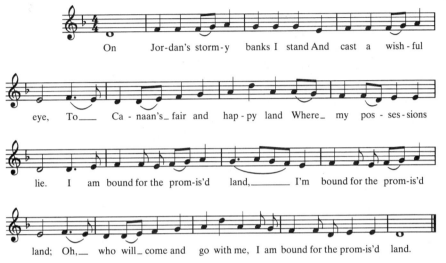

Transcription 10.4
"The Promised Land"

A further stage in the "revivalizing" of this hymn is illustrated in "On the Other Side of Jordan" (Transcription 10.5), in which a one-line refrain is interpolated after every line of the text. Both the words and the music of the refrain then become the basis for an added chorus. The whole appears in *The Revivalist* of 1868, set to a folkish tune that has a decidedly Irish lilt.

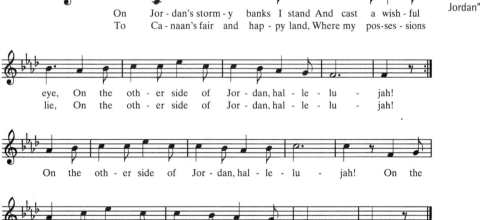

Transcription 10.5
"On the Other Side of Jordan"

Repetition was carried even further through the use of a form in which a single word is changed to make each new stanza, as can be seen in "Way Over in the Promised Land," from *The Social Harp* of 1855 (Transcription 10.6). According to George Pullen Jackson, this spiritual was probably sung with "fathers" only in the first verse, then "mothers" in a second. Further multiplication of verses was easy, using "brothers," "sisters," "friends," "neighbors," and so on. This pattern was to persist in vernacular religious song, especially among African Americans; it proved useful in the "freedom songs" of the civil rights movement of the 1960s—songs that were most often adaptations of old spirituals and hymns. (See "Ain't Gonna Let Nobody Turn Me Around," CD 2/11, p. 103.)

Transcription 10.6
"Way Over in the Promised Land"

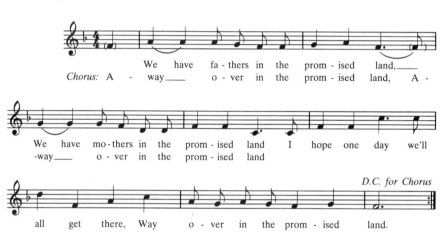

The revival spirituals were also distinguished by the import of their texts. These emphasized the basic themes of the prevailing theology—especially salvation, its attendant joys, and the glories of a heaven that was far removed from the present life. The examples already cited have been replete with expressions that pervade the spirituals: "promised land," "Canaan," "the other side of Jordan." Along with the descriptions of heaven and its joys is a dissatisfaction with this present life that is so pronounced as to amount at times to a rejection of the world and, if not actually a wish for death, at least a poignant anticipation of the joys and release from pain it would bring to the righteous saints who had been converted.

Our bondage it shall end, by and by, by and by.
I am a stranger here below.
This world is not my home.
How blest the righteous when he dies!

How gently heaves the expiring breast,
How mildly beams the closing eyes
When sinks a weary soul to rest.
Sweet home! Oh, when shall I get there?

Parallel Traditions: White and Black Spirituals

The African American spiritual was treated extensively in Chapter 2, where the expressiveness of this folk form, together with its unmistakably African features, have been amply illustrated. Parallel traditions of these "spiritual songs" existed among blacks and whites. Unfortunately much pointless and often heated controversy as to which tradition influenced the other has been generated, some of it, on both sides, regrettably tainted with racism. It is not necessary to denigrate white spirituals, much less to deny their existence, in order to praise black spirituals, and the same applies the other way around as well. *Black Song: The Forge and the Flame* is an exhaustive work on the black spiritual by the African American author John Lovell, Jr. Though the book is often polemical, the writer does not deny that there is a "blend of African and American elements." He goes on to say that "the blend is a fair compound of equal elements, not a strong superior mixed with a weak inferior. . . . There is hardly any doubt that the Afro-American songmaker borrowed from the hymns he heard, and from the Biblical stories he picked up. In putting them into his African-like setting he created something quite new, with obvious characteristics of both original traditions" (84–86).

Though there is still some controversy over where and how this blending did occur, it seems reasonable that it did not occur in the large slave-holding areas of the South, or through the master-slave relationship, but precisely in those regions and under those conditions that nurtured the folk hymn and the revival spiritual among whites—in the uplands and on the frontier, among the plain folk and at the camp meeting. Whether it was a matter of black singers listening to white singers, or the other way around, both were present, and the camp meeting, a frontier institution, was probably the site of as uninhibited a meeting of the races as could be encountered in that time. Many of the early camp-meeting preachers, such as Lorenzo Dow and Peter Cartwright, preached against slavery and were, in fact, among the earliest abolitionists.

MUSIC AMONG SMALLER INDEPENDENT AMERICAN SECTS

Conditions in America have been such as to nurture from the beginning, despite glaring episodes of intolerance and persecution, a lively tradition of

CD 3/2 (1:08)
"'Tis the Gift to Be Simple," Sister Mildred Barker and others at The United Society of Shakers, Sabbathday Lake, Maine. Recorded between 1965 and 1976.

religious independence and nonconformity. Many sects either have been transplanted to the United States or have sprung up here, where, especially in the eighteenth and nineteenth centuries, they found the space necessary to provide the measure of isolation and self-sufficiency they so deeply desired. Mention must be made at least of the Moravians (of central European origin, with a strong classical-music tradition) and the Shakers (originating in the English Midlands, with a self-generated tradition of folklike music). It is fitting to close this chapter on early American religious music with one of its great masterpieces, the Shaker spiritual "'Tis the Gift to Be Simple" (CD 3/2, Transcription 10.7).

Transcription 10.7
"'Tis the Gift to Be Simple"

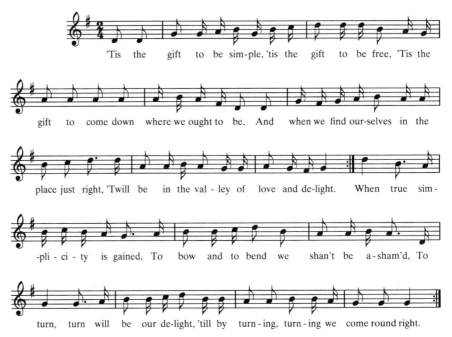

This song (the melody of which was borrowed by Aaron Copland for his *Appalachian Spring*) gives expression to the basic Shaker themes of simplicity and humility, and stands as a consummate achievement of innocent religious art. It is included in the hope that it will be *sung* as well as listened to.

■ PROJECTS

1. Find three psalm tunes (*besides* "Old 100th"!) that are still in use and appear in modern hymn collections in this country. Find out as much as you can about the origins of the

tunes, and in which early psalters they appeared. Find and consult early versions of the tunes if possible. (Most hymnals have a good index of composers and sources, which can help, as can the index of tune names. The *Hymnal of the Protestant Episcopal Church in the U.S.A.*, for example, is rather rich in tunes from the old psalters of the sixteenth and seventeenth centuries.)

2. Read William Billings's prefaces to his *Continental Harmony* (see Additional Reading)—both "To the several Teachers of MUSIC, in this and the adjacent States" and "A Commentary on the preceding Rules: by way of Dialogue, between Master and Scholar." Comment on what these treatises seem to say about Billings himself: his sense of humor, his ability and ingenuity as a teacher, and his views on music, especially vocal music.

3. Find three revival spirituals in present-day hymnals. Find out what you can about the tunes and put together a brief commentary. The Lorenz book in the reading list may be helpful.

4. Write a brief paper comparing the camp meetings of the Kentucky Revival with the large outdoor rock festivals of the 1960s.

ADDITIONAL LISTENING

Early Shaker Spirituals. Rounder 0078.

The New England Harmony: A Collection of Early American Choral Music. Smithsonian/Folkways 32377.

Urban Revivalism and Gospel Music

The opening decades of the nineteenth century witnessed the beginnings of a growing cultural cleavage between the city and the country. The products of America's native school of church composers were progressively cast aside by those dedicated to what they saw as the improvement of church music, who turned to Europe not only for "rules" as to what was correct but also for actual tunes. *The Boston Handel and Haydn Society Collection of Church Music,* compiled by Lowell Mason and published in 1822, was a landmark. Gone were the fuging tunes; there was not a single piece by Billings, Ingalls, or Swan. Instead, there were European hymn tunes, as well as adapted tunes by Handel, Mozart, Haydn, and Beethoven. The inexorable divergence between "highbrow" and "lowbrow" in American tastes after 1800 applied to religious music as well. For the worship services of the urban churches that had a pronounced liturgical bent, coupled with a substantial tradition and an intellectual, even aesthetic, dimension to their appeal (Episcopal, Lutheran, Presbyterian to some degree, as well as Roman Catholic), a hymnody continued to develop along the lines Lowell Mason helped to establish—cultivated and eclectic, selecting and adapting from a wide range of traditions. Any recent hymn book of these denominations (such as *The Hymnal of the Protestant Episcopal Church in the United States of America* [1940]) will illustrate this. Here medieval plainchant, Lutheran chorales, Calvinist psalm tunes, and melodies by classical and modern composers rub shoulders with American folk hymns such as "Kedron."

On the other hand, after 1800 the broadly popular evangelical denominations and sects continued to demand a popular type of song, particularly for special occasions such as revival meetings, which incorporated many features of the old camp-meeting spiritual.

URBAN REVIVALISM AFTER THE CIVIL WAR: THE MOODY-SANKEY ERA OF GOSPEL HYMNS

Robert Stevenson has called hymn tunes "pre-eminently the food of the common man," and nineteenth-century America had a seemingly insatiable hunger for that food. In the period following the American Revolution, the demand for popular hymnody was met by drawing upon the wealth of folk music in the possession of the rural people, thereby creating the folk hymn. After the Civil War, folk music, no longer a very vital part of the lives of a much larger and increasingly citified populace, could not be drawn upon to satisfy that demand. Instead, it was met by a large number of hymn writers and composers, most of whom had only a modest amount of formal training but had an instinctive feel for what would best appeal to the great numbers of Christian believers, many of them new converts. These hymn writers and composers maintained a prodigious output of what have come to be known as gospel songs or gospel hymns. The production of these became especially copious after the revivalism of Dwight L. Moody and Ira Sankey swept the country beginning in 1875. In that year Sankey published, with P. P. Bliss, a volume called *Gospel Hymns*. This was followed by five sequels, culminating in *Gospel Hymns Nos. 1 to 6 Complete* in 1895, a compendium of more than seven hundred hymns and songs that typify the genre. As comprehensive as such a collection might seem, it represents only a small fraction of the simple, homely songs and hymns produced. As an example, Fanny Jane Crosby (1820–1915), using hundreds of pen names in addition to her real name, worked for years under a contract that called for the production of three hymns (words only) a week. How far she exceeded even that is indicated in her own statement: "I have often composed as many as six or seven hymns in one day." It is no wonder that her total output has been estimated at more than eight thousand hymns.

The models for these gospel songs did not come from the European-influenced collections of Mason and others; rather, their lineage was from the earlier camp-meeting song through the Sunday school songs for children that began to be published in the mid-nineteenth century. Their optimistic stance is revealed in the titles of collections such as *Happy Voices, The Sunny Side,* and *Golden Chain.* A new feature of revivalism was that singing the gospel became as important as preaching the gospel; therefore, to reach the masses the gospel hymn had to be of the utmost simplicity, governed by a conventionality that virtually amounted to a formula. With extremely rare exceptions, all the tunes were in the major mode, in contrast to the dour minor and modal tunes of the old rural folk hymns. The major mode was thought to be more cheerful and optimistic, and reinforced better the millennial spirit of the revivalist preaching of the day—preaching that replaced the grim pessimism and preoccupation with death and eternal judgment that had characterized antebellum "hell-fire" preaching and the songs that went with it. The tunes were harmonized with the three most basic chords, embellished occasionally with some chromaticism in the style that has since become known as "barbershop harmony."

The form of the gospel song is nearly always that of verse and chorus. The chorus is a feature that not only shows a direct descent from the earlier revival spiritual but also relates the music to the commercial secular songs of Tin Pan Alley. This chorus often embodies a sort of polyphony even more rudimentary than that of the old fuging tunes; the lower, or men's, parts simply repeat short phrases that have just been sung by the upper, or women's, parts, thus illustrating the perennial delight that the most naive manifestations of counterpoint have for the musically innocent. The chorus of "Sweet By-and-By" (CD 3/3), one of the best-known hymns of the 1895 collection *Gospel Hymns Nos. 1 to 6 Complete,* illustrates this feature (see Figure 11.1). As this example shows, the music was written on two staves in four-part harmony. The tune was now on top, in the soprano: this made it more prominent for congregational singing. The four-part harmonizations were also eminently convenient for the mixed solo quartet of soprano, alto, tenor, and bass (often paid professionals) that was such a popular feature in churches from the Civil War on.

The words, as might be expected, show the same preoccupation with the central theme of salvation as did those of the revival spiritual, though there is less gloomy dwelling upon death and, with the increased cheerfulness that pervaded popular theology, a great deal more sentimentality.

CD 3/3 (1:07)
"Sweet By-and-By" (excerpt). 1867. The Harmoneion Singers.

Figure 11.1
Verse and chorus form in "The Sweet By-and-By." A quote from the Book of Isaiah (given just below the title) sets the proper context for one of the best-known hymns from the end of the nineteenth century.

What can these simple gospel songs mean in American experience? The following account by Charles Ives has particular resonance in relation to the attack on the World Trade Center on September 11, 2001.

> The morning paper on the breakfast table gave the news of the sinking of the *Lusitania* [a passenger liner torpedoed and sunk by a German submarine in the North Atlantic on May 7, 1915—an event that led to the entry of the United States into World War I]. I remember, going downtown to business, the people on the streets had something in their faces that was not the usual something. . . . As I came on the platform [of the elevated], there was quite a crowd waiting for the trains . . . and while waiting there, a hand-organ or hurdy-gurdy was playing in the street below. Some workmen sitting on the side of the tracks began to whistle the tune, and others began to sing or hum the refrain. A workman with a shovel over his shoulder came on the platform and joined in the chorus, and the next man, a Wall Street banker with white spates and a cane, joined in it, and finally it seemed to me that everybody was singing this tune, and they didn't seem to be singing in fun, but as a natural outlet for what their feelings had been going through all day long. . . . Now what was the tune? It wasn't a Broadway hit, it wasn't a musical comedy air, it wasn't a waltz tune or a dance tune or an opera tune. . . . It was (only) the refrain of an old Gospel Hymn that had stirred many people of past generations. It was nothing but—*In the Sweet Bye and Bye.* It wasn't a tune written to be sold, or written by a professor of music—but by a man who was giving out an experience. (92–93)

Ives not only quoted this hymn tune but also described in music the entire experience in the last movement of his *Orchestral Set No. 2*, subtitled "From Hanover Square north, at the end of a tragic day, the voices of the people again rose." (See Additional Listening.)

Despite the cultural cleavage between city and country noted at the beginning of this chapter, in the field of popular religious music there was considerable urban and rural interchange. Country music, for example, got much of its material not only from Tin Pan Alley (as noted on p. 113) but from urban gospel songs as well. "Sweet By-and-By" as sung and played by traditional musicians Harry and Jeanie West is an example of the nineteenth-century gospel hymn "ruralized" (CD 3/4).

CD 3/4 (1:06)
"Sweet By-and-By" (excerpt), Harry and Jeanie West, vocal, guitar, and banjo

From a religious song of the 1890s came the title and melody of "Can the Circle Be Unbroken" (CD 3/5). A. P. Carter converted it into one of the Carter Family's best-known songs by filling out, in country-music fashion, the scene of the hearse coming to carry the mother away. Note the inclusion of

CD 3/5 (0:53)
"Can the Circle Be Unbroken" (excerpt), Carter Family. Recorded in 1935.

the phrase "by-and-by," perennial by this time in popular usage. (For more songs by the very influential Carter Family, listen to CD 1/4, pp. 9–10, and CD 2/15, pp. 112–13.)

Following the tragedy of September 11, 2001, Sheryl Crow flew up from Florida to New York to sing for the employees of American Express, who had lost eleven fellow employees in the World Trade Center. She sang not only "God Bless America" but also "Will the Circle Be Unbroken" (the title by which the song has long been known.) (See *Rolling Stone* magazine's special issue of October 25, 2001.)

THE BILLY SUNDAY–HOMER RODEHEAVER ERA: FURTHER POPULARIZATION

CD 3/6 (1:03) "Brighten the Corner Where You Are." Recorded in 1915. Homer Rodeheaver, vocal, and brass band.

The turn of the century saw further popularization and even secularization of evangelical song. There was a greater emphasis on informality and entertainment in revival meetings; the piano replaced the old reed organ, and Homer Rodeheaver (associated from 1909 to 1929 with the evangelist Billy Sunday) added trombone solos to his singing and piano playing to liven up the proceedings. In mid-career Rodeheaver made full use of the new media of radio and recordings; he also published extensively, through the Rodeheaver Company of Winona Lake, Indiana. His *Christian Service Songs* (for which practical orchestrations were available) went through many editions. It included older traditional material (standard tunes by Handel, Mendelssohn, and the like, and by

The evangelist Billy Sunday virtually leaps off the stage in this depiction of one of his spirited and energetic sermons. Varied reactions from the congregation further charged the atmosphere of his urban revival meetings. Here we find the full range of human emotion—from smugness to outright despair.

Courtesy of the Boston Public Library

the Americans Mason and Root) but is best known for the popular sacred and semisacred songs that characterized the era, among them "Brighten the Corner Where You Are" (Charles Gabriel, 1913; CD 3/16), "In the Garden" (C. Austin Miles, 1912), and "The Old Rugged Cross" (George Bernard, 1913).

After a decline during the Depression era, urban revivalism again began attracting attention with the activities of Billy Graham. The music accompanying his meetings was conservative, with a return to the repertoire represented in the Moody-Sankey *Gospel Hymns*. (Appropriately, Ira Sankey's reed organ is now in the possession of the Billy Graham Evangelistic Association.) With the advent of television evangelism, the emphasis, as in the Sunday-Rodeheaver era, is again on entertainment, eclecticism, and commercialism.

GOSPEL MUSIC AFTER THE ADVENT OF RADIO AND RECORDINGS

Following the course of jazz, blues, and country music, what Charles Wolfe has called "the fourth great genre of grass roots music"—gospel music—entered the commercial arena of the radio and the phonograph in the mid-1920s, and was profoundly influenced by both media. In the eighty years since, two parallel traditions, black and white, have developed, both drawing to a significant degree on the same reservoir of nineteenth-century gospel hymnody, but each reacting in its own way to popular secular currents of the times—white gospel music to those of white country music, and black gospel music to those of blues and jazz.

Southern White Gospel Music

Twentieth-century white gospel music in the South had its musical roots in the rural shape-note tradition described in the preceding chapter, and, instrumentally, in the folk music of that region. Its religious roots were in evangelical revivalism and in the Holiness and Pentecostal movements that about the turn of the century began to sweep across the whole country, taking root especially in the South, the Midwest, and California, where they made converts among the poor, both black and white. The terms "Holiness," "Sanctified," and "Pentecostal" are sometimes used interchangeably to describe this general movement, which was actually made up of several distinct movements and many sects, as manifested in many practically independent denominations and churches. The term "Pentecostal" is not universally applicable to the movement as a whole, since it connotes a particular emphasis on the phenomenon of glossolalia, or "speaking in tongues," which not all Holiness churches or adherents practice. The terms "Apostolic," "Church of the Nazarene," "Church of God" (or "Church of God in Christ") are frequently encountered as names of the Holiness churches. The Holiness and Pentecostal denominations were frequently racially integrated early in the century but have since become largely segregated. (See Anderson.)

At first the musical fare in the white churches was that of the rather staid gospel hymns of the Moody-Sankey era, which began to reach rural southerners in shape-notes as early as 1890. By that time the four-shape system, as preserved in *Southern Harmony* and *The Sacred Harp*, had largely given way to a seven-shape system, which had been introduced in the mid–nineteenth century and which persists in publications to this day. See the refrain of "Give the World a Smile" (Figure 11.2) and compare it with the four-note notation used in "Wondrous Love" (Figure 10.3, p. 187).

The influence of the commercial process has been a major part of the story of gospel music in this century, both black and white. In white gospel music the process reached a new level early in the twentieth century. Publishers such as James D. Vaughan of Lawrenceburg, Tennessee, whose business was to sell songbooks, found many ways to promote their wares. As Bill Malone has written, "Vaughan [a devout member of the Church of the Nazarene] and his gospel cohorts preached an otherworldly message, but they very astutely utilized the techniques of this world to popularize that vision" (67–68). This included by 1910 the formation of professional male quartets that toured churches and conventions, the formation of a school of music in 1911, the formation of a record company in 1922 and of a radio station, WOAN, in 1923. The Stamps-Baxter firm of Dallas, Texas, outstripped Vaughan and, according to Malone, "dominated much of the white gospel market until World War II, particularly in the region west of the Mississippi River."

CD 3/7 (3:10)
"Give the World a
Smile," by Deaton and
Yendall. The Stamps
Quartet. Recorded in
Atlanta, Georgia, 1927.

The influence of popular music was noticeable in the singing of the many male quartets that publishers sponsored. Recordings of the famous Stamps Quartet from the late 1920s show the addition of piano accompaniments that introduce ragtime figures in the breaks. The choruses (which since the days of the eighteenth-century fuging tunes had tended to involve contrapuntal devices of one kind or another) often indulged in tricky instrumental-like afterbeat effect. Sometimes whole choruses were repeated with the voices imitating banjos, as heard in the very popular "Give the World a Smile" (CD 3/7, Transcription 11.1). This banjo imitation is the kind of onomatopoeic effect for which black barbershop quartets had been famous for years, along with *a cappella* imitations of boat whistles, church bells, locomotives, brass bands, and steam calliopes (Abbott 303; for more on barbershop quartets, see pp. 210, 275–76).

Figure 11.2
"Give the World a Smile," refrain

(continued)

Figure 11.2
(continued)

Text, "Give the World a Smile"

Verse 1   Are you giving to the world a smile (sunny smile),
Helping lessen someone's dreary mile (dreary mile)?
Do you greet the world with song as thru life you pass along,
Cheering those whom you may meet along life's way?

(Refrain)

Verse 2   Just a bright and sunny smile will win (it will win)
Many souls from dreary paths of sin (paths of sin),
Lift them up on higher plain, where they hear the glad refrain
Of the smiling band of workers on life's way.

Verse 3   (voices imitating plinking sound of banjos)

The popularity of bass soloists in gospel music, still apparent in 1980s recordings of male gospel groups, goes back to this period of the publishing-house quartets. As Malone has put it, "The gospel singers learned much of their four-part harmony from the shape-note singing schools, but they also picked up elements from the barbershop quartets, the black gospel quartets, and other popular quartets of their day" (69).

The texts emphasized more down-to-earth, homely, and even topical meta-phors. As in secular country music and the blues, the train motive appeared in songs such as "Life's Railway to Heaven" by Charlie D. Tillman (who also composed that song associated more than any other in the popular mind with southern white gospel music, "Old Time Religion"). "The Glory Train" hailed Jesus as "our great conductor" who "has been this way before." The faithful are admonished: "Get your ticket and be ready, / For this train may come today . . . Have your baggage checked for glory, / So you'll meet with no delay."

Another favorite motif was the newly invented telephone, which also figured in the blues (see p. 135.) In "The Royal Telephone" of 1919 we find this chorus:

Telephone to glory, O what joy divine!
I can feel the current moving on the line;
Built by God the Father for his loved and own,
We may talk to Jesus thru this royal telephone.

Text, "The Royal
Telephone"

A close variant of "The Royal Telephone," called "Telephone to Glory," was recorded several times by black gospel singers in the 1920s (Oliver 205). The metaphor lives on: the Mighty Clouds of Joy, a present-day black gospel quartet, recorded a distant variant with the title "Call Him Up."

In place of the dour warnings that the words of the earlier four-shape-note hymns conveyed, there was more of a tendency to anticipate the joys of heaven, as in "Where We'll Never Grow Old" (1914), "When the Roll Is Called Up Yonder (I'll be there)" (1921). As previously noted in the urban revivalism of the Billy Sunday era, there was an emphasis on the semisacred "message" song, which simply advocated cheerful optimism, as in the popular "Give the World a Smile," or indulged in sentimentality, as in "If I Could Hear My Mother Pray Again."

By the 1960s, with the rewards of commercial success becoming ever larger, as the careers of successful country and rock groups showed, two distinct motivations for performing gospel music had emerged. As Malone puts it, "The sense of religious mission no doubt still burned brightly in the lives of many gospel singers, but an increasing number viewed the music as just another facet of popular music, or as an avenue for entrance into different kinds of performing careers" (113).

By the 1980s popular commercial gospel groups such as the Florida Boys, a male quintet, were most typically purveying a slick, studio-produced product, with a large pop/soft-rock backup group with drums and a mixture of electric and acoustic instruments, strangely at odds with the very conservative old-line evangelical message of the words.

On the other hand, a return to tradition is evidenced in the work of "Christian bluegrass" groups such as Doyle Lawson & Quicksilver, with their unaccompanied traditional arrangements, who are reviving, as in their *Heaven's Joy Awaits*, some of the Stamps-Baxter and James D. Vaughan songs. (See

Additional Listening.) And outside the gospel movement itself, some folk revivalists have taken a renewed interest in songs from the old seven-shape-note repertory, and it is not unusual to hear, in the old singing style, with string-band accompaniment, songs such as "The Lonesome Road," "Can the Circle Be Unbroken" (CD 3/5) in its more recent variant, "Will the Circle Be Unbroken," and of course the perennial "Amazing Grace." *The Prairie Home Companion* radio show is a good place to listen for some of these.

Black Gospel Music: The Roots

African American gospel music had its religious roots in the turn-of-the-century Holiness movement, as described in the introduction of white gospel music (see pp. 201–2). The Holiness sects are based on a highly personal, vivid, and emotional religious experience—an experience that involves, ultimately, possession by the Holy Spirit. This possession shows itself in emotionally charged expression and movement—moaning, singing, speaking in tongues, and dancing (the term *shout* can refer to a dance as well as a song). This seemingly unbridled expression—the one and only outlet for pent-up emotions in the lives of the poor of both races, who made up the majority of adherents of the Holiness sects—elicited amusement and scorn from the world at large. The derogatory term "Holy Rollers" was frequently heard. Since these believers were already among the outcasts of society, the contempt only strengthened the sense of community they felt in their worship. Though the Holiness and Pentecostal adherents were always in a minority numerically among church members, the freedom of expression that they encouraged, especially in music, had a special appeal and gave them, eventually, an influence disproportionate to their numbers. The singular fact is that it was just these scorned modes of worship, this rejected music of the disinherited, that ultimately came to influence not only a large segment of American religious music, white and black, but indirectly a great spectrum of popular music as well.

We cannot go very far in understanding the conditions under which black gospel music developed unless we understand something of the role of the black preacher. W. E. B. Du Bois said, "The Preacher is the most unique personality developed by the Negro on American soil. A leader, a politician, an orator, a 'boss,' an intriguer, an idealist—all these he is, and ever, too, the center of a group of men, now twenty, now a thousand in number" (Du Bois, Chapter 10; Oliver 140). Heilbut has pointed out the capacity for showmanship, even "clowning" on occasion (Ferris and Hart 103). In the Holiness church, all that was required to be a preacher was that one have the combination of qualities enumerated by Du Bois and that one feel the "call" to preach. An indispensable gift was the ability to elicit a response from the congregation.

As, in the course of his exhortation, the responses became more frequent and more intense, the sounds of preacher and congregation together gradually merged into song. Early entrepreneurs recorded many of these sermons-into-songs, in conditions not unlike those of the storefront churches where the actual services took place. It is estimated that over seven hundred "sermons" were recorded in the 1920s and early 1930s. Recordings in archival collections, such as "Jesus the Lord Is a Savior," give some flavor of what the Sanctified services were like. (See Additional Listening.)

The black Holiness churches welcomed the use of instruments. There were the characteristic percussion instruments (the tambourine, the triangle, and later the drums) as well as the guitar and its urban replacement, the piano. But the services could also include, especially on the recordings of the 1920s, the trumpet, the trombone, and the string bass, as can be heard in "I'm on the Battlefield for My Lord" (CD 3/8). The music, in fact, often has the sound and feel of early jazz.

CD 3/8 (2:06) "I'm on the Battlefield for My Lord," Rev. D. C. Rice and his Sanctified Congregation. Vocal group with piano, trumpet, trombone, string bass, drums, and triangle. Recorded in 1929.

To conclude that jazz influenced the music of the Sanctified churches is to get the picture as much backward as forward; they grew up together, and jazz may well owe as much to the music of the Holiness churches as it does to the streets and brothels of New Orleans. One small clue is that the traditional jazz standard "When the Saints Go Marching In" is actually a Sanctified shout. Early gospel singers such as guitar-playing Rosetta Tharpe, who came out of the Church of God in Christ, recorded "Daniel in the Lion's Den" with bass, drums, and boogie-woogie piano; and Sister Ernestine Washington recorded, among other pieces, "Does Jesus Care?" with Bunk Johnson's jazz band. (See Additional Listening.)

Black gospel music, unlike its white counterpart, was a music of the cities. Its roots can be found not only in what preachers and their congregations were doing in many humble storefront Holiness churches but also in the music of many blind street evangelists. Blind Willie Johnson (1902–50) was a street singer in Dallas. His "God Moves on the Water" is one of many songs based on the sinking of the *Titanic* in 1912. (See Additional Listening.) Paul Oliver points up an interesting contrast between the races in their responses to the *Titanic* disaster: for whites it could be accounted for by "human error or folly," whereas blacks attached far more metaphorical significance to it as "indicating the inevitability of God's judgment on the arrogance of those who believed themselves invincible" (223). Blind Willie Johnson was the religious counterpart, in style and guitar technique, to blues singers such as Blind Lemon Jefferson. Some blues singers did record gospel songs, usually under different names. Blind Lemon Jefferson's recording of "I Want to Be Like Jesus in My Heart" was released under the name of Deacon L. J. Bates, and Charley Patton recorded gospel songs as Elder J. J. Hadley. There were token releases by other blues singers as well (Oliver 202–4).

Memphis, world headquarters of the Church of God in Christ, the largest black Sanctified denomination, was a center for Sanctified music in the 1920s. For further evidence of the influence of Sanctified singing on jazz, listen to the singing of Sister Bessie Johnson, who together with Sister Melinda Taylor recorded "He Got Better Things for You" as the Memphis Sanctified Singers (CD 3/9). The growling, rasping vocal quality is exactly what jazz musicians were imitating on trumpet and trombone.

The Methodist minister and composer Charles Albert Tindley (1851/59–1933) has been called the "progenitor of black-American gospel music." In the first decade of the twentieth century he was writing songs in what became the prototypical form and style of gospel music—simple melodies and harmonies, in verse-and-chorus form. Among these were "I'll Overcome Some Day" of 1901 (the chorus of which entered, by a circuitous route, the civil rights struggle a half-century later as "We Shall Overcome") (CD 2/12, p. 103), "What Are They Doing in Heaven" of the same year (one of several songs to cross over into the white gospel tradition), "We'll Understand Better By and By" (1905), and "Stand By Me" (also 1905). The center of Tindley's work was Philadelphia, where he wrote songs for "new arrivals in the North who poured in daily, most of them poor and illiterate, and who valued highly the simple, direct, and emotional life style of which Tindley spoke" (Boyer, *Black Perspectives* 113).

By the 1920s the gospel music indigenous to the Holiness churches was beginning to be introduced to other African American denominations as well. But the phenomenal growth of modern gospel music as it is known today did not begin until the 1930s.

Modern Black Gospel Music's First Phase: The 1930s, 1940s, and 1950s

The one person most responsible for the initial propagation of modern gospel music was Thomas A. Dorsey (1899–1993). After an early career as a blues singer, composer, and pianist—as "Georgia Tom" he had played and recorded blues with Ma Rainey and Tampa Red—he was first drawn to gospel music in 1921. For a while he continued to play and record blues, but from 1932 on he devoted himself wholly to the blues' sacred counterpart. It was in that year, a year of personal tragedy, that he wrote his most famous song, "Precious Lord." Dorsey proved to be an indefatigable promoter, organizer, and manager, as well as composer, of gospel music. He published his own compositions, and went from church to church in Chicago, and later from city to city, with singers such as Sallie Martin and later Mahalia Jackson, performing and promoting gospel music. Dorsey published his songs not in book collections, as had been the case with popular sacred music up to that time, but rather (in the

manner of Tin Pan Alley) as sheet music. In his capacity as organizer and promoter, he started with Sallie Martin the National Convention of Gospel Choirs
and Choruses. "I'll Tell It Wherever I Go," which Sallie Martin recorded with
Dorsey at the piano, illustrates the seminal style of "gospel blues" in its early
stages. (See Additional Listening.)

The Era of the Gospel Divas   Thanks in part to Dorsey's promotional activity, the solo gospel singer began to assume more importance. During this first
phase of modern gospel music, it was women singers who dominated, just as in
the 1920s female singers had dominated the classic urban blues. In fact, the
two greatest influences on the first two generations of women gospel soloists
were the music of the Holiness churches and the singing of blues singers such
as Ma Rainey and Bessie Smith. (Of women singers prominent in the first
three decades of gospel music Mahalia Jackson, Rosetta Tharpe, Marion
Williams, and Ruth Davis either came out of Holiness backgrounds or were
strongly affected by the music, and Willie Mae Ford Smith joined a Holiness
church in 1939, at the age of 33.)

The first generation of singers included Roberta Martin (1907–69), who
began as the pianist for Dorsey's chorus, Mahalia Jackson (1911–72), with
whom Dorsey toured as pianist from the mid-1930s until about 1950, Willie
Mae Ford Smith (1906–94), and Sister Rosetta Tharpe (1915–73). The
second generation included such singers as Clara Ward (1924–73), Marion
Williams (1927–94), Ruth Davis (1928–70), and Albertina Walker (b. 1930).
These women developed distinctive styles that were individual blends of certain enduring characteristics of gospel singing: the bending of notes, the sliding into or between pitches, the bending of rhythms (in common with jazz
singers), the repetition of syllables or words, the interpolation of extra words
or exclamations, and a range of vocal effects that included shouting, falsetto,
and a hoarse, rasping, or growling vocal quality. Mahalia Jackson's "Didn't It
Rain" (CD 3/10) is illustrative of her distinctive style.

In the beginning the basic accompanying instrument was the piano, played
in a "gospel" style, which, quite unlike the accompaniments played for congregational hymn singing, owed a great deal to ragtime, stride piano, and other
popular styles. Soon it was common to add bass and drums to the piano; in the
1950s the electric organ became an indispensable part of the ensemble. A small
vocal group (mostly female, but occasionally including men) was frequently
added, but the soloist tended to dominate; the vocal backup group merely
added support, and reiterated key phrases of the soloist for emphasis. When
gospel music began to enter the commercial arena with recordings, radio
appearances, and tours, many soloists formed their own groups, such as the
Roberta Martin Singers, the Davis Sisters, the Clara Ward Singers, and later
the Caravans.

CD 3/10 (2:37) "Didn't It
Rain," Mahalia Jackson,
vocal, with The Mildred
Falls Trio

The Gospel Quartets   The foregoing capsule description helps to define the traditional gospel group led by the female "diva," but the other type of group important in gospel music's first phase was the male ensemble—usually a quartet that sang unaccompanied, dressed in suits and ties. The unaccompanied male gospel quartet predated modern gospel music; early quartets in what Boyer has termed the "folk" phase, up until 1930, were built on the nineteenth-century tradition of the Fisk Jubilee Singers and others. (Boyer, "Black Gospel Music"). In the period 1930–45, termed by Boyer the "gospel" or "jubilee" period, groups adopted mannerisms from the more rhapsodic aspects of Holiness singing and from the rhythmic aspects of jazz; a characteristic number would start slowly, with florid improvisation, and then work up to a highly rhythmic ending. Characteristic of this "jubilee" period is "Swing Down Chariot" of 1946 by the Golden Gate Quartet (CD 3/11).

CD 3/11 (3:29)
"Swing Down Chariot."
Golden Gate Quartet.
Vocal quartet with
piano, guitar, string
bass, and drums.
Recorded in 1946.

The roots of black gospel music in the spiritual are illustrated in comparing this with "Low Down the Chariot and Let Me Ride" (CD 1/10). The black gospel quartet is in some ways the sacred counterpart of the black barbershop quartet. In fact, the Golden Gate Jubilee Quartette (which later became the Golden Gate Quartet) originated in Eddie Griffin's Barber Shop in Norfolk, Virginia in 1930 (Abbott 292). (The secular barbershop quartet is treated in Chapter 14, pp. 275–76.)

The "jubilee" period male quartet merged imperceptibly into Boyer's next phase, that of "sweet" gospel, in which a lead singer emerged as dominant, with the rest of the group forming a close-harmony background and responding to the lead. The Dixie Hummingbirds' "When the Gates Swing Open" is representative. (See Additional Listening.)

Styles in Black Gospel Music Since Midcentury

Since the mid–twentieth century, and especially beginning in the 1970s, gospel music has evolved along two fairly distinct lines: "contemporary" and "traditional." Underneath the difference in style and sound, the basic distinction between the two types lies in the way each regards its public. For "contemporary" gospel, the public is an audience to be entertained, and perhaps soothed and comforted; for "traditional" gospel, it is a congregation to be charged with religious ecstasy.

Traditional gospel music, even on recordings, always conveys the ambience of an actual service. Even though the location may be Carnegie Hall (and it is much more apt to be an actual church), the congregation is palpably there, and participating. The "sermonette" before the song (an innovation evolved out of the old recorded preachers' sermons by Willie Mae Ford Smith, Dorothy Norwood, Inez Andrews, and other old-line gospel singers) or the pastor's exhortation is delivered over an instrumental background that merges into the next song. The instrumentation of piano, electric organ, electric guitar, electric bass, and drums is in the direct line of the tradition evolved since the 1930s. The choir, singing in an altogether homophonic texture, is an important element. Numbers now appear for chorus alone, representing a resurgence of actual choral singing in gospel music. More frequently the chorus is used for backing up the soloist, singing a verse or a chorus of the song, or sometimes repeating short phrases, in the background, under the soloist's improvisation. The soloists tend to sing in a "hard gospel" style, highly charged emotionally. The fast numbers, driven by the accompaniment (all the instruments except the organ can be considered a rhythm section), are highly rhythmic and syncopated, and often incorporate hand clapping. "I Feel the Spirit" (CD 3/12) illustrates features of traditional gospel music today.

LISTENING GUIDE

"I Feel the Spirit," Clarence Eggleton and choir.

0:00	*Instrumental introduction*
0:23	I feel the Spirit movin' in this place; [2X]
0:33	It's all over me, I can't hold my peace.
0:38	I feel the Spirit movin' in this place; [3X]
0:52	It's all over me, I can't hold my peace.
0:56	I feel the Spirit movin' in this place;
1:00	*Instrumental break*
1:20	I feel the Spirit movin' in this place; [2X]
1:30	It's all over me, I can't hold my peace.
1:34	I feel the Spirit movin' in this place; [3X]
1:49	It's all over me, I can't hold my peace.
1:53	I feel the Spirit movin' in this place;
1:58	I feel like Jeremiah; in his heart there's a burning fire; Shut up in my bones; Spirit won't leave me alone. [2X]

At this point there is a vamp, in which typically, as a means of increasing the intensity, the text becomes more condensed, with more repetition.

2:22	I feel the Spirit movin' . . . [4X]
2:40	movin' . . . [6X]
2:55	I feel like Jeremiah; in his heart there's a burning fire; Shut up in my bones; Spirit won't leave me alone. [2X]

(continued)

CD 3/12 (5:35)
"I Feel the Spirit,"
Clarence Eggleton
and choir

LISTENING
GUIDE
(continued)

3:18   I feel the Spirit movin' . . . [8X]

3:58   movin' . . . [6X]

4:09   in this place.

At this point there is an apparent *end, with applause, but the instruments pick up the momentum, and there is a reprise with even more repetition.*

4:24   I feel the Spirit movin' . . . [10X]

5:12   movin' . . . [6X]

5:25   in this place.

The intensity and momentum built up has to be heard (preferably live) to be appreciated. During the vamp the leader may go down and circulate among the congregation, and the congregation may respond to the highly charged emotional momentum established by the music and go into a shout, dancing or moving rhythmically. In a live situation this may go on for as long as half an hour before leader and ensemble bring it to a close; recordings obviously must edit these vamps.

Although there is a considerable overlap between traditional and contemporary gospel music, the latter tends to sound as if it is more at home in the concert hall than in church, and often more in the recording studio than either. The singing style and the vocal quality of both soloists and choir tend to be smoother, more polished, and more pop-oriented, with less of the emotion-driven "edge" that characterizes traditional gospel singing. Solo cuts may have a soft-rock or soft-rhythm-and-blues background, with velvet-voiced studio backup singers replacing the incisive and committed voices of the historic gospel choir. Instrumentally there is a heavy reliance on a battery of electronic keyboards and on studio electronic manipulation. Brass instruments and even a full orchestra augment or replace the basic piano-organ-drums sound of traditional gospel. Heilbut has summed it up in these words: "The eclecticism of 'contemporary gospel' derives from several sources: the academic training of many young choir directors; the example of the highly complex recording techniques of a Stevie Wonder or Michael Jackson; and the simple financial lure" (Ferris and Hart 113). "Contemporary" gospel is a product in which there is indeed a fine line, often subtly crossed, between the sacred and the secular. The secularization of which Heilbut speaks sometimes involves not only adopting the "highly complex recording techniques of a . . . Michael Jackson" but also imitating, in a muted way, the latter's sex appeal as well, as album photos of Al Green or Edwin Hawkins, with open shirt and necklace, show.

In live performances and on live recordings, "audience" has replaced "congregation." Perhaps the trend toward multiracial concert audiences accounts in part for Boyer's observation that congregational response during many contemporary gospel concerts consists of smiling, soft weeping, and clapping, most often on a primary rather than a secondary beat—that is, shunning the "backbeat" so traditional in black music. Where a section of a song would have previously elicited a moan, shout, or vocal utterance, the audience response is only applause at concerts of contemporary gospel. Boyer goes on to note the loss of "participation"—a passive role has replaced the formerly active one ("A Comparative Analysis" 143).

Andraé Crouch, one of the leaders of contemporary gospel, goes so far in the lyrics of one of his songs as to disown gospel's roots in the worship of the Holiness churches:

> You don't have to jump no pews,
> Run down no aisles,
> No chills run down your spine;
> But you know that you've been born again.
> Don't you know my hands didn't shake,
> The earth didn't quake,
> No sparks fell from the sky;
> But I know that I've been born again.

Secularization and Commercialization in African American Gospel Music

The evolution of "contemporary" gospel style, so briefly described above, is only one manifestation of what has been happening to African American gospel music since mid-century. In 1961 two significant events occurred: Mahalia Jackson sang at one of John F. Kennedy's inauguration parties, and Clara Ward and the Ward Singers started singing in nightclubs. Mahalia Jackson's appearance symbolized the widespread acceptance of gospel music, Clara Ward's its secularization. Recent developments include black gospel's move from shabby store-front churches to concert extravaganzas; the appearance of black gospel stars and groups at jazz festivals and in nightclubs; a secularizing of the material, whereby "message" songs, expressing optimistic or altruistic sentiments but avoiding the word "God" or "Jesus," could be sung to a broader audience, and thus earn both popularity and money; and a "song exchange" between gospel and secular pop music, wherein pop songs could be "gospelized" and their popularity appropriated. It must be noted however that some gospel songs have social or political "messages" having nothing to do with entertainment; "Move on Up a Little Higher," "Surely God Is Able (to carry you through)," "I'm Climbing Higher and Higher (and I won't come down)," all by the Reverend W. Herbert Brewster, and "How I Got Over" by

Clara Ward, as sung during the civil rights struggle of the 1950s, carried more than religious implications, just as spirituals had before Emancipation.

Gospel music today presents a pluralistic picture. In its commercial aspect, as represented by contemporary gospel, it now accounts for a significant segment of the American popular-music industry. At the grassroots level of church and community choirs, on the other hand, traditional gospel music is flourishing; ensembles such as the New Jerusalem Baptist Church Choir in Flint, Michigan, and the Sacramento Community Choir in California are giving live performances and producing "live" recordings that have a resounding authenticity. Gospel has become multiracial, and other Christian denominations, including such liturgically conservative ones as the Roman Catholic Church, have instituted gospel choirs, as have many colleges and universities. A network of teachers, workshops, and conventions (especially the large Gospel Music Workshop of America) is active in propagating and offering instruction in gospel music, not only in the United States, but in other countries as well. Gospel music, following jazz and rock 'n' roll, now belongs to the long succession of exports of American popular music—all of which have stemmed from African American roots.

PROJECTS

1. Make a survey of "Christian music" in the urban churches today, with emphasis on your own area if you live in a city. For each church you survey, characterize the basic repertory as being, for example, "revivalist," "traditional, with strong European influence," "folk," "pop," "ethnic," "consciously multiethnic," or whatever. Determine whether there is more than one *constituency* for music in the same church, and hence more than one distinct repertory, with perhaps even separate services for each.
2. Using W.E.B. Du Bois's description of the African American preacher in *Souls of Black Folk* as a point of departure, carry this into our own time by writing a paper on the social and political roles of the black preacher since the mid–twentieth century. Has the relationship of preacher to congregation carried over into the relationship of speaker to audience? In what ways?
3. Make a study of the music in the black churches in your area. How does it relate to the gospel music described in this chapter? What part do older hymns or spirituals play in the repertory? Are there differences in musical preferences between one denomination and another?

ADDITIONAL LISTENING

"Does Jesus Care?" Perf. Sister Ernestine Washington with Bunk Johnson's band. *The Asch Recordings 1939–1947*. Smithsonian/Folkways AA001.

"God Moves on the Water." Perf. Blind Willie Johnson. *Country Gospel Song.* Smithsonian/Folkways RF019.

Heaven's Joy Awaits. Perf. Doyle Lawson & Quicksilver. Sugarhill 3760.

"I'll Tell It Wherever I Go." Perf. Sallie Martin, vocal; Thomas A. Dorsey, piano. *Precious Lord: The Great Gospel Songs of Thomas A. Dorsey.* Sony 57164.

"Jesus the Lord Is a Savior." *An Introduction to Gospel Song.* Smithsonian/Folkways RF005. Includes three more sermons. The *Anthology of American Folk Music* (Smithsonian/Folkways 40090) includes two sermons by the Reverend Gates and one each by the Reverend McGee, the Reverend Moses Mason, and the Reverend D. C. Rice.

Orchestral Set No. 2. By Charles Ives. Polygram Records 466745.

"When the Gates Swing Open." Perf. The Dixie Hummingbirds. *The Essential Gospel Sampler.* Sony 57163.

PART IV

POPULAR SECULAR MUSIC

A by-product of the growth of cities, and the consequent specialization of human endeavor, is the evolution of a popular culture (produced for the masses of the people by specialists) as distinct from a folk culture (made for people in smaller groups, or cultural "villages," by people who are themselves members of the village). If we illustrate this by an analogy with the production of another commodity we consume in great quantities—our daily bread—a first stage in this evolution is reached when the home-baked is replaced by the store-bought. A second stage is reached when that baked in the neighborhood bakery is replaced by the mass-produced plastic-wrapped article for sale in the supermarket; large, efficient baking plants serve huge areas, and the bread looks and tastes about the same whether we buy it in Arizona or Vermont.

Popular music requires a certain critical mass of population to support the commercial process devoted to its production. It will emerge whenever sufficient numbers of people are willing to pay for an art that has the look or sound of the familiar (it almost always has some points of resemblance either with folk art or with the well-accepted fine art that people know), that is made easily available by the mechanisms of its commercial distribution, and that adds something desirable and even necessary to their lives without being too difficult to understand. Its primary purpose is to entertain.

Except for the products of the Yankee singing-school composers described in Chapter 10, Americans did not begin to make their own distinctive kind of popular music until the Jacksonian era—an era of cultural as well as political populism. It was not until the end of the nineteenth century that the making of popular music became an industry—an industry in which the United States has for a century been the undisputed leader.

Popular art is no longer ignored by scholars and observers of culture. Popular music (as a component of popular culture) is a sensitive indicator of the temperament and preoccupations of a people. Nor is popular art ignored any longer by "serious" artists. It has become subject matter itself. We have seen this come about fairly recently in the visual arts, but Charles Ives was already composing music that was "about" popular music in the first two decades of the twentieth century.

Because of the vast market, those who can successfully create this kind of music are naturally very well paid for it. But the gift of creating something that many people will regard as memorable, and that will be immediately and

State Historical Society of Missouri, Columbia

The boatman's reputation for merrymaking in spite of a grueling occupation inspired popular secular art such as George Caleb Bingham's *The Jolly Flatboatmen* (1846), and the minstrel tune "De Boatman's Dance."

widely in demand, is mysterious and rare, and there are never very many around at any given time who can do it extremely well.

The distinctions made between popular music and folk, ethnic, or classical music are distinctions of *function*, not of quality or ultimate value. The superlative popular song, the "evergreen"—the one song in perhaps a hundred thousand that transcends the ephemeral nature of the genre, and has that imponderable property of resonating in the memory and feelings of generation after generation—is surely one of the glories of American music.

12 Secular Music in the Cities from Colonial Times to the Jacksonian Era

Musical life in the largest American cities (Philadelphia, New York, Boston, Charleston, and Baltimore) during the colonial and federal periods was by no means primitive or dull. Music historians, together with performers specializing in the re-creation of early music, have illuminated the existence of a lively and varied musical culture in our growing urban centers. To re-create a sense of what this musical life was like will be the purpose of this chapter.

CONCERTS AND DANCES

The giving of public concerts for which people pay admission presupposes a certain critical mass of population that will include enough people with the means, the leisure, and the inclination to support such endeavors. For the first hundred years of eastern-seaboard settlement, that was not the case. But by the middle of the eighteenth century, public concerts were being given fairly regularly in Philadelphia, New York, Boston, and Charleston. (Oscar Sonneck, pioneer historian of American music, determined that the first "concert of music on sundry instruments" was given in Boston in 1731.)

What were these concerts like? Many of the early ones would hardly fit our notion of a formal concert of classical music; the music itself was varied and popular, but in addition the program could include dramatic recitations, card tricks, balancing acts ("a dance upon wire"), and other "Manly Feats of Activity." Another pleasurable aspect of concert life was the outdoor concert in the summer months, modeled after English practice. Two attractions existed then that have been familiar to patrons of outdoor summer concerts ever since — fireworks and ice cream!

Dancing in the Eighteenth and Early Nineteenth Centuries

That the range of pleasures offered by these events was agreeably broad is demonstrated by the fact that the concert proper was nearly always followed by "proper music . . . to wait upon such ladies and gentlemen, as may choose to dance." "The concert will terminate by a ball" was the pleasant and in fact

nearly obligatory promise put forth in most advertisements. The kind of dancing that would have gone on at these balls varied with time and place. In colonial times, especially among the landed gentry of the southern colonies, it is
likely that the elegant *minuet,* and possibly also the more intricate *gavotte,* would
be danced. After the Revolution, these dances, with their suggestions of
monarchy and aristocracy, fell out of favor. The *country dances,* on the other
hand, enjoyed the widest popularity throughout the period. Of English origin,
they were done in all the colonies and states, by all classes of society, in urban
as well as rural settings. A French importation, the *cotillion,* became the
quadrille (which in time gave rise to the more typically rural *square dance*). Both
the country dance, with its typical lining up of dancers in opposing rows (as in
the later *Virginia reel*), and the quadrille, with its square set of eight dancers,
were social dances, as contrasted with later couples dances such as the *waltz*
and the *galop.*

The music for country dances came from a variety of sources. Fortunately
some of it has been preserved in manuscript books, mainly for the use of the
fifers and fiddlers who played for dancing. Many tunes used for eighteenth-
century dancing are still familiar to us today, including "The Rakes of Mal-
low," "The Irish Washerwoman," "Soldier's Joy" (which in its countless
variants became a staple in the fiddler's repertory; see p. 13 and CD 1/6), and
"The College Hornpipe," better known to us today as "The Sailor's Hornpipe"
(CD 3/13, Transcription 12.1).

CD 3/13 (1:09)
"College Hornpipe,"
Rodney Miller, fiddle

Transcription 12.1
"College Hornpipe"

The binary form is exactly that of "Soldier's Joy" (Listening Guide, p. 14): An 8-bar first strain, repeated, followed by a "high" strain, repeated, then the whole thing played again. There is a noticeable "swing" to Rodney Miller's interpretation—that is, there is an emphasis on, and an almost imperceptible lengthening of, the first of each pair of eighth notes. This varies with individual fiddlers.

The Performers

Who were the musicians that furnished the music for the first hundred years of American urban musical life? Contemporary advertisements show those who plied the trade of "music master" to have been of a hardy, resourceful, and versatile breed. In addition to being music masters, many were also dancing masters and fencing masters; they were thus equipped to minister to more than one need of the polished aristocrat of the day, especially in the southern colonies. Many also offered a variety of musical instruments for sale—as well as tobacco and other sundries. It is known that a great many African Americans were accomplished musicians and played for dances in the northern as well as the southern colonies and states. Some of the scant information we have on this subject comes from contemporary newspapers, in advertisements about slaves—either "for sale" or "runaway." These indicate that the most common instrument played was the fiddle, but the fife, the drum, the flute, the banjo, and the French horn also appear in the lists (Southern, Chapters 2 and 3).

The child prodigy was evidently a great attraction at concerts, promoted by parents who were professional performers and who seized the opportunity to capitalize on an unsophisticated public's curiosity and eagerness to be amazed. The ages of such children were naturally featured in their announcements. A concert by "P. Lewis, Professor of Music," who presented an entire program in Boston in 1819 in which his children—aged 8, 7, and 4—were the sole performers, was exceptional only because the children were so young and so numerous.

The century 1730–1830 was a period of gradual transition from the amateur to the professional. Though the word "amateur" does not appear at first, his identity was made plain by the use of the word "gentleman," as distinguished from the professional, who was designated as "professor." By this the "gentleman amateur" not only maintained his distinction of class but also insulated himself from judgment by professional standards. An advertisement of a concert in Charleston in 1772 makes both these points plainly: "The vocal part by a gentleman, who does it merely to oblige on this occasion." After the privations of the Revolution had passed, the flow of professional immigrants increased, mostly on account of the increased appetite for musical theater in the cities. This resulted in the gradual reduction of the amateur, "gentleman" or not, to a distinctly subordinate role in the growing musical life of the cities (Crawford).

The Composers

Who were the composers of this music? Late in the eighteenth century it began to be common to print programs, especially in the newspapers. We find, as might be expected, that the composers were mostly European; Haydn, Pleyel, Handel, Stamitz, and Corelli appear frequently. After the Revolution, with the coming into prominence of the professional musician, we find the names of those, either immigrants or native-born, who must be recognized as the first American composers, including among the native-born Francis Hopkinson, Samuel Holyoke, and Oliver Shaw, and among the immigrants Alexander Reinagle, James Hewitt, and Rayner Taylor.

Concert Music

The programs played at these concerts were much more varied than we are accustomed to today. As the frequent appearance of the phrase "Concert [earlier spelled "Consort"] of Vocal and Instrumental Musick" indicates, songs were nearly always included. The instrumental pieces were overtures, symphonies (not usually performed in their entirety, as later audiences would come to expect), sonatas, and concertos or solos for various instruments. Popular solo instruments were the violin, the guitar, the "German flute" (the transverse flute, in contrast to the recorder), the French horn, and the harp.

Programmatic pieces intended to depict momentous events began to appear toward the end of the eighteenth century. (Those events were usually battles but sometimes were travels by sea or land, which in those days were also momentous and could be equally hazardous.) *The Battle of Prague,* by the Bohemian-born Frantisek Koczwara (Franz Kotzwara), showed up on numerous programs for half a century and was a kind of prototype. American contributions to the genre were represented by *The Battle of Trenton,* a pastiche arranged from various sources by James Hewitt (when French titles became popular, this or a similarly inspired piece appeared on programs as *La Bataille de Trenton*), and after the French Revolution *The Demolition of the Bastille,* by John Berkenhead. These programmatic pieces persisted well into the nineteenth century. The best sampling of concert music of the period is to be found on *Music of the Federal Era* (New World 80299), which treats both vocal and instrumental music, including an excerpt from the ubiquitous *The Battle of Prague.* It does not accurately reflect the *proportion* of American music on concert programs of the colonial period, which were dominated by European music.

The Audiences

What were the audiences for these concerts like? For one thing, they could be noisy—though not as noisy as theater audiences. Nevertheless, the admonition by the performer who "finds himself obliged to request that silence may be observed during his performance" was not unusual. Audiences could even be rowdy; one concert manager advertised that "every possible precaution will be used to prevent disorder and irregularity," and another promised that a "number of constables will attend to preserve order."

On another point, it is clear that audiences did not represent the broad spectrum of the populace at large—an advertisement in Charleston in 1799 makes it clear that "persons of color" will not be admitted, for example. And from the same city in 1782 we find an announcement to the effect that "gentlemen of the navy, army [referring to officers during the British occupation of the city] and the most respectable part of town" would be admitted. It is clear that concerts, at least in the early part of the period, were primarily for "gentlemen." "Ladies" typically were admitted on the "gentleman's" ticket, sometimes two for each.

BANDS AND MILITARY MUSIC

CD 3/14 (1:12)
"Lady Hope's Reel,"
American Fife Ensemble

The functions of military music throughout history have been manifold: to dignify ceremonial functions, to lift morale, to enable soldiers to march in step together, and, of supreme practical importance, to convey signals and commands. The last two needs, essential but utilitarian, were met by the simplest means—that which has long been known as *field music*. For eighteenth-century foot soldiers this meant drums and fifes, which were incorporated into each company unit. The fifers were often young boys. Collections of music for the fife existed in print and manuscript in the eighteenth century, and the tunes were often those of songs or dances of the period. "Lady Hope's Reel" (CD 3/14) was one such tune. It is shown in the first two lines of Figure 12.1 as it was written down by a fifer in the Revolutionary War, Giles Gibbs, Jr., who was seventeen years old when he copied out these tunes in the summer of 1777. He was captured and killed by a British raiding party in 1780. Transcription 12.2 presents the tune as edited, with reference to other sources, for a modern edition of *Giles Gibbs, Jr.: His Book for the Fife*.

CD 3/15 (1:24)
"Washington's March."
1794. The Liberty Tree
Wind Players: two
oboes, bassoon, two
French horns.

To fulfill more elaborate functions, larger ensembles, known as *bands of music*, were formed. The basic makeup was a pair of oboes, a pair of French horns, and one or two bassoons, often with a pair of clarinets either replacing or supplementing the oboes. "Washington's March" (one of many to bear this title) illustrates the sound (CD 3/15).

Figure 12.1
"Lady Hope's Reel"—a song-and-dance tune turned military field music—as written down by fifer Giles Gibbs, Jr. during the Revolutionary War.

(From His Fife Book, Giles Gibbs, Jr. Facsimile courtesy The Connecticut Historical Society.)

The Connecticut Historical Society, Hartford

Transcription 12.2
"Lady Hope's Reel" in modern notation

This was a kind of ensemble well known in Europe, and masters such as Haydn and Mozart wrote a considerable amount of what was basically out-door music for this ensemble, or augmented versions of it. "Bands of music" were usually employed by the regimental officers themselves and were used on social as well as military occasions. Made up of fairly skilled musicians, who often played stringed instruments as well, they came to play a rather promi-nent role in the musical life of the times, especially during the time of the Rev-olution, which, in the cities (especially those occupied by the British), was not always marked by great austerity. These bands played for military ceremonies and parades, at which the public were often spectators. They also played for dances for the officers and their ladies, and even gave public concerts, and on occasion played in the theaters.

This is but the first installment on the subject of the American band, an ensemble of importance throughout our history. For the continued story of the band in America after the Jacksonian era, see page 277.

MUSICAL THEATER

The musical theater, in its many varied forms, was the institution upon which most of the musical life in the cities centered in this period, especially after the Revolution. It was usually the theater that employed those professional musicians who were active in the United States, and that attracted performers, composers, and impresarios from Europe (mostly from England).

In the eighteenth century, music was a nearly universal accompaniment to theatrical performances of all kinds. Even what we would regard today as straight drama (the plays of Shakespeare, for example) was usually presented with interpolated songs, dances, and incidental music. What is generally regarded as the first theater in the colonies was built in Williamsburg, Virginia, in 1716, and there is evidence that musicians were employed in this enterprise from the very beginning (Mates 40). Furthermore, it has been shown that the majority of stage works produced were actually "musicals"—belonging to one of the many various, confusing, and overlapping types that will be alluded to presently.

But if music was nearly always present in the theater, and its presence taken for granted, it was the most ephemeral ingredient of any production, and its providers were subordinate and often anonymous. The music for operas, or related musical genres, was often appropriated from other sources to begin with; it was also frequently changed from production to production, and from city to city, as the show traveled. The music was not usually published, and it was subsequently often lost altogether. From the truly impressive number of musical stage works presented in America in the century between 1730 and 1830 a disappointingly small amount of the actual music has survived.

Theatrical Genres

There existed in this period a vast array of entertainments in which music was a major ingredient. Until about 1800, the forms we would most recognize today as "musicals" were the famous ballad opera and its often less precisely defined successors, the pastiche opera and the comic opera. What they had in common was spoken dialogue, which was interspersed with songs, and sometimes with dances and choruses. The music was in a style familiar to its public. For the most part the characters and the situations were drawn from everyday life.

The original ballad opera was the famous *The Beggar's Opera,* first performed in London in 1728. With its already-popular tunes, its memorable low-life characters, and its satirization of the conventions of the imported upper-class Italian opera of its day (which it nearly put out of business for a time), it was an instant success and was soon widely imitated. Though the initial intensity of its popularity, and the heyday of ballad opera in general, was over in London in a decade or so, a certain few operas of this genre proved to be amazingly long-lived, especially in America. *The Beggar's Opera* itself was performed in Providence, Rhode Island, by a "Sett of Inhabitants" (amateurs) at least as early as 1746, and by a professional company in New York by 1750 (McKay 140; Sonneck 15). Julian Mates has written that "it was *The Beggar's Opera,* in most places, which introduced the musical to America" (142). It was a staple of the repertory through the remainder of the eighteenth century and has been revived, in various forms, ever since.

By 1800 ballad operas and pastiches were no longer being written, and a new genre, the *melodrama,* appeared that coexisted with comic opera for the rest of the period with which this chapter deals. The melodrama introduced wordless instrumental music as an accompaniment to stage action. An American "Operatic Melo-Drame" that has survived is *The Indian Princess, or La Belle Sauvage,* first performed in Philadelphia in 1808. It is based on an American subject—the story of Captain John Smith and Pocahontas.

Captain John Smith and his band of English adventurers have landed on the banks of the Powhatan River, in what is now Virginia. They sing a chorus of rejoicing on their safe arrival (CD 3/16).

> CD 3/16 (2:02)
> "Chorus of Adventurers," from *The Indian Princess.* Music by John Bray. Text by James Nelson Barker.

Alice (wife of one of Smith's yeomen) *Chorus*	Jolly comrades, join the glee,
	Chorus it right cheerily, (*etc.*)
	Jolly comrades, join the glee,
	Chorus it right cheerily, (*etc.*)
	For the tempest's roar is heard no more,
	But gaily we tread the wish'd-for shore:
	Jolly comrades, join the glee,
	Chorus it right cheerily, (*etc.*)
	For past are the perils of the blust'ring sea. (*etc.*)

> Text (Barker), "Chorus of Adventurers," from *The Indian Princess*

In each of the three acts of *The Indian Princess* there is, as the defining feature of melodrama, music to accompany stage action, as for example "Smith brought in prisoner," "Smith is led to the block," "The Princess leads Smith to the throne," "She supplicates the King for his pardon," and "Smith is pardoned—general joy diffused." Also of interest is the inclusion of the Irishman, Larry, and his lament—an early appearance of the ethnic characters that were such a feature of the popular musical theater in the late nineteenth century. (See Additional Listening.)

Political independence of the colonies from England was declared in 1776, but cultural independence evolved much more slowly. For three-quarters of a century more, the legacy of English comic opera, with its comic characters, its homely but pungent satire, and its popular, folklike songs, was entertaining Americans, if not continuously in the large cities of the eastern seaboard, then in crude, sparsely documented, but keenly enjoyed performances in frontier towns and cities. The tenacity of the pieces themselves was amazing. An example is *The Poor Soldier* (a favorite of George Washington), written by an Irish playright, John O'Keeffe, and first performed in London in 1783. It reached the United States in 1785, and after a successful New York run of nineteen performances by the famous Old American Company, it was taken on the road by that company. Thereafter, until the end of the eighteenth century, hardly a year went by without a performance of *The Poor Soldier* somewhere, by some company. In 1801 it was done in Cincinnati—the first play performed in the Northwest Territory—and continued to be played throughout the Ohio Valley for twenty years. *The Poor Soldier* was part of the American theatrical scene in one form or another almost until the Civil War; the same was true of *Love in a Village*, both thriving alongside the circus and the minstrel show (see pp. 231ff.).

In addition to the comic operas, there was a bewildering variety of theatrical entertainments, all of which employed music in some form. Theatrical presentations hardly ever consisted of just a single play, and could go on for four or five hours! There were shorter "afterpieces," sometimes known as *farces*, that followed the main play or opera. *Interludes* were even slighter pieces that went between the acts of longer works. In addition there were forms such as the *pantomime*, in which stage action and speech were accompanied by wordless music. A species of pantomime popular in America featured the old stock comic figures of the *commedia dell'arte*, especially that of Harlequin. Like a character in a sitcom, Harlequin appears in many settings, in pieces with titles such as "Harlequin Doctor," "Harlequin Barber," "Harlequin Balloonist," "Harlequin Pastry-cook."

Theaters and Audiences

The first theatrical performances in the colonies were given in buildings made for other purposes—often in taverns or warehouses (though not, of course, in churches). The first musical in America, in 1735, was given in the Courtroom in Charleston, South Carolina. By midcentury, theaters had been built in most cities. The space for the audience, according to a plan that remained basically unaltered to the twentieth century, was divided into three distinct parts: at the bottom level was the "pit" (now called the "orchestra"); above that, in a horse-shoe shape around the walls, were one or more tiers of boxes; and above the boxes was the gallery. The distribution of the audience was rigidly defined: "ladies and gentlemen in the boxes, the pit occupied almost entirely by unattached gentlemen, and the gallery 'reserved for the rabble'" (Mates 64). An announcement of 1759 quotes the following prices: "Box, 8 shillings. Pit, 5 shillings. Gallery, 2 shillings" (Sonneck 26).

The behavior of audiences was, by our standards, notoriously bad. There was loud talking and often card playing in the boxes, and coming and going, with the slamming of doors. Prostitutes, who used the theater (in Sonneck's words) "as a kind of stock exchange," were by custom assigned the upper boxes. Liquor was served to the "unattached gentlemen" in the pit. It was not until the end of the century that the custom of allowing some of the audience to sit on the stage during the performance was abolished. But the greatest disturbances came from the gallery. It was customary for people in the gallery to interrupt the orchestra's performance by shouting down requests for popular tunes—requests that, if not complied with to their satisfaction, would result in loud demonstrations. A letter to a New York newspaper as late as 1802 describes the behavior of the gallery "gods": "The mode by which they issue their mandates is stamping, hissing, roaring, whistling; and, when the musicians are refractory, groaning in cadence." The habit of the gallery's throwing objects at the orchestra, and into the pit, was notorious. "As soon as the curtain was down, the *gods* in the galleries would throw apples, nuts, bottles and glasses on the stage and into the orchestra." Mates quotes a report of a performance in 1794 "when half the instruments in the orchestra were broken by missiles from the upper reaches of the theater" (73). Thieves and pickpockets in the theaters were common. Feelings in the audience (often motivated by the volatile political issues of the day) ran high, especially in the federal era and after the French Revolution; certain tunes were associated with certain factions (pro- or anti-Federalist, pro- or anti-French, and so on), so that managers and orchestra leaders had to be extremely judicious in the choice of music, in order not to provoke the riots that were all too common in the theaters of the day.

POPULAR SONG

Popular song—enjoyed by the general populace and not associated with the stage or the concert hall—is at once the most widespread kind of music making and the most difficult to chronicle. Secular songs were not published complete with lyrics and music together until the last decade of the eighteenth century. Before that time, popular songs were disseminated in print for the most part by the publication of the words alone, either as single-sheet *broadsides,* or in collections called *songsters* (see p. 11). By the time of the Revolution, newspapers, of which there were a great many in the colonies, had become another medium for the publication of lyrics, especially topical verses dealing with the patriotic and political matters that were of so much concern at the time. Gillian Anderson, examining issues of 126 newspapers, found nearly 1,500 such lyrics printed during the ten-year period 1783–93 (Anderson). It is not possible to determine now whether all these versifications (often crude by literary standards) were in fact meant to be sung, but the strength of the ballad tradition, the number of tunes known to be in wide circulation, and the fact that in many cases the names of the tunes were given justify our including this vast output in our consideration of popular song. Many patriotic songs, including "Yankee Doodle" and the many sets of words associated with it, were first disseminated in this manner.

One very popular song that was parodied in broadsides of the time was "The Dusky Night" or "A-Hunting We Will Go." The tune is given in Figure 12.2 as it appeared in a copybook of 1797.

The Connecticut Historical Society, Hartford

Here is the text of the original version of the song, as used in a revival of *The Beggar's Opera* in England:

> The Dusky Night rides down the Sky,
> When wakes the Rosey Morn,
> The Hounds all join the Jovial cry, (2X)
> The Huntsman winds his Horn. (2X)
>
> *(Chorus)*
>
> Then a Hunting let us go. (4X)

The broadside parody, attacking the British desire to raise more revenue from the colonies, appeared in journals of the day in New York and Philadelphia. Known as the "Junto Song" (CD 12/5), it substitutes "A-taxing we will go" for the original words of the chorus.

Sidebar (left margin):

CD 3/17 (0:50)
"Junto Song" (excerpt), a parody on "A-Hunting We Will Go." 1775. Seth McCoy, tenor; James Richman, harpsichord.

Figure 12.2
A version of "The Dusky Night" ("A-Hunting We Will Go") as it appears in a copybook dated 1797. Later transformed into "A-Taxing We Will Go," the popular tune was among many that served as models for parody in the nineteenth century.

Text, "The Dusky Night" ("A-Hunting We Will Go")

'Tis money makes the member vote,
And sanctifies our ways;
It makes the patriot turn his coat (2x)
And money we must raise. (2x)

Text, "Junto Song"
("A-Hunting We
Will Go")

(Chorus)

And a-taxing we will go,
A-taxing we will go. (3x)
One single thing untax'd at home,
Old England could not shew,
For money we abroad did roam, (2x)
And thought to tax the *new*. (2x)

(Chorus)

This is a colonial example of a protest song (see p. 97). It is another example of the parodying of an already familiar song, as with the "Pittsburgh" parody of the "Crawdad Song" (CD 2/10, pp. 100–101).

There was no very clear dividing line between sacred and secular in this period, and religion was often invoked in political and military struggles. William Billings's "Chester," especially with the updated topical verses added for its second version of 1778, is said to have been the most popular song of the Revolutionary War. (See CD 2/35, p. 181.)

The turn of the century saw the beginnings of change, gradual but significant, in American urban secular music. The publishing of songs individually, rather than in sets, marked the beginning of sheet music, which became, during the nineteenth century, the basis for the entire popular-music industry, known later as Tin Pan Alley. In the first quarter of the nineteenth century, the growth in sheer volume of music published was in marked contrast to the last quarter of the eighteenth; in the period 1801–25 nearly ten thousand titles appeared of secular music alone (Wolfe). The range of songs was broad—from topical songs on political or patriotic themes, crude but timely, to settings of the poetry of Shakespeare, Sir Walter Scott, or Thomas Moore. This very breadth was symptomatic of a divergence of taste that was to lead, as the century progressed, to the fragmentation of our musical culture.

▬ PROJECTS

1. As revealed in the chapter, audiences in the eighteenth century were often inconsiderate and ill-behaved. From personal observation, write a paper on the behavior of present-day audiences for a variety of events in a variety of locations: a classical concert, a jazz concert, a rock concert, a concert of folk music, and so on. To what would

you attribute the differences, both between the eighteenth and the twentieth centuries, and between various kinds of contemporary events?

2. Sketch a plot and scenario for a modern-day "ballad opera," dealing in a comical and even satirical way with some current issue or event. Read the texts of several ballad operas in preparation for this; the scenes should be short and the characters few, and allowance should be made for the inclusion of "airs," which can be parodies of existing popular songs.

3. Study the modern edition of *Disappointment: or, The Force of Credulity* (Madison, WI: A-R Editions, 1976), an eighteenth-century ballad opera that was not performed until 1937! Read the two articles on the subject by Carolyn Rabson in *American Music* (vol. 1, no. 1 [Spring 1983], pp. 12ff, and vol. 2, no. 1 [Spring 1984], pp. 1ff). Write an article, in a lively journalist style, describing the piece and its history.

▬ ADDITIONAL LISTENING

The Birth of Liberty: Music of the American Revolution. New World 80276.

Come and Trip It: Instrumental Dance Music 1780s–1920s. New World 80293.

John Bray: The Indian Princess. New World 80232.

Music of the Federal Era. New World 80299.

CHAPTER

13 Popular Musical Theater from the Jacksonian Era to the Present

The age of Andrew Jackson (president 1829–37) was characterized by westward expansion and a new degree of political populism and marked the beginning of a new era of *cultural* populism as well. One useful yardstick of this new populism was the music publishing industry, which was expanding rapidly and catering to a much broader segment of the people. New methods of lithography made possible the use of black-and-white illustrations in sheet music in the late 1820s, and colored illustrations in the 1840s—developments that were clearly linked to a growing popular market, as can be seen in the popular nature and appeal of illustrated sheet music published in the 1820s and 1830s. Thus the period from 1820 to 1840, which saw the admission of three new western states into the union (Missouri, Arkansas, and Michigan), the opening of the Erie Canal, and the construction of the Baltimore and Ohio Railroad to carry paying passengers as far west as Harpers Ferry, also saw the mass publication of sentimental popular favorites such as "Woodman! Spare That Tree!"—and also, for less genteel tastes, "Massee Georgee Washington and General Lafayette," "My Long-Tail Blue," "Jim Crow," and "Zip Coon"—all illustrated with blackface figures with exaggerated features, dress, and poses (Nathan 35–58).

As the country was expanding westward, so were its cities growing rapidly, both on the more settled eastern seaboard and in the Ohio and Mississippi valleys. And as the cities grew, so did the number and size of the theaters, and the audience for the vast array of theatrical entertainments that we noted in the last chapter—comic operas, musical romances, melodramas, farces, and pantomimes. Two forms in particular—the *olio*, a kind of variety show that predated vaudeville, and the *circus*, which had incorporated comic song-and-dance acts into its original format—prepared the way for the first of a succession of truly indigenous forms of popular musical entertainment.

MINSTRELSY AND MUSICAL ENTERTAINMENT BEFORE THE CIVIL WAR

The first of these indigenous forms, and one that swept the country by mid-century, was the blackface minstrel show. It was based on what had become by then a common source of entertainment among the broader masses, both in America and in England: the exaggerated portrayal of any exotic people—rural people, Irish people, German people, Jewish people, and, as early as the eighteenth century, African people.

The faculty of black people for spontaneous song and dance, and for unbridled comedy, was well known to observers such as Lewis Paine. A white man from Rhode Island, Paine went to the South for an extended stay on business and was sentenced to prison there for helping a slave to escape. In Georgia in the 1840s, he described the festivities after a corn shucking.

> The fiddler walks out, and strikes up a tune; and at it they go in a regular tear-down dance; for here they are at home. . . . I never saw a slave in my life but would stop as if he were shot at the sound of a fiddle; and if he has a load of two hundred pounds on his head, he will begin to dance. One would think they had steam engines inside of them, to jerk them about with so much power; for they go through more motions in a minute, than you could shake two sticks at in a month; and of all comic actions, ludicrous sights, and laughable jokes, and truly comic songs, there is no match for them (Southern 91).

It is clear from this that there was abundant material here for imitation by white entertainers, once they saw its potential. The original black minstrelsy was an informal, spontaneous, and exuberant affair of the plantation. But its reputation spread. Thus it came about that the native songs, dances, and comedy of the slaves first reached the general American public in the form of parodies by white entertainers.

Blackface Minstrelsy in Current Critical Scholarship

Before dealing in some detail with a form of entertainment that enjoyed unprecedented popularity for over half a century, especially among the American working class, and the shadow of whose influence in American culture can be traced for another half-century (and as some would have it, can be detected even today), let us note another phenomenon: blackface minstrelsy has claimed an unprecedented amount of attention from scholars in the last half-century, and especially from those whose works have been published just within the past decade. A glance at the reading lists for this chapter in the Additional Reading, by no means exhaustive, reveals the inclusion of five books on the subject published in the 1990s, each by a prestigious university press. All include the word "blackface" in their titles. Why this intense interest, and what are the conclusions to be drawn from it?

The word "blackface," in all its ramifications, is surely the key to the answer, which has to do with a broadening, and brooding, concern over racism, and more recently over class and gender discrimination. Current scholarly writing exhibits a wide gamut. Nearly universal condemnation is typified in some of the generalizations made by Eric Lott, who begins the first chapter of his *Love and Theft* by hailing as the "current consensus on the subject" Frederick Douglass's assessment of blackface imitators as "the filthy scum of white society, who have stolen from us a complexion denied to them by nature, in which to make money, and pander to the corrupt taste of their white fellow citizens." To this are added the ingredients of racial politics—"half a century of inurement to the uses of white supremacy" (a quote from Alexander Saxton)—and sexual politics—characterizing blackface minstrelsy as arising "from a white obsession with black (male) bodies" (Lott 3).

Indeed, the popular form did employ the most negative and repugnant racial stereotypes. This is visibly evident in the nineteenth century songbook and sheet-music covers. (See Bean 111–19, with examples from 1827 to 1902.) The stereotypes are not entirely absent even from late-nineteenth-century stage works by African American composers themselves—works that represented a significant step *out* of minstrelsy. (For some rather uncomfortable-to-listen-to evidence, hear "Darktown Is Out Tonight" from *Clorindy, the Origin of the Cakewalk* of 1898, by Will Marion Cook; see Additional Listening.) The shadow of blackface minstrelsy was still present in *Shuffle Along* of 1921, by Sissle and Blake.

But minstrelsy, as America's first popular mass entertainment of the nineteenth century, is, like rock in the twenty-first, too pervasive and complex to be adequately characterized by a single solely negative view. As for the long and mixed harvest for African Americans themselves, Mel Watkins writes that "few readily affirm that it was partially through opposition to [minstrelsy's] distortion of black cultural forms that authentic African-American arts evolved and flourished as perhaps the most influential cultural expression of the twentieth century. . . . The minstrel stage established the platform on which the authentic African American would evolve within America's oppressive racial environment, and nearly all early twentieth-century black performers cut their teeth in that venue" (Bean ix–x).

Another point is that white minstrelsy incorporated satire and commentary on other minorities as they came into notice, and other issues as well—and this without giving up the blackface, an important function of which had been "to give the minstrel a position similar to the classical fool" (Toll 161). Even before the Civil War, minstrels had lampooned opera and classical drama (through parody), women's rights, the Irish, the Chinese, the Gold Rush, and public figures such as P. T. Barnum and Jenny "Leather-lungs" Lind. After the Civil War there were many other targets—the Germans, the American Indians, the Japanese, "city slickers," immoral and filthy urban conditions ("at least there was not a single bug in the house; all of them were married and had children"). (See Toll 160–87.)

Then the musician will always, in assessing the legacy of minstrelsy, remember the host of good tunes, both sprightly and sentimental, without which American music would be much the poorer: "Old Zip Coon" (better known as "Turkey in the Straw"), "Buffalo Gals," "The Yellow Rose of Texas," "Old Dan Tucker," "The Blue Tail Fly," "De Boatmen's Dance," and the many familiar songs by Stephen Foster, the most popular on the early minstrel stage being "Camptown Races," "Old Folks at Home," "Nelly Bly," "Old Uncle Ned," "Nelly Was a Lady," and "Hard Times" (CD 3/30, pp. 266–67). (See Winans in Bean 141ff.)

Finally, we must return to the basic fact of blackface minstrelsy's popularity among the mass of the American people over a span of generations. Living for a time as a teenager in a rural working-class community, the author remembers taking part in plans to put on, for a benefit of some sort, an amateur minstrel show. Had the performance actually come off, the likelihood is that the reaction would have been simply good-natured enjoyment, by audience and performers alike, of a culturally familiar entertainment and that we would have been too innocent to realize that we were supporting white supremacy or participating in a "theft" of black culture, much less that we were experiencing "white racial dread" of black male bodies.

The Beginnings of Minstrelsy

Impersonations on the stage of the black man by the white were already taking place in the eighteenth century, both here and in England. Dale Cockrell has broadened considerably the conventional received opinion on this subject by substantiating that there was indeed a tradition of blackface on the early American stage, both in comedy and in tragedy (13–29). (Shakespeare's *Othello* was "the most popular legitimate blackface entertainment" of the period Cockrell surveyed, 1716–1843. He found 425 documented performances, dating from 1751, in most of which a white actor would play the hero in blackface.) But even more fascinating is Cockrell's documenting of "blackface in the streets." For example, white *callithumpians* (riotous working-class bands) "often masked in chimney soot and grease, regularly took to the byways of New York, Philadelphia, Boston, and elsewhere during the 1820s–1840s, generally at the time of New Year's." Outlandishly dressed, and with drums, whistles, and noisemakers, they raised havoc of all kinds. This was but one of a number of festivities, some particularly associated with either Christmas or the pre-Lenten season of Carnival. In "inversion" festivities (seasonal rituals in which a slave selected by the slaves themselves would become "master"), some of the black retinue would wear whiteface masks (Cockrell 32).

Two American entertainers, George Washington Dixon (1808–61) and Thomas Dartmouth "Daddy" Rice (1808–60), did blackface song-and-dance routines in the 1820s and 1830s. Dixon introduced the songs "Long Tail Blue" (referring to the blue swallowtail coat associated with the black urban dandy) and "Coal Black Rose." Rice was famous for his song-and-dance routine "Jim Crow," which he introduced in 1832 and which, according to a well-known story, he adapted from the singing and movements of a black man he encountered in Cincinnati (Hamm 118–21).

Familiar and very popular as single acts in olios and circuses, the impersonation of blacks had, by the 1830s, evolved into two stage types. One, typified by Gumbo Chaff or Jim Crow, portrayed the ragged plantation or riverboat hand, joyous, reckless, uncouth. The other, typified by Zip Coon or Dandy Jim, was a citified northern dandy, with exaggeratedly elegant clothes and manners.

The minstrel show itself was put together in the early 1840s. It consisted of songs (both solo and "full chorus"), dances, jokes, conundrums, satirical speeches, and skits. The performers, only four in number at first, seated themselves in a rough semicircle on the stage. In the middle were the banjo player and the fiddle player. The two "end-men" played the tambourine and the bones, and these, along with the inevitable foot tapping of the banjo player, provided a kind of primitive "rhythm section." It was the end-men who indulged in the most outrageous horseplay. The bones, which were in the beginning actually just that, were held one pair in each hand and rattled together. The fiddle played the tune more or less straight, while the banjo, instead of merely strumming chords, as it would in the later jazz band, played an ornamented version of the tune. Since the banjo music was eventually written down and published, we know not only that it presupposes a good deal of agility but also that the lively and syncopated rhythms were similar to those that would appear later in ragtime. What did the early minstrel band actually sound like? Hans Nathan has this to say:

> The volume of the minstrel band was quite lean, yet anything but delicate. The tones of the banjo died away quickly and therefore could not serve as a solid foundation in the ensemble. On top was the squeaky, carelessly tuned fiddle. Add the dry, "ra, raka, taka, tak" of the bones and the tambourine's dull thumps and ceaseless jingling to the twang of the banjo and the flat tone of the fiddle, and the sound of the band is approximated: it was scratchy, tinkling, cackling, and humorously incongruous. (128)

Robert Winans, banjoist who has led and recorded a re-created minstrel band, disagrees with this and has written in rebuttal, "I think that the sound was much more solid than that, that the instruments blended surprisingly well, with a more mellow and melodic sound than Nathan suggests" (Bean 143). Listen to CD 3/18 and come to your own conclusions.

The coming to town of the touring minstrel show was as eagerly anticipated as the coming of the circus, with which it had a good deal in common. The troupe's arrival was signaled by the inevitable parade through town, winding up at the theater where the evening performance was to be given. At this performance the public's expectations of an evening of vivid and diverting entertainment were seldom disappointed; they laughed hard at the comic songs, repartee, conundrums, and grotesque antics of the end-men, and at the skits and parodies that made up the second half of the show. But there also may have been some moist eyes in the crowd at the close of the sentimental songs, ranging from "Old Black Joe," "My Old Kentucky Home," and "Old Uncle Ned" to such later (and less slave-oriented) songs as "She May Have Seen Better Days" or "Just Tell Them That You Saw Me."

Dan Emmett

Daniel Decatur Emmett (1815–1904) was a pioneer performer in minstrelsy, and one of the most important composers and authors of its early folkish and rough-hewn material. Born in a small Ohio town just emerging from the backwoods, Emmett grew up in a frontier society similar to that in which Abraham Lincoln was raised, with all its virtues and vices—its examples of courage and fierce independence, its violence and prejudices, and, above all, its rough-and-ready humor. At 18 he enlisted in the army, where he mastered the drum and the fife. In the late 1830s he began appearing in circuses, singing and playing the drums and, later, the banjo and the fiddle.

Blackface singing and dancing with banjo accompaniment was by that time common in the circus; of the four performers who formed the original Virginia Minstrels in New York City in 1843 (Dan Emmett, Frank Brower, William Whitlock, and Richard Pelham), at least three had had experience in touring circuses. The Virginia Minstrels, the first group to use the classic instrumentation described earlier (fiddle, banjo, tambourine, and bones) and the first to put together a whole evening of minstrel music, dancing, and skits, caught on with both public and press in New York and Boston. The popularity of this entertainment in the United States was so great that many imitators and competitors soon appeared—E. P. Christy and his troupe among them. Emmett himself was active for over twenty-five years as an "Ethiopian" performer, and as composer-author of songs and skits, especially for the shows' finales, the "walk-arounds." His song "De Boatman's Dance" (CD 3/18, Transcription 13.1) became so well known as to achieve the status of a folk song. A lively pentatonic tune, with its emphatic repetition of short motives, it is typical of the exuberant songs of early minstrelsy.

CD 3/18 (2:40)
"De Boatman's Dance," attributed to Dan Emmett. Vincent Tufo, fiddle; Percy Danforth, bones; Matthew Heumann, tambourine; Robert Winans, banjo.

Transcription 13.1
"De Boatman's Dance"

(From *Dan Emmett and the Rise of Early Negro Minstrelsy*, by Hans Nathan. Copyright © 1962 by the University of Oklahoma Press. Reprinted by permission.)

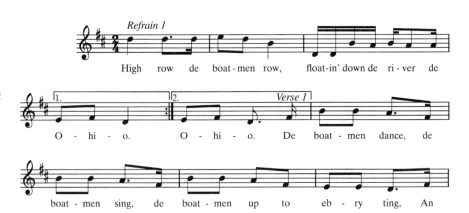

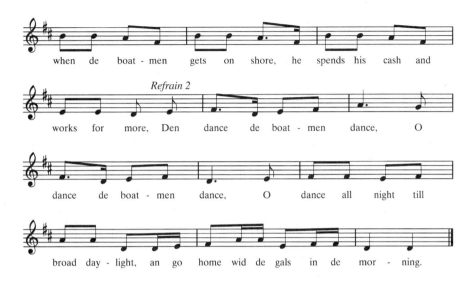

when de boat-men gets on shore, he spends his cash and

Refrain 2

works for more, Den dance de boat - men dance, O

dance de boat - men dance, O dance all night till

broad day - light, an go home wid de gals in de mor - ning.

Refrain 1	High row . . .
Verse 2	I went on board de odder day
	To see what de boatmen had to say;
	Dar I let my passion loose
	An dey cram me in de callaboose.
Refrain 2	Den dance . . .
Refrain 1	High row . . .
Verse 3	When de boatman blows his horn,
	Look out old man your hog is gone;
	He cotch my sheep, he cotch my shoat,
	Den put em in a bag an tote em in de boat.
Refrain 2	Den dance . . .
Refrain 1	High row . . .
Verse 4	De boatman is a thrifty man,
	Dars none can do as de boatman can;
	I neber see a putty gal in my life
	But dat she was a boatman's wife.
Refrain 2	Den dance . . .

Listen to CD 4/24, "The Banjo," by Louisiana-born composer Louis Moreau Gottschalk for a skillful evocation of banjo sound and texture on the piano.

It was for Bryant's Minstrels that Dan Emmett wrote "Dixie" (full title, "I Wish I Was in Dixie's Land") in 1859. Perhaps the most phenomenally popular song of the nineteenth century, it was minstrelsy's greatest legacy to

American music. It soon acquired a significance entirely unintended and even resented by its composer, when it was adopted by the Confederacy at the outbreak of the Civil War.

Stephen Foster and Minstrelsy

Stephen Collins Foster (1826–64) was minstrelsy's best-known composer. He was not, as Emmett was, a minstrel performer himself, but in 1845 he began writing "Ethiopian songs," at first for the enjoyment of a group of friends. In Cincinnati he met a member of a professional minstrel troupe (the Sable Harmonists) who introduced his "Old Uncle Ned" in one of their programs. In 1848 he wrote "Oh! Susanna," selling it outright to a Pittsburgh publisher for one hundred dollars. It became enormously popular. The next year he signed a contract with the leading New York publisher, Firth, Pond & Co., and committed himself to a songwriting career. In 1852 he made a brief steamboat trip down the Ohio and the Mississippi to New Orleans—his only visit to the South. Stephen Foster will be considered more fully in the next chapter, in connection with American popular song.

Zenith and Decline

The minstrel show reached its zenith in the years just before the Civil War. After the war, minstrelsy lost much of its original flavor and character, becoming, as Nathan has said, "an efficient large-scale variety show which favored less and less the dry, tough humor of Emmett's texts and tunes and the primitive style of his performances" (276). The *review* indeed did replace the minstrel show almost completely in New York in the 1860s. But the latter continued strong in smaller centers of population and in rural America. After the Civil War, African American musicians and entertainers themselves began to participate, and all-black minstrel companies, such as the Georgia Minstrels, the Original Black Diamonds (of Boston), Haverly's Genuine Colored Minstrels, and W. S. Cleveland's Colossal Colored Carnival Minstrels, toured for another half-century or so. Minstrelsy thus became both a training ground and a source of employment for many black musicians who later branched out in the direction of blues or jazz. W. C. Handy was one, as was "Ma" Rainey, who toured widely in the South with various minstrel shows and circuses in the first two decades of the twentieth century. Other jazz figures who played for a time in minstrel bands include Bunk Johnson, Lester Young, and Jelly Roll Morton (Stearns, Chapter 11).

Despite the (nominally) free status of blacks and the drastically changed social and economic conditions in the South after the Civil War, the basic content and characterization of black people in postwar minstrel songs remained virtually the same as during slavery, with continued nostalgic references to idyllic plantation life. These were performed, and often also composed, by blacks themselves. The songs of James Bland (1854–1911), the best-known black songwriter for the minstrel stage, are typical in this regard. "Oh, Dem Golden Slippers," "In the Evening by the Moonlight," and "Carry Me Back to Old Virginny" were all composed about 1880; from their characterization of black people and depiction of conditions in the South, they could have been written thirty years earlier. But the nostalgically clothed stereotype was what audiences continued to want to hear.

Less than a generation later, there were the beginnings of change. About the turn of the century, performers such as the team of Bert Williams (1874–1922) and George Walker (c. 1872–1911), black singer-comedians who also wore blackface makeup, helped to bring new standards of integrity to the stage portrayal of the black man. As George Walker said in 1906:

> The one hope of the colored performer must be in making a radical departure from the old "darkie" style of singing and dancing. . . . There is an artistic side to the black race, and if it could be properly developed on the stage, I believe the theatergoing public would profit much by it. . . . My idea was always to impersonate my race just as they are. The colored man has never successfully taken off his own humorous characteristics, and the white impersonator often overdoes the matter (Gilbert 284).

Playing eventually in shows such as *In Dahomey* (1902) and *In Bandana Land* (1907), Williams and Walker were part of the first wave of black shows with black performers at the turn of the century, as we shall see.

FROM THE CIVIL WAR THROUGH THE TURN OF THE CENTURY

Immediately after the searing and costly War Between the States, the popular musical stage entered a period of exuberant growth, characterized by foreign importation and native experimentation. With the great leaps in industry and transportation, and the heterogeneous, enriching inflow of immigrants, a new and energetic era was beginning. Above all, the cities grew, and with them the wealth and expectations of all but the poorest of their inhabitants. In an era of affluence and expansion, the public was in the market for—and got—new theatrical diversions.

The New York Stage in the 1860s

New York City's dominance as America's entertainment capital was well established by the mid–nineteenth century. It was the first stop for touring artists and companies from Europe, and already the magnet toward which all native talent was drawn. Beginning in the 1860s, it became the fantasy-land of that dream of every producer, the "Broadway hit." Let us, very briefly, pay our respects to the first of these, *The Black Crook*. Produced in 1866 in Niblo's Garden, the best-appointed theater in New York, with its stage completely rebuilt for the occasion, the original production lasted five and a half hours and was a spectacle lavish beyond anything that had been seen previously. Its thin, derivative melodramatic plot was overwhelmed by huge ensemble numbers, costumes, extremely elaborate scenic effects and changes, and, as a significant ingredient, the dancing of no fewer than two hundred French ballet dancers in "immodest dress." *The Black Crook* actually looked more to the past than to the future. None of its ingredients was new; what *was* new was the prodigally lavish scale of the production (said to have cost more than $35,000, an astounding outlay for the time), and the fact that it ran for 474 performances and grossed more than a million dollars.

Vaudeville

After the impetus of *The Black Crook*, the New York stage became the arena for continued experiment on a new scale. One form emerged that was to become a prominent and typically American entertainment for half a century—*vaudeville*. Its antecedents were to be found in the minstrel theater, the English music hall, and, more immediately, the lowbrow entertainments offered in beer halls and saloons to which the name "burlesque" had come to be applied. But in the 1880s Tony Pastor, called the "father" of vaudeville, successfully turned it into clean, family entertainment. Vaudeville typically was a succession of individual acts, including dancers, acrobats, jugglers, magicians, and animal acts, usually headlined by a well-known comedian or singer.

Importations from London, Paris, and Vienna

The American popular stage languished musically until the importation of comic opera of exceptionally high quality from London, Paris, and Vienna beginning in the last quarter of the century. W. S. Gilbert and Arthur Sullivan in London, Jacques Offenbach in Paris, Johann Strauss, Jr., in Vienna—each of these represented a peak of achievement in English, French, and German comic opera, all coming about the same time. It was an unprecedented era of concentrated brilliance, which cast beams on this side of the Atlantic as well.

The London "invasion" came first; *H.M.S. Pinafore* was heard (in a stolen version) in Boston in 1878 and became prodigiously popular at once. After *Pinafore*, there followed in short order *The Pirates of Penzance* (premiered in New York by the author's own company, to protect their rights), and then *Iolanthe, The Sorcerer,* and *Princess Ida,* climaxed by the phenomenal success of *The Mikado* in 1885.

The new popularity of English comic opera created a popular audience for other European light operas as well, and both French *opéra bouffe* and Viennese operetta (which had been given in the United States earlier in their original languages) were presented in English translations. After a lull in the 1890s, Viennese operetta again enjoyed a great period of popularity in the United States with the advent of *The Merry Widow,* by Franz Lehar, in 1907 and *The Chocolate Soldier,* by Oskar Straus, in 1909. A host of operettas more or less on the Viennese model were subsequently produced by immigrant composers, a development that will be taken up in due course.

The Americanization of the Musical

While these foreign importations were enjoying their popularity, there was gradually emerging a more indigenous kind of musical show. The Harrigan and Hart comedies of the period represented an important early step toward the Americanization of the musical. Portraying with humor the Irish, the Germans, and the African Americans in believable comic situations growing out of the everyday lives of everyday people, they were an immediate success. The first was *The Mulligan Guard Ball* (1879), and this was followed by many Mulligan Guard sequels with the same characters, much in the manner of a television situation-comedy series. The songs, all by David Braham (1834–1905), a London-born musician who came to the United States at the age of 15, became popular at the time in their own right and were sometimes borrowed for other shows. Songs such as "The Babies on Our Block" (CD 3/19) from *The Mulligan Guard Ball* illustrate the Irish flavor that was brought to the musical stage by these shows. (Irish characterization had been introduced to the American popular musical stage at least seven decades earlier in the melodrama *The Indian Princess,* as we saw in the preceding chapter (pp. 225–26).

CD 3/19 (2:00) "The Babies on Our Block" (excerpt), by David Braham and Edward Harrigan. 1879. Max Morath, tenor; Dick Hyman, piano, and vocal ensemble.

Verse 1		
A strain	If you want more information or in need of merriment,	
	Come over with me socially to Murphy's tenement.	
A strain	He owns a row of houses in the first ward near the dock,	
	Where Ireland's represented by the babies on our block.	

Text, "The Babies on Our Block"

B [bridge]	There's the Phalens and the Whalens from the sweet Dunochadee,
	They are sitting on the railings with their children on their knee,
A strain	All gossiping and talking with their neighbors in a flock,
	Singing "Little Sally Waters" with the babies on our block.

Refrain (choral)

C strain	"Oh, little Sally Waters, sitting in the sun,
[derived from A]	A-crying and weeping for a young man;
C strain	Oh, rise, Sally, rise, wipe your eye out with your frock";
[ends like A]	That's sung by the babies a-living on our block.

Verse 2

Of a warm day in the summer, when the breeze blows off the sea,
A hundred thousand childeren [sic] lay in the Battery;
They come from Murphy's building,
Oh, their noise would stop a clock!
Oh, there's no perambulatory with the babies on our block.
There's the Clearys and the Learys from the sweet Blackwater side,
They are laying on the Batt'ry and they're gazing at the tide;
All royal blood and noble, all of Dan O'Connell's stock,
Singing "Gravel, Greeny Gravel" with the babies on our block.

Refrain (choral)

"Oh, Gravel, Greeny Gravel, how green the grasses grow,
For all the pretty fair young maidens that I see";
Oh, "Green, Gravel Green," wipe your eye out with your frock;
That's sung by the babies a-living on our block.

In the verse we have an example of the fully developed 32-bar song form, with bridge—a form basic to American popular music for a century. We will encounter it again in the show songs of Jerome Kern, Kurt Weill, and Leonard Bernstein. The choral refrain in "The Babies on Our Block" is only half as long as the verse; it has not assumed the importance that the full 32-bar chorus will subsequently, with the verse becoming the part of the song hardly anyone remembers.

The movement toward the Americanization of the musical comedy of this period culminated in the shows and songs of George M. Cohan (1878–1942), an energetic and ambitious showman who came up from vaudeville to become an author, composer, stage director, and performer who dominated the musical stage in the first two decades of the twentieth century. The one word inevitably used by writers to describe Cohan is "brash." The directness of his style, his informality, and above all his fast pace (Heywood Broun described him as "a disciple of perpetual motion") brought new vitality to the theater. Cohan was right for his time, and fittingly marked the last stage in the adolescence of American popular musical theater, sounding a decisive note of independence from Europe. His three most important and characteristic shows came early in the century: *Little Johnny Jones* in 1904 (which included "The Yankee Doodle Boy"), *Forty-five Minutes from Broadway* in 1906, and *George Washington, Jr.*, also in 1906. (*The Little Millionaire*, the last of this genre, came in 1911.) Of the first three, each has its American hero (a jockey, a reformed gambler, a young superpatriot), and the three shows together contain the best of Cohan's show tunes. The verse in CD 3/20 is made out of snatches of popular tunes: "Yankee Doodle," "Dixie," "The Girl I Left Behind Me," and "Star-Spangled Banner."

CD 3/20 (1:12)
"The Yankee Doodle Boy" (excerpt), from *Little Johnny Jones*, by George M. Cohan. 1904. Richard Perry, vocal.

(*Verse*)	I'm the kid that's all the candy,
	I'm a Yankee Doodle Dandy;
	I'm glad I am
	(So's Uncle Sam).
	I'm a real live Yankee Doodle,
	Made my name and fame and boodle
	Just like Mr. Doodle did,
	By riding on a pony.
	I love to listen to the Dixie strain,
	"I long to see the girl I left behind me."
	And that ain't a josh,
	She's a Yankee, by gosh.
	(Oh, say can you see
	Anything about a Yankee that's a phoney?)
Chorus	I'm a Yankee Doodle Dandy,
	A Yankee Doodle do or die.
	A real live nephew of my Uncle Sam,
	Born on the Fourth of July.
	I've got a Yankee Doodle sweetheart,
	She is my Yankee Doodle joy,
	Yankee Doodle came to London
	Just to ride the ponies,
	I am that Yankee Doodle Boy!

Text, "That Yankee Doodle Boy"

By this time the chorus, which has the "main tune," has assumed the importance it will hold from now on in American popular music.

What is American about Cohan's songs? Contributing factors are the "bragging" lyrics, the fast tempi (characteristic of Cohan's most typical songs), the predominance of the major mode, and the syncopation of a fairly rudimentary kind, as on the words "I'm glad I am—so's Uncle Sam." This is the kind of syncopation typical of up-tempo popular music of this era and is also found in "Dixie," "Camptown Races," "The Yellow Rose of Texas," and in Cohan's "Over There." It is also in Sousa marches such as "High School Cadets" and "Manhattan Beach." It is not as concentrated a syncopation as is found in ragtime. (For an explanation of syncopation, with examples, see the chapter on ragtime, pp. 292–95.)

THE FIRST HALF OF THE TWENTIETH CENTURY

Black Musicians on Broadway: The Emergence from Minstrelsy

Late in the nineteenth century it began to be apparent that the contributions of black musicians to America's popular musical stage need not—in fact, *could* not—be forever limited to the caricatured renditions of the minstrel stage. Change, however, was painfully slow.

Two important landmarks came in 1898. Robert Cole produced the first full-length all-black musical show, *A Trip to Coontown.* But more successful and memorable was an all-black musical comedy sketch, *Clorindy, the Origin of the Cakewalk,* with music by the talented and classically trained musician Will Marion Cook (1869–1944). With its characteristic music, dancing, and choral singing, *Clorindy* created a sensation and opened the doors for black music and musicians on the Broadway stage, performing for predominantly white audiences. The first wave of black musicals followed. Will Marion Cook himself wrote a succession of shows; the next three were unsuccessful, but *In Dahomey* (1902), satirizing the scheme to colonize American blacks in Africa; *In Abyssinia* (1906), an extravaganza laid in Africa; and *In Bandana Land* (1908), set in the American South, were all hits. The team of Cole and the Johnson brothers wrote two musicals, *The Shoo-Fly Regiment* (1906) and *The Red Moon* (1908), and J. Rosamund Johnson wrote the music for *Mr. Lode of Koal* (or *Kole*), of 1909. Thus the first period of activity of the black musical lasted for a decade.

After a lull during the second decade of the century, a second era of black musical shows was inaugurated in 1921 by the famous *Shuffle Along,* with lyrics by Noble Sissle and music by Eubie Blake. It was essentially a revue. Some of its fast numbers (of which "I'm Just Wild about Harry" was the most famous) are imbued with the ebullient but easygoing momentum of ragtime and early jazz; some (such as "Bandana Days") are almost pure George M. Cohan. Of its slow songs, some are close to the blues ("Daddy, Won't You Please Come Home"), and one in particular is in the style of the standard sentimental show tune. "Love Will Find a Way" the authors feared, needlessly, might not be accepted by a white audience from black singing actors.

Shuffle Along is credited with helping to initiate the Harlem Renaissance of the 1920s—a period of unprecedented cultural activity and rising intellectual and artistic self-esteem among American urban blacks. From that time until the Depression, many all-black shows played Broadway. Blake and Sissle wrote three more, and among others of note were *Keep Shuffling* (1928) and *Hot Chocolates* (1929), with music by Thomas "Fats" Waller (1904–43). A more recent black idiom, rhythm-and-blues, was brought to Broadway in a lavishly staged black adaptation of a classic (*The Wizard of Oz*) called *The Wiz* (1975).

Operetta, and Three Immigrant Composers

Building on the basic style, form, and approach of operetta, three immigrant composers brought a consistently high level of competence to the popular musical stage. During the forty years from Victor Herbert's first success, *The Wizard of the Nile* (1895), to Sigmund Romberg's last Viennese piece, *May Wine* (1935), there was hardly a time when there was not an American operetta on the Broadway stage. Its three great American exponents were Victor Herbert, Rudolf Friml, and Sigmund Romberg. All three were European-born, and all received there a thorough musical training (though Romberg's was more practical than formal, gained by hanging around the very epicenter of German-language operetta, the Theater-an-der-Wien in Vienna). All came to America, thus fully trained and equipped, in their twenties.

Victor Herbert (1859–1924), born in Dublin and trained in Germany, had the broadest musical experience and competence of the three. He entered the field of the popular musical show at the relatively late age of 35, but once in, he knew that the theater was his métier. He was extraordinarily facile, composing over forty operettas. His major contributions were made in the two decades between *The Wizard of the Nile* (1895) and *Eileen* (1917), and included *The Fortune Teller* (1898), *Babes in Toyland* (1903), *Mlle. Modiste* (1905), *The Red Mill* (1906), *Naughty Marietta* (1910), and *Sweethearts* (1913). In addition to his gift for producing a memorable melody, Herbert's virtuosity as a composer enabled him to handle ensemble and choral scenes (e.g., the opening scene of *Naughty Marietta*, with its street cries) with a skill and inventiveness theretofore associated only with opera.

Rudolf Friml (1879–1972), born in Prague, was another thoroughly schooled musician, who was in his early years a concert pianist. His range was somewhat narrower, but between 1912 (*The Firefly*) and 1928 (*The Three Musketeers*) he produced some enduring operettas, including *Rose Marie* (1924) and *The Vagabond King* (1925).

Sigmund Romberg (1887–1951) was more versatile than Friml. He identified himself completely with the popular musical theater, writing music for numerous revues for the Shuberts and others, including annual "editions" of

The Passing Show between 1914 and 1924. But his forte was operetta, with a pronounced Viennese flavor, and his main contributions were *Maytime* (1917), *The Student Prince* (1924), *The Desert Song* (1926), *The New Moon* (1928), and *May Wine* (1935).

From the works of these three composers, we can arrive at a working definition of that form so popular in America from the Gay Nineties to the Depression—the operetta, or "light opera." Its setting was exotic, belonging to another place and time—Vienna, Heidelberg, Hungary, Paris, even eighteenth-century New Orleans. The characters often included royalty or nobility, frequently incognito, but gypsies, brigands, and opera singers were also favorites. The plot usually involved either concealed identity or concealed fortune, and the hoary theatrical device of look-alikes was employed. The music was tuneful, often memorably so, and like its Viennese counterpart, it placed its greatest faith in its waltzes, which really epitomized the genre.

The Revue

Thriving during the same period as the operetta was the revue, an even lighter form of entertainment, usually associated with the late spring or summer portion of the season. The trade names were many: "passing show," "follies," "scandals," "vanities." It was a succession of single acts, usually lacking even a pretense of dramatic thread or interest. Into it went the ancient elements of song-and-dance, burlesque, spectacle, and the display of feminine beauty.

THE MUSICAL IN ITS MATURITY: *SHOW BOAT* TO *WEST SIDE STORY*

The musical show had its period of greatest achievement in the thirty years that began with *Show Boat* (1927) and ended with *West Side Story* (1957). During this time the musical had set itself new musical-dramatic problems (the term "musical *comedy*" was no longer appropriate), and had solved them, without ceasing to captivate and entertain its audience. It was a period of sustained creation by major writers devoting their talents principally to the live musical stage, and it was, moreover, a period when the popular stage still had its audience. Broadway was in a clear position of leadership and supplied America (and much of the world) with its best popular music.

A glance at the thirty years under consideration reveals the domination of five superbly equipped and successful composers: Jerome Kern (1885–1945), Irving Berlin (1888–1989), George Gershwin (1898–1937), Richard Rodgers (1902–79), and Cole Porter (1891–1964), each of whom wrote music for at least a dozen shows. Four others also made important contributions: Kurt Weill (1900–50), and near the end of the period, Frederick Loewe (1901–88), Frank Loesser (1910–69), and Leonard Bernstein (1918–90). During those thirty years, only one year passed without the appearance of a new show by at least one of these nine composers; in most years there were two or three. Their shows and the best known of their hundreds of songs are so familiar that a mere listing would be pointless. It will be more profitable here to consider certain aspects of the musical itself—areas in which innovation and evolution occurred during its era of greatest achievement.

The Evolution of Dramatic Values   During this period there was a great widening and deepening of the dramatic dimensions of the musical—a gain in both range and verisimilitude, without compromising the musical's essential nature as entertainment. Subject matter, plot, characterization, and range of emotion were all broadened. A brief look at six shows of the era should substantiate this.

Show Boat (1927: music by Jerome Kern, book and lyrics by Oscar Hammerstein II) was adapted from Edna Ferber's novel. It put real characters in believable situations—Magnolia, the sheltered daughter of the Mississippi showboat's owner, who survives a broken marriage with a riverboat gambler to make her way to the top as a musical comedy star; the half-caste Julie, singing two love songs that shattered the conventional sentimental mold, "Can't Help Lovin' Dat Man" (CD 3/21) and "Bill" ("an ordinary boy"). Also worthy of note is the realistic and sympathetic portrayal of African Americans on the stage. Joe's song "Ol' Man River" is especially famous in its interpretation by Paul Robeson. A poignant but minor plot element in the novel, the story of Julie has been emphasized in our time as groundbreaking for a novel written eighty years ago, as is her song about her love for an anti-stereotypical man ("dere ain't no reason why I should love dat man"). There are no "perfect men" in this story.

CD 3/21 (3:45) "Can't Help Lovin' Dat Man" from *Show Boat*. 1927. Music by Jerome Kern. Lyrics by Oscar Hammerstein II. Helen Morgan, vocal.

Verse, 12 bars

Oh, listen <u>sister</u>,
I love my <u>mister</u> man
And I can't tell yo' why.
Dere ain't no reason why I should love dat <u>man</u>.
It must be sumpin' dat de angels done <u>plan</u>.

Chorus, standard 32-bar form

[*A* strain]   Fish got to swim and birds got to <u>fly</u>,
I got to love one man till I <u>die</u>,
Can't help lovin' dat man of mine.

Text, "I Can't Help Lovin' Dat Man"

(Words and Music by Jerome Kern, Oscar Hammerstein, II. © copyright 1927 Universal Polygram International Publishing, Inc. [ASCAP] International Copyright Secured. All Rights Reserved.)

Culver Pictures

Helen Morgan created the role of Julie in the first production of *Show Boat* (1927).

[*A* repeated]	Tell me he's <u>lazy</u>,
	tell me he's <u>slow</u>.
	Tell me I'm <u>crazy</u>,
	maybe I <u>know</u>.
	Can't help lovin' dat man of mine.
[Bridge]	When he goes <u>away</u>
	Dat's a rainy <u>day</u>,
	And when he comes back dat day is <u>fine</u>!
	De sun will <u>shine</u>!
[*A* strain]	He kin come home as late as kin <u>be</u>,
	Home widout him ain't no home to <u>me</u>!
	Can't help lovin' dat man of mine!

Often neglected is the art of the lyricist. Oscar Hammerstein II set a high standard; note not only the economy and the aptness of the imagery but also the interest sustained by the interior rhymes.

Pal Joey (1940: music by Richard Rodgers, lyrics by Lorenz Hart, book by John O'Hara) was based on O'Hara's stories, which the author himself had suggested as a framework for a musical. It is strongest in characterization: the hero is a crass, selfish opportunist, finally abandoned by the two women who

have, each in her own way, been used by him. The shoddy nightclub milieu of
Chicago marked a new venture into the seamier aspects of realism. Vera's
unsentimental love song, this time to a real heel, "Bewitched, Bothered, and
Bewildered," gained musical force through a characteristic Rodgers device of
the almost obsessive development of a small melodic motive. Here again note
the art of the lyricist, Lorenz Hart, as shown in the sequence of interior rhymes
in the choruses.

I'm wild again!
Beguiled again!
A simpering, whimpering child again.
Bewitched, bothered, and bewildered am I.

Couldn't sleep
And wouldn't sleep
Until I could sleep where I shouldn't sleep.
Bewitched, bothered, and bewildered am I.

A pill he is,
But still he is
All mine and I'll keep him until he is
Bewitched, bothered, and bewildered like me.

Seen a lot;
I mean a lot!
But now I'm like sweet seventeen a lot.
Bewitched, bothered, and bewildered am I.

I'll sing to him
Each spring to him
And worship the trousers that cling to him.
Bewitched, bothered, and bewildered am I.

Vexed again,
Perplexed again,
Thank God I can be over-sexed again.
Bewitched, bothered, and bewildered am I.

Text, Excerpts from
"Bewitched, Bothered,
and Bewildered"

So novel for 1940 were the elements thus introduced into a Broadway
musical that *Pal Joey* did not succeed with the public until its revival twelve
years later.

Lady in the Dark (1941: music by Kurt Weill, lyrics by Ira Gershwin, book
by Moss Hart) plunges us into the realm of psychosis and the dream fantasy.
The theme was not new to the musical; Rodgers and Hart had explored it in
1926 in *Peggy-Ann,* as did Romberg in *May Wine* (1935). But *Lady in the Dark*

Two excerpts from
Lady in the Dark. 1941.
Music by Kurt Weill.
Lyrics by Ira Gershwin.
Book by Moss Hart.
CD 3/22 "Glamour
Dream" (0:30).

CD 3/23 "Childhood
Dream: My Ship" (2:43).

presents an almost clinical treatment of the subject, as the heroine, Liza, undergoes psychoanalysis. The dream sequences, more than mere surrealistic burlesque, have a genuine bearing on the heroine's problems, and the three men among whom she must choose are real, three-dimensional characters. As for the role of the music in this "new musical and lyrical pattern in the American Theatre," Moss Hart in his preface to the musical score writes that he and composer Kurt Weill decided to do "a show in which the music carried forward the essential story and was not imposed on the architecture of the play as a rather melodious but useless addenda." As the most notable illustration of this, the dramatic resolution in the play is neatly paralleled by a musical one; the mysterious tune Liza remembers from childhood, which has haunted the play as a fragmentary motive, appears at the end, completed and harmonized, as "My Ship."

Text, "My Ship"

A   My ship has sails that are made of silk,
The decks are trimmed with gold,
And of jam and spice
there's a paradise
in the hold.

A   My ship's a-glow with a million pearls
And rubies in each bin,
The sun sits high
in a sapphire sky
When my ship comes in.

Bridge   I can wait the years
Till it appears
One fine day in spring,
But the pearls and such
They won't mean much
if there's missing just one thing.

A   I do not care if that day arrives,
That dream need never be,
If the ship I sing
Doesn't also bring
My own true love to me.

It is interesting to note that for the final resolution of the drama, Weill does not hesitate to resort to the comfortable tradition of the 32-bar chorus, in *aaba* form.

Carousel (1945: music by Richard Rodgers, lyrics and book by Oscar Hammerstein II, based on the play *Liliom* by the Hungarian playwright Ferenc

Molnar) has elements of tragedy and symbolic fantasy, with a finale built on the age-old theme of redemption—heavy fare for a musical show. The hero is an outcast who must conceal his tenderness beneath a bullying, swaggering exterior. Thus he cannot, in life, communicate his love to Julie, nor can she to him—"*If* I loved you" is as much as they can ever say to each other. His suicide brings an opportunity for redemption; stealing a star that he gives to the daughter he has never seen in life, he conquers, for them both, the alienation that was threatening to warp her existence as it had his. Music has an ample role; the entire prelude is pantomimed to a carousel waltz, and there is a ballet-pantomime sequence in the second act.

Two more Rodgers and Hammerstein collaborations brought innovations in theme and setting. *South Pacific* (1949), one of the best-crafted musicals of the period, was able to deal in song with one of the play's basic themes, inter-racial marriage, in "You've Got to Be Taught" ("to hate and fear"). These virtuosos of the form were able next to execute the remarkable feat of bringing an exotic Oriental setting to the stage (*The King and I*, 1951) and treating it tastefully, without resorting either to crude spectacle or to caricature, and without subjecting the audience to imitations of Oriental music. They also showed the extent to which sentimental convention could be discarded by authors with sufficient talent and daring, in depicting a relationship between two principals in which the love interest is present only by muted implication.

(Five years later the authors of *My Fair Lady*, an otherwise nearly perfect piece, felt obliged to make a concession to conventional sentimentality—even more persistent than "middle-class morality," it seems—in bringing Eliza back to Henry Higgins in a dénouement that is weak and unconvincing dramatically, and that George Bernard Shaw had specifically ruled out in the preface to a play written after his *Pygmalion*, on which *My Fair Lady* was based.)

Satire and "Social Significance"   In the troubled political and economic climate of the 1930s, the theater did what it has always done in such times—it assumed the role of commentator, satirist, and gadfly. Political satire had never been completely absent from musical comedy, here or abroad, as a close look at Gilbert and Sullivan reveals. What was new was that the musical show, hitherto the realm of entertainment, fantasy, and escape, became involved to an extent previously unknown. The treatment given this theme represented a wide spectrum of approaches.

Three shows by the team of George Gershwin (music), Ira Gershwin (lyrics), and George S. Kaufman and Morrie Ryskind (book) were brilliantly acidic and made use of outrageous fantasy. The shows were *Strike Up the Band* (1930), *Of Thee I Sing* (1931), and *Let 'Em Eat Cake* (1933). *Of Thee I Sing*, with its right combination of the fantastic (a beauty contest to determine who is to be the new First Lady, "Miss White House"), good show songs, and genuinely humorous satire (the vice president is such an anonymous figure that he cannot get a library card because he cannot produce two references), was the most successful of the three, and the first musical to win the Pulitzer Prize.

Two shows of this period had an even more conscious emphasis on "social significance." *Pins and Needles* (1937) was a very successful revue produced by the garment workers' union and ran (with updating) for three years. *The Cradle Will Rock* (1938: music, lyrics, and book by Marc Blitzstein) was a hard-hitting propaganda piece.

At the other end of the spectrum were shows that treated their themes with a lighter touch—musicals making use of satire, rather than satire taking the form of musicals. The veteran Irving Berlin wrote the music and lyrics for *Face the Music* (1932) and *As Thousands Cheer* (1933), both with books by Moss Hart, and *Louisiana Purchase* (1940), with book by Morrie Ryskind. Rodgers and Hart's one venture into this field was *I'd Rather Be Right* (1937). Cole Porter successfully satirized not only American politics but also the Soviet Union in *Leave It to Me* (1938). The hit of the show was the very nonpolitical "My Heart Belongs to Daddy," which brilliantly etched one of Cole Porter's favorite hard-bitten female types. Porter returned to political satire, again of the Soviet Union, in *Silk Stockings* (1955).

Increased Sophistication of Musical Resources   During the period under consideration, the Broadway show utilized more fully and freely the musical means that had long been at the disposal of classical composers. One of these was counterpoint—the sounding together of two or more melodies. By nature an undramatic device, it was utilized in a form where words are important and where the attention, for greatest dramatic effect, should be focused on only one thing at a time. But carefully introduced, it can be effective, if only as a foil for the otherwise constant monody. This is the basis for the ensemble number, which involves two or more characters. For example, the superb and witty "Marry the Man Today," from *Guys and Dolls*, incorporates a quasi-canonic echoing effect between two voices; and in the superbly crafted ensemble near the end of the first act of *West Side Story*, five characters present three different interpretations of what "tonight" means to them. Occasionally even imitative counterpoint has its place: Kern included a fugue in *The Cat and the Fiddle* as early as 1931, and the "Fugue for Tinhorns" (actually a three-part canon) in *Guys and Dolls* of 1950 (CD 3/24) is one of the most effective opening numbers in any musical.

CD 3/24 (1:25) "Fugue for Tinhorns," from *Guys and Dolls*. 1950. Music and lyrics by Frank Loesser, after a story by Damon Runyon.

Text: "Fugue for Tinhorns"

Nicely-Nicely Johnson:	I got the horse right here, The name is Paul Revere,
	And here's a guy that says if the weather's clear,
	Can do, can do, this guy says the horse can do. (etc.)

Benny Southstreet:	I'm picking Valentine 'cause on the morning line
	The guy has got him figured at five to nine,
	Has chance, has chance, this guy says the horse has
	chance. (etc.)
Rusty Charley:	But look at Epitaph, he wins it by a half
	According to this here in the Telegraph.
	Big threat, big threat, this guy calls the horse big
	threat. (etc.)

Beyond an increased broadening and sophistication of technique, the musical during this period came gradually to assign a far greater role to music itself; there was more of it, and it was given more work to do. Instead of being called upon only when it was time for a song or a dance, it underscored dialogue, accomplished transitions, or arranged itself in a sequence of movements that became the equivalent of the operatic scene. Furthermore, in the best musicals the entire score had a unity to it. Jerome Kern took a large step in this direction in the score of *Show Boat* when he employed a few key motives, associated with certain characters, at appropriate moments in the background. This was a technique long known to opera but new to the musical.

Increased Importance of the Dance   Another evolutionary development was the increased attention lavished on the dance. Song and dance had always gone together on the entertainment stage. But a new era was begun when George Balanchine, noted Russian-born choreographer and ballet master who had come to the United States in 1933, was called upon to create a special jazz ballet for the Rodgers and Hart show *On Your Toes* (1936). The result was the famous "Slaughter on Tenth Avenue," an extended "story" ballet sequence within the musical. From that time forward, choreography and dance, in whatever style is appropriate, have become integrated ingredients in the best musicals, especially telling in drama and fantasy sequences, as in *Carousel* and *Allegro*. For *Oklahoma!* (1943) a new orientation for the dance was required, and Agnes De Mille created what were essentially folk-ballet sequences. The musical *On the Town* (1944), with score by Leonard Bernstein, had actually originated as a ballet, *Fancy Free*, by the same composer, with choreography by Jerome Robbins.

Robbins also contrived the dance and movement for *West Side Story*, in which it played an important role in the unfolding of the action—indeed, that was one of the few musicals conceived and directed by a choreographer. The score itself is nearly a succession of dances, with dance rhythms underlying even the love song. The two contrasting types (jazz-rock and Latin) in juxtaposition express the essential conflict that is the basis of the modern urban plot derived from Shakespeare's *Romeo and Juliet*.

Beethoven, *Great Fugue* String Quartet, Op. 133 (excerpt)

Fugue theme enters at

CD 3/25 (1:11)
Beethoven, *Great
Fugue* String
Quartet, Op. 133
(excerpt), opening
part

0.04	
0:23	
0:30	cello (lowest part)
0:51	viola
0:58	cello again
1:06	2nd violin

CD 3/26 (3:56)
"Cool," from *West
Side Story.* 1957.
Music by Leonard
Bernstein. Lyrics by
Stephen Sondheim.
Book by Arthur
Laurents. Based on
a conception of
Jerome Robbins.

Leonard Bernstein, classically trained musician with a special admiration for Beethoven (1770–1827), used as a model in crafting the music for the dance sequence "Cool" (CD 3/26) one of Beethoven's greatest works, the *Great Fugue,* for string quartet (CD 3/27). Not only did he derive his theme for his "Fugue" (so titled in the score) from Beethoven's, but also the whole feeling of barely restrained tension, achieved by the interruption of silence with brief fragments of music, now loud and now soft, is the same feeling of uneasy anticipation that pervades the opening of the Beethoven fugue as well.

The fugue in "Cool" begins at approximately 1:00.

West Side Story offers yet another example of sophisticated musical resources being put to work in the service of the drama itself. An obvious feature of the classical operatic ensemble is that more than one person is singing at once, often with different words, and with a wholly different attitude toward the situation at hand. Bernstein adapts the technique of the operatic ensemble to "Tonight," which is the climax of Act I. The characters, each voicing his or her own feelings about what will happen "tonight," are (1) Jets and Sharks, in duet, ("The Jets [the Sharks] are gonna have their day Tonight"); (2) Anita ("Anita's gonna get her kicks Tonight"); (3) Tony, and then Maria ("Tonight, tonight won't be just any night").

"Tonight," from *West Side Story*

0:07	Riff (Jets)
0:12	Bernardo (Sharks)
0:17	Riff
0:24	Bernardo

0:44	Jets and Sharks together	LISTENING GUIDE *(continued)*
1:08	Anita	
1:25	Tony [full 32-bar song form]	
2:24	Riff	
2:41	Maria [full 32-bar song form finishes the number, but from here on other voices come in with their individual themes]	
2:42	Riff	
2:54	Bernardo	
2:56	Anita [barely audible; from here to end all are singing]	

Note once again that the "hit tune" "Tonight" is cast in the time-honored 32-bar-chorus form. An interesting bit of sophistication that Bernstein adds is putting the repeat of "A," the first 8-bar strain, in a new key a third higher than the original, and then working his way back to the original key in the bridge.

THE MUSICAL SINCE THE ADVENT OF ROCK

Almost fifty years have passed since *West Side Story,* and those decades have wrought profound changes in the American popular musical stage. Late in the 1950s, Broadway began to lose the ear of its hitherto large public—an ear it had been able to take for granted in the three decades we have just been considering, when the best of America's popular tunes were from Broadway shows. Partly to blame was the decline of the big bands, which were no longer there to function as a medium for the dissemination of these tunes. The "hit parade" was over, partly because Broadway itself was in something of a slump—a dry transitional period, when the great composers were gone or were past their most productive period, and the new talent had not yet matured. (When a new generation did arrive, it would strike out in dramatically new directions.) But the greater reason was that receptiveness to show tunes, and to the whole ambience of the musical, was narrowing, especially among younger people, as the new and affluent youth market turned to rock 'n' roll, no longer interested in the wares of Broadway. Radio first, and eventually the record industry, followed the market; a gulf began to open up between the musical and the broad public. At least partly in response to that situation, several things happened to the musical show as a new generation of practitioners took over.

The Broadening of Sources and Subjects of the Musical

In the second half of the twentieth century, the musical continued to mine the familar sources of ore for subjects: books, plays, and even operas (*La Bohème* for *Rent*, 1996). But it also searched further and further afield for its stories and ideas, from the Bible to the comic strip and the fairy tale. In a reversal of the usual process of producing a film version of a musical, older films became the basis for new musicals. Two spectacle musicals, *Grand Hotel* (1989) and *Sunset Boulevard* (1993), are only among the latest, both based on classic American films decades old. Show business itself has been a favorite subject—often in portrayals of the more selfish, ruthless, insensitive, and pathetic side of what goes on behind the scenes. Beginning in the 1960s there has been a special reliance on the show built around a striking female personality (whether real or fictional), and often designed as a vehicle for one star. As lighter entertainment, the revue, which virtually died out during the heyday of the story musical, has again been cultivated, often as a retrospective of the work of a single composer, lyricist, or choreographer.

As a final gesture in what amounted to a progressive elimination of a plot as an ingredient in the musical, a show can simply be based on a *concept*. The concept could be the tangled relationships of sex, love, and marriage (*Company*, 1970); it could be the trauma of dancers desperately trying to be hired for shows (*A Chorus Line*, 1975); it could be the painter and his painting, and hence the relationship of art to life (*Sunday in the Park with George*, 1984). Or it could simply be the elaborately costumed setting of a series of descriptive verses by a well-known poet about a well-known domestic animal (*Cats*, 1981).

Not only has there been a steadily widening range of sources, settings, and concepts, but also, following trends in literature and on the legitimate stage, *themes* new to the popular musical stage have been introduced in the past decade. There could be mentioned in passing the onstage horror and bloodthirstiness of *Sweeney Todd*. Of deeper contemporary significance is the theme of homosexual love, which appeared in *La Cage aux Folles* (1983) and was central to *Falsettos* (1992, by William Finn), a musical that brought together two earlier works by the same author, *March of the Falsettos* (1981) and *Falsettoland* (1990), with the same sets of characters. These works of the early 1990s deal with AIDS, as does the 1996 rock musical *Rent*.

The Diminished Role of Music in the Musical Show

The music of the musicals has acquired, in most shows, increased sophistication: a more supple handling of form, a more ingenious use of ensembles, more effective scoring, a capacity for integrating into the whole a greater variety of musical styles, and so on. But with all this polish, it is paradoxical that, in the musical after mid-century, the *music itself* has mattered less in the whole scheme of things. It is no longer the most significant ingredient, especially in regard to what had formerly been the most memorable part of the earlier musicals—the singable, hummable song. There might actually be more music (it is practically continuous in *Sweeney Todd* and *Dreamgirls*), but it is subservient to other elements. On the decline of the overall role of music, and hence of the composer, observers are generally in agreement. Gerald Bordman has written, "Emphasis on composers in earlier shows has now passed to librettists, directors, and choreographers" (36)

What has taken the place of music as a prime ingredient in the musical? For one thing, *words*. Lyrics have acquired new brilliance, wit, and sophistication. Penetrating and urbane, at times earthy, the best are replete with clever rhymes, especially internal ones. In our time, the worthiest successor to Ira Gershwin as a lyricist is Stephen Sondheim (b. 1930). An example of exceptional intricacy of both meter and rhyme scheme is found in his "Beautiful Girls," the opening number of *Follies*. Although each chorus (there is no verse) adds up to a standard 32 bars (with a customary extension at the end) made up of 4-bar phrases, the lyrics are highly asymmetric as to the number of syllables per phrase, varying from seven to seventeen. The rhyme scheme is one of elegant complexity, with no fewer than four different rhyming "distances" used simultaneously. As Figure 13.1 shows, the widest distance is one of 16 measures of music. Most striking are the internal rhymes—those at a distance of less than the standard 4-measure phrase. Of these there are three kinds: five at 2 measures, two at 1 measure, and two ear-catching rhymes at a half-measure. The entire song is worth a close look, as a vivid illustration of the way in which

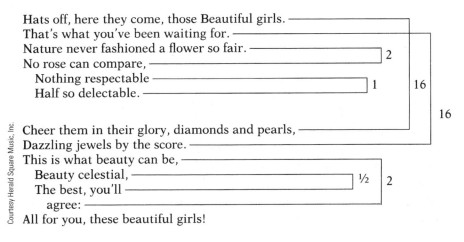

Courtesy Herald Square Music, Inc.

Figure 13.1
Rhyming scheme for "Beautiful Girls" from *Follies* (music and lyrics by Stephen Sondheim).

the sophisticated musical can sound catchy and familiar, and yet embody the most subtle intricacies in musical form, prosody, and rhyme.

Elaborate scenic and stage effects have become an integral (and expensive) ingredient in the musical. Shows such as *The Wiz* (taking us from Kansas to the fantasy land of Oz), *Sweeney Todd* (with its overwhelming portraying of London at its seamiest), and *Barnum* (putting us *in* the circus) were notable for their stunning visual elements. By the time of *Sunday in the Park with George* (where an artist's painting is assembled in its brilliant color before our eyes), so far had staging preempted the song that one critic mused that the audience might well leave the theater "humming the scenery" (Watt). Yet in 1984, that was only the beginning. Since then the series of spectacle shows—shows in which stage effects are possibly the most memorable ingredient, have followed one upon another, each striving to outdo the last in overwhelming the audience: *Les Misèrables, Phantom of the Opera, Grand Hotel, Sunset Boulevard, Miss Saigon,* and what next?

Among the new musicals today there is a cleavage between, on one hand, the sophisticated shows, with far-out subjects, treatments, and messages, high critical acclaim, and small audiences and, on the other hand, the more popular shows—mostly the spectacles such as *Les Misèrables* and *Phantom of the Opera*. These two types of shows are epitomized by the two most powerful figures in the business today. As John Lahr has put it, the musical today is "caught between the boulevard nihilism of Stephen Sondheim, which doesn't send in the crowds, and the boulevard bravado of Lloyd Webber, which does" (Lahr).

The audience has a third choice—the revivals. A scanning of the periodicals during the last five years or so reveals that of the shows that are reviewed, mostly in New York, approximately one-fourth are revivals—revivals going back seventy-five years to *Show Boat*. And of course the percentage of revivals is much higher in other cities throughout the country, and on the stages of college and community theaters—perhaps, after all, more accurate indicators of American taste at large in any period than what occupies the more fashionable and trendier stages of Manhattan.

In Conclusion, a New Live Musical

In the current confused, fragmented, and generally moribund state of the American musical— what critic John Lahr has described as "once a glorious fun machine, now yet another fabulous theatrical invalid" (Lahr)—a new production has recently created a good deal of excitement.

The media have labeled it a "rock opera," but there is far more to *Rent*, by Jonathan Larson (1960–96), than just another trendy low-life musical. Drugs, homosexuality, AIDS, poverty, the homeless, and incidentally, those two four-letter words (as well as support groups, phone machines, and cellular tele-phones) place it unequivocally in our time. But they are part of the *setting*; it is the realistic portrayal of believable characters on the stage, and their experi-ences and feelings, that ultimately engages our attention. Like many successful musical shows, *Rent* is based on a story that has already been staged—in this case, the opera *La Bohème* by Puccini, to which it pays homage not only in its basic plot but also in specific crucial scenes as well, most notably the meeting of Mimi and Roger (Puccini's Rudolfo) and, in the final scene, Mimi's death. (Larson actually quotes Puccini here, but it is Musetta's Waltz that we hear.) The music is well crafted and combines the timbres, textures, and vocal styles of contemporary popular music (not exclusively rock) with well-established compositional techniques, as exemplified by a canon in "Will I?" and a ground bass (actually as basic to rock as to seventeenth- and eighteenth-century music) in "Seasons of Love." "Santa Fe" is a song of visionary escape from the dreary life of New York City. A real *tour de force* is the finale, in which three previously heard tunes and lyrics are combined, two at a time, in a moving cli-max. This finale reiterates the essential message of the show. Benny, a former fellow bohemian turned entrepreneur, has declared in the first act that "this is Calcutta, Bohemia is dead." The rest of the extended Bohemian family have been determined to prove him wrong, and the last words are those of one of the three songs recapitulated in the finale: "There's only now, there's only here; give in to love or live in fear. No other path, no other way, no day but today." Having neither the "boulevard nihilism" of a show by Sondheim nor the sur-face glitter, the spectacular sets, and the "boulevard bravado" of a show by Webber, *Rent* may, with its directness, its sympathetic portrayal of believable characters, and its craftsmanship, open up new possibilities and give new hope to the currently chaotic and ailing stage musical. (The finale of *Rent* was unavailable for inclusion in the CD set; see Additional Listening.)

▬ PROJECTS

1. Compare the text of an original play with the "book," or libretto, of a musical show based on that play. Note technical changes and changes of plot, emphasis, and charac-terization. What do you think were the reasons for the changes? (For example, com-pare *Oklahoma!* with *Green Grow the Lilacs*; *Carousel* with *Liliom*; *The Most Happy Fella* with *They Knew What They Wanted*; or *My Fair Lady* with *Pygmalion*.)
2. Make a brief study of the use of the popular musical theater as an instrument of pro-paganda in any given age.
3. Select two show songs of the 1920s or 1930s and two show songs of the 1980s or 1990s, and do a comparative study of their lyrics; include a comparison of their lan-guage and subject, as well as of their form, prosody, rhyme scheme, and so on.

■ ADDITIONAL LISTENING

"Beautiful Girls." *Follies (Original Broadway Cast)*. Music and lyrics by Stephen Sondheim. Angel Classics 64666.

"Bewitched, Bothered, and Bewildered." *Pal Joey (Original Cast)*. Music by Richard Rodgers, lyrics by Lorenz Hart, book by John O'Hara. DRG 94763.

"Darktown Is Out Tonight" (from *Clorindy*). *Don't Give the Name a Bad Place: Types and Stereotypes in American Musical Theater 1870–1900*. NW 80265.

The Early Minstrel Show. NW 80338.

Finale. *Rent* Dreamworks DRMD2-50003, disc 2, track 17.

I Wants to Be a Actor Lady: and Other Hits from Early Musical Comedies. NW 80221.

14 Popular Song, Dance, and March Music from the Jacksonian Era to the Advent of Rock

A half-century ago, when little serious attention was given to the study of popular culture, a writer began his history of popular music with the assertion that it "is an index to the life and history of a nation" (Spaeth 3). The songs that are enjoyed and sung by a broad segment of the populace do indeed afford a vivid picture not only of the life and history but also of the attitudes, feelings, motivations, prejudices, mores—in fact, the dominant *worldview*—of an era. Popular songs fulfill this role even better than does the popular musical stage. Musical theater, for all its popularity, could not possibly reach and be enjoyed by the masses to the extent that popular song could. An age that numbered its theatergoers in the tens of thousands would number in the millions those who sang its songs.

POPULAR SONG FROM THE 1830s THROUGH THE CIVIL WAR

At the beginning of the preceding chapter we noted the changes that were then under way in what has been called the Jacksonian era (1829–37) in American social, political, and cultural life, and the developments in music printing that went hand in hand with the growth of a mass market for sheet music. The growth of this market, however, and with it the birth of distinctively American song, was related to far more than technology. Nicholas Tawa begins his book *A Music for the Millions* by observing:

> A turbulent era in American history opened with Andrew Jackson's election to the presidency and his passionate attack on privilege. It closed with Lincoln's election and the onset of the Civil War. From 1828 to 1861, new democratic beliefs and practices interspersed themselves aggressively among older aristocratic ways of thinking. . . . Inevitably, music reflected the social, economic, and political upheaval of these years. The once-dominant European-derived composition mirroring a narrow, leisured constituency was soon overwhelmed by a different type of musical work, one imbued with ideas favored by the common citizenry and exposed in the simplest verbal and melodic terms—the American popular song. (1)

The Parlor Song

The most flourishing genre of the period was what has become known as the parlor song. Parlor songs were purchased by, and sung in the living rooms of, the rapidly expanding numbers of middle-class families in cities and towns—to the accompaniment (kept purposely simple) of the piano, the *harmonium* (or *reed organ*), or the guitar. Indeed, simplicity and directness of expression were values that were prized in these songs, even when they were performed by professionals.

Melodies from Italian operas, principally those of Rossini (1792–1868), Donizetti (1797–1848), and Bellini (1801–35), were in circulation with English words and were more popular in America in the antebellum period than is generally supposed (Hamm, Chapter 4). But the basic models for the new popular song are to be found much closer to oral tradition. Irish folk melodies, especially as adapted and given new words by the Irish poet Thomas Moore (1779–1852), were popular in the United States throughout the nineteenth century, beginning with the first printing of Moore's famous collection, *Irish Melodies*, in 1808. The unadorned attractiveness and accessibility of the melodies (some of which are clearly related to dance tunes) helped win them wide acceptance. Then, too, Moore's new words often struck a note of melancholy and nostalgia that somehow, paradoxically for a new country with ever-widening possibilities, seemed in accord with nineteenth-century sentiments. Much of Moore's large collection is unfamiliar today, but a few of the songs have entered permanently into the body of American song, including "Believe Me, If All Those Endearing Young Charms," "The Minstrel Boy," "The Last

Rose of Summer," and "The Harp That Once Through Tara's Halls." Other imports from the British Isles were popular and helped set the American parlor song on its course. The most popular of these were "Home, Sweet Home" (1823), "Long, Long Ago" (1833), and a pathetic song of parting, "Kathleen Mavourneen" (1841).

Surveying native-born American songs, we find many that were sentimental or nostalgic in tone—often having to do with separation, usually by death. "Flow Gently, Sweet Afton" (1838), with music by the American J. E. Spilman on a poem by Robert Burns, was one. (Scottish influence on the American parlor song was significant—probably second only to that of Ireland.) "The Ocean Burial" (1850), a "favorite and touching ballad" with music by George N. Allen to words by Rev. Edwin H. Chapin, was another. The words to "The Ocean Burial," which begin "O! bury me not in the deep, deep sea," were later brought ashore and transformed into the text for one of the most popular of all cowboy songs, "O Bury Me Not on the Lone Prairie."

George Frederick Root wrote such songs on the subject of death as "The Hazel Dell" (1853) and "Rosalie, the Prairie Flower" (1855). The best known of the songs of love, separation, and death by Stephen Foster began to appear in the 1850s, including "The Village Maiden" (1855), "Gentle Annie" (1856), and, perhaps his most famous song in this vein, "Jeanie with the Light Brown Hair" (1854). "Beautiful Dreamer" (1862 or 1864) is ambiguous as regards death. Stephen Foster himself, and the breadth of his song output, will be dealt with in due course (pp. 265–67).

Touring Professionals: Henry Russell and the Hutchinson Family

Parlor songs were not confined to the parlor; in the period before the Civil War, professional singers were on the road giving concerts. These performers played an important role in shaping public taste, in acquainting the public with new songs, and in promoting them. That even songs for the "parlor" could profit by such promotion is shown by the sheet-music covers, which frequently advertised songs as having been "sung by," or even "sung with distinguished applause by," some popular singer.

One of the most successful and influential of these was the Englishman Henry Russell (1812–1900 or 1901), who visited the United States twice between 1836 and 1844. A most effective singer who also played his own piano accompaniments, he pioneered as a "one-man show" at a time when few other performers could hold the interest of an audience for an entire evening by themselves. His style and his material (he performed mostly his own songs) were designed to be spellbinding. His diction was such that every word was understood. Thus he was eminently fitted for popularity at a time when the main purpose of both singer and song was to arouse the emotions.

His songs tell us much about what was popular with antebellum audiences. Of his sentimental songs the best known are "The Old Arm Chair" (1840) and "Woodman! Spare That Tree!" (1837). Both have as their basis a special kind of sentimentality prevalent in the nineteenth century—sentimental attachment to a particular object. (This kind of sentimentality has survived in American popular culture and is frequently found in country music, as shown in songs such as "Picture on the Wall" [possibly identical with an 1864 song by Henry Clay Work] and "Send Me the Pillow That You Dream On.")

> Woodman! spare that tree!
> Touch not a single bough;
> In youth it sheltered me,
> And I'll protect it now;
> 'Twas my forefather's hand
> That placed it near his cot,
> There, woodman, let it stand,
> Thy axe shall harm it not!

More overtly dramatic songs of Henry Russell were such extended scenic monologues as "The Ship on Fire" and "The Maniac." Real spellbinders that depended for their effect on acting ability as well as singing, these were almost like one-man operatic scenes. Though it is clear that in the case of "Woodman! Spare That Tree!" the plea to save the tree was on sentimental, not ecological, grounds, many of Russell's songs did espouse social causes. The emotions so effectively aroused in his hearers were meant to be directed toward the alleviation of some current evil. That accorded with a prevalent view of the time as to the *moral* function of art, and especially of song. "The Maniac" was not merely a melodramatic scene; it also called attention to the wretched conditions in the mental asylums of his day. "The Dream of the Reveller" (1843) dealt with the evils of alcohol abuse, and after his return to England Russell wrote many antislavery songs. Thus, what Russell's compatriot Charles Dickens was aiming to do by literary means Russell *apparently* aimed to do with song. (It is disenchanting, however, to note that Henry Russell's sincerity may have been simply part of his act. As Richard Crawford has pointed out, George Frederick Root was disillusioned to find that Russell, in the privacy of his dressing room, was "much amused at the grief of his weeping constituents." [153]).

Among the foremost American performer-composers to follow Henry Russell's example were the Hutchinson Family Singers (Figure 14.1). From a rural New England background of strong convictions, they composed and

CD 3/28 (1:46) "Woodman! Spare That Tree!" by Henry Russell. 1837.

Text, "Woodman! Spare That Tree!"

New York Library for the Performing Arts

Figure 14.1
The Hutchinson Family Singers. The stiff postures and assured facial expressions in this lithograph reflect their strong convictions and beliefs.

CD 3/29 (2:41)
"Get Off the Track!"
Words by Jesse Hutchinson, to the tune of "Old Dan Tucker." 1844. The Hutchinson Family Singers (present-day group).

sang songs supporting many of the causes in which they so firmly believed. The cause that most absorbed them during the 1840s, their period of greatest activity, was the abolition of slavery. They sang frequently at antislavery meetings and rallies, appearing with the most radical abolitionists of the time, Wendell Phillips and William Lloyd Garrison. They participated in street marches, and on their tours they refused to sing in halls that would not admit blacks. They were well acquainted with Frederick Douglass, the escaped slave who settled in Lynn, Massachusetts, and they traveled with him to England. Abolition was by no means a universally popular cause, even in the North, and the Hutchinsons were hissed on occasion when they sang songs deemed "political." Their most famous abolitionist song, "Get Off the Track" (CD 3/29), was often sung to mixed reactions; it inspired wild enthusiasm among abolitionist sympathizers, and abuse, vocal and sometimes physical, from others.

Text "Get Off the Track!"

(*First verse*)   Ho! the car Emancipation
Rides majestic thro' our nation,
Bearing on its Train, the story,
Liberty! a nation's glory
Roll it along, Roll it along,
Roll it along thro' the nation
Freedom's Car Emancipation.

(*Last verse*)   Hear the mighty car wheels humming,
                 Down the track the engine's coming.
                 Church and statesmen hear the thunder,
                 Clear the track or you'll fall under.
                 "Get off the track! Get off the track!
                 Get off the track!" All are singing,
                 While the Liberty Bell is ringing.

This early protest song is not folk music, but otherwise it certainly fits into the context of Chapter 6 as an "instrument of advocacy." Like many protest songs, it uses an already existing tune. The irony in this particular case is that it is set to the tune of a blackface minstrel song, "Old Dan Tucker." The message of "getting off the track" was picked up over a century later by Bob Dylan in "The Times They Are a-Changin'" (1963). For a lively account in the press of a particularly spirited performance of the song at an antislavery society convention, see Cockrell, *Excelsior,* page 254.

Stephen Foster

Without doubt the best-known composer of the entire century was Stephen Collins Foster (1826–64). Although the popular Foster image is based on a good deal of misinformation and misinterpretation, the facts, insofar as modern objective scholarship can determine them, are more interesting than the fiction, and his accomplishments, his legacy, and his influence are undeniably impressive.

Foster was born as the ninth child into a fairly prosperous family in Pittsburgh. It was not to be expected, either of his family or of the mercantile environment of Pittsburgh in the 1830s, that his aptitude for music would be especially encouraged. Pursuing music in spite of that, Foster achieved enough success with some of his songs in the late 1840s (notably "Oh! Susanna") to induce him to sign contracts with publishers in New York and Baltimore. He actually became a professional songwriter in the 1850s and was able, for a time, to support himself in that way. His contracts provided for the payment of continuing royalties on sales—potentially a very favorable arrangement. But by the mid-1850s, serious problems began to surface, as manifested in his being persistently in debt (mostly to his brothers); in periodic, and ultimately prolonged, separations from his family; in a failure to manage prudently such resources as he had; and finally, in the alcoholism that defeated him in his last years in New York.

Foster's output of songs can be divided roughly into two categories: parlor songs and songs for the minstrel stage. As for the parlor songs, those dealing with love, separation, and death have been mentioned briefly in connection with similar songs by other composers of the period (p. 262). Many of his songs from 1862 on are about the Civil War ("Better Times Are Coming," "We Are Coming, Father Abraham, 300,000 More," both in 1862; and, as the war dragged on, "When This Dreadful War Is Ended" and "Willie Has Gone to the War," both in 1863). Foster's postminstrel humorous songs ("There Are Plenty of Fish in the Sea," 1862; "My Wife Is a Most Knowing Woman," 1863; "If You've Only Got a Moustache," 1864) lack the tang and bite of minstrelsy and draw on that perennial fund of comic material based on the pitfalls of courtship and marriage.

The songs he wrote for the minstrel stage (described variously on their covers—"plantation melody," "plantation song," "Ethiopian melody") are with few exceptions his most enduring. The comic songs, with their inherent rhythmic vitality and their simple but catchy melodic lines, show, of all his output, the closest relationship to the rough-hewn folk songs, sacred and secular, of the antebellum frontier. These exuberant, high-spirited songs for the minstrel stage include "Oh! Susanna" (1848), "Camptown Races" (1850), "Nelly Bly" (1850), "Way Down in Ca-i-ro" (1850, with its original piano part marked "a la banjo"), "Ring de Banjo" (1851), and "The Glendy Burk" (1860). The dialect so typical of minstrel material was used in Foster's early songs (such as "My Brudder Gum," and "Ring de Banjo"), but he dropped this mannerism in his later songs, rightly thinking that it would restrict the universality of their appeal.

The sentimental minstrel songs (Foster himself used the word "pathetic," in the sense of evoking pathos), unlike the comic songs, portray blacks with a profound sympathy, as human beings capable of feeling the pain of separation and the unending weariness of a life of servitude—a weariness to be relieved only by an often welcome death. The grief of separation—whether from loved ones or from an irrevocable past—is uppermost in the four best-known "pathetic plantation" songs: "Old Folks at Home," "My Old Kentucky Home," "Old Black Joe," and "Old Uncle Ned."

CD 3/30 (2:00)
"Hard Times Come Again No More" (excerpt), 1855. Poetry and music by Stephen Foster. The Hutchinson Family Singers (present-day group), with melodeon.

Text, "Hard Times Come Again No More"

The misery and hopelessness of poverty were not often dealt with in the parlor song, but one example, suffused with a degree of genuine sympathy, stands out: Stephen Foster's "Hard Times Come Again No More" (1855). Though there is no mention in the poetry of blacks or the implications of slavery itself, the song was a hit on the minstrel stage.

(*Verse*)   Let us pause in life's pleasures and count its many tears
             While we all sup sorrow with the poor:
             There's a song that will linger forever in our ears:
             Oh! Hard Times, come again no more.

(*Chorus*)	'Tis the song, the sigh of the weary;
	Hard Times, Hard Times, come again no more:
	Many days you have lingered around my cabin door,
	Oh! Hard Times, come again no more.
(*Verse*)	While we seek mirth and beauty and music light and gay
	There are frail forms fainting at the door:
	Though their voices are silent, their pleading looks will say
	Oh! Hard Times, come again no more.

(Chorus)

This song exhibits the typical nineteenth-century form of verse and chorus. It is an indication of the popularity of quartet singing by informal groups, in the home and other social gatherings. The chorus was frequently arranged and printed for four-part chorus of two sopranos, tenor, and bass, as it is sung on CD 3/30. Though this convivial practice had declined by the 1890s, to judge from the printed music, the *name* "chorus," as applied to the more familiar part of the song, has survived into the present. The *melodeon,* also known as the harmonium, or reed organ, is a keyboard instrument operated by foot-powered bellows. Developed in the first part of the nineteenth century, it was very popular as a parlor instrument until the 1920s.

A consideration of Foster's "pathetic plantation songs" would be incomplete without taking account of the appearance in 1852 of Harriet Beecher Stowe's novel *Uncle Tom's Cabin,* the central theme of which is slavery. The novel achieved instant popularity and was almost immediately adapted for the stage; William Austin writes that nine versions of it were produced in New York before the end of 1852. Foster originally conceived "My Old Kentucky Home" with the play in mind, though he changed his final version, deleting the name Uncle Tom. At one time or another, however, at least four of his plantation songs—"Old Folks at Home," "My Old Kentucky Home," "Massa's in de Cold Ground" (sung by chorus), and "Old Black Joe"—were sung in stage versions of *Uncle Tom's Cabin.* (William Austin has thoroughly explored Foster's relation to the Stowe novel, and the plays that were made from it, in his *"Susanna," "Jeanie," and "The Old Folks at Home": The Songs of Stephen Foster from His Time to Ours.* In this book, indispensable to a deeper understanding of the meaning of Foster's songs, Austin traces the preoccupation with these songs on the part of an impressive array of musicians, from Antonin Dvořák and Charles Ives to Pete Seeger, Ray Charles, and Ornette Coleman.)

Songs of the Civil War

Uncle Tom's Cabin was only one of many portents of the tragedy of epic proportions that America was to live through in the next decade. Her greatest national trauma (more lives were lost in the Civil War than in all of America's other wars combined) left an indelible mark on all aspects of the culture. Popular song was quick to mirror the war's events, its ideals, its motivations, its slogans, and, of course, its anguish. By the time of the Civil War, the popular-music publishing industry was in place and functioning. It was able to get songs to the public with an immediacy that rivaled that of the newspapers. Within a few days of the Confederate bombardment of Fort Sumter, which began the war, George F. Root's "The First Gun Is Fired!" was in print. More than in any other period in our history, popular song was the journalism of the emotions.

To fill the immediate need for songs, both sides rushed to fit new words to existing tunes. New verses to "The Star-Spangled Banner" were attempted by both sides. "The Yellow Rose of Texas" (Turner) became "The Song of the Texas Rangers," and Henry Russell's famous "Woodman! Spare That Tree! (touch not a single bough)" became "Traitor! Spare That Flag! (touch not a single star)." (The fascinating story of "The Yellow Rose of Texas," a durable song that apparently originated during the Mexican War, is told in Turner.) The ambivalence of Maryland as a border state was illustrated by the fact that both sides converted the German song "O Tannenbaum" into "Maryland, My Maryland," but with two sets of words urging diametrically opposed loyalties. At a time when secessionist feelings were running high, "Dixie" was used in a show in New Orleans (with no credit given to Dan Emmett as the composer); from there it spread rapidly throughout the South, becoming virtually the musical symbol of the Confederacy. It was not exclusively the property of the South, however; it could be found, with appropriate words, in virtually every state.

The other song most often associated with the Civil War is "The Battle Hymn of the Republic." It made its way, by gradual transformation, from a camp-meeting song with the words, "Say, brothers, will you meet us on Canaan's happy shore?" to a marching song used by Union regiments, growing out of that famous incident at Harpers Ferry in 1859, with the somewhat crude words "John Brown's body lies a-mouldering in the grave," to the loftier hymn, with words by Julia Ward Howe, that we know today. (For a capsule history see Heaps and Heaps 50–54.) As rallying songs, the South had "The Bonnie Blue Flag" (1861), a "southern patriotic song" with an Irish lilt, by Harry Macarthy.

CD 3/31 (0:45) "The Battle Cry of Freedom." 1862. Words and music by George Frederick Root. First Brigade Band (formed in 1964).

The North had George F. Root's "The Battle Cry of Freedom" (1862), an immensely popular song. The First Brigade Band (performer on CD 3/31) is a "portrayal" of a band that left Brodhead, Wisconsin, in 1864 to participate in General Sherman's campaign in Georgia. For more on the wind band in America after the Revolution (a period that was covered in Chapter 12, pp. 222–24), see pages 277–81 later in this chapter.

The importance of this song in the Union armies is attested by the fact that on the printed sheet music of another of Root's songs there appears this note: "In the Army of the Cumberland, the Soldiers sing the Battle-Cry when going into action, by order of the Commanding general."

Verse 1	Yes, we'll rally round the flag, boys, we'll rally once again,
	Shouting the battle cry of Freedom,
	We will rally from the hillside, we'll gather from the plain,
	Shouting the battle cry of Freedom.
Chorus	The Union forever, Hurrah boys, hurrah!
	Down with the Traitor, Up with the Star;
	While we rally round the flag, boys, Rally once again,
	Shouting the battle cry of Freedom.

Text, "The Battle Cry of Freedom"

As the war dragged on and hopes for an early end were cruelly disappointed, the tenor of the new songs that appeared began to change. Among sober songs put into the mouths of soldiers in the field were "Just Before the Battle, Mother," by Northern composer George F. Root, and another by one of the best composers who cast in their lot with the South, John Hill Hewitt. Setting a poem by a northern woman, Ethel Lynn Beers, of Goshen, New York, Hewitt produced in "All Quiet Along the Potomac Tonight" (CD 3/32), a song that transcended sectionalism and treated with a combination of sympathy and irony the death of a lone soldier on guard duty.

CD 3/32 (1:28) "All Quiet Along the Potomac Tonight" (excerpt). 1863. Words by Ethel Lynn Beers. Music by John Hill Hewitt.

All quiet along the Potomac tonight,
Except here and there a stray picket
Is shot as he walks on his beat to and fro,
By a rifleman hid in the thicket:
'Tis nothing, a private or two now and then
Will not count in the news of the battle:
Not an officer lost, only one of the men,
Moaning out all alone the death rattle.
All quiet along the Potomac tonight.

Text, "All Quiet Along the Potomac Tonight"

A subject only recently explored is the attitude toward African Americans portrayed in popular songs of the time. One researcher, Caroline Moseley, has found it mostly negative, even in the Unionist and abolitionist songs of the North. (See Moseley.) The attitudes of black people themselves toward the war and ultimate emancipation was inferred in songs written by white songwriters. The very popular "Kingdom Coming" (1862), a dialect song by Henry Clay Work, couched in jubilant terms the anticipation of freedom.

CD 3/33 (0:36) "Kingdom Coming." 1862. Words and music by Henry Clay Work. First Brigade Band.

Text, "Kingdom
Coming"

Verse 1   Say, darkeys, hab you seen de massa, wid de muffstash on his face,
             Go long de road some time dis mornin', like he gwine to leab de place?
             He seen a smoke, way up de ribber, whar de Linkum gumboats lay;
             He took his hat, an' lef berry sudden, an' I spec he's run away!
Chorus   De massa run? ha, ha! De darkey stay? ho, ho!
             It mus' be now de kingdom comin', an' de year ob Jubilo!

The song was indeed written by a white man (one whose father had been jailed in Illinois for helping runaway slaves to escape), but it is also known to have enjoyed wide currency among blacks; entering oral tradition, it achieved something of the status of a folk song, along with "Steal Away" and other songs that had specific reference to freedom in this present life.

POPULAR SONG FROM THE CIVIL WAR THROUGH THE RAGTIME ERA

The half-century between the Civil War and World War I witnessed changes that marks it as the beginning of the modern age. As such it presents contradictory images. Westward expansion, epitomized by the completion of the transcontinental railroad in 1869, a scant four years after Lee's surrender at Appomattox, was perceived as progress; yet it was accomplished at the shameful cost of killing off many of the original inhabitants who had lived on the land for millennia, and destroying the survivors' way of life. Industry and invention flourished, manufacturing and selling goods undreamed of in any previous time, and raising the material standard of living (for most) far above what it had been; this was perceived as progress, and was celebrated in the many fairs and expositions that were held. Yet it was achieved only with a frightful waste of natural resources; and in many cases workers who produced the goods were exploited beyond the point of endurance, and strife between management ("the bosses") and the newly formed and struggling labor unions reached shockingly bloody proportions. Cities grew and prospered, as did the nation overall; yet corruption among those who governed was all too common. Immigrants poured into the country from both Europe and Asia; their hopes and prospects for a better life were on the whole justified, yet discrimination, and worse, degraded many and worked against their entering the "mainstream" of American life.

The Gilded Age (to use Mark Twain's famous term) has been given many interpretations. For all its excesses—its "crass materialism" and flagrant examples of corruption and waste—the age of "rowdy adolescence" was also a time of solid accomplishments; schools, colleges, and libraries were built as well as bridges and railroads, and there was Chautauqua as well as burlesque.

Popular Song before Tin Pan Alley

Popular song, which had itself become an industry by the end of the century, did not mirror the full range of the contradictory images just described. The most popular topical songs were those that presented the positive aspects of events; Henry Clay Work's enthusiastic tribute to progress, "Crossing the Great Sierra" (published in 1869 after the completion of the railroad), was more successful than his sympathetic and prophetic lament, "The Song of the Red Man" (1868), which has the following lines:

Driven westward we came, but the paleface was here,
With his sharp axe and death-flashing gun;
And his great Iron Horse now is rumbling in the rear;
O my brave men! your journey is done.

Text, "The Song of the Red Man." (See Additional Listening.)

A few well-established songwriters wrote songs about social issues. Work, the composer of "The Song of the Red Man," also wrote one of the most popular temperance songs, "Come Home, Father" (1864). George Frederick Root wrote "The Hand That Holds the Bread" in 1874, in support of the Grange movement rallying farmers against middlemen and monopolists. Septimus Winner wrote "Out of Work" in 1877, reflecting one of the frequent depressions of the period. But except for a few of the temperance songs, songs of social comment were not big items in the general marketplace. Songs such as "No Irish Need Apply," "Drill, Ye Tarriers, Drill," "The Dodger," and "The Farmer Is the Man Who Feeds Them All" (CD 2/8, p. 97) are all from this period, and have survived doggedly only in the quasi–oral tradition of their constituencies.

The Civil War left a legacy of bitterness, war-weariness, sorrow, and a general depletion of spirit. Songs of gentle sentiment were popular. "Whispering Hope (Oh how welcome thy voice)," by Septimus Winner (1868), speaks of comfort after sorrow—a mellifluous duet in waltz time. There was a preoccupation with growing old; three typical songs of love and remembrance in old age are all still well known: "When You and I Were Young, Maggie" (1866), "Sweet Genevieve" (1869), and "Silver Threads Among the Gold" (1873). Even the waltzing exuberance of "The Flying Trapeze" (1868), with its gracefully arching melody expressive of the swings of the aerialist and its ruefully comic final verses, is tinged with the sadness and hopelessness of lost love.

Once I was happy, but now I'm forlorn,
Like an old coat that is tattered and torn.

Text, "The Flying Trapeze"

In many ways the popular song of the period was linked more to the past than to the future. There was (relatively) an innocence, a sincerity, and, above all, an artistic and business climate in which the individual, regardless of location or commercial connections, could still succeed. Thomas Westendorf, who wrote "I'll Take You Home Again, Kathleen" in Plainfield, Indiana, in 1876, was later sent a check for fifty dollars each month for many years "in gratitude" by the publisher, who, having bought the song outright, was under no contractual obligation to do so (Hamm 264). (The publisher, John Church & Co., was based not in New York, but in Cincinnati.) The whole story (beginning with a "hit" coming out of Plainfield, Indiana!) would have been, if not unthinkable, at least highly unlikely two decades later.

Tin Pan Alley: Popular Music Publishing Becomes an Industry

As American cities became larger, wealthier, and more sophisticated in the last two decades of the nineteenth century, two things happened that affected popular music. One was the increased vitality, and ultimately the Americanization, of the popular musical stage, as we saw in the last chapter. The other was the gradual emergence of a centralized industry for the publication and promotion of American popular songs. Both phenomena were centered in New York City.

Broadway and Tin Pan Alley were interrelated in complex ways but were never one and the same. They cohabited the same area in the beginning—what was then the theater district of East 14th Street in Manhattan, where Tony Pastor's famous Opera House, the home of vaudeville, was located. But the close relationship exemplified in this proximity grew looser over time, and as the musical theater developed, under the powerful influence of the great show composers of the new century, the *stratification* of American popular song took place. In craftsmanship and sophistication, Broadway show songs, from Victor Herbert to Jerome Kern, were at the top. George Gershwin discovered this early in his career. James Maher describes Gershwin's "almost ecstatic sense of revelation when he first heard music by Jerome Kern"—music that made him conscious that most popular music was of inferior quality, and that musical-comedy music was made of better material (Maher). Beginning in the 1890s, theater songs dominate the great canon of American popular song, which includes most of the "evergreens" such as "Smoke Gets in Your Eyes."

Slightly below the theater songs was a class of songs that began to appear in the 1930s, the movie songs. This category also includes a number of evergreens: "The Way You Look Tonight," "You'd Be So Nice to Come Home To," "Over the Rainbow," and "Laura" are among them.

Beyond theater songs and movie songs was that vast category of songs purveyed by what James Maher has called "the marketplace-oriented music publishing companies known collectively as Tin Pan Alley." Its songs issued forth in prodigious quantities, only the tiniest fraction of which attained "hit" status. Most of them were short-lived, manufactured to conform to the passing fashions of the year, the season, the month. Yet here too, as we shall see, were some "evergreens." (Though it was not uncommon to find composers contributing to two of the three strata here defined, Irving Berlin was virtually the only song-writer to contribute to all three—composing extensively and successfully for Broadway, Hollywood, and Tin Pan Alley.)

New York's dominance in popular-song publishing was not achieved at the hands of the old-line publishers—certainly not at the hands of publishers who would send monthly checks to songwriters out of sheer gratitude. As Sanjek has put it,

> Much as would the post–World War II music houses when faced with the annoying presence of hillbilly and race music, the established arts- and parlor-music publishers failed to perceive the future. It was in the hands of music publishers specializing in new popular American music—first formed around 1885, whose founders . . . were, as one of them, Isidore Witmark, remembered, "youngsters who had caught on and had a fair notion of the direction in which they were headed. What they knew least about was music and words, what they cared about least might be answered in the same phrase. They discovered that there was money in popular song. (7–8)

The basic vehicle for the dissemination of the popular song, and therefore the basic commodity of the industry, continued, until the 1920s, to be sheet music. The money in popular song, it was realized by these new entrepreneurs, was in songs that sold not in thousands of copies but in millions. In the 1880s sales began to climb toward that goal, and in 1892 the song that perhaps more than any other symbolizes the era—"After the Ball," by Charles K. Harris—sold over two million copies in its first few years, with sales eventually reaching over ten million.

For a song to reach anything even approaching that volume of sales (few did, and most barely paid for their printing costs), of course it had to be publi-cized, and that became a profession in itself, in which ingenuity and brashness paid off. The exploits of song "pluggers" (who profited from the example set by that early master of "public relations," P. T. Barnum) included, but were not limited to, bribing performers across a wide spectrum, from professionals (who could be credited as coauthors of a song, with their picture on the cover), to hopefuls who sang on the popular amateur-nights, to the Italian *padrone* who leased street organs to immigrant organ-grinders. The novelist Theodore Dreiser (brother of songwriter Paul Dresser) left a valuable account of how the whole process worked in an 1898 article quoted at some length in Isaac Goldberg's *Tin Pan Alley: A Chronicle of American Popular Music.* (See Additional Readings.)

As to the form of the songs themselves, the earlier four-part chorus, typical of the Stephen Foster era, was replaced by the solo "chorus" (the older name stuck, though it was no longer literally accurate). In the conventional Tin Pan Alley song, it was the "chorus" that had the identifiable "tune"; the "verse," with its lead-in narration, was the part hardly anyone remembered, and it was frequently omitted, especially when the tunes were later used as jazz "standards." The squarer 4/4 meter of the typical antebellum song had given way to 3/4; the waltz-song dominated the field—songs such as "After the Ball" (1892, by Charles K. Harris), "Daisy Bell," better known as "A Bicycle Built for Two" (1892, by Harry Dacre); "The Band Played On" (1895, by Charles Ward); and "Meet Me in St. Louis" (1904, a promotional song for the world's fair of that year by Kerry Mills).

CD 3/34 (0:57)
"My Gal Sal," by
Paul Dresser. 1905.
Don Meehan, vocal;
Dave Corey, piano.

There was a broad range of songs that played quite deliberately on the sentiments, written out of sincere feelings (here we think of Paul Dresser) or out of shrewd calculation as to what would sell (and here we think of Charles K. Harris), or, as is more likely in most cases, a combination of the two. Perhaps, as has been suggested, these songs offered an opportunity for emotional release, even if vicarious, at a time when the outward display of emotion was not acceptable in Protestant middle-class society. Prominent in this genre were the songs about women either bought or betrayed—women not as objects of romance but as objects of pity. So much have these songs been associated with the period that their very titles have entered the language as phrases symbolic of the late Victorian age: "She May Have Seen Better Days" (1894), "Mother Was a Lady" (1896), "Take Back Your Gold" (1897), "She Is More to Be Pitied Than Censured" (1898), "Only a Bird in a Gilded Cage" (1900). Songs about separation by death were numerous; familiar are "Dear Old Girl" (1903) and "My Gal Sal" (Paul Dresser's most famous song, of 1905).

Many a song that is actually about death reveals the fact only in the verse; the better-known chorus has more general sentiments. Examples are "When You Were Sweet Sixteen" (1898), "You Tell Me Your Dream, I'll Tell You Mine" (1899), and "In the Shade of the Old Apple Tree" (1905). More blatantly pathetic "tearjerkers" are represented by "In the Baggage Coach Ahead" (where "baby's cries can't waken her"), published in 1896. The cover of this crowning example of bathos gives a picture and a byline to Imogene Comer, "Queen of Descriptive Vocalists," while at the same time taking opportunistic advantage of the scenario to advertise "The Empire State Express of the New York Central . . . Fastest Train in the World."

The Ragtime Song

The nature and origins of ragtime, whose brief but intense flowering began in the 1890s and was over before 1920, will be considered in the next chapter. Ragtime, in its revival, has come to be regarded as essentially music for solo piano. In its day, however, ragtime had a far broader meaning. The ragtime or "coon" song we tend now to see as a vulgarized offshoot of pure ragtime, with its essential characteristics diluted. Both in the crudity of its words and in the grotesque caricatures of its sheet-music covers, the coon song appears today as grossly insulting to black people. In its day, however, the ragtime song was a popular manifestation of the "ragtime craze," and these songs were written and sung by black as well as white performers. With all its vulgarity, it brought a new dimension to American popular song. As Arnold Shaw has said, "Coon songs were an infusion into the pop music scene of high spirits, revelry, and rhythmic drive, much as Rhythm and Blues was later in the 1950s," and he also makes the point that, as in the case of rhythm-and-blues half a century later, the coon song was as much a style of singing as it was a type of song (42). The lineage of the female "coon shouter" starts perhaps with Mama Lou, in Babe Connors's St. Louis brothel, who, according to Shaw, may have been the writer of "Ta-Ra-Ra Boom-De-Ay" and "The Bully," songs that were later popularized on the New York stage by the white singer May Irwin (1862–1938).

The white composer Frederick Allen ("Kerry") Mills produced a memorable little "ragtime cakewalk" called "At a Georgia Camp Meeting" (CD 4/5, p. 292) published in 1897 as a piano piece, and in 1899 as a song. The tune, with its ragtime syncopations, became very popular and was much associated with a dance craze called the cakewalk, which swept America and even invaded Europe. (The cakewalk, originally a plantation slave dance, had appeared in exaggerated form as the minstrel show "walk-around" for years.)

So persistent, and evidently popular, was the "darky" image in song that it was present even in songs whose well-known *choruses* gave little hint of it. "Ida! Sweet as Apple Cider" (1903) and "Coax Me" (1904) have faint traces of dialect, and references to a "dusky maid" and "dusky lovers" in their verses. Even the well-known "Mighty Lak' a Rose" (1901, by Ethelbert Nevin—a song that did not come out of Tin Pan Alley), in spite of the "eyes so shiny blue," has dialect (including the endearing term "Mammy") that shows a clear relationship to the long tradition of black dialect songs reaching back to the 1840s and before.

The Barbershop Quartet, Black and White

Flourishing about the same time as ragtime was another form of entertainment (popular at least as much for the performer as for the listener), the barbershop quartet. The relation of the barbershop itself to the quartet was mentioned in connection with origin of the black gospel quartet, to which the black barbershop quartet is closely related (p. 210). James Weldon Johnson (who edited *The Book of American Negro Spirituals*) wrote in the preface:

Pick up four colored boys or young men anywhere and the chances are ninety out of a hundred that you have a quartet. . . . In the days when such a thing as a white barber was unknown in the South, every barber shop had its quartet, and the men spent their leisure time playing on the guitar—not banjo, mind you—and 'harmonizing'. . . . When I was a very small boy [about 1880] one of my greatest pleasures was going to concerts and hearing the crack quartets made up of the waiters in the Jacksonville hotels sing. . . . When I was fifteen and my brother was thirteen we were singing in a quartet which competed with other quartets. (35–36)

W. C. Handy, famous "father of the blues," as soon as he became a tenor, sang in the quartet that Florence, Alabama had. (Nearly all Southern towns had such a quartet.) White barbershop quartets flourished somewhat later. (The distinctions in repertoire, style, and history between black and white quartets has not been adequately studied, so far as is known. The photo [Figure 14.2] of the Atlanta University Quartette shows two guitars present, and Johnson's mention of the guitar in his early recollections of the barbershop suggests the possibility that the black quartets were accompanied.) By the 1920s the growing popularity of jazz, radio, and sound films led to a decline in at least the professional quartets that had been formed. The recognition by

Figure 14.2
James Weldon Johnson (far right) with other members of the Atlanta University Quartette, early 1890s. The two guitars suggest that early black quartets were accompanied.

1938 that barbershop quartet singing had become in need of preserving resulted in the founding of the Society for the Preservation and Encouragement of Barber Shop Quartet Singing in America (SPEBSQSA), in the beginning an essentially white organization. The texture of the barbershop quartet is made up of a tenor, singing the melody, another tenor harmonizing above, a bass on the bottom, and a baritone supplying the other notes of the chords, as needed. It is "close" harmony in that the voices sing in a tight texture, generally as close together, except for the bass, as the chord will allow. The repertoire probably consisted mainly of the parlor songs and hymns popular in the late nineteenth century. (See Abbott in Additional Readings.)

We have briefly sketched the rich mix that was popular song in the two decades surrounding the turn of the century—years when the "marvelous hit-machine" was being built. Before we follow popular song further into the twentieth century, let us look at another important ingredient in our popular musical culture: the American band.

THE BAND IN AMERICA AFTER THE JACKSONIAN ERA

Bands and Band Music to the Time of Sousa

As was noted in Chapter 12, the wind band was an important part of the American musical scene in the colonial and federal periods. Subsequent European experiment and invention resulted in improvements in brass instruments, making them more flexible and capable of producing the full range of chromatic tones. These improvements, as well as the greater durability and carrying power of brass instruments (important for outdoor functions) led to the gradual elimination of clarinets, oboes, and bassoons, and the rise of the *brass band*, which dominated the scene until well after the Civil War. A sampling of the music played by these bands includes quicksteps, polkas, schottisches, and waltzes—a fair reflection of the dances that were popular at the time.

With the Civil War came the need for brass bands in ever-greater numbers. The standard Civil War band was small by present-day standards, consisting of a dozen brass players and five drummers. But even before hostilities ceased, there was a portent of things to come. When Patrick Gilmore, then in New Orleans, was asked by General Banks to provide music for the inauguration of the new governor there, he assembled a band of five hundred and a chorus of six thousand (including schoolchildren), and put on the first of his many mammoth concerts, climaxed by the firing of fifty cannon (electrically controlled from the podium) and the ringing of all the church bells in the city.

After the war, Gilmore expanded on the concept of the concert event of huge proportions. The ultimate came in 1872 as a World Peace Jubilee in Boston, for which he assembled two thousand instrumentalists and choruses of twenty thousand in a specially built, one-hundred-thousand-seat coliseum. This jubilee lasted eighteen days, and to augment the entertainment, Gilmore invited bands from England, France, and Germany, as well as Johann Strauss and his orchestra from Vienna. Patrick Gilmore never again assembled anything on this scale (in its day the equivalent, in complexity and the sheer numbers involved, to the modern Olympic Games), but the "jubilee" concept—under the more modern designation "festival"—is still a related cultural phenomenon worldwide; and the assembling of large instrumental forces survives in the "massed bands" heard today wherever school bands and bandsmen gather.

Less spectacular but ultimately more significant was the work that Gilmore did beginning in 1873 in developing his 22nd Regimental Band in New York into a combination concert and touring band. He was to establish a pattern for bands that lasted half a century. He played summer concerts at Manhattan Beach, and winter concerts in Gilmore's Garden. (This establishment, originally P. T. Barnum's Hippodrome, ultimately became Madison Square Garden, and under that name moved later to a succession of new locations.) In the spring and fall, Gilmore's band toured.

A typical band program of the late nineteenth century would show a judicious mixing of classical favorites, numbers by featured "headline" soloists, and popular songs and hymns. The classical ingredient consisted of transcriptions from the orchestral repertoire, mostly operatic overtures. Classical selections were always balanced by popular numbers; the soprano soloists who appeared with the bands might sing operatic excerpts but would be sure to include songs such as "Silver Threads Among the Gold," and even popular hymns such as "Nearer, My God, to Thee." Touring concert bands such as Gilmore's, and later Sousa's, played much the same role in the dissemination of popular songs as did the big dance bands of the 1930s and 1940s. Featured instrumental soloists were big attractions; these included accomplished performers on the saxophone, the baritone horn, and the trombone. But by far the most popular "stars" with the bands were the cornet soloists. The cornet had developed into an extremely facile virtuoso instrument that was to the band what the violin as a solo instrument was to the orchestra.

Gilmore tempered the sound of the brass band with the gradual reintroduction of woodwind instruments, which in time became numerically dominant, until by the end of the century the concert band consisted, in rough proportion, of one-third clarinets (the equivalent of the orchestra's violins), one-third other woodwinds, and one-third brass; the percussion section was somewhat smaller in proportion than in the brass-band days. Under Gilmore and Sousa, who were both very discriminating and demanding musicians, the professional concert touring band developed into an ensemble that in dynamic range, tone quality, blend, phrasing, and precision was comparable to the best orchestras of its day.

John Philip Sousa (1854–1932) and the Band from the 1890s to the 1930s

The most important figure in the development of the American band and its music began his independent professional career as an orchestral violinist (he played under the popular French composer and conductor Jacques Offenbach in Philadelphia in 1876) and a conductor with traveling musical shows. In 1880 he was invited to direct the U.S. Marine Band. By that time he had heard, and been impressed by, Gilmore's band, and he perceived the potential of the wind band. He reorganized the Marine Band and its repertoire thoroughly and raised it to a position of excellence and renown, even securing permission to take it on tour. In 1892 he formed his own independent band, which he conducted, except for an interval of training bands for the navy during World War I, until his death in 1932.

Paying and treating his musicians well, Sousa at the same time made of his band a profitable business, with stockholders. It was essentially a touring ensemble, and except for a very few regular engagements (such as those at Manhattan Beach, New York, and Willow Grove, Pennsylvania), the band was on the road a great deal. He followed Gilmore's example in balancing his programs between popular and classical selections; furthermore, he kept up with developments in popular music. His solo trombonist, Arthur Pryor, was from Missouri, the cradle of ragtime, and he arranged and taught the band to play this new music. (Pryor's composition "Lassus Trombone," in this vein, was long a popular band number, especially with trombonists.) Sousa's band took ragtime to Europe in 1900, and his turn-of-the-century programs, with their "plantation songs and dances" and "coon songs," show that contemporary popular derivatives of black American music had a place on his programs. (See CD 4/5, p. 292.) He later incorporated some form of jazz into his programs.

Considering his active public life, Sousa's creative output was phenomenal. He completed 12 operettas, 11 suites, 70 songs, nearly 100 other instrumental pieces of various kinds, and over 200 arrangements and transcriptions, as well as three novels and an autobiography. But he is best known for his marches. "The Washington Post," a march composed in 1889 for a ceremony honoring the student winners of an essay contest sponsored by that newspaper, attained instant and widespread popularity, and became indelibly associated with a new dance, the two-step. Between 1877 and 1931, Sousa composed 136 marches, an imposing proportion of which (one could cite "The Washington Post," "Semper Fidelis," "The Thunderer," "The Liberty Bell," "King Cotton," "El Capitan,"

Figure 14.3
"A medal for every march!" seems to be the message behind this caricature of John Philip Sousa. With over 130 marches to his credit, it is no wonder the artist thought to place a humorous "medal annex" just behind the prolific composer!

and "The Stars and Stripes Forever") have, along with some of the songs of Stephen Foster, entered the domain of permanent national music. Nor is their popularity limited to America; like the Foster songs and the waltzes of Johann Strauss, Jr., they have become part of a world music.

Sousa had a flourishing grassroots tradition on which to build. The 1890s, when his own band was touring and establishing its reputation, was the great era of American bands, especially in the towns and small cities in the Midwest. Town bands furnished music both functional and entertaining, and they were a strong focus of community pride. Before the advent of movies and later of radio, it was town bands, along with singing and theatrical groups, that accounted for most of what local entertainment and culture existed; these attractions were augmented by such traveling entertainments as circuses, minstrel shows, lecturers and performers on the Chautauqua circuit, and occasional visits by the bands of Alessandro Liberati, Frederick Innes, Thomas Brooke, Patrick Gilmore, and even Sousa himself. A lively and sympathetic description of the town bands of the period is given by H. W. Schwartz, who quotes ads placed in music papers and business magazines for the purpose of attracting musicians to small communities that could offer them steady employment as well as a position in the local band. Of the twenty-three ads quoted, all but five are from towns in the Midwest (170–76).

The Band from the 1930s to the Present

The decline of the professional concert/touring band began about the time of Sousa's death in 1932. Subsequently there were two significant developments. The first was the passing of leadership to the *academic*-band movement; college and university bands developed in size, in excellence, and in general esteem, especially in the Midwest. The second development, the creation of new works specifically for wind band, was related to this but was also the outgrowth of the work of Edwin Franko Goldman (1878–1956), whose professional band countered the general trend of decline. The Goldman Band performed continuously from 1918 to 1979, after Edwin Franko Goldman's death, under the leadership of his son Richard Franko Goldman (1910–80). In the 1950s

Richard Franko Goldman began to commission new works. Thus it was that works for the newly developed "symphonic band," or "symphonic wind ensemble" began to come from established composers. This flow of new works for band reached its peak in the 1950s and 1960s; there was hardly a major American composer of the time who did not contribute at least one work for band, including Virgil Thomson, William Schuman, Walter Piston, Peter Mennin, Vincent Persichetti, Howard Hanson, Paul Creston, and Ross Lee Finney.

POPULAR SONG FROM RAGTIME TO ROCK

We now return to popular song where we last left it, at the close of the ragtime era, to describe the three decades between 1920 and 1950—decades that have generally been regarded as the "golden years" of Tin Pan Alley.

The Major Media Shift and the Role of the Big Bands

These "golden years" began with three technological developments that drastically changed the *media* by which popular song reached the public and thus brought fundamental changes to the entire industry. The phonograph recording became a significant factor after the turn of the century, radio in 1922, and the sound movie in 1929. What took place after 1920, then, was a gradual shift in the consuming public from an active to a passive role, as the phonograph and the radio replaced the parlor piano as a source of music in the home. Even that intermediate stage represented by the player piano ("canned" music produced by a "live" instrument) was edged out, sales of player pianos having reached their peak in 1923.

As the Depression arrived in the early 1930s, radio and the new talking pictures became the dominant media, dealing a severe blow to the phonograph, which did not really recover its position until the end of the decade, with recordings of the popular swing bands. Radio thus became a prime means for the dissemination and plugging of songs, as it has remained to this day (in changed form, and with a more specialized audience and material). Many of the prominent bands performed on weekly broadcasts in the 1930s, either from a permanent base or by remote hookup while on tour. Singers with the bands became increasingly important as purveyors of new popular songs. Some bandleaders were themselves composers, and a few of the best songs in this period came from the bands.

Stability and Pluralism in Popular Music between the Wars

Although the big technological media shifts had profound effects on the popular-music industry, the nature and style of popular song itself changed little in this period. But if popular song was essentially static during this period, it was also pluralistic. The stratification referred to earlier in relation to the beginnings of Tin Pan Alley was a fact of American cultural life throughout this period. Sanjek points up this cleavage in taste—this pluralism—in describing the policies of Tin Pan Alley publishers in the 1930s:

> Well-written songs possessing any poetic qualities were rejected immediately, because it was the general Tin Pan Alley feeling that true sheet-music buyers had little or no interest in them and therefore they were "not commercial." Those "great" songs of the 1930s, beloved by cultural elitists and social historians, were well known only to a minority of Americans—those who were better educated and more affluent than the average radio "fan" and who had access to the Broadway stage and other sophisticated entertainment. (19)

This view does seem to be borne out by a few statistics. Hamm has compiled a list of the "top forty" songs between 1900 and 1950, those being the ones most often recorded. Of these, only twelve (30 percent) are from plotted Broadway shows, six (15 percent) are from revues (a form descended from vaudeville), and the other twenty-two (55 percent) are nonshow Tin Pan Alley songs (487–88). (Any list is apt to have its own self-contained bias, of course; a list of recorded songs may reflect the popularity of a particular dance band, or the popularity of their particular version of a song, as well as the inherent popularity of the song itself.)

Tin Pan Alley songs about the real life that surrounds us were a rarity; one that did become popular appeared in the Depression era, from a topical review called *New Americana*. CD 3/35 is an early recording by Bing (Harry Lillis) Crosby (1904–77), one of the most popular entertainers in twentieth-century America, just about the time he was beginning his movie and radio career.

The mainstay of Tin Pan Alley in this period was the ballad (not the same as the folk ballad treated in Part I), a type of love song providing most of the "standards"—those few songs that in quality and appeal transcended the quantities of ephemera produced. As a sample of the best the Alley had to offer in these three decades (again excluding show and movie tunes), here is a select list of half a dozen independent songs: "I'll See You in My Dreams" (1924, Isham Jones; one of many songs by bandleader-composers); "Blue Skies" (1927, Irving Berlin); "Star Dust" (1929; Hoagy Carmichael; this perennial, one of the most frequently recorded of all popular songs, began as a quasi-ragtime piano piece, which was later slowed down and given lyrics by Mitchell Parish); "Stormy Weather" (1933, Harold Arlen; written by this veteran Broadway composer for Harlem's Cotton Club, where it was introduced by Ethel Waters);

CD 3/35 (3:14)
"Brother, Can You Spare a Dime?" 1932. Lyrics by E. Y. Harburg. Music by Jay Gorny. Bing Crosby, vocal. Recorded in 1932.

"Blue Moon" (1934, Richard Rodgers; one of his few songs not introduced in a show or a movie); and "You Go to My Head" (1938, J. Fred Coots).

The popular singers of the period invariably sang with the bands, live, on the radio, and on recordings. The gifted and troubled Billie Holiday (1915–59) sang first as vocalist with the bands of Count Basie and Artie Shaw, and later with her own ensembles, which included in "You Go to My Head" as pianist Claude Thornhill, well-known leader and arranger. See CD 3/36.

CD 3/36 (2:52)
"You Go to My Head."
1938. Music by J. Fred
Coots. Lyrics by Haven
Gillespie. Billie Holliday,
vocal. Recorded in
1938.

TIN PAN ALLEY AND ITS RELATION TO JAZZ AND BLACK VERNACULAR MUSIC

Many of the leaders of the dance orchestras and big bands of the period composed and introduced songs. Duke Ellington contributed many, most of which are decidedly instrumental in character. "I'm Beginning to See the Light" (1944), a collaborative effort of Duke Elllington, Johnny Hodges, and Harry James, is a typical song to come out of the stylistic milieu of the big band in that its melody is made up of *riffs*—short melodic fragments repeated over changes of harmony.

Aside from these songs by bandleaders of the period, the typical popular song between the wars (whether from Broadway, Hollywood, or Tin Pan Alley) had little relationship to jazz or other black vernacular music. The one exceptional bridge was the blues. Harold Arlen was perhaps the closest to jazz and blues of any of the major songwriters of this period. As Alec Wilder has written, "He, more than any of his contemporaries, plunged himself into the heartbeat of the popular music of his youth, the dance band." Wilder goes on to show how Arlen's "don't-worry-about-the-mud-on-your-shoes attitude," characteristic of blues and jazz, is illustrated in songs such as "Sweet and Hot" (1930), "Between the Devil and the Deep Blue Sea" (1931), "I Gotta Right to Sing the Blues" (1932), "That Old Black Magic" (1942), and especially the memorable "Blues in the Night" (1944) (Wilder 257–74). (See CD 3/37.)

Though they were distinct, the one from the other, there was a symbiotic relationship between jazz and popular music in this period. Jazz was heavily indebted to Broadway, Hollywood, and Tin Pan Alley for its "standards"— songs whose melodies and chord progressions became the basis for its arrangements and improvisations. Consider jazz without the hundreds of renditions of "Star Dust," without Coleman Hawkins's "Body and Soul," without Charlie Parker's "Embraceable You," and without the score of bebop versions of "How High the Moon."

For its part, popular music was indebted to jazz for a continuously revitalized rhythmic basis and for the jazz arrangements by popular hot bands that contributed their flavor to, and helped promote, the songs. Performances by such singers as Bing Crosby, Ethel Waters, Mildred Bailey, Jack Teagarden, Billie Holiday, Lena Horne, Sarah Vaughan, and Ella Fitzgerald, backed up by bands such as those of Benny Goodman, Teddy Wilson, Artie Shaw, Harry James, and Duke Ellington, impart, through interpretation, a jazz or blues flavor to songs that do not necessarily possess it inherently.

Finally, the relation of black vernacular dance to popular music in this period is crucial. Since the turn of the twentieth century, innumerable vernacular dances have entered the mainstream of popular dance. The Charleston, the shimmy, the Black Bottom, and various "animal dances," such as the turkey trot, the grizzly bear, and the bunny hug, began, despite opposition, to coexist with and gradually replace the older polkas, schottisches, and waltzes. (One animal dance—possibly made up by the popular and influential team of Vernon and Irene Castle before World War I—was the fox trot, which became "respectable" and survived well into the period under consideration.) The toddle was danced to Dixieland jazz. But the dance that became indelibly associated with swing jazz came out of places like the Savoy Ballroom in Harlem in the late 1920s (the home ground of many of the hottest bands). First known as the lindy hop (after Charles Lindbergh's famous flight), it became more broadly familiar as the jitterbug. Although most of the young could and did do it, when performed by accomplished jitterbuggers in its more flamboyant and elaborate form it was a dance to watch as well. It was the dance symbol of hot jazz, and the interaction and mutual stimulus between a hard-driving swing band and a group of equally hard-dancing, frenzied jitterbuggers on the dance floor were undeniable.

The Decline of Tin Pan Alley and the Dispersion of the Popular-Music Industry

After midcentury, an upheaval in the popular-music industry, leading to its dispersion and decentralization, began in the "provinces," far removed from the creaking but still functioning Broadway–Hollywood axis. Regional and ethnic musics began to account for significantly larger shares of the market. Coming out of teeming and troubled urban areas such as Chicago, Detroit, and Philadelphia was black rhythm-and-blues; from the South and the West came white hillbilly music, given the trade name country-and-western. As an offspring of both came rock 'n' roll.

There is an interesting parallel between this development and the beginnings, half a century earlier, of Tin Pan Alley. Although the birth of Tin Pan Alley was marked by the centralization of the industry, and the rock era by its decentralization, there is a sense in which the advent of rock marks the completion of another cycle in the periodic *democratization* of American popular music. It was with the beginning of another such cycle, in the Jacksonian era of a century and a half ago, that we began the long story that this chapter has attempted to tell.

Going back to midcentury for our closing example, when the big bands and the great singers were in their heyday, let us listen to one of the best and most extended (at fifty-eight measures) of Harold Arlen's blues-tinged collaborations with lyricist Johnny Mercer, as interpreted by that masterful, and versatile jazz singer, Ella Fitzgerald (1917–96). Beginning by winning an amateur contest at Harlem's Apollo Theater, Ella Fitzgerald sang with the Chick Webb band, which she later led for three years after his death before starting a long solo career.

CD 3/37 (7:11) "Blues in the Night." 1941. Music by Harold Arlen. Lyric by Johnny Mercer. Ella Fitzgerald, vocal; Billy May's Orchestra. Recorded in 1960.

▮ PROJECTS

1. Sigmund Spaeth restated a thought expressed many times when he wrote that our popular song "captures the civilization of each period far more accurately than do many of the supposedly more important arts." Taking any decade in our history, make a survey of its popular songs, and assess the extent to which this statement applies, and how it applies.

2. Songs about separation by death were common in the nineteenth century. They have always been a staple of country music (which inherited some of its songs from the sentimental repertory of the nineteenth century), and made a brief appearance in the teenage death songs of early rock 'n' roll. But such songs were almost totally absent from the output of Tin Pan Alley during its "golden years." Putting together what you know, write a paper discussing possible reasons for this.

3. If you come from a relatively small community in which a town or city band has been an important entity, assemble some recollections (either your own or those of relatives or acquaintances) of the band's activities and significance in the life of the community.

▮ ADDITIONAL LISTENING

American Popular Song: Six Decades of Songwriters and Singers. Smithsonian Collection of Recordings, Cassette RP 0007.

Brother, Can You Spare a Dime? American Song During the Great Depression. NW 80270

"Song of the Red Man, The." *The Hand That Holds the Bread: Progress and Protest in the Gilded Age.* NW 80267.

Songs of the Civil War. NW 80202

Where Home Is: Life in Nineteenth-Century Cincinnati. NW 80251

Jazz occupies a unique and not easily classifiable position in the panorama of American music. It has never, except in the brief heyday of the swing bands, been what could be called broadly popular music. The terms "folk" and "classical" have also been used in trying to place it in the larger picture of American music. It cannot be forced under any of these verbal umbrellas; it can only stand alone—sui generis. Jazz has been thought by many to be the most distinctive American music—indeed, by some, *the* American music. This perception, even if exaggerated, is all the more remarkable in that of the six streams we have chosen to identify, jazz, though now a century old, is still the newest.

Jazz, like blues and rap, came into being as unmistakably the musical expression of African Americans. But jazz, to a greater extent than either of the others, has long since transcended exclusive racial *identity*—in the sense that, for example, only black musicians can play jazz. Jazz and classical music have come to be our two most "serious" forms of music making—serious in their sophistication, in the intellectual as well as musical qualifications demanded in their practice, and in the low priority that their most dedicated practitioners assign to the profit motive—hence the survival of both genres largely independent of mass appeal, and their inherent resistance to being commercialized. Virgil Thomson's characterization of jazz as a "persecuted chamber music" makes the point deftly.

If jazz and classical music have this much in common, it is natural that there should have been many serious attempts to fuse them—attempts that have yielded interesting if not ultimately satisfactory results. For the ways in which they differ are also fundamental. Although there have been classical improvisers (a few) and jazz composers (many), the most basic difference is that classical music is a comprehensive manifestation of the art of the composer, and jazz a stylistically unique manifestation of the art of the improvising performer.

Frank Driggs Collection

A virtuoso jazz combo focuses intently on their music-making in this recording session for RCA Victor.

CHAPTER

Ragtime and Pre-Jazz

15

THE CONTEXT OF RAGTIME
FROM ITS ORIGINS TO ITS ZENITH

In the early years of the twentieth century, the terms *ragtime* and *jazz* both had broader and looser definitions than the more purist ones we find applied today. In the case of ragtime, we find that our idea of it as exclusively solo piano

CD 4/1
(1:13) "Hello! Ma Baby" (chorus), by Joseph Howard and Ida Emerson. 1899. Don Meehan, vocal; Dave Corey, piano.

Bettmann/CORBIS

Jelly Roll Morton

music is at variance with its contemporary perception. The dominant form of American popular music has always been the song, and as Edward Berlin has pointed out, it was the ragtime songs—songs such as "You've Been a Good Old Wagon but You've Done Broke Down" (1895), "A Hot Time in the Old Town" (1896), "Mister Johnson, Turn Me Loose" (1896), "All Coons Look Alike to Me" (1896), "At a Georgia Camp Meeting" (in its version as a song, 1899; see CD 4/5), "Hello! Ma Baby" (1899), and "Waiting for the Robert E. Lee" (1912)—that were more often recognized as "ragtime" in their day than the now-familiar piano pieces. (The ragtime song was introduced briefly in the preceding chapter; see p. 274.) This even raises the possibility that the piano versions of these ragtime songs played some part in the evolution and popularization of piano ragtime itself (Berlin 1–7). "Hello! Ma Baby" (CD 4/1), a ragtime song from 1899, uses as the basis of its lyrics the then-novel invention of the telephone, as had the blues and gospel songs of that period as well. (See pp. 135 and 205.)

The Origins of Ragtime

The roots of ragtime in our vernacular music are broad. Its most easily identifiable feature—a syncopated melody against a steady, marchlike bass in duple meter—can certainly be found in music published in the 1880s, not in the middle Mississippi Valley (generally considered to be the cradle of ragtime), but in New York. And the distinctive rhythms (including the syncopations) of the banjo tunes of the early minstrel show had appeared in print before the Civil War. (For reference to a piano piece with ragtime syncopations published in 1886, see Berlin 107–8, and for a discussion of the banjo's contribution to piano ragtime, see Lowell H. Schreyer, "The Banjo in Ragtime" in Hasse 54ff.)

Both the ragtime songs and the dances of the period had their role in the development of ragtime. The earliest known ragtime instruction book, written in 1897 as the ragtime craze was just beginning, gives an alternative name for "rag time" as "Negro Dance time," and for the next two decades the names of specific dances were associated with published rags (Berlin 115). The *march* could be used as dance music; many early rags include "march" or "two-step" or both in their titles or subtitles. A specialty dance that also contributed to ragtime was the *cakewalk*. A march involving an exaggerated kind of strutting, it presumably originated on the plantations, with slave couples competing for the prize of a cake. It was taken over into the minstrel show and was on Broadway by the 1870s; by the 1890s it had become a popular, though strenuous and exacting, dance for the general public (Shaw 43–44). Many early rags also incorporated the term "cakewalk" in their titles.

Caribbean dance rhythms—rhythms of the danza, the habanera, or the *seguidilla*—have been cited as one of the sources of ragtime rhythms. (See p. 70.) Louis Moreau Gottschalk (1829–69) incorporated these rhythms into most of his piano pieces with West Indian associations, including his "Danza" (1857), "La Gallina" (copyright 1869), and "Ojos Criollos" (no copyright date), the last two of which carry the subtitle "Danse cubaine." (For more on Gottschalk, and his piece "The Banjo," see CD 4/24, pp. 340–41.) The earliest collections of Creole songs from Louisiana also contain syncopations identical to those found in ragtime. (See "Miché Bainjo" in Allen, Ware, and Garrison.) The actual extent to which this music could have influenced ragtime itself is debatable, however. The whole question of Latin American influence (principally rhythmic) on the origins of both ragtime and jazz is often overlooked and is in need of more investigation—investigation that might convince us, for example, that a piece like Scott Joplin's "Solace" (1909, subtitled "A Mexican Serenade"), an exquisite example of a rag with a habanera bass, is not the isolated anomaly that it may appear to be. (See Berlin 115–18.)

CD 4/2 (1:18)
"Solace—A Mexican Serenade" (first strain), by Scott Joplin, 1909. John Hasse, piano.

Ragtime as Piano Music and the Work of Scott Joplin

Despite the breadth of interpretations given the term *ragtime,* it was as music for solo piano that it ultimately achieved significance and endured. The dissemination of piano ragtime is widely thought to have been given considerable impetus by the gathering of ragtime pianists (before the term had been applied to the genre) at the World's Columbian Exposition in Chicago in 1893. There, according to Blesh and Janis, "hundreds of the itinerant piano clan had gathered" (including Scott Joplin, 1868–1917, and Ben Harney, 1871–1938), presumably to be heard on the "Midway" and in the red-light district; but more informative documentation as to what music was played will probably never come to light (Blesh and Janis 18, 41). Not long afterward—in the same year (1896) in which Ben Harney moved to New York from his native Louisville, and began introducing ragtime through his highly successful playing and singing—Scott Joplin moved to Sedalia, Missouri, where for the next five years he composed, played, and published the first of the approximately three dozen piano pieces that he and his publisher referred to as "classic rags." Thus Ben Harney, the white Brooklynite Joseph Lamb (1877–1960), and others in New York, and Scott Joplin, Tom Turpin (1873–1922), Arthur Marshall (1881–1968), Scott Hayden (1882–1915), James Scott (1886–1938), and others in the Midwest, helped to launch ragtime as we know it into what became, in the next two decades, a national craze.

Ragtime for the piano assumed in its initial stages three forms: piano renditions of ragtime songs; the "ragging" of unsyncopated music; and original compositions for the piano. The piano compositions began to be published in 1897—William Krell's "The Mississippi Rag" was possibly the first, with "Harlem Rag" by the St. Louis composer Tom Turpin coming out the same year. It is probable that at least three thousand rags were published between 1897 and 1920; estimates have run as high as ten thousand. As could be expected most of these were mediocre musically, and were simplified in their published versions to be more suited to the modest pianistic abilities of the many who bought them and attempted to play them at home. What are today regarded as the masterpieces of piano ragtime were not necessarily best-sellers; Scott Joplin's most famous work, "Maple Leaf Rag" (1899), was virtually the only one of his works to become widely popular in his lifetime, and it was the work that justified his being heralded on sheet-music covers as "the king of ragtime writers."

Scott Joplin has emerged as the most important ragtime composer of the period. A versatile musician (he played the cornet and the piano and led a band) with high musical standards and determined ambition, he lavished a great deal of effort and resources on composing and producing large-scale works for the stage, none of which were successful in his lifetime. But his most enduring and influential works are his rags, whose musical inventiveness and craftsmanship set a standard against which others are measured and validate the term that he and his publisher applied to them—"classic."

The association of the piano with the ragtime era is no coincidence; figures show that the sales of pianos rose sharply after 1890, and declined just as steeply in the 1920s. But a modified form of the piano, the mechanical player piano, was also an important feature of the era; after 1900, player-piano sales also rose steeply, reaching a peak before the ragtime era was completely over (Hasse 15). Thus a great deal of ragtime (as did its successor, "novelty" piano music) came into American homes in the form of piano rolls. These rolls could be either "hand-played," often by the composer himself, or "arranged" by the calculated punching of the paper rolls. In fact, many rags, including one by Joplin himself, appeared only in piano rolls, and were never published in sheet-music form (Hasse 90ff).

Those who bought the sheet music, however, intent on playing it at home, soon discovered that ragtime is not easy to play. To aid the learner and cash in on the boom, instruction books in ragtime began to appear—the earliest by Harney himself in 1897. One truly valuable document is an all-too-brief set of six exercises by Scott Joplin, published as *School of Ragtime* in 1908, with accompanying explanations and admonitions. (Joplin concentrates most on accurate rendering of the rhythm, and warns the performer, as he was to do over and over again in his published rags: "Never play ragtime fast at any time.") To provide personal instruction, studios were opened to accept pupils—and, yes, the first advertisement for "Ragtime Taught in Ten Lessons" appeared in Chicago in 1903.

In its heyday the creation and publication of ragtime was not, like Tin Pan Alley and the popular-song industry, concentrated in New York City. The mid–Mississippi Valley and the Ohio Valley were strong areas for ragtime, and an examination of sheet music shows that rags were published not only in St. Louis, Kansas City, Columbia, and Sedalia, Missouri, but also in Indianapolis, Cincinnati, Memphis, Nashville, Chicago, Detroit, New Orleans, Dallas, and San Francisco, and even in such places as Temple, Texas (for early Joplin pieces); Moline, Illinois; New Albany, Indiana; Kiowa, Kansas; and Oskaloosa, Iowa. John Hasse, who has been both a researcher into and a performer of Indiana ragtime, has termed the ragtime era "the golden age of local and regional music publishing." Piano ragtime was also a genre to which women composers contributed significantly; May Aufderheide (1890–1972), of Indianapolis, was only the best known among many (Hasse 154ff, 368ff).

Ensemble Ragtime

CD 4/3 (0:41)
"St. Louis Tickle"
(introduction and first
strain), by Barney and
Seymour. C.1904.
Ossman-Dudley Trio:
banjo, mandolin, and
guitar.

CD 4/4 (0:31)
"Dill Pickles Rag" (first
strain), by Charles L.
Johnson. 1912. Clark
and Luches Kessinger,
fiddle and guitar.

CD 4/5 (1:10)
"At a Georgia Camp
Meeting" (introduction
and first two strains),
by Kerry Mills. 1899.
The Sousa Band.
Recorded in 1908.

The performance of ragtime was not limited either to the solo piano version or to the song; as soon as it became popular, this music began to be played by many kinds of ensembles, including brass bands, concert bands, dance bands and orchestras, and smaller groups that included mandolins, guitars, and banjos. "St. Louis Tickle" (CD 4/3) was recorded in 1904 with a banjo, mandolin, and guitar trio.

The crossover of ragtime into fiddle music is shown in "Dill Pickles Rag," in a 1912 recording for fiddle and guitar (CD 4/4). Notice the metric freedom observed as typical of country music and rural fiddle music in general—the last bar of the first 8-bar phrase has an extra beat added. (Listen to "El Chotis," CD 1/30.) This is but another warning, if one were needed, not to take the author's treatment of American music in parallel "streams" as implying in any way the isolation of one from another.

"Stock" arrangements for bands and orchestras (mostly for dancing) were issued by publishers; and sheet-music publications of rags for piano often advertised versions of the same piece "published for band, orchestra, mandolin, guitar, etc." John Philip Sousa was quick to recognize the popularity of ragtime. He began to program it in the 1890s, and on his first tour of Europe in 1900 he gave most of his audiences there their first taste of ragtime with arrangements of such pieces as "Smoky Mokes" and "Bunch o' Blackberries" (Hasse 268). Sousa's band recorded in 1908 an instrumental version of Kerry Mills's well-known ragtime song "At a Georgia Camp Meeting" (CD 4/5).

THE MUSICAL CHARACTERISTICS OF RAGTIME

Ragtime Rhythm

Syncopation is so basic to the rhythmic life of much American music that we shall devote some space to an examination of it as it occurs in ragtime, as a basis for understanding it as encountered elsewhere. Syncopation is the displacing of accents from their normal position in the musical measure, so that they contradict the underlying meter. Syncopation assumes a steady beat, stated or implied, and cannot be said to exist without it. This is normally supplied in ragtime by the "oom-pah" of the left hand, while the right hand has the melody, with its characteristically displaced accents. This displacement is done simply by arranging the succession of long and short notes to make *some* of the longer notes begin at rhythmically weak spots in the metric continuum, so that the accent they create at the moment of their attack serves to contradict rather than reinforce the prevailing background meter.

Some examples will illustrate how this works. Transcription 15.1 is the rhythm of the first two measures of the fiddler's tune "Turkey in the Straw." Here all the notes except the last are the same length, so that there can be no accents by virtue of note length, and hence no syncopation. The running notes constitute a continuous background made up of what might be called the "lowest common denominator" of durations, since they are the shortest notes used. They occur in groups of four to a beat. This is the same metric background that is used in ragtime.

Transcription 15.1
Rhythmic excerpt from "Turkey in the Straw"

Let us observe the ways in which longer notes can be superimposed on this background. If we want a longer note to reinforce the meter, it will do this most strongly if its beginning coincides with the first note of a rhythmic subdivision.

(Background   )

Transcription 15.2
Syncopation I

This is the normal position of the lowest, and hence the "heaviest," of the left-hand bass notes. Somewhat weaker, and creating a mild contradiction, or syncopation, would be a note beginning on the third of the sixteenth notes of our background.

Transcription 15.3
Syncopation II

This mild syncopation, called by Berlin "augmented syncopation," had been in wide use in American popular song since the earliest days of the minstrel show. (Berlin, in his *Ragtime*, pp. 82–89, includes a rather thorough treatment of ragtime syncopation that is consistent with the author's explanation.) It is the only type of syncopation found in "Dixie," for example; and it is found in a number of other songs of the same genre, such as "Camptown Races" and "The Yellow Rose of Texas." It persisted to the end of the nineteenth century and was a feature of many of the ragtime songs described earlier (including "A Hot Time in the Old Town" and "Hello! Ma Baby"). It flavored some Sousa marches of the 1890s, such as "High School Cadets" and "Manhattan Beach," and in the early years of the twentieth century it was characteristic of some of the peppier songs of George M. Cohan, including "Yankee Doodle Boy" and "Over There."

But this mild form of syncopation was never an important feature of ragtime itself, which characteristically used the still jauntier kind of syncopation created by having longer notes beginning on parts of the beat that are even weaker inherently—either the second or the fourth of the background sixteenths.

Transcription 15.4
Syncopation III

These, or variants of these, are the typical syncopations that may be found on every page of ragtime. Berlin makes a distinction between the two forms in Transcription 15.4. The first he calls "untied" syncopation, and he notes that it was more typical of earlier ragtime; the second, which he calls "tied" syncopation, seems to appear with greater frequency in the more mature phase of ragtime.

If we now observe the way these syncopations are placed in genuine ragtime, we get an idea of the fine balance the best composers achieved between contradiction and affirmation of the meter within the phrase. In Transcription 15.5 from the first strain of Scott Joplin's "The Entertainer" (1902), the contradictions, or syncopations, are marked with an S. This well-known rag shows a typical number and distribution of syncopations. Rags of what might be called the classic period usually have between two and four to a phrase, fairly evenly distributed.

Transcription 15.5
Rhythmic excerpt from
"The Entertainer"

It will be readily apparent that given the subdivision of the beat into four parts, the variety of syncopated figures available to the composer is rather limited, and that rhythmically ragtime can all too easily take on the character of a series of clichés. As ragtime strove to evolve, there was a tendency in some works of the middle and late periods to crowd more syncopations into the phrase. Some of Joseph Lamb's compositions reveal this, such as Transcription 15.6, from the first strain of his "American Beauty Rag" (1913). Here there are seven syncopations in the first phrase—six of them within the first two measures, including four in immediate succession. When we listen to the actual music, it is apparent that Lamb uses these syncopations with ease and grace, but there is a certain air of ripeness about it that suggests a genre that has almost reached the limits of its refinement.

Transcription 15.6
Rhythmic excerpt from
"American Beauty Rag"

A rhythmic feature to appear in late ragtime (Berlin places it about 1911, see pp. 147–52) is the dotted rhythm in Transcription 15.7, which actually amounts in performance to an unevenness in playing the lowest-common-denominator durations, with the first of each pair being longer than the second (though not, in actual practice, three times as long, as a strict interpretation of the rhythm as written would indicate).

Transcription 15.7
Dotted rhythms of
late ragtime

This unevenness was a performance practice that would later, after the advent of jazz, be applied to the performance of earlier ragtime. A comparison between Scott Joplin's performance, on a piano roll, of his "Maple Leaf Rag" in 1916 (CD 4/6) with an interpretation of the same piece by Jelly Roll Morton in 1938 (see Additional Listening) shows this clearly. The relation of the uneven performance of background notes to the "swung" eighths of swing jazz is evident; the appearance of dotted rhythms in ragtime pieces of the teens may be an indication that the practice of swing had earlier precedents than has been generally assumed.

Ragtime Form

It is in its standardized form that ragtime shows most clearly its relation to the march and the two-step; in fact, the name "march" or "two-step" is incorporated into the titles of many piano rags. The following Listening Guide shows the form of Joplin's famous "Maple Leaf Rag" of 1899 in relation to Sousa's "The Washington Post" of 1889—the march that popularized the two-step. It shows both the similarities and the differences.

The form of both rag and march is based (like the fiddle tune, and most other dance music) on a succession of musically independent "strains" of uniform length (sixteen measures), most of which are repeated. An introduction is optional; Joplin, except in his most famous rag, almost invariably uses one. After two strains in the main key, there follow two strains in the related key of the subdominant, called the "trio" in both the march and the rag. The differences of the rag from the march are mainly three: the march almost invariably ends in the subdominant key, a different key from that in which it began, whereas the rag often (but not always) returns to the principal key at the end; in the rag, it is common to close the first part with another statement of the A strain before going to the trio; and in the march, the second strain of the trio often consist of a "breakup" strain (familiarly called the "cat fight"), whose function is to prepare for the return, often in grandiose style, of the main theme

LISTENING GUIDE	Comparison of Joplin's "Maple Leaf Rag" with Sousa's "The Washington Post" March			
	"Maple Leaf Rag"		"The Washington Post" March	
		Exceptionally, no introduction		
CD 4/6 (3:10) "Maple Leaf Rag," by Scott Joplin. 1899. Scott Joplin, piano. Recorded in 1916.	0:00	*A* strain	0:00	Introduction
	0:22	*A* repeated	0:07	*A* strain
	0:43	*B* strain	0:22	*A* repeated
	1:04	*B* repeated	0:36	*B* strain
	1:25	*A* strain restated	0:51	*B* repeated
CD 4/7 (2:24) "The Washington Post," by John Philip Sousa. The Advocate Brass Band, George Foreman, director.		Trio in subdominant key		Trio in subdominant key
	1:46	*C* strain	1:06	*C* strain
	2:08	*C* repeated	1:21	*C* repeated
	2:29	*D* strain (back in the tonic key)	1:35	*D* short "break-up" strain
	2:49	*D* repeated	1:43	*C* repeated
			1:57	*D* repeated
			2:05	*C* final statement

of the trio, which is usually the most memorable tune. The march is in this regard a more "public," and hence a more "theatrical," form.

A delightful reference to "Maple Leaf Rag" in contemporary music is in *The Bushy Wushy Rag* (CD 4/20), a Continental Harmony project celebrating two icons of mid-America, ragtime and baseball. The first five notes of "Maple Leaf Rag" are heard here, stretched out and repeated in different keys.

The Mingling of African American and European American Traits in Ragtime

Ragtime represents an interesting intersection of musical traits that can be identified as European and African in origin and approach. Its rhythm is derived from African American sources. On the other hand, ragtime form, melody (except for syncopation), and harmony are clearly related to those of the American popular song and dance music of the time — European-derived, by way of Tin Pan Alley. The harmonies, where they depart from the basic three chords, employ for the most part the familiar "barbershop" type of chromaticism. A rare intersection of African Americanism and European Americanism is found in the first trio (subdominant) strain of Joplin's "Pine Apple Rag" (Transcription 15.8), where the quintessential blues harmony (the subdominant chord with a flatted seventh) appears in the same phrase with a conventional modulation to the mediant key. (This rag was copyrighted in 1908, four years before the first published blues appeared.)

Transcription 15.8
Excerpt from
"Pine Apple Rag"

THE DECLINE AND DISPERSION OF RAGTIME

Ragtime's original heyday was brief, in retrospect; scarcely a generation had elapsed between its full-fledged appearance in the 1890s and its decline and metamorphosis into other styles. Recognizing the dual forms, vocal and instrumental, that ragtime assumed, Berlin has noted that by the mid-1910s vocal ragtime (as the ragtime song) "merged with the mainstream of popular music, while piano ragtime inclined toward what became known as jazz" (61). Piano ragtime, in its dispersion, assumed several forms and affected several distinct genres. Foremost, of course, was its merging with jazz. For a time, the two terms were used almost interchangeably.

Jelly Roll Morton

Ferdinand Joseph ("Jelly Roll") Morton (1890–1941), a New Orleans–born pianist and bandleader, was a key figure in this transition. His own works (variously and somewhat imprecisely titled "rags," "blues," and "stomps," among other designations) date mostly from the post-ragtime era. In these we can see that Morton's own style had superseded classic ragtime, while reinterpreting some of its elements. Morton's identity as a bandleader is also evident; not only did many of the pieces exist as band numbers, but also Morton often wanted his piano itself to "sound as much like a band as possible." Nevertheless, he drew a clear distinction between the new jazz and older ragtime, which he had grown up with and knew thoroughly. His historic recordings, with commentary, made for Alan Lomax at the Library of Congress in the late 1930s, illustrate these distinctions and are a valuable source of information about the transition from ragtime to jazz. Though Morton makes his first appearance in our panoramic survey in connection with ragtime, it is really for his work in the formative stages of jazz that he is most important. After extensive traveling from 1904 to 1922, he went to Chicago, where he recorded, both as piano soloist and as bandleader, the works by which he is known (Lomax; Hasse 257ff).

Two Offshoots of Ragtime: Stride Piano and Novelty Piano

CD 4/8 (3:11)
"If Dreams Come True,"
by James P. Johnson.
1939. James P. Johnson,
piano.

As classic piano ragtime itself declined, two other offshoots appeared—descendants of the parent form, but not to be confused with it. One was the largely New York phenomenon of "stride piano," also known as "Harlem piano." This genre, cultivated by James Price Johnson (1894–1955) and Fats Waller (1904–43) in the 1920s and 1930s, retains some of ragtime's characteristics, most notably a steady left-hand rhythmic pulse (expanded to wide-reaching "strides" between low bass notes and midrange offbeat chords), with syncopated right-hand figuration. Basically a virtuoso form developed by pianists with phenomenal facility, stride piano is often faster than ragtime, with a driving beat and very elaborate melodic line. James P. Johnson's ebullient "If Dreams Come True" as recorded in 1939 (CD 4/8), is a fine example.

The atmosphere and function of the Harlem rent party of the 1920s and 1930s is succinctly described by Marshall Stearns when he calls it "an unstable social phenomenon that was stimulated by Prohibition and made necessary by the Depression." He continues: "The object of such a party is to raise the rent, and anybody who can pay a quarter admission is cordially invited. The core of the party usually centers around a pianist whose style was shaped by many similar situations: he plays very loud and very rhythmically" (122).

Another offshoot of ragtime was the so-called novelty piano music of the early 1920s; anyone familiar with such pieces as "Nola," "Canadian Capers," "Kitten on the Keys," or "Dizzy Fingers" knows the style. A "show-off" kind of piano music (carefully made to sound more difficult than it actually is), it has been described by Ronald Riddle as "a refined, white suburban extension of ragtime" (Hasse 285). The "novelty" itself was an attraction in tune with the times; such words as "tricky," "sparkling," and "scintillating" were used to describe and sell it. It was ideal for the medium of the player piano during the last few years of that instrument's popularity; before being replaced by the phonograph and the radio, the player piano made this novelty music accessible to people without the technical ability to play it themselves. But the sheet music itself also sold extremely well; Zez Confrey's "Kitten on the Keys" (which first appeared as a piano roll played by the composer) outsold "Maple

Leaf Rag" when it was issued as sheet music in 1921. Musically, novelty piano shared the basic underlying features of ragtime but emphasized greater speed, an obviously exhibitionist kind of virtuosity, and a particular species of syncopation known as "secondary rag," in which the regular quadruple subdivisions of the basic pulse are grouped in threes. Secondary rag can be heard in "Dill Pickles Rag" (CD 4/4).

Transcription 15.9
Secondary rag

The composer most closely associated with the genre was Edward E. "Zez" Confrey (1895–1971). Novelty piano, for all of its short-lived superficiality, had in its technical aspects—especially its secondary rag—an unmistakable influence on certain piano music of the 1920s and 1930s, especially that of George Gershwin. Riddle has mentioned Confrey's influence, by way of the popular "Kitten on the Keys," on Gershwin's *Rhapsody in Blue*. (Confrey played in the same famous Aeolian Hall concert that introduced the *Rhapsody* in 1924!) He has also pointed out its influence on European composers such as Ravel and Martinu, when they wrote in an obviously "jazzy" style; in fact, some aspects of novelty piano were taken by outsiders to be synonymous with jazz at the time. Riddle's excellent article on the subject closes with the observation that "in the end, the piano novelty suffered a sad but predictable fate: it lost its novelty. While it lasted it was great fun . . . but it was too hot *not* to cool down."

THE RAGTIME REVIVAL

It was only in revival that ragtime regained its integrity and distinctiveness. This selective revival, focusing almost exclusively on piano rags, which began about midcentury, has now lasted far longer than did the ragtime era itself.

The revival of traditional jazz, under the umbrella name of "Dixieland," began in the 1940s. Working backward chronologically, the next step, given the obvious relationship of ragtime to early jazz, was the rediscovery and study of ragtime itself, which was then generally viewed as a quite dated and old-fashioned precursor of jazz. Writers Rudi Blesh and Harriet Janis and performer, entertainer, and scholar Max Morath were among the first to give ragtime serious attention. There were discovered in the best of the piano rags musical excellences that had largely escaped the public in the ragtime era itself. Joshua Rifkin made studio-quality recordings, on a concert grand piano, of the rags of Scott Joplin in 1970; with his first best-selling record he separated ragtime from its association with the tinny, out-of-tune barroom piano and its accompanying stereotypical milieu, and focused on its musical values. In 1972 Gunther Schuller reinstated instrumental ragtime when he refurbished old stock arrangements (notably those found in the famous "Red Back Book") and founded and rehearsed the New England Conservatory Ragtime Ensemble. William Bolcom and John Hasse are among those who not only have continued to perform and record piano ragtime but also have composed rags of their own. This renewed attention to the musical aspects of ragtime has made the works of some of the early composers of what has now become known as "classic" ragtime, especially Scott Joplin, James Scott, and Joseph Lamb, stand out in perspective against the mass of mediocrity perpetrated in the ragtime era itself. Thus a few dozen rags emerge as small gems, illustrative of the potential for investing miniature and highly circumscribed forms such as the rag with refinement, craftsmanship, and vitality.

PRE-JAZZ

Minstrelsy, ragtime, and the blues were only the most public and audible forms of black (or black-derived) music that came before jazz. Behind them, mostly unheard and unheeded by white Americans, were all the varied musical manifestations of what has been called the "black experience." Where and when, from all this background, did actual jazz begin to emerge? This is a complex question, the first part of which cannot be adequately answered with the single place name New Orleans. It will be necessary to take a broader look geographically, for there were musical developments in all the cities and towns of the South and in the larger cities of the North (in other words, wherever there was a sizable population of African Americans) that set the stage for the emergence of jazz.

James Reese Europe and African American Bands at Home and Abroad

An important forerunner of jazz in New York was orchestral ragtime, which from the late 1890s until after the first World War was heard both in stage shows and as played by black dance orchestras. In many parts of the country it had long been the role of black musicians to furnish music for dancing. As Eileen Southern has said, "In many places the profession of dance musicians was reserved by custom for Negroes, just as was, for example, the occupation of barber. [See pp. 275–77 with regard to the origins of the barbershop quartet.] Consequently, black dance orchestras held widespread monopolies on jobs for a long period in the nation's history—even after World War I" (Southern, *Music* 338).

In the early 1900s New York's Black Bohemia (an area in West Manhattan around 53rd Street) furnished the "syncopated dance orchestras" that were much in demand for all occasions. Such an orchestra gave a public concert in 1905, and by 1910 James Reese Europe (1881–1919) had founded the famous Clef Club, whose orchestra gave public concerts, including a famous and highly successful one at Carnegie Hall in 1912. Europe, a pioneer in jazz orchestration, aimed at developing an orchestra that "is different and distinctive, and that lends itself to the playing of the peculiar compositions of our race." Two features that distinguished this orchestra from the standard white orchestra of the time were the increased importance, and often dominance, of drums and other percussion, and the presence of proportionately large numbers of banjos and mandolins, which, as Europe explained, took the place of the second violins, and gave "that peculiar steady strumming accompaniment to our music. . . ." James Weldon Johnson, the well-known black poet, wrote of the Carnegie Hall concert: "New York had not yet become accustomed to jazz; so when the Clef Club opened its concert with a syncopated march, playing it with a biting attack and an infectious rhythm, and on the finale bursting into singing, the effect can be imagined. The applause became a tumult!" Europe's 1914 recording of his "Castle House Rag" with his Society Orchestra is illustrative of what New Yorkers were hearing, especially the surprising and famous final strain, which Lawrence Gushee describes as "ferociously raggy" (Badger 51; for a recording of "Castle House Rag," see Additional Listening).

With the entry of the United States into World War I in 1917, African Americans joined the armed forces in large numbers, and bands were formed of black musicians whose services were much in demand. The most famous of these bands was formed and led by James Reese Europe himself. In France the band was enormously popular, not only with the American troops, but with the French as well (Little, in Southern, *Readings*). Europe was commissioned as a line officer, and he and the members of his band fought as combat soldiers in the all-black 369th Infantry Regiment (the "Hellfighters"), one of the most highly decorated units of the war.

Was Europe's band playing jazz? Perhaps not in the strictest sense, since he laid great stress on the musicians' reading the music accurately. (Eubie Blake, who had played with Europe in 1916, described "that Europe gang" as "absolute reading sharks. They could read a moving snake, and if a fly lit on that paper he got played.") Europe's own description of the band's playing is illuminating:

We accent strongly . . . the notes which originally would be without accent. It is natural for us to do this; it is, indeed, a racial musical characteristic. I have to call a daily rehearsal of my band to prevent the musicians from adding to their music more than I wish them to. Whenever possible they all embroider their parts in order to produce new, peculiar sounds. (Southern, *Music* 352)

James Reese Europe and the band had a triumphant return to the States in 1919, and almost immediately embarked on a world tour. Had he not been killed in May of that year (stabbed by a mentally ill band member during a concert in Boston), he surely would have played a still more prominent role in the evolution of the nascent jazz. More formally educated and more commercially successful than most early jazz musicians, he has tended to be dismissed as a mere popularizer. Yet, as J. Reid Badger has pointed out, "by recognizing the achievements of Jim Europe, we can better understand the musical and historical context that eventually produced such major jazz orchestrators as Fletcher Henderson and Duke Ellington" (60). (For a recording of "Memphis Blues" by Europe, see Additional Listening.)

Brass Bands

Better known as precursors of jazz were the smaller, more informal black brass bands that took part in the nationwide flourishing of bands noted in the preceding chapter. New Orleans, possibly owing to French influence, had an exceptional number of bands, as well as dance orchestras. The French interest in the military, or brass, band goes back to Napoleonic times. There were also trained musicians playing in the French Opera House who regularly taught the instruments.

The bands were not large by present standards, consisting of only ten or twelve pieces, including trumpets or cornets, alto and baritone horns, trombones, tuba, clarinets, and drums. They could furnish music for concerts as well as parades; in addition, there was often a smaller group affiliated with the band that played for dances, since many of the men doubled on stringed instruments. The repertoire of both groups had of necessity to be broad, and by no means consisted entirely of the new ragtime but included quadrilles, polkas, waltzes, and mazurkas.

It was for their parade music that black bandsmen in the South ultimately became most famous, and not the least important job of these bands was playing for funerals. The lodge or secret society (often more than one) to which the deceased belonged would engage the band. In the legendary and often-described scene, the band would march solemnly to the graveyard, playing hymns such as "Nearer, My God, to Thee" or "Come, Ye Disconsolate," or "any 4/4 played very slow." After the burial the band would re-form outside the cemetery and march away to the beat of the snare drum only. After it was a block or two away from the graveyard, it would burst into ragtime — "Didn't He Ramble," or a "ragged" version of a hymn or spiritual. It was then that the "second line" of fans and enthusiastic dancing bystanders would fall in behind the band (Stearns 50–51).

The Excelsior and the Onward were the most famous bands. No recordings exist of those bands. But recordings by the surviving Eureka Brass Band (an organization dating from the 1920s), which were made in the 1950s, give some idea of the sound. The juxtaposition of "Eternity," the kind of piece that would have been played in the solemn march to the graveyard, and "Just a Little While to Stay Here," the kind of jazzed version of a hymn tune that would have been played on the way back, furnish a kind of aural synthesis of this experience. (See CDs 4/9 and 4/10.)

There was keen competition among the bands, and "cutting" or "bucking" contests were common. A few legendary names emerge from this period — none larger than that of Charles "Buddy" Bolden (1877–1931), the New Orleans trumpet player. He was a versatile musician, reading music when necessary but preferring to play by ear. Bolden played "sweet" music for the general public and "hot" music for the "district" and its patrons. It was for the latter that he became most famous, introducing his "hot blues" about 1894. Was Buddy playing jazz, that far back? Earwitnesses like Bunk Johnson (1889–1949) say that he was. It is certain that he was heavily imbued with the blues. The New Orleans bass player "Pops" Foster has written of him, "He played nothing but blues, and all that stink music, and he played it very loud" (Cook 88). Here was ample evidence at an early date of the perennial and symbiotic relationship between blues and jazz.

CD 4/9 (0:54)
"Eternity" (first strain), by C. W. Dalbey. Between 1900 and 1910. Recorded by the Eureka Brass Band in New Orleans, 1954.

CD 4/10 (1:53)
"Just a Little While to Stay Here" (traditional; three strains). Eureka Brass Band, 1954

▰ PROJECTS

1. A broad and general sensitivity to the feelings of any group perceived as a minority (whether defined by race, color, religion, or any other basis) is fairly recent and still imperfect, as our jokes and our songs reveal. The study of popular art is a study not of what later periods may select but of what is actually popular in contemporary culture, and therefore revealing of its nature. This precept leads a scholar such as Vera Brodsky Lawrence to include sheet-music covers in her edition of the works of Scott Joplin, and Edward Berlin and Arnold Shaw to discuss the "coon song" in their treatises. If you were doing an illustrated lecture on American popular culture since the Jacksonian era, think about how you would treat the minstrel skit, the coon song, the Irish (or Jewish, or Chinese) song, the Polish (or Italian, or Catholic, or Mormon) joke. Discuss your views in a paper. Is censorship justifiable, and under what circumstances?

2. Write a paper comparing the role of women in ragtime (you could begin with Max Morath's article "May Aufderheide and the Ragtime Women" in Hasse, *Ragtime: Its History, Composers, and Music*) with the role of women in jazz (consulting such works as *American Women in Jazz, 1900 to the Present: Their Words, Lives, and Music* by S. Placksin or

Stormy Weather: The Music and Lives of a Century of Jazz Women by L. Dahl [New York: Pantheon, 1984]).

3. The musical relationship between blues and ragtime was, in the classic period of ragtime, somewhat noticeable but not great. Investigate the relationship between the *texts* of ragtime songs (such as those mentioned in the chapter) and those of early blues. For ragtime songs, consult Edward Berlin's chapter "Ragtime Songs" in Hasse, *Ragtime: Its History, Composers, and Music*; Blesh and Janis's *They All Played Ragtime*; and song collections such as *Favorite Songs of the Nineties* (see the previous chapter). For blues lyrics, see Chapter 8 and such sources as the W. C. Handy anthology and Paul Oliver's *The Meaning of the Blues*.

▰ ADDITIONAL LISTENING

"Castle House Rag," by James Reese Europe. *And the Beat Goes On.* CDI 38.

Come and Trip It: Instrumental Dance Music 1780s–1920s. New World 80293. Includes reconstructions of ragtime by modern orchestras.

"Maple Leaf Rag." Perf. Jelly Roll Morton. *Smithsonian Collection of Classic Jazz.*

"Memphis Blues" (James Reese Europe). *Ken Burns Jazz: The Story of America's Music.* Sony 61432.

Ragtime, I: *The City.* Smithsonian/Folkways RF017.

Ragtime II: *The Country.* Smithsonian/Folkways RF018.

"The Washington Post" (John Philip Sousa). *The Washington Post & Other American Newspaper Marches.* Advocate Brass Band Recordings 820. An interesting album of 18 marches, all named for American newspapers, imitating the very successful "The Washington Post."

CHAPTER

16   Jazz

THE NEW ORLEANS STYLE: THE TRADITIONAL JAZZ OF THE EARLY RECORDINGS

The most representative early jazz recordings date from about 1923. By that time the style known as "traditional" or New Orleans jazz was well established, though that city was no longer at the center of its development. Because those early recordings were so important in defining what jazz was and in laying the groundwork for what it was to become, we shall begin by examining an early recording in some detail, using it as a point of departure for a brief description of the basic nature and structure of jazz.

Photo by Herman Leonard

A contemporary jazz group in an intimate setting. Notice the players' concentration, the *listening* to each other during a saxophone solo, the drummer's brush on the ride cymbal, and the pianist's exuberance.

Traditional Jazz as Illustrative of Jazz Method and Structure

Our example is the famous "Dippermouth Blues." Though recorded by King Oliver's Creole Jazz Band in the north in 1923, it is representative of the New Orleans style in instrumentation, form, and manner of performance. (The fact that this New Orleans group made recordings of this piece in Chicago and in Richmond, Indiana, shows the state of dissemination and transition that jazz had already entered by 1923.)

The essence of jazz has been from the beginning, and remains, a *way* of playing and singing—a style of performance with many *intangible* features, but whose tangible aspects can be defined by accent, phrasing, tone color, the "bending" of pitch and rhythm, and the freedom of the individual player to improvise within well-understood limits. The basic *procedure* of jazz, from the traditional to much of the most recent, is to produce a series of variations on a standard formal harmonic plan, whether that of a popular song (a "standard"), or simply the "ground plan" of the blues, as outlined below.

A perception of *form* (whether they use the term or not) is something all jazz performers have; they always know at any given moment exactly where they are in the phrase, and in the chorus. Listeners can enrich their perception of jazz by developing this skill as well. Keeping track of the 8-bar phrases gives the listener a feel for the 3-phrase blues form, and also where the boundaries are between the choruses. Not all jazz is in blues form, of course, but whether

LISTENING GUIDE

CD 4/11 (2:17) "Dippermouth Blues," by Joe Oliver. 1923. King Oliver's Creole Jazz Band. Recorded in Chicago, 1923.

"Dippermouth Blues," King Oliver's Creole Jazz Band

0:00   Introduction

1st chorus: Polyphonic chorus (all front-line instruments playing)

0:05   Phrase 1
0:10   Phrase 2
0:15   Phrase 3

2nd chorus: Polyphonic chorus

0:19   Phrase 1
0:25   Phrase 2
0:29   Phrase 3

3rd chorus: Clarinet solo, other instruments supporting

0:34   Phrase 1
0:39   Phrase 2
0:44   Phrase 3

4th chorus: Clarinet solo, other instruments supporting

0:49   Phrase 1
0:53   Phrase 2
0:59   Phrase 3

5th chorus: Polyphonic chorus

1:03   Phrase 1
1:08   Phrase 2
1:13   Phrase 3

6th chorus: Muted cornet solo, other instruments supporting

1:18   Phrase 1
1:23   Phrase 2
1:27   Phrase 3

7th chorus: Muted cornet solo, other instruments supporting

1:32   Phrase 1
1:37   Phrase 2
1:42   Phrase 3

8th chorus: Polyphonic, clarinet and cornet dominating

1:46   Phrase 1
1:51   Phrase 2
1:56   Phrase 3

9th chorus: Polyphonic chorus

2:01   Phrase 1

2:06   Phrase 2

2:10   Phrase 3

2:15   Coda—Concluding 4 bars

the prevailing form is based on three, four, or any other number of phrases, this orientation skill serves well for most jazz listening, and it also makes it apparent when the standard form is deviated from, or abandoned entirely, as in modern or free jazz.

Form and Harmony

In its form, "Dippermouth Blues" is an apt illustration of the fundamental variation technique of jazz. After the 8-bar introduction, each of the nine choruses is an exposition of the 12-bar blues form. It appears in its simplest, most standard form in the sixth chorus (the first solo chorus by King Oliver on cornet):

Phrase 1:	I	—	—	I7
Phrase 2:	IV7	—	I	—
Phrase 3:	V7	—	I	—

Close listening discloses subtle variations in the harmony from chorus to chorus. The first two choruses of the piece show the kind of embellishing of the harmony that is typical of jazz versions of the blues—embellishments that, in the second and third phrases, show the influence of the European-based harmonies of ragtime:

Phrase 1:	I	IV7	I	I7
Phrase 2:	IV	#ivd7	I	VI7
Phrase 3:	II7	V7	I	—

Countless other blues are variations on some version of this basic blues pattern. But the blues as performed is more than simply a formal and harmonic plan; a manner of performance is implied that includes the inflection of certain notes—the blue notes, as described in Chapter 2. It can be heard in King Oliver's lowered thirds of the scale at the beginning of his solos, and clarinetist Johnny Dodds's blues sevenths at the beginning of his.

(Though we are not through yet with what we can learn from "Dippermouth Blues," it will be useful to look ahead a little and point out an interesting way to trace the evolution from traditional to big-band jazz by comparing this 1923 recording with a New York recording of 1925 of the same piece, called "Sugar Foot Stomp," by the noted pianist and arranger Fletcher Henderson [see Additional Listening], and then with the 1937 arrangement, made by Henderson, for the Benny Goodman band, as CD 4/15, p. 316.)

Instrumentation   The instrumentation of "Dippermouth Blues" is two cornets, one clarinet, one trombone, and a rhythm section of piano, banjo, and drums. Except for the addition of a second cornet, innovative for its time, that is a typical makeup for traditional jazz. (The cornets, played by King Oliver and Louis Armstrong, were only later replaced by trumpets, which have a more incisive sound.) For a detailed overview of the changes in jazz instrumentation over the years, see Table 16.1, The Growth and Evolution of the Jazz Band, pages 312–313.

Texture   In describing the texture, we can make an analogy with ragtime. The melody, or "front-line," instruments (in this case, the cornets, the clarinet, and the trombone) correspond to the right hand, to which is entrusted the melody, or the simultaneous overlayering of melodies. The rhythm section corresponds to the left hand, which has the job of keeping the beat going and of outlining the harmonies. If we grasp this division of function between front-line, or melody, and rhythm sections, it will serve us well in understanding jazz texture throughout the decades to follow. The front line will later increase, in the big band, to complete sections of saxophones, trumpets, trombones, and whatever additional melody instruments may be employed. The rhythm section, on the other hand, will remain to a remarkable degree the same as we hear it in these early recordings, only dropping the antiquated banjo and adding the string bass (in place of the tuba that was sometimes used in early jazz). The rhythm section is to remain the most stable and indispensible element of the jazz ensemble.

Ragtime, as a solo piano form, had a single melody (at most lightly harmonized) in the right hand. Traditional jazz, on the other hand, exhibits in its most typical choruses a complex layering of melodic lines, with the cornet(s) in the middle, the trombone below, and the clarinet adding a more ornate and decorative line on top of it all. "Dippermouth Blues" shows this texture in all but the solo choruses, in which the clarinet and later the first cornet emerge as soloists.

Improvisation

Another vital ingredient of jazz is improvisation. Upon a formal and harmonic ground plan such as the one illustrated above, the musicians are free to invent, in an appropriate jazz style, their own melodic lines that fit with, and express, that harmony and that form. Ideally, as improvisation, it never sounds exactly the same twice. Depending upon the talent and the mood of the performer, the improvisation can be fresh, spontaneous, and loaded with new ideas, or it can follow patterns already established in previous performances or by other performers. But jazz improvisation is never a matter of "anything goes." It is a product (as is all good art) of a fine balance between discipline and freedom—in the case of the jazz solo, between the discipline imposed by the preset form and harmony and the freedom to create within these limitations.

Louis Armstrong (1898–1971) has been deemed the first great improvising soloist in jazz. He was one of the performers who defined the "hot" style of playing in the 1920s, and was an early master of "swing." Swing is not easily described, but all its elements amount to contradictions or dislocations, in one way or another, of a regular metric pattern—playing pairs of shorter notes unequally within a beat so as to give more length and stress to the first, displacing accents, or playing notes slightly behind or ahead of the beat. His solos, with their melodic inventiveness, rhythmic drive, and variety of tonal color, especially during the period from the 1920s through the late 1930s, were models that had a great influence on the course of jazz as it moved out of the traditional period. Also noteworthy was Armstrong's "scat" singing—wordless improvising of complete choruses. All of this is well illustrated in "Hotter Than That" with Armstrong's Hot Five, recorded in Chicago in 1927 (CD 4/12). There is a clarinet solo by Johnny Dodds (who was also the clarinetist in "Dippermouth Blues"), and added to the "Five" is Lonnie Johnson on the guitar, with an interesting interplay with Armstrong's cornet near the end (Schuller, *Early Jazz* 111).

CD 4/12 (2:58)
"Hotter Than That,"
by Lillian Hardin
Armstrong. 1927.
Louis Armstrong and
His Hot Five. Recorded
in 1927.

DISSEMINATION AND CHANGE: THE PRE-SWING ERA

Chicago

There were two jazz styles in Chicago in the 1920s, black and white, both played by musicians from New Orleans. There were the white bands such as the Original Dixieland Jazz Band, which had begun to record in Chicago in 1917, and the New Orleans Rhythm Kings. Young white musicians in Chicago who began to play jazz had heard the Original Dixieland Jazz Band, but not necessarily King Oliver's Creole Jazz Band, and it was the white bands that were their model. King Oliver and Louis Armstrong and other black musicians were recording and playing on Chicago's South Side—but necessarily playing in places where the young white musicians weren't supposed to go. Mezz Mezzrow, a Jewish jazz player from Chicago who tried his best to *become* black, writes of the white Chicago jazz, "Chicago style is an innocent style. It's the playing of talented youngsters just learning their ABC's, and New Orleans was its source, but you can't expect any derivative to be as good as the source. New Orleans was simple, but not innocent" (Mezzrow and Wolfe 307).

One very talented Chicago youngster with a musical family background who grew up knowing his musical ABCs, was Bix Beiderbecke (1903–31). He listened to King Oliver and Louis Armstrong as well as the Original Dixieland Jazz Band, played cornet jobs around Chicago as early as 1921, and formed his own band (the Wolverines) in 1923. Bix's cornet solos are unique landmarks and attest to the talent of the "youngster" who was, in Gunther Schuller's words, "the greatest white jazz musician of the twenties." It is interesting to hear the progression from what Frederic Ramsey, Jr., has described as "the fluid, relaxed music of the King Oliver Jazz Band" in "Sweet Lovin' Man" of 1923, through "the variant but nevertheless stimulating New Orleans music played by white musicians from the Crescent City, the New Orleans Rhythm Kings" recording of the same piece in the same year, to "the choppy, youthful and provocative jazz played by the mid-western Wolverines," in "Jazz Me Blues" of 1924. (See Additional Listening.)

What was the milieu of jazz in the 1920s? Musicians played a great deal for and among themselves, after hours, but for the paying public (a rapidly growing constituency) the home of jazz was the nightclub and its orbit of related establishments. This was to constitute its basic environment, physically and economically, for years to come. One effect of Prohibition was to relegate the public dispensing of liquor to the tough guy—the mobster who could either dictate to the law or take it into his own hands. Consequently, especially in Chicago and places like it, jazz came under the aegis of the gangster (Morris; Mezzrow and Wolfe). For a fuller understanding of jazz, its environment must be kept in mind, not only its effects on the lives of its musicians, but the whole set of prejudices that grew up around it. The nightclub and its milieu is still basic to the day-by-day support of a sizable core of players who earn wages playing it.

Two New York Developments

New York became the scene of intense jazz activity in the 1920s. But the stage had been set for this long before, as we saw in the preceding chapter. Two important developments began to emerge in New York before 1930. The first was the "Harlem piano" described in Chapter 15 (CD 4/8, p. 298.) The second was the evolution of the big band. This led directly into the period of jazz's greatest stability, popularity, and economic security—an era that lasted until the end of World War II, and that has been designated as the *swing era*. New York can claim no monopoly in the development of the big bands. (For documentation of the development of the big bands elsewhere, notably in Chicago, St. Louis, Kansas City, and San Antonio, see New World 217 and 256.) But it did serve as a magnet to draw talented musicians from New Orleans (often by way of Chicago), from Chicago itself, from Kansas City, and elsewhere—musicians who helped forge the new ensemble that was to carry jazz to every part of the land and, ultimately, of the world.

Early Steps in the Evolution of the Big Band

The term *big band* may be misleading. Compared with a full orchestra, the bands were still small—scarcely more that about fifteen musicians (see Table 16.1, pp. 312–313). But that was twice the size of a New Orleans–style band, and many players and jazz fans considered the "big" bands a betrayal of the very essence of jazz. We can see the big bands today as a pragmatic solution to the problem of balancing the demand for a fuller, larger, and more varied sound with the need to retain the sine qua non of jazz—improvisational freedom, and the elusive hot quality that goes with it.

We have examined "Dippermouth Blues" as recorded by King Oliver's Creole Jazz Band, with only seven musicians. Fletcher Henderson (1897–1952), a pianist and leader-arranger from Georgia, recorded the same piece, with slight additions, in New York in 1925, calling it "Sugar Foot Stomp." The differences constitute an interesting documentation of the beginnings of the big band. There are now eleven musicians, the most significant addition being two saxophones. The individual hot solos are still there, the most memorable being the choruses played by Louis Armstrong himself, who had come from Chicago to join Henderson's band and who plays essentially the same solos as in the earlier, King Oliver version. But the new trend toward *arranged* jazz is apparent in the way the instruments play predetermined figures together at the "breaks" (the fill-in passages at the ends of the phrases), in the tightly disciplined and rehearsed (if not written-down) clarinet ensemble playing, and especially in the almost choralelike presentation of the blues progression near the end. (This piece, important for a fuller appreciation of the development of the big band, is available from several sources; see Additional Listening.)

THE SWING ERA AND THE BIG BANDS

The big-band style, as it evolved in the East, drew on the New Orleans archetypal style, either directly or by way of Chicago. The swing era, virtually synonymous with the heyday of the big bands, is usually thought to have

Table 16.1
The Growth and Evolution of the Jazz Band

	RHYTHM					Brass
King Oliver (1923)	Piano		Banjo	Drum set		Cornet Cornet
Duke Ellington (1927)	Piano	Acoustic bass	Banjo	Drum set		Trumpet Trumpet
Duke Ellington (1940)	Piano	Acoustic bass	Guitar	Drum set		Trumpet Trumpet Cornet
Stan Kenton (1958)	Piano	Acoutic bass		Drum set		Trumpet Trumpet Trumpet Trumpet Trumpet
Gil Evans (1973)	Piano [Electric piano]	Electric bass	Guitar	Drum Set	Symphonic percussion Synthesizer	Trumpet Trumpet Flugelhorn
American Jazz Orchestra (1989)	Piano	Acoustic bass	Guitar	Drum set		Trumpet Trumpet Trumpet Trumpet

begun in the early 1930s, to have come to full flower about 1935, and to have bloomed gloriously for nearly a decade. By that time, after the repeal of Prohibition and partial recovery from the Depression, the mob-controlled nightclubs no longer constituted the nearly exclusive support and environment for jazz. Dance halls, which by the mid-1930s had grown into large, well-appointed, and well-attended ballrooms, gave jazz a new forum and a broader popular base. The big "name" bands toured these, as well as giving stage

MELODY					
Brass	**Reeds**				
Trombone	Clarinet				
Trombone	Alto sax [Soprano sax]* [Baritone sax]		Tenor sax [Clarinet]		Baritone sax [Alto sax] [Clarinet]
Trombone Trombone Valve trombone	Alto sax	Alto sax	Tenor sax	Tenor sax	Baritone sax
Trombone Trombone Trombone Trombone French horn French horn	Alto sax	Alto sax	Tenor sax		Baritone sax
Trombone (Tuba) Tuba French horn French horn	Alto sax		Tenor sax [Flute]	Baritone sax	Baritone sax [Soprano sax] [Flute]
Trombone Trombone Trombone Bass Trombone	Alto sax	Alto sax [Clarinet] [Flute]	Tenor sax	Tenor sax [Clarinet]	Baritone sax [Clarinet] [Flute] [Bass clarinet]

*Reed doublings are common, but not standardized, and will vary over time, from band to band, and even from one piece to another.

shows in theaters. Recordings sold extremely well by that time, and could be heard on phonographs at home, in the jukeboxes that soon provided a ubiquitous accompaniment to nearly all public eating and drinking in the land, or on the new popular mass medium of the day, radio. The disc jockey, with his enormous influence, came into being. There were also weekly broadcasts of live bands. Movies featured jazz bands. This was the period when jazz enjoyed its widest public.

Three Significant Bands

Duke Ellington   Of all the jazz musicians who came into prominence with the big band, none had a more influential career than Edward Kennedy "Duke" Ellington (1899–1974), whose creative activity spanned half a century. He was a pianist, but his medium of expression was the band itself, and as leader, arranger, and composer he made music with a group that held together with exceptional consistency and continuity throughout the years. A famous early piece is "East St. Louis Toodle-Oo," which shows already the smooth and disciplined playing and the use of instrumental effects and colors typical of Ellington's essentially orchestral approach to jazz. (See Additional Listening.)

The Ellington band's unique use of instrumental color is the product of two factors: the imagination of Ellington himself (joined, from 1938 on, by his arranger, Billy Strayhorn) and a succession of remarkable players that Ellington had in his band. Trumpet players Bubber Miley, Cootie Williams, and Ray Nance (who was also a violinist); trombonists Joe Nanton, and Juan Tizol; clarinetist Barney Bigard; and saxophonists Johnny Hodges (soprano and alto), Ben Webster (tenor), and Harry Carney (baritone) are a few whose expansion of the tonal possibilities of their instruments, together with Ellington's use of those new possibilities, contributed to the Ellington sound. From the crucial period of the 1940s is "Ko-ko" (CD 4/13).

In addition to being a noteworthy example of the tone colors for which the Ellington band was famous, "Ko-ko" is formally a 12-bar blues in the less usual minor mode (actually E-flat minor). Much of its rhythmic structure is an expression of the familiar call-and-response pattern found so often in African American music.

As a composer, Duke Ellington had a broad range. He was primarily an instrumental composer, writing for his band, but he also was responsible for a fairly large output of songs—some of which began as such, and some of which resulted from words being put to his band numbers—*Concerto for Cootie* of 1940, for example, later becoming the basis for the song "Do Nothing Till You Hear from Me." He pioneered in writing more extended works for jazz ensemble, beginning as early as 1931 with *Creole Rhapsody* (which filled two sides of a ten-inch 78-rpm record), and including *Black, Brown and Beige* (1943, a multimovement commentary on the history of black people in America) and many suites, from the *Deep South Suite* of 1946 to the *Togo Brava Suite* of 1971. He also wrote musicals, film scores, a ballet, incidental music to a Shakespeare play, and, in the late 1960s and early 1970s, a series of *Sacred Concerts*.

CD 4/14 (2:49)
"Taxi War Dance," by
Lester Young and
Count Basie. 1939.
Count Basie and His
Orchestra.

The Midwest and Count Basie   There was another part of the country to be heard from in the 1930s. This was "the West" to easterners, but it was actually the heartland, and in particular Kansas City. In the days before mass media

"Ko-ko," Duke Ellington and His Orchestra

LISTENING
GUIDE

CD 4/13 (2:39)
"Ko-ko," by Duke
Ellington. 1940.
Duke Ellington and
His Orchestra.
Recorded in 1940.

Introduction: 8 bars

0:00   Baritone sax call; brass rhythmic figure response

1st chorus: 12 bars

0:12   Valve trombone (Juan Tizol) call, saxes response

2nd chorus: 12 bars

0:31   Trombone with plunger mute (Joe Nanton); brass, afterbeat figure;
        walking bass pizzicato becomes prominent

3rd chorus: 12 bars

0:49   Same plan as 2nd chorus

4th chorus: 12 bars

1:07   Piano solo (Ellington); saxes have repeated figure (riff)

5th chorus: 12 bars

1:25   Whole band in antiphonal (call-and-response) chorus

6th chorus: 12 bars

1:43   Whole band in 2-bar segments, answered by 2-bar solos in bass

7th chorus: 12 bars

2:01   Whole band in antiphonal chorus

Coda: 12 bars

2:20   Begins with repeat of 8-bar intro, expands to full 12 bars with 4-bar tag
        at end

threatened to blanket the whole country and induce a homogenized culture suffocating to regional artistic identity, it was possible for different areas to develop artistic dialects as distinctive as their speech. What we are calling attention to here may seem like a fine distinction to the beginning listener to jazz, but listen to the hard-driving beat — "jump," it was called, or "four heavy beats to a bar, and no cheating" (to quote Count Basie) — of "Taxi War Dance" of 1939 (CD 4/14), with its steady, insistent four-beat under the tenor saxophone solo of Lester Young. You will then get a notion of that Kansas City ingredient that went into big-band jazz after the arrival in the East of Bennie Moten (1894–1935), William "Count" Basie (1904–84), Lester Young (1909–59), and a host of other players from "the West." It was closely akin to the drive of boogie-woogie, which had come from the same part of the country. (Notice, incidentally, the sly repeated reference in the trombones to the first four notes of the "On the Trail" theme from the *Grand Canyon Suite* by Ferde

Grofé, who was in the 1920s pianist and arranger for Paul Whiteman's jazz orchestra.)

Benny Goodman   Anyone born before 1925 has lived through this most opulent period in the history of jazz and can call up a litany of the big bands and their star players. To name a few is to leave out many, but for the purposes of our brief survey the bands of Duke Ellington, Count Basie, and Benny Goodman have been taken as at least representative. Benny Goodman (1909–86), clarinetist and bandleader, was an important white musician of the swing era was. His highly skilled band of fourteen to sixteen musicians played an essentially hot style closely derived from that of black jazz artists of the time. Goodman acknowledged this heritage, using arrangements written for him by Fletcher Henderson, some of which were based on traditional New Orleans originals by King Oliver or Jelly Roll Morton. In addition, Goodman was one of the first to incorporate black musicians into his ensembles, using them at first as featured performers in his trio, quartet, and sextet. The disciplined but driving swing of his band helped to bring jazz to a new plateau of popularity and acceptance as dance music.

CD 4/15 (2:20) "Sugar Foot Stomp" (based on "Dippermouth Blues"), Benny Goodman and His Orchestra. Recorded in 1937

Typical of this Goodman swing style is the Fletcher Henderson arrangement of Oliver's "Sugar Foot Stomp" (CD 4/15). It is especially interesting for two reasons: first, because it was one of the Henderson arrangements that helped to accomplish the historic breakthrough for swing in 1935, and second, because of the comparison it affords with two earlier versions of the work already cited: the original 1923 recording of "Dippermouth Blues" (CD 4/11, pp. 306–7, with Listening Guide) and the 1925 Fletcher Henderson New York recording of "Sugar Foot Stomp" (p. 311; see Additional Listening). The Henderson arrangement is adapted to include solos by Benny Goodman.

In this recording from a live concert (see Listening Guide), we get the sense of the audience excitement and participation, not only in the applause at the beginning and end, but also in the applause for Harry James's trumpet solo. This was a performance "on the road," and presumably for a dancing audience; but it was common in those days during certain favorite numbers for the dancers to stop dancing and gather in front of the bandstand to get closer to the band and cheer them on.

Four More Aspects of the Swing Era

The Great Jazz Singers   Though jazz is fundamentally instrumental music, the period of its greatest popularity—the era of the big bands, their tours, their live radio shows, their recordings, their movies—was also the period of the great jazz singers. In Chapter 14 we were able to include three of the greatest:

"Sugar Foot Stomp," Benny Goodman and His Orchestra   LISTENING GUIDE

Introduction: 4 bars

0:05

1st chorus: 12 bars

0:09   Full ensemble

2nd chorus: 16 bars

0:24   This "irrelevant" (according to Martin Williams) addition, made in the 1920s by arranger Don Redman, is here retained, and divided into two 8-bar sections, the first for clarinets, and the second for a Goodman solo.

3rd, 4th, and 5th choruses: 36 bars

0:43–1:24   Harry James trumpet solo closely modeled on original solos by King Oliver and Louis Armstrong

6th chorus: 12 bars

1:25   Goodman clarinet solo

7th chorus: 12 bars

1:40   Full band

8th chorus: 12 bars

1:54   Full band, last bar of which overlaps as 1st bar of 8-bar Coda. (This is what Henderson had done in his 1925 version.)

2:08   Coda, 7 bars

Bing Crosby, Billie Holiday, and Ella Fitzgerald. (We wanted to include Frank Sinatra, but his music was not available to us.) The songs they sang were mostly from the great musical shows, which flourished during the same period, as we saw in Chapter 13. But there were some memorable nonshow tunes as well—"Star Dust" (1929, Hoagy Carmichael, with words by Mitchell Parish); "Sophisticated Lady" (1933, Duke Ellington); "Stormy Weather" (Harold Arlen); "You Go to My Head" (1938, J. Fred Coots, CD 14/9); and "Blues in the Night" (1941, Harold Arlen, CD 3/37).

Latin Influence   Latin bands were very popular at the time. The rumba craze was no less intense than that of the tango earlier, or the mambo, samba, or chachachá later. What the purely Latin bands played was not jazz, but it illustrates and reminds us of the perennial Latin presence and influence in American music. Jazz was by no means unaffected by it, and Latin drummers were soon to be incorporated into jazz ensembles (as were those from Africa, which has quite a different tradition, albeit with similar instruments). See Chapter 4, and CDs 1/35, 1/36, and 1/37.

The Small Combo   The second aspect is the simultaneous cultivation of the small ensemble in the era of the big band. This was no longer the old-time jazz ensemble (which did indeed enjoy a revival) but the intimate group of three to seven players that was the vehicle for developing some of the newest ideas in jazz. Its commercial aspect was represented by the "cocktail combo" playing in small bars, but there were important artistic dimensions to the small combo as well. The Benny Goodman Sextet's recording of "I Found a New Baby" (1941) is a particularly good example because of the solo for electric guitar by Charlie Christian. Actually the small combo has always been present at every phase in jazz evolution; it was not an invention of the post–World War II "cool" or "progressive" schools. Louis Armstrong had recorded with from two to six musicians in the 1920s. The solo pianist also flourished; Earl Hines (1903–83), Art Tatum (1909–56), Bud Powell (1924–66), and Erroll Garner (1921–77) were leading figures.

The Traditional Revival   The traditional, or New Orleans, style of jazz has shown a persistent vitality. An early copy of New Orleans style (mostly white and more or less New York–oriented), known generally as "Dixieland," was translated into big band terms in the work of such white bandleaders Bob Crosby ("South Rampart Street Parade," 1937) and Eddie Condon ("Somebody Loves Me," 1944). But a real revival of the older style was one of the landmarks of the 1940s as well. In an episode in American music replete with both nostalgia and human interest, players who had been active in the very early days of jazz (some of whom had never before been recorded) were located, sometimes with considerable difficulty, and reinstated with honors in the kingdom of jazz, for the purpose of re-creating the authentic traditions and music of the long-gone New Orleans beginnings. How authentic such re-creations can be in an art so basically improvisational, and so dependent upon the player's subjective impressions of a *total* environment, may be open to question. But the documents are there now, recorded a generation after the fact, for all time. For examples, listen to Bunk Johnson, legendary symbol of this revival, in "Down by the River" (1942; see Additional Listening), or Kid Ory, in any number of revival recordings. Younger musicians, including Lu Watters and Turk Murphy, also became interested in the old style.

Wartime and the Seeds of Change

With the entry of the United States into World War II there came a freezing of the status quo. The feeling of security that a repetition of the accustomed can give was what was needed and sought. During the war, people flocked to ball-

rooms to hear the name bands and bought the latest records; and overseas soldiers, sailors, airmen, and marines heard the same bands and the same pieces.
(Notwithstanding that, wartime hardships, including shortages of gasoline for
touring, took their toll among the bands, some of which disbanded even before
the war was over.) Meanwhile, underneath the desperately needed continuity
of the surface, changes were being wrought that would profoundly alter the
jazz scene once the war was over.

THE EMERGENCE OF MODERN JAZZ: BOP AS A TURNING POINT

In the decades since the end of World War II, the whole fabric of occidental
music has frayed into so many different strands that it has become a daunting
task to keep track of them. Jazz has been no exception. Beginning in the 1940s
a combination of factors wrought evolutionary changes in jazz that brought a
whole new set of leaders to the fore and made significant alterations, not only
in the music itself, but also in the function of jazz, in its audience, and in the
way it was perceived. From the beginning of the 1930s through the end of
World War II, there had been, for most fans, one kind of jazz—that of the big
bands. The best-known names were Benny Goodman, Glenn Miller, Artie
Shaw, Tommy Dorsey, Harry James, and the like. (White bandleaders all, to
be sure. Even then, the bands of Duke Ellington, Count Basie, Billy Eckstine,
Lionel Hampton, Jimmie Lunceford, and other black jazzmen, who were
regarded by aficionados as playing "real jazz," had a smaller public.) Jazz,
however attenuated by the popular bands in the minds of its devotees, came as
close in this period to being synonymous with America's popular music as it
has ever been or is ever likely to be again. After the war, all was different; the
place of jazz in our culture changed. It lost its mass following, especially
among the young, who have shown repeatedly that what they really like most
is music with a strong beat that they can dance to (a need that was soon to be
met by black rhythm-and-blues, and white rock 'n' roll). At the same time, jazz
began to be considered seriously as *art* music, not only by its fans and critics,
but by some of its practitioners as well. Jazz became bohemianized.

It began with *bop* (a shortening of "rebop" or "bebop"). The first outstanding exponents of the new style were the trumpeter John "Dizzy" Gillespie
(1917–93) and the alto saxophonist Charlie Parker (1920–55), together with
pianist Thelonious Monk (1917–82) and drummer Kenny Clarke (1914–85).
Gillespie and Parker had keenly creative minds and extremely facile techniques on their respective instruments. Bop developed as the first jazz to
demand an entire ensemble of virtuoso performers. (In this sense, bop bore the
same relationship to swing jazz that bluegrass did to country music.) The

ensemble was characteristically small—a quintet or a sextet made up of a rhythm section (piano, bass, and drums) and a front line of just two or three instrumentalists. In addition to an astounding virtuosity, there was an obscuring of the familiar melodies jazz fans had grown accustomed to hearing. Bop continued to use the harmonic basis (the "changes") of certain jazz standards (Gershwin's "I Got Rhythm" was a favorite), but free, elaborate, and very difficult new melodic variations were invented on the original harmonies, often overlapping phrase endings. Frequently the harmonic plan itself, the very basis of jazz, would be changed through the use of substitute chords. Tempi were usually very fast, and the supporting rhythm section became much lighter. The cymbal, with its bright, insinuating tone, and the string bass, now "walking" at a fast pace, together took over from the drums the job of keeping the beat, and the drums could now be used both less frequently and more effectively for accentuation, or for the superimposing of cross-rhythms that made the rhythmic texture more complex and tended at times to obscure the beat. From then on, the jazz rhythm section was permanently transformed, in an evolutionary development that would outlast bop itself. This lightening and obscuring of the beat, together with the fast tempos, discouraged dancing to bebop; it became instead a music for *listeners*, and this encouraged its being perceived as an art music.

It has been customary to call the advent of bop a revolution in jazz. Bop *can* be seen as a "black backlash" to the "white synthesis." (For one view of the whole racial situation that prevailed in jazz in the 1930s and 1940s, see Shaw 158–63.) Ignoring the *evolutionary* aspects of the music itself, however, distorts the picture of the origins of this crucial development. In fact, bop's antecedents could be found across a fairly broad spectrum of the jazz of the 1940s, including some of the innovative playing and arranging going on in a few of the big bands themselves, notably those of Count Basie (especially the rhythm section) and Earl Hines. Other big bands that were playing convincingly in bop style before the end of the 1940s were those of Billy Eckstine, Boyd Raeburn, Claude Thornhill, and Woody Herman. Some writers have cautioned against viewing bop as a revolt against the big bands, and stress its evolutionary rather than revolutionary origin (Morgenstern; Gridley 139).

Bebop's musical ingredients had their precedents in the work of individual players as well, and bop certainly could not have assumed the sound it did had it not been for the playing of such important jazz figures as Art Tatum, Lester Young, and Roy Eldridge. Early bop was not well documented in commercial recordings, which began to pick it up after its influence among jazz players had spread to a considerable extent. There is no more typical or frequently cited example of early bop than Charlie Parker's "KoKo" of 1945 (not to be confused with Ellington's "Ko-ko"), a superb distillation of the essence of the style. (There many sources; see Additional Listening.) There are only four performers: Charlie Parker, alto saxophone; Dizzy Gillespie, trumpet and piano; Curley Russell, bass; and Max Roach, drums. Note the unison passages used to open and close the pieces. (These passages possibly had their origins in the rigorous practice sessions Parker and Gillespie had in the early days, playing etudes in unison in all keys as fast as they could.) The unisons were new to jazz, and were a contradiction of the old spirit of heterophony and polyphony that underlay the traditional jazz of the 1920s and 1930s. The unison lines became in turn a tradition that stuck, reappearing in post-bop works.

In due course bop was translated into big-band terms, just as traditional jazz had been before it. In "Things to Come" (1946), Gillespie records with a band of seventeen pieces (large even for the big-band era) a work that transfers to the large ensemble the drive and virtuosity of bop. "Oop-Pap-a-Da" (1947) and "Lemon Drop" (1948) show another characteristic, vocalizing on nonsense syllables (which provided titles for many of these pieces). The singing exhibits the same fluidity and virtuosity that we hear in the instrumental solos. (Scat singing, as this is called, was not new to jazz; Louis Armstrong, as we heard in CD 4/12, was doing it in the 1920s.)

The Progeny of Bop

Cool Jazz   What has become known as "cool" jazz followed so closely on the heels of bop that it can almost be regarded as the other side of the same coin — the same dispassionate objectivity (symbolized by the typical avoidance of instrumental vibrato), the same underlying complexity, the same careful avoidance of the obvious that tends to obscurity. But now these features were exhibited in a music of understatement, of restraint, of leanness. What had been interpreted by some as an attitude of disdain in bop became in cool jazz one of detachment.

Many of the same musicians played both bop and cool, and a lineage can be established. An early example, in a transitional stage, is "Boplicity" (1949), with Miles Davis (trumpet), J. J. Johnson, (trombone), and Kenny Clarke (drums) — all of whom were influential in the development and spread of bop. The tempo has been slowed, but many bop characteristics remain: the light style of drumming, with the emphasis on the cymbal; the important role of the bass in keeping the beat; and, an important trademark of bop, the unison playing at the beginning of the piece (in this case harmonized by the arranger, Gil Evans; see Additional Listening).

"Criss-Cross" (1951), by Thelonious Monk, reveals more characteristics of the cool trend. The vibraphone appears, here played by Milt Jackson (1923–99). The tone of the "vibes" — warmed somewhat by its mechanical vibrato, but still restrained and detached — made it almost a symbol of cool jazz.

CD 4/16 (2:53) "Criss-Cross," by Thelonious Monk. Thelonious Monk Quintet. Recorded in 1951.

One of the most influential small combos in this style was the Modern Jazz Quartet, with piano (John Lewis, also a composer), vibes (Milt Jackson, heard in "Criss-Cross"), bass (Percy Heath), and drums (Connie Kay). With no wind instruments (in fact, this entire ensemble is really a rhythm section), their small combo epitomized the restrained understatement toward which cool jazz tended. "Django," a funeral processional for the Belgian guitarist Django Reinhardt, is one of the group's most famous works, which exists in many recorded versions. (See Additional Listening.)

"Cool" jazz dominated what was *new* in jazz of the 1950s—not what was popular. Its adherents were to be found mostly in intellectual circles—on college campuses, among both students and professors. There was an intellectual ferment about jazz that affected critics, fans, and some composer-performers themselves. If jazz was *art*, then there was no reason why it shouldn't appropriate whatever it took a fancy to in fine-art music, learning and borrowing from both the forms and the technical procedures of European or European-derived classical music. For example, John Lewis, whose Modern Jazz Quartet represented the quintessence of "cool" jazz, in the late 1950s, became interested in the music of the Italian Renaissance and the *commedia dell'arte*. (*Piazza Navona*, 1960, by John Lewis, illustrative of his interest in the Renaissance composer Giovanni Gabrieli [1557–1612], is on NW 216.)

Hard Bop and Funk   Evolving directly from bop in the 1950s and 1960s, and often regarded as a reaction to the restraint and intellectualism of cool jazz, was a development known as *hard bop*. It represented a pull back toward the roots of jazz, especially its roots in black gospel music. Pianist and composer Horace Silver (b. 1928) and drummer Art Blakey (1919–90) were leaders in the evolution of hard bop. Many of the features of bop are present (the texture of the rhythm section, the unison or homophonic openings and closings). But hard bop tended to relax the frenetic tempi of bop, and the rhythmic basis of the newer *funky jazz*, as it was called, often showed a return to the characteristically black backbeat. There was a preference for darker, "earthier" tone colors; for that reason the huskier tenor saxophone was preferred over the lighter alto (as had been the case also in the visceral rhythm-and-blues). This is illustrated in "Now's the Time," by a quartet that includes Sonny Rollins, tenor sax, and Herbie Hancock, piano (NW 242).

Modal Jazz   Another successor to bop in which many of the same musicians were involved has been called *modal jazz*. It represented a new venture for jazz both harmonically and structurally, in that it no longer used the chord progressions of standard tunes as the basis for improvisation; what replaced these was simply a succession of scales on which the performer improvised. One very seminal set of pieces that set a precedent for jazz in this direction were those on the 1959 album *Kind of Blue*. The trumpeter Miles Davis (1926–91), who had a hand in influencing new developments and indicating new trends in jazz for more than three decades, beginning in the late 1940s, was the leader and stimulator of the small combo that produced this album, but Bill Evans, piano; John Coltrane, tenor saxophone; and Julian Adderley, alto saxophone, contributed significantly to the realization of its concepts and went on to develop the style further. The nine-minute "So What" from this album is a good introduction to the style, and also to the work of John Coltrane, who has a long and seminal solo. (It is widely available; see Additional Listening.)

John Coltrane (1926–67) was a crucially important voice in the jazz of the decade 1955–65. A commanding player technically, he was also one of the most serious-minded composer-performers in jazz. "Out of This World" (CD 4/17), a fourteen-minute meditation on the tune by Harold Arlen, with pianist McCoy Tyner, bassist Jimmy Garrison, and drummer Elvin Jones, was a landmark work recorded in 1962. In a reversal of the traditional jazz *modus operandi*, instead of following the chord changes of the song, the harmony is virtually static for the whole piece, with a rocking back and forth between two chords in a mode that suggests Dorian on E-flat. There are brief venturings out into brighter domains harmonically (the first is about two minutes into the piece, into a mode vaguely on E-natural), but the static quality still dominates throughout. But this static background is a perfect foil for Coltrane, who weaves an increasingly involved and tense commentary, on the prevailing modal scale, on the Arlen tune. When Tyner, the pianist, takes over, after six minutes or so, he maintains the same texture, with the same chords in the left hand, against which he also spins out a single-line commentary. Coltrane returns about nine minutes into the piece, working the music up to a still more frenetic mood, with strange and even nonmusical sounds. All is brought to a conclusion, with a brief "bow" by the bassist and the drummer for their indispensable contributions to the whole. Space limitations forbid the inclusion of more than an excerpt here, but the importance of hearing the whole piece cannot be too highly emphasized. (Those interested in the jazz of the 1960s and beyond have had to get used to hearing pieces longer, sometimes much longer, than the three-minute pieces of the former age, confined to the limits of the old 78-rpm records. The models became increasingly the dimensions of serious classical music.)

CD 4/17 (4:00) "Out of This World" (excerpt). John Coltrane. 1962.

Free Jazz   A small proportion of Coltrane's later work fell into the category of one of the most extreme, least understood, and least popular movements in jazz history—*free jazz*. Ornette Coleman's album *Free Jazz* of 1960 gave the concept its name and was as seminal in this regard as Miles Davis's *Birth of the*

Cool (1949–50) had been for that genre, and as his *Kind of Blue* (1959) was for so-called modal jazz. Free jazz exhibits one or more of the following characteristics: (1) collective improvisation; (2) freedom from preset chord progressions and/or established tonality; (3) extension of the sonorous range of instruments (especially the saxophone) by playing extremely high pitches, or making the instruments squeal, shriek, or groan; (4) playing deliberately "out of tune" in relation to conventional intonation; (5) expansion of form, by creating pieces in which the length of the sections, and hence the overall length, is not predetermined, and which may thus be quite extensive. ("Free Jazz" lasts thirty-six minutes, Coltrane's "Ascension" nearly forty, Cecil Taylor's "3 Phasis" nearly an hour.) The Art Ensemble of Chicago's "Certain Blacks" (early 1970s), with its spoken or chanted additions, is typical of the more theatrical, satirical, and racially specific aspects of the genre.

Fitting into the category of free jazz is the work of Cecil Taylor (b. 1933), which in many ways is in a class by itself. A gifted absorber of many musical influences, including the whole range of jazz styles, he has stated a desire to *use* European influences rather than try futilely to reject them. In collaboration with a small ensemble, known as the Cecil Taylor Unit, he has produced music of exceptionally high intensity, energy, and turbulence, characterized by long periods of unrelieved tension. "Holiday en Masque" (NW 201) is representative.

The relationship of all the jazz of the 1960s in which black musicians played a leading role (hard bop, modal jazz, free jazz, and so on) to the social turmoil of the times has been emphasized by some writers who also point out the identification of many of the young black jazz musicians such as Albert Ayler (1936–70) and Archie Shepp (b. 1937) with one aspect or another of the black nationalism movement (Jones; Roberts; Kofsky).

A turning away from extremism and experimentalism, and a reaching out to a larger audience, began to occur in both jazz and classical music in the 1970s. The overtly and even militantly racial overtones that characterized some black jazz of the 1960s abated in the 1970s, and many of its proponents began to adopt (or re-adopt) more accessible and popular styles such as rhythm-and-blues.

The "Third Stream" and Other Developments Parallel to Bop

Parallel to the lineage of bop to cool to modal to free jazz there were other related developments. What these developments had in common was the incorporation of musical elements, procedures, and actual instruments (violins, cellos, flutes, and French horns, for example) that had hitherto been considered foreign to jazz. The term "third stream" was invented and applied by Gunther

Schuller (b. 1925) shortly after midcentury to the merging of elements from the jazz and "classical," or European, traditions to form a new "stream" in music. (It is useful to consult Schuller's own writings on the subject, especially since in the 1980s he broadened the meaning of the term *third stream* to include the synthesis of "the essential characteristics and techniques of contemporary Western art music and various ethnic or vernacular musics"—in other words, including other musics in addition to jazz ("Third Stream Revisited").

Small combos playing a species of "cool" jazz began to incorporate materials derived from the European classical tradition. The so-called West Coast school of jazz (mostly white performers, including such men as Dave Brubeck [b. 1920], Paul Desmond, Gerry Mulligan, Chet Baker, Bob Brookmeyer, and Shorty Rogers) is illustrative of this.

One aspect of these explorations was rhythmic innovations that took jazz out of the duple or quadruple grouping of pulses (expressed by the meters 2/4 and 4/4) that had characterized it since its earliest associations with the march and the two-step. The first change in this direction was the introduction of triple meter, typified by the waltz. Then followed so-called asymmetrical meters, in which groupings of two, three, and four pulses were mixed in recurring sequence. "Take Five," by Paul Desmond, is illustrative (see Additional Listening).

Gunther Schuller himself worked toward a synthesis of avant-garde European procedures and sounds (including twelve-tone technique) with jazz styles and improvisation, over a considerable period of time between the late 1940s and the early 1960s; several of his resulting compositions were included in the album *Jazz Abstractions*.

THE PLURALISM OF THE LAST QUARTER-CENTURY

Rock Fusions and Electric Jazz in the 1970s and 1980s

As a strategically important point of departure for comprehending the fusions of the 1970s and 1980s, let us return to the bop lineage and examine what was happening in the bands that Miles Davis assembled during the late 1960s. From the album *Nefertiti* of 1967 to the landmark album *Bitches Brew* of 1969, a fairly rapid and direct transition can be observed. The piece "Bitches Brew" (CD 16/8) hints at the *jazz-rock fusion* that was to be further explored in the 1970s. The piano and the guitar have been completely replaced by their electric counterparts, and there is a change in the *rhythmic* basis of the music—always an indicator of major developments in jazz. The beat is now mostly the "square" beat of rock—that is, with evenly spaced subdivisions. With very little swing to it, it has the static effect of both rock and classical minimalism.

CD 4/18 (2:32) "Bitches Brew" (excerpt), by Miles Davis. Miles Davis and Ensemble. Recorded in 1969.

"Out of This World" (CD 4/17) was fourteen minutes long. Seven years later, "Bitches Brew" (the piece, not the album) was twenty-seven minutes long — the whole side of an LP. We observed in the Coltrane piece the repetition of essentially static harmony, which held the piece together. "Bitches Brew" uses an older and more basic device — that of the *ground bass*. After a long, two-and-a-half-minute introduction, featuring a collage of apparently random unmeasured sounds and electronically induced echo effects in Davis's trumpet sound, the bass lays down an insistent ostinato that, except for the return of the introductory material at the end, will underlie the rest of the 27-minute piece. We have encountered the ostinato in boogie-woogie; "Bitches Brew" extends that device through hundreds of repetitions, in the manner of the passacaglia of the seventeenth and eighteenth centuries.

Many of the players on these Davis recordings of the late 1960s became important in further developments in the jazz-rock fusion of the 1970s, including pianists Herbie Hancock, Chick Corea, and Joe Zawinul, guitarist John McLaughlin, and saxophonist Wayne Shorter.

The group Weather Report, formed in 1971 by Josef Zawinul (b. 1932), reflected with a high degree of competence a broad range of trends and influences. Indeed, their work can serve as an index of the ingredients of much of what has been called *electric jazz*, or the fusion music of the 1970s.

The New Virtuosity, the Return to Acoustic Jazz, and the Reconnection with Tradition

One of the most significant developments in the last two decades has been the post-fusion resumption of the acoustic jazz tradition. Like the bebop of fifty years before, this new resurgence has been led by a new generation of virtuosos — highly skilled performers who are also composers and who, in addition, have a thorough understanding of jazz traditions. A well-known example is that of the young trumpet player Wynton Marsalis (b. 1961), who has demonstrated a remarkable fluency in both jazz and classical music — a flexibility and catholicity not uncommon among today's young musicians.

There has been a resurgence — a reinterpretation — of bebop, to the extent that the term *neo-bop* has, not surprisingly, been applied to this stage of jazz. The unison openings and closings are there, and as an occasional alternative to the prevailing small combo, "big bands" (big in sound, at least) have been formed, made up of virtuoso performers throughout, and reminiscent of the Gillespie bands of the 1940s. Tempi that are fast even by the standards of bop in the 1940s and 1950s make the term *super-bop* appropriate; perhaps the stretching of the limits of human capacity, so pervasive in athletics, is a characteristic of our times.

Using the quarter note, typically defined in bop by the walking bass, as a basis, the up-tempo bop performances of the mid-1940s hovered around 300 to the minute. Gillespie and Parker's famous "Shaw 'Nuff" of 1945 (NW 271) was played at 288; Parker pushed this to 312 in his "KoKo" of the same year (NW 271). The Gillespie band played "Things to Come" (NW 271), in 1946, at a frenetic 340, which was fast even for the up-tempo bop of the day, and the performance was not uniformly clean. By contrast, Ricky Ford's ensemble played his "One Up, One Down" (NW 204) in 1977 *cleanly* at 344. To set these tempi in context, the standard fast-tempo numbers of the swing bands of the late 1930s were considerably slower; Benny Goodman played Fletcher Henderson's "Down South Camp Meeting" at 216 to the minute, and the Basie band performed "Doggin' Around" at 256. But even in the 1930s there were extraordinary precursors of bop tempos in the Midwest bands; Bennie Moten's famous "Toby" (NW 217) was played at an amazing 316 to the minute in 1932—faster than Parker's "KoKo"!

A COMPARISON OF TEMPI IN FAST JAZZ

The new post-fusion acoustic jazz is not revivalism; new aspects, new additions, new influences are evident. The palette of instrumental color has been expanded; Jaco Pastorius (1951–87), for example, in addition to presenting the electric bass as a jazz solo instrument (a troublesome exception, perhaps, to labeling this development acoustic jazz), has also introduced virtuoso harmonica (as played by "Toots" Thielemans) and virtuoso steel drum (as played by Othello Molineaux) with his band Word of Mouth, in "Invitation" (1983).

Although players can still find interesting things to do with the chord progression of "I Got Rhythm" (as Marsalis does in "Hesitation," on his first album), the choice of harmonic basis is much wider than it was in the bop of midcentury. Irregular phrase lengths and more sophisticated formal schemes, including the use of a succession of different tempi, meters, and styles in the same piece, have been employed. In the matter of rhythm, the most crucial element of jazz, cross-rhythms are often superimposed that can confound the sense of the prevailing meter for measures at a time. In "Skain's Domain," for example (CD 4/19), there is a basic relaxed bop beat of about 230 per minute, which, even as the ear tries to follow and grasp its organization, shifts tantalizingly back and forth between groupings of four and three (expressible as 4/4 and 3/4, respectively). Superimposed on these fluctuations are cross-rhythms of a different order, based on a triple grouping of the shorter values (expressible as 3/8, 6/8, 12/8, and so on), as shown in Transcription 16.1. All of this is done with an ease and fluency that dazzles the ear even as it mystifies it.

CD 4/19 (3:55)
"Skain's Domain" (excerpt). Wynton Marsalis. 1985.

Transcription 16.1
Some of the rhythms in "Skain's Domain"

Paying Homage to, and Conserving, the Past   Accompanying the return to acoustic jazz has been the appearance of a number of albums that pay homage to the composers, performers, and songs of the past. This homage takes the form of reinterpretations of jazz standards by song and show composers such as Gershwin, Rodgers, Kern, Porter, and Arlen, and of instrumental composi-tions by jazz performers such as Charlie Parker, Thelonious Monk, and Ornette Coleman. Along with the *reinterpretation* on their own terms of jazz standards by present-day artists, there is also the actual *conservation* of jazz classics as live music. There are a growing number of *repertory bands*—bands whose function it is to re-create specific pieces, just as a symphony orchestra re-creates a Beethoven symphony. Unlike a Beethoven symphony, however, a jazz piece may have come into being with little or no written notation associ-ated with it, and what little was written out may have been lost. The recon-struction therefore may have to rely largely on transcribing existing recordings—an extremely arduous undertaking. Repertory bands began to develop in the 1970s, as a result of the independent work of Gunther Schuller and of Martin Williams, noted jazz critic. In the 1980s the American Jazz Orchestra and the Lincoln Center Jazz Orchestra began playing in New York, and in 1990 the Smithsonian Jazz Masterworks Orchestra was founded in the nation's capital. Also involved in their own way with the conservation of the jazz of the past as live music are the "ghost bands" that continue to tour with the repertory that they played when their leaders were still alive—those of Count Basie, Tommy Dorsey, and Glenn Miller, for example. There are also the numerous school workshops and clinics, such as those established by Stan Kenton and Maynard Ferguson, which have helped to make jazz programs in schools and colleges effective conservators of the big-band tradition.

Jazz is nearly a century old. It is fitting that we close this chapter on this remarkable music on two notes: the concern for its conservation by serious musicians, and the openness to change and evolution on the part of equally serious musicians. Often they are the same people. This tells us something about the maturity of jazz, as well as that of its devotees. The place where you find jazz records in the typical large record store of today is indicative of its place in our culture. It is *not* in the main section, with pop and rock. In the store I go to, jazz happens to be in the same room with folk, ethnic, and classical music—whose devotees are equally comfortable with their passions in music and the knowledge that these have little to do with what is popular. Relatively seldom in its history has jazz actually been popular music. Yet it has endured, and will continue to endure, growing in breadth, excluding nothing that is true to its essence, and thriving in its own way for those who have come to know and love it.

▰ PROJECTS

1. Make an assessment of jazz in your local area. Is there music being played that is recognizably jazz, as distinct from rock or merely pop music? Where is it being played, and for whom? What styles can one hear—are there bands playing in a revival of the big-band style? of traditional (Dixieland) jazz? of cool?
2. If the calendar of musical events in your area allows, or your travel capabilities permit, attend three live jazz performances. Try for a variety of experiences. Write a commentary on the music of each, placing it in the general framework of contemporary jazz as outlined in this chapter.
3. If your area has a radio show devoted to jazz (on a public radio station, for example), interview the commentator or disk jockey on one of the following topics: (*a*) his or her assessment of the current trends in jazz; (*b*) what mail or telephone responses tell about local tastes in jazz; (*c*) his or her own list of the five best new releases of the past year or so, with reasons for the choice; (*d*) a topic of your own invention.
4. If there is a retired jazz musician in your community, interview him/her about his/her experiences, recollections of noted jazz figures, working conditions, comparisons of jazz *now* with jazz *then*, and so on.

▰ ADDITIONAL LISTENING

"Boplicity." Miles Davis. *Smithsonian Collection of Classic Jazz.*

"Django." Perf. Modern Jazz Quartet. *Ken Burns Jazz: The Story of America's Music.* Sony 61432.

"Down By the River." Perf. Bunk Johnson. *Jazz, Vol. 3: New Orleans.* Smithsonian/Folkways 02803.

"East St. Louis Toodle-Oo." Perf. Duke Ellington. See "Django"; see also *Smithsonian Collection of Classic Jazz.*

History of Jazz, A: The New York Scene. Smithsonian/Folkways RF003.

"Jazz Me Blues." Perf. Wolverines. *Jazz, Vol. 6: Chicago, No. 2.* Smithsonian/Folkways 02806.

"KoKo." Perf. Charlie Parker. See "Django"; see also *Smithsonian Collection of Classic Jazz,* and *And The Beat Goes On* CD II 17.

"So What." Perf. Miles Davis Sextet. See "Django"; see also *Smithsonian Collection of Classic Jazz.*

Study in Frustration, A Thesaurus of Classic Jazz. Perf. Fletcher Henderson. Sony 57596.

"Sugar Foot Stomp." Perf. Fletcher Henderson. See "Django"; see also Smithsonian/Folkways FH-RBF 37 CD.

"Sweet Lovin' Man" (two versions). See "Jazz Me Blues."

"Take Five." By Paul Desmond. See "Django."

Yardbird Suite: The Ultimate Collection. Rhino Records 72260. 38 tracks of Parker on 2 CDs.

AP/Wide World Photos

A dedicated young
student, Tseng
Yu-ting, receives
inspiration and
instruction from the
hands of master
cellist Yo-Yo-Ma.
Far from an "old dead
tradition," classical
music lives on!

PART VI   CLASSICAL MUSIC

It is self-evident that no survey of American music would be complete without a discussion of American classical music (known variously as concert music, art music, or fine-art music). Encompassing the breadth of approaches that American composers have taken to writing classical music, our attention will be as broadminded as it is broad. And having designed Part VI with that ideal in mind, the author says to those who are tempted to scrimp on it, or even to skip it altogether—"Try it!"

Although there are distinctions between the six streams we have identified in this panorama, there are no barriers. As we shall see, creative classical musicians have not hesitated to acknowledge American vernacular music. Louis Moreau Gottschalk made music out of his impressions of the banjo, and Aaron Copland out of his impressions of the blues. Conversely, creative composers of jazz and popular music believed that the forms and techniques of classical music belonged to them as well. Frank Loesser wrote canons; Jerome Kern wrote a fugue; George Gershwin wrote a piano concerto. To Leonard Bernstein, the composer of *West Side Story* (as well as operas and symphonies), the music of Beethoven was as relevant as the rhythms of New York City's Hell's Kitchen in the twentieth century (just as Shakespeare was certainly relevant to those who conceived the show). To John Lewis of the Modern Jazz Quartet, the Italian Renaissance was as much a part of his artistic heritage as the music of jazz guitarist Django Reinhardt. And those interesting student-teacher relationships that our popular composers dreamed of but never achieved add interest to the panorama: George Gershwin wanted to study with Maurice Ravel, and Charlie Parker with Edgard Varèse.

Thus the impoverishing notion that classical music is either elitist or irrelevant, or both, is itself both irrelevant and out of touch with the real attitudes of musicians themselves. To demonstrate this, we begin our consideration of classical music not with music that is old (which should not on that account be undervalued, and will be given its due) but with music that was written to celebrate the new millennium.

Photo by Jim Steere / Courtesy of the Chicago Symphony Orchestra

A musician with the Chicago Symphony Orchestra plays the bassoon—a double-reed woodwind instrument that produces a slightly nasal, but deep and rich tone.

Classical Music and the Contemporary World

In the final years of the twentieth century, the American Composers Forum, a leading and innovative composers' organization (based, significantly, not in New York City but in St. Paul, Minnesota, in the "grassroots" heartland of the country), conceived the idea of having each of the fifty states produce a new work to celebrate the opening of the new millennium. The project was called, appropriately, Continental Harmony. (Readers may recall from Chapter 10 that this was the title of one of William Billings's tunebooks, published a little over two hundred years earlier.)

We will consider four of these Continental Harmony works in this chapter. Written for and performed in areas of the country as diverse as St. Louis, Missouri; the San Francisco Bay Area, California; Grand Forks, North Dakota; and Madison County, Mississippi, each illustrates a different aspect of the relevance of classical music's techniques and breadth of vision to the contemporary world.

The Continental Harmony project stipulated that each work relate in specific ways to the history and the culture of the community for which it was written and in which it was performed. Thus the project as a whole illustrates the diversity of American music, and each individual work in itself bears witness to the *sense of place* that, though certainly recognized as vital to the legitimacy of a novel or a drama, is also vital to certain kinds of music, regardless of style or medium. What is interesting is that most of the composers did not live in the communities they composed for; they did, however, spend a considerable amount of time in residence in those communities. The works, then, represent the careful observation and commentary of a thoughtful "outsider" on the culture and history of the community.

ST. LOUIS, MISSOURI

CD 4/20 (3:10)
The Bushy Wushy Rag (excerpt), by Phillip Bimstein. 2000. Equinox Chamber Players and tape.

The Bushy Wushy Rag (CD 4/20), by composer Philip Bimstein (who is also mayor of a small town in Utah), celebrates two cultural icons of St. Louis and the mid–Mississippi Valley—baseball, and, in a subtler musical way, ragtime. After the initial sports announcer speaking over the crowd, the "narrator" is Robert Logan, long-time vendor at the games of the St. Louis Cardinals. The music begins with a slowed-down version (called in music augmentation) of the first five notes of the "Maple Leaf Rag" played by the Equinox Chamber Players, a woodwind quintet comprising flute, oboe, clarinet, bassoon, and French horn. (For a detailed treatment of the "Maple Leaf Rag," see CD 4/6, pp. 295–96.) Toward the end of the excerpt it is not hard to recognize part of the "St. Louis Blues." The piece also illustrates the modern techniques of the electronic manipulation of sounds used today in all styles of music. In this case, it is obvious in the collage of live crowd sounds and in the tape-loops of Robert Logan's voice. Less obvious is that the rhythmic punctuations heard between the phrases of the "Maple Leaf Rag" are actually the sounds, captured and manipulated in the manner of *musique concrète,* of a baseball hitting the catcher's glove!

THE SAN FRANCISCO BAY AREA, CALIFORNIA

The Navigator Tree (CD 4/21), by New York composer, mathematician, computer scientist, and futurist Jaron Lanier (who invented the term "virtual reality"), shows how twenty-first-century classical music has the capability of bringing together in one work diverse musical instruments, musical ensembles, and musical cultures. In this case, the participants are the Sonos Hand Bell Choir from Oakland, California, a Japanese taiko drum group (the San Jose Taiko), and an Indonesian gamelan ensemble (the Pusaka Sunda Gamelan; see the section in Chapter 5 on Asian music, and CD 2/6, pp. 93–94). All are part of the musical scene in the San Francisco Bay Area. The difficulties and complexities of combining these diverse ensembles are illustrated by the fact that they represent not only different tuning systems but also altogether divergent approaches to music. For example, only the handbell ringers learn and perform music by reading standard notation. The piece is about the last day in the life of the Navigator Tree, a towering redwood tree that used to loom over the Oakland hills across the bay from San Francisco and served to guide ships through the Golden Gate. The Navigator Tree, along with many other huge redwoods, was cut down sometime between 1845 and 1860—as the conductor of the work's premier put it, an example of our "cutting down the things that sustain us."

CD 4/21 (1:55)
The Navigator Tree (excerpt), by Jaron Lanier. 2000.

GRAND FORKS, NORTH DAKOTA

In 1996, in the upper Midwest, the first blizzard of the season arrived on November 17. There followed seven more, breaking all records. On April 4, the most brutal of all brought rain, which turned to sleet, and ended with twenty inches of wet snow. On April 19, 1997, the Red River of the North crested in Grand Forks at fifty-four feet above flood stage. The permanent dike gave way, whole sections of the city were flooded, massive evacuation took place, and a fire consumed eleven buildings in the core of the city. Help began to materialize immediately. Chuck Haga, a journalist who moved back home to Grand Forks from Minneapolis for a while to "live some of the recovery," wrote:

CD 4/22 (2:00)
"Red River, remember me" (excerpt), from *What the River Says*, by Steve Heitzeg. 2000. Grand Forks Master Chorale, Dr. James F. Rodde, director.

> Major disasters tend to blur traditional roles. Part-time mayors work around the clock. High school students become heroes. Retired teachers and sales clerks from distant places suspend their normal lives for a week or a month to help feed and comfort people who will not know normal again for years, if ever. . . . The roster of volunteers who came to

Eric Hylden/Grand Forks Herald

What the River Says. The fires that gutted these buildings were only part of the devastation wreaked upon Grand Forks, North Dakota, when the Red River of the North crested at fifty-four feet above flood stage on April 19, 1997.

muck out basements is one of the flood's most remarkable and reassuring consequences. Those volunteers came singly and by the planeload, from all over the country, from corporations, unions, colleges, police departments, and professional associations. . . . The volunteers came even from Kenya, the Sudan, and the Kurdish region of Iraq: refugees themselves, brought to Minnesota by a relief agency, and quick to see a way to give something back. (Haga)

Laurel Reuter, whose life's work has been the North Dakota Museum of Art in Grand Forks, schooled herself "to remember that a cultural life sustains people awash in disaster" (Reuter). So when the American Composers Forum announced the Continental Harmony project of one work from each of the fifty states, the Grand Forks Master Chorale proposed as North Dakota's project "the creation of a choral work which reflects the hopes and spirit of a community which has gone through a major natural disaster—the 1997 flooding of the Red River—and must now not only rebuild but face new questions about living in this river valley." The proposal was accepted, and Steve Heitzeg was selected as the composer. His composition, *What the River Says,* is a three-movement work for chorus, piano, and percussion consisting of river driftwood (two pieces to be tapped together), river stones (to be struck together), and a sunflower seed and wheat rattle. Some idea of what the music meant to the community is indicated by what Pat Owens, the mayor of Grand Forks, wrote to the composer: "Your tribute gives us the strength to carry on. Keep the faith!" Members of the chorale worried aloud, "How do you keep singing well when you're crying?" The following excerpt is an abridgment of the third movement, "Red River, remember me," with words by the composer. (See CD 4/22.)

> You flow through the Dakotas north through Grand Forks to Pembina and weave
> your way to Winnepeg to rest in Canada.
> Floods and droughts, regret,
> Things we can't forget.
> My love is a river, although changing, always there.
> Driftwood for some jewelry, wild grasses as flowing hair.
> Where two rivers meet
> Is sacred and bitter-sweet.
> The Red River, lonely river,
> The Red River flows through me.
> Red River Valley,
> O, lonely valley,
> Red River Valley remember me.

Text, "Red River, remember me"
(Excerpt reprinted by permission of Stone Circle Music.)

MADISON COUNTY, MISSISSIPPI

Not until composer Anne LeBaron, with the support of many in the community under the leadership of the Madison County Cultural Center, conceived and realized *Traces of Mississippi* had the northern, predominantly black communities of Madison County, Mississippi, and the southern, predominantly white communities, worked together. It was thought that such a thing simply could never happen, and the expressions of joy and wonder on the part of many of the community following the multiracial premier of *Traces of Mississippi* proved that the principal goal of the work had been realized.

Traces of Mississippi is in fourteen parts, for chamber orchestra, children's chorus, mixed chorus, performance poets, and rap artists. The arrival of the Illinois Central Railroad in the 1850s was an important event in this cotton-producing area in Mississippi, and the train functions as a motive in the work. (The Illinois Central sent a special train through Madison County as part of the festivities of the premier.) "And We Ride," written and spoken by performance poet Jolivette Anderson, appears four times in *Traces of Mississippi* and constitutes the entire thirteenth section of the work. Notice the musical evocation of the train whistle at about 1:05 into the excerpt (CD 4/23).

These four new-millennium pieces have illustrated the flexibility and technical resources of the classical music of our time. More important, it is the

CD 4/23 (2:15)
"And We Ride . . . (#4),"
Traces of Mississippi.
Music by Anne LeBaron.
Words by Jolivette
Anderson.

Main Street, Canton, Mississippi, as it looked a century and a half before the performance of *Traces of Mississippi.* Prior to the coming of the Illinois Central Railroad in the 1850s, bales of cotton for market had to be shipped by wagon.

Madison County Library, Mississippi

author's hope that they convince the reader that classical music is neither irrelevant nor elitist. At its best, and at the "grassroots" level, this music can indeed be both relevant and moving, meeting the needs of the human spirit in a deeper and more inclusive way than can music made purely to entertain.

Having made this point, let us take a brief look at the background of America's classical music, and then at its various strands in the twentieth century.

▬ PROJECTS

1. Your community would like to apply for a grant from the American Composers Forum for a Continental Harmony project. Draft a design for a project that would fit your community, spelling out what sort of piece you would like a composer to write that would relate in specific ways to its history and culture.

▬ ADDITIONAL LISTENING

American Composers Forum. *http://www.composersforum.org/.*

Continental Harmony Project. *http://www.continentalharmony.org/* and *http://www.pbs.org/harmony/community/index.html,* an interactive Web site.

innova Recordings *http://www.innovarecordings.com/.* The label of the American Composers Forum: *"innova* Recordings, chronicles today's significant and radical directions in creative music. By welcoming ground-breaking artists and launching their work to the farthest corners of the planet, *innova* champions the unheard."

Accomplishments from the Jacksonian Era to World War I

When in 1828 General Andrew Jackson was swept by a substantial majority into the presidency—the first president from west of the Appalachians—he was riding the combined wave of two related movements that were to bring fundamental changes to American politics and society, and ultimately to American music. These were the rise of political populism and the increasing importance of the West.

The soldier-politician who gave his name to the era was not himself so much the *instrument* as the *symbol* of these related movements of geographical expansion and an increased degree of political democracy. As an indication of how geographical expansion coincided with increased political democracy, between the battle of New Orleans in 1815 (in which Jackson's frontier militia defeated the British regulars) and Jackson's election in 1828, the union admitted six new states, all except Maine west of the Appalachians, and five of them granting more liberalized suffrage rights. The relationship of American democracy to American music—a relationship that will have considerable relevance to this chapter—has been commented on by the noted American musicologist Irving Lowens, who has pointed out that it is the interaction of two tendencies, equalitarianism on the one hand and libertarianism on the other, that defines American democracy. He further writes: "It is my contention that the past history of the United States has demonstrated a certain correlation between the dominance of the equalitarian urge and the vitality of popular music, and a similar correlation between the dominance of the libertarian urge and the vitality of fine-art music" (267).

It is Lowens's general observation that there was a balance between the two up to about 1830, that equalitarianism was dominant from the Jacksonian era to the Civil War (accompanied by the concurrent vitality of popular music) and that libertarianism dominated between the Civil War and World War I (accompanied by a corresponding vitality of classical music). Though this is an obvious oversimplification, it can serve as a point of departure for interesting discussion. There can be little doubt of the equalitarian urge of the age of Jackson, and we have already observed in Chapters 13 and 14 the growth and vigor of American "vernacular" music, represented by developments in popular song and theater. As a counterbalance to this musical populism (typified for many by the lowbrow "minstrel ditties"), voices had begun to be raised, even earlier in the century, on behalf of reform, of education, of the propagation of "good music" as being morally and spiritually uplifting. (It would never have occurred to earlier composers or commentators to think in those terms.) Should music (and with it all art) improve, educate, and *enlighten* us, or is it enough that it merely *entertain* us? Those were fundamental questions that arose in the nineteenth century—and that still arise. It is on those lines that the boundaries of the categories *classical* and *popular* were set—boundaries that are not particularly constructive today and that this book has sought at least to cause to fade in importance.

LOUIS MOREAU GOTTSCHALK AND THE VIRTUOSO IN NINETEENTH-CENTURY AMERICA

In 1853 there appeared in New York, just arrived from Europe, a brilliant pianist. He had recently completed a triumphant concert tour of Spain, where the queen had made him a Cavalier of the Order of Isabella the Catholic; Chopin had predicted a great future for him; the great French composer Hector Berlioz was his friend and mentor.

The most gifted American musician of the era, Louis Moreau Gottschalk (1829–69) did not so much bridge this just-emerging gap between classical and popular music as walk a careful line between them, both as a composer and as a virtuoso performer. He was thoroughly familiar with the European classics of his time but knew that American audiences were not attuned to them in sufficient numbers to constitute the audiences that he needed to attract.

Born in New Orleans, he had learned all that he could from any musician there by the time he was 11; when he was 13, his parents sent him to Paris to study. The director of piano classes at the Paris Conservatoire in 1842 rejected him without even hearing him play, because, in his opinion, "l'Amérique n'était qu'un pays de machines à vapeur" ("America was nothing but a country of steam engines"). That Gottschalk, seven years later at the age of 20, was invited to sit as a judge at examinations at this same conservatory is a fitting sequel, and suggests how rapidly he took his place among the leading young pianists of the day. His remarkable appearance, stage presence, and charm were universally commented upon throughout his life; he was to become, in effect, one of the first "matinee idols."

By the time Gottschalk returned to the United States, he had already established himself as a composer. His compositions, in accord with his needs as a concert artist in the nineteenth century, fall into three main categories. First, there are the pieces based on vernacular American music, such as "The Banjo" (CD 4/24).

This *tour de force* is an example of classical music using popular music (in this case the music of the minstrel show) as "subject matter." (Listen again to

CD 4/24 (3:53) "The Banjo," by Louis Moreau Gottschalk. 1854–55. Eugene List, piano.

Louis Moreau Gottschalk assaults the the piano keys with a whirlwind of fingers in this caricature from 1869, one of many tributes to his virtuosity.

the banjo in the minstrel band in CD 3/18, "De Boatman's Dance.") The piano here not only imitates the rhythmic drive and repeated-note figurations of the banjo but also invokes one of the most popular minstrel tunes—"Camptown Races" by Stephen Foster. The introduction hints at the verse: "De Camptown ladies sing dis song, Doodah! Doodah!" and near the end of the piece is invoked the chorus: "Gwine to run all night! Gwine to run all day!" (It should be noted that the tune of the chorus is nearly identical with that of the black spiritual "Roll, Jordan, Roll.")

Of this same type were three piano pieces Gottschalk had written when still in his teens in Paris, based on folk tunes of the Louisiana blacks that he remembered from his childhood—"Le Bananier: Chanson nègre"; "La Savane: Ballade créole"; and "Bamboula: Danse des Nègres." A second class of compositions is the virtuoso concert pieces, or "paraphrases," consisting of medleys of operatic airs, or popular tunes that were often patriotic. *The Union*, for example, so popular during the Civil War, includes "The Star-Spangled Banner," "Hail Columbia," and, as a final *tour de force*, "Hail Columbia" and "Yankee Doodle" played at the same time! A third class is the so-called salon pieces. These Gottschalk liked the least, but as a popular artist and "matinee idol" he had to write, play, and publish them. They are sentimental creations, with titles such as *The Dying Poet*. The most famous of these is *The Last Hope: Religious Meditation*. It became almost an obligatory ritual for him to end his concerts with it, head bowed and eyes closed. (The main theme from *The Last Hope* lives on in a different guise. Almost two decades after Gottschalk's death, a Congregational minister put sacred words to it, and it has since led an independent existence as the hymn tune "Mercy.")

Gottschalk's years in the United States were twice interrupted by sojourns in the West Indies. The second of these, beginning in 1857, lasted five years—years in which Gottschalk virtually dropped out of sight. He himself describes them as

> years foolishly spent, thrown to the wind, as if life were infinite, and youth eternal; six years, during which I have roamed at random under the blue skies of the tropics, indolently permitting myself to be carried away by chance, giving a concert wherever I found a piano, sleeping wherever the night overtook me—on the grass of the savanna, or under the palm-leaf roof of a *veguero* (a tobacco-grower) with whom I partook of a tortilla, coffee, and banana, which I paid for on leaving in the morning, with *"Dios se lo pague"* (God repay you); to which he responded with a *"Vaya usted con Dios"* (God go with you)—these two formularies constituting in this savage country, the operation so ingeniously perfected among civilized people, that is called "settling the hotel bill." (39–40)

The year he embarked upon his long West Indian rambling, Gottschalk began a journal, published as *Notes of a Pianist.* They are brilliantly written (in French) and are reminiscent of the essays and memoirs of his older mentor, Berlioz, in their wit and insight. As valuable descriptions and commentaries on American life of the time, they rank with the journals and writings of Frances Kemble, Frederick Law Olmsted, and Alexis de Tocqueville. Who knew better, or could better have expressed, the American state of mind with regard to the fine arts a century ago than Gottschalk, writing in 1862?

> There is no doubt that there are immense lacunæ in certain details of our civilization. Our appreciation of the *beaux-arts* is not always enlightened, and we treat them like parasites occupying a usurped place. The wheels of our government are, like our managers, too new not to grate upon the ear sometimes. We perhaps worship a little too much the golden calf, and do not kill the fatted calf often enough to feast the elect of thought. Each of us thinks himself as good as (if not better than) any other man—an excellent faith that engenders self-respect but often leads us to wish to reduce to our own level those to whose level we cannot attain. These little faults happily are not national traits; they appertain to all young societies. We are, in a word, like the beautiful children of whom Montaigne speaks, who bite the nurse's breast, and whom the exuberance of health sometimes renders turbulent. (52)

1830–1865: EDUCATION AND REFORM IN A TIME OF EXPANSION

To return to the evolution of American classical music of the time, we should note that the most significant endeavors of this antebellum period had to do with the teaching of music to the broad masses of people, and especially to children. Three men were representative of this movement: Lowell Mason (1792–1872), Artemas Nixon Johnson (1817–92), and George Frederick Root (1820–95, whom we met in Chapter 14 as the composer of some enormously popular Civil War songs. Listen again to "The Battle Cry of Freedom" as played by a reconstructed Civil War band, CD 3/31. What is most important to note is that the teaching of music, the establishing of music schools, the publication of numerous graded collections of music, and the founding of choral societies (all in a way outgrowths of the singing-school movement described in Chapter 10) did not cater to a musical elite, but, on the contrary, sought to bring what were seen as the benefits of music to the broadest possible public. Neither Mason nor Root had exaggerated pretensions as composers, but they wrote songs, hymns, anthems, and cantatas that were accessible to singers of modest abilities, an accomplishment of which they were justly proud. Both became shrewd businessmen, and by successfully reaching this broad public, they became wealthy (both were connected with their own publishing firms). But they never abandoned the ideal of supplying what Root called the "people's song." As Root explained, "It was not, until I . . . went more among the people of the country, that I . . . respected myself, and was thankful when I could write something that all the people would sing" (83).

George Frederick Root composed many works in the then-popular genre of the cantata. *The Haymakers* (1857), a large-scale secular work, deals in a naive and idyllic way with one episode of farm life—a life that Root knew well from his personal background. Although Root grew up with the strong opposition to the theater on moral grounds still prevalent in New England in his time, he did call *The Haymakers* "An Operatic Cantata" and included directions for simple staging. Unjustly forgotten, *The Haymakers* shows Root to have been a more accomplished composer than would be evident from his popular songs. His music is expressive, even on occasion dramatic, while remaining well within the capabilities of the amateur singers for whom it was intended (no mean accomplishment). The work is as authentic as it is unpretentious; Root composed the work on the same farm in Massachusetts where he had labored as a boy. He later wrote that "by stepping to the door, I could see the very fields in which I had swung the scythe and raked the hay, and in which I had many a time hurried to get the last load into the barn before the thunder-storm should burst upon us" (113).

CD 4/25 (2:49)
"But See! In the West
a Cloud Appears," from
The Haymakers, by
George Frederick Root.
1857.

Root's treatment of this very aspect of haymaking can be heard in "But See! In the West a Cloud Appears" (CD 4/25). As the sultry day wears on, a threatening cloud grows into a monstrous thunderhead in a way that could have been described only by someone who had had firsthand experience with New England summer weather. (Root wrote his own text.) "Yes! to the work!" describes the hurry to get the hay in, while the cloud rises fast, and the wind and the rain come on. But the hay will be brought in, and there is old-fashioned optimism in the farmers' assertion that "We shall not lose the day." This "operatic cantata" is from an age far removed in many ways from ours, but its somewhat dated language should not keep us from enjoying it as an attractive and well-wrought bit of authentic Americana—in addition to providing an extremely rare example of attention paid in the arts to the life and work of the American farmer.

Text, "But See! In the
West a Cloud Appears"

But see! in the west a cloud appears,
Higher and higher mounts its crest,
See! it spreads its ample fold,

Look! its deepening fringe of gold;
Ha! behold the lightnings play.
Spare not your muscles now, good lads,
But quick to the work,
And rest not until within the barn
Our spoil be safely housed.

Yes! to the work! to the work! a shower! a shower!
Hurry, hurry, etc.

Come follow while quickly we rake up the hay
The cloud rises fast, let us make no delay.
Hurry, hurry, etc.

'Tis spreading and rising, come make no delay
Faster! yet faster! come, rake up the hay
Hurry, hurry, etc.

The cloud rises fast, 'tis spreading and rising,
Roll the winnow, roll!
Roll it faster, for the black cloud is here
Hurry, hurry, etc.

On the wagon quickly load it away,
Pitch it faster, for the rain will not stay.
Pile it higher, so we'll not lose the day,
Hurrah! we shall not lose the day.

OUTSPOKEN "NATIVISTS" OF THE MID-NINETEENTH CENTURY AND THE DEBATE OVER NATIONALITY

Given the cultural background of the adolescent nation, it was understandable, even inevitable, that most of those concerned with improvement, education, and reform in music should turn for their source to "the courtly muses of Europe," to use Ralph Waldo Emerson's 1837 phrase from "The American Scholar." (Though his remarks referred to the activity of the scholar, and hence primarily to literature, his themes of embracing what is common and prizing what is at hand were later applied to music by one of his most fervent admirers, Charles Ives. (See p. 389.) There was, especially in intellectually and culturally sophisticated circles in Boston, New York, and Philadelphia, an increased regard for Europe as the fount of all art, including music. However, a few voices of the time, in harmony with Emerson's views, were heard in support of the ideal of self-reliance in American music. Anthony Philip Heinrich (1781–1861—dubbed "The Loghouse Composer of Kentucky"), William Henry Fry (1813–64—practicing journalist and opera composer), and George Frederick Bristow (1825–98—competent, versatile professional who spent his entire life in and around New York City) had this in common as composers: they were among America's most outspoken "nativists." They wanted to see flourish a distinctive American music, written by American composers and, equally important, actually *performed* for American audiences. Bristow, who composed four symphonies and a full-length opera, *Rip Van Winkle*, complained in a letter published in 1853:

> During the eleven years the Philharmonic Society [of which Bristow was a member] has been in operation in this city, it played once, either by mistake or accident, one single American composition, an overture of mine. As one exception makes a rule stronger, so this single stray fact shows that the Philharmonic Society has been as anti-American as if it had been located in London during the Revolutionary War, and composed of native-born British tories. (Chase 308)

The Debate over Nationality

These three composers, different as they were, all espoused a "nativist" view— that there should evolve a distinctively American music, developing a life of its own not in the shadow of European tradition, together with an audience to appreciate and support such music. There were critics, however, who took an opposite view—a view that has been called "expatriate." These critics were imbued with a reverential attitude toward those European masters—mainly Germanic—whose music was just beginning to be performed in the culturally adolescent republic. Theirs was an idealistic dedication to the *cosmopolitan*, the *universal*, the expression that seeks to transcend place and time. This competed with an equally idealistic desire to express the *national*, the *specific*, the unique sense of *this* place and *this* time. This is a debate that takes place in all eras, but at this time it was played out against the background of our period of greatest national expansion, between the Louisiana Purchase and the Civil War. It was a time of fierce national pride; "Manifest Destiny" was its appropriate motto.

AFTER THE CIVIL WAR: THE PURSUIT OF CULTURE IN A TIME OF INDUSTRIALIZATION

After the trauma of the Civil War, the patterns of American life changed. The changes were wrought by the westward movement of a substantial portion of the population, by settlement and cultivation of the land, by the building of towns and cities, by the exploitation of natural resources, and by industrialization. The telegraph was quickly followed by the railroad in linking east and west. Great wealth began to accrue to a new class of men—the builders of a new industrial society, entrepreneurs in growing new enterprises: coal and iron mining, steelmaking, railroad building, engineering, construction, manufacturing, and the extracting and refining of petroleum.

With this new wealth came the desire to advance education and culture. Educational and cultural enterprises conceived in the earlier part of the century, which hitherto had led a struggling existence, now prospered on a scale impossible before the industrial age. Colleges and universities were founded and endowed, as were libraries and art museums. In the larger cities, the two most expensive forms of music making—opera and the symphony orchestra— began to flourish conspicuously.

The passage of opera from an unassimilated alien to an indigenous American art form is chronicled in Chapter 22. The symphony orchestra became "naturalized" much sooner than did opera. Not just New York and Boston, but Philadelphia, Pittsburgh, Cincinnati, St. Louis, and even Los Angeles had established symphony orchestras by 1900. A reasonably complete account of the growth of the symphony orchestra in America would have to take into account the work of an immigrant boy from a small town in north Germany, who came here as an accomplished violinist at the age of 10, and went on to become the leading founder and conductor of American symphony orchestras. The unremitting pioneering work of Theodore Thomas (1835–1905) is encountered again and again in the story of the American music of his era. (See Additional Reading.) Today there are more than a thousand orchestras in cities throughout the United States, including not only major professional orchestras but also semiprofessional, community, and college orchestras.

Though perenially beset by financial crises (and the last decade has been a difficult time for orchestras), the symphony orchestra, however its role and character may evolve to fit the times, will continue to have a place in American musical life.

African American Performers and Composers

Sometime in 1876 in New York, there appeared as soloist with Theodore Thomas's orchestra a Cuban violinist of African parentage, José White (Southern 250). White was trained in Paris and was recognized in Europe as a distinguished violinist and composer. Though he was not an American, his accomplishments, and those of others of African descent who had succeeded in Europe, could not but have been an inspiration to black musicians here. Not until quite recently has there been a general awareness of the activities of these musicians in American concert life following the Civil War. Among the best known of them was the phenomenal Thomas Greene Bethune, known universally in his lifetime (1849–1908) as "Blind Tom." Tom was born in slavery on a plantation near Columbus, in Harris County, Georgia; his extraordinary musical abilities were recognized when he was 4 by the Columbus journalist-politician James Bethune, who had purchased him in 1850. He began to be taken on tours and "exhibited" as early as 1857. After the Civil War the Bethune family continued to manage and control Tom's professional career, both in America and in Europe. He appeared last on the Keith Circuit, as a vaudeville attraction, in 1905. He had a phenomenal memory for both words and music; he could play long and difficult pieces after a single hearing, and recite lengthy poems and orations. He also composed and played his own works, which numbered at least one hundred, including another in the long line of "battle pieces," *The Battle of Manassas*. John William Boone, known as "Blind Boone" (1864–1927), another outstanding black pianist and composer, was more fortunate than Blind Tom in having a black manager who was also a devoted friend. He wrote a great deal of brilliant and difficult piano music, some of which incorporated African American themes. The work of many other black concert artists of the nineteenth century is now becoming better known (Sears 135; Southern 246–50).

THE SECOND NEW ENGLAND SCHOOL

Boston, the hub of New England life, has always been an important cultural center, but it occupied an especially commanding position of leadership from the mid–nineteenth century to World War I. Including in its orbit Cambridge and nearby Concord, its intellectual life had already, by the time of the Civil

War, been marked by the great literary and philosophical tradition that included Emerson, Hawthorne, Longfellow, Whittier, and Thoreau.

Musically the ground had been cultivated by the the First New England School, the eighteenth-century singing-school composers, including William Billings, Justin Morgan, Timothy Swan, Supply Belcher, and others (see Chapter 10). In 1815 the Handel and Haydn Society was formed, followed by the Boston Academy of Music, founded under the aegis of Lowell Mason in 1833. In 1867 the New England Conservatory (today one of America's leading music schools) was founded; and in 1881 the Boston Symphony Orchestra was formed. It was a time of great patrons and patronesses. The two most notable were Henry Lee Higginson, who founded and supported (for long nearly single-handedly) the Boston Symphony and built Symphony Hall for it in 1900, and Mrs. Isabella Stewart Gardner, a colorful and generous patroness who surrounded herself with a large circle of artists and musicians to whom she gave help. She engaged musicians to give chamber music concerts, orchestral concerts, and even operas at her two successive palatial Boston establishments, 152 Beacon Street and the even more sumptuous Fenway Court (Kenny).

It is not surprising, then, that Boston should have nurtured during this fifty-year period a tradition of musical composition and a group of composers who are often (conveniently, though inaccurately) considered together as a "school." What these composers had in common was a dedication to excellence of musical craftsmanship and to the highest ideals of serious composition as they saw them. The musicians of the Second New England School broke ground for the American composer, helped to establish the place of music in our colleges and universities, and left behind an impressive body of music.

John Knowles Paine   Because he came earliest and was gifted with tenacity and a sense of purpose, to John Knowles Paine (1839–1906), competent and dedicated, fell the role of pioneer. At 19, already an accomplished organist, Paine was giving subscription organ concerts to raise money for study in Europe. Important ground was broken for the place of American music in her colleges when Paine received the first full professorship of music at Harvard—and the first in the United States—in 1875. A good introduction to the works of John Knowles Paine is his ten-minute overture *As You Like It*, after Shakespeare. (Additional Listening)

George Chadwick   Another New England pioneer, George Chadwick (1854–1931), was brought up in a typical Yankee musical atmosphere: his father, in his spare time from his varied pursuits, taught singing schools and organized a community chorus and orchestra. George, after some study at the New

England Conservatory, went to Germany at the age of 23 for three years of study. In 1897 he became director of the New England Conservatory, a post he occupied until his death. The range of Chadwick's compositions was broad. He wrote a comic opera, *Tabasco*, and a serious opera, *The Padrone* (an operatic precursor of *The Godfather*), which "tells a realistic story of poor Italian immigrants whose lives are ruined by a small-time mafioso figure who controls them." His works exhibit qualities of exuberance, vitality, and humor.

Perhaps his best-known work is a suite for orchestra titled *Symphonic Sketches*, written between 1895 and 1904. A good introduction to the works of Chadwick is the third of these, the six-minute "Hobgoblin," which the composer designates a "Scherzo Capriccioso," elucidating it with a quote from Shakespeare's *Midsummer Night's Dream* describing Puck: "That shrewd and knavish sprite called Robin Good-fellow."

The movement is a scherzo that, in the composer's words, was intended to portray "the rascally imp that frightens maidens of the villagery, skims milk, mocks the breathless housewife at the churn, misleads night wanderers, disconcerts sorely the wisest aunt telling the saddest tale." *Scherzo* is an Italian word meaning "joke." *Capriccioso* simply means "capricious." In listening to "Hobgoblin," the main thing is just to enjoy the musical equivalents that Chadwick invents for "mischievous," "quirky," "knavish," "mocking," "misleading," "disconcerting," "rascally." Secondarily, the Listening Guide may be helpful in pointing out some features of the form and in identifying some of the instruments that appear prominently.

CD 4/26 (5:50) "Hobgoblin," from *Symphonic Sketches*, by George Chadwick. 1904. Eastman-Rochester Symphony Orchestra, Howard Hanson, conductor.

LISTENING GUIDE

"Hobgoblin," *Symphonic Sketches*, by George Chadwick

	Instruments	Form and Rhythm
0:00	French horn	*A* theme—call-and-response between horn (call) and high strings and woodwinds (response)
0:17	Full orchestra	Transitional passage based on opening horn tune
0:27	Mainly woodwinds	*B* theme—reminiscent of the rhythm of *A* but busier
0:55	Strings	Fast scale passage, leading to . . .
1:04	Horns	Augmentation* of scherzo rhythm, over *B* theme

*__Augmentation__ has already been encountered in Philip Bimstein's treatment of "Maple Leaf Rag" in his *Bushy Wushy Rag*, CD 4/20. Here it refers to the slowing down of the basic one/two/three rhythm of the scherzo, so that ONE TWO THREE is superimposed on One/two/three/One/two/three as shown here.

One two three One two three
ONE   TWO   THREE

(continued)

LISTENING GUIDE *(continued)*	1:09	Strings	*B* theme—development; listen for frequent references to the rhythms and shape of the *B* theme
	1:38	Violins & violas	*A* theme—complete form of the theme that the horns began at 0:00
	1:50	Full orchestra	Augmentation of scherzo rhythm
	1:53	Harp	
	2:14	Horns & trumpets	*A* theme—grandiose statement in full brass sound
	2:32	Woodwinds	*B* theme—listen for the bassoon and, again, the development of the *B* theme.
	3:26	Horns	Call-and-response, as in the beginning
	3:39		Full stop, then big scale passage into *B* theme
	4:09	Strings	Fast scale passage (as at 0:55)
	4:19	Horns	*A* theme—complete form (as played by strings at 1:38)
	4:30	Full orchestra	Augmentation of scherzo rhythm
	4:34	Harp	
	4:55	Horns & trumpets	*A*—grandiose statement of *A* (as at 2:14)
	5:39		Two "Grand Pauses" (empty measures), before final rush to end

Amy Marcy Cheney Beach   One of the most precocious, talented, and energetic composers of this time and place was also America's first prominent woman composer, Amy Marcy Cheney Beach (1867–1944). She was composing piano pieces at the age of 4, playing public recitals at 7, and performing as soloist with the Boston Symphony Orchestra before she was 18. Unlike Paine and Chadwick, who went to Europe to study, Amy Beach acquired her musical training entirely in Boston. She composed many songs and piano pieces, as well as chamber music, choral music, and larger works that included a piano concerto, an opera, and the splendid thirty-minute *Gaelic Symphony* (1894). (See Additional Listening.) Persistent and resourceful in securing performances of her own works, she was also generous in helping young musicians, and assumed leadership in many musical organizations, including the cofounding of the American Association of Women Composers in 1926.

FIVE INDIVIDUALISTS AROUND
THE TURN OF THE CENTURY

Roughly contemporaneous with the Second New England School were five composers—Edward MacDowell, Charles Martin Loeffler, Henry F. Gilbert, Charles Tomlinson Griffes, and Arthur Farwell—who had little in common except that each had a highly individual background and artistic stance.

America's first success story in producing a composer of truly international recognition was the career of Edward MacDowell (1860–1908). MacDowell had gone to Europe to study at the age of 15. While still in his twenties he had become a successful pianist, teacher, and composer there, and had virtually settled in Germany when he was persuaded to return to the United States and take an active part in its rapidly developing musical life. In 1888 he came back and settled in Boston, then a center of intense cultural activity. For the next eight years he concertized, composed, and had his works widely performed. From that period come many songs; many solo piano pieces, including the famous *Woodland Sketches;* and some of his most important orchestral compositions, including the *Indian Suite,* published in 1897 (see Additional Listening).

MacDowell's use of genuine Indian themes in this suite represents one of the earliest, and perhaps most successful, attempts to use material of this kind in a symphonic composition. Yet even though the *Indian Suite* is one of Mac-Dowell's strongest works, it was untypical in that he otherwise seldom used indigenous material. He was no "nativist." He declared in a lecture that "purely national music has no place in art"; and he disparaged as "childish" what he regarded as artificial "means of 'creating' a national music." MacDowell's range of expression we can now see to have been rather narrow. Perhaps his talent for art gives us a clue to his musical nature; he was fundamentally a pictorialist, and one who was most at home in miniature forms.

Charles Martin Loeffler (1861–1935) was born either in Berlin or in Alsace, and came to America as an accomplished violinist in 1881. Trained in composition in Europe before his arrival, he wrote a large number of works here that reflected his broad interests, especially in literature. His music reveals an awareness of Russian and especially French music of the time. Although overt "Americanism" in his music is practically confined to one movement of his Partita for Violin and Piano, he had a little-known but genuine enthusiasm for jazz, and enjoyed a friendship and correspondence with George Gershwin (Knight 452). A widely read man who was esteemed in intellectual as well as artistic circles, Loeffler was often a beneficiary of the patronage of Mrs. Isabella Stewart Gardner. Among works of his currently available, the moody and exotic *La Mort de Tintagiles,* completed in 1897, is representative of his forward-looking harmonic language and use of orchestral color (see Additional Listening).

Henry F. Gilbert (1868–1928), like Loeffler, had a broad range of tastes (they shared an interest in French literature), but Gilbert's leanings were distinctly nativist. He incorporated African American melodies, Indian melodies, and ragtime into his compositions. Impressed with the work of the photographer Edward S. Curtis and his pioneering studies of American Indians, Gilbert transcribed phonograph recordings Curtis had collected in the field, and wrote a score, performed by an orchestra of twenty-two musicians, to accompany Curtis's photographic presentation "The Story of a Vanishing Race," which opened at Carnegie Hall in 1911. Gilbert gave full rein to his impulsive curiosity, traveling to Chicago to hear exotic music at the Columbian Exposition of 1893. Illustrative of Gilbert's interest in America's vernacular musical sources is his eleven-minute symphonic poem *The Dance in Place Congo,* composed 1906–8 (see Additional Listening). The setting, the tunes, and the title are taken from George Washington Cable's 1886 articles on African American music making in New Orleans during the Reconstruction era (see Additional Reading). The principal tune is the one Gottschalk had also used a half-century earlier as the basis for one of his best-known piano works, "Bamboula."

Charles Tomlinson Griffes (1884–1920), in a productive period as a composer that lasted a bare thirteen years, managed to create an amazingly large body of works, many of which have increased in stature and significance with the passage of time. His early works reflected the influence of German Romanticism; later he produced some remarkable pieces that have become the prime American examples of Impressionism, including *Roman Sketches* and *The White Peacock.* Toward the end of his life Griffes produced a group of "Oriental" works, including his ten-minute *The Pleasure-Dome of Kubla Khan,* based on the poem by Coleridge (see Additional Listening). Less well known are his *Three Poems of Fiona MacLeod* of 1918. In these songs, which exist in versions for voice and orchestra, Griffes turned his attention, and his penchant for the exotic, to Celtic lore. That his further development as a composer might have taken him into still other realms of expression is shown by his striking Piano Sonata of 1917–18, which is forward-looking in its dissonance and its neoclassical avoidance of any programmatic associations.

Arthur Farwell, Idealistic Promoter of a Native Music

At the same time that MacDowell and the Boston classicists were at their honorable work of cultivating in America what were basically European musical forms and modes of expression, there were other musical winds stirring in the land. To understand these, it is necessary to recall a few things that had happened meanwhile on the broad musical scene. In the 1870s the Fisk Jubilee Singers (followed soon by other groups) had begun to open up a reservoir of

African American musical culture vastly different from the popular caricatures of the minstrel stage. In the 1880s American Indian music was beginning to be seriously collected and studied. On the popular musical stage about the same time, Harrigan and Hart were presenting plays with music that dealt with a cross-section of the everyday life of the people of New York. Ragtime arrived from the Midwest in the 1890s. From 1892 to 1895 the great Czech composer Antonin Dvořák (1841–1904) was in America as director of the National Conservatory in New York. His African American student Harry Thacker Burleigh (1866–1949), later to become a prominent composer, arranger, and concert singer, was a frequent visitor to his New York apartment, and repeatedly sang spirituals for him. Dvořák heard the songs of Stephen Foster; he spent summers in Iowa, where he heard Indian music. He issued what was in effect a challenge to American composers, to look to their own native music as a foundation on which to establish in America what he termed "a great and noble school of music." And there were composers of the time who were more than ready to accept that challenge. A spirit of ferment and optimism accompanied the advent of the new century, which seemed to portend a new era. One pioneer composer, writing in 1903, addressed himself to "all composers who feel the pulse of new life that marks the beginning of an era in American music," inviting them to join those workers who had been striving

> to draw out of the dawning, though widely distributed realities and possibilities of American musical life, the elements and forces necessary to form a definite movement which shall make for the untrammeled growth of a genuine Art of Music. Such an art will not be a mere echo of other lands and times, but shall have a vital meaning for us, in our circumstances, here and now. While it will take the worthier traditions of the past for its point of departure, it will derive its convincing qualities of color, form, and spirit from our nature-world and our humanity. (A. Farwell)

So wrote Arthur Farwell (1872–1952), a man of his time, whose initiative, enterprise, and integrity of ideals made him a leader and a mover. A native of the Midwest, he settled in Newton Center, Massachusetts, after a period of study that included the study of American Indian music, and entered upon a significant venture for American music. Having tried unsuccessfully to get his *American Indian Melodies* published, and having met other American composers who suffered similar rejections, he resolved to try to overcome the resistance to American music by founding a composers' press. The Wa-Wan Press came into being late in 1901. (The name "Wa-Wan" is that of an Omaha Indian ceremony of peace and brotherhood.) The emphasis was on quality—quality not only of the music chosen but of design and typography as well. In this Farwell was inspired by the examples of such predecessors as William Blake and William Morris. The press was in existence for ten years, during all of which time it remained Farwell's venture. During the decade of its existence it published the work of thirty-six American composers, including nine women. A glance at the complete output of the Wa-Wan Press shows that it maintained exceptional standards of workmanship and appearance. Like William Morris before him, Farwell eschewed commercialism, aware of the extent to which it could perpetuate and surround peoples' lives with shabbiness and mediocrity. For that reason, Farwell's work has special meaning for today.

A second aim of the Wa-Wan Press, and of Farwell himself, is less easily stated, but it had to do with developing an American music more in touch with American life. "It must have an American flavor," he wrote. "It must be recognizably American, as Russian music is Russian, and French music, French." Arthur Farwell sounded for American music the same note that Emerson, two generations earlier, had sounded for American literature: first, find your own voice, cultivate your own field; second, do not divorce art from life.

Farwell's concern with making music an active part of the lives of the great mass of the people expressed itself in many novel ideas, which his abilities as a leader and organizer enabled him to bring to fruition. While working in New York, he organized with Harry Barnhart the New York Community Chorus, which eventually grew to 800 singers. In 1916, using this chorus, he collaborated in the production of a Song and Light Festival on the shores of a lake in Central Park. The lighting effects, spectacular for their day, were described in a contemporary account:

> One-half million candle power of illumination shining through hundreds of artistic panels and huge globes gave the lake at the end of the Mall a fantastic aspect of colorful fairyland. No two of the colored panels were alike. The reflections of delicate red, blue, green and gold shades twinkled in the water, which was dotted with gray boats carrying passengers through the festival of song and light. (B. Farwell 85)

An orchestra and the 800-voice chorus performed some standard works by Handel, Wagner, and others, but integrated with these were songs such as "Old Black Joe" and "Nearer, My God, to Thee," in which the entire assembled audience of 25,000 gathered on the opposite shore of the lake participated. The total effect must have been impressive.

In California, where Arthur Farwell lived and worked from 1918 to 1927, he was connected with many projects for involving people more directly with music than the conventional concert format would allow, often in an outdoor setting. While teaching at the University of California in Berkeley, he wrote *California*, a masque of song, given in the Greek Theater with audience participation; later, in Southern California, he was instrumental in the establishment of the Hollywood Bowl, and he wrote music for *La Primavera*, a "Community Music Drama" produced in Santa Barbara in 1920. In 1925 he organized a series of outdoor concerts in a natural amphitheater that he named The Theater of the Stars, near Big Bear Lake, in the mountains of Southern California.

CONCLUSION

The period of nearly a hundred years with which this chapter has been concerned represents a great deal of ground covered. It began in an ebullient age of expansion and democratization, of fierce and sensitive national pride—an age of artistic innocence in which Heinrich, the "Loghouse Composer," could be dubbed "the Beethoven of America." It closed on the eve of a cataclysmic war involving profound changes in the order of a world more tightly bound together—an age of closer ties with the Europe from which American composers felt compelled to seek both *guidance* and *independence*. To use Blake's pair of terms, in art America had traversed the ground from "innocence" to "experience"—from Heinrich's idyllic *Dawning of Music in Kentucky* to the realistic *Padrone* of Chadwick.

At this point we proceed not simply to a new chapter but to a series of parallel chapters, depicting the parallel progress of tradition and innovation.

▬ PROJECTS

1. In this chapter the nineteenth century has been identified as the age in which, for a variety of reasons, the cleavage between classical and popular music became most pronounced. Considering the phenomena of "third stream" music, "minimalism," and the current concern with "accessibility" in classical music circles, has this cleavage grown less in our time? Has it become irrelevant? Give your considered views in a brief but well-documented paper.
2. Sample the coverage given the arts in a local newspaper for a period of several weeks. Observe the proportion of space given to local artists and local live performances, as compared with space devoted to "name" artists or stars, whose work is accessible mostly through the media of records, films, or television. Write a paper on how your findings relate to the "nativist" versus "expatriate" controversy dealt with in this chapter.
3. Read Louis Moreau Gottschalk's *Notes of a Pianist* (see References), and write a paper on any of a number of subjects suggested by this brilliant diary—e.g., "The Life of a Concert Artist in Mid-Nineteenth-Century America" or "Music in the Mining Towns of the West."

■ ADDITIONAL LISTENING

Beach, Amy Marcy Cheney. Symphony in E minor (*Gaelic*), Op. 32. Detroit Symphony Orchestra. Cond. Neeme Jarvi. Chandos 8958.

——. Symphony in E minor (*Gaelic*), Op. 32. Royal Philharmonic Ensemble. Cond. Karl Krueger. Bridge 9086.

Gilbert, Henry F. Symphonic poem, *The Dance in Place Congo,* Op. 15. Los Angeles Philharmonic Orchestra with Zita Carno. Cond. Calvin Simmons. New World Records 80228.

Griffes, Charles Tomlinson. *The Pleasure-Dome of Kubla Khan,* Op. 8, for piano (or orchestra). *American Masterpieces.* Andre Kostelanetz Orchestra. Cond. Andre Kostelanetz. Sony 63034. Boston Symphony Orchestra. Cond. Seiji Ozawa. NW 80273.

Loeffler, Charles Martin. *La Mort de Tintagiles,* Op. 6, for viola d'amore and orchestra. *La Mort de Tintagiles / Five Irish Fantasies.* Indianapolis Symphony Orchestera with Jennie Hansen. Cond. John Nelson. New World Records 80332.

MacDowell, Edward. Suite No. 2 (*Indian*), Op. 48, for orchestra. *American Orchestral Music. American Composers Series.* Vox (Box 2 Classical) 5092.

——. Suite No. 2 (*Indian*), Op. 48, for orchestra. *Edward MacDowell: Suites Nos. 1 and 2 / Hamlet and Ophelia.* Ulster Orchestra. Cond. Takuo Yuasa. Naxos 8559075.

——. Suite No. 2 (*Indian*), Op. 48, for orchestra. *Edward MacDowell Suites.* Bohuslav Martinu Philharmonic Orchestra. Cond. Charles Anthony Johnson. Albany Troy 224. Also includes Suite No. 1, Op. 41, and *Sea Pieces* (orch. Johnson).

Paine, John Knowles. *Overture to Shakespeare's As You Like It, Op. 28 / Symphony No. 1 in C Minor.* New York Philharmonic. Cond. Zubin Mehta. New World Records 80374.

CHAPTER

19 The Evolving Tradition, 1920–70

To the listener in the adventurous period that began in the 1920s, *all* American art music seemed new, and stirred interest and controversy. It is only from the vantage point of a later time that we can see how tradition and innovation were being cultivated simultaneously. For example, *Intégrales* by Edgard Varèse, the Symphony for Organ and Orchestra by Aaron Copland, and *Rhapsody in Blue* by George Gershwin were all premiered in New York in 1924–25; each was perceived as *new* music, yet each bore quite a different relationship to the current state of musical evolution. What was most readily accepted and absorbed during this period was the music that was evolving along traditional lines. It is with such music that this chapter will be concerned. The less readily approachable innovations of the twentieth century will be treated in the next chapter.

SOME BACKGROUND FOR THE "FERVENT YEARS"

The qualities that unmistakably characterized the period were enthusiasm, energy, and optimism. As David Owens put it, "America was taking stock, really for the first time, of its cultural assets, and it can be said that nothing before or after in the country's aesthetic history has exhilarated it to such a degree" (Owens). For it was then that an indigenous fine-art music (the coming of which had been prophesied—and in part made possible—by so many of the pioneers we encountered in the last chapter) began to flourish. The two decades between the wars, especially, were years of ferment and change—"fervent years," as they have been called.

Partly this was the result of the existence of a group of young musicians who fairly early in their lives made the irrevocable decision to become composers, and who dedicated themselves fully and knowledgeably to preparing themselves for productive careers. As Roger Sessions put it:

> The striking fact is that those who aspired to genuine and serious achievement, no longer a handful of ambitious individuals who remained essentially isolated, were young Americans who had begun to learn what serious accomplishment involved. They were determined to find their way to it. Such seeking had not occurred before in the United States, but they did not find what they sought within the then existing framework of American music life. (16)

Americans in Paris

Not finding "what they sought within the then existing framework of American music life," most did turn once more to Europe, but a far different Europe from what had existed previously. It was not merely that the Great War and its aftermath had weakened German dominance—it was also that more venturesome things were taking place elsewhere. Arthur Farwell had already noted, two decades earlier, the greater musical inventiveness of France and Russia. By the third decade of the twentieth century, the Russian Revolution had created a climate that was not inviting to composers. France was in all ways more hospitable, and France, specifically Paris, fostered an atmosphere of fervent concern for music (and for the arts generally) that was evidenced in a burst of new music being performed and in new artistic movements. Dada, for example, was a rejection of artistic formalism and rationality. This ferment attracted younger composers. The young French group of *Les Six*—Darius Milhaud, Francis Poulenc, Arthur Honegger, Georges Auric, Louis Durey, and Germaine Tailleferre—in the artistic company of the older iconoclast Eric

Satie, held together and motivated by the writer Jean Cocteau, was making itself heard. There was also important music by non-French composers: Igor Stravinsky, Arnold Schoenberg, Paul Hindemith, Béla Bartók, Serge Proko-fiev. Serge Koussevitzky (1874–1951), noted Russian conductor, began in 1921 in Paris the "Concerts Koussevitzky," at which many new works were performed.

Among the young émigrés American composers formed a particular con-tingent. In the same year that Koussevitzky began his celebrated concerts, a music school for Americans was established in the palace at Fontainebleau. Although Paul Vidal of the Paris Conservatory was the composition teacher, it was an exceptional woman in her thirties, Nadia Boulanger (1887–1979)—an organist and a teacher of harmony, counterpoint, and composition—who was destined to have the most influence on a host of American composers who came to her for instruction, guidance, and encouragement throughout the 1920s and 1930s. A list of these young "Americans in Paris" who studied at least for a time with Mlle. Boulanger, gaining not only perceptive criticism but also the confidence to find and strike out on their own paths, included many of the most important composers of the period.

Americans Back Home

American composers returning from Europe in the 1920s found reasons for both pessimism and optimism. Certainly there was as yet no great audience cre-ating a demand for the music of American composers, and many could justifi-ably join H. L. Mencken in condemning Americans' tendency to shallow materialism and their lack of interest in, or understanding of, the arts. Some of the young émigrés therefore stayed away for good; but many composers did not. As Aaron Copland, with characteristic optimism, pointed out, positive forces (mostly generated by the composers themselves) were at work. The International Composers' Guild and its offshoot, the League of Composers, were active and gave concerts of new music. In 1924 Serge Koussevitzky, whose celebrated concerts in Paris had introduced many new works, was appointed conductor of the Boston Symphony, beginning a long tenure during which he not only played many new American works but was also often responsible, through commissions, for their creation. The decade before the crash of 1929 was a time of opulence in American life, and there were patrons of the arts. In the mid-1920s the Guggenheim Memorial Foundation was estab-lished. When in 1929 the RCA Victor Company offered an unprecedented award of $25,000 for a symphonic work, the competition was such that the prize had to be split five ways. These were what Claire Reis (1888–1978), an indefatigable and indispensable supporter of new music in this period, called the "crusading days." Virgil Thomson identified five composer "commandos": Aaron Copland (1900–90), Roger Sessions (1896–1985), Roy Harris (1898–1979), Walter Piston (1894–1976), and Thomson himself (1896–1989). With a camaraderie born of combat (note the use by both Reis and Thomson of military terms) that momentarily submerged their differences, they were fighting to establish a "beachhead" both for American composers and for new music in general.

The Drive toward an "American" Music

However they might interpret the term, it was natural that composers of the time should be seeking to write music that was "recognizably American." In this they were responding to the same urges that had been expressed two and three decades earlier by Farwell, Gilbert, and others. As Roger Sessions stated,

> The principal concern of music in the twenties was the idea of a national or "typically American" school or style and, eventually, a tradition which would draw to a focus the musical energies of our country which, as Rosenfeld once said to Aaron Copland and the author, would "affirm America." (140)

For the new generation of composers it was no longer a matter of simply incorporating folk material into compositions or using it as a basis for symphonic elaborations, although those practices are perfectly valid. As Copland put it,

> Our concern was not with the quotable hymn or spiritual: we wanted to find a music that would speak of universal things in a vernacular of American speech rhythms. We wanted to write music on a level that left popular music far behind — music with a largeness of utterance wholly representative of the country that Whitman had envisaged. (*Music and Imagination* 104)

There was much experimentation in this search for "a music that would speak of universal things in a vernacular of American speech rhythms." It was natural, for example, that as earlier composers had looked to American Indian music, African American spirituals, and minstrel tunes, composers in the third decade of the twentieth century should look to jazz and the attendant popular music influenced by it.

John Alden Carpenter   The generation that preceded the young "commandos" had not all left the scene, and John Alden Carpenter (1876–1951) was one of the older composers who made use of the idioms of the Jazz Age in some of his works. His thirteen-minute "jazz pantomime" *Krazy Kat,* based on the George Herriman comic-strip character, was first performed as a ballet-pantomime in New York in 1922. Its success led the Russian impresario Diaghilev to commission another work, *Skyscrapers* (see Additional Listening). It is subtitled "a ballet of modern American life," and its scenes alternate between depictions of "work" and depictions of "play." Produced in New York in 1926, it was something of a landmark in its balletic treatment of modern urban life.

Copland composed his jazz-based *Music for the Theater* in 1925, and the next year utilized jazz motifs again in his Concerto for Piano and Orchestra. George Gershwin's *Rhapsody in Blue,* Piano Concerto in F, and *An American in Paris* (the last two commissioned by Walter Damrosch for the New York Symphony) date from this period also. After the 1920s the tendency to turn to jazz as a stylistic source for American classical music waned.

The American Composer Finds a Public

With the onset of the Depression decade before World War II, American fine-art music entered a period in which it became noticeably more functional, possibly more so than in any other period before or since. American composers had a public, and there was an actual need for their music. Copland wrote:

> In all the arts the Depression had aroused a wave of sympathy for and identification with the plight of the common man. In music this was combined with the heady wine of suddenly feeling ourselves—the composers, that is—needed as never before. Previously our works had been largely self-engendered: no one asked for them; we simply wrote them out of our own need. Now, suddenly, functional music was in demand as never before in the experience of our serious composers. Motion-picture and ballet companies, radio stations and schools, film and theater producers discovered us. . . . No wonder we were pleased to find ourselves sought after and were ready to compose in a manner that would satisfy both our collaborators and ourselves. (*The New Music* 161–62)

This new practical direction for American classical music tended to take the form of linking music functionally with other arts: film, dance, and poetry. As an introduction to the traditionally evolving classical music after World War I, we shall consider each of these, and then turn to the more "abstract" forms of composition—the sonata, the quartet, the symphony—that also flourished.

MUSIC WITH FILM

The 1930s saw the rise of the symphonic film score, with lush orchestral music mostly by European composers brought up in the European symphonic-operatic tradition. Film scoring rapidly became a very specialized job. Not until 1936 did a major American composer write film music, and then it was in the field of the documentary, a genre that is independent to a degree of the pressures of the entertainment industry.

A Realistic Film of the American West

In the mid-1930s the Resettlement Administration, a United States government agency, wanted a documentary film to propagandize on behalf of its program to aid farm families driven out of drought-stricken areas—mainly the Dust Bowl of the Southwest. Pare Lorentz, a film reviewer turned filmmaker, was engaged to make this, his first movie. The result was a powerful documentary called *The Plow That Broke the Plains.* The film still makes a stunning visual impact today, with its expressive footage of prairie grasslands; devastated, dust-blown farms; and hard-hit, long-suffering farm families; and its visual analogies, as for example between military tanks and mammoth harvesters, or between a collapsed ticker-tape machine and bleached bones on the plowed-over, denuded land.

Virgil Thomson, an individualistic composer and a highly influential writer and critic during this entire period of American musical history, was engaged to write music for the film. Both Thomson and Lorentz felt the rightness of "rendering landscape through the music of its people," as the composer put it. The music therefore integrates material representative of the vastness and variety of American vernacular music, including a Calvinist psalm tune, cowboy songs, African American blues, and World War I songs. The music is available in the form of a thirteen-minute suite for orchestra in six movements fashioned by the composer himself, and is quite effective apart from the film, in which it is actually covered at times by the narration. Of the six movements of the suite, the third, labeled "Cattle," is the one in which the landscape is most clearly rendered through the music of its people, for we hear versions of three authentic cowboy tunes: "I Ride an Old Paint," "The Cowboy's Lament" (also known as "The Streets of Laredo"), and "Whoopie Ti Yi Yo, Git Along, Little Dogies." The fourth movement of the suite is "Blues," appropriately conventionalized and urbanized in the style of 1920s commercial jazz, to underscore the brash and ruinous exploitation of the land. Toward the end the music becomes progressively more dissonant (it is marked "Rough and violent"), and the themes more and more incoherent, climaxed by a final jangling chord that has as its underpinning, appropriately, the diminished triad. The sixth and last movement, "Devastation," brings back the material of the first, to complete the archlike structure. It goes on to include a fugue exposition, and ends this documentation of "the most tragic chapter in American agriculture" with a gigantic tango on a stretched-out version of the fugue theme (Additional Listening).

Two Films about the Small Town and the Big City

Aaron Copland began his career, as did many other composers of his generation, with a period of study in France in the 1920s with Nadia Boulanger. He returned to become one of the original "commandos" working on behalf of American music and its composers. He went on, in succeeding decades, to compose music in virtually every medium, and to become one of the most prominent and influential American composers, not only through his music but through his writing as well. Copland wrote two film scores for the industry, the second of which was *Our Town*, for the movie based on Thornton Wilder's play about life and death, the commonplace and the universal, dramatized in episodes in the lives of two families in a small New England town. Much of the music is available in an orchestral piece called simply *Our Town: Music from the Film Score* (Additional Listening).

Quite different from the music for *Our Town* is the score Leonard Bernstein created for the Elia Kazan film *On the Waterfront* (1954). This film is about a longshoreman who is possessed of a degree of sensitivity and moral integrity that seems irreconcilably at odds with the harsh, brutal world of the waterfront in which he has always lived. The quiet opening melody, unaccompanied (one of the main themes of the score), has a spacious diatonic simplicity about it, until the introduction of the one "blue note" (a master stroke of inflection and timing) at once affects the whole feel of the music. For all the spareness of its opening, and its references to jazz (appropriate to the urban setting and the theme of alienation), it is soon apparent that this is a "symphonic film score," which has been adapted into a 23-minute symphonic suite (Additional Listening).

MUSIC WITH DANCE

The "Americanization" of ballet began about this time, with the search for new material and fresh approaches. Forerunners of this, as noted previously, were John Alden Carpenter's *Krazy Kat* of 1922 and *Skyscrapers* of 1926. In 1937 Lincoln Kirstein commissioned for his Ballet Caravan a score from Virgil Thomson for his ballet *Filling Station*—a score with copious references to popular dances (the waltz, the tango, the Big Apple) and other Americana, "all aimed," as Thomson has written, "to evoke roadside America as pop art."

A Western Ballet: *Billy the Kid*

The next year, Kirstein brought into being, with Aaron Copland as composer, the first "western" ballet, *Billy the Kid*. A more unequivocally "American" theme could hardly be imagined. (Musical comedy did not take up the American west until five years later, with *Oklahoma!*) If it seems strange that a composer born in Brooklyn, and, as Arthur Berger called him, a "thorough-going New Yorker," should compose a ballet set in the arid western prairie, Berger goes on to remind us of the psychologically not-so-different solitude and aridness of the teeming city streets.

As Virgil Thomson had done in *The Plow That Broke the Plains*, Copland made extensive use of authentic cowboy tunes in *Billy the Kid*, especially in the scene labeled "Street in a Frontier Town" (CD 5/1). The ballet begins with an introduction labeled "The Open Prairie," with a vast, static quality about it that evokes the loneliness of the prairie. If it can be called a dance, it is a lean, somewhat harsh, but majestic *sarabande*—a huge dilation upon its basic rhythm that dwarfs merely human figures.

Kirstein himself devised the scenario for *Billy the Kid*, around the short career of the legendary William Bonney (1859–81).The scenario for the street scene is given in the score as follows:

> The first scene is a street in a frontier town. Familiar figures amble by. Cowboys saunter into town, some on horseback, others with their lassoes. Some Mexican women do a Jarabe which is interrupted by a fight between two drunks. Attracted by the gathering crowd, Billy is seen for the first time as a boy of twelve with his mother. The brawl turns ugly,

CD 5/1 (5:36) "Street in a Frontier Town," from *Billy the Kid*, by Aaron Copland. 1938. The Philadelphia Orchestra, Eugene Ormandy, conductor.

Photo by Roy Stevens

Ballet meets the Wild West in Aaron Copland's *Billy the Kid* (1938).

LISTENING GUIDE

Copland, "Street in a Frontier Town,"
from *Billy the Kið Ballet Suite*

0:00   The solo piccolo plays a slight, fragile, little tune based on the folk tune "Great Granddad," emphasizing the smallness of the human figures when they appear.

"Great Granddad"

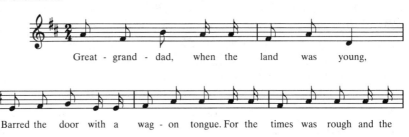

Great - grand - dad,   when the   land   was   young,

Barred the   door   with a   wag - on   tongue. For the   times   was   rough   and the

red - skins mocked, And he   said   his   prayers with his   shot - gun   cocked.

0:21   A distillation of "Git Along, Little Dogies" intrudes and alternates with phrases of "Great Granddad." Occasional disagreements among the instruments about the right notes of the tune — and the hiccuping grace notes — enchance the rough-edged, drunken effect.

"Git Along, Little Dogies"

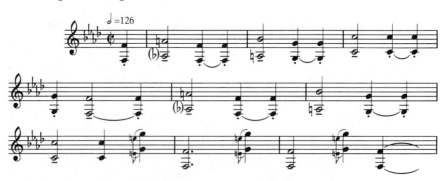

1:55   A brisk introduction leads to a square-dance treatment of "The Old Chisholm Trail."

"The Old Chisholm Trail"

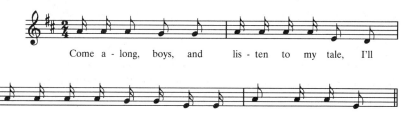

Come a - long, boys, and   lis - ten to my tale,   I'll

tell   you   of   my   trou - bles   on   the   old   Chis - holm   trail.

2:13   The trombones play a highly modified version of "Goodbye, Old Paint."

"Goodbye, Old Paint"

My   foot   in   the   stir - rup,   my   pon - y   won't

stan',___   Good - by,   old   Paint,   I'm   a   leav - in'   Chey -

-enne.   I'm   a - leav - in'   Chey - enne,   I'm   off   for   Mon -

-tan',___   Good - by,   old   Paint,   I'm   a - leav - in'   Chey - enne.

2:21   "The Old Chisholm Trail"—then in quick succession . . .

2:29   "Git Along, Little Dogies"

2:46   "Great Granddad"

2:59   A brief interlude leads to . . .

3:13   "Come Wrangle Your Bronco"—a fairly extensive treatment in an
        asymetrical rhythm of five.

3:58   "Goodbye, Old Paint"—an extensive treatment with the last part of the
        song first.

Words for all the cowboy tunes above are from *Cowboy Songs and Frontier Ballads*, by John and
Alan Lomax, a collection first issued in 1910.

guns are drawn, and in some unaccountable way, Billy's mother is killed. Without an instant's hesitation, in cold fury, Billy draws a knife from a cowhand's sheath and stabs his mother's slayers. His short but famous career had begun.

From the end of our excerpt to the end of the suite, there is a long slow section devoted to "The Dying Cowboy" (or "Bury Me Not on the Lone Prairie") that, except for an expressive lengthening of the stressed notes, is quite faithful to the original song.

Transcription 19.1
"The Dying Cowboy"

A gun battle and a drunken celebration of the Kid's escape follow. After this extended sequence, the music of the suite omits the escape scene, the music of the lovers' *pas de deux* in the desert, and the death of Billy at the hands of the posse, and goes directly to the recapitulation of the impressive "open prairie" music. The complete *Billy the Kid: Ballet Suite* is a twenty-minute orchestral piece, frequently heard in live performances, and readily available on CD (Additional Listening).

MUSIC WITH POETRY

Music for Solo Voice

The song for a single voice with accompaniment has been an important form of musical expression since the Middle Ages. In America the art song, as it is called, has developed parallel to the vigorous popular-song tradition. The distinction is not one of quality but one of the level of sophistication. The art song is not bound by the conventions that have long dictated to popular song its form, its degree of difficulty, its subject matter, and, above all, its *approach* to that subject matter. The accompaniment is more independent of the vocal line than in the popular song; it is more developed musically; and, most important, it is fully written out by the composer. Finally, the art-song composer usually works with a text that is more sophisticated and developed *as poetry*. American composers have set verses by Walt Whitman (one of the most frequently used poets), Sara Teasdale, Vachel Lindsay, Edwin Arlington Robinson, Archibald MacLeish, E. E. Cummings, Emily Dickinson, Tennessee Williams, Langston Hughes, Mark Van Doren, Wallace Stevens, and James Agee.

Music for Solo Voice and Piano   Songs tend to be composed in groups, most often to poems by the same author. From the wealth of American songs, five such groups for voice and piano are suggested as an introduction; most are settings of poems by significant American poets. The first is *Three Poems by Edwin Arlington Robinson,* a series of settings by John Duke (1899–1984) of some of the concise and cryptic verse portraits of that American poet (1869–1935). "Richard Cory" is from Robinson's *Children of the Night,* written before the turn of the century (Additional Listening).

The second group is *Songs of Separation,* by William Grant Still (1895–1978). Still was the first African American composer to have his music published and played widely. He played oboe in the orchestra of Eubie Blake's *Shuffle Along* (see pp. 244–45), and while on tour in Boston took composition lessons from George Chadwick (see pp. 348–50). Still went on to compose numerous instrumental and vocal works, including five symphonies. The best known of these is the famous *Afro-American Symphony.* One of the *Songs of Separation,* composed in 1949, is "A Black Pierrot" (CD 5/2), to a poem by the African American poet Langston Hughes, a prominent figure in the Harlem Renaissance. (For a source of this and other songs from the group, see Additional Listening.)

CD 5/2 (2:26)
"A Black Pierrot." 1949. Music by William Grant Still. Poem by Langston Hughes. Robert Honeysucker, baritone; Vivian Taylor, piano. Recorded at the African Meeting House, Boston.

I am a black Pierrot:
She did not love me,
So I crept away into the night and the night was black, too.
I am a black Pierrot:
She did not love me,
So I wept until the red dawn dripped blood over the eastern hills
And my heart was bleeding too.
I am a black Pierrot:
She did not love me,
So with my once gay colored soul shrunken like a balloon without air,
I went forth in the morning to seek a new brown love.

Text, "A Black Pierrot"

(From *The Collected Poems of Langston Hughes* by Langston Hughes, copyright © 1994 by The Estate of Langston Hughes. Used by permission of Alfred A. Knopf, a division of Random House, Inc., and Harold Ober Associates Incorporated.)

CD 5/3 (2:24)
"Heavenly Grass," from
Blue Mountain Ballads.
1946. Music by Paul
Bowles. Poem by
Tennessee Williams.
William Sharp, baritone;
Steven Blier, piano.

Text, "Heavenly Grass"

(Words by Tennessee
Williams. Music by Paul
Bowles. Copyright © 1964
(Renewed) by G. Schirmer,
Inc. (ASCAP). International
Copyright Secured. All
Rights Reserved. Reprinted
by permission.)

The third group is *Blue Mountain Ballads,* by Paul Bowles (1910–99), to poems by playwright Tennessee Williams. Bowles spent a good deal of his life in North Africa, where he composed, wrote novels, and did ethnomusicological research. He composed incidental music to several of Williams's plays. (For recordings of *Blue Mountain Ballads,* see Additional Listening.)

My feet took a walk
In heavenly grass
All day while the sky shone clear as glass,
My feet took a walk
In heavenly grass.
All night while the lonesome stars rolled past,
Then my feet come down to walk on earth
And my mother cried
When she give me birth.
Now my feet walk far
And my feet walk fast,
But they still got an itch for heavenly grass.

The fourth group is *Hermit Songs,* by Samuel Barber (1910–81). Barber is probably best known for his Adagio for Strings, which is frequently played on occasions, many of them memorial in nature, where serious and thoughtful music is needed. Barber has been called a neoromantic, and his works, in all media, have found a favorite place in the repertoire of American music. The *Hermit Songs* are ten songs for voice and piano on poems by medieval Irish poets, composed in 1953 (Additional Listening).

The fifth group is *Twelve Poems of Emily Dickinson* set to music by Aaron Copland—another instance of the setting by American composers of the most distinguished American poets. Of these poems Copland wrote, "The poems centre about no single theme, but they treat of subject matter particularly close to Miss Dickinson: nature, death, life, eternity" (see Additional Listening.)

Music for Solo Voice and Orchestra

For voice with orchestra, composers will often set a single longer text. This was the case with the sixteen-minute *Knoxville: Summer of 1915,* by Samuel Barber, on a text by James Agee. An American masterpiece, it represents a rare coincidence of gifted poet and first-rate composer, each at the height of his powers. The text, a fragment of the prologue to Agee's novel *A Death in the Family,* consists of the wonder-filled observations, through the eyes of childhood, of an uneventful summer evening. Barber, a composer noted for his lyricism, manages to evoke an innocence and nostalgia that perfectly complement the text (Additional Listening).

Music for Chorus   As a nation America has grown up with choral singing. Psalm tunes were sung by whites and blacks both; the singing schools early implanted among Americans a vigorous tradition of part-singing and fostered a native school of choral music; the urban singing societies of the nineteenth century saw to it that the major works of the cultivated tradition were heard; the singing of the Fisk Jubilee Singers and similar groups from other black colleges started the choral singing of spirituals among blacks and whites alike. Large-scale choral works were composed by native composers in the nineteenth century, as we heard in the case of *The Haymakers* (1857), by George F. Root (CD 4/25, pp. 343–44).

Two contrasting works are suggested as an introduction to American choral music of the second half of the twentieth century. The first is *The Peaceable Kingdom* (1936), by Randall Thompson (1899–1984), a sequence of choruses for unaccompanied mixed voices on biblical texts from Isaiah. The title is that of a famous piece of folk art by the American painter and Quaker preacher Edward Hicks (1780–1849), illustrating the millennial text of Isaiah 11: 6–9, which begins, "The wolf also shall dwell with the lamb, and the leopard shall lie down with the kid; and the calf and the young lion and the fatling together; and a little child shall lead them." The music shows a mastery of choral writing and exhibits a wide range of textures and devices, including the biting dissonance of "their faces shall be as flames," the quiet desolation of "the paper reeds by the brooks," the delicious word-painting of "the trees of the field shall clap their hands," and the exuberant polyphony of "as when one goeth with a pipe to come into the mountain of the Lord." (See Additional Listening.)

A more recent choral work of a different character is a setting by Roger Sessions of Walt Whitman's poem *When Lilacs Last in the Door-yard Bloom'd* (Additional Listening). It is a 42-minute cantata for soprano, contralto, baritone, mixed chorus, and orchestra, completed in 1970. Whitman's poem is a dirge on the death of Lincoln. The first four stanzas form a kind of prologue, introducing Whitman's "trinity" of "Lilac blooming perennial and drooping star in the west,/ And thought of him I love." It also introduces the symbol of the mourning bird. The second section describes the procession of the coffin, and the tribute of the poet: the sprig of lilac, the perfume ("sea-winds") for the grave, and the pictures—broad Whitmanesque scenes with people—to adorn the burial-house. The third section is the bird's carol of death ("dark mother," "strong deliveress"), Whitman's retrospective view of a Civil War battlefield, and a final passing beyond and leave-taking. Roger Sessions, one of the original "commandos," became an influential teacher, as well as a composer of well-wrought works that demand much of both performer and listener.

MUSIC INDEPENDENT
OF FILM, DANCE, OR POETRY

Music for Solo Piano

We begin with three sets of short piano pieces by George Gershwin, Aaron Copland, and Samuel Barber. Each is an *interpretation*, filtered, we might say, through the artistic temperament of each composer, of one or more of the vernacular idioms explored earlier in this book.

George Gershwin composed five piano preludes in 1926. Of the five, three were published the next year—two bright movements flanking a central blues-like "Andante con moto e poco rubato," the best known of the three. The first prelude uses the jazz-Latin rhythm of the Charleston (very close to a speeded-up tango) with variants. The catchy asymmetry of its rhythms is matched by simultaneous cross-relations in the chords (for example, A-natural against A-flat), which constitute realizations in piano terms of the blue notes of the scale.

The second of Aaron Copland's *Four Piano Blues*, marked "soft and languid," dates from 1934. A highly attenuated interpretation of the blues, it is sophisticated *play*, with piquant polyharmonies (in the first section) against stylized blues sonorities.

On the flyleaf of Samuel Barber's four *Excursions*, written in 1945, appears the following note: "These are 'Excursions' in small classical forms into regional American idioms. Their rhythmic characteristics, as well as their source in folk material and their scoring, reminiscent of local instruments, are easily recognized." The first is an excursion into the realm of boogie-woogie (see pp. 339–40). The second is a slow, restrained blues, with four variations on the classic 12-bar form. The third evokes a cowboy ballad sung to a guitar accompaniment. The fourth is an excursion into the realm of the hoedown—a lively evocation of fiddle and banjo figuration. It is interesting to compare this with Louis Moreau Gottschalk's "The Banjo" (CD 4/24, p. 340), a similarly polished "translation" of banjo idioms into a piece for the concert hall a century earlier. (For all three sets of piano works, see Additional Listening.)

Chamber music

We can make but a few suggestions for the exploration of American chamber music. For the string quartet, a good beginning might be George Gershwin's pleasantly soporific 11-minute *Lullaby for String Quartet* (written about 1920). In contrast to that, there is the serious and energetic 23-minute String Quartet No. 3 (1939) by William Schuman (1910–92). For wind chamber music, a good introduction to the medium of the *woodwind quintet* (consisting of flute, oboe, clarinet, bassoon, and one brass instrument, the French horn; remember the *Bushy Wushy Rag*, CD 4/20, p. 334) would be Samuel Barber's *Summer Music*, of 1956. In contrast to this would be the austere but impressive Concerto for Piano and Woodwind Quintet by Wallingford Riegger, composed in 1953. (See Additional Listening for all.)

The Symphony

The symphony evolved as an important musical form in the eighteenth century, and by the time of the death of Beethoven (1827) it had come to represent the ultimate vehicle for the expression of serious musical thought in terms of "absolute" or "pure" music. American composers who wrote from the 1920s on regarded the symphony in this classical sense, and the typical American symphony since then has been a nonprogrammatic work, generally in several independent movements, and usually regarded as a vehicle for the composer's most serious musical thoughts.

The Third Symphony of Roy Harris

Roy Harris (1898–1979) is the last of the five "commandos" active from the 1920s to be considered here. He tended to be a peripatetic loner, imbued with a sense of his own destiny to express "the American spirit" and, like the poet Robert Frost, caught up in his own legend—that of a man close to the soil—for Frost, New England, for Harris, the Plains. (Roy Harris was indeed born in a log cabin in Lincoln County, Oklahoma, on Lincoln's birthday, but he moved to California at the age of 5.) His undoubted gifts and his authentic contribution are best represented by his Third Symphony (1939), one of the strongest and most compact of American symphonies.

Before conducting you on a guided trip through the seventeen-minute symphony, it will be well to introduce you to three characteristics of Harris's musical language. The *first* is his use of the drama inherent in the simple but fundamental conflict between the major and the minor triad. Purge your ears of complex sounds for the moment, and sensitize yourself to this basic tension.

Harris makes much of this tension, changing through the movement of one voice (that entrusted with the third of the chord, the harmonic "coloring agent") the inflection of the entire chord.

CD 5/4 (17:13).
Third Symphony, by Roy Harris. 1939.
New York Philharmonic, Leonard Bernstein, conductor.

Transcription 19.2
The major and the minor triad

Alternatively, the change in the coloring agent can appear in a melodic line, as in the very opening of the piece.

Many such shifts occur in the melodic line. Harris, in fact, developed a theory of light and dark in musical sonority based on the "coloring" of chords and entire scales through these inflections.

The *second* characteristic of Harris's musical language is the juxtaposition of distantly related simple chords (triads). This is shown in a passage for full orchestra near the climactic end of the symphony, at about 16:22 (see Listening Guide).

The *third* characteristic is the use of very long, flowing melodic lines, which go on for pages and pages in the score. The melody at the very opening, in the cellos, lasts a whole minute (Transcription 19.4). (Until the advent of minimalism, thirty years later, a minute was a long time in music.)

As another illustration of a long melodic line, Transcription 19.6 notates the first appearance of the violins in the symphony.

Transcription 19.6
Harris, Third Symphony, measures 60–97

(By Roy Harris. Copyright © 1939 (renewed) by Associated Music Publishers, Inc. (BMI). International Copyright Secured. All Rights Reserved. Reprinted by permission.)

At this point the woodwinds enter with the same theme a major 6th higher, while the violins continue

All the violins are playing in unison, and the line, beginning about 2:35 into the piece, goes on for over a minute. After the entrance of the trombones, the violins continue their line for another minute and a half, ending by themselves on a high unison *fff* (as loud as possible) at about 5:12. In the meantime, at about 4:08, all the woodwinds, except for the flutes, have played the melody as a counterpoint to the violins. Near the very end of the piece, this melody is repeated (about 13:30) in a canon between all the strings (except the basses), and all the woodwinds (except the piccolo), in a passage that lasts again for a whole minute.

Seventeen minutes in length, the Third Symphony is in one continuous movement, though divided rather clearly into sections, as Harris has outlined

LISTENING GUIDE

CD 5/4 (17:13). Third Symphony, by Roy Harris. 1939. New York Philharmonic, Leonard Bernstein, conductor.

Harris, Third Symphony

I. Tragic — Low string sonorities

0:00   Cellos play long melody with major vs minor triads (see Transcription 19.4).

0:31   Violas and cellos play a melody with both major and minor triads, lending a faint blues quality to the color shift.

2:25   Brass enter — listen to all four horns playing in unison.

2:35   Violins enter with long melody (see Transcription 19.6). Try to follow the violin line all the way to 5:12.

4:08   Woodwinds enter with same melody at a new pitch level.

II. Lyric — Strings, horns, woodwinds

5:41   A faster-flowing theme with wide leaps implies a single chord (A major) and marks the beginning of the lyric section. It is sounded in all strings except the basses. Elements of this theme will appear later.

Measures 152–158

III. Pastoral

7:15   This middle section has a distinctive texture heard nowhere else in the symphony. Against an undulating background of string sound, woodwind and brass solos occur in order: English horn, clarinet, oboe, bassoon and bass clarinet together, flute, English horn, clarinet, bassoon, clarinet and bass clarinet together, and so on. Rapid scales in woodwinds and strings lead to the next section.

for us. Now is the time to listen to the whole work, noting the landmarks already pointed out as we go along.

The symphony is not programmatic in a literal sense, but it will be noted that Harris himself has attached to each section a word whose significance goes beyond the purely musical ("Tragic," "Lyric," "Pastoral," "Dramatic"). Like Arthur Farwell (see pp. 352–55), who was one of Harris's early teachers and in a sense his "discoverer," Roy Harris consistently and consciously sought the

IV. Fugue—Dramatic

10:02   **A.** Brass and percussion dominate. All strings except basses play the dramatic fugue theme *ff*.

Measures 416–421

     Timpani solos punctuate subsequent entrances of the fugue subject.

10:16   Trombones

10:30   Horns

10:43   Trumpets

11:14   Trombones and trumpets, in canon (twice, with percussion entrance in between)

11:38   Horns and trumpets in canon

11:55   Trumpets/trombones and horns in canon. A contrasitng section follows.

12:12   **B.** Woodwinds develop theme from Section II in canon (see transcription at 5:41).

12:46   Fugue theme reappears.

13:22   Brass play a new rhythmic, repeated-note figure with dramatic silences.

V. Dramatic—Tragic

13:30   **A.** Restatement of violin theme from Section I (see Transcription 19.6): all strings in canon with all woodwinds against punctuating brass and percussion motif heard at 13:22.

14:30   **B.** Coda over repeated note in timpani. Woodwinds and horns play suggestions of lyric theme (see transcription at 5:41).

16:22   Timpani stops. Full orchestra plays chordal passage (see Transcription 19.5). Percussion punctuations lead to final g minor chord, *fff*.

expression of human states of mind and even cultural values, especially those belonging to what he called "the American spirit," according to his credo that the "creative impulse is a desire to capture and communicate feeling." The form of the work, according to Harris's own description, is sufficiently clear to allow the listener to follow the unfolding of its essential musical drama, even on first hearing. It has been, and continues to be, widely performed; Virgil Thomson called it "to this day America's most convincing product in that form."

Two Other, Contrasting American Symphonies   For further acquaintance, two other American symphonies are suggested. Here we confront a contrast between two modes of expression within the same broad tradition and in the same general period. The first is a fairly early work, the Symphony No. 2 (*Romantic*) by Howard Hanson (1896–1981). Written in 1930, it was a virtual manifesto by its composer, intended in his words to be "lyrical and romantic in temperament," as opposed to what he saw as the tendency toward "cerebral" music. The next work is another Second Symphony—that of Roger Sessions, dating from 1946. The Sessions work is dense, complex, and dissonant; it fits the classic notion of "modern music," and the adjectives called up to describe it might well have been applied more than thirty years earlier to Stravinsky's *The Rite of Spring.* It is "modern music" in the good old-fashioned scandal-creating sense—the kind that used to cause riots among audiences in the days when concertgoers were less inhibited. Yet this four-movement work has strength, expressiveness, moments of fascinating, beguiling sound, and a "difficult" kind of beauty that is more apt to make its greatest impression in retrospect—after the sounds themselves have died away. (See Additional Listening for both symphonies.)

In Conclusion

Our survey of traditionally evolving classical music existing independent of the other arts began with George Gershwin's Preludes for Piano, and has ended with the Second Symphony of Roger Sessions—a considerable journey showing the range of American music in the period 1920–70 between two extremes of technical difficulty, accessibility, and compositional Americanism. The Gershwin speaks to us with wit, in an urbane and colloquial accent; the Sessions, devoid of any conscious regionalism or nativism, brings us into the rarefied atmosphere of the avant-garde that is our next concern. Backing up somewhat in time so as to follow the developments of our experimental and innovative wing through the twentieth century, we enter the restless, challenging arena—sometimes harsh, sometimes quixotic, but nearly always stimulating—of individualism and exploration that is the subject of the next chapter.

▨ PROJECTS

1. Interview a composer in your community who has written music for a film or a ballet, concerning the problems peculiar to the medium, and the methods used to solve them.
2. Interview a concert pianist on the subject of American works in the active repertory. Prepare by becoming acquainted with at least three such works. (There are many touring artists, as well as artists-in-residence at colleges and universities. Consulting

the offerings of local concert series and contacting the artist's management well ahead of time will make this go more smoothly and be more productive.)

3. Attend a concert that includes the performance of an American symphony. Write a brief essay on any aspect or aspects of it that you wish. Your own observations and impressions are important. As supporting material, you may find it possible (if it is a local orchestra) to interview the conductor with regard to why he or she chose that particular symphony, some of the problems involved in its preparation, and the place of the American symphony (in general) in the active repertory of American symphony orchestras.

4. If there is a symphony orchestra in your community (a college or university orchestra, an amateur community orchestra, or a professional or semiprofessional orchestra), survey the entire season's programs; report on the percentage of American works included, and their type and vintage. You may want to include an interview with the orchestra's musical director on the subject of programming American music.

■ ADDITIONAL LISTENING

Samuel Barber

Excursions, Op. 20. On *Adagio for Strings, Violin Concerto, Orchestral and Chamber Works*. Angel Classics 74287.

Excursions, Op. 20. On *American Ballads*. Lara Downes, piano. Postcards 2002.

Hermit Songs, Op. 29, for voice and piano. Leontyne Price, soprano; Samuel Barber, piano. Sony 46727.

Hermit Songs, Op. 29, for voice and piano. On *Leontyne Price Sings Barber*. Leontyne Price, soprano. RCA 61983.

Knoxville: Summer of 1915, Op. 24 (rev. for voice and chamber orchestra). Eleanor Steber, soprano. Dunbarton Oaks Orchestra. Cond. William Strickland. Sony 46727.

Knoxville: Summer of 1915, Op. 24. On *Leontyne Price Sings Barber*. Leontyne Price, soprano. RCA 61983.

Summer Music, Op. 31. On *Adagio for Strings, Violin Concerto, Orchestral and Chamber Works*. Angel Classics 74287.

Leonard Bernstein

On the Waterfront, symphonic suite. On *Candide/West Side Story/On the Waterfront/Fancy Free*. New York Philharmonic. Cond. Leonard Bernstein. Sony 63085.

Paul Bowles

Blue Mountain Ballads. On *Love's Secret and Other Songs by American Composers*. Vox (Classical) 5129.

Blue Mountain Ballads. On *William Sharp, Baritone*. William Sharp, baritone; Stephen Blier, piano. New World Records 80639.

John Alden Carpenter

Skyscrapers, ballet for chorus and orchestra. London Symphony Orchestra. Cond. Kenneth Klein. Albany Troy 235.

Aaron Copland

Billy the Kid, orchestral suite from the ballet. On *Copland*. Philadelphia Orchestra. Cond. Eugene Ormandy. RCA Victor 6802.

Four Piano Blues. On *Aaron Copland: Piano Music.* Sony Classics 66345.

Four Piano Blues. On *American Ballads.* Lara Downes, piano. Postcards 2002.

Four Piano Blues. On *Copland: Works for Piano.* WER 6211.

Four Piano Blues. On *Mark Anderson Plays Copland/Gershwin.* Nimbus 5585.

Our Town, music from the film score. On *Copland Conducts Copland*. London Symphony Orchestra. Sony 42429.

Twelve Poems of Emily Dickinson, song cycle for voice and piano. Phyllis Curtin, soprano; Aaron Copland, piano. Video Arts International 1194.

John Woods Duke

"Richard Cory." On *But Yesterday Is Not Today—The American Art Song 1927–1972*. Donald Gramm, bass; Donald Hassard, piano. New World Records 80243.

George Gershwin

Lullaby for String Quartet. On *American Adagios*. Cincinnati Pops Orchestra. Cond. Erich Kunzel. Telarc 80503.

Preludes (3) for Piano. On *George Gershwin Plays George Gershwin*. Pearl 9483.

Preludes (3) for Piano. On *Sweet and Low-Down: Richard Dowling Plays George Gershwin*. Klavier 11117.

Howard Hanson

Symphony No. 2 *(Romantic)*, Op. 30. St. Louis Symphony Orchestra. Cond. Leonard Slatkin. Angel Classics 7850.

Symphony No. 2 *(Romantic)*, Op. 30. On *Music of Howard Hanson*, Vol. 1. Seattle Symphony Orchestra. Cond. Gerard Schwarz. Delos 3905.

Wallingford Riegger

Concerto for Piano and Woodwind Quartet, Op. 53. On *Music for Piano and Winds*. Bridge 9068.

William Schuman

String Quartet No. 3. On *American String Quartets 1900–1950*. Vox (Classical) 5090.

Roger Sessions

Symphony No. 2. On *Roger Sessions Symphonies Nos. 1, 2 and 3*. New York Philharmonic. Cond. Dimitri Metropoulos. CRI 573.

When Lilacs Last in the Door-yard Bloom'd, cantata for soloists, chorus, and orchestra. Boston Symphony Orchestra. Cond. Seiji Ozawa. Tanglewood Festival Chorus. Cond. Michael Steinberg. New World 80296.

William Grant Still

Songs of Separation, song cycle for voice and piano, Nos. 1–5 (complete). On *Works by William Grant Still*. New World 80399.

Randall Thompson

The Peaceable Kingdom. On *Alleluia: A Randall Thompson Tribute.* Michael O'Neal Singers. Aca Digital 20065.

Virgil Thomson

The Plow That Broke the Plains, film score and suite for orchestra. Symphony of the Air. Cond. Leopold Stokowski. Vanguard Classics 1.

The Plow That Broke the Plains, film score and suite for orchestra. On *American Ballads.* Postcards 2002.

Twentieth-Century Innovation

"To experiment and to explore has never been revolutionary for an American; he is unaffectedly at home in the unregulated and the untried" (Cowell and Cowell 3). So wrote Henry and Sidney Cowell in the first chapter of their influential book on Charles Ives. The story of the "unregulated and the untried" in twentieth-century American music is long and complex, with many aspects. We begin with two stubbornly independent New Englanders.

CHARLES IVES (1874–1954)

The Life and Career

For all of what appears to us as his modernity, and the relevance of many of his ideas today, Charles Ives inhabited a world quite different from ours. Essentially his world was, and remained for him, that of nineteenth-century America, which can be thought of as ending with World War I. (The period 1890 to 1918 has been called the Progressive Era, and Ives has been called a "progressive," in the tradition of Theodore Roosevelt, John Dewey, and others [Crunden].) His boyhood in Danbury, Connecticut, a growing manufacturing town in the southwestern corner of the state, was of exceptional significance to his work; he drew upon its impressions throughout the whole of his fairly short creative life. Pervading nearly all these impressions, according to Ives himself, was the extraordinary figure of his father. George Ives (1845–94) is somewhat sketchily known to us today, mainly through the recollections of his son Charles, but he was a well-trained musician of broad practical experience who also had an inquiring mind and the spirit of an explorer, especially in musical acoustics. He was the youngest bandmaster in the Union army during the Civil War. (For a famous and amusing anecdote concerning President Lincoln, General Grant, and George Ives's Brigade Band of the First Connecticut Heavy Artillery, see Cowell and Cowell 15.) George returned to Danbury to become the versatile town musician. Yet Danbury, a microcosm of growing industrial America, held these musical activities in low esteem. Music, except for the most popular, earthy variety (such as country fiddling), was an effeminate pursuit and no fit profession for a man—that was the prevailing attitude in nineteenth-century middle-class America. Charles dealt with the burden of that attitude all his life.

We have Charles's word for many experiments in musical sound made by his father, and for many musical experiences, planned or unplanned, that made a lasting impression on him. There were two complementary sides to Charles Ives's early musical background. On one hand there was the curiosity, the open-mindedness toward tinkering and experimentation. On the other hand there was the solid grounding in musical rudiments that the boy received from his father and from others. Ives, in common with many other New England composers, was a church organist. He got his first permanent job at 14, and worked steadily at it for the next fourteen years in Danbury, New Haven, and New York City. Ives, then, was no musical amateur, no dilettante, in no sense any sort of "primitive." His innovative and experimental tendencies showed up early (as in his *Variations on "America,"* for organ, which he wrote in 1891), but his father insisted that this sort of thing be supported by an underpinning of solid knowledge and technique.

At 20, Ives entered Yale. He studied with the renowned composer Horatio Parker, a strict taskmaster and academician. Though Ives said that he soon gave up showing Parker his more adventurous essays, it is now clear that Parker's teaching was essential to his growth as a composer.

It is unlikely that Ives ever considered becoming a professional musician. As a product of the Yale of his time, he went into business when he graduated in 1898. For the next twenty years he was to pursue under full steam two careers at once: that of life insurance executive and that of composer. His creative and humane approach to the former (he pioneered in the field of estate planning and the training of insurance agents) made him and his partnership (Ives and Myrick) enormously successful.

The entry of the United States into the First World War in 1917 was a severe blow to Ives. (As an aside, it must be noted that Ives was unreservedly opposed to war, but once his country was in, he worked in practical ways for the war effort—selling bonds [he advocated a new small-denomination bond of fifty dollars so that more people could participate, in accord with his philosophy of involving the masses of common people, whether in art, politics, or business] and making a gift to the government of two completely equipped ambulances.) At that time his health broke severely. As early as 1919, sensing and accepting the change in his life, Ives began to make plans for the future of some of his most cherished compositions. He finished the important *Concord Sonata* and had it published at his own expense. To accompany the sonata he wrote a prologue, four essays (on Emerson, Hawthorne, the Alcotts, Thoreau), and a lengthy epilogue. Called *Essays Before a Sonata,* they constitute an artistic and philosophical manifesto, and the most valuable documentation of Ives's thought. Shortly afterward, he prepared an edition of *114 Songs,* again published at his own expense and distributed free of charge.

Ives was far from idle in his long retirement. He supported attempts to get his work, and that of other composers of new music, before the public. He supervised the editing of his own music by other devoted musicians, and it is thanks to their intensive and exhausting labors that much of Ives's music has reached the public. He disdained the copyrighting of his music, and exclaimed, in connection with the publication of part of his Fourth Symphony, "If anyone wants to copy or reprint these pieces, that's FINE! This music is not to make money but to be known and heard" (Cowell and Cowell 121). In later years, he returned royalty checks or gave them away. It is said that when he received the Pulitzer Prize for his Third Symphony (written mostly in 1904; first performed in 1947), he told the committee, "Prizes are for boys. I'm grown up," and gave the money away.

The precise chronology of Ives's creative life, including the dating of many of his most important compositions, is clouded with a degree of uncertainty that may never be dispelled. In the 1920s, when he was "discovered" and his works began to be performed, did he then add more of the dissonances and complexities for which they, and he, became famous? Did he "adjust" the chronology of some of his more adventurous works, assigning them earlier dates so as to validate the role of innovator that his younger contemporaries, especially Henry Cowell, were eager to bestow on him? When his health was still good, did he actually avoid going to concerts, or was he a more normal participant in the musical life of his time? Was he so completely uninfluenced by the then "modernists" such as Wagner, Debussy, Mahler, and Stravinsky, of whom he was so contemptuously dismissive in his writings?

These questions only serve to caution us against a naive acceptance at face value of *all* aspects of the considerable Ives *lore*—a lore to which Ives himself was evidently willing to contribute. The questions are simply evidence of an understandable desire to know more about the complex and enigmatic man who left such a prodigious legacy of important works. The indisputable *reality* of Ives for us must be in the works themselves, and it is to these that we now turn.

The Music

Ives's Range as Revealed in the Songs

Ives wrote nearly 150 songs, his output spanning his entire creative career. The songs are an excellent introduction to his music. Their range is large musically—from the simple to the complex and dissonant—and textually—covering nearly every aspect of human experience. We start with six songs arranged in approximate order of difficulty and dimension. (See Additional Listening.)

"At the River" (1916), one of four songs based on hymn-tune themes published in the *114* collection, shows Ives reworking some of the musical material he liked best. The hymn by Robert Lowry is seen as it passes through the prism of Ives's unique musical imagination; it emerges fractured and colored with unusual harmonies.

"Tom Sails Away" (1917), with a text by Ives himself, is set in Ives's more expansive and dissonant "prose" style. One of three war songs in the *114* collection, it includes a quote from George M. Cohan's "Over There" in the vocal line, while the piano quotes a tune apparently always in the back of Ives's mind when it turned (as it so often did) to thoughts of his country—David Shaw's "The Red White and Blue" ("O Columbia, the Gem of the Ocean").

Some of the songs make a more philosophical comment on the human condition. In "The Cage" (1906) the voice intones Ives's short prose text, using mostly the noncommittal whole-tone scale, while the piano, in a rhythmically independent part, uses severe sonorities based on the interval of the perfect fourth to depict the restless pacing of the leopard in the cage. (See CD 5/5.)

CD 5/5 (1:00)
"The Cage," by Charles Ives. 1906.

Text, "The Cage"

A leopard went around his cage from one side to the other side; he stopped only when the keeper came around with meat. A boy who had been there three hours began to wonder, "Is life anything like that?"

Several songs reflect Ives's social idealism. The song Ives placed first in the *114* is a startling work, big in conception, which he titled "Majority" or "The Masses" (1914). The text, by Ives, expresses one aspect of his complex and sometimes contradictory idealism—a deep faith in democracy. "Majority" is a

Transcription 20.1
Ives, "The Cage,"
opening measures

A leop-ard went a-round his cage

thesaurus of Ives's harmonic vocabulary; in addition to a few plain triads, it uses extended chords built in thirds, fourths, and fifths, and also—possibly with programmatic connotations—appropriately massive, all-embracing tone "clusters" (chords built in seconds), two octaves in extent, combinations that strike not only the ear but the eye as well.

Transcription 20.2
Ives, "Majority,"excerpt
(Merton Music, Inc.
1935. Used by
permission.)

Many of the recipients of the *114 Songs* were put off, or puzzled, by this opening song, with its strident dissonances. (The album was the butt of many contemporary jokes.) The fact is that Ives felt very strongly about the use of dissonance. It was, in a way, an indication for him of *manliness* in music. He complained vociferously about the "sissies, that couldn't stand up and take the full force of dissonance like a man." Recalling his boyhood, and the traumatic conflict between his natural bent for music (a form of activity dominated by "nice ladies") and his love of sports and natural honest regard for his peers (among whom music was a "sissy" thing to be spending one's time on), we can begin to understand at least one of the possible sources of Ives's whole set of attitudes on the emasculation of art.

There was also a sense for Ives in which dissonance, if used in the service of an art that emphasizes "substance" rather than "manner" (a favorite Ivesian polarity), can be virtuous. In his *Essays Before a Sonata* he wrote, "Beauty in music is too often confused with something that lets the ears lie back in an easy chair." Ives was always contemptuous of any "easy way" (97).

Finally, there are the longer narrative songs, which have their roots in the vernacular. *Charlie Rutlage* (1920 or 1921) is a cowboy ballad. The poem, attributed to D. J. "Kid" O'Malley, appeared in John Lomax's *Cowboy Songs*. In the middle three stanzas, the narrative itself, Ives reverts to melodrama; behind the recitation of the singer, the piano works up bits and pieces of "Whoopie Ti Yi Yo, Git Along Little Dogies" (with the words in the score) to a frenzied climax on the words "fell with him." (Compare with Copland's tipsy version of the same cowboy tune in the street scene of *Billy the Kid*, CD 5/1 p. 363; and unnumbered transcription "Git Along Little Dogies" in Listening Guide, p. 364.)

General William Booth Enters into Heaven (1914) is Ives's best-known song. General William Booth (1829–1912) was the founder, in England in 1878, of the Salvation Army, a religious philanthropic organization that officially began operations in the United States in 1880. As a means of reaching and helping the poor and downtrodden, the Salvation Army made considerable use of its

CD 5/6 (6:00)
*General William Booth
Enters into Heaven.*
1914. Music by Charles
Ives. Text adapted from
Vachel Lindsay.

uniformed street bands, which became a familiar sight and sound in American cities. The text is a portion of Vachel Lindsay's poem (minus six lines), which Ives read in a review. The drama and imagery of the imaginary scene put into play all of Ives's powers of musical characterization. The opening alliteration, "Booth led boldly with his big bass drum," furnished Ives with a motive that begins the piece and also frames it; the ending is a faint dying away of the drumbeats in the distance. (One cannot help remembering here that Ives as a boy had played the drum parts on the piano for his father's band during their practices.)

Vachel Lindsay had noted that his poem was "to be sung to the tune of 'The Blood of the Lamb,'" but Ives chose instead a tune called "Fountain" ("There is a fountain filled with blood"), by Lowell Mason, whose hymn tunes he recalled frequently in his music.

The tune is overtly present only at the very end of Ives's song; before that, it is a kind of shadowy presence — Ives's settings of "Are you washed in the blood of the Lamb?" are based on a derivative of the tune, which is also present, unobtrusively, in the piano left hand under the words "Jesus came from the court house door." Other touches of text-painting are evident: the "banging banjo" tune, the trumpets, the memorable treatment of "round and round and round and round." *General William Booth* is a vivid musical drama in miniature on the theme of salvation.

Transcription 20.3
Ives, *General William Booth Enters into Heaven*, opening measures

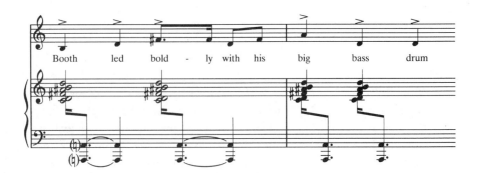

Bettmann/CORBIS

Charles Ives

Booth led boldly with his big bass drum
        (Are you washed in the blood of the Lamb?
        Are you washed in the blood of the Lamb, of the Lamb?)
        Hallelujah
Saints smiled gravely, and they said: "He's come"
        (Are you washed in the blood of the Lamb? The blood of the Lamb?)
Walking lepers followed, rank on rank,
Lurching bravoes from the ditches dank
Drabs from the alleyways and drug fiends pale
Minds still passion-ridden, soul-powers frail:
Vermin-eaten saints with mouldy breath,
Unwashed legions with the ways of Death
        (Are you washed in the blood of the Lamb?
        Are you washed in the blood of the Lamb?)

Text, *General William Booth Enters into Heaven*, adapted from poem by Vachel Lindsay (Merton Music, Inc., 1935. Used by permission.)

Ev'ry slum had sent its half-a-score
The round world over. (Booth had groaned for more.)
Ev'ry banner that the wide world flies,
Bloomed with glory and transcendent dyes.
Big-voiced lassies made their banjos bang, bang, bang, made their banjos,—
Tranced, fanatical they shrieked and sang:
> 'Are you? Are you washed in the blood? In the blood of the Lamb—
>   of the Lamb?
>
> Hallelujah! Hallelujah Hallelujah, Lord, Hallelujah, Lord, Hallelujah!

It was queer to see
Bull-necked convicts, Bull-necked convicts with that land make free.
Loons with trumpets blowed a blare,
On, on, upward thro' the golden air!
> (Are you washed in the blood in the blood of the Lamb,
>   in the blood of the Lamb, the Lamb of the Lamb, the Lamb?)

Jesus came from the court house door,
Stretched his hands above the passing poor.
Booth saw not, but led his queer ones,
Round and round—round and round and round and round and round
    and round and round and round, the mighty court-house square,
Yet! in an instant all that blear review
Marched on, marched on marched on march on marched on marched on
    marched on spotless, clad in raiment new.
The lame were straightened, withered limbs uncurled
And blind eyes opened on a new sweet world—
> Are you washed in the blood of the Lamb?
> Are you washed in the blood of the lamb?

Ives and Programmaticism   Ives was fundamentally a composer of program music. Much of his music is "about" something, often with its roots in a vivid impression of a scene. Two sets of orchestral compositions illustrate this particularly well: *Three Places in New England* and *Four New England Holidays*. In the latter, each of the holidays is associated with one of the seasons. For *The Fourth of July* (summer), we have Ives's own description:

It's a boy's '4th. . . . His festivities start in the quiet of midnight before, and grow raucous with the sun. Everybody knows what it's like—if everybody doesn't—Cannon on the Green, Village Band on Main Street, fire crackers, shanks mixed on cornets, strings around big toes, torpedoes, Church bells, lost finger, fifes, clam-chowder, a prize-fight, drum-corps, burnt shins, parades (in and out of step), saloons all closed (more drunks than usual), baseball game (Danbury All-Stars vs Beaver

Brook Boys), pistols, mobbed umpire, Red, White and Blue, runaway horse—and the day ends with the sky-rocket over the Church-steeple, just after the annual explosion sets the Town-Hall on fire. All this is not in the music—not now. (*Memos* 104 n)

The multitude of impressions, seemingly random, crowding one another, superimposing themselves—all this is startlingly parallel to Ives's musical composition. Everywhere he looks, there is something to record; he cannot get it all down. There is a quiet opening in which the violins and the string basses begin "Columbia, the Gem of the Ocean," the tune that is to be the mainstay of the movement. There is a gradual gain of momentum, as bits and pieces of a dozen other tunes are heard; there is an explosion of fireworks; the band finally comes on with a great tumultuous rendition of the main theme, wrong notes, missed beats, and all; there is a final explosion—and again quietness. The sound of the band in full swing in this movement is one of the most vividly realized moments in all of Ives's music: the tunes ("Columbia, the Gem of the Ocean," "The Battle Hymn of the Republic," and "Yankee Doodle" all at once), recklessly off-key, are heard through the buzz and roar of the crowd noises. Originally thought unplayable, even by Ives himself, these are some of his grandest and most successful pages. (See Additional Listening.)

Simultaneity and Perspective   There are many manifestations of simultaneity in Ives's music. His impressionistic bent—his fidelity to his model, which was life itself as experienced—led him to try to render the sense of two or more things going on at the same time. In *Putnam's Camp* (the second of *Three Places in New England*), we hear one march beat established, and presently another—in a different tempo, marked "as a distant drum beat"—is heard superimposed. There are many examples of even more complex simultaneous meters in Ives's music, but this one is particularly clear and has a direct relationship to his boyhood experience of hearing two bands marching in opposite directions around the park in Danbury, each playing a different tune, in a different key, and at a different tempo. (See Additional Listening.)

The concept of *perspective* finds its way into Ives's work as well—a sense of relative nearness and distance. Ives himself wrote, "As the distant hills, in a landscape, row upon row, grow gradually into the horizon, so there may be something corresponding to this in the presentation of music." This spatial sense can be heard in *The Unanswered Question, A Cosmic Landscape*, a work that has philosophical connotations. As Henry Cowell describes it:

The orchestra is divided, the strings playing very softly throughout off-stage, representing the silence of the seers who, even if they have an answer, cannot reply; the wind group, on stage, is dominated by the trumpet, which asks the Perennial Question of Existence over and over in the same way, while "the Fighting Answerers (flutes and other people)" run about trying in vain to discover the invisible, unattainable reply to the trumpet. When they finally surrender the search they mock the trumpet's reiteration and depart. The Question is then asked again, for the last time, and the "silence" sounds from a distance undisturbed. (176–77)

Ives's Attitude Toward the Performance of His Music   Charles Ives had as a young man the normal composer's desire to hear his works realized in performance. He occasionally hired individual performers to play with him, and groups of musicians from theater orchestras. But after some bitter and humiliating experiences with performances and readings, his attitude toward performance seemed gradually to change. His music itself became less and less geared to actual realization in sound—less in touch with practical problems. Concerning the music's difficulties and enormous complexities, Ives manifested a curiously dualistic attitude. On one hand, he sometimes freely castigated the laziness, indifference, and lack of ability of performers who would not come to grips with the difficulties of new or hard music. On the other hand, at times he seemed quite ready to acknowledge that some of his music was possibly unplayable. In the postface to the *114 Songs* he wrote, "Some of the songs in this book, particularly among the later ones, cannot be sung, and if they could, might perhaps prefer, if they had a say, to remain as they are; that is, 'in the leaf'—and that they will remain in this peaceful state is more than presumable."

His detachment sometimes dealt with a reality of music that transcended any actual realization in sound, a realization that he seemed actually to disdain at times. His famous "My God! What has sound got to do with music!" is his most succinct and often-quoted statement of this attitude. He continues cogently:

> The waiter brings the only fresh egg he has, but the man at breakfast sends it back because it doesn't fit his egg cup. Why can't music go out in the same way it comes in to a man, without having to crawl over a fence of sounds, thoraxes, catguts, wire, wood, and brass? (*Essays* 84)

Idealism versus Professionalism in Music   One aspect of Ives's idealism regarding art is his attitude toward professionalism and what it does to an artist's independence and self-reliance. He wrote:

> It may be possible that a day in a "Kansas wheat field" will do more for [the American composer]than three years in Rome. . . . If for every

thousand-dollar prize a potato field be substituted, so that these candi-
dates of Clio can dig a little in real life, perhaps dig up a natural inspiration, art's air might be a little clearer. (*Essays* 93)

And again, in a strong statement that summarizes his attitude:

Perhaps the birth of art will take place at the moment in which the last
man who is willing to make a living out of art is gone and gone forever.
(*Essays* 88)

Ives apparently never regretted his decision to go into business rather than
become a professional musician, but he saw a relationship between his daily
work in the world and his art that tended to develop a "spiritual sturdiness"
that showed itself in "a close union between spiritual life and the ordinary business of life." Emerson said: "There is virtue yet in the hoe and the spade, for
learned as well as for unlearned hands." Ives said:

I have experienced a great fulness of life in business. The fabric of existence weaves itself whole. You cannot set an art off in the corner and
hope for it to have vitality, reality and substance. There can be nothing
exclusive about a substantial art. It comes directly out of the heart of
experience of life and thinking about life and living life. My work in
music helped my business and work in business helped my music.
(Cowell 97)

Ives's Music and the World

The music of Charles Ives was not suddenly discovered after his death; the
process of bringing it before the public was a protracted one, and the list of
hardworking and courageous protagonists in "the Ives case" is long and distinguished. Some recognition came as early as the 1920s. Mostly composers, and
a few critics, championed Ives's music in the 1930s, and then in the 1940s
important performers followed. A landmark event, touching off much of the
success of the 1940s, was the first complete public performance of the *Concord
Sonata*, in 1939 by John Kirkpatrick. This performance marked the beginning
of widespread favorable critical acclaim of Ives's music; Lawrence Gilman
called the *Concord Sonata* "the greatest music composed by an American." In
1946 Lou Harrison premiered the Third Symphony; the next year it was
awarded the Pulitzer Prize. By that time Ives's music was well on its way, and
the 1950s saw its acceptance and acclaim by a far greater segment of the general musical public, who now had a chance to hear a fair amount of it.

For Ives the man there is no lack of admiration; his idealism, his grit, his humor, and his generosity have fired the imagination of succeeding generations. For the music there is admiration and love—tempered, for many who know it well, with certain reservations. Copland pointed out the deleterious effect on Ives's music of his having worked in virtual isolation—"cut off from the vitalizing contact of an audience." Elliott Carter points to the "large amounts of indifferentiated confusion" and is forced, reluctantly, to the conclusion that Ives's work often "falls short of his intentions." Virgil Thomson pointed out the need to distinguish purely musical quality from the wealth of not-strictly-musical associations that have grown up around Ives's work: "When time shall have dissolved away his nostalgias and ethical aspirations, as they have largely done for Beethoven and for Bach and even for the descriptive leitmotifs of Wagner, what sheer musical reality will remain in Ives's larger works?" (27).

A good deal, one suspects. Ives's most cogent, most nearly perfect realizations—many of the songs, *The Unanswered Question*, *The Housatonic at Stockbridge*, practically all the *Holidays*—have been indispensable to our music. Virgil Thomson, speaking for all subsequent composers, hailed Charles Ives as "whether we knew it or not, the father of us all" (photo caption).

CARL RUGGLES (1876–1971)

Carl Ruggles is often mentioned with Ives. Indeed, they had much in common; they were nearly exact contemporaries, and both were New Englanders of a highly independent spirit and temperament. Although they did not meet until 1930, when both were over 50 (Ruggles was involved at the time with a particular New York wing of the avant-garde that held a disparaging view of Ives), they immediately became fast friends and great admirers of each other's music. Both were uncompromising idealists in music and indifferent to popularity, and when each struck out to find new paths, those paths (though quite different) led into the domain of dissonant and "difficult" musical utterance.

The picture most us have of Carl Ruggles is that of a craggy New Englander working in a remodeled schoolhouse in Vermont, known for his voluble, opinionated talk laced with salty profanity. (He was descended from a seafaring family on Cape Cod.) He had an extremely small output; the complete works (those he allowed to survive) could be performed in a single program of less than two hours. There is no nostalgic or impressionistic display of Americana; in fact, Ruggles's music has no discernible relationship to American popular music, and very little to any other music. Ruggles was a most meticulous craftsman, and he was not in a hurry. With the support of a patron and in good health, he was able to work in his Vermont studio, dividing his time between painting (his abstract canvases have been exhibited in several museums), composing (he often covered the walls like a mural with his music, written with different colored crayons on huge staff paper, so that he could see an entire section at once), and entertaining a vast range of friends.

Ruggles's music never overtly reflects outward scenes—any more than do his abstract paintings. His melodies are often long, sweeping lines, gathering in intensity and covering a great range. He is usually very careful not to repeat a note too soon (a tendency that is part of the basic dogma of serialism; see p. 411). The opening melody of *Portals* shows these features (Transcription 20.4).

Transcription 20.4
Ruggles, *Portals*, opening melody

When Ruggles pauses on a chord, it is often complex. Of the two sonorities in *Portals* shown in Transcription 20.5, the first involves seven "pitch classes" (pitches without reference to the octave or register in which they occur) with only one doubling, and the second eleven, with only two doublings.

Transcription 20.5
Two chords from *Portals*

Ruggles's music, in both its sound and its *gesture*, leaves an unmistakable impression. It is dissonant and often dense, but it sings in a way much dissonant music does not, and it never seems to falter or lose its way. Charles Seeger referred to Ruggles's work as a "distinct type of artistic effort—the attempt to convey the most approved ideal by the least approved means" (18).

NEW YORK AND EUROPE-RELATED "FUTURISM" AND "MODERNISM"

Much of the excitement and activity connected with innovation in America between the two World Wars was to be found in and around New York City — always more closely in touch with Europe than any other part of the country. New York, long established as a trend-setting capital, attracted composers and other artists from all parts of the United States, and eventually from Europe itself as well. *Modernism* became in the twentieth century an imprecise term much used and abused by many. It is with us still, in the even less precise term *postmodernism*. It first came into very broad use in the 1920s, fed by the Dada and "futurism" of the Europe of the 1910s. (Dadaism was a nihilist artistic movement, characterized by the rejection of existing artistic standards and the cultivation of the deliberately outrageous.) As Carol Oja has written, "Ellis Island became one of the passageways through which early modernism entered America" (12). Three immigrant composers played significant parts in the propagation of modernism here. The name of Leo Ornstein (1892–2002) is not especially well known in American music, though more attention has been paid to him recently. He arrived in the United States in 1907, established himself as a piano virtuoso and as a composer of "futurist" music that included the "clusters" found in the music of both Ives and Henry Cowell (see Transcriptions 20.2 and 20.6), and then virtually dropped out of sight in the early 1920s. Carlos Salzedo (1885–1961), harpist and composer, arrived in 1909 and became immediately involved in the activities of the modernists. With Edgard Varèse, who arrived in 1915, Salzedo founded the International Composers Guild in 1921. The more traditional Ernest Bloch (1880–1959) arrived in 1916.

EDGARD VARÈSE (1883–1965)

Edgard Varèse quickly became one of the most influential of the modernist immigrants. Though he had already begun to establish his career in Europe, he started it afresh when he arrived in the United States at the age of 32. But though he is almost universally considered an American composer, he always perceived himself as European, and was so perceived in his time by others as well (Oja 27). This is but another potent reminder of the close ties of New York to Europe, and especially to France in the period between the wars—a fact noted in the previous chapter (pp. 357–58).

At that time, technology, and especially machines themselves, were a preoccupation with artists, including composers. The "Machine Age" manifested itself in many ways, not least in the use of "noise" in music, which meant the enlargement of and new emphasis on the percussion section in ensembles, and the introduction of noisemakers such as typewriters, electric bells, sirens, anvils, and propellers. Varèse's *Hyperprism*, first performed in 1923, is an early example of Machine Age music. There are ten wind instruments (a flute, a piccolo, a clarinet, three horns, two trumpets, and two trombones), with a large percussion section consisting of three drums, a tambourine, a pair of crash cymbals, two suspended cymbals, a tamtam (a large unpitched gong), a triangle, an anvil, a slapstick, two Chinese blocks, a big and small rattle, sleigh bells, a siren, and a "lion roar" (a cord attached to the membrane of a large drum, which when grasped between pieces of leather and pulled produces an unforgettable imitation of the real thing).

CD 5/7 (4:10)
Hyperprism, by
Edgard Varèse.
1922–23. Columbia
Symphony Orchestra,
Robert Craft, conductor.

Varèse himself described some of his conceptions of music. He strongly advocated composers' making use of the latest scientific developments.

> . . . If you are curious to know what . . . a machine could do that the orchestra with its man-powered instruments cannot do, I shall try briefly to tell you: whatever I write, whatever my message, it will reach the listener unadulterated by "interpretation" . . . after a composer has set down his score on paper by means of a new graphic, similar in principle to a seismographic or oscillographic notation, he will then, with the collaboration of a sound engineer, transfer the score directly to this electric machine. After that anyone will be able to press a button to release the music exactly as the composer wrote it—exactly like opening a book. (Varèse 190–91)

This remarkable forecast of electronic-tape music was written in 1939. (Twenty years later, Varèse qualified somewhat his apparent rejection of the performer.)

Varèse conceived of music as spatial, and of musical sounds as analogous to masses in space, with quasi-geometrical characteristics. In a lecture given in 1936 he described his projected "corporealization" of music in a startlingly illustrative paragraph.

> When new instruments will allow me to write music as I conceive it, the movement of sound-masses, of shifting planes, will be clearly perceived in my work, taking the place of linear counterpoint. When these sound-masses collide, the phenomena of penetration or repulsion will seem to occur. Certain transmutations taking place on certain planes will seem to be projected onto other planes, moving at different speeds and at different angles. There will no longer be the old conception of melody or interplay of melodies. The entire work will be a melodic totality. The entire work will flow as a river flows. (197)

In 1928 Varèse went to France for five years, during which time he completed only one work, the famous *Ionisation* (1930–31; see Additional Listening). For this five-minute work he used nothing but percussion—an orchestra of thirteen percussionists playing thirty-seven instruments (though not all at once). There followed a hiatus in his composing. He lived in the West for a while, returned to New York for the war years, and did do some work on a vast project called *Espace* ("Space"). In theme it was the counterpart of Beethoven's Ninth Symphony, or Ives's "Majority" ("Theme: TODAY, the world awake! Humanity on the march. . . . Millions of feet endlessly tramping, treading, pounding, striding, leaping."). Varèse at one time imagined a performance of it broadcast simultaneously from all the capitals of the world, with a choir in each singing in its own language!

Varèse's eagerly awaited liberation, which he had long asked of science, from the limitations of the human performer and traditional acoustical instruments came in 1958. He was given the opportunity to create eight minutes of sound to be projected literally *in space* through the medium of 425 loudspeakers in the Philips Pavilion designed by Le Corbusier for the Brussels International Exposition in 1958. (*La Poème électronique* was actually the title of the entire concept, which included visual projects designed by Le Corbusier; the pavilion was simply the "vessel" to contain both.) Here the sound masses (a montage made up of a combination of manipulated "real" and synthesized sound carefully assembled by Varèse, who worked for eight months in the Philips laboratory in Eindhoven, Holland) could literally move in space, thanks to a three-track tape and an elaborate "routing" of the sound channels through the maze of speakers installed in the roof of the pavilion. (See Additional Listening.)

The technology that finally made *La Poème électronique* possible added a lively new electronic wing to the edifice of music in the post–World War II years. These developments will be considered in due course.

Ballet Mécanique   We return briefly to the Machine Age of the 1920s, to take note of a "happening" in Carnegie Hall in April 1927. George Antheil (1900–59), a composer who was born in Trenton, New Jersey, "across the street from a very noisy machine shop" (Oja 73), had written his first modernist piece in 1921, *Second Sonata: "The Airplane."* In 1923 he began his *Ballet Mécanique* in Europe. (Modernism in the 1920s was a very transatlantic phenomenon.) He envisioned its production, after much extravagant and boastful promotion, as a triumph after which, in his words, the "rest of my career will take care of itself." Though the actual event was a fiasco instead (see Oja 71), it has a secure reputation as a landmark circuslike piece typifying Machine Age music. Its full title was *Ballet pour Instruments Mécaniques et Percussion,* and the score originally called for three xylophones, three propellers, a tamtam, four bass drums, a siren, two pianos, and a pianola (player piano). But for the Carnegie Hall performance "he expanded the scoring to six xylophones and ten pianos . . . reportedly also adding whistles, rattles, sewing machine motors, and two large pieces of tin"(Oja 90). In a manifesto "My Ballet Mécanique: What It Means," he began by stating: "My *Ballet Mécanique* is the new FOURTH DIMENSION of music" (qtd. in Oja 83). Fernand Léger, the Dada artist, directed a film entitled *Ballet Mécanique* that was to accompany the music, but they were not performed together until 1935, with a version of the music for pianola. The film, with its rapidly changing collage effects, is still in existence.

After the dismal failure of *Ballet Mécanique,* which followed its extravagant publicity campaign (one thinks of P. T. Barnum), Antheil virtually dropped out of sight, and the music he wrote subsequently was in a much more conservative vein. (The author remembers seeing him take a modest bow in the audience in Pasadena, California, in the late 1940s, after the performance of one of his works.)

RUTH CRAWFORD (SEEGER) (1901–53)

The modernism of the 1920s and 1930s had many aspects, some of which present seeming incongruities. The "fourth dimension" touted by Antheil in connection with his *Ballet Mécanique* was an aspect of the *hyperspace theory,* which attracted intellectual attention in the first two decades of the twentieth century. Some held it as applying to time, and others to space itself—indeed, the combination *time-space* was a concept alluded to by avant-garde composers in their rationalizations well into midcentury, as we shall see. (It is not impossible that the title of Varèse's *Hyperprism,* like many other of his titles—*Ionisation,* for example—is related to the general preoccupation among the modernists with the expanding concepts of the science of that time.) But another aspect of modernism was, as Oja puts it, the "association of dissonance with spirituality" (97). Both Ives and Ruggles had expressed this; Ives coupled it with manliness, and Ruggles with his pursuit of the sublime. But it was the French American composer and philosopher Dane Rudhyar (1895–1985) who was its quiet but insistent spokesman and who, incidentally, was one of the earliest to turn the attention of American musicians to the music and philosophy of Asia. He referred to much of the modernist music of his day as *metaphysically aimless.* Ives and Ruggles would have agreed. But it was a young woman composer from the Midwest who was most strongly influenced by Rudhyar's views and by the spiritual ingredient in music.

Ruth Crawford was a gifted composer whose breadth of interests and abilities resulted in her leaving, at her early death, a fairly small but important body of original compositions. She came to New York in 1929, and soon became a part of the modernist musical scene there, in association with Henry Cowell (who befriended and aided her, as he did so many), Carl Ruggles, and Edgard Varèse. Her early String Quartet (1931), a work lasting barely ten minutes, is prophetic of later developments. In sheer sound and texture, the most remarkable is the slow third section. Melody in the usual sense does not exist; our attention is held by what has replaced it: surging dynamic accents, and harmonies, mostly dissonant, that are constantly shifting in register and color. It would not sound out of place had it been composed fifty years later. (See Additional Listening; highly recommended.)

Ruth Crawford's work in advanced idioms of the time is also well represented by her remarkable *Three Songs* (1930–33) to poems of Carl Sandburg. Crawford became a close friend of Sandburg's (initially through teaching piano to his daughters), and Sandburg's involvement with American folk music probably contributed to making this another of Crawford's avid interests. She made many transcriptions and arrangements of folk songs, including some for children. One of Crawford's teachers was Charles Seeger (1886–1979), whose perceptive mind and broad range of interests made him one of the most articulate and influential teachers, writers, and musicologists of this century in America. Ruth Crawford became Seeger's second wife, and their shared interest in folk music has been carried on by her stepson Pete, and by her own children Mike and Peggy. (See CD 2/13.)

THE WEST: COWELL, HARRISON, CAGE, AND PARTCH

Henry Cowell (1897–1965)

Henry Cowell came into the world gifted with the kind of observant, eagerly absorbing mentality that was able to reap the full benefit of growing up in the richly polyglot atmosphere of the San Francisco Bay area just after the turn of the century—the same milieu that a generation earlier had nurtured Jack London and Gertrude Stein. Unencumbered by even modest means, and free of any predetermined set of cultural values, Cowell was free to accept his musical stimulus where he found it—in Irish folk tunes (from his family), Gregorian chant (from a neighbor), Oriental music, and rural American hymnody (from early sojourns in Kansas and Oklahoma). In San Francisco, young Cowell heard Chinese opera more frequently than Italian. When he got hold of a battered old upright piano, he soon found he had an instrument that would open up new possibilities, and he began experimenting. In 1912, at the age of 15, he played in public in San Francisco a piece called *The Tides of Manaunaun;* it was a prelude to an opera he was writing based on Irish mythology. Manaunaun was the maker of great tides that swept through the universe; to convey the sense of this vast motion, Cowell, interestingly enough, hit upon the same device that Ives, on the other side of the continent and at about the same time, was using to convey the sense of the masses in Majority—huge groups of tones sounded together that could be played only with the entire forearm. (See Transcription 20.6.) These became known as tone clusters. Cowell used them in many of his piano works—became notorious for them, in fact—but nowhere more effectively than in this very early piece. (See Additional Listening.)

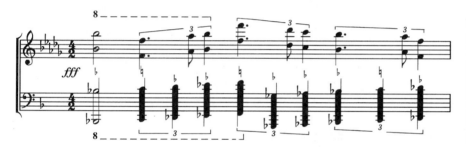

Transcription 20.6
Cowell, *The Tides of Manaunaun*, opening

(Copyright © 1922 (renewed) by Associated Music Publishers, Inc. (BMI). International Copyright Secured. All Rights Reserved. Reprinted by permission.)

By the time he was 20, Cowell had composed 199 pieces, including an opera and a symphony. Convinced of the value of some systematic study, he found an ideal person to supervise it in Charles Seeger, then teaching at the University of California. Cowell's formal education had ended with the third grade, but he was a voracious learner: at the age of 20 he was seeing Seeger for lessons in music every morning in Berkeley, studying English with Samuel Seward every afternoon at Stanford, working at night as a janitor—and writing a book! Cowell went east to New York for further study and began appearing in concerts playing his own works on the piano. Between 1923 and 1933 he made five important tours of Europe (including a trip in 1928 to the Soviet Union, which he was the first American composer to visit).

There are many sides to Cowell's work. There is Henry Cowell the teacher—one of our best, and an important influence on such composers as Lou Harrison, John Cage, and other free spirits of the musical "left wing."

There is Henry Cowell the tireless worker for new music, and new ideas in music. In 1927 he founded the important periodical *New Music Quarterly,* which published a great many new scores (though not a note of his own). It was through this that he met Charles Ives, becoming his first important discoverer, his lifelong promoter, with his wife Sidney Cowell his first biographer, and after Ives's death his musical executor.

There is Henry Cowell the imaginative theorist and inventor. The book he had virtually finished when he was 22 (not published until eleven years later, in 1930) was a slim but important volume called *New Musical Resources*.

There is Henry Cowell the student of a worldwide range of musical cultures. In 1931–32 he studied comparative musicology in Berlin with Professor Eric Moritz von Hornbostel. Oriental music he had already heard a great deal of in his youth. His works subsequently bore witness to the detailed study of musical cultures as widely separated as those of Japan, Persia, and Iceland.

And finally there is, as our major concern, Henry Cowell the prolific composer. We left him as the 15-year-old composer of a remarkable piano piece. His subsequent output was as varied as the interests of the man himself. The experimental works—those that place him in this chapter as one of our innovators—were for the most part early works. Of these, the short works for piano are the most accessible and open up the most interesting possibilities.

CD 5/8 (2:33)
The Banshee, by Henry Cowell. 1925. Henry Cowell, piano.

About 1923 Cowell began to produce works calling for the performer to play directly on the strings of the piano. In *Aeolian Harp* (1923, named after a small "harp" whose silk strings are played upon by the wind), the performer silently depresses the keys of the successive chords, releasing their dampers; the strings are then swept with the other hand, in the manner of the autoharp. They are also plucked. (See Additional Listening.) In *The Banshee* (1925; see Figure 20.2) the dampers are all released, and the performer, standing in the crook of the piano, plays directly upon the strings—at times sweeping across them in various ways, at times sweeping lengthwise on one or more strings, at times plucking them.

The changes that occurred in the twentieth century in the way music is written down make a fascinating study in itself. Standard musical notation had evolved gradually in Europe since the Middle Ages to accommodate music of a far less complex and freewheeling nature. This led composers of new music in some cases to try to adapt standard notation to new demands, and in other cases, as we shall see, to abandon it entirely. (For an example of the abandonment of standard notation in favor of graph notation, see Figure 20.1, p. 413.) Cowell's notation of *The Banshee* represents an intermediate step. The piece as conceived is obviously more suited to improvisation than to being played from notation, and his use of standard notation (one suspects just for the purposes of copyright and publication) is highly ambiguous, even when accompanied by a full page (not shown) of explanation of the alphabetical symbols. In fact, if one tries to follow the notation, one finds it bears very little resemblance to the way Cowell himself performed it for the recording. The improvisatory nature of the piece makes it probable that no two performances would be alike.

Still other possibilities in the use of the piano were explored by Cowell in a piece called *Sinister Resonance*, written about 1930. It involves further direct

3. The Banshee

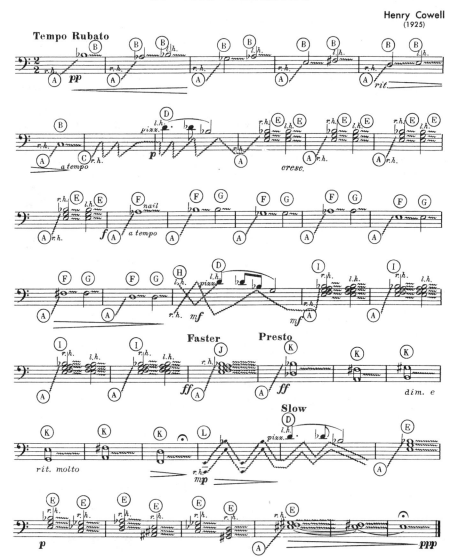

Henry Cowell
(1925)

Figure 20.1
The Banshee (1925) by Henry Cowell is played directly on the piano strings. Wavy lines in the score tell the performer to sweep across the strings in a particular manner to produce bone-chilling effects.

manipulation of the strings; playing several pitches on one string by "stopping" the string; "muting" strings with the hand; and playing harmonics by lightly touching the strings at one of the nodes while they are played from the keyboard. The muted, damped, and otherwise manipulated sounds of the piano strings in *Sinister Resonance* led directly into the sounds of the "prepared piano" of John Cage. (See Additional Listening.)

CONLON NANCARROW (1912–97) AND THE PLAYER PIANO

CD 5/9 (2:00)
Study No. 1, *Studies for Player Piano*, by Conlon Nancarrow

In his book *New Musical Resources*, Henry Cowell had suggested another piano possibility—the use of the player piano to achieve hitherto unheard-of effects. By the early 1900s, the player piano as we know it was popular and in full production. The way it worked was that a roll of paper with holes punched in it would pass over a "tracker bar," which resembled an elongated harmonica, with each hole representing a specific piano key. When a vacuum was created within the mechanism, each punched hole in the roll would allow air into the corresponding hole in the tracker bar (as with the harmonica), which would then force the hammer to strike the corresponding string. Thus was an already familiar and ubiquitous parlor instrument converted into an automaton that could execute, without a performer, anything available on commercial piano rolls, from popular songs to the most difficult solos in the repertory. With a little thought it becomes evident that the holes on the roll can be punched not only to reproduce preexisting music (the original aim of the inventors) but also to allow for *any* combination of pitches and rhythms, including combinations that could not possibly be performed by a live pianist. Conlon Nancarrow, born in Texarkana, Arkansas, seized upon these possibilities and began, in the 1940s, actually to "compose" for the instrument, by punching out the rolls in accordance with a preconceived plan. His modestly titled "Studies," on which he worked in relative seclusion in Mexico City for over forty years, number over forty. It is clear that when the physical limitations of the human pianist are removed, numerous possibilities exist, including very rapid passages, many simultaneous notes (far more than the pianist's ten fingers could reach), wide leaps, and complex rhythmic organization. His interest in the temporal dimension led him to develop pieces in which two or more tempi are going on simultaneously. This is reminiscent of some of Ives's works; but Nancarrow, freed from the limitations of human performers, was able to go much further in the direction of complex ratios of tempi, from a fairly simple 4:5, for example, to irrational relationships such as $2:\sqrt{2}$. These rhythmic relationships no doubt interested Cowell (if indeed he knew about them), since he had made similar experiments, leaving it to human performers to deal with them. This early study displays the complexities possible to this medium, and the melodic lines show the influence of the contemporary vernacular of jazz and blues.

Cowell and World Music   In 1956–57 Cowell went on a world tour, sponsored in part by the Rockefeller Foundation and the United States government. He spent a considerable amount of time in Iran and in Japan, both studying their music and bringing a knowledge of American music to them. This marked the beginning of a series of works based on Persian music (*Persian Set*, 1957, and *Homage to Iran*, 1959) and Japanese music (*Ongaku* for orchestra, 1957). Later his interest expanded to include the music of Iceland; his Symphony No. 16 (1962) is subtitled *Icelandic*. In these works, as in the works inspired by American and Celtic music, Cowell only rarely uses traditional tunes but writes his *own* Persian, Japanese, or Icelandic music. Always skillfully scored, even to suggesting the timbres of national instruments or the voicing of national choral singing, it nevertheless has a flavor of pleasant musical tourism, of the same type that issued forth in the nineteenth century when Russian and French composers were writing Spanish music.

Henry Cowell's mind was inventive but quite literal, at times almost childlike. He worked prodigiously at a complicated craft in an uncomplicated way. It was his role to suggest new sound resources without troubling deeper musical waters. But because of his relentless efforts in so many directions (as composer, publisher, editor, impresario, teacher, propagandist, and traveling ambassador), American music and American composers are much in his debt.

Henry Cowell was the first American composer to remind us that the West Coast of the United States is, culturally as well as geographically, farther from Europe, and closer to Asia, than is New York. The orientation of the East Coast to Europe continues to survive the colonial period (which lasted much longer culturally than politically); the West Coast, with more tenuous European ties and a greater variety of influences, has been more open to choices. In music, this openness to a large vocabulary of sounds, which we first noted in Cowell, has been carried further by Lou Harrison and John Cage, both of whom were students of Cowell.

Lou Harrison (b. 1917)

Lou Harrison, born in Portland, Oregon, went east in the 1940s to become, for a time, an important part of the New York musical scene. But he has always remained a West Coast man in his independence of "establishment" music and thinking. Harrison has been a dancer, painter, playwright, conductor, and maker of musical instruments.

There have been three main foci of Lou Harrison's work, and these are interrelated. The *first* is his cultivation of percussion instruments, showing up as early as 1941 in his *Fugue for Percussion*, and through the years in a variety of ensemble pieces and concertos. The *second* is his interest in a return to the pure intonation of just intervals (a topic that will be discussed in connection with Harry Partch), as exemplified in his *Four Strict Songs for Eight Baritones and Orchestra*, on his own text, patterned after the "making-things-right-and-good-again songs of the Navaho." The *third* is his knowledge of and love for the music of the Pacific Basin, particularly that of the Indonesian gamelan, an ensemble of percussion instruments. Lou Harrison and his colleague William

Colvig have built and performed on their own gamelans, each with its own unique name and tuning. Harrison has often combined in his works Oriental and Western instruments, as in his *Pacifika Rondo* of 1963, and in many smaller pieces. His *Threnody for Carlos Chavez* (1978; see CD 2/6, p. 94) for solo viola and gamelan is typical of his wide-ranging musical concerns, since it combines Javanese and European medieval practices with engaging sonorous results. These works stand as unique manifestations of the inclusiveness and breadth of spirit characteristic of Lou Harrison.

John Cage (1912–92)

CD 5/10 (1:29)
"Sonata V," from
Sonatas and Interludes for Prepared Piano, by
John Cage. 1946–48.
Yuji Takahashi, prepared piano.

John Cage, another of Cowell's students, was a West Coast composer who formed an early attachment to percussion instruments and to the dance. This latter came about partly because some of his earliest jobs consisted of playing for dance classes and partly because he soon discovered that in the 1930s, when it was difficult otherwise to find an audience for percussion music, dancers were eager for new sounds to accompany their new choreographic creations. It was in Seattle that Cage first hit upon the idea of the "prepared piano." A dancer had requested a score for a new ballet, *Bacchanale*, to empha-size percussion. Since the company could not afford a whole percussion orchestra, Cage (who was the son of an inventor) followed up on some of Cowell's experiments and modified the sound of a grand piano by muting or damping the strings with various objects, thereby in effect creating a percus-sion orchestra inside the piano, at the control of a single player. That was in 1938, and it was followed by many works for prepared piano, mostly for the dance. In 1946–48, after he had moved to New York, he returned to the pre-pared piano, writing the well-known *Sonatas and Interludes for Prepared Piano*.

Beginning in the 1950s, electronics, with its new sound sources, engaged him. Also, Oriental teachings, as he understood and interpreted them, were leading him in the direction of indeterminacy as to musical results and an abdi-cation of the role of composer. These developments belong to a later section of this chapter, beginning on page 414.

Harry Partch (1901–74)

There was another westerner, born at the turn of the century, who also struck out on his own—the embodiment, as a musician, of Blake's dictum "I must cre-ate a system, or be enslaved by another man's." Harry Partch, working for years alone and virtually unknown, rejected three of the most basic elements of his immediate musical heritage: conventional instruments, a scale of twelve equidistant notes to an octave, and counterpoint. His musical influences, as he himself listed them, are, like Cowell's, varied and typical of the West: "Christian hymns, Chinese lullabyes, Yaqui Indian ritual, Congo puberty ritual, Cantonese music hall, and Okies in California vineyards." Yet Partch did not become a "collector," either of exotic instruments or of exotic systems. Instead, he found what he needed as a base for his own music in two ancient ideas that had become eclipsed in Western music: purely tuned intervals and monophony (the singing or reciting of a single voice). And he soon saw that his return to pure intervals would draw him into another endeavor—that of building his own instruments.

Harry Partch, the son of apostate former missionaries to China, was born in Oakland, California, but soon moved with his family into the southwestern desert area of Arizona and New Mexico. His father, who understood Mandarin Chinese, worked for the immigration service, moving frequently from one small railroad-junction town near the Mexican border to another. Thus the boy grew up, lonely and largely self-educated, among the polyglot people of "the declining years of the Old West," as he put it—including the Yaqui Indians, the Chinese, and the hoboes and prostitutes his father and mother occasionally brought home. He read a great deal, enjoying Greek mythology especially. Musical instruments, obtained by mail order, were in the household. At 14 Partch began to compose seriously. At 21 he found Hermann von Helmholtz's famous book on musical acoustics, *On the Sensations of Tone*, and began writing works using pure, or "just," intonation. At about 26 he wrote the first draft of his own treatise and manifesto, *Genesis of a Music*. At 28 he burned, in a big iron stove, all the music he had written up to that time and set out with determination and (as he described it) "exhilaration" on new paths.

His first instruments were an Adapted Viola (a viola to which has been attached a longer cello fingerboard, marked so as to facilitate playing the smaller just intervals), an Adapted Guitar, a Chromelodeon (an adapted reed organ), and a Kithara (a lyre-shaped plucked-string instrument with movable bridges, allowing for a sliding tone). With these Partch wrote his first major work, *U.S. Highball*. "A hobo's account of a trip from San Francisco to Chicago," it is to a great extent autobiographical, for Partch's life between 1935 and 1943 consisted in large measure of hoboing, dishwashing, WPA jobs, and wandering. *U.S. Highball* has a Subjective Voice (the protagonist) and several Objective Voices, whose words consist of "fragments of conversations, writings on the sides of boxcars, signs in havens for derelicts, hitchhikers' inscriptions"—all of which Partch had recorded in a notebook he always carried during his wanderings. *The Letter*, an early work, was one received unexpectedly from an old companion of his in 1935. It was recorded in 1950, with Partch himself reading.

In succeeding years Partch built many new instruments, and rebuilt many earlier ones. The percussion instruments feature various marimbas. The Marimba Eroica is the largest; its lowest tone, below any of the notes on the

CD 5/11 (2:45)
The Letter, by Harry Partch, for Intoning Voice, Kithara I, Adapted Guitar, Diamond Marimba, and Bass Marimba

Harry Partch playing the Kithara, an instrument of his own design. Listen for the distinctive sound of its plucked strings and sliding tone on CD 5, Track 11, a recording of Partch's composition *The Letter.*

Harry Partch Foundation

piano, is produced by a Sitka spruce plank more than seven feet long suspended over a resonator eight feet long and four feet high. The smallest and softest is the Mazda Marimba, made of twenty-four light bulbs "with their viscera removed," yielding a sound, according to Partch, like the "bubbling of a coffee percolator." Other percussion include a Gourd Tree, Cone Gongs, and the bell-like Cloud-Chamber Bowls—the tops and bottoms of twelve-gallon glass carboys suspended. Appealing in sound, his instruments, especially as he redesigned them, came to have a great visual appeal as well; they are very much "part of the set" of a Partch performance, which, in accord with the composer's ideas of corporeal music, has always, and increasingly in the later works, a strong element of theater in it. The players themselves (who must be specially trained) are also aware at all times that they are "on stage."

Partch's *Genesis of a Music* (first published, after many drafts, in 1947, with a revised and enlarged second edition completed in 1972) is both manifesto and treatise. Unlike Cowell's earlier and comparable smaller work, *New Musical Resources*, it is not a suggestion of what *might* be done but a painstakingly thorough description of what Partch spent a lifetime doing—together with his reasons for doing so. The theoretical portions include, with respet to the *ratios* that Partch used to express intervals, a complete description and derivation of his scale of forty-three tones to the octave.

It takes a bold, energetic, and singularly dedicated and single-minded composer to develop and commit himself to a system of intonation impossible to produce on existing instruments; to build new instruments to the new specifications; and then to create new works exploiting the resources of both the intonation and the instruments. The most poignant limitation in such a lifework is that Partch's music can be performed only by specially trained performers, and only on his own instruments—one of a kind, and difficult and expensive just to maintain, let alone duplicate. Although a few recordings of his works were made in the late 1990s, most available recordings were made when Partch was still alive. It is not certain what the future of his music—*live*—will be. But it is likely that this was of little concern to Harry Partch. He had done his work. In 1972 he wrote:

> I am not trying to institute a movement in any crypto-religious sense. If I were, *idea* would soon turn into something called form, and the world is already plagued with its ephemera. . . . [The pathbreaker's] path cannot be retraced, because each of us is an original being. (xi)

Pure Intonation: A Postscript   It is interesting to note that three of the individualists treated in this chapter were concerned with pure, or just, intonation—that is, with the musical intervals resulting from simple and rational mathematical frequency ratios, in contrast with the irrational ratios and the "clouding" of all intervals except the octave that results from the compromise of twelve equal-tempered semitones to the octave. (The comparison of a purely tuned fifth on a violin, a viola, or a cello, or a purely tuned fourth on a guitar, with the same interval played on a piano will demonstrate that this seemingly theoretical distinction is actually quite apparent to the ear.) Cowell dealt theoretically with the concept in his *New Musical Resources*. Lou Harrison has written music to be played in pure intonation, and Partch committed himself to it wholly. There are others who have further explored it, including Ben Johnston

(b. 1926), who studied with Partch. Johnston's *Sonata for Microtonal Piano* (first performed in 1965) uses a piano specially tuned to a complex scale of eighty-one different pitch classes, seven of which appear in octave duplications. (The piano, with its eighty-eight keys, can be tuned to eighty-eight different pitches. In Johnston's very complex tuning, there are eighty-one different pitch classes, instead of the twelve of the conventionally tuned scale. This means that octave duplication is limited to just seven pitch classes. See Additional Listening.)

MIDCENTURY MODERNISM

At the conclusion of World War II, the modernism that emerged, both in the United States and in Europe, grew in evolutionary fashion, of course, out of the innovations that have already been encountered (the use of noise, the use of machines as musical instruments, the studied use of dissonance, and so on). But the modernist parameters took on new dimensions. For one thing, the new technologies that resulted inevitably from the fruits of wartime research became available to composers.

The visible machines—the typewriters, electric bells, sewing-machine motors, sirens, metal "thunder sheets," wind machines, airplane propellers— were no longer there as interesting visual objects enhancing the percussion section. They were replaced by the invisible machinery of electronics, the only visible components of which were loudspeakers. But there were also new aesthetic concepts added to the ever spicier soup, challenging the very definitions of what constituted music, for a time polarizing its practitioners, and giving rise to ever more *talk* about music—more rationalizing and preaching.

In view of all this, let us be aware that the most direct and ultimately the most enlightening approach to the music of the modernism that emerged after World War II is through simply listening to the sounds themselves. Roger Sessions, a composer who long championed the avant-garde, wrote:

> One cannot insist too strongly or too frequently that, in the arts generally and in music in particular, it is only productions that really count, and that only in these—music, written or performed—are to be found the criteria by which ideas about music, as well as music itself, must finally stand or fall: not the converse. (71–87)

CD 5/12 (0:37)
Phonenema, for soprano and piano (excerpt), by Milton Babbitt. 1969–70. Lynn Webber, soprano; Jerry Kuderna, piano.

One can observe in the music of midcentury modernism certain pervasive traits in the sound patterns—a vocabulary of sound types and gestures. This vocabulary is to a considerable degree independent of the philosophies, systems, and rationales behind the music, and even to an extent of how the sounds are produced. No clearer example of the interchangeability, in regard to style, of the live and electronic music of modernism can be cited than the two alternative realizations of Milton Babbitt's *Phonemena* of 1969–74 (CD 5/12 and 5/13).

Milton Babbitt (b. 1916) is a composer and mathematician who has been among the most influential of the midcentury modernists, both in the domain of twelve-tone serial music and in electronic music. Genial and witty, he has composed popular songs and one (unsuccessful) Broadway musical. More will be heard about him in connection with the composer's "maximum rational control" over his material.

The foregoing examples show that the *styles* of modernism, quite apart from either the medium employed or the genetic procedures used to create the music, asserted an autonomous existence. Much of the new music invites this approach—confining one's attention purely to the aural surface. If we take John Cage, the genial guru of the other aspect of modernism ("minimum rational control") at his word, "nothing takes the place but the sounds." Unlike Ives's ideal music, for the listener what it sounds like *is* what it is.

The Surface Features

One consistent characteristic of the sounds is that they tend to avoid the middle portion of what had previously been the usual range in any parameter. Thus, in pitch they are often either very high or very low; in volume, either very soft (as in the case of many of Morton Feldman's compositions throughout) or very loud (George Crumb has specified that the dynamic level of his electrified string instruments in *Black Angels* be "on the threshold of pain"); and in duration, either very short or very long indeed, avoiding the medium-length durations upon which traditional music is based. (See Additional Listening.)

Rhythmic complexity (engendered by the consistent use of a complicated and nonrepeating series of durations) is a crucial characteristic. This complexity is of the type used by Ives, as shown in the rhythmic pattern from "In the Night"—considered unplayable by most performers in his day.

With the advent of electronic music, it became possible to realize such complexities in the laboratory, so to speak. But there has arisen a new generation of virtuoso performers (challenged, like the John Henry of the ballad, to compete with the machine) who can execute these rhythms manually, and these performers are now given complex series of durations to realize, such as this example from Elliott Carter's Double Concerto of 1961 (see Additional Listening).

CD 5/13 (0:33) *Phonemena*, for soprano and tape (excerpt), by Milton Babbitt. 1974.

Transcription 20.7 Rhythmic excerpt from "In the Night," by Charles Ives

Transcription 20.8
Rhythmic excerpt from
Elliott Carter's Double
Concerto

It is important to note, as a feature of modernist music, that rhythmic complexity has often obscured, or eliminated, the sense of *pulse*.

New Sounds and New Sound Sources

The search for *new* sounds, following up on the music of the Machine Age, continued to be a concern in most avant-garde music since midcentury, and this search has added to the tonal palette sounds that include extended possibilities with traditional instruments (including the human voice), as well as electronically generated and/or processed sound. After midcentury, advanced amplifying and recording techniques made accessible previously unheard sounds—human brain waves, for example. Alvin Lucier based his *Music for Solo Performer* (Davis, California, 1965) on the amplification of the alpha current, a low-voltage brain signal. Moral and ethical concerns are also reflected in the choice of noises. The new compelling environmental awareness has found expression in the increased use of the sounds of nature, such as the fascinating "songs" of the humpback whale. Technology is giving us access to worlds of ever tinier sounds; "plant music," for example, already exists (Cope 316–17). Amplification has also made possible the conversion of ordinary objects into "instruments" that can be played; Miles Anderson, for example, with a degree of whimsy refreshing in the often too-deadly-serious world of contemporary music, adds to his Caravan ensemble the sounds produced by plucking the spines of an amplified cactus.

New modes of simultaneity have also produced new sounds. The combining of a few tones in dissonant relationships has been extended to the practice of heaping together a great many pitches—often all the available pitches in a certain range. This is a further development of the "cluster" chords of Ives and Cowell. The perception of dissonance, especially at soft dynamic levels, has been replaced by what is perceived as a *sound mass*.

Another option is *no* sound. Silence is an important element—a more pronounced structural feature than in traditional music. As early as 1952 Cage himself preempted the ultimate position in the use of silence with his famous piece *4' 33"*, in which no intended sounds whatever are produced, and which may therefore be performed by "any instrument or combination of instruments." (It must be added that in contrast to Antheil's use of silence, as in his *Ballet Mécanique*, as simply another structural ingredient in music, Cage and others of his modernist persuasion view silence as a window through which ambient sounds may be heard as part of the composition.)

Finally, there has been a concern with the spatial aspects of sound — specifically, in the musical effects created by separating sound sources and placing them in various ways in the performance space. Ives experimented with this; among many more recent examples of the use of spatial dimension in live performance could be cited Donald Erb's short *Spatial Fanfare for Brass and Percussion* and the final movement of John Corigliano's Concerto for Clarinet and Orchestra (1977) — works of which the spatial dimension cannot be experienced by listening to a conventional recording.

New Approaches to the Ordering of Sounds

Modernism also changed the way in which sounds are organized. There was a discernible tendency away from what was perceived in more traditional music as coherent (and therefore somewhat predictable) structure — away from the perception of a musical passage, apprehended as some kind of moving line (a melody perhaps) progressing toward some kind of goal or climax. Replacing the sense of movement or progression is the sense either that the music is static — resembling an unchanging field or a stationary object — or that it consists of a succession of individual *moments*, not perceptibly connected with one another. This discontinuity is congruent with, and was very probably influenced by, two technological media developments: film and tape. In both of these media, the *splice* has made the instant juxtaposition of discontinuous "moments" possible, and this proved to be a pervasive mode of organization for much of the new music since midcentury.

THE TWO DOMINANT RATIONALES OF MIDCENTURY MODERNISM

If the surface of midcentury modern music, as the ear alone perceived it, gave the impression of having simply appropriated more sounds into its vocabulary and devised new ways of relating them to one another, the situation in the 1950s and 1960s was far less simple from the composer's point of view. He or she had, as never before, to *rationalize*. Innocence was no longer possible; the new "advanced" composer had to know too much. There lay in wait for the serious young aspiring composer a maze of ideas, ideologies, methods, dogmas, and intellectual abstractions and justifications. The European intellectual climate had made European composers more prone to rationalization, but American composers had also become involved, despite a certain ineradicable residue of independence and distrust of hierarchical systems. Among composers dedicated to advanced music, a fortunate few, such as Morton Feldman, succeeded in extricating themselves and confronting autonomously once more the basic function of the composer—to make music. Feldman himself said in the late 1960s, "Unfortunately for most people who pursue art, ideas become their opium. The sickness that you feel about the situation today is a piling up of multitudinous suggestions and multitudinous misconceptions, each tumbling over the other. There is no security to be one's self" (Schwartz and Childs 365).

In rationale and method, the paths that composers took varied in detail with each individual, but two fairly clear general routes were followed—routes that diverged widely. Cage, in an address given in 1957, pointed up rather clearly the difference in the amount of *rational* control exercised by the composer over the aural result: the production.

> One has a choice. If he does not wish to give up his attempts to control sound, he may complicate his musical technique towards an approximation of the new possibilities and awareness. (I use the word "approximation" because a measuring mind can never finally measure nature.) Or, as before, one may give up the desire to control sound, clear his mind of music, and set about discovering means to let sounds be themselves rather than vehicles for man-made theories or expressions of human sentiments. (*Silence* 10)

(The notion of "letting sounds be themselves" is strikingly reminiscent of the Polish philosopher Wronsky's definition of music as "the corporealization of the intelligence that is in sounds"—a definition that greatly influenced Varèse.)

The almost diametrically opposed positions represented by the ideal of maximum rational control on the one hand (Milton Babbitt: "I believe in cerebral music, and I never choose a note unless I know why I want it there" [Bruno 22] and a minimum of such control on the other (John Cage: "Discovering means to let sounds be themselves") polarized the new music in the 1950s and 1960s to the extent that the two approaches were given separate labels: *avant-garde* for the first and *experimental* for the second.

Toward Maximum Rational Control by the Composer

The trend toward ever greater control over the end result of musical composition was manifested in two distinct but related areas. The first was the control over every aspect of performance, going beyond the historically basic specifications of pitch, rhythm, and tempo (which evolved historically in that order) to include the most detailed instructions regarding tone color and dynamic nuance. The ultimate realization of control, of course, is the composition directly on tape (electronic music), which eliminates the performer entirely.

A second, and more fundamentally crucial, area of increased control was that governing the myriad of choices the composer makes in writing the piece to begin with. In the twentieth century the greatest degree of predetermined control of choices was represented by the technique of *serial organization.* "Classical" serial technique, derived from the work of Arnold Schoenberg and other German-Austrian composers beginning in the 1920s, consists of organizing music according to a series, or *set,* consisting of all of the twelve pitches (or *pitch classes*) arranged in a certain invariable order that persists (allowing for permutations) throughout the work. Serial technique applied to pitches alone has been used by many American composers, including Milton Babbitt, Ben Weber, George Perle, Ross Lee Finney, until the late 1960s George Rochberg, and, in some works, Aaron Copland.

Ultimately, on both sides of the Atlantic, the move was taken toward subjecting the *total* aural result of a composition to the intellectual predetermination of serial procedures. What has become popularly known as *total serialization* involves a procedure by which the ordering of all the other measurable dimensions of sound—duration, intensity, timbre, and register—is serially determined. This procedure results in a composition that has been called "the unpremeditated result of comprehensive premeditation" (Krenek 673). The idea itself has become well known, although actual pieces in which all the so-called *parameters* of music (a term borrowed, significantly, from mathematics) have been serially predetermined are relatively rare. One such piece is Milton Babbitt's *Three Compositions for Piano,* in which dynamics, rhythm, and pitch are serialized. The early date (1947) is testimony to the independent leadership of American composers in this field. (See Cope 42–44.)

Around serial music, and the theorizing that went with it, a rarefied atmosphere was created in which the layman was made to feel not only uncomfortable but also unwelcome and inferior. The pronouncements of some composers were not calculated to dispel this. Charles Wuorinen said, "Composers have always been 'intellectuals' and this stance is absolutely unavoidable today, for music has grown too rich and complex to be handled by the illiterate" (Schwartz and Childs 375). The fact that the universities tended to be the centers for the cultivation of serialism helped to foster the analogy of this type of composition to pure scientific research. This view was cogently expressed by Milton Babbitt himself in a now-famous article, circulated under the title "Who Cares If You Listen?" Written for a magazine with broad circulation (*High Fidelity*), and in this case in terms any intelligent layman can understand, it is one of the most lucid and unequivocal statements of the viewpoint of the composer-as-research-specialist. (For the entire article see Schwartz and Childs, or Chase.) (The title is the source of gross popular misunderstanding, since it was chosen not by Babbitt but by the magazine's editor, who was unwilling to change it at the author's request, and therefore chose to misrepresent, for popular consumption, Babbitt's carefully stated position.)

The composer's attempt to achieve total rational control over the compositional process had two acknowledged limitations. The first stemmed from the basic premise of serialism that all the pitches, durations, intensities, and other properties constituting the predetermined series must be heard before any can be repeated. But, as the proverb has it, the more things change, the more they are the same, and the aural result of this constant change was actually a kind of *static* quality. As the German avant-gardist Karlheinz Stockhausen put it, "If from one sound to the next, pitch, duration, timbre and intensity change . . . one is constantly traversing the entire realm of experience in a very short time, and thus one finds oneself in a state of suspended animation, the music 'stands still'" (Nyman 23).

A second limitation was the built-in tendency of serialism to defeat the avowed purpose of those adopting it as a means of achieving totally predetermined control; the music comes to resemble, to a remarkable degree, that generated by opposite procedures of deliberate randomness. As Krenek said of serialism, "It is reasonable to assume that in pursuing this concept beyond certain limits one would reach a point of diminishing returns, for the internal organization of the final product would become so complicated that its outward appearance would be hardly distinguishable from that of organized chaos" (673).

(In explaining the phenomenon of maximum order resembling disorder, composer George Rochberg has invoked the aid of the physical concept of *entropy*, "the measure of the tendency of nature toward disorder, non-differentiation, and a final state of static equilibrium," in a fascinating essay too long to quote from effectively. See "Indeterminacy in the New Music" in Rochberg, *The Aesthetics of Survival*.)

The paradoxical similarity between the results of procedures designed to give the composer maximum control and those designed to give him minimum control have been noted by many observers. This leads us to the consideration of the other dominant rationale of midcentury modernism.

Toward Minimum Rational Control by the Composer

The second path of the new music after midcentury was that of progressive relinquishment of rational control by the composer. Here, as at the opposite extreme of serialism, the musical result cannot be envisioned in full, but for a different reason—the composer has deliberately willed it so. Increasingly, aspects of the whole result are left either to the performer or to the operation, in some form or other, of chance.

Improvisation   A certain degree of planned relinquishment of control to the performer (quite aside from the ever present element of interpretation) exists in the realm of improvisation. Improvisation was revived in very special instances in avant-garde music of midcentury. In the case of the Improvisation Chamber Ensemble, a small group founded by Lukas Foss in 1957, it involved wide performer choices within a carefully planned structure, and the interaction of players who were highly skilled, experienced in this type of performance, and used to working together. It was therefore rare.

Limited Indeterminacy   In view of the limitations of true improvisation, composers have sought other related means of applying indeterminacy within controlled limits. Indeterminate notation is one means used, supplying performers with a basic idea of the sound intended and specifying certain guides and limitations to its production. Graph notation, for instance, an early idea that survives in various forms, was used by Morton Feldman to produce such works as *Projection 3* (1951) for two pianos. Most indeterminate notation must continue to rely heavily upon explanatory directions, which are sometimes as lengthy as the notation itself. (See Cage, *Notations*.)

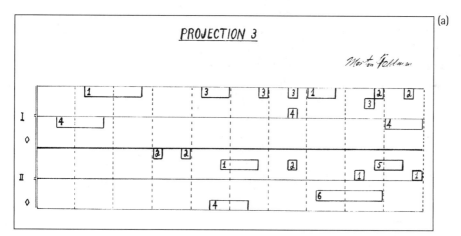

(a)

(b)

Relative pitch (high, middle, low) is indicated. ⊏⊐ high; ⊐⊏ middle; ⊓ low. Any tone within these ranges may be sounded. The limits of the ranges may be freely chosen by the player. Duration is indicated by the amount of space taken up by the square or rectangle, each box (♩) being potentially 4 icti. The single ictus, or pulse, is at the tempo of 72 or thereabouts. Dynamics are very low. Each pianist reads two parts simultaneously, with the lower part (◊) making of the piano a source of sympathetic resonance. Numbers in the piano parts indicate the amount of sounds to be played simultaneously.

Figure 20.2
In *Projection 3* Morton Feldman provided only general guidelines for performace by way of sparse graph notations (a), and explanatory directions (b). In this exciting, largely unpredictable medium, each performer assumes the creative role of co-composer.

Another practice was that of giving the performers (including the conductor) certain choices in the performance—choices relating to the order of musical events (including how many of all those possible are to be performed at all) and to the duration of those events. Earle Brown's *Available Forms I* (1961) furnishes an example of this procedure. This is a work for chamber ensemble in which the conductor moves at will from one to another of six "events," the notations for all of which are available to all the performers at all times. To such procedures Brown has given a name: "open form." It is significant that Brown was influenced by the work of the sculptor Alexander Calder. There is a certain correspondence between *open form* in music and the *mobile* in art; in both, the individual components are predetermined by the artist, but their relationship at any given moment (or in any given performance) is unpredictable.

Unlimited Indeterminacy

The progression toward a minimization of control by the composer may be thought of as a continuum, beginning with improvisation. As we move further along the continuum in the direction of ever-decreasing control over the realized sound itself, we become involved with significant changes in the aesthetic concepts of what constitutes the essence and function of music, and of art in general. With Cage's "my purpose is to remove purpose," we encounter at once a fundamentally different attitude and aesthetic. If the traditional role of the composer is eliminated, there is no alternative but to leave the artistic results, literally, to *chance*. This is the alternative path that experimental music pursued, in the elevation of chance to a position in which it replaces altogether what has been called imagination, intuition, inspiration. In this we encounter once again (as with indeterminacy's complementary opposite, total organization) the goal of removing artistic decisions from the domain of human memory, experience, and intuition, the effects of which are to be expurgated much as (in another context) would be the consequences of "original sin."

John Cage's *Music of Changes* (a piano piece written in 1951, lasting forty-three minutes) is an early example of this, having been arrived at through an elaborate process of using charts and coin tosses in accord with the Chinese oracular book of wisdom *I Ching* ("Book of Changes"). With this type of new music, the scope of the composer in determining the actual sounds is reduced to that of merely setting up systems or arranging for the unpredictable to happen. The occupation of the composer *as creative artist* is deliberately eliminated. Cage himself, in a one-man dialogue, asked himself the ultimate question—"Why bother, since, as you have pointed out, sounds are continually happening whether you produce them or not?"—but avoided answering it.

NEW TECHNOLOGY AND THE NEW MUSIC

The present sophisticated state of electroacoustic music can be understood as a composite of the following capabilities: the ability to record any sound or succession of sounds, the ability to synthesize (to build up from the electronic scratch of the basic sine tone, as it were) any imaginable sound or succession of sounds, and the ability to manipulate sounds obtained from either of these two processes in various ways, including slowing them down or speeding them up, raising or lowering their pitch, reversing their direction in time, changing their timbre by filtering out certain frequencies, combining any number of them simultaneously, introducing echo effects, making them endlessly repeat, and juxtaposing them in any way. *Sampling* constitutes a synthesis of all three of these capabilities, in that a sound from *any* source can be "listened to," analyzed, synthesized, and subjected to any of the aforementioned manipulations.

In its first stages (roughly the 1950s), nearly all efforts were directed toward the production of the sound on tape as the sole end product. To attend a "performance," all you did was be in the presence of loudspeakers and listen. The first program of such music in the United States was given at the Museum of Modern Art in New York in 1952, and was the work of two of the pioneers of electroacoustic music, Otto Luening and Vladimir Ussachevsky. Because of the amount and cost of the equipment involved, universities were both the centers and the patrons of the development of electronic music—at first Columbia and Princeton, later joined by the Universities of Michigan and Illinois, and Stanford University.

From the beginning both "live" and synthesized tones were used as raw material. Performerless tape music has continued to be cultivated; *La Poème électronique* (1958) by Edgar Varèse, mentioned earlier in this chapter, was a landmark. Subsequent carefully crafted compositions—some of them large-scale, and by no means inexpressive—by Luening and Ussachevsky, and after them Mario Davidovsky, Mel Powell, Kenneth Gaburo, Charles Wuorinen (whose *Time's Encomium* of 1969 won the Pulitzer Prize), and Morton Subotnick, gave indications of what was possible. Since it soon became evident that the recording, playable at home, and not the public "concert," was the important mode of dissemination for this music, it is not surprising that in the 1960s record companies themselves were commissioning electronic works (for example, Subotnick's *Silver Apples of the Moon* and *The Wild Bull*, commissioned by Nonesuch).

But by and large the elimination of the performer did not prove to be the altogether worthwhile liberating advance it was at first thought to be. For one thing, for all the inventiveness that was applied, there seemed to be still a pervasive *sameness* to electronic sounds—the result of what Mel Powell described as tape music's "perilously limited array of options." Probably a more decisive limiting factor was the absence of a human performer—a vital ingredient to the essentially human transaction that is live musical performance. As early as 1953 Luening and Ussachevsky were combining live performers and tape sounds, and they produced two works for orchestra and tape the next year (*Rhapsodic Variations* and *A Poem in Cycles and Bells*).

This has proven to be the most prevalent use of electronic music, and works for tape and a single performer or small group of performers are very numerous. The degree to which live performers must synchronize with the tape varies considerably, from situations in which they are completely independent (John Cage's *Aria with Fontana Mix*) to pieces in which the interaction is highly organized (Mario Davidovsky's various pieces appropriately called *Synchronisms*).

OTHER ASPECTS OF MIDCENTURY MODERNISM

Toward Theater and the Combination with Other Media

The tendency of many of the endeavors of modernism was toward the involvement of other senses than the auditory, and hence other media. The extension of the new music into the "multimedia" realm is actually a fairly complex subject, for the heading embraces many essentially different kinds of endeavors. In regard to the combination of live and electronic music, the quasi-dramatic situation inherent in the juxtaposition of performer and inanimate loudspeaker—"man versus the machine"—has been deliberately exploited in some works. Another type of multimedia piece came out of the desire to "theatricalize" the basic concert situation. Making "theater" out of a concert situation makes actors out of the performers. The late works of Harry Partch illustrate this. A more passive kind of theatricalism is represented by a piece such as *Vox balaenae* (*Voice of the Whale*) (1971), by George Crumb, wherein three musicians playing electrified instruments (flute, cello, and piano) and making music "inspired by the singing of the humpback whale" are directed to wear masks and to play in a deep blue light. In this case, the music clearly exists independent of the visual setting, which merely adds an atmospheric dimension to the live performance. (See Additional Listening.)

A more recent theatricalism, using a mixture of media, is the "performance art" of the 1980s and 1990s, centered on a solo performer who may play, sing, speak, act, dance, in any combination, aided by a battery of visual displays and props. Laurie Anderson is perhaps the best-known performer in this vein. "Performance art" is apt to verge on pop, its visual aspect related to the video.

Very elaborate attempts were made in the late 1960s and early 1970s to create whole artistic "environments" that would actively involve the audience. A short environmental piece, *Souvenir* (1970) by Donald Erb, presented close coordination of the aural, visual, and tactile components in a "happy" and "non-neurotic" (in the composer's words) piece for dancers, instrumental ensemble of winds and percussion, electronic tape, projections, and "props" that include weather balloons (bounced around in the hall by the audience), and Ping-Pong balls, which the audience afterward carries away as "souvenirs" (Cope 232–35).

Once the traditional concert situation was superseded, the temptation to expand multimedia works to gargantuan proportions proved irresistible to some. Robert Moran's *39 Minutes for 39 Autos*, done in San Francisco in 1969, involved a "potential of 100,000 performers, using auto horns, auto lights, skyscrapers, a TV station, dancers, theater groups, spotlights, and airplanes, besides a small synthesizer ensemble." Such mammoth one-time happenings have their counterpart in the visual arts in the works of Boris Christo.

Multimedia works in which there was little or no coordination between the elements were best described in their heyday as "happenings," a large portion of which were the result of chance operations of one kind or another. With John Cage and his followers and collaborators in the 1960s, the combination of multimedia experiments and indeterminacy led to the production of happenings such as *HPSCHD*, a vastly complex work by Cage and Lejaren Hiller. The sound alone was a dense overlaying of fifty-two electronic sound tapes and seven amplified harpsichords played by five live performers. The basic source material for the harpsichordists was *Introduction to the Composition of Waltzes by Means of Dice*, attributed to Mozart (the witty diversion of a genius at play, which was cited again and again with singular seriousness by theorists of twentieth-century indeterminacy in search of antecedents). The choice of nearly all the sound material, live and electronic, was controlled by chance—in this case, by a computerized version of *I Ching*. The whole performance (which took place in the huge Assembly Hall of the University of Illinois in 1969, and lasted four and a half hours) was accompanied by visual projections from sixty-four slide projectors and eight movie projectors going simultaneously, as well as miscellaneous light beams and the reflected light from spinning mirrored balls—a manufactured "kinetic environment," and the most complex embodiment up to that time of Cage's dictum that "the more things there are, as is said, the merrier."

Anti-Art, and the Confusion of Art with Life

The restlessly experimental fever among the indeterminacy wing of modernism during its most active phase, in the 1960s, led some composers on the fringes to adopt a quasi-philosophical stance, to direct their energies to exercises whose aim seemed to be to question the nature and function of music itself, and to undermine the assumptions and the *modus operandi* on which it is based. The ideas of John Cage appeared to provide the cues for much of this. Cage himself, though working with craftsmanlike diligence in realizing his own "happenings," as a leader hardly went beyond being a genial, witty, and provocative questioner and storyteller. But there were those in the next generation who took Cage's "purpose . . . to remove purpose" with an intense earnestness that showed itself in a variety of manifestations.

One was the conscious use of human responses normally unrelated to the perception of art as the basis for a "composition." *Danger* was one ingredient (danger to hearing from very loud sounds). *Boredom* (the very thing that all but the most doggedly experimental artists seek to avoid) was studied and exploited by Cage and others. La Monte Young's *Composition 1960 No. 7* consists of two notes forming the interval of a perfect fifth, to be held a "long time"; Philip Corner's *The Barcelona Cathedral* consists of the loud clang of ten metallic percussion instruments being sounded together every few seconds, for half an hour. Minimalism, treated in the next chapter, grew at least partly out of this domain.

"Concept" music consists merely of *ideas* for "pieces," or "happenings," the actual realization of which would be either impossible or, as expressions of the philosophy motivating them, ambiguous or manifestly pointless. Of the first type would be pieces that would take several hundred years to perform, for example. Representative of the second type would be La Monte Young's *Composition 1960 No. 9*, which, in his words, "consists of a straight line drawn on a piece of paper. It is to be performed and comes with no instructions."

The "pieces" often consisted *merely* of instructions ("word-scores"), some of which were gentle invitations to become aware of the beauties of the environment or to relinquish some of the egotism of the "performer." Pauline Oliveros's *Sonic Meditations* includes instructions to "Take a walk at night. Walk so silently that the bottoms of your feet become ears" and "Become performers by not performing." But if everything of which we are aware is to be regarded as art, then art has no distinctive existence and is meaningless. This anti-art stance was generally related to a confusion of art with life itself. John Cage insisted on the confusion: "Art's obscured the difference between art and life. Now let life obscure the difference between life and art" (*A Year* 19).

The purely musical aspects of modernism—those aspects having to do with sound itself—have left their mark on American music and will continue to be adapted and used. But the extremism, the rigid dogmatism, and the contempt for the wider audience, and for art itself, that characterized the 1950s and the 1960s were doomed to fade, and fade they did, in favor of a more inclusive, humane, and richly varied musical art that transcended modernism. It is to that that we turn our attention next.

PROJECTS

1. Review thoughtfully Ives's statements about "idealism versus professionalism in music" in the section so labeled in this chapter, and read Ives more fully in this regard (starting with the complete Epilogue of the *Essays*). In what ways do you agree or disagree with his stance? Is this stance possible today? Make this the subject of a brief talk or paper.

2. Henry Cowell and Harry Partch both began fairly early to write treatises on their conceptions of the directions and resources required of the "new music"—Cowell in *New Musical Resources*, and Partch in *Genesis of a Music*. Make a brief comparative study of these.

3. In his *Genesis of a Music*, page 9, Harry Partch clarifies his distinction between Corporeal and Abstract music, giving instances of each from a broad range of music. Read this and the material leading up to it, ponder this distinction, and think about your own listening habits and preferences. Of which type is the music that most (and least) appeals to you? Make an annotated diary of the music you listen to for a week or a month, describing the degree of Corporeality or Abstractness of each piece, giving your reasons for making the distinction, and describing your reaction to the music with regard to this distinction.

4. Write a well-reasoned critique of Milton Babbitt's important essay "Who Cares If You Listen?" (reprinted in both Chase, *The American Composer Speaks*, and Schwartz and Childs, *Contemporary Composers*). Deal with as many of its implications as you can fathom. For example, what do you think would happen if all "advanced" composers of "specialized" music withdrew in isolation from the "public life of unprofessional compromise and exhibitionism"? Or, related to this, what would be the ramifications of the "complete elimination of the public and social aspects of musical composition"?

ADDITIONAL LISTENING

Elliott Carter

Double Concerto for Harpsichord and Piano with Chamber Orchestra. Contemporary Chamber Ensemble with Paul Jacobs and Gilbert Kalish. Cond. Helmuth Kolbe and Arthur Weisberg. WEA/Atlantic/Nonesuch 79183.

Henry Cowell

Aeolian Harp, for piano. On *Henry Cowell: Piano Music*. Henry Cowell, piano and vocals. Smithsonian/Folkways 40801.

Aeolian Harp, for piano. On *New Music—Piano Compositions by Henry Cowell*. Sorrel Hays, piano. New Albion Records 103.

Aeolian Harp, for piano. On *Sound Forms for Piano*. New World Records 203.

Sinister Resistance. On *Henry Cowell: Piano Music*. Henry Cowell, piano and vocals. Smithsonian/Folkways 40801.

The Tides of Manaunaun. On *Henry Cowell: Piano Music*. Henry Cowell, piano and vocals. Smithsonian/Folkways 40801.

The Tides of Manaunaun. On *New Music—Piano Compositions by Henry Cowell.* Sorrel Hays, piano. New Albion Records 103.

Ruth Crawford (Seeger)

String Quartet (1931). Pellegrini Quartet. CPO 999 670-2.

String Quartet (1931). On *Ruth Crawford Seeger Portrait.* Schoenberg Ensemble. UNI/ Deutsche Grammophon 449925.

George Crumb

Black Angels. Kronos Quartet. WEA/Atlantic/Nonesuch 79242.

Black Angels. On *American String Quartets (1950–1970).* The Concord String Quartet. Vox (Classical) 5143.

Vox balaenae (Voice of the Whale), Suite for 3 Masked Players: electric flute, electric cello, and electric piano. University of Pennsylvania Chamber Players. Cond. Richard Wernick. New World Records 80357.

Charles Ives

"At the River," Kz101, for voice and piano. On *Charles Ives Songs.* Jan De Gaetani, vocal; Gilbert Kalish, piano. WEA/Atlantic/Nonesuch 71325.

"At the River," Kz101, for voice and piano. On *My Native Land: A Collection of American Songs.* Jennifer Larmore, vocal; Antoine Palloc, piano. Elektra/Asylum 16069.

"At the River," Kz101, for voice and piano. On *Songs of Charles Ives and Ernest Bacon.* Helen Boatwright, vocal; John Kirkpatrick, piano. CRI 675.

"The Cage" for voice and piano. On *Charles Ives Songs.* Marni Nixon, vocal; John McCabe, piano. Nonesuch H 71209.

Charlie Rutlage, for baritone and orchestra. On *Ives: An American Journey.* Thomas Hampson, vocal. San Francisco Symphony and Chorus. Cond. Michael Tilson Thomas. RCA 63703.

The Fourth of July, from *Four New England Holidays.* Chicago Symphony Orchestra. Cond. Michael Tilson Thomas. Sony 42381.

General William Booth Enters into Heaven, Kz98, for voice and piano. On *Charles Ives Songs.* Marni Nixon, vocal; John McCabe, piano. Nonesuch H 71209.

"Majority," Ky36 (Kz131), for voice and piano. On *Charles Ives Songs.* Jan De Gaetani, vocal; Gilbert Kalish, piano. WEA/Atlantic/Nonesuch 71325.

"Majority," Kz45, for voice and piano. On *My Native Land: A Collection of American Songs.* Jennifer Larmore, vocal; Antoine Palloc, piano. Elektra/Asylum 16069.

Putnam's Camp, from *3 Places in New England,* Kv30, for orchestra. On *Ives: An American Journey.* San Francisco Symphony and Chorus. Cond. Michael Tilson Thomas. RCA 63703.

"Tom Sails Away," Kz106, for voice and piano. On *Ives: An American Journey.* Thomas Hampson, vocal. RCA 63703.

"Tom Sails Away," Kz106, for voice and piano. On *Songs of Charles Ives and Ernest Bacon.* Helen Boatwright, vocal; John Kirkpatrick, piano. CRI 675.

Ben Johnston

Sonata for Microtonal Piano. On *Sound Forms for Piano.* New World Records 203.

Conlon Nancarrow

Studies for Player Piano, Nos. 1, 27, and 36. On *Sound Forms for Piano.* New World Records 203.

Edgard Varèse

Ionisation, for 13 Percussion Instruments. On *Ionisation Music of Varèse, Penderecki, Ligeti.* Riehe Ensemble. Cond. Friedrich Cerha. Vox (Classical) 5142.

Ionisation, for 13 Percussion Instruments. On *Varèse: Arcana/Ameriques/Ionization/Density 21.5/Octandre/Intégrales.* New York Philharmonic. Cond. Pierre Boulez. Sony 45844.

Ionisation, for 13 Percussion Instruments. On *Varèse: The Complete Works.* Royal Concertgebouw Orchestra. Asko Ensemble. Cond. Riccardo Chailly. Polygram Records 460208.

La Poème électronique, for tape. On *Varèse: The Complete Works.* Royal Concertgebouw Orchestra. Asko Ensemble. Cond. Riccardo Chailly. Polygram Records 460208.

CHAPTER

Toward a More Hospitable Music 21

Developments as early as the 1960s pointed to the fact that modernism was beginning to lose its hegemony. By the 1980s, it was clear to the general musical public that modernism had already reached its outermost limits and receded. Three manifestations attest to this: first, there was greater *autonomy* for the composer (who no longer felt an outsider if not fully committed to one of two highly exclusive schools, serialism and experimentalism); second, the music had *assimilated* more from a wide range of sources, including older European music, ethnic musics from around the world, and popular and folk musics; and third, the music was more *hospitable*—that is, capable of being enjoyed by a broader audience, an audience that had been left out, and hence turned off, by the excesses of a music born of an aesthetic that disdained this broader audience as "illiterate."

Predictably, new names (such as "postmodern" and "neoromantic") have been applied to the fine-art music that emerged with the recession of modernism. But the transcending of modernism is a transcending of categories and "schools" as well. As William Bolcom put it:

> We are in the 1980s, and it is generally accepted among most artists that modernism is on the wane. What is happening now is less a new movement—although critics have been quick to name it postmodernism—than it is a movement away from movements, those schools and isms that have bedeviled art and led towards its current sclerotic self-consciousness. (Rochberg, *Aesthetics* vii)

Thus a label such as "New Romanticism," current in New York and elsewhere during the 1980s, itself connotes a fashion, and at best can characterize only a portion of the phenomenon. The situation is better described as Michael Walsh has done:

> During the 1960s the horizons of American music suddenly expanded. . . . The decline of Darmstadtism freed composers once again to give voice to individual modes of expression; while initial reactions were tentative and uncertain, within fifteen years a thousand flowers had bloomed. (Walsh)

(Darmstadt, Germany, was host to annual summer convocations of the avant-garde after World War II, and had been called the "citadel of serialism." In designating the 1960s as the watershed, Walsh assigns a fairly early date to the initial reactions to modernism, this pointing up the increasing overlapping of artistic trends in our time.)

MINIMALISM: A RADICAL ANTIDOTE TO MODERNISM

Towering over the thousand blooms like a colossal sunflower was minimalism, a hardy plant that spread its seeds far and wide. Minimalism, in music as in the other arts, has as its "underlying impulse the radical reduction of composi-tional materials" (Dreier). Its most familiar manifestation is a musical texture in which short, simple patterns are repeated for long periods of time, either without variation, or subjected to subtle changes that gradually alter the melodic, rhythmic, or timbral content. In simple repetition, minimalist works had their predecessors. Eric Satie's *Vexations*, a Dadaist product of the last decade of the nineteenth century, instructed the performer to play a simple 32-bar piece very slowly and softly 840 times—hence it was essentially "concept music." Such pieces involving unrelieved repetition, with no subtle changes, represented experiments in boredom and the hypnotic effects of repetition, and forecast the similar essays of the Cagean experimentalists of midcentury modernism. (See "boredom" as treated in the preceding chapter, p. 418.) Rep-etition as a means of making a piece of art appeared in the domain of the visual arts as well, as in Andy Warhol's multiplication of such popular icons as the image of Marilyn Monroe.

But minimalism as a way of making music to be taken seriously began to appear prominently in the 1960s. It was associated with two trends of the times. One was an increased interest in Asian and African music, in which repetition plays a very significant role. (Much Asian and African music that involves repetition exists for purposes fundamentally different from that of Western music, including ritual and the inducement of altered states of consciousness. These functions, along with elements of Eastern philosophy and religion, have been adopted by some Western composers. The need, in our time, to understand more about Asian and African music is clear but is beyond the scope of this book.) The other trend was a reaction, on the part of some composers born in the 1930s, to midcentury modernism itself, especially the serialism of the dominant academic East Coast/European "establishment."

Minimalism as merely simple repetition taken to extremes began to be modified in various ways in the 1960s. One approach was to treat music as a gradual, perceptible *process*, and one that the listener can hear happening throughout the music. Steve Reich explains it by three analogies:

> Performing and listening to a gradual musical process resembles: pulling back a swing, releasing it, and observing it gradually come to rest; turning over an hour glass and watching the sand slowly run through to the bottom: placing your feet in the sand by the ocean's edge and watching, feeling, and listening to the waves gradually bury them. (9)

The technology of tape recording suggested one means of treating music as a process. This included the splicing of tapes into loops so that fragments of speech or music could be recycled in a repeated pattern that could be played endlessly or combined with other loops in various ways. Many of the ideas and possibilities of sound manipulation and musical structure were originally *suggested* by experimentation with tape. Steve Reich tells of an accidental discovery that was to have far-reaching consequences for minimalism. This happened as he was working with the recording he had made of a young black Pentecostal preacher, Brother Walter, in Union Square, San Francisco, which eventually became *It's Gonna Rain* (1965).

> In the process of trying to line up two identical tape loops in some particular relationship, I discovered that the most interesting music of all was made by simply lining the loops up in unison, and letting them slowly shift out of phase with each other. As I listened to this gradual phase shifting process I began to realize that it was an extraordinary form of musical structure. . . . It was a seamless, continuous, uninterrupted musical process. (50)

Thus *phase shifting* came into being. Born of tape technology, the process was soon applied to pieces for human performers, as in Reich's *Piano Phase* (1967) for two pianos, and *Clapping Music* (1972) for performers clapping hands. The rights could not be obtained to include *It's Gonna Rain* and other early examples of phase shifting in the CD set, but as a sample of this early phase of minimalism, they are recommended (Additional Listening).

Reich abandoned this kind of very gradual phase shifting in the early 1970s, when he began the serious study of African and Asian music. But the structural method of having two or more voices repeat patterns in changing relationships—an idea that originated with tape loops—continued to be used in works by other composers. John Adams (b. 1947) used this device in his 28-minute *Shaker Loops* (1978), with seven "loops" for seven string players, wherein the shifting phases create what he has called a "congenial friction." (See Additional Listening.)

What minimalism brought *back* to classical music was *tonality, pulsation,* and *repetition.* These elements were certainly not new, but, as John Adams has pointed out, "in the context of what had happened in contemporary classical music since the time of Schönberg [the leading pedogogical proponent of twelve-tone serialism], and particularly John Cage's developments, *reintroducing* them was in itself a revolutionary act" (Adams). This reintroduction—this "emphatic embracement of the most essential ingredients of what was most familiar"—propelled minimalist music into an immediate and unanticipated popularity, especially among those who had little previous experience with contemporary classical music. It became at once both influential and controversial. Minimalist composers became the new "stars" of classical music.

La Monte Young (b. 1935), in his work with long sustained sounds (either acoustic or electronic) dating from the late 1950s, was an early influence on minimalism. The cross-cultural aspect of minimalism, and its curious juxtaposition of mysticism and technology, is projected in the almost Dadaist flavor of such titles as La Monte Young's *The Tortoise Recalling the Drone of the Holy Numbers as They Were Revealed in the Dreams of the Whirlwind and the Obsidian Gong and Illuminated by the Sawmill, the Green Sawtooth Ocelot and the High-Tension Line Step-down Transformer,* of 1964. Composers contemporary with Young who have become better known as proponents of minimalism are Terry Riley (b. 1935), Steve Reich (b. 1936), and Philip Glass (b. 1937). As Ruth Dreier has pointed out, they have many things in common. After a more or less traditional musical education, each rejected serialism; each discovered and studied Asian or African music; each became interested in exploring the physical properties of sound; each was involved with other arts in addition to music; and each founded his own performing group (Dreier). In addition, each uses or has used electronic means (synthesizers or tape).

In addition to African and Asian music, another palpable influence on minimalism, as John Adams has pointed out, is the machine itself. "Composers began to notice that machines, whether old-fashioned mechanical ones, or new electronic ones, tended to operate in interesting and often expressive modes of repetition."

Riley's *In C* (1964) was something of a landmark work. Its relation to modernism is in its indeterminacy; the number and type of instruments is optional, as is the total length (the first performance, in San Francisco, lasted over an hour and a half). The simple design of this type of minimalism is the repetition of individual elements that in themselves are not varied but simply added to and then subtracted from the texture. There is a single tempo, governed by the steady repetition of a "C" two octaves above middle C on the piano throughout. Each performer plays his or her way through a sequence of fifty-three musical fragments, precisely notated, repeating each as many times as desired before going on to the next. When all the performers have gone through all the fragments, the piece is over. The total aural result is that of a static, relatively consonant sound mass, with constant but slight changes in its details. To fully savor it as a kind of sonic "event" one needs to hear a live performance in its totality. (For recordings of this work, see Additional Listening.)

The move away from electronics to live performers in the 1970s was a feature not only of minimalism but of all of classical music, as modernism waned. Reich wrote as early as 1970:

> In any music which depends on a steady pulse, as my music does, it is actually tiny micro-variations of that pulse created by human beings, playing instruments or singing, that gives life to the music. . . . Electronic music as such will gradually die and be absorbed into the ongoing music of people singing and playing instruments. (25, 28)

Another, and perhaps more familiar, type of minimalism is that in which short fragments are repeated, but gradually undergo transformation in the process—notes may be changed, or notes may be added to the pattern as it is repeated. The "Violin Solo Music" from *Einstein on the Beach* by Philip Glass (CD 5/14) is an example of this.

Einstein on the Beach is an opera lasting nearly five hours, without intermission, and is treated in the next chapter. It is interesting to note that minimalist composers, having taken their vow of poverty in submitting to a "radical reduction in compositional materials" (including for the most part chromaticism, modulation, and closed forms), have had recourse, whether intentionally or not, to compositional devices found in older music—music that had not yet embraced the more recent musical language of Romanticism, for instance. Thus we find in the Glass example the use of a "ground bass"—a recurring pattern of notes that, in itself, constituted in the seventeenth and eighteenth centuries a kind of minimalism! The sequence of notes is set out in

CD 5/14 (1:35)
"Violin Solo Music," from *Einstein on the Beach*, by Philip Glass. 1976.

Transcription 21.1, a pattern of four pitches, with one repeated, to make a five-beat rhythm that is most of the time adhered to in the excerpt.

Transcription 21.1
Five-note ground bass from Glass's *Einstein on the Beach*

In the 1980s minimalism began to mellow considerably: the obstinately uncompromising ultralong stretches of repetition were modified; the harmonic changes were more frequent and the harmonic palette became richer; traces of chromaticism and functional harmony made their appearance (the last movement of Adams's *Grand Pianola Music* of 1982 includes, probably with parodistic intent, a great deal of dominant-to-tonic progression—see Additional Listening); there was greater variety of instrumental color; and there were settings of English-language texts, especially by American poets, including Walt Whitman, Emily Dickinson, and William Carlos Williams. (The operatic works of John Adams, Philip Glass, and others are treated in Chapter 22.) Minimalism's great popularity, and the attendant star status of composers such as Reich, Glass, and Adams, led to commissions and performances by major orchestras.

CD 5/15 (4:35)
Tehillim, Part I (excerpt), by Steve Reich. 1981.

Reich's *Tehillim* of 1981 (CD 5/15) is illustrative of the adaptations that minimalism had undergone by that time. It is a setting of four Psalms in ancient Hebrew for four women's voices and a small ensemble featuring percussion. The first of the four has as its text the first four verses of Psalm 19. The pitch material is strictly diatonic (the tones of the d minor scale), but of these only four (d, e, g, and a, together with the d and the e in the upper octave) are much used. The limited pitch material, and especially the repeated emphasis on the high d and e, contributes to the minimalist feel of the piece. We have already noted the resorting to older structural devices (ground bass in *Einstein on the Beach*) in music made out of simple minimal material. In this case, the ancient device of canon is a basic structural feature. (Recall CD 2/36, the canon on "Jesus Wept" by the eighteenth century composer William Billings.)

At the beginning of this excerpt, the first voice sings alone, with a clapping background reminiscent of Reich's *Clapping Music*, for about the first 1:14, at which time the second voice joins with the opening material, and the two sing in a canon at a very close time interval. At 1:53 the string bass enters with long sustained notes. The other voices enter subsequently. At about 3:07, the tempo starts to slow.

This excerpt includes a little more than a third of the first movement. As is the case with *In C*, the texture thins out again, and the movement ends with percussion alone on the "clapping" theme. (For a recording of the complete work, see Additional Listening.)

More recent minimalist works manage to retain the quintessentials of pulsation, repetition, and tonality—the last somewhat expanded. Most clearly a translation into orchestral terms of earlier minimalism's procedures and overall affect are pieces such as John Adams's 28-minute *Fearful Symmetries* (1988) and Steve Reich's 15-minute *Three Movements for Orchestra* (1986). Adams's orchestral works without text tend to be more "symphonic" and often parodistic. But repetitition (though not tonality or pulsation) is a less prominent feature in Adams's highly expressive and moving works set to English texts, including the 32-minute *Harmonium* (1980–81), for large orchestra and chorus, with texts by John Donne and Emily Dickinson, and his 19-minute *The Wound-Dresser* (1988), for baritone and orchestra, a setting of a portion of Walt Whitman's graphic and wrenching poem of the same name from his *Drum-Taps*, a memoir of the Civil War. (See Additional Listening for recordings of these works.)

At the start of the new century, minimalism remains with us, as a still recognizable but now less abrasive and less segregated part of the whole panorama of American classical music. It is to the rest of this panorama that we now turn.

MODERNISM GIVES WAY TO ASSIMILATION AND RECONNECTION

Reconnection with Classical Music of the Past

That "the past is dead and must be buried" has been identified as "the chief tenet of modernism" (Bolcom, in Rochberg, *Aesthetics* viii). But as modernism has receded, there has emerged a marked tendency for music to reestablish connections with the past. The composer Billy Jim Layton wrote, as long ago as 1965:

> The best hope for the world today, the direction, I am fully confident, of the important, vital music to be written, is that of a responsive and enlightened liberalism. . . . Today there is need for a new, rich, meaningful, varied, understandable and vital music which maintains contact with the great central tradition of humanism in the West. (Layton)

George Rochberg has said, "If it appears that a large part of the music of the twentieth century was a *music of forgetting,* the music of the end of the century and beyond must become a music of remembering" (*Aesthetics* 87). This "remembering" takes many forms.

The first is outright quotation. Quotation in the new music is handled in highly individual ways and varies greatly in extensiveness. It can be obscure and fragmentary, as in the twelve-minute *Contra Mortem et Tempus* (1965) by

George Rochberg (see Additional Listening). Similarly, in the first movement of his twenty-minute Piano Quartet (1976), William Bolcom makes a very oblique reference to the music of Chopin. Less obscure is the type of quotation in which recognizable phrases of older music appear. In *Ancient Voices of Children* (1970), by George Crumb, a toy piano plays a portion of a phrase from the eighteenth-century Anna Magdalena Bach Notebook, which slows to a stop before its end, "like clockwork . . . running down." (See Additional Listening.) A similar feeling is evoked in Crumb's twenty-minute *Black Angels* (also 1970) for amplified string quartet, which quotes eleven measures of Schubert's *Death and the Maiden* as "a fragile echo of an ancient music."

CD 5/16 (4:35)
"1 after Marc-Antoine Charpentier," from *Prism*, by Jacob Druckman. New York Philharmonic, Zubin Mehta, conductor.

A somewhat different effect is achieved in the 22-minute *Prism* (1980), by Jacob Druckman, in which recognizable snatches of older music are interrupted or overlaid with dissonant and/or atonal material. This is illustrated in the first movement, which is based on music from the seventeenth-century opera *Médée* (Medea, 1694) by Marc-Antoine Charpentier. (Similar tendencies exist in the other arts. A precisely parallel example of such "quotation" in the visual realm can be seen in the work of Doug and Mike Starn [b. 1961], who, in *The Christ Series*, have produced a great number of pieces based on reworked photographic images of *The Dead Christ*, a painting done by Philippe de Champagne about 1650, in the same century as the Charpentier opera quoted by Druckman.) Through the dissonant and somewhat fragmented texture of the symphonic score, the seventeenth-century music, the motives of which are hinted at, comes into full focus for only a few seconds at a time at 0:48, 1:07, 1:24, only to become engulfed in the mist and chaos each time. At 2:08 the older music is allowed to sound uninterruptedly for almost a minute, only to be virtually swallowed up for the remainder of the movement. The two subsequent movements are also based on music from older operas on the subject of Medea from Greek mythology: *Il Giasone* (Jason, 1648), by Francesco Cavalli, and *Medea* (1797), by Luigi Cherubini.

Eclecticism and the Assimilation of Other Musics

Composers have also been influenced by the traditional music of cultures from other continents. We have already noted the influence of African, Indian, and Indonesian music on composers such as Lou Harrison and Steve Reich. But American composers have also incorporated into their works references to various genres of Western popular music, as did Charles Ives nearly a century ago. References to jazz and blues are not as common or as overt as they were in the 1920s and 1930s, but they are present in very attenuated form in works such as the appropriately titled *Déjà Vu* (1977) of Michael Colgrass, and the final movement of John Harbison's Symphony No. 1. References to other genres of vernacular music are fairly widespread. William Bolcom's thirteen-minute Quintet for brass (1980) is a tribute to his various ancestors, and in it are snatches of a waltz (rendered momentarily with a Mexican flavor), a march, a gospel hymn, and a bravura cornet solo, as well as a Renaissance canzona. It is all done in the spirit of "remembered fathers," as Ives would have done. But references in more recent works have tended to be distinctly parodistic, even satirical, in manner. In this vein could be mentioned *From the Other Side* (1988) by Donald Martino, *Quartetset* (1995) by Sebastian Currier, and, even more extreme, *Carny* (1992) by John Zorn.

MUSIC WITH ASSOCIATIVE CONNOTATIONS

Although the term *program music* is not in favor, there has been a marked resurgence of music that has, in one way or another, associations beyond the music itself. As a significant sampling of works, approximately half of the compositions awarded the Pulitzer Prize in the 1970s through the 1990s show some extramusical impetus or association. The very use of a title for a work (a practice now increasingly common) suggests the desire to communicate something more than can be done by the generic term "quartet" or "symphony," or clinical titles such as *Synchronism* or *Phonemena*. In an age of sophistication, titles may be indirect in their significance; as George Crumb has said in one case, they are "metaphors chosen more for poetic values rather than for specific meanings."

A text, of course, constitutes a strong associational element. In the new music, there is a notable return to practices of word-setting that are more lyrical than the jagged and fragmented lines of modernism, and show attention to natural word rhythms and inflections and a concern to let the words be understood. Composers have shown a deeper concern and commitment both to the poetry and to the poet. Rather than setting a text for a single work and letting it go at that, some composers have developed more profound relationships with the works of particular literary figures, extending over a considerable period of time and encompassing a series of works. This has been the case with George Crumb and the works of Federico García Lorca, with David Del Tredici and the *Alice* books of Lewis Carroll, and with Stephen Albert and the works of James Joyce.

In the case of music without text (the domain of traditional program music), composers have in some instances made public the extramusical associations attached to their works, thereby validating them for the listener. Mysticism in various forms has been the point of departure for many of George Crumb's purely instrumental works: numerology, for example, in the case of *Black Angels* (completed on Friday the 13th, 1970); astrology and the zodiac for *Makrokosmos I* (1974). Christian mysticism is the impetus for *Black Host* (1967) for organ, by William Bolcom, based on the occult "black mass."

Buddhist concepts of earth, man, and heaven are the stimuli for each of the three movements of the Piano Concerto of Peter Lieberson. Dreams, or the state of dreaming, may be taken into account, according to the composers themselves, by listeners who seek an explanation of the nature and form of George Rochberg's *Music for the Magic Theater* (1966) and William Bolcom's *Whisper Moon* (1971). All of this can be interpreted as evidence of composers seeking, and indeed needing, to relate their music, and art itself, to larger issues of life—neither (in Rochberg's words) "to seal art off from life" nor to *confuse* art with life, as some of the experimentalists had done. As Rochberg wrote of his *Contra Mortem et Tempus* (1965), composed after the death of his son:

> It . . . became clearer than ever before that the only justification for claiming one was engaged in the artistic act was to open one's art completely to life and its entire gamut of terror and joys (real and imagined); and to find, if one could, new ways to transmute these into whatever magic one was capable of. (Notes)

The New Relationship to the Public

The following statements by two composers of the same generation (John Corigliano, b. 1938; David Del Tredici, b. 1937) represent the new attitude toward the audience and the reassessed view of the function of the composer:

> I don't understand composers with what I call an eternity complex, people who ignore today's audiences and think of themselves as misunderstood prophets whose masterpieces will be seen as such in a century or so. That, I think, reveals a basic contempt for audiences. . . . I wish to be *understood*, and I think it is the job of every composer to reach out to his audience with all means at his disposal. Communication should always be a primary goal. (Corigliano, emphasis in original)

> Composers now are beginning to realize that if a piece excites an audience, *that doesn't mean it's terrible.* For my generation, it is considered vulgar to have an audience really, *really* like a piece on a first hearing. But why are we writing music except to move people and to be expressive? (Del Tredici, qtd. in Rockwell 83, emphasis in original)

The new accessibility and commitment to *communication*, however interpreted, has with some composers taken the form of *music as social statement*. Steve Reich's *Come Out* (1966) is a tape composition based on the recorded statement of a black man injured by the police. Christian Wolff, an early associate of John Cage and Morton Feldman, has since his *Changing the System* (1972–73) turned his attention mostly to political subjects, using labor and protest songs as material; examples of his work in this vein are his *Wobbly Music* (1975–76), *The Death of Mother Jones* (1977), and *Peace Marches 1, 2,* and *3* (1983–84). An eclectic composer who has turned to social statement is the pianist Frederic Rzewski; *Coming Together* and *Attica* (1972) both had as their source and inspiration a letter from an inmate at the New York state prison in Attica at the time of the prison uprising there. Best known is his *The People United Will Never Be Defeated!,* a long set of variations for piano on a leftist Chilean song. In this turning to social statement, there is an interesting parallel with the folk-protest movement of the 1930s and 1940s. Both movements suffered from the same kind of limitation: that of using (in Rockwell's words) "an idiom that speaks to a far different social and racial group than the victims of the oppression that is being protested."

IN CONCLUSION

The closing years of the twentieth century in American fine-art music were a time of the full blooming of the "thousand flowers"—a time of unprecedented diversity and contrast. As we conclude the exploration of this music, the point needs to be made that *not all works* that have the capacity "to move people and to be expressive," as David Del Tredici puts it, make use of quotation, nor are they all in any overt way referential to the music of the past, or to the music of other cultures. To cite individual works of which this is true is to leave out many more, but as a mere hint of the riches there to be explored, there is the dreamlike exoticism of *Aftertones of Infinity* (1978) and *Music of Amber* (1981) by Joseph Schwantner (b. 1943); the often mercurial indulgence of virtuosity of the Concerto for Clarinet and Orchestra (1977) by John Corigliano (b. 1938); the striking and sometimes sudden contrasts of the expressive Symphony No. 4 (1986, see Additional Listening), with its text by Theodore Roethke, by William Bolcom (b. 1938); and the sheer musicality and sustained interest, moment by moment, of the 23-minute *Passages* (1981), on poems of A. R. Ammons, and the Symphony No. 1 (1982) by Ellen Taaffe Zwilich (b. 1939). "Way to Go" (CD 5/17), the sixth and last song of *Passages,* makes a fitting close to our consideration of the transcendance of modernism.

> West light flat on trees:
>   bird flying
>   deep out in blue glass:
>   uncertain wind
> stirring the leaves: this is
>   the world we have:
>   take it

CD 5/17 (3:46)
"Way to Go," from *Passages.* Music by Ellen Taaffe Zwilich. Poem by A. R. Ammons. 1981. Janice Felty, vocal, with The Boston Musica Viva.

Text "Way to Go," A. R. Ammons

(Copyright © 1964 by A. R. Ammons, from *Collected Poems 1951–1971* by A. R. Ammons. Reprinted by permission of W. W. Norton & Company, Inc.

■ PROJECTS

1. Listen to a fairly extended minimalist piece (perhaps one mentioned in the chapter) and write a brief paper examining your own reactions, both as you listen and afterwards. Could they best be described as "boredom," "restless annoyance," "trance," or some other? Did they change as you listened? Was there another distinct reaction when the piece was over?

2. If you are acquainted with contemporary developments in one of the other arts, write a brief paper comparing its current state with that of music, as described in this chapter. Has there been a move to transcend modernism?

3. Write a brief paper on the use of titles in contemporary music. Include examples of composers who use them, and composers who don't. Does a title alter your expectations of a piece of music? Consider your perception, for example, of George Crumb's *A Haunted Landscape* (NW 326) if it were simply known as *Piece for Orchestra;* or of George Rochberg's Concerto for Oboe and Orchestra (NW 335) if it were called *A Haunted Landscape.*

4. Does it bother you to hear a piece by a contemporary composer that might possibly be mistaken for the music of some previous century? Why? Write a brief but well-thought-out essay on this.

5. The composer Carl Ruggles became concerned when audiences at contemporary music concerts in New York earlier in the twentieth century actually increased, viewing it as a sign that contemporary music was "selling out." And Milton Babbitt, in his famous (and mistitled) article "Who Cares If You Listen?" of 1958, suggested the "very real possibility of complete elimination of the public and social aspects of musical composition." On the other hand, John Corigliano, as quoted in this chapter, says that he does not "understand composers . . . who ignore today's audiences and think of themselves as misunderstood prophets." Write a brief essay explaining where you stand on this issue, and why.

■ ADDITIONAL LISTENING

John Adams

Fearful Symmetries, for orchestra. Orchestra of St. Luke's. Cond. John Adams. WEA/Atlantic/Nonesuch 79218.

Fearful Symmetries, for orchestra. On *The John Adams Earbox* (10-CD box set). Orchestra of St. Luke's. Cond. John Adams. WEA/Atlantic/Nonesuch 79453.

Grand Pianola Music, for 3 sopranos, 2 pianos, winds, brass, and percussion. London Sinfonietta. Cond. John Adams. WEA/Atlantic/Nonesuch 79219.

Grand Pianola Music, for 3 sopranos, 2 pianos, winds, brass, and percussion. On *The John Adams Earbox* (10-CD box set). Orchestra of St. Luke's. Cond. John Adams. WEA/Atlantic/Nonesuch 79453.

Harmonium. San Francisco Symphony Orchestra. Cond. Edo de Waart. ECM Records 821465.

Harmonium. On *The John Adams Earbox* (10-CD box set). Orchestra of St. Luke's. Cond. John Adams. WEA/Atlantic/Nonesuch 79453.

Shaker Loops, for 7 strings or string orchestra. Orchestra of St. Luke's. Cond. John Adams. WEA/Atlantic/Nonesuch 79360.

Shaker Loops, for 7 strings or string orchestra. On *The John Adams Earbox* (10-CD box set). Orchestra of St. Luke's. Cond. John Adams. WEA/Atlantic/Nonesuch 79453.

The Wound-Dresser, for baritone and orchestra. Sanford Sylvan, baritone. Orchestra of St. Luke's. Cond. John Adams. WEA/Atlantic/Nonesuch 79218.

The Wound-Dresser, for baritone and orchestra. On *The John Adams Earbox* (10-CD box set). Orchestra of St. Luke's. Cond. John Adams. WEA/Atlantic/Nonesuch 79453.

William Bolcom

Symphony No. 4. Joan Morris, vocal. St. Louis Symphony Orchestra. Cond. Leonard Slatkin. New World Records 80356.

George Crumb

Ancient Voices of Children, for mezzo soprano and boy soprano, oboe, mandolin, harp, amplified piano and toy piano, and 3 percussionists. Contemporary Chamber Ensemble. Cond. Arthur Weisberg. WEA/Atlantic/Nonesuch 79149.

Steve Reich

It's Gonna Rain, for tape. On *Steve Reich 1965–1995*. WEA/Atlantic/Nonesuch 79451.

Tehillim. London Symphony Orchestra. Cond. Michael Tilson Thomas. WEA/Atlantic/Nonesuch 79295.

Three Movements for Orchestra. London Symphony Orchestra. Cond. Michael Tilson Thomas. WEA/Atlantic/Nonesuch 79295.

Three Movements for Orchestra. On *Steve Reich 1965–1995*. WEA/Atlantic/Nonesuch 79451.

Terry Riley

In C, for instrumental ensemble, choir, and solo voice. On *Terry Riley In C*. State University Center of Creative and Performing Arts, New Music Center, with Terry Riley, saxophone. Sony 7178.

In C, for instrumental ensemble, choir, and solo voice. On *Terry Riley: 25th Anniversary Concert In C*. New Albion Records 71.

George Rochberg

Contra Mortem et Tempus. Aeolian Quartet. CRI 768.

CHAPTER

22

Opera

Why a chapter on opera? There are at least two reasons. First, significant American operas have been written and produced over the past seventy years that are worthy of our acquaintance; and second, at the turn of the millennium American opera not only is thriving but also has become a fascinating arena for the exploration of the new and different approaches to both drama and music.

Opera *is* drama. It is drama expressed *through* music. As the most complex and comprehensive of all musical forms, it also encompasses literature. There is (in most opera) a story, told through the poetry (indifferent, good, or superb) of the libretto. There is certainly a stage, with all the movement, setting, and, above all, acting that a stage implies. But it is the music (usually continuous) that is the most compelling element—that makes it an expressive whole. There is, of course, singing, by one, two, or a stage full of performers, but there are times when there is just instrumental music, which can effectively project a mood, build suspense, or accompany or actually further the action.

What about opera's opposite number, the popular musical theater, which we explored in considerable detail in Chapter 13? It certainly has some of the same elements, but it is a different mix and serves a different function. It began as spoken drama of a distinctly popular nature, with songs interspersed, and despite the evolutions through which we traced it, it remains essentially that. It is popular entertainment, with its own clientele. That clientele has certain expectations, and if popular musical theater is to *be* popular, those norms must be satisfied without too much experimentation or departure from its norms. It must have, first and foremost, popular songs—songs that can be hummed by the audience as they leave the theater, and that may become "hits"—the writing of which requires a rare talent indeed! It must feature dance as a vital element. And it must (usually) have a happy ending. Popular musical theater, as we saw in Chapter 13, has adopted some of opera's techniques. But it has not *become* opera; nor is there any reason why it should. Each has its own valued place in American culture.

OPERA IN AMERICA BEFORE THE 1930s: AN UNASSIMILATED ALIEN

For two hundred years, between the performance of the ballad farce *Flora, or the Hob in the Well* in Charleston in 1735 and the premiers of *Four Saints in Three Acts* (1934) and *Porgy and Bess* (1935), opera was essentially an exotic import—an immigrant form, often performed in a foreign language. *Rip Van Winkle*, by George Frederick Bristow, was an opera on a thoroughly American tale by one of America's most competent composers, but its successful run of seventeen performances in New York in 1855 hardly set a precedent for American opera in its day. Scott Joplin's *Treemonisha*, a remarkable work based on African American life and musical idioms, had only a barely noticed performance with piano accompaniment in 1915. (It was lavishly staged and recorded in 1975, and was awarded the Pulitzer Prize in 1976.)

TRADITIONAL AMERICAN OPERA BEGINNING IN THE 1930s

Some Forerunners

There were some harbingers of change early in the twentieth century. When the Metropolitan Opera of New York, already the nation's leading company, acquired a new general manager in 1908—the Italian Giulio Gatti-Casazza— his enlightened idea of a proper repertory embraced a blend of the old and the new, including new operas by native composers. In 1910 he produced the first American opera that the Metropolitan, already more than a quarter of a century old, had ever performed: *The Pipe of Desire,* by Frederick Converse. Before Gatti-Casazza left in 1935, he had produced a total of sixteen American operas in twenty-seven seasons. Among these were *Natoma* (1911), on an American Indian theme, by Victor Herbert; *Mona* (1912) by Horatio Parker; *Shanewis* (1918), another Indian opera, by Charles Cadman; and *The King's Henchmen* (1927) and *Peter Ibbetson* (1931), two operas by Deems Taylor that had considerable success. Louis Gruenberg's *The Emperor Jones* (1933), as appropriate to its subject (it is based on the play by Eugene O'Neill), uses African American musical elements. *Merry Mount* (1934), an opera by Howard Hanson after a story by Hawthorne, was the last American opera of the Gatti-Casazza regime. Some of these operas were worthy forerunners of what was to come in the "definitive decade" of the 1930s. The quarter-century 1910–35, under Gatti-Casazza, were the best years for American opera by the nation's highest-budgeted opera company; in the thirty-eight years following, under the next three managers, the number of American operas produced fell to a mere nine!

THREE LANDMARKS OF THE 1930s

The innovations of the 1930s were decidedly not happening at the Metropolitan, or at any other major opera house. Of the three very different operas we will now examine, one was premiered in Hartford, Connecticut, one in Boston, and the other in a small theater in New York.

The Devil and Daniel Webster

The first two, despite their vast differences, were both designated by their authors as "folk operas." The one-act opera *The Devil and Daniel Webster* (1938), by Douglas Moore (1893–1969), is an operatic version of the fanciful short story of the same title by the Americanist writer Stephen Vincent Benét. (Daniel Webster appears in another opera, with a libretto by Gertrude Stein,

CD 5/18 (2:42)
"I've Got a Ram Goliath," from *The Devil and Daniel Webster,* by Douglas Moore. 1938.

The Mother of Us All—Americanist, but in quite a different vein. See p. 440.)
Though no actual folk tunes are used, the musical language of New England
fiddle tunes and folk hymns is reflected in the lively rhythms and simple triadic
harmonies. There are solo "arias" in the operatic tradition; "I've Got a Ram
Goliath" (CD 5/18) is Daniel Webster's boasting assurance to the frightened
Jabez Stone and his wife, Mary, that the devil (to whom Jabez has sold his
soul) is no match for him.

Text, "I've Got a Ram
Goliath" (Douglas
Moore)

I've got a ram Goliath,
He was raised on Marshfield grain.
He's got horns like a morning-glory vine
And he butts like a railroad train.
I've got a ram Goliath,
Named for the Philistine.
And I wrestle him ev'ry Tuesday night
With these two hands of mine.
I've got a bull, King Stephen,
A bull with a rolling eye.
When he stamps his foot, the stars come out
And the lightening blinks in the sky.
I've got a bull, King Stephen,
With a kick like a cannon ball.
But he acts like a suckling turtle-dove
When I go into his stall.
I'm not an idle boaster.
Let this be said of me.
I was born in old New Hampshire
And always fought for the free.
They know about Daniel Webster
Wherever the eagle flies,
And they know he stands for the Union,
And doesn't stand for lies.
Ask at the workmen's cottage,
Ask at the farmer's gate!
They know about Daniel Webster,
The pride of the Granite State.
They know about Daniel Webster
As only neighbors can.
And he'll fight ten thousand devils
To save a New Hampshire man!

Porgy and Bess

It is quite a different American world that we enter in George Gershwin's folk opera, *Porgy and Bess* (1935). In Charleston, South Carolina, in the early part of the twentieth century, there was a crippled black beggar named Samuel Smalls who got himself around by means of a cart pulled by a goat, and thus acquired the name of Goat-Sammy. A white Charleston writer, Du Bose Heyward, wrote a short novel—his first—based on this character, whom he renamed Porgy. He set the story in Catfish Row (originally Cabbage Row), a large ancient mansion with a courtyard that had become a black tenement. Through his knowledge of his city and its black people, he surrounded Porgy with thoroughly believable characters, and spun a tale of humor, foreboding, violence, brief joy, and desolation. The novel appeared in 1926. George Gershwin read it, liked it, and wrote to the author proposing that they collaborate in making an opera out of it. (Heyward was at the time working with his wife on a play adaptation, which was staged in 1927. The play, in turn, *nearly* became a musical produced by Al Jolson, with music by Jerome Kern.)

Gershwin had many commitments at that time; after many delays, there was a period of intensive effort. Gershwin went to Charleston during the winter of 1934, and spent the summer of that year on one of the Sea Islands off its coast—composing, observing, and absorbing all he could of the atmosphere and the black people's music, with which he felt a great affinity. (See CD 1/9 for an African American spiritual recorded in the Sea Islands.)

For those acquainted only with some of the superb songs of the opera (and who does not know "I Got Plenty o' Nuthin'"; "Bess, You Is My Woman Now"; "It Ain't Necessarily So"; and, above all, "Summertime"?), the experience of the opera as a whole must come as something of a revelation. *Porgy and Bess* is a full-fledged, full-scale opera, in the realistic tradition. The story has been transformed into a tightly knit tragedy, though not without elements of joy, optimism, and especially (a thing Gershwin insisted upon) humor. The volatile central figure is Bess, around whom the action revolves.

Although Gershwin used no actual African American folk music, there are touches of unmistakable realism and authenticity in the music. These lesser-known treasures are worth the experience of hearing the complete opera. For instance, the dramatic situation in which more than one thing is going on at the same time onstage is reflected musically in "Summer time/Seven come, seven come to pappy!" (Act 1, Scene 1). In the opening street scene, Clara is singing ("Summer time") to quiet her baby while the men are shooting craps. In the second scene, after Robbins's murder by Crown, his widow and her friends are mourning and hoping that enough money will be put into the saucer to pay for his burial. The call-and-response of "Come on, sister . . ." (Act 1, Scene 2) establishes the atmosphere of an impromptu church service, in which Porgy chants the exhortations of a preacher. The Street Cries of the Strawberry Woman, the Honey Man, and the Crab Man in Act 2, Scene 3, are colorful bits of authentic street lore. The "hurricane bell" and the fervent prayers of the terrified people awaiting the storm (Act 2, end of Scene 3, and Scene 4) include a passage for voices alone in which six solo singers chant freely over a background of continuous humming—inspired by what Gershwin heard while standing outside a black church in Hendersonville, South Carolina. Gershwin thoroughly immersed himself in the musical ambience of the South Carolina blacks. Du Bose Heyward described how, on a visit to a meeting of the Gullah blacks on a remote Carolina Sea Island, Gershwin joined wholeheartedly in the "shouting." Of his whole South Carolina experience Heyward said, "To George it was more like a homecoming than an exploration."

Four Saints in Three Acts

CD 5/19 (1:40)
Vision of the Holy
Ghost: "Pigeons on
the Grass Alas," from
*Four Saints in Three
Acts*. Music by Virgil
Thomson. Libretto by
Gertrude Stein. 1934.

In 1934 an opera was premiered in Hartford, Connecticut, that broke new ground for the American lyrical stage and that forecast, in interesting ways, the nonnarrative musical theater that was to come into being more than forty years later. *Four Saints in Three Acts* with music by Virgil Thomson was described by its scenarist, Maurice Grosser, as "both an opera and a choreographic spectacle." The text is by Gertrude Stein, a formidable talent of forceful originality in the use of language. The opera dispenses with plot in the conventional sense in favor of atmosphere, achieved through a series of "imaginary but characteristic incidents." It is set in Spain, and its principal characters are Saint Teresa and Saint Ignatius. Literal expectations must be laid aside; there are actually fifteen saints in all, in four acts, and one of the saints is represented by two singers identically dressed. The text is simply and beautifully set by Thomson to a light and transparent orchestral accompaniment so that every word can be heard and understood. It was Thomson's idea, daring in its day, that an all-black cast of singers could best interpret the words and music. The memorable sets for the first production were of draped cellophane. Act 1 takes place at Avila; Act 2 is a garden party in the country near Barcelona; Act 3 is set in the garden of a monastery on a sea coast. Act 4 takes place in heaven. CD 5/19 is an excerpt from Act 3's "Pigeons on the Grass Alas" which is, according to Stein, St. Ignatius's Vision of the Holy Ghost.

Virgil Thomson had this advice for the listeners:

> Please do not try to construe the words of this opera literally or to seek in it any abstruse symbolism. If, by means of the poet's liberties with logic and the composer's constant use of the simplest elements in our

musical vernacular, something is here evoked of the childlike gaiety and mystical strength of lives devoted in common to non-materialistic end, the authors will consider their message to have been communicated. (Thomson)

Saint Ignatius:	Pigeons on the grass alas.
Chorus I, II:	Pigeons on the grass alas.
Saint Ignatius:	Short longer grass short longer longer shorter yellow grass. Pigeons large pigeons on the shorter longer yellow grass alas pigeons on the grass.
Chorus I, II:	If they were not pigeons what were they.
Saint Ignatius:	If they were not pigeons on the grass alas what were they.
Compère:	He had heard of a third and he asked about it.
Chorus I, II:	It was a magpie in the sky.
Saint Ignatius:	If a magpie in the sky on the sky can not cry if the pigeon on the grass alas can alas and to pass the pigeon on the grass alas and the magpie in the sky on the sky and to try and to try alas on the grass alas the pigeon on the grass the pigeon on the grass and alas.

Chorus I, II:	They might be very well very well very well they might be they might be very well they might be very well very well they might be.
	     Let Lucy Lily Lily Lucy Lucy let Lucy
	     Lucy Lily Lily Lily Lily Lily let Lily Lucy
	     Lucy let Lily: Let Lucy Lily.

Compère:	Scene One.

AMERICAN OPERA IN RELATION TO AMERICAN CULTURE AFTER THE 1930s

Two of the three operas selected for attention from the 1930s had American subjects and settings. This is noted not as an incitement to chauvinism but because any dramatic form takes root and flourishes best in the soil of its native culture. Composer and writer Charles Hamm, in a 1961 essay critical of American opera composers up to that time, made that point with regard to

Italy, Germany, and Russia—countries that developed strong operatic traditions *and indigenous repertoire*. He wrote: "The history of opera tells us, clearly and repeatedly, that the popularity of opera in those countries can be traced back to successful attempts by composers to create operas completely comprehensible to audiences in those countries, comprehensible not merely because they are written in the vernacular but because *they have something to do with the culture of the country"* (Hamm 289, emphasis added).

Earlier operas had dealt with American subjects (recall *The Indian Princess* of 1808, based on the story of Pocahontas, and Bristow's *Rip Van Winkle* of 1855), but the derivative nature of their musical idioms (English in the first case, Italian in the second) mitigated their validity as authentic expressions of American culture. Given the state of American musical development when they were composed, one could hardly have expected otherwise. By the 1930s, however, America was developing its own diverse musical voices. In the years that followed, a number of operas were composed that had a valid and palpable relation to the culture of the country. None fits this description better than Virgil Thomson's *The Mother of Us All* (1947), with libretto by Gertrude Stein, who had written the text of *Four Saints in Three Acts,* and who, despite her self-exile, continued to feel a strong identification with her native land. Thomson explains in his preface to the score: *"The Mother of Us All* is a pageant. Its theme is the winning in the United States of political rights for women. Its story is the life and career of Susan B. Anthony (1820–1906). Some of the characters are historical, others imaginary. They include figures as widely separated in time as John Quincy Adams and Lillian Russell." As in the earlier *Four Saints in Three Acts,* the vocal writing is exceptionally true to the rhythms of speech; and the music, of a self-effacing simplicity, reinforces its relevance through the use of nineteenth-century-style waltzes, marches, and hymnlike tunes.

After *The Mother of Us All,* the floodgates were opened for a multitude of works having "something to do with the culture of the country." Actual historical figures were the basis for two more operas by Douglas Moore. The first was *The Ballad of Baby Doe* (1956), based on the lives of Horace Tabor, Augusta Tabor, and Baby Doe, from Colorado's fabulous mining era. The second was *Carry Nation* (1966), based on events in the life of the turn-of-the-century Prohibitionist that led her to launch her crusade. Marc Blitzstein, who had written a famous leftist opera, *The Cradle Will Rock,* in 1937, was at work on *Sacco and Vanzetti,* an opera based on that famous case, when he died in 1964. Operas based on novels included *Regina* (1949), by Marc Blitzstein, on Lillian Hellman's *The Little Foxes,* and *Of Mice and Men* (1970), by Carlisle Floyd, on John Steinbeck's novel of the same name. A shorter work by Lukas Foss is *The Jumping Frog of Calaveras County* (1950) on the Mark Twain story. Robert Ward's *The Crucible* (1961) is based on the Arthur Miller play about the Salem witch hunts. Carlisle Floyd's best-known work is *Susannah* (1954), which transfers the apocryphal story of Susannah and the Elders to rural Tennessee, where it is thus played out in a setting of rural and primitive southern orthodoxy—stern, intolerant, and hypocritical. Floyd's more recent *Willie Stark* (1981) is an adaptation of the novel *All the King's Men* by Robert Penn Warren, based on the career of the legendary Louisiana politician Huey Long. Thomas Pasatieri made an opera out of *The Trial of Mary Lincoln* (1972), and Jack Beeson used a famous American murder as the basis for *Lizzie Borden* (1965).

NEW OPERA IN THE LAST QUARTER OF THE CENTURY

Beginning in the 1970s, new approaches to the combining of music and drama began to be tried out, resulting in new genres of serious musical theater. The chapter on opera is the place to consider them in all their variety, because explorers who have gone in directions that differ as widely as Meredith Monk, whose wordless dramas of music and gesture require a live audience, and Robert Ashley, whose word-laden dramas for television eliminate a live audience, have elected to *call* their productions operas. They can be considered, very roughly, as representing two approaches, with enough gray areas and overlapping to challenge effectively the division.

Remaking Traditional Genres in Traditional Venues

A public symposium in 1994 involving four opera composers had as its title "Remaking American Opera." The verb is an apt one. It became clear by the 1990s that "grand opera," meaning opera given with lavish staging and full orchestras in major opera houses, was not to be written off after all by innovative American composers, but had been "remade." New American operas in the old tradition of opulent production, though they constitute a minute proportion of the repertoire, do appear from time to time in the major opera theaters. They are not commissioned and produced altogether out of a sense of artistic altruism; the amazing rise in popularity (referred to in the preceding chapter) of minimalist composers such as Philip Glass and John Adams led the big houses to produce, for sellout crowds, Glass's *Einstein on the Beach* (1976), *Satyagraha* (1980), *Akhnaten* (1984), and *The Voyage* (1992); and Adams's *Nixon in China* (1987) and *The Death of Klinghoffer* (1991). All but *Einstein on the Beach* are full-scale "grand operas."

Einstein on the Beach, ultimately responsible for Glass's sudden fame, was written as a mixed-media theater piece to be accompanied by Glass's small amplified ensemble, which played onstage. Musically, *Einstein* is thoroughly minimalist; Andrew Porter, in reviewing the first U. S. performance, described

Photo © Beatriz Schiller

A scene from Philip Glass's mixed-media theater piece, *Einstein on the Beach* (1976).

the music as "in essence a series of extended moto perpetuos, each of them lasting longer than Ravel's 'Bolero'." (*Bolero* is an orchestral piece written by the French composer Maurice Ravel in 1929. In a sense an early minimalist piece, that lasts about fourteen minutes, its melodic material consisting of just two tunes, each of which is played nine times.) The "Violin Solo Music" from *Einstein on the Beach* (CD 5/14, p. 425) conveys the essence. *Einstein* is a four-act opera lasting nearly five hours, without intermission. (Members of the audience come and go during the performance.) The orchestra was the Philip Glass Ensemble of five instrumentalists, the solo violinist who plays the role of Einstein (all heavily amplified), and a sound engineer. Like Thomson's *Four Saints in Three Acts*, a seminal opera of forty years earlier (CD 5/19, pp. 438–39), *Einstein* has no plot in the conventional sense. Glass has designated the genre as "non-literary theater"; the "libretto" consists largely of numerals sung or spoken, and sol-fa syllables. The staging, décor, and direction of Robert Wilson were as responsible for its memorability as was the music. According to Porter, there were "three basic images: a train, a courtroom that dissolves into a prison, and a field of dancers with a spaceship in the sky above them." A transcribed panel discussion between Virgil Thomson and Philip Glass in 1987 included a comparison between *Four Saints in Three Acts* and *Einstein on the Beach*. *Einstein* was described as "pictures set into motion, rather than narratives acted out on stage," and *Four Saints* as "words set into motion in the same way" (Clark).

John Adams went directly into full-scale opera with a commission from the Houston Grand Opera for *Nixon in China* (1987), with a libretto by Alice Goodman. The first act fulfills all the expectations of grand opera. President Nixon and Chairman Mao have bestowed on them, in late-twentieth-century musical and stage terms, all the operatic ceremony associated in eighteenth- and nineteenth-century operas with kings and pharaohs. The spectacle everyone remembers, the landing onstage of the Spirit of 76 and the emergence of Nixon and his wife, Pat, is the equivalent, as Adams has wittily observed, of the onstage elephants in *Aïda* or the burning of Valhalla in *Die Götterdämmerung*—"the things people pay big bucks to see." The second act is, as Adams says, devoted to the women. One of the most expressive moments in the opera comes as something of a surprise in the opera's context; it is Pat's Whitmanesque soliloquy "This is prophetic!" The repetitiousness of the music becomes gentler as the better time she foresees appears as a vision realized in homely terms of everyday life in her own country. In Act 3, statecraft is forgotten, and the leading couples communicate only with each other in private reflections of the past. The opera ends with a soliloquy by Chou En-lai. Repetitive music seems to work well in *Nixon in China*. Here the music, without notable climaxes, stays in the background (as in traditional Chinese opera), changing harmony and color at appropriate times, and letting the vocal lines, which fit the inflections of the text, stand out in relief.

Other grand operas in recent years have also had as their subjects present-day people and events. Adams treated a notorious assassination in the Middle East in *The Death of Klinghoffer* (1991), an opera he sees as "creating a dramatic experience that found a location on the globe within a stone's throw of the birthplace of the three great Western religions, with an incredible historical expanse between the almost biblical timeless past and the painful and invasive present." Anthony Davis's opera *X: The Life and Times of Malcolm X*, on the assassinated black leader, was produced in 1986. It is in a nonminimalist, dissonant idiom. Davis subsequently composed an opera on the Patty Hearst saga. Another opera having to do with assassination is *Harvey Milk* (1995), by Stewart Wallace, which deals with the fatal shooting of San Francisco Mayor George Moscone and Supervisor Harvey Milk, San Francisco's first openly gay elected official, in 1978.

Thus new American operas on American subjects have found themselves a niche, however narrow, in those prestigious halls devoted to the cultivation of that most expensive of all musical genres, "grand opera." But a place in this niche comes at the price of adherence to grand opera's strict traditions and priorities. And operas on current figures and events, however much attention they may attract, are not without their problems, legal, financial, and political. John Adams's *The Death of Klinghoffer* was picketed in San Francisco, and sold-out performances in Los Angeles were cancelled because management feared the loss of support from large and powerful contributors. These factors have caused innovative composers to look to other venues and to create other genres. It is to these that we now direct our attention.

Opera for Less "Grand" Venues

Productions (not always called "operas") that call for more modest resources in more modest venues (in any stage production it is what you *see* that costs the most) have flourished and have invited venturesome and imaginative treatments. *Ravenshead* (1995–98, by Steve Mackey and Rinde Eckert) is one example. There is only one singer/actor (Rinde Eckert, who also wrote the libretto), and a small onstage ensemble of six instrumentalists, only two of which are not electrified. With these resources and a "set" consisting of a single resourcefully designed boat, the story of *The Strange Last Voyage of Donald Crowhurst* is enacted. It is based on the true story of a British businessman who attempted to sail solo in a race around the world; all that was found of him was his empty boat and two sets of logs, one true and the other a fake. The whole is an absorbing *tour de force*.

Creating New Operatic Genres

Meredith Monk (b. 1943) is a multifaceted artist who is composer, singer, dancer, choreographer, and filmmaker but who practices none of those in conventional ways, preferring to work "between the cracks," as she has said, and in the process creating new genres. Though she sparingly uses *spoken* text, she has almost never set words to music, preferring instead to make use of what she calls the *abstract* property of the human voice. Freed from language, which is always specific to a particular culture, she seeks a more direct expression of emotion through wordless vocal sounds. She has mastered and taught to the members of her Meredith Monk Vocal Ensemble a wide variety of what have been called "extended vocal techniques." Asserting that "the body doesn't lie," she bypasses words in dealing with the narrative elements in her pieces, using situations that are simple enough that their emotional aspect is dealt with through gesture, dance, and textless voice. Her music, especially the accompaniments, which are usually done with piano or organ, is minimalist, so that the vocal parts stand out in relief.

CD 5/20 (2:30)
"Choosing Companions" (excerpt), from *Atlas*, by Meredith Monk. 1991.

A recent long work is *Atlas* (1991). It was inspired by the travels of Alexandra David Neel, the explorer who was the first woman to go into Tibet. The basic "poem," as Monk expresses it, is about exploration, as a metaphor for following our *inner* voices no matter what the *outside* world is saying. "Choosing Companions" (CD 5/20) is an early section of the work in which the young heroine is "auditioning" applicants to accompany her on her journey. For more information and background on *Atlas*, "Opera from Elsewhere: Meredith Monk's *Atlas*" is extensive and valuable (Lassetter).

Although Meredith Monk uses film, she stresses the importance of live performance, valuing the "energy" that flows between audience and live performers. In combining different mediums, she seeks "ways of integrating all human resources into one life affirmative form—a healing ritual."

Meredith Monk has said that when sound was added to film, something was lost. Philip Glass, an admirer of Meredith Monk's work, has *removed* the soundtrack from a 1946 film by Jean Cocteau, *La Belle et la Bête* (Beauty and the Beast), and added his own music performed by his seven-piece ensemble and four singers who are placed on the stage in front of the large screen on which the film is projected. The music is composed so that the voices are synchronized as closely as possible with the images on the screen.

Perfect Lives (1979–84) is an opera for television in seven half-hour episodes by Robert Ashley (b. 1930). There are characters, and a scenario, though the "story" is difficult to find and follow through the maze of continuous monochromatic stream-of-consciousness narration by Ashley himself. As to the actual "events" of the scenario, Ashley has said, "There's very little of that in *Perfect Lives*, of people actually doing things." There is a sense of *place* (the Midwest) in the work, which is expressed in the language, the visual images, and the music. Ashley describes the episodes as "songs about the Corn Belt." The music is continuous, and minimalist. The term "cocktail" has been applied (or misapplied) to it; its ingredients derive from pop-rock, boogie-woogie, and jazz. Ashley himself did not write all of the music; he put great emphasis on the work as collaborative effort. Visually the work is a rapidly shifting collage, its chief ingredients being Ashley himself as narrator, the pianist, "Blue" Gene Tyranny (Robert Sheff) performing, the two *dramatis personae* (Isolde and "D," the Captain of the Football Team), and location shots, all manipulated with the techniques available to the video craft of its time.

In view of what has been touched on in the foregoing brief summary, it should be clear that American opera, as we enter the twenty-first century, is *work in progress*.

In Conclusion: *Eric Hermannson's Soul*

American opera today is rich, varied, and vital. It is an encouraging sign of this richness that there are still, when all is said and done, valuable things to be done in its "grand" form. With music by Libby Larsen and a libretto by Chas Rader-Shieber, *Eric Hermannson's Soul* (CD 5/21), leaping over abstract modernism, does what only opera at its best can do: give us richly sung drama, dealing with genuine human emotions on the part of believable human beings in believable situations. Furthermore, it is based, like some of the best in Amer-

CD 5/21 (6:56)
Eric Hermannson's Soul (excerpt). 1998. Music by Libby Larsen. Libretto by Chas Rader-Shieber, after the short story by Willa Cather. Premier performance by Opera Omaha.

ican opera, on some of the best in American literature, and literature not from either the East Coast or the West Coast but from the plains of mid-America.

The opera is based on a short story of the same name by Willa Cather. There are many themes, but the principal one is the conflict of two American cultures—one urban, sophisticated, jaded, dominated by what is seen in this case as the artificiality of the New York art world, and the other rural, simple, but grindingly harsh, dominated by both the beauty and the constant peril of the world of nature. It is a theme dealt with many times by Cather.

Margaret Elliot is, in Cather's words, "beautiful, talented, critical, unsatisfied, tired of the world at twenty-four." She is a captive of her class and position, engaged to Jack, a New York art dealer, whom she will marry out of a sense of duty, of what is expected of her. Eric Hermannson is "handsome . . . a giant in stature," afraid of nothing but the devil. (In this case, the devil as invoked by the possessed preacher Asa Skinner is far more potent and menacing than the New England "Scratch" we met in *The Devil and Daniel Webster*.) Eric is a locally renowned fiddler and dancer, with a previously unrevealed sensitivity to the music of Margaret's world, but beaten down and sobered by the toil and isolation of the Nebraska plains. Margaret finds herself in Eric's world very briefly, as she visits her late father's ranch, in a last adventure before her marriage. In spite of (or perhaps equally because of) the seemingly insurmountable differences in their background, experience, and expectations (Cather says of Margaret that "there were greater distances between her life and Eric's than all the miles which separated Rattlesnake Creek from New York City"), Margaret and Eric fall in love, deeply and equally hopelessly. The poignancy of their love is heightened by the realization that each is in fact an outsider in his and her own community. But the "impossible" union is in fact not to happen. Margaret realizes it first, and in their final climactic scene together tells him that she must return to New York and marry Jack, and both realize they will never see each other again.

Text, *Eric Hermannson's Soul* (excerpt) (Chas Rader-Shieber)	Margaret:	How sweet the corn smells tonight.
	Eric:	Yes, like the flowers in paradise I think. You go away tomorrow? They tell me you go back.
	Margaret:	Yes, we have stayed longer than we should.
	Eric:	You not come back any more?
	Margaret:	No, I expect not.
	Eric:	You forget about this country I guess? Forget about us?
	Margaret:	No Eric. I will not forget. But you must understand. This country isn't for me. And it's not for my husband to be. It was wrong Eric. It was wrong to invite you to the dance. I'm to be married in New York. Soon . . . very soon. All my life I've searched the faces of men, city men, with money and silver success in their eyes. I

searched for the look I found in your eyes. They shine, Eric. They shine for me the way that no eyes will ever shine for me again on earth. I searched in dreams and found that look in this perfect and impossible place . . . this was you . . . you were my great moment and in a moment it will be all gone. Back to the city.

[*Quartet:*]   Dear love, What of all things that be is ever worth one thought from you or me?
Quartet not active participants in the scene.

Margaret: And you won't be sorry you danced tonight?

Eric: I never be sorry. I was never happy before. I never be so happy again, ever. You will be happy many times, I only one.

Margaret: No, Eric, you have your music back . . . your love . . . your great moment is just beginning.

Eric: You are not always happy too?

Margaret: No, not always, not very often I think.

Eric: If I own all the world I give him you!

Margaret (*simply*):   Thank you Eric.
They sit peacefully a moment. They kiss.

PROJECTS

1. As regards opera composed in a language other than English, the controversy between presenting such operas for English-speaking audiences in English and presenting them in the original language still rages. Write a brief paper presenting reasoned arguments in support of either practice. Support your arguments with specific examples in which the language of performance either enhances or detracts from the opera's effectiveness.

2. If there is a producing opera company in a city near you, make a survey of the percentage of American operas produced in this season's programming.

3. Read a story or a play that has been made into an opera by an American composer, comparing the original with the opera. Note the changes that have been made, and try to determine if they were made to fulfill the requirements of opera. For example, you could compare Du Bose Heyward's novel *Porgy,* or the play adapted by the author and his wife, with the opera *Porgy and Bess* (score available in many music libraries, many recorded versions available); Emily Brontë's *Wuthering Heights* with Carlisle Floyd's opera of the same title (score available in many music libriries, no current recording available); or Arthur Miller's play *The Crucible* with the opera of the same title by Robert Ward (score in many music libraries, one recorded version available).

4. Douglas Moore's opera *The Ballad of Baby Doe* and Meredith Willson's musical *The Unsinkable Molly Brown* have the same setting (Colorado), and both deal with actual historical figures, women who faced the challenges of the mining-camp era of the West. Compare these two works, as a means of pointing out some of the differences—musical, dramatic, and in overall approach—between opera and popular musical theater.

5. In a brief paper, assess the pros and cons from your point of view of producing operas on current "newsworthy" happenings, especially murders or assassinations. Include a consideration of both the motivations and the dangers involved.

ADDITIONAL LISTENING

Adams, John. *John Adams Earbox* (10-CD Box Set). Includes *Nixon in China*. Orchestra of St. Luke's. Cond. Edo de Waart. WEA/Atlantic/Nonesuch 79453.

——. *Nixon in China*. Orchestra of St. Luke's. Cond. Edo de Waart. WEA/Atlantic/Nonesuch 79177.

Gershwin, George. *Porgy and Bess* (cast recording). Houston Grand Opera. Cond. John DeMain. RCA 2109.

Thomson, Virgil. *The Mother of Us All*. Libretto by Gertrude Stein. Santa Fe Opera. Cond. Raymond Leppard. New World Records 80288.

American Music in Your Own Backyard

The 1990 edition of *American Music: A Panorama* introduced for the first time a concluding chapter on "Regionalism and Diversity." Since then, "diversity" has become a word as constantly in our ears and before our eyes in print as are the manifestations of it that surround us. We swim in diversity. Regionalism has received less attention. In one sense the two are antithetical. A strong regional culture, rooted in a sense of *place*, can inhibit diversity, as has happened in the southern Appalachians or in the Cajun triangle. And diversity can dilute regionalism. *Klezmer* music sounds pretty much the same wherever it is cultivated, resisting to a certain extent regional influence.

Yet "place" will, in the end, leave its distinctive mark. The regional differences inherent in the sheer physical vastness of the country, and the complexity of its geography and its history, account in large measure for the heterogeneity (or, if you prefer, the "diversity") that we are aware of in America as a whole. In this sense regionalism and diversity are but two ways of looking at the same phenomenon.

In some areas, diversity has *become* a regional characteristic in itself, where there are a number of relatively small, self-sufficient communities whose members continue to cultivate music and customs that in the more recent past originated elsewhere — in Latin America, in Europe, or in Asia. These cultural pockets, often virtually unknown to those of the cultural "mainstream," are found most often in, or on the fringes of, huge urban areas. New York City, with its large ethnic enclaves — villages, towns, and cities within the super-city — is the most outstanding example of this, but these pockets can be found in any of our metropolises. They are areas that have in many cases received substantial refugee populations or that have drawn workers by virtue of powerful but capricious economic magnets such as mining. These pockets can occur in rural as well as urban areas. California is a well-known example, but a substantial amount of cultural diversity, under the surface, can be found even in states such as Wyoming.

Most of this short chapter will be devoted to an overview of a certain specific place, viewed as a sample of the complex overlaying of cultures typical of most American places. The choice of places is beside the point; this one just happens to be where the author lives. Any other place would do as well; in fact, the whole idea of this chapter is to inspire the reader to look around wherever he or she may be, and become aware of how many different kinds of music, made by people of how many different histories and places of origin, can be found in his or her own backyard.

THE SACRAMENTO VALLEY: A RICH MIX OF CULTURES

The study of a people and their culture cannot be divorced from some knowledge of the land they inhabit. The Sacramento Valley of California is a broad alluvial valley between two mountain ranges—a low coastal range to the west, and the Sierra Nevada to the east. From the high, snow-trapping barrier range of the Sierra flow down into the valley a series of tumultuous rivers that, until barely a century ago, spread wide out of their banks in the spring, flooding the valley, depositing rich alluvial soils and clays, and filling the huge old basins with half a million acres of water from January to May. Tamed now by scores of dams and hundreds of miles of levees and canals, they furnish the water that allows a multitude of crops to grow through the long hot season from May to October, when no rain falls.

Unlike Louisiana and the upper Midwest (two places studied in Chapter 5)—which are longer-settled regions whose cultural identity, bearing the characteristics of one or two dominant immigrant groups, has been established for well over a century—the Sacramento Valley presents a picture of a complex "cross-bedding" of successive migrations from many directions. This has left a rich mix of cultures, many of them still distinct and unassimilated. The phase of greatest influx is so recent that the sense of transiency has still not been replaced by one of settled permanency, and there is nothing that can be identified as a single distinctive regional culture. Each wave of newcomers has come with its own culture, in its own time, and for its own reasons. Trappers, mission founders, would-be empire builders, gold seekers, agricultural barons, land speculators, laborers imported en masse for railroad building or harvesting, networks of immigrants bringing relatives from foreign countries, military, defense, and government workers, wealthy entrepreneurs, and refugee populations—all have formed part of the picture.

A Thumbnail Cultural Chronology of the Valley

A peaceful Indian population with a culture singularly well adapted to the unique region were the original inhabitants; they and their way of life have been all but gone for a century. The Spaniards scarcely penetrated the valley to any extent, and the Mexican government, heir to Spain's territorial claim in 1822, could exercise only a tenuous hold on an area where American trappers and adventurers roamed freely. (The significant Mexican influence and presence was destined to come much later.) The discovery of gold in the Sierra foothills in 1848 brought sudden, irreversible, and drastic change. With the rapid influx of easterners (accompanied by significant immigration from Europe, Central and South America, and Asia), acquisition by the United States and statehood (in 1850) were inevitable. The population soared, and when the easily obtainable placer gold ran out (about 1853), large corporations took over the mining, and individual miners left or went into farming, which was destined to become the fertile valley's major industry. Railroad building in the 1860s brought in the first of the great laborer populations, the Chinese; as an immigrant labor population the Chinese were replaced by the Japanese beginning about 1900.

From 1900 to 1920 was the time of the great land boom, and the period saw further diversification of the valley's population. Land companies bought up large tracts (many upon the dissolution of the huge holdings that had originally been Mexican land grants) and advertised heavily in the East. Colonization projects brought more immigrants.

As agriculture in the valley changed from the growing of wheat, which could easily be harvested mechanically, to fruit and vegetable crops, which required handpicking, the need for seasonal labor grew, and this has made a large transient population of farmworkers, with the social problems attendant on it, a part of the Sacramento Valley scene since very early in the twentieth century. Since as early as 1919, Mexicans have been coming to do this work.

The Depression and drought of the 1930s brought many from the Dust Bowl areas of Texas, Oklahoma, and Kansas (thus adding to the constituency for country music, which became especially strong in the adjoining San Joaquin Valley to the south). World War II brought further shifts in population throughout the nation; many who came to the valley during the war stayed or returned to it, thus beginning another period of population growth, which is still going on. Significant recent additions are large refugee populations from Southeast Asia.

An Incomplete Cultural and Musical Inventory of the Sacramento Valley

Among the American Indians there is, as described in Chapter 3, a new movement under way to restore and revitalize their native dance, music, crafts, and culture. This movement is strong in the Sacramento Valley, even though few of the Indians there may be descended from the original tribes. There are frequent intertribal powwows, often under the auspices of a college or university. There is considerable mutual cooperation and support between the American Indian and the Chicano movements (see pp. 59–60).

Many Chinese came to the valley and worked as miners during the gold rush, until driven out of this occupation by the Americans. Many more were brought in in the ensuing decade to build the railroad. Hardworking, canny, thrifty, keeping to themselves and to their own traditions, they were the object of scorn and persecution. Their numbers in the valley declined after 1890. In the decades since World War II, many Chinese have become fully integrated into the social, economic, and cultural life of the valley, but small groups cultivate Chinese culture, language, and music. Beginning in the 1960s the influx of Chinese as refugees from Vietnam and other parts of Southeast Asia increased dramatically.

Another early immigrant group was the Portuguese, who were among the first Europeans to settle in the Sacramento area, some arriving with the gold rush. Coming mostly from the Azores, they established small family farms. Following a familiar pattern, the immigrants, once established, encouraged others from the same areas to come, and provided for them upon their arrival. The Portuguese tended to form tightly knit communities, their social activities centering on the church (St. Elizabeth's in Sacramento still celebrates a Portuguese Mass) and its holy days. The *festas* are colorful celebrations, including a procession with music, followed by a feast. For years there were radio programs with a live band playing Portuguese music. Portuguese dances and songs are performed in the social halls in the community, accompanied by traditional *violas de arames, violãos,* and *guitarras.* A popular folk song from the Azores known and sung by the Portuguese in Sacramento is "Lira" (Transcription 23.1).

Text, "Lira"

A shepherd came down from the hills
And knocked on my door.
He brought a sealed letter [with the news]
That my Lira was dead.

CD 5/22 (1:33)
Hokkai bon uta (Dance song from the island of Hokkaido) (excerpt)

The Japanese began immigrating in significant numbers around the turn of the century, many coming from Hawaii after its annexation by the United States. Replacing the Chinese as a source of labor, they too were targets of persecution and mistrust until after World War II. Members today of a highly visible and well-integrated component of valley population, a few Americans of Japanese descent are now making conscious efforts to keep alive their own rich traditions of music, dance, and drama. Of special interest is the cultivation

Do ma - to veio un pas - tor_____
Tra - zi - a car - ta cer - ra - da_____

Do ma - to veio un pas - tor_____
Tra - zi - a car - ta cer - ra - da_____

Do ma - to veio un pas - tor_____
Tra - zi - a car - ta cer - ra

á min - ha por - ta ba - teu._____
-da que_a min - ha Li - ra mor - reu._____

of *minyo*, or folk music and dance (as distinct from *buyo*, or the highly cultivated classical dance). This costumed dance for multiple dancers is accompanied by a solo singer (either man or woman), one or several *shamisens* (a plucked stringed instrument of three strings), a *yokobue* (transverse flute), a *kane* (small bell), and a *taiko* (drum). Also accompanying the performance is the *hayashi*, a chorus of women's voices which "responds" to the solo singer's phrases with high-pitched rhythmic vocables that have no literal meaning. Their refrains have been referred to as "cheering calls." These are audible on the recording of "Hokkai bon uta" (CD 5/22), a folk song from the northern island of Hokkaido highly popular among dance groups in the United States. The dance movements of *minyo odori* consist largely of stylized interpretations of the body motions of *work* performed in the various localities from which the songs come—for example, work in the rice fields, coal mining, fishing, rice pounding, and cattle driving.

The major influx of Mexicans, and their considerable contribution to the cultural mix, is fairly recent, beginning with the harvests of the early 1920s. Their music today is mainly of the musica norteña tradition described in Chapter 4, with strong Chicano overtones.

Immigrants from Greece, coming primarily from Peloponnesus, began arriving in the early 1900s and built their first church in Sacramento in 1921. Though the Greeks are thoroughly integrated into the community, they have preserved a good deal of their culture, focused on the Greek Orthodox Church. Since the 1950s and 1960s there has been a renaissance of Byzantine liturgical music in California. This was followed in the 1970s and 1980s by a renewed interest in Greek folk dance and costumes, and consequently in authentic Greek folk music, with regional distinctions preserved. Folk-dance festivals, in which many young people take part, are frequent events. Several Greek bands are active, playing popular American as well as traditional Greek music. The traditional *klarino* (a type of clarinet) is no longer much used in the bands in Sacramento, but the *bouzóuki*, a fretted lutelike instrument with a long neck, has appeared in ensembles with greater frequency since the popularity of the film *Zorba the Greek*. It keeps company in the bands with electric guitar, drums, and electric keyboards. Greek music is flourishing but adapting—or, rather, flourishing *by* adapting.

Immigration from Ukraine to the United States has occurred in five waves, beginning in the 1870s. The latest wave, in the late 1980s and 1990s, followed *glasnost* and the breakup of the Soviet Union, and consisted mostly of Ukrainian Baptists and Pentecostals who were escaping religious persecution. This wave added substantially to the 120 families that previously constituted the population of Ukrainian descent in Sacramento. Today there are in the Sacramento area Ukrainian Catholic, Baptist, Evangelical, and Pentecostal churches, each with a choir and a cantor, and some with a small orchestra. The Ukrainian Heritage Club of Northern California promotes Ukrainian culture, including music, as does the School of Ukrainian Studies, which has a children's choir.

Of special interest is the cultivation of the Ukrainian *bandura*, a plucked stringed instrument that was originally used to accompany the singing of epic folk ballads as early as the seventh century. Enlarged and perfected, it has become, in the hands of accomplished bandurists such as Ola Herasymenko Oliynyk of Sacramento, a concert instrument. She performs numerous solo and ensemble works for bandura, and has formed and leads the Bandura Ensemble of Northern California. "Zelenyi Dubochku" (The Green Oak) and "Chy Ya Tobi Ne Kazala" (Did I Not Tell You?) are Ukrainian folk songs, accompanied by the bandura. (See CDs 5/23 and 5/24.)

CD 5/23 (0:45) "Zelenyi Dubochku" ("The Green Oak") (one verse). Ola Herasymenko, voice and bandura.

Text, "Zelenyi Dubochku" ("The Green Oak")

Green oak—why do you bend down your bough?
Soldier—why do you worry so much?
Soldier—why do you worry so much?
Soldier—why do you worry indeed?
Did your horses slow down on you?
Or did you lose your way?

CD 5/24 (0:44) "Chy Ya Tobi Ne Kazala" ("Did I Not Tell You?") (two verses). Ola Herasymenko, voice and bandura.

Did I not tell you, did I not remind you?
Not to send your match-makers, and not to show up yourself any more,
Because my mother will not let me marry you anyway?

If my mother wanted me to marry the likes of you,
I would have been married a long time ago.

Text, "Chy Ya Tobi Ne Kazala" ("Did I Not Tell You?")

To be complete, this inventory of ethnic cultures of the Sacramento Valley and their musics would have to include many other communities as well. Among those that have active organizations devoted to preserving and celebrating their customs and their cultures, in addition to those treated above, are the Filipinos, the Laotians, the Vietnamese, the Koreans, the Sikhs, the Pacific Islanders, the Armenians, the Serbs, the Croats, the Norwegians, the Poles, and the Italians.

CONCLUSION

We have concluded our sweeping glance over the panorama of American music by trying to convey a sense of two of its most characteristic attributes — regionalism and diversity. As this is written, the author senses a renewed concern on the part of many, both in and out of arts councils, commissions, and boards — a concern that could be only sparsely documented here — for the health of our culture. He senses an awareness of the impoverishment that would come with the loss of regional and traditional musics through their complete absorption in mass culture, and he finds generous-minded patrons, producers, scholars, and performers working to see that this does not happen. The economics of the entertainment industry — the great "hit machine" — does indeed depend upon the mass production and marketing of a technically perfect, homogenized product devoid of regional eccentricities, and upon a public devoted to consumption rather than participation. But what the hit machine cannot do is to reflect, to serve, or to place value on these eccentricities — the very things that give us our individuality. As Woody Guthrie sang, looking out from the sixty-fifth floor of one of the mass culture machine's chic and insulated bastions:

It's a long way's from here to th'U.S.A. (293)

◼ PROJECTS

1. Look around in your own community and make an inventory of the various cultures that are not in the "mainstream," that have retained their culture and perhaps their language as well, and that have their own distinctive and identifiable music and musical tradition.

2. Pick one culture in your own community that fits the description in project 1, and make a study (through interviews, attendance at social and religious events, etc.) of their music and the way it functions in their culture.

3. Find out about any national holidays that are celebrated by ethnic groups in your community, and attend and report on them. These are usually celebrations of national independence like the American Fourth of July; Mexicans, for example, celebrate *Cinco de Mayo* (May 5), and Norwegians *Syttende Mai* (May 17).

4. Find out about and report on the support your own state government gives to folk, ethnic, or regional arts, through a state folklorist, or a state arts board or arts council.

REFERENCES

1. Anglo-Celtic-American Tradition

Child, Francis James. *The English and Scottish Popular Ballads*. 5 vols. Boston, 1882–98. New York: Dover, 1965. A historic collection, with extensive scholarly notes comparing multiple versions of the same ballads, establishing the "Child canon." Attention is on texts only; a very few tunes appear in an appendix.

Christeson, R. P. *The Old-Time Fiddler's Repertory*. Columbia: Univ. of Missouri Press, 1973.

Cohen, John, and Mike Seeger. *Old-Time String Band Song Book*. New York: Oak, 1976.

Laws, G. Malcolm, Jr. *Native American Balladry*. Philadelphia: American Folklore Society, 1964. A significant study of native balladry outside the Child canon, dealing with an area of American folk song indispensable to a comprehensive picture.

Lomax, Alan. *The Folksongs of North America*. Garden City, NY: Doubleday, 1960. This excellent broad collection surveys the entire field of American folk songs in the English language. The introduction and the notes are especially valuable.

Nathan, Hans. *Dan Emmett and the Rise of Early Negro Minstrelsy*. Norman: Univ. of Oklahoma Press, 1962.

Owens, William A. *Texas Folk Songs*. Dallas: SMU Press, 1976.

Randolph, Vance. *Ozark Folksongs*. Ed. and abr. Norm Cohen. Urbana: Univ. of Illinois Press, 1982.

Seeger, Charles. "Versions and Variants of the Tunes of Barbara Allen." *Selected Reports*, no. 1, Institute of Ethnomusicology, Univ. of California, Los Angeles, 1966.

Sharp, Cecil. *English Folk-Songs from the Southern Appalachians*. Ed. Maud Karpeles. London: Oxford Univ. Press, 1932. 2 vols. reprinted in 1, 1966. Not only is the collection a rich source of ballads and their variants in pure form from oral tradition, but also the introduction is a valuable essay on both the folk and their songs.

Thede, Marion. *The Fiddle Book*. New York: Oak, 1967.

Thomas, Jean. *Ballad Makin' in the Mountains of Kentucky*. New York: Oak, 1964.

Twain, Mark. *Life on the Mississippi*. New York, London: Harper & Brothers, c. 1923.

Wimberly, Charles. *Folklore in the English and Scottish Ballads*. New York: Dover, 1965.

2. African-American Tradition

Allen, William Francis, Charles Pickard Ware, and Lucy McKim Garrison, eds. *Slave Songs of the United States*. New York, 1867. (There have been many reprints.) A classic, of permanent importance as the first such collection published.

Courlander, Harold. *Negro Folk Music, U.S.A.* New York: Columbia Univ. Press, 1963. Includes forty-three complete songs.

Epstein, Dena J. *Sinful Tunes and Spirituals: Black Folk Music to the Civil War*. Urbana: Univ. of Illinois Press, 1977. A valuable study, with extensive citations from contemporary sources.

Jackson, George Pullen. *White and Negro Spirituals*. New York: Da Capo, 1975.

Johnson, James Weldon, and J. Rosamund Johnson, eds. *The Books of American Negro Spirituals*. 2 vols. in 1. New York: Viking, 1940. Originally issued as two books, the first in 1925, this is a standard collection. James Weldon Johnson was a novelist and poet, author of *God's Trombones (Seven Negro Sermons in Verse)*. His brother, J. Rosamund Johnson, created the piano arrangements.

Katz, Bernard, ed. *The Social Implications of Early Negro Music in the United States*. New York: Arno, 1969. A collection of important articles and excerpts from books, dating from 1862 to 1939, most of which include a generous number of examples.

Laws, G. Malcolm, Jr. *Native American Balladry*. Philadelphia: American Folklore Society, 1964. A significant study of native balladry outside the Child canon, dealing with an area of American folk song indispensable to a comprehensive picture.

Lomax, John A., and Alan Lomax. *Our Singing Country*. New York: Macmillan, 1941.

Maultsby, Portia K. "West African Influences and Retentions in U.S. Black Music." *More Than Dancing: Essays on Afro-American Music and Musicians*. Ed. Irene Jackson. Westport, CT: Greenwood, 1985.

Murphy, Jeannette Robinson. "The Survival of African Music in America." *Appleton's Popular Science Monthly* Sept. 1899.

Sandburg, Carl. *The American Songbag*. New York: Harcourt Brace & World, 1927.

Southern, Eileen. *The Music of Black Americans*. 2nd ed. New York: Norton, 1983. A comprehensive, *indispensable* study of the entire field.

——, ed. *Readings in Black American Music*. 2nd ed. New York: Norton, 1983. Excerpts from important source material ranging over the entire field.

3. American Indian Tradition

Densmore, Frances. *The American Indians and Their Music*. New York: Women's Press, 1926. An early comprehensive work by a pioneer researcher. It is supplemented by numerous tribal studies published between 1910 and 1939, and reprinted by Da Capo Press. More than mere transcriptions, they treat the customs, ceremonies, and legends of the tribes.

Heth, Charlotte. Notes. *Music of the Yurok and Tolowa Indians*. NW 80297.

Levine, Victoria Lindsay. "Musical Revitalization among the Choctaw." *American Music* 11.4, (Winter 1993).

Lornell, Kip, and Anne K. Rasmussen, eds. *Musics of Multicultural America*. New York: Schirmer Books, 1997.

McAllester, David P. *Peyote Music*. Viking Fund Publications in Anthropology, no. 13. New York: Viking, 1949. 85.

"Native." *Random House Dictionary*. Unabr. ed. 1967.

Nettl, Bruno. "Indians, American/Music/Styles." *The New Grove Dictionary of American Music*. Vol. 2. London: Macmillan, 1986. 464–68.

——. *North American Indian Musical Styles*. Philadelphia: American Folklore Society, 1954. An important brief study, somewhat technical, of regional characteristics. Includes some musical examples.

O'Kane, Walter Collins. *Sun in the Sky*. Norman: Univ. of Oklahoma Press, 1950.

"Primitive." *Random House Dictionary*. Unabr. ed. 1967.

Rhodes, Willard. "Acculturation in North American Indian Music." *Acculturation in the Americas*. Chicago: Univ. of Chicago Press, 1952.

Robb, J. Donald. *Hispanic Folk Music of New Mexico and the Southwest*. Norman: Univ. of Oklahoma Press, 1980.

4. Hispanic and Latin Traditions

Aparicio, Frances R. *Listening to Salsa: Gender, Latin Popular Music, and Puerto Rican Cultures*. Hanover: Wesleyan Univ. Press, 1998.

Aztlán 17.1 (Spring 1986). Includes "Unraveling America's Hispanic Past: Internal Stratification and Class Boundaries" by Ramón Gutiérrez, and "Mexicanos, Chicanos, Mexican-Americans, or Pochos . . . Qué somos? The Impact of Nativity on Ethnic Labelling" by Aída Hurtada and Carlos H. Arce.

Contreras, Maximiliano. *Crossing: A Comparative Analysis of the Mexicano, Mexican-American and Chicano*. San Pedro, CA: International Universities Press, 1983.

Fernández, Joaquin. Note to the author. Robert L. Vialpando, of Alcalde, New Mexico, is a collector and researcher of alabados.

Geijerstam, Claes af. *Popular Music in Mexico*. Albuquerque: Univ. of New Mexico Press, 1976.

Koegel, John. *Inter-American Music Review* 13.2 (Spring–Summer 1993). Includes "Mexican and Mexican-American Musical Life in Southern California, 1850-1900" and "Calendar of Southern California Amusements 1852–1897; Designed for Spanish-Speaking Public."

——. "Spanish and Mexican Dance Music in Early California." *Ars Musica*. Lamont School of Music, Univ. of Denver. Fall 1994.

Lornell, Kip, and Anne K. Rasmussen, eds. *Musics of Multicultural America*. New York: Schirmer Books, 1997.

Loza, Steven. *Barrio Rhythm: Mexican American Music in Los Angeles*. Urbana: Univ. of Illinois Press, 1993. A well-done treatment of the subject, from 1769 to the present, with emphasis on developments in popular music over the past fifty years. Some transcriptions and complete texts of recent works. Includes index, bibliography, and discography.

Robb, John Donald. *Hispanic Folk Music of New Mexico and the Southwest: A Self-Portrait of a People*. Norman: Univ. of Oklahoma Press, 1980. More extensive than his 1954 *Hispanic Folk Songs of New Mexico*, this is the major summary in published form of many years of collecting. The anthology (891 pages) includes many types of music—sacred, secular, and instrumental—with informative notes on each type. The songs include texts and English translations.

Roberts, John Storm. *The Latin Tinge: The Impact of Latin American Music in the United States*. New York: Oxford Univ. Press, 1979.

Singer, Roberta. "Tradition and Innovation in Contemporary Latin Popular Music in New York City." *Latin American Review* 4.2 (Fall–Winter 1983).

Stark, Richard B. *Music of the Spanish Folk Plays in New Mexico*. Santa Fe: Museum of New Mexico Press, 1969. Songs and texts of various versions of *Los*

Pastores transcribed from recordings made between 1940 and 1968. Includes some songs from *Las Posadas* and from another folk play, *El Niño Perdido*.

Stevenson, Robert. *Music in Aztec and Inca Territory: Contact and Acculturation Periods*. Berkeley and Los Angeles: Univ. of California Press, 1977.

Stevenson, Robert Louis. "The Old Pacific Capital." *Across the Plains*. New York: Scribner's, 1903.

Steward. Sue. *¡Musica!: The Rhythm of Latin America*. San Francisco: Chronicle Books, 1999.

Sturman, Janet. *Zarzuela: Spanish Operetta, American Stage*. Urbana: Univ. of Illinois Press, 2000.

Titon, Jeff Todd, ed. *Worlds of Music*. 4th ed. New York: Schirmer Books, 2002.

Waxer, Lise, ed. *Situating Salsa*. Routledge, 2002.

5. Other Traditions

Allen, William Francis, Charles Pickard Ware, and Lucy McKim Garrison, eds. *Slave Songs of the United States*. New York, 1867. New York: Oak, 1969. Seven Louisiana songs in patois are included in this famous early collection.

Bergmann, Leola Nelson. *Americans from Norway*. Philadelphia: Lippincott, 1950.

Cable, George Washington. "The Dance in Place Congo" and "Creole Slave Songs." Reprinted in *The Social Implications of Early Negro Music in the United States*. Ed. Bernard Katz. New York: Arno, 1969.

Lornell, Kip, and Anne K. Rasmussen, eds. *Musics of Multicultural America*. New York: Schirmer Books, 1997.

Stearns, Marshall. *The Story of Jazz*. New York: Oxford Univ. Press, 1956.

Whitfield, Irène Thérèse. *Louisiana French Folk Songs*. New York: Dover, 1969. An important collection in this area. Because of its uniqueness, its few weaknesses are all the more unfortunate: the musical transcriptions are, it must be suspected, not always trustworthy, and there is a lack of uniform documentation as to where, and especially when, the songs were collected. There are translations of the texts into standard French but not into English.

6. An Instrument of Advocacy

Denisoff, R. Serge. *Sing Me a Song of Social Significance*. Bowling Green, OH: Bowling Green State Univ. Press, 1983.

Hampton, Wayne. *Guerrilla Minstrels: John Lennon, Joe Hill, Woody Guthrie, Bob Dylan*. Knoxville: Univ. of Tennessee Press, 1986.

Jackson, George Pullen. *Spiritual Folk-Songs of Early America*. 1937. New York: Dover, 1964.

Wilgus, D. K. *Anglo-American Folksong Scholarship Since 1898*. New Brunswick, NJ: Rutgers Univ. Press, 1959.

7. Country Music

Cash, Wilbur J. *The Mind of the South*. New York: Knopf, 1941.

Gentry, Linnell, ed. *A History and Encyclopedia of Country, Western, and Gospel Music*. 2nd ed. Nashville: Clairmont, 1969.

Giddins, Gary. Notes. *Shake, Rattle & Roll: Rock 'n' Roll in the 1950s*. New World 249.

Green, Archie. "Hillbilly Music: Source and Symbol." *Journal of American Folklore*. July–Sept. 1965.

Malone, Bill C. *Country Music, U.S.A.* Rev. ed. Austin: Univ. of Texas Press, 1985. The best comprehensive work available.

8. Blues and Soul

Baraka, Amiri (Le Roi Jones). *Blues People*. New York: Morrow, 1963. A survey by an eminent black writer, who uses music to illustrate and illuminate the history of his people in America.

Cohn, Lawrence, ed. *Nothing But the Blues: The Music and the Musicians*. New York: Abbeville, 1993. A compilation of eleven chapters by various authors; at 432 pages in large format this is a comprehensive general work on the subject.

Cook, Bruce. *Listen to the Blues*. New York: Scribner's, 1973.

Gillett, Charlie. *The Sound of the City: The Rise of Rock 'n' Roll*. New York: Dell, 1970.

Handy, W. C., ed. *Blues: An Anthology*. New York, 1926. New York: Macmillan, 1972. A famous collection of early published blues by Handy and others. A 1949 edition includes a rather extensive and valuable essay, "The Story of the Blues" by Abbe Niles. This is included in the most recent edition, which also incorporates additional blues, and guitar-chord symbols.

Keil, Charles. *Urban Blues*. Chicago: Univ. of Chicago Press, 1966. Still an indispensable study, and one of the few to deal adequately and from a variety of angles with the modern urban component of the blues. His annotated outlines of blues styles (Appendix C) is valuable.

Oliver, Paul. *The Meaning of the Blues*. New York: Macmillan, 1960. An exhaustive and perceptive study of blues subjects and the milieu of its people, in the form of extensive commentary on 350 blues texts arranged according to subject. Most of the blues texts used as examples in this chapter are quoted in Oliver's work.

9. Rock

Bayles, Martha. *Hole in Our Soul*. New York: Free Press, 1994.

Belz, Carl. *The Story of Rock*. 2nd ed. New York: Oxford Univ. Press, 1972. Valuable, in spite of its age.

Charlton, Katherine. *Rock Musical Styles: A History*. Dubuque, IA: Wm. C. Brown, 1989.

Eisen, Jonathan. *The Age of Rock 2*. New York: Random House/Vintage Books, 1970.

Fernando, S. H., Jr. *The New Beats*. New York: Doubleday/Anchor 1994.

Frith, Simon. "Folk or Popular? Distinctions, Influences, Continuities." *Popular Music*. Vol. 1. Ed. Richard Middleton and David Horn. Cambridge: Cambridge Univ. Press, 1987.

———. *Sound Effects: Youth, Leisure, and the Politics of Rock 'n' Roll*. New York: Pantheon, 1981.

Helander, Brock. *The Rock Who's Who*. 2nd ed. New York: Schirmer Books, 1996. 849 tightly packed yet readable pages, with extensive discography, and a comprehensive index listing individuals, groups, and songs, and an extensive bibliography by individuals.

Gillett, Charlie. *The Sound of the City*. Rev. ed. New York: Pantheon, 1984.

Gracyk, Theodore. *Rhythm and Noise: An Aesthetics of Rock*. Durham and London: Duke Univ. Press, 1996.

Melly, George. *Revolt into Style*. Garden City, NY: Anchor/Doubleday, 1971.

Rose, Tricia. *Black Noise: Rap Music and Black Culture in Contemporary America*. Hanover and London: Wesleyan Univ. Press, 1994.

Shaw, Arnold. *Dictionary of American Pop/Rock*. New York: Schirmer Books, 1982.

———. *Honkers and Shouters*. New York: Macmillan, 1978.

Stuessy, Joe. *Rock and Roll: Its History and Stylistic Development*. Englewood Cliffs, NJ: Prentice Hall, 1990.

Worster, Larry. Correspondence with the author.

10. Psalm Tune to Rural Revivalism

Buechner, Alan. Annotations. *The New England Harmony*. Smithsonian/Folkways 2377 LP. This excellent 32-page booklet has much valuable information on the singing school tradition. The booklet is available separately from Folkways, although the record album is nearly indispensable as well.

Chase, Gilbert. *America's Music*. Rev. 3rd ed. Urbana and Chicago: Univ. of Illinois Press, 1987.

Johnson, Charles A. *The Frontier Camp Meeting*. Dallas: SMU Press, 1955. 64–65.

Lovell, John, Jr. *Black Song: The Forge and the Flame*. New York: Macmillan, 1972.

McKay, David P., and Richard Crawford. *William Billings of Boston: Eighteenth-Century Composer*. Princeton, NJ: Princeton Univ. Press, 1975. A fine and very readable addition to work in the field of the Yankee singing school. It includes much valuable background information, including a complete survey of sacred music in New England to the time of Billings.

Patterson, Beverly Bush. *The Sound of the Dove: Singing in Appalachian Primitive Baptist Churches*. Urbana and Chicago: Univ. of Illinois Press, 1995.

Stevenson, Robert. *Protestant Church Music in America*. New York: Norton, 1966; paperback, 1970. A brief but invaluable survey, written with a broad perspective of the subject by a noted scholar. Begins with the all-but-forgotten Huguenot settlements in Florida more than half a century before the landing of the Pilgrims. Excellent bibliography.

11. Urban Revivalism and Gospel Music

Abbott, Lynn. "Play That Barber Shop Chord": A Case for the African-American Origin of Barbershop Harmony." *American Music* 10.3 (Fall 1992).

Anderson, Robert Mapes. *Vision of the Disinherited: The Making of American Pentecostalism*. New York: Oxford Univ. Press, 1979.

Boyer, Horace Clarence. "Black Gospel Music." *New Grove Dictionary of American Music*. ii, 254–59. This can be compared with Heilbut's chronology in Chapter 3 of *The Gospel Sound*.

———. "C. A. Tindley: Progenitor of Black-American Gospel Music." *Black Perspectives in Music* 11.2 (Fall 1983).

———. "A Comparative Analysis of Traditional and Contemporary Gospel Music." *More Than Dancing*. Ed. Irene Jackson. Westport, CT: Greenwood, 1985.

Du Bois, William E. B. *The Souls of Black Folk: Essays and Sketches*. Chicago: McClurg, 1903.

Ferris, William, and Mary L. Hart, eds., *Folk Music and Modern Sound*. Jackson: Univ. Press of Mississippi, 1982.

Heilbut, Tony. *The Gospel Sound*. 3rd Limelight Ed., 1989.

Ives, Charles. *Ives-Memos*. Ed. John Kirkpatrick. New York: Norton, 1972.

Malone, Bill C. *Southern Music: American Music*. Lexington: The Univ. Press of Kentucky, 1979.

Oliver, Paul. *Songsters and Saints*. New York: Cambridge Univ. Press, 1984. Well-documented and well-written study of blues and gospel recordings made in the late 1920s.

12. Early Secular Music in the Cities

Anderson, Gillian. *Freedom's Voice in Poetry and Song*. Wilmington, DE: Scholarly Resources, 1977. This compendious "inventory of political and patriotic lyrics in colonial American newspapers" concludes with a songbook with ninety-two songs and eight poems.

Crawford, Richard. Notes. *Music of the Federal Era*. New World 80299.

Mates, Julian. *The American Musical Stage Before 1800*. New Brunswick, NJ: Rutgers Univ. Press, 1962.

McKay, David. "Opera in Colonial Boston," *American Music* 3.2 (Summer 1985).

Sonneck, O. G. *Early Opera in America*. 1915. New York: Benjamin Blom, 1963.

Southern, Eileen. *The Music of Black Americans*. 2nd ed. New York: Norton, 1983.

Wolfe, Richard J. *Secular Music in America, 1801–1825: A Bibliography*. New York: New York Public Library, 1964.

13. Popular Musical Theater

Bean, Annemarie, et al., eds. *Inside the Minstrel Mask: Readings in Nineteenth-Century Blackface Minstrelsy*. Hanover, NH: Wesleyan Press, 1996.

Bordman, Gerald. *American Musical Comedy from "Adonis" to "Dreamgirls."* New York: Oxford Univ. Press, 1982.

Cockrell, Dale. *Demons of Disorder: Early Blackface Minstrels and Their World*. Cambridge, England: Cambridge Univ. Press, 1997.

Gilbert, Douglas. *American Vaudeville*. Reprint, New York: Dover, 1963.

Hamm, Charles. *Yesterdays: Popular Song in America*. New York: Norton, 1979.

Lahr, John. "Spellbound." Rev. of *Sunset Boulevard*. *The New Yorker*, 26 July 1993: 74–76.

Lott, Eric. *Love and Theft: Blackface Minstrelsy and the American Working Class*. New York: Oxford Univ. Press, 1993.

Nathan, Hans. *Dan Emmett and the Rise of Early Negro Minstrelsy*. Norman: Univ. of Oklahoma Press, 1962. A most important study of the early minstrel show, as well as of Emmett himself. Nearly half the work consists of a valuable anthology of all types of minstrel material by Emmett and others, including, for example, the complete text of a skit or "extravaganza."

Southern, Eileen, ed. *Readings in Black American Music*. 2nd ed. New York: Norton, 1983.

Stearns, Marshall. *The Story of Jazz*. New York: Oxford Univ. Press, 1956.

Toll, Robert C. *Blacking Up: The Minstrel Show in Nineteenth Century America*. New York: Oxford Univ. Press, 1974.

Watt, Douglas. "Sunday in the Park Is Pretty." *New York Daily News* 3 May, 1984.

14. Popular Song, Dance, and March Music

Cockrell, Dale. *Excelsior: Journals of the Hutchinson Family Singers, 1842–1846*. Stuyvesant, NY: Pendragon, 1989.

Crawford, Richard. *The American Musical Landscape*. Berkeley and Los Angeles: Univ. of California Press, c. 1993.

Hamm, Charles. *Yesterdays: Popular Song in America*. New York: Norton, 1979. This well-documented work has chapters relevant to nearly every aspect of the present chapter.

Heaps, Willard A. and Porter W. Heaps. *The Singing Sixties: The Spirit of Civil War Days Drawn from the Music of the Times*. Norman: Univ. of Oklahoma Press, 1960.

Johnson, James Weldon. *The Book of American Negro Spirituals*. New York: Viking, 1969.

Maher, James T. Introduction. Wilder xxxiv.

Moseley, Caroline. "'When Will Dis Cruel War Be Ober?' Attitudes Toward Blacks in Popular Song of the Civil War." *American Music*, 2.3 (Fall 1984).

Sanjek, Russell. *From Print to Plastic: Publishing and Promoting America's Popular Music (1900–1980)*. I.S.A.M. Monograph no. 20. Brooklyn: Inst. for Studies in American Music, 1983.

Schwartz, H. W. *Bands of America*. Reprint, New York: Da Capo, 1975.

Shaw, Arnold. *Black Popular Music in America*. New York: Schirmer Books, 1986.

Spaeth, Sigmund. *A History of Popular Music in America.* New York: Random House, 1948.

Tawa, Nicholas. *A Music for the Millions.* New York: Pendragon, 1984.

Turner, Martha Anne. *The Yellow Rose of Texas: The Story of a Song.* El Paso, Texas: Western Press of the Univ. of Texas Press at El Paso, 1971.

Wilder, Alec. *American Popular Song: The Great Innovators 1900–1950.* New York: Oxford Univ. Press, 1972. This subjective but highly respected book by a songwriter-author treats in considerable detail a great number of songs by all the significant songwriters of the period.

15. Ragtime and Pre-Jazz

Allen, William Francis, Charles Pickard Ware, and Lucy McKim Garrison. *Slave Songs of the United State.* 1867. Various publishers.

Badger, J. Reid. "James Reese Europe and the Prehistory of Jazz." *American Music* 7.1 (Spring 1989).

Berlin, Edward A. *Ragtime: A Musical and Cultural History.* Berkeley and Los Angeles: Univ. of California Press, 1980. An excellent study, with probably the best analysis of the musical elements of ragtime.

Blesh, Rudi, and Harriett Janis. *They All Played Ragtime.* 4th ed. New York: Oak, 1971. The first book on the subject, and still the source of a wealth of information.

Cook, Bruce. *Listen to the Blues.* New York: Scribner's, 1973.

Gushee, Lawrence. Notes. *Steppin' on the Gas: Rags to Jazz 1913–1927.* NW 269.

Hasse, John, ed. *Ragtime: Its History, Composers, and Music.* New York: Schirmer Books, 1985. A valuable collection of articles on various aspects, including some by Hasse himself. Extensive bibliography and discography, well organized.

Lomax, Alan. *Mister Jelly Roll: The Fortunes of Jelly Roll Morton, New Orleans Creole and "Inventor of Jazz."* 2nd ed. Berkeley and Los Angeles: Univ. of California Press, 1973.

Shaw, Arnold. *Black Popular Music in America.* New York: Schirmer Books, 1986. See especially Chapter 3, "My Ragtime Baby."

Southern, Eileen. *The Music of Black Americans: A History.* 2nd ed. New York: Norton, 1983.

———. *Readings in Black American Music.* 2nd ed. New York: Norton, 1983.

Stearns, Marshall. *The Story of Jazz.* 1956. New York: Oxford Univ. Press, 1974. This standard work, still valuable, has excellent chapters on "Ragtime,"

"The New Orleans Background," and "The Transition to Jazz."

16. Jazz

Gridley, Mark. *Jazz Styles: History and Analysis.* 6th ed. Englewood Cliffs, NJ: Prentice Hall, 1996.

Jones, LeRoi. *Blues People.* New York: Morrow, 1963.

Kofsky, Frank. *Black Nationalism and the Revolution in Music.* New York: Pathfinder, 1970.

Mezzrow, Mez, and Bernard Wolfe. *Really the Blues.* Garden City, New York: Anchor, 1972.

Morgenstern, Dan. Notes. *Bebop.* NewWorld 271.

Morris, Ronald L. *Wait Until Dark: Jazz and the Underworld 1880–1940.* Bowling Green, OH: Bowling Green Univ. Popular Press, 1980.

Roberts, John Storm. *Black Music of Two Worlds.* New York: Schirmer, 1972.

Schuller, Gunther. *Early Jazz: Its Roots and Musical Development.* New York: Oxford Univ. Press, 1968.

———. "Third Steam Revisited." *Musings.* New York: Oxford Univ. Press, 1986.

Shaw, Arnold. *Black Popular Music in America.* New York: Schirmer Books, 1986.

17. Classical Music and the Contemporary World

Haga, Chuck. "A Journalist Comes Home." *Under the Whelming Tide: The 1997 Flood of the Red River of the North.* Grand Forks, North Dakota Museum of Art, 1998. N. pag.

Reuter, Laurel. "A Flood of Fire and Ice." *Under the Whelming Tide: The 1997 Flood of the Red River of the North.* Grand Forks, North Dakota Museum of Art, 1998. N. pag.

18. Jacksonian Era to World War I

Chase, Gilbert. *America's Music: From the Pilgrims to the Present.* 3rd ed. Urbana: Univ. of Illinois Press, 1987.

Farwell, Arthur. "A Letter to American Composers." *The Wa-Wan Press* (reprint, New York: Arno Press/New York Times, 1970), 1: xvii.

Farwell, Brice, ed. *A Guide to the Music of Arthur Farwell.* Privately printed by Brice Farwell, Briarcliff Manor, New York, 1972.

Gottschalk, L. M. *Notes of a Pianist.* New ed. Trans. and with notes by Jeanne Behrend. New York: Knopf, 1964. One of the most perceptive and brilliant documents that we have of nineteenth-century American life as seen by a musician.

Kenny, Herbert. Notes. *Mrs. H. H. A. Beach.* . . . NW 268.

Knight, Ellen. "Charles Martin Loeffler and George Gershwin: A Forgotten Friendship." *American Music* 3.4 (Winter 1985): 452.

Lowens, Irving. *Music and Musicians in Early America.* New York: Norton, 1964.

Root, George F. *The Story of a Musical Life.* Cincinnati: John Church, 1891.

Sears, Ann. "Keyboard Music by Nineteenth-Century Afro-American Composers." *Feel the Spirit: Essays in 19th Century Afro-American Music.* Ed. George Keck. Westport, CT: Greenwood, 1988. 135–55.

Southern, Eileen. *The Music of Black Americans: A History.* 2nd ed. New York: Norton, 1983.

19. Evolving Tradition, 1920–1970

Copland, Aaron. *Music and Imagination.* Cambridge: Harvard Univ. Press, 1952.

———. *The New Music.* New York: Norton, 1968.

Owens, David. "American Music's 'Golden Age.'" *The Christian Science Monitor* 12 May 1982.

Sessions, Roger. *Reflections on the Music Life in the United States.* New York: Merlin, 1956.

20. Twentieth-Century Innovation

Bruno, Anthony. "Two American Twelve-Tone Composers." *Musical America* 71.3 (Feb. 1951).

Cage, John. *A Year from Monday.* Middetown, CT: Wesleyan Univ. Press, 1963.

———. ed. *Notations.* New York: Something Else Press, 1969.

———. *Silence* Cambridge: MIT Press, 1966.

Chase, Gilbert, ed. *The American Composer Speaks.* Baton Rouge: Louisiana State Univ. Press, 1966.

Cope, David, *New Directions in Music.* 4th ed. Dubuque, IA: William C. Brown, 1984.

Cowell, Henry, and Sidney Cowell. *Charles Ives and His Music.* Rev. ed. New York: Oxford Univ. Press, 1969.

Crunden, Robert M. "Charles Ives's Place in American Culture." *An Ives Celebration.* Ed. H. Wiley Hitchcock. Urbana: Univ. of Illinois Press, 1977.

Ives, Charles. *Charles E. Ives: Memos.* Ed. John Kirkpatrick. New York: Norton, 1972. This book and *Essays* (see next entry) may be considered well-nigh indispensable primary sources for Ives's life, work, and, most important, thought. With some regrettable exceptions (such as the "Conductor's Note" to the Fourth Symphony), they contain nearly everything Ives wrote. The *Memos,* in addition, carefully and knowledgeably edited, contain some almost equally valuable appendices, including an annotated list of all Ives's compositions.

———. *Essays Before a Sonata, and Other Writings.* New York: Norton, 1961; paperback, 1964.

Krenek, Ernst. "Serialism." *Dictionary of Contemporary Music.* Ed. John Vinton. New York: Dutton, 1971.

Nyman, Michael. *Experimental Music: Cage and Beyond.* New York: Schirmer Books, 1974.

Oja, Carol J. *Making Music Modern: New York in the 1920s.* New York: Oxford Univ. Press, 2000.

Partch, Harry. *Genesis of a Music.* 2nd ed. New York: Da Capo, 1974.

Schwartz, Elliott, and Barney Childs, eds. *Contemporary Composers on Contemporary Music.* New York: Holt, Rinehart & Winston, 1967.

Seeger, Charles. "Carl Ruggles." Reprint in *American Composers on American Music,* by Henry Cowell. Palo Alto: Stanford Univ. Press, 1961.

Sessions, Roger. *Roger Sessions on Music: Collected Essays.* Princeton, NJ: Princeton Univ. Press, 1979.

Thomson, Virgil. *American Music Since 1910.* New York: Holt, Rinehart & Winston, 1970.

Varèse, Edgard. "Freedom for Music." *The American Composer Speaks.* Ed. Gilbert Chase. Baton Rouge: Louisiana State Univ. Press, 1966.

21. Toward a More Hospitable Music

Adams, John. "Living on the Edge: The Composer in a Pop Culture." Address. California State Univ., Sacramento. 9 Nov. 1996.

Corigliano, John. Notes. *John Corigliano: Concerto for Clarinet and Orchestra.* NW 309.

Dreier, Ruth. "Minimalism." *The New Grove Dictionary of American Music.* Vol. 3. London: Macmillan, 1986. 240.

Layton, Billy Jim. "The New Liberalism." *Perspectives of New Music* 3.2 (Spring–Summer 1965).

Reich, Steve. *Writings about Music.* New York: New York Univ. Press, 1974.

Rochberg, George. *The Aesthetics of Survival: A Composer's View of Twentieth-Century Music.* Ann Arbor: Univ. of Michigan Press, 1984.

Rochberg, George. Notes. *George Rochberg: Contra Mortem et Tempus.* CRI 231.

Rockwell, John. *All American Music: Composition in the Late Twentieth Century.* New York: Knopf, 1983. This incisive and readable book by an eminent critic covers many areas; Chapters 6 and 7 are especially relevant to this chapter.

Walsh, Michael. Notes. *George Rochberg: Concerto for Oboe and Orchestra*. New World 80335.

22. Opera Old and New

Clark, J. Bunker, ed. "The Composer and Performer and Other Matters: A Panel Discussion with Virgil Thomson and Philip Glass, Moderated by Gregory Sandow." *American Music* 7.2 (Summer 1989): 181–204.

Hamm, Charles. "Opera and the American Composer." *The American Composer Speaks*. Ed. Gilbert Chase. Baton Rouge: Louisiana State Univ. Press, 1969.

Lassetter, Leslie. "Opera from Elsewhere: Meredith Monk's *Atlas*." *Sonneck Society Bulletin* 20.3 (Fall 1994): 10–14.

Thomson, Virgil. Notes. *Four Saints in Three Acts*. RCA Victor 09026-68163-2.

American Music in Your Own Backyard

Guthrie, Woody. *Bound for Glory*. New York: Dutton, 1943.

ADDITIONAL READING

1. Anglo-Celtic-American Tradition

Bronson, Bertrand Harris. *The Singing Tradition of Child's Popular Ballads*. Princeton, NJ: Princeton Univ. Press, 1976. A single-volume abridgment of Bronson's four-volume work *The Traditional Tunes of the Child Ballads*. The extensive introduction includes a description of the modes used in the tunes. There is a monumental bibliography.

Fife, Austin, and Alta Fife. *Cowboy and Western Songs: A Comprehensive Anthology*. New York: Clarkson N. Potter, 1969.

Krassen, Miles. *Appalachian Fiddle*. New York: Oak, 1973.

Laws, G. Malcolm, Jr. *American Balladry from British Broadsides*. Philadelphia: American Folklore Society, 1957.

Sandburg, Carl. *The American Songbag*. New York: Harcourt Brace & World, 1927. An early landmark collection by an American writer famous for his enthusiasm for folklore, song, and poetry. The notes have the Sandburg touch, and make good reading.

2. African-American Tradition

Baraka, Amiri. *Blues People*. New York: Morrow, 1963. A perceptive social study of African American music by a prominent black writer (known as LeRoi Jones when the book was first published). The first six chapters are applicable to folk music.

Lovell, John, Jr. *Black Song: The Forge and the Flame*. New York: Macmillan, 1972. A major comprehensive survey (686 pages long) of the spiritual. Though no aspect is excluded, Lovell, a literary scholar, devotes his major attention to the texts and to their social background and implications.

3. American Indian Tradition

Burton, Bryan. *Moving within the Circle*. Danbury, CT: World Music Press, 1993. A fairly broad survey, in popular style, with musical transcriptions, instructions for dances and making instruments, a discography, and one CD.

Heth, Charlotte. "Update on Indian Music: Contemporary Trends." *Sharing a Heritage*. Los Angeles: UCLA American Indian Studies Center, 1984.

Waldman, Carl. *Encyclopedia of Native American Tribes*. New York and Oxford: Facts On File, 1988. A useful reference work in popular style, with drawings. Arranged alphabetically by tribe.

4. Hispanic and Latin Traditions

Flores, Richard R. *Los Pastores: History and Performance in the Mexican Shepherds Play of South Texas*. Washington, DC: Smithsonian Inst. Press, 1995.

Gerard, Charley, with Marty Sheller. *Salsa: The Rhythm of Latin Music*. Crown Point, IN: White Cliffs Media Company, 1989. Deals with the music itself, with many musical examples (including the full score of an arrangement), an index, a discography, and a glossary.

Gutiérrez, Ramon. "Unraveling America's Hispanic Past: Internal Stratification and Class Boundaries." *Aztlán: A Journal of Chicano Studies* (UCLA Chicano Studies Research Center) 17.1 (Spring 1986).

Herrera-Sobek, Maria. *Northward Bound: The Mexican Emigrant Experience in Ballad and Song*. Bloomington: Indiana Univ. Press, 1993.

Hurtado, Aída, and Carlos H. Arce. "Mexicanos, Chicanos, Mexican-Americans, or Pochos . . . Qué somos?: The Impact of Nativity on Ethnic Labelling." *Aztlán: A Journal of Chicano Studies* 17.1 (Spring 1986).

Paredes, Americo. *A Texas-Mexican Cancionero: Folksongs of the Lower Border*. Urbana: Univ. of Illinois Press, 1976. The sixty-six songs are interesting in themselves, but the extensive and informal prefaces to each section, and to each song, make this a valuable introduction to this whole regional music. The photographs are an extra bonus.

——. *"With his pistol in his hand."* Austin: Univ. of Texas Press, 1958. An extensive documentation of a ballad ("El Corrido de Gregorio Cortez") and its hero, which supplies valuable background information on the Texas-Mexico border country.

Peña, Manuel. *The Texas-Mexican Conjunto: History of a Working-Class Music*. Austin: Univ. of Texas Press, 1985.

Steward, Sue. *¡Musica!: The Rhythm of Latin America*. San Francisco: Chronicle Books, 1999.

Tinker, Edward Larocque. *Corridos and Calaveras*. Austin: Univ. of Texas Press, 1961. Although this deals specifically with the corrido and related forms as found in Mexico, it is excellent background reading for the corrido as a genre. Especially fascinating are the reproductions of the old broadsides themselves, with their drawings by the famous artist José Guadalupe Posada, a forerunner of Rivera and Orozco. A delightful book, in a very artistic format.

Waxer, Lise, ed. *Situating Salsa*. Routledge, 2002.

Weigle, Marta. *Brothers of Light, Brothers of Blood: The Penitentes of the Southwest*. Albuquerque: Univ. of New Mexico Press, 1976. A well-documented, thorough, and sympathetic treatment of this brotherhood, counteracting the often exaggerated and sensational accounts that had appeared earlier.

5. Other Traditions

Ancelet, Barry Jean. *The Makers of Cajun Music*. Québec: Presses de l'Université duQuébec, 1984. A beautifully prepared treatise, in both English and French, with many fine color photos.

Broven, John. *South to Louisiana: The Music of the Cajun Bayous*. Gretna, LA: Pelican, 1983.

Krehbiel, Henry Edward. *Afro-American Folksongs: A Study in Racial and National Music*. New York: Ungar, 1914; reprint, 1962. Krehbiel collaborated with Cable and with Lafcadio Hearn in collecting and studying black folk music in Louisiana in the nineteenth century. Chapters 9, 10, and 11, on "Creole" music, are the results of this collaboration.

Leary, James P. "Old Time Music in Northern Wisconsin." *American Music* 2.1 (Spring 1984). A valuable documentation of the current state of old-time music in the Chequamegon Bay area, a region of rich ethnic diversity.

Takaki, Ron. *Strangers from a Different Shore: A History of Asian Americans*. Boston, Toronto, and London: Little, Brown, 1989.

6. An Instrument of Advocacy

Broadside (periodical, New York 1962–88). The leading publication for topical songs, its editorial policy was to include songs by a variety of writers, thus giving new writers a chance to be published. It was started in 1962 by Pete Seeger, Malvina Reynolds, and Agnes Cunningham to serve this purpose, and to include more topical songs than the earlier *Sing Out!*

Carawan, Guy, and Candie Carawan, comp. *We Shall Overcome: Songs of the Southern Freedom Movement*. New York: Oak, 1963.

Denisoff, R. Serge. *Great Day Coming: Folk Music and the American Left*. Urbana: Univ. of Illinois Press, 1971; Penguin, 1973.

Fowke, Edith, and Joe Glazer. *Songs of Work and Protest*. New York: Dover, 1973. One hundred songs with extensive commentary.

Goldsmith, Peter D. *Making People's Music: Moe Asch and Folkways Records*. Washington and London: Smithsonian Inst. Press, 1998.

Greenway, John. *American Folksongs of Protest*. Philadelphia: Univ. of Pennsylvania Press, 1953. New York: A. S. Barnes, 1960. A rather detailed account of protest songs, especially those used in the labor movement. Many examples, including music.

Lomax, Alan, comp. *Hard-Hitting Songs for Hard-Hit People*. With notes by Woody Guthrie; music transcribed and edited by Pete Seeger. New York: Oak, 1967. Probably the best collection concentrating on the period of the 1930s. Illustrated with fine photographs made under the auspices of the Farm Security Administration by Walker Evans and others.

Yurchenko, Henrietta. "The Beginning of an Urban Folk-Song Movement in New York: A Memoir." *Sonneck Society Bulletin* 8.2 (Summer 1987). A brief, vivid account of this movement in New York in the 1930s, including firsthand impressions of Woody Guthrie, by one who participated in it.

7. Country Music

Dunson, Josh, and Ethel Raim, eds. *Anthology of American Folk Music*. New York: Oak, 1973. Transcriptions from the Folkways three-cassette recorded anthology with the same title. Commentary and photographs are especially good. Includes blues and gospel music. This and the Seeger below constitute the basic anthologies in notation of old-time music, much of which has never been transcribed in this form.

Editors, Country Music Magazine. *The Comprehensive Country Music Encyclopedia*. New York: Times Books, 1994.

Green, Archie. "Austin's Cosmic Cowboys: Words in Collision." *"And Other Neighborly Names": Social Process and Cultural Image in Texas Folklore*. Ed. Richard Bauman and Roger D. Abrahams. Austin: Univ. of Texas Press, 1981.

Linn, Karen. *That Half-Barbaric Twang: The Banjo in American Popular Culture.* Urbana and Chicago: Univ. of Illinois Press, 1991.

Rosenberg, Neil V. *Bluegrass: A History.* Urbana: Univ. of Illinois Press, 1987.

Seeger, Mike, and John Cohen, eds. *The Old-Time String Band Songbook.* New York: Oak, 1976; now in Music Sales Corp. catalog. An important collection of transcriptions from recordings of songs popular in the 1920s and 1930s. Documentation, commentary, and photographs make this especially valuable.

Tichi, Cecilia. *High Lonesome: The American Culture of Country Music.* Chapel Hill: Univ. of North Carolina Press, 1994.

8. Blues and Soul

Charters, Samuel. *The Bluesmen.* New York: Oak, 1967.
———. *Sweet as the Showers of Rain.* New York: Oak, 1977. This and *The Bluesmen* constitute a 2-volume expansion of the author's earlier *The Country Blues* (New York: Rinehart, 1959).

Ferris, William, Jr. *Blues from the Delta.* 1979. New York: Da Capo, 1984.

Handy, W. C. *Father of the Blues.* New York: Macmillan, 1941. In spite of the obvious kind of exaggeration implicit in its title, Handy's autobiography contains a wealth of background information, written from the standpoint of firsthand professional experience, on America's popular music business during the first four decades of the twentieth century.

Harrison, Daphne Duval. *Black Pearls: Blues Queens of the 1920s.* New Brunswick, NJ: Rutgers Univ. Press, 1988.

Oliver, Paul. *The Story of the Blues.* New York: Chilton, 1969. A comprehensive study, profusely illustrated with photographs, this is a basic source, though concentrating mainly on the rural and "classic" blues. There is a fine bibliography and discography.

Shaw, Arnold. *Black Popular Music in America.* New York: Schirmer Books, 1986.

Southern, Eileen. *The Music of Black Americans.* 2nd ed. New York: Norton, 1983. A comprehensive, *indispensable* study of the entire field.

Taft, Michael. *Blues Lyric Poetry: An Anthology.* New York: Garland, 1983. Lyrics of more than two thousand blues songs, transcribed from reissue LPs. Published with a companion three-volume concordance.

Titon, Jeff Todd. *Early Downhome Blues: A Musical and Cultural Analysis.* Urbana: Univ. of Illinois Press, 1977. In addition to cultural background, photographs, and reproductions of contemporary advertisements, this study includes transcriptions from forty-eight blues recordings of the 1920s, with musical analysis, thus making it one of the most musically thorough and useful studies in the field.

See also various works in the reading lists for Chapter 2 (additional background on the folk phase) and Chapter 15 (jazz, especially the early jazz so closely related to blues).

9. Rock

Gore, Tipper. *Raising PG Kids in an X-rated Society.* Nashville: Abingdon, 1987.

Pattison, Robert. *The Triumph of Vulgarity: Rock Music in the Mirror of Romanticism.* New York: Oxford Univ. Press, 1987.

Stambler, Irwin, ed. *Encyclopedia of Pop, Rock, and Soul.* Rev. ed. New York: St. Martins, 1989.

Walser, Robert. *Running with the Devil: Power, Gender, and Madness in Heavy Metal Music.* Hanover and London: Wesleyan Univ. Press, 1993.

10. Psalm Tune to Rural Revivalism

Cobb, Buell E., Jr. *The Sacred Harp: The Tradition and Its Music.* Athens: Brown Thrasher Books, Univ. of Georgia Press, 1989.

Jackson, George Pullen. *White Spirituals in the Southern Uplands.* 1933. New York: Dover, 1965. The basic history of the shape-note movement and its background. It includes the seven-shape branch. It also includes a listing, with initial-phrase quotations, of the eighty most popular tunes in the tradition.

Lorenz, Ellen Jane. *Glory, Hallelujah! The Story of the Campmeeting Spiritual.* Nashville: Abingdon, 1978. Includes music and words for forty-eight "northern campmeeting spirituals."

Lowens, Irving. *Music and Musicians in Early America.* New York: Norton, 1964. Chapters 2, 3, 8, 14, 18. A collection of valuable articles by one of the most eminent scholars in American music.

Sewall, Samuel. *Samuel Sewall's Diary.* Ed. Mark Van Doren. New York: Russell & Russell, 1963. "The most intimate record now available of life in New England during the important period which it covers" (1674–1729).

Titon, Jeff Todd. *Powerhouse for God: Speech, Chant, and Song in an Appalachian Baptist Church.* Austin: Univ. of Texas Press, 1988.

11. Urban Revivalism and Gospel Music

Boyer, Horace Clarence. "Contemporary Gospel Music." *Black Perspectives in Music* 7.2 (Spring 1979).

Goodspeed, Rev. E. J. *A Full History of the Wonderful Career of Moody and Sankey in Great Britain and America*. 1876. New York: AMS Press, 1973.

Harris, Michael W. *The Rise of the Gospel Blues: The Music of Thomas Andrew Dorsey in the Urban Church*. New York and Oxford: Oxford Univ. Press, 1992. A serious and well-documented study of a seminal figure, including transcriptions illustrating musical style. The work's thoroughness sheds light on many aspects of black gospel music.

Reagon, Bernice Johnson, ed. *We'll Understand It Better By and By: Pioneering African American Gospel Composers*. Washington and London: Smithsonian Inst. Press, 1992. Ten scholars, musicians, and educators contribute substantial articles on six major figures, plus an overview. There are many musical examples.

Sizer, Sandra S. *Gospel Hymns and Social Religion: The Rhetoric of Nineteenth-Century Revivalism*. Philadelphia: Temple Univ. Press, 1978.

12. Early Secular Music in the Cities

Borroff, Edith. "Origin of Species: Conflicting Views of American Musical Theater History." *American Music* 2.4 (Winter 1984).

Brooks, William. "*Pocahontas*: Her Life and Times." *American Music* 2.4 (Winter 1984).

Camus, Raoul F. *Military Music of the American Revolution*. Chapel Hill: Univ. of North Carolina Press, 1976. Basic work by a leading authority.

Hamm, Charles. *Yesterdays: Popular Song in America*. New York: Norton, 1979. The first five chapters deal with this period.

Hoover, Cynthia Adams. "Music in Eighteenth-Century American Theater." *American Music* 2.4 (Winter 1984).

Keller, Kate Van Winkle, and Ralph Sweet, eds. *A Choice Selection of American Country Dances of the Revolutionary Era, 1775–1795*. New York: Country Dance and Song Soc. of America, 1976. Twenty-nine dance tunes on single staff, with directions for performing the dances.

Lambert, Barbara, ed. *Music in Colonial Massachusetts. 1630–1820*. 2 vols. I: *Music in Public Places*. II. *Music in Homes and in Churches*. Charlottesville: Univ. Press of Virginia, 1980, 1985.

Lowens, Irving. *Music and Musicians in Early America*. New York: Norton, 1964. Articles on various topics, from the seventeenth century to the mid–nineteenth.

Mates, Julian. "The First Hundred Years of American Lyric Theater." *American Music* 1.2 (Summer 1983).

Porter, Susan L. *With an Air Debonair: Musical Theatre in America 1785–1815*. Washington, DC: Smithsonian Inst. Press, 1991. Unquestionably the most thorough and comprehensive work on the subject. Includes a painstaking clarification of the various confusing genres. Appendix A consists of a checklist of musical entertainments performed in the United States during the period, giving librettist, composer, genre, and the date and place of the first performance in America. Appendix B gives a list of theater performances in five American cities, 1801–15.

Shapiro, Anne Dhu. "Action Music in American Pantomime and Melodrama, 1730–1913." *American Music* 2.4 (Winter 1984).

Sonneck, Oscar George. *Early Concert-Life in America (1731–1800)*. 1906. New York: Musurgia, 1949. An indispensible work by a pioneering scholar in American music; all the quotes in the chapter from contemporary newspaper accounts are from this book or *Early Opera in America*. Sonneck's painstaking study of contemporary newspapers up to 1800 is being expanded in a project carried out by the Sonneck Society that bears his name.

13. Popular Musical Theater

Bordman, Gerald. *American Musical Revue: From The Passing Show to Sugar Babies*. New York: Oxford Univ. Press, 1985.

———. *American Musical Theatre: A Chronicle*. 2nd ed. New York: Oxford Univ. Press, 1992.

———. *American Operetta: From H.M.S. Pinafore to Sweeney Todd*. New York: Oxford Univ. Press, 1981.

Ferber, Edna. *Show Boat*.

Lhamon, W. T., Jr. *Raising Cain: Blackface Performance from Jim Crow to Hip Hop*. Cambridge: Harvard Univ. Press, 1998.

Mahar, William J. *Behind the Burnt Cork Mask: Early Blackface Minstrelsy and Antebellum American Popular Culture*. Urbana: Univ. of Illinois Press, 1999.

Mates, Julian. *America's Musical Stage: Two Hundred Years of Musical Theatre*. Westport, CT: Greenwood, 1985.

Riis, Thomas L. *Just Before Jazz: Black Musical Theater in New York, 1890 to 1915*. Washington, DC, and London: Smithsonian Inst. Press, 1989. Thorough piece of work, with lists of songs by shows, many photos, and sixty-nine pages of sheet music facsimiles.

Shakespeare, William. *Othello*; *Romeo and Juliet*.

14. Popular Song, Dance, and March Music

Abbott, Lynn. "'Play That Barber Shop Chord': A Case of the African-American Origin of Barbershop Harmony." *American Music* 10.3 (Fall 1992): 289–325.

Austin, William W. *"Susanna," "Jeannie," and "The Old Folks at Home": The Songs of Stephen Foster from His Time to Ours*. New York: Macmillan, 1975. A perceptive study of the complex array of meanings that Foster's songs have had in a variety of contexts.

Goldberg, Isaac. *Tin Pan Alley: A Chronicle of American Popular Music*. New York: Ungar, 1961. Includes introduction by George Gershwin.

Levy, Lester. *Give Me Yesterday: American History in Song, 1890–1920*. Norman: Univ. of Oklahoma Press, 1975.

———. *Grace Notes in American History: Popular Sheet Music from 1820 to 1900*. Norman: Univ. of Oklahoma Press, 1967. Arranged by topic, with background for each of the songs. Includes single-line tunes, and photo reprints of covers.

Pessen, Edward. "The Great Songwriters of Tin Pan Alley's Golden Age: A Social, Occupational, and Aesthetic Inquiry." *American Music* 3.2. (Summer 1985).

Shapiro, Nat. *Popular Music, 1920–1979: A Revised Cumulation*. Detroit: Gale, 1985. This is a three-volume rearrangement of an earlier ten-volume collaboration with Bruce Pollock.

Tawa, Nicholas. *Sweet Songs for Gentle Americans: The Parlor Song in America, 1790–1860*. Bowling Green, OH: Bowling Green Univ. Popular Press, 1980. Includes music to many songs.

15. Ragtime and Pre-Jazz

Berlin, Edward A. "Scott Joplin's *Tremonisha* Years." *American Music* 9.3 (Fall 1991).

Kenney, William H. "James Scott and the Culture of Classic Ragtime." *American Music* 9.2 (Summer 1991).

Riis, Thomas L. *Just Before Jazz: Black Musical Theater in New York, 1890 to 1915*. Washington, DC and London: Smithsonian Inst. Press, 1989.

Schafer, William J. *Brass Bands and New Orleans Jazz*. Baton Rouge: Louisiana State Univ. Press, c. 1977.

Schafer, Willim J., and Johannes Riedel. *The Art of Ragtime: Form and Meaning of an Original Black American Art*. Baton Rouge: Louisiana State Univ. Press, 1973.

Schuller, Gunther. *Early Jazz: Its Roots and Musical Development*. New York: Oxford Univ. Press, 1968. See Chapter 2, "The Beginnings."

16. Jazz

Lomax, Alan. *Mister Jelly Roll: The Fortunes of Jelly Roll Morton, New Orleans Creole and "Inventor of Jazz."* 2nd ed. Berkeley and Los Angeles: Univ. of California Press, 1973. Based on an extensive series of interviews recorded at the Library of Congress.

Hodeir, André. *Jazz: Its Evolution and Essence*. Trans. David Noakes. New York: Grove, 1956. Valuable in spite of its age

Sargeant, Winthrop. *Jazz: A History*. Rev. ed. New York: McGraw-Hill, 1964.

Schuller, Gunther, *The Swing Era: The Development of Jazz 1933–1945*. New York: Oxford Univ. Press, 1988. A valuable sequel to *Early Jazz*. These two works are the most substantial general works on jazz from the beginning to the end of the big-band era.

Stearns, Marshall. *The Story of Jazz*. 1956. New York: Oxford Univ. Press, 1974. Recommended, especially for its treatment of the beginnings of jazz.

18. Jacksonian Era to World War I

Block, Adrienne Fried. *Amy Beach: Passionate Victorian*. New York: Oxford Univ. Press, 1998.

Cable, George Washington. "The Dance in Place Congo" and "Creole Slave Songs." Reprinted in *The Social Implications of Early Negro Music in the United States*. Ed. Bernard Katz. New York: Arno, 1969.

Chase, Gilbert, ed. *The American Composer Speaks*. Baton Rouge: Louisiana State Univ. Press, 1966. Includes writings by Heinrich, Fry, Gottschalk, John Hill Hewitt, MacDowell, Farwell, and Gilbert.

Crawford, Richard. *The American Musical Landscape*. Berkeley and Los Angeles: Univ. of California Press, 1993. See Chapter 1 on Farwell, among others, and Chapter 5 on Root.

Katz, Bernard, ed. *The Social Implications of Early Negro Music in the United States*. New York: Arno, 1969. Includes George Washington Cable's 1886 articles on African American music making in New Orleans.

MacDowell, Edward. *Critical and Historical Essays*. Reprint, New York: Da Capo, 1969.

Schabas, Ezra. *Theodore Thomas: America's Conductor and Builder of Orchestras, 1835–1905*. Urbana and Chicago: Univ. of Illinois Press, 1989.

Tawa, Nicholas. *The Coming of Age of American Art Music: New England's Classical Romanticists*. New York: Schirmer Books, 1991.

19. Evolving Tradition, 1920–1970

Cowell, Henry, ed. *American Composers on American Music: A Symposium*. Palo Alto, CA, 1933. New intro. New York: Ungar, 1962. An essential collection.

Reis, Claire R. *Composers, Conductors and Critics*. 1955. New intro. by the author and pref. by Aaron Copland. Detroit: Detroit Reprints in Music, 1974. Largely a personal account; the author was director of the influential League of Composers for twenty-five years.

Sessions, Roger. *Roger Sessions on Music: Collected Essays*. Princeton, NJ: Princeton Univ. Press, 1979.

Tawa, Nicholas E. *Serenading the Reluctant Eagle*. New York: Schirmer Books, 1984. Perceptive and detailed overview of the period, including attention to the audiences for American music.

Thomson, Virgil. *American Music Since 1910*. New York: Holt, Rinehart & Winston, 1970. Another essential book by a well-known participant and observer of the period.

20. Twentieth-Century Innovation

Chase, Gilbert, ed. *The American Composer Speaks*. Baton Rouge: Louisiana State Univ. Press, 1966. Included are pieces by Ives, Cowell, Cage, Partch, and Varèse.

Cowell, Henry, ed. *American Composers on American Music: A Symposium*. 1933. New intro. New York: Ungar, 1962. The prototype of such collections, this excellent "symposium" of the early 1930s, focusing on the contemporary scene, includes thirty-one articles on American composers and on general tendencies.

Duckworth, William. *Talking Music*. New York: Schirmer Books, 1995.

Gagne, Cole, and Tracy Caras, eds. *Soundpieces: Interviews with American Composers*. Metuchen, NJ: Scarecrow, 1982.

Rochberg, George. *The Aesthetics of Survival: A Composer's View of Twentieth-Century Music*. Ann Arbor: Univ. of Michigan Press, 1984. A thoughtful critique of modernism.

Rockwell, John. *All American Music: Composition in the Late Twentieth Century*. New York: Knopf, 1983.

Includes perceptive individual chapters on Babbitt, Cage, Rzewski, Ashley, Glass, and others.

Schwartz, Elliott, and Barney Childs, eds. *Contemporary Composers on Contemporary Music*. New York: Holt, Rinehart & Winston, 1967.

Thomson, Virgil. *American Music Since 1910*. New York: Holt, Rinehart & Winston, 1970; paperback ed., 1972. In addition to supplying insightful background, this work has summaries and assessments of Ives, Varèse, and Cage.

21. Toward a More Hospitable Music

Rothstein, Edward. "The Return of Romanticism." *New Republic* 27 August 1984.

Strickland, Edward. *Minimalism: Origins*. Bloomington: Indiana Univ. Press, 1993.

Tawa, Nicholas. *A Most Wondrous Babble: American Composers, Their Music, and the American Scene, 1950–1985*. Westport, CT: Greenwood, 1987. See especially Chapter 8, "Reconciliations," and its many notes and references.

22. Opera Old and New

Dizikes, John. *Opera in America: A Cultural History*. New Haven and London: Yale Univ. Press, 1993. There is a distinction between "opera in America" and "American opera." Although this book devotes a good deal of space to singers, managers, and buildings (opera in America), there is also good coverage of American opera composers and their music.

Gagne, Cole, and Tracy Caras. *Soundpieces: Interviews with American Composers*. Metuchen, NJ, and London: Scarecrow, 1982. Includes interviews with Robert Ashley and Philip Glass.

Rockwell, John. *All American Music: Composition in the Late Twentieth Century*. New York: Knopf, 1983. Though the period covered is no longer so "late," this is a collection of still-interesting essays, including material on Glass, Reich, Monk, Ashley, and Laurie Anderson.

Tomalin, Nicholas, and Ron Hall. *The Strange Last Voyage of Donald Crowhurst*, 2nd ed. New York: McGraw-Hill, 2001.

GLOSSARY

accent   Emphasis placed on a single note or chord.

acoustic   Not powered by electricity. Refers to an instrument that produces sound naturally when it is plucked, strummed, bowed, struck, or has air blown through it.

acoustics   The scientific study of the production and perception of sound.

afterbeat   A beat that follows the metrically stronger pulse in a bar of music—for example, beats 2 and 4 in 4/4 meter ("march time").

atonal   Without a tonal center. Describes music that does not center on any particular **key.**

augmentation   An increase in the duration of a note.

backbeat   A strong accent on a beat that is normally in a weaker position—for example: "oom-PAH-oom-PAH" rather than "OOM-pah-OOM-pah" in 4/4 meter ("march time").

bar   A unit of musical time (also called a *measure*) consisting of a certain number of pulses that have been grouped together. In written music, the boundaries of these units are indicated by vertical marks through the **staff** called *barlines*.

beat   A steady pulse that divides musical time into even segments.

bending   A technique used with stringed instruments (especially the guitar) in which the sound of a note is made higher or lower by pulling on the string as a note is sounding.

binary form   "Two-part form." Describes a musical work that is made up of two complementary sections.

break   A brief instrumental interlude that occurs in an ensemble piece; often an improvised solo passage in a work for a group of instruments.

bridge   A transitional passage that connects to more musically important sections.

cadence   A point at which melodic and harmonic activity comes to a pause or a halt.

chord   Two or more notes sounded simultaneously.

chord progression   A succession of two or more chords.

chromatic scale   A collection of twelve adjacent rising pitches or twelve adjacent falling pitches in which the distance between each pitch and the next is a half step.

clef   A sign placed on the musical staff that indicates the positions and names of pitches.

color   The character and quality of a note. Also called *timbre*.

consonance   Describes pitches that sound stable and agreeable.

counterpoint   The art of combining two or more independent melodic lines.

cross-rhythm   A rhythm in which the regular or expected pattern of accents in a measure is contradicted by a new and conflicting set of accents.

diatonic scale   A collection of seven adjacent rising pitches or seven adjacent falling pitches in which the whole steps and half steps are arranged to form the **major scale** or the **minor scale.**

diminished triad   See **triad.**

diminution   A reduction in the duration of a note.

dissonance   Describes pitches that sound unstable and in need of resolution.

dominant   The fifth pitch (ascending) of a scale in any given **key.** A chord built on this pitch is the *dominant chord.*

dotted rhythm   A rhythm in which the addition of a dot after a note has augmented the note's value by half. The effect is such that pulses that usually unfold evenly and steadily are altered to unfold in staggered, uneven time values.

drone   A long, sustained sounding of one or more fixed pitches.

dynamics   The degrees of loudness or softness in music.

falsetto   A high, soprano-like voice produced by an adult male.

form   The organization of a musical work as composed by the artist or as perceived by the listener.

genre   A "type" of music as determined by factors including style, form, performing medium, and performance venues.

ground bass   A pattern of notes in the lowest part of a musical work for two or more voices or instruments that is repeated over and over.

half step   The smallest interval in Western music. On the piano, this interval is sounded by any two immediately adjacent keys (white or black).

harmonic progression   See **chord progression.**

harmony   Pitches sounded simultaneously (chords) that provide support for a melodic line or create the overall soundscape of a work.

heterophony   A musical texture in which two or more versions of the same essential melody are sounded simultaneously.

homophony   A musical texture in which the melodic interest is invested in one voice or instrument while other parts provide a subordinate accompaniment.

indeterminacy   Music created at least in part by random, or chance, elements. Also called *chance music* or *aleatory music.*

interval   The distance between two pitches.

intonation   In theory, a system of tuning; in performance, the degree to which a musician sounds a pitch accurately; also, the first few introductory notes in a piece.

key   A tonal center built on a fundamental note called the **tonic.**

major scale   A collection of seven notes that ascend in the following order of whole steps and half steps: 1–1–1/2–1–1–1–1/2. The character of this scale might be described as bright or happy.

major triad   See **triad.**

measure   See **bar.**

melody   A distinctive series of pitches forming a recognizable, often memorable, musical unit. This is usually what we whistle or hum in recalling a piece of music.

meter   Musical time organized into groups of steady pulses. Most pulses in Western music are organized into groups of two (duple meter) or groups of three (triple meter). Unusual groups not equally divisible by two or three (groups of five or seven pulses, for example) are called *asymmetrical meters.*

metronome   A mechanical or electronic device that sounds steady beats as clicks or beeps, which help musicians keep steady time while practicing or recording a piece.

minimalism   A style of composition in which only the smallest amounts of musical materials are used and repeated over and over, sometimes with only very subtle variations between repetitions.

minor scale   A collection of seven notes that ascend in the following order of whole steps and half steps: 1–1/2–1–1–1/2–1–1. The character of this scale might be described as dark or sad.

minor triad   See **triad.**

modal   A term often used to describe the character of a musical work that does not fall neatly into the soundscapes of either the **major scale** or the **minor scale.** See also **mode.**

mode   The quality or character of a scale (pitches organized into fixed ascending and descending patterns of half steps and whole steps). The primary modes in Western music are major and minor.

modulation   The process of changing from one tonal center (**key**) to another.

monody   Music that consists of a single melodic line.

monophony   A musical texture in which there is one melodic line with no accompaniment.

monotone   A single pitch on which a text is recited.

motive   A short, sharply defined melodic idea that can stand alone—for example, the four notes that open Beethoven's well-known Fifth Symphony.

offbeat   Any subdivision or a beat other than the initial one, which is usually the strongest.

ostinato [Italian, "obstinate"]   Any musical figure (it can be a particular melody, motive, chord, or rhythm) that is repeated over and over.

overtones   Secondary tones that naturally emanate from a fundamental pitch when it is sung or played on an instrument. Also called *harmonics.*

pentatonic scale   A collection of five pitches that ascend and descend in a fixed order. Its characteristic sound may be heard by playing any five consecutive black keys on the piano.

phrase   A self-contained musical idea that forms part of a larger unit of expression, such as a melody or a theme.

phrasing   In performance, the realization of self-contained musical ideas that form part of a larger unit of expression, such as a melody or a theme.

pitch A musical sound that can be represented as a single point on a measurable range from high to low — for example, a single point on a **staff** or in a **scale**.

pitch class Designates all pitches having the same name, without regard to their relative positions, low or high. For example, the pitch named "C" sung by an adult male, and the pitch named "C" sung by a child are in two different ranges; thus, strictly speaking, they are not the same pitches. They are both "C's" in the most general sense, however, and therefore belong to the same pitch class.

polyphony A musical texture in which several independent melodic lines are presented simultaneously in **counterpoint.**

program music Any musical work that aims to re-create in sound the events, characters, emotions, and overall impressions of a nonmusical source, such as a story, a painting, or the experience of walking through the woods.

recitative A dramatic form of speech that is musically heightened by placing emphasis on natural rhythms and inflections.

refrain A block of text and/or music that is repeated at regular intervals in the course of a piece.

rhythm Organized patterns of movement through time.

riffs Short, sometimes stereotypical, melodic phrases that are repeated over changing harmonies either as the main tune or as an accompaniment.

ritornello [Italian, "little return"] The section of music (most often presented at the beginning of a work) that comes back in part, or in its entirety, in the course of a performance.

scale A collection of pitches organized in a fixed ascending and descending pattern of whole steps and/or half steps.

scat singing A virtuosic manner of vocalizing nonsensical syllables that tends to emphasize fast, complex, "tongue-tying" rhythms.

score A written representation of a musical work in which the notated parts for all instruments and voices involved in its performance are shown simultaneously.

serial music Music in which pitches, rhythms, or other components are arranged in a certain order (series), then redeployed in that exact order throughout a composition.

solmization A manner of designating pitches by a set of syllables rather than fixed letter names — for

example, "do-re-mi-fa-sol-la" rather than "C-D-E-F-G-A." Solmization is a useful tool in the instruction of singing, because the syllables indicate where the half steps and whole steps occur.

staff The graph of five horizontal lines upon which pitches and rhythms are indicated.

stanza A unit of song text or poetry usually consisting of at least four lines of verse unified by a regular rhyme scheme and meter.

strophe See **stanza.**

strophic form A form in which successive **strophes** or **stanzas** are set to the same music.

subdominant The fourth pitch (ascending) of a scale in any given **key**. A chord built upon this pitch is the *subdominant chord.*

syncopation The momentary contradiction of a prevailing meter brought about by placing accents on beats or parts of beats that normally would not receive strong emphasis.

tempo The speed at which beats move forward through time.

tetratonic scale If this isn't an established musical term . . . well, it should be! Here it refers to a collection of four pitches that ascend and descend in a fixed order.

texture The musical "fabric" of a composition — that is, how individual lines interact with one another. Basic textures include **monophony, heterophony, homophony,** and **polyphony.**

timbre See **color.**

tonal Having a tonal center. Describes music that centers on a **key**.

tonality The organization of tones (pitches) around a definite **key** center.

tone A sound that has a definite and consistent **pitch.** When this term is preceded by an adjective, it describes the character or quality of sound produced by a musician with the voice or on an instrument (e.g., "smooth tone," "uneven tone").

tone cluster A very densely packed and dissonant collection of pitches. Its characteristic sound may be heard by simultaneously pressing several keys on a piano with the full palm or even the forearm.

tonic The first pitch (ascending) of a scale in any given **key**. A chord built on this pitch is the *tonic chord.* The tonic pitch (and the chord built upon it) is the most important in any given key — all harmonies and melodies gravitate toward it.

triad A chord consisting of three pitches with adjacent pitches separated by the interval of a third. A *major triad* is composed of a major third between the bottom and middle notes, and a minor third between the middle and top notes; its sound could be described as bright or happy. A *minor triad* is composed of a minor third between the bottom and middle notes, and a major third between middle and top notes; its sound could be described as dark or sad. A *diminished triad* is composed of two minor thirds; its sound is very tense and unstable.

tuning A system of pitches arranged according to certain intervals; also, the act of adjusting the sounds produced by the voice or an instrument to bring them into accord with predetermined pitches.

vibrato The ornamental wavering or wobbling of a pitch to intensify and enrich the sound quality.

vocables Utterances that are used in an ornamental fashion.

whole step An **interval** made up of two half steps.

ILLUSTRATION CREDITS

This page constitutes an extension of the copyright page. We have made every effort to trace the ownership of all copyrighted material and to secure permission from copyright holders. In the event of any question arising as to the use of any material, we will be pleased to make the necessary corrections in future printings. Thanks are due to the following authors, publishers, and agents for permission to use the material indicated.

xii: Illustration by Francis A. Beckett, ca. 1880. Photograph © 2002 Board of Trustees, National Gallery of Art, Washington
xii: Printed by permission of the Norman Rockwell Family Agency. Copyright © 1940 the Norman Rockwell Family Entities. Photo courtesy of the Berkshire Museum, Mass.
xiv: Albright Knox Gallery, Buffalo, New York / Bridgeman Art Library, London / Superstock

Part I. 1: Photo by David Gahr **13:** State Historical Society of Missouri, Columbia **21:** Photo by Frederick Ramsey, Jr. From *Been Here and Gone*, Rutgers University Press **37:** Photo by R.H. Lowie, Courtesy Dept. of Library Services, American Museum of Natural History **54:** Courtesy DRT Library, the Alamo, San Antonio **85:** Elemore Morgan, Jr. **100:** Photo courtesy of The New York Library for the Performing Arts at Lincoln Center. Reprinted with permission of Warner Brothers

Part II. 107: Southern Historical Society / University of North Carolina at Chapel Hill **115:** Frank Driggs Collection **136:** Archive Photos / PictureQuest **146:** © Roger Ressmeyer / CORBIS

Part III. 173: Dorothea Lange / Library of Congress
174: The Music of Henry Ainsworth Psalter **177:** Reproduced from the preface to the Bay Psalm Book : A Facimile Reprint of the First Edition of 1620, Chicago: Univ. of Chicago Press, 1956 **187:** Source unknown **190:** Courtesy of The New York Historical Society, New York City **198:** Courtesy Da Capo Press **200:** Courtesy of the Boston Public Library

Part IV. 217: State Historical Society of Missouri, Columbia **225:** The Connecticut Historical Society, Hartford **228:** The Connecticut Historical Society, Hartford **248:** Culver Pictures **257:** Herald Square Music, Inc. **264:** Photo courtesy of The New York Library for the Performing Arts at Lincoln Center **276:** Library of Congress **280:** Photo courtesy of The New York Library for the Performing Arts at Lincoln Center

Part V. 287: Frank Driggs Collection **288:** © Frank Driggs / Archive Photos / PictureQuest **305:** Photo by Herman Leonard **331:** AP / Wide World Photos

Part VI. 333: Photo by Jim Steere. Courtesy of the Chicago Symphony Orchestra **336:** Eric Hylden / Grand Forks Herald **338:** Madison County Library, Mississippi **341:** Photo courtesy of The New York Library for the Performing Arts at Lincoln Center **363:** Photo by Roy Stevens **385:** Bettmann / CORBIS **399:** From a facsimile by Associated Music Publishers, Inc., New York **404:** Harry Partch Foundation **413:** Performance instructions (page 4) and following page 1 of score, Feldman's Projection 3, C.F. Peters Corporation **442:** Photo © Beatriz Schiller

INDEX